Slovenia

Steve Fallon

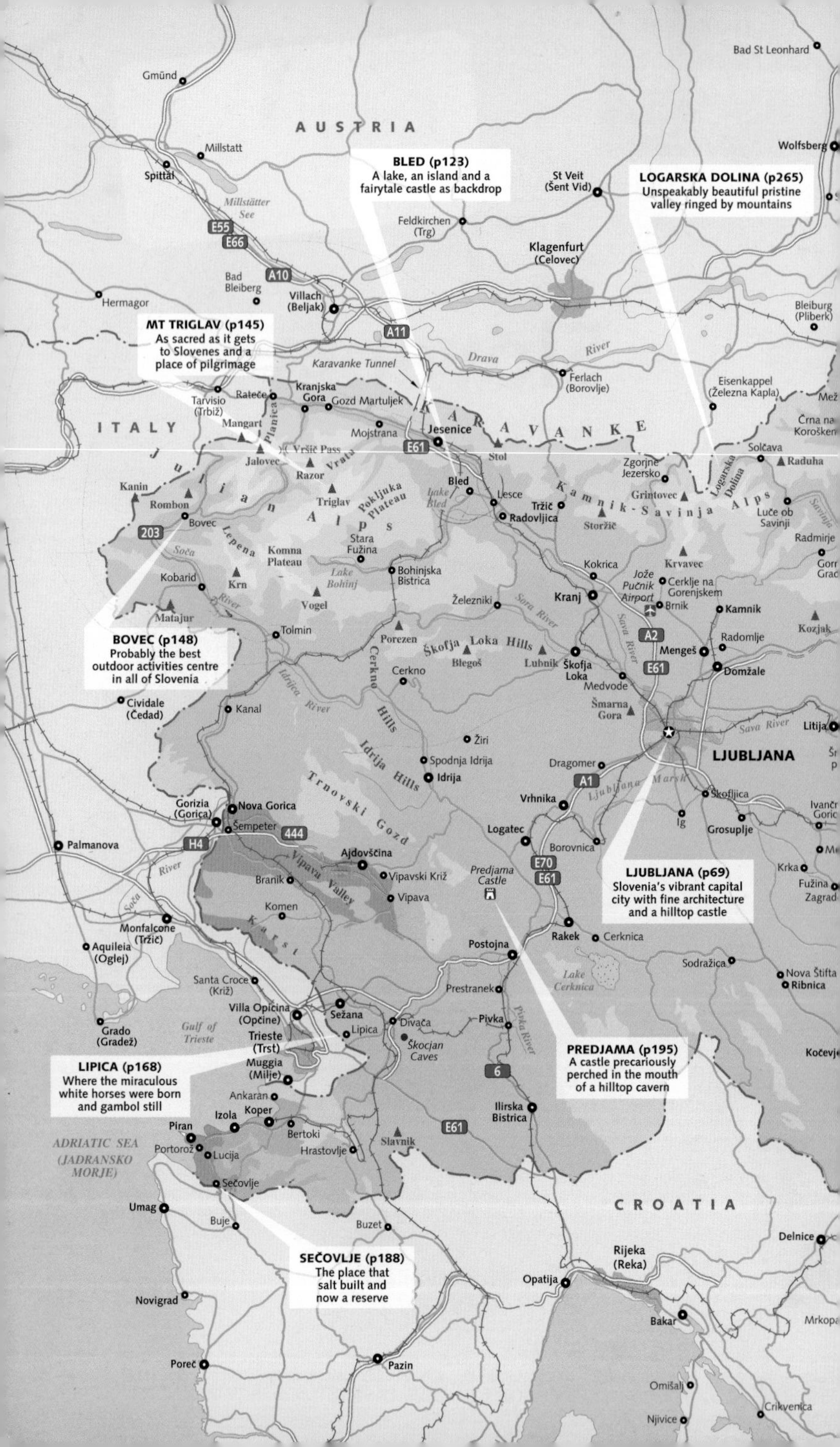

AUSTRIA
ITALY
CROATIA
BLED (p123)
A lake, an island and a fairytale castle as backdrop
LOGARSKA DOLINA (p265)
Unspeakably beautiful pristine valley ringed by mountains
MT TRIGLAV (p145)
As sacred as it gets to Slovenes and a place of pilgrimage
BOVEC (p148)
Probably the best outdoor activities centre in all of Slovenia
LJUBLJANA (p69)
Slovenia's vibrant capital city with fine architecture and a hilltop castle
PREDJAMA (p195)
A castle precariously perched in the mouth of a hilltop cavern
LIPICA (p168)
Where the miraculous white horses were born and gambol still
SEČOVLJE (p188)
The place that salt built and now a reserve
Gmünd
Bad St Leonhard
Millstatt
Spittal
Millstätter See
Wolfsberg
St Veit (Šent Vid)
Feldkirchen (Trg)
Klagenfurt (Celovec)
Bad Bleiberg
Hermagor
Villach (Beljak)
Bleiburg (Pliberk)
Karavanke Tunnel
Drava River
Ferlach (Borovlje)
Eisenkappel (Železna Kapla)
Tarvisio (Trbiž)
Rateče
Kranjska Gora
Gozd Martuljek
Mojstrana
Jesenice
Mangart
Planica
Vršič Pass
Jalovec
Razor
Vrata
K A R A V A N K E
Stol
Julian Alps
Kanin
Rombon
Bovec
Triglav
Pokljuka Plateau
Bled
Lake Bled
Lesce
Radovljica
Tržič
Storžič
Zgornje Jezersko
Grintovec
Kamnik-Savinja Alps
Solčava
Raduha
Logarska Dolina
Luče ob Savinji
Lepena
Soča
Komna Plateau
Stara Fužina
Lake Bohinj
Bohinjska Bistrica
Krn
Kobarid
Matajur
Vogel
Tolmin
Porezen
Kokrica
Kranj
Krvavec
Jože Pučnik Airport
Cerklje na Gorenjskem
Brnik
Kamnik
Železniki
Sora River
Škofja Loka Hills
Blegoš
Lubnik
Škofja Loka
Medvode
Radomlje
Mengeš
Domžale
Sava River
Cerkno
Cerkno Hills
Idrijca River
Cividale (Čedad)
Kanal
Šmarna Gora
Žiri
Spodnja Idrija
Idrija
Idrija Hills
Trnovski Gozd
Litija
LJUBLJANA
Dragomer
Ljubljana Marsh
Vrhnika
Škofljica
Ig
Grosuplje
Gorizia (Gorica)
Nova Gorica
Šempeter
Palmanova
Logatec
Borovnica
Ajdovščina
Vipavski Križ
Vipava
Vipava Valley
Branik
Predjama Castle
Komen
Karst
Soča River
Monfalcone (Tržič)
Rakek
Cerknica
Krka
Fužina
Aquileia (Oglej)
Postojna
Lake Cerknica
Sodražica
Nova Štifta
Ribnica
Santa Croce (Križ)
Prestranek
Villa Opicina (Opčine)
Sežana
Divača
Pivka
Pivka River
Grado (Gradež)
Gulf of Trieste
Trieste (Trst)
Lipica
Škocjan Caves
Muggia (Milje)
Ankaran
Kočevje
Izola
Koper
Ilirska Bistrica
Piran
Bertoki
Slavnik
ADRIATIC SEA (JADRANSKO MORJE)
Portorož
Lucija
Hrastovlje
Sečovlje
Umag
Buje
Buzet
Delnice
Rijeka (Reka)
Opatija
Novigrad
Bakar
Poreč
Pazin
Omišalj
Njivice
Crikvenica

BOGOJINA (p274)
A town of flowers, storks and a church designed by Plečnik
ŠEMPETER (p263)
An almost complete
man-era 'city of the dead'
PTUJ (p243)
A medieval town of history and cultural monuments
ADLEŠIČI (p232)
Slovenia's folk 'heart' on the banks of a warm river
KOČEVSKI ROG (p211)
Virgin forest where bears and WWII ghosts do roam
HUNGARY
CROATIA
MARIBOR
ZAGREB
Feldbach
Szentgotthard (Monošter)
Zalalövő
Šalovci
Őriszentpéter
Goričko Hills
Mačkovci
Deutschlandsberg
Leibnitz (Lipnica)
Moravske Toplice
Cesztreg
Bad Radkersburg (Radgona)
Murska Sobota
Bogojina
Gornja Radgona
Dobrovnik
Lenti
Bakovci
Rédics
Beltinci
Lendava (Lendva)
Ljutomer
Tornyiszentmiklós
Bučkovci
Podturen
Selnica ob Muri
Mura River
Slovenske Gorice
Lenart
Kobansko Hills
Muta
Radlje ob Dravi
Dravograd
Vuzenica
Vuhred
Drava River
Selnica ob Dravi
Lovrenc na Pohorju
Ruše
Žigartov
Slovenj Gradec
Spodnje Hoče
Pohorje Massif
Rogla
Mislinja
Dornava
Ptuj
Ormož
Središče ob Dravi
Čakovec
Slovenska Bistrica
Šoštanj
Zreče
Pragersko
Kidričevo
Goričak
Velenje
Ptujska Gora
Cirkulane
Slovenske Konjice
Letuš
Poljčane
Haloze Hills
Varaždin
Rogaška Slatina
Donačka Gora
Šempeter
Žalec
Celje
Rogatec
Šentjur
Trbovlje
Laško
Podčetrtek
Krapina
Zidani Most
Kozjansko
Radeče
Bistrica ob Sotli
Senovo
Podsreda
Zabok
Boštanj
Sevnica
Sava
Brestanica
Mokronog
Krško
Krka River
Brežice
Vrbovec
Šmarješke Toplice
Šmarjeta
Kostanjevica na Krki
Terme Čatež
Šentjernej
Mokrice
Obrežje
Kostanjevica Cave
Otočec ob Krki
Novo Mesto
Pleterje Monastery
Kostanjevica Castle
Samobor
Gorjanci
Dolenjske Toplice
Uršna Sela
Jastrebarsko
Božakovo
Metlika
Mirna Gora
Podzemelj
Kanižarica
Črnomelj
Dragatuš
Adlešiči
Karlovac
Žuniči
Vinica
River
Vrbovsko
Ogulin
A1
E57
E70
H1
3
4
6
105
ELEVATION
2000m
1500m
1000m
500m
100m
0
LEGEND
Freeway
Freeway under construction
Primary Road
Secondary Road
Tertiary Road
0
20 km
0
12 miles

On the Road

STEVE FALLON Coordinating Author

They say you're not really a Slovene until you've climbed Mt Triglav and got 'spanked' at the summit, so after a decade of stalling I decided it was time. Of course we did it the hard way – up and down in a day – but being on top of the Slovenian world looking down on creation was worth every ache and all the pains.

DON'T MISS

More often than not, even serial visitors to Slovenia like myself just stop and stare, mesmerised by the sheer beauty of this land. With so much splendour strewn across the country, it's nigh on to impossible to choose a *številka ena* (No 1) ab-favourite top place. OK, OK, it's got to be the Vršič Pass (p145), which stands (literally) head and shoulders above the rest and leads me from alpine Gorenjska, past Triglav and down to sunny Primorska and the bluer-than-blue Soča River. All in a hair-raising, spine-tingling hour.

ABOUT THE AUTHOR

Steve has been travelling to Slovenia since the early 1990s, when a well-known travel publishing company initially refused his proposal to write a guidebook to the country because of 'the war going on' (it had ended two years before) and an influential US newspaper told him their readers weren't interested in 'Slovakia'. Never mind, it was his own private Idaho for over a decade. Though *on še govori slovensko kot jamski človek* (he still speaks Slovene like a caveman), Steve considers part of his soul to be Slovenian and returns as often as he can for a glimpse of the Julian Alps in the sun, a dribble of *bučno olje* (pumpkinseed oil) and a dose of the dual.

SLOVENIA STARS

You might be forgiven for thinking that anything of beauty in this greenest of green lands is, well, all natural. But it ain't necessarily so. Yes, there are verdant mountains begging to be scaled, gin-clear rivers crying out for the stroke of an oar and mighty caves with their mouths agape in welcome. But humankind's touch has beautified Slovenia too, as you'll soon see in its varied architecture, its excellent wines and traditional dishes and its vibrant folk culture.

JOHN ELK III

Attitude for Architecture

Slovenia boasts a great wealth of architecture, from Romanesque chapels to its share of postmodern monstrosities. But don't expect everything to be in the nation's towns and cities. Look too to wayside shrines, farmhouses and even mountain huts for a touch of inspiration and even extravagance.

❶ Medieval Squares

The core of most Slovenian towns and cities forms a symphony of colourful residences and civic buildings dating back to the Middle Ages. Among the finest are Škofja Loka and Radovljica in Gorenjska, Koper and Piran in Primorska and Ptuj in Štajerska.

❷ Castles

Slovenia was once known as the 'land of castles' and counted more than a thousand of them. Many of them remain – and are remarkably intact. Among the oldest is Podsreda (p240) in Štajerska, but for sheer visual impact nothing compares with Predjama (p195) in Notranjska.

❸ Churches

Houses of worship run the gamut of architectural styles in Slovenia (even the intensely religious Plečnik got into the act at Bogojina, p274, in Prekmurje) but baroque (such as Ljubljana's Franciscan Church of the Annunciation, p76, or the Church of St James, p80) is the calling card.

❹ Ljubljana

No place in Slovenia waltzes through architecture so adroitly as the 'beloved' capital, from its ancient hilltop castle (p80) to the pair of splendid art nouveau banks (p76) on Miklošičeva cesta.

❺ Plečnik

No discussion of Slovenian architecture can start or end without mentioning Jože Plečnik (p86), a man who left his architectural mark across the nation but especially in Ljubljana with projects including the Triple Bridge (p76) and the National and University Library (p81).

❸

In with the Outdoors

People here live very active, very outdoorsy lives; according to a recent government survey, every third Slovene takes part in active leisure pursuits. That's not surprising. Skiing was invented here, they say you're not Slovene until you've scaled the 2864m of Mt Triglav and no place has embraced the newfangled sport of canyoning like Slovenia.

❶ Hiking & Climbing

Hiking and climbing is a religion in Slovenia and the principal place of pilgrimage is Mt Triglav (p144). But it's not the only place of worship and there is an excellent system of trails – some 10,000km of them – criss-crossing the country.

❷ Water Sports

You can't consider a visit to Slovenia complete without a trip down the Sava Bohinjka River (p127) in Gorenjska or the sapphire-blue Soča River (p151) in Primorska in a canoe, kayak or raft.

❸ Spas

Nothing beats taking to the waters after a day of skiing or hiking and Slovenia counts almost two dozen thermal spa resorts. Some are very flash indeed with all the mod cons, but if you want an old-world-style spa town choose Dolenjske Toplice (p208) in Dolenjska or Rogaška Slatina (p240) in Štajerska.

❹ Skiing

They say it all started somewhere in the hills of Notranjska (barrel staves usually figure largely in the story) and nowadays some 300,000 people visit the almost 50 ski grounds in Slovenia every year.

❺ Caving

Abseiling and wearing a torch in your helmet is not a requirement to visit some of Slovenia's most awe-inspiring caves. The Jules Verne vision that is the Škocjan Caves (p167) can be visited easily on foot and Postojna Cave (p192) sails past as you sit on a mini-train.

1

Supping & Sipping

For its size, Slovenia offers an extremely varied (and healthy) cuisine, with as many dishes borrowed from neighbouring Italy, Austria and Hungary as home-grown ones. And wine is a way of life here, with three major wine-growing regions divided into three times as many districts.

2

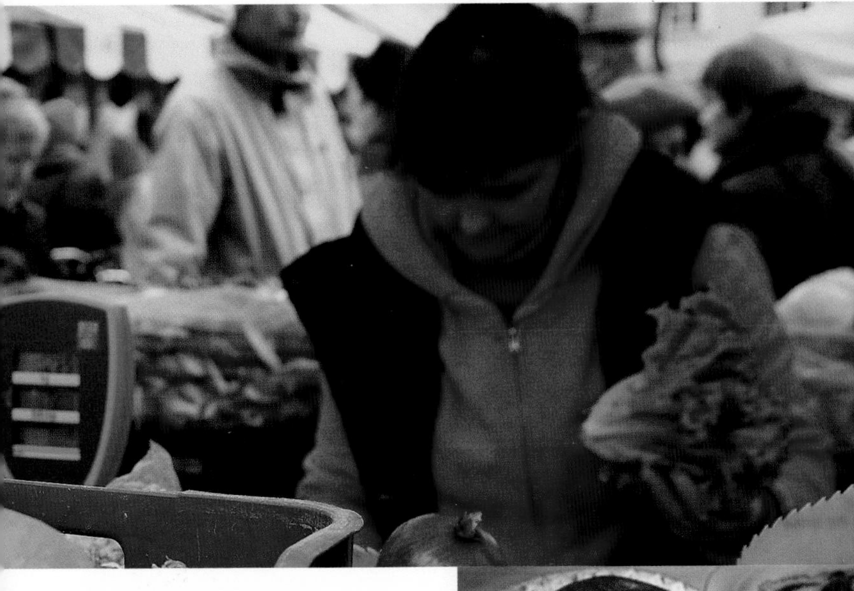

❶ Markets
Markets throughout Slovenia, but especially the large outdoor one in Ljubljana (p95), are cornucopias offering a bounty of seasonal goodness: from strawberries, raspberries and cherries through all the stone fruits to apples, pears and nuts. Dried wild mushrooms, honey and *bučno olje* (nutty pumpkinseed oil) are good buys.

❷ Goriška Brda
The red wines of the Vipava Valley (p166) may vie in popularity and the wine region of Jeruzalem-Ljutomer (p249) is also idyllic, but no place in Slovenia is so redolent of vines and wines and the art of viticulture as Goriška Brda (p159) in Primorska.

❸ Potica
Potica (a kind of nut roll) is as much an icon in Slovenia as the *kozolec* (hayrack) seen in hilly areas in most parts of the country. *Potica* is also made with savoury fillings and is eaten after a meal or at teatime.

3

❹ Podravje
Once upon a time Slovenian wine (p50) was all about big reds from Primorska, but now the nation is looking to the northeast and its whites, especially sauvignon blanc, which is being compared to that of New Zealand.

❺ Bread
Nothing is more Slovenian than *kruh* (bread), and it is generally excellent. Real treats are the braided loaves made at holiday times and *pisan kruh* (mottled bread), in which three types of dough (usually buckwheat, wheat and corn) are rolled up and baked.

1

It's Party Time!

Slovenes, although not the most spontaneous people, let their hair down at festivals, both traditional and of a more recent inspiration, around the country throughout the year. Expect lots of booze, colourful costumes and – we're sorry – accordion music.

❶ Street Theatre

You're likely to encounter outdoor performances in cities and towns throughout Slovenia in the warmer months, but no festival is better organised and more anticipated than Ljubljana's week-long Ana Desetnica International Street Theatre Festival (p89) in late June/early July.

❷ Cows' Ball

Traditionally marking the return of the cows to the valleys (p138) around Bohinj in September, this zany fair is a day-long knees-up of folk dance and music, eating and drinking. And, yes, if pigs can fly, cows can dance.

❸ Kurentovanje

The best known (though hardly the only) rite-of-spring festival (p247) celebrated at Ptuj in the days leading up to Shrove Tuesday and the start of Lent involves hairy creatures in frightening leather masks that look and act as evil as the spirits they're meant to scare off.

❹ St Martin's Day

The day on which *mošt* (must; essentially fermenting grape juice) officially becomes wine and can be sold as such is an important traditional holiday (though not a public one) here. Families enjoy a Martinovanje dinner of goose and new wine accompanied by folk music on 11 November.

Contents

Regional Map Contents

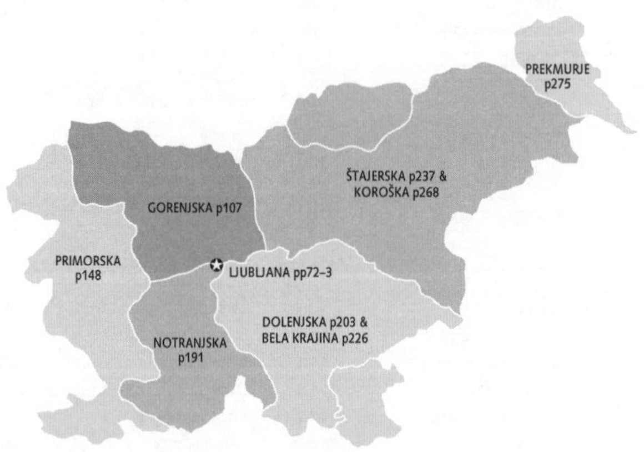

Destination Slovenia

It's an undeniably tiny place, with just over 2 million people. But good things come in small packages and never was that old chestnut more appropriate than in describing Slovenia, an independent republic bordering Italy, Austria, Hungary, Croatia and the Adriatic Sea.

Slovenia has been dubbed a lot of things since it separated from Yugoslavia in 1991 – 'Europe in Miniature', 'The Sunny Side of the Alps', 'The Green Piece of Europe'. They may sound like PR sound bites but they're all true.

From the Venetian harbour towns of the coast to the Hungarian-style farmhouses of Prekmurje; from the subterranean magic of the Škocjan Caves to *The Sound of Music* scenery of the Julian Alps; and from the opera and concert halls of Ljubljana to the WWII Partisan bases hidden in the hills of Dolenjska – Slovenia has it all. Its incredible mixture of climates brings warm Mediterranean breezes up to the foothills of the Alps, where it can snow even in summer. And with more than half of its total area covered in forest, Slovenia really is one of the greenest countries in the world.

And in this land of the great outdoors the list of activities on offer is endless; throughout the year you'll encounter locals engaged in decidedly active pursuits – canoeing and kayaking in spring, swimming and water-skiing in summer, hiking and climbing in autumn, and skiing and snowboarding in winter.

But Slovenia ain't paradise. Like everywhere, it has its own share of difficulties.

Take the economy. Slovenia joined the EU in 2004, exchanged the tolar for the euro in 2007. And while Slovenia remains the most prosperous country in 'transition Europe', the average annual inflation rate has jumped from 2.5% to more than 6% in just a few years, a result of pricing in the new euro and the effects of the global credit crunch. Job loss is another big (and relatively new) worry here; at the time of writing 90,000 people were unemployed out of a labour force of just under a million.

And then there's the problem with the neighbour to the south… Since the collapse of Yugoslavia, Slovenia and Croatia have been battling over where to draw their border in Piran Bay and the dispute could lead to the former's blocking the latter's bid to join the EU. The two haven't actually gone to war – in fact, they never have in their history and the issue is now in arbitration – but the dispute has sparked the so-called Facebook Wars, with tens of thousands of Croatians joining a group on the site calling for a boycott of Slovenian products and Slovenia.

Mind you, it would take them a month of Sundays to get here nowadays. Road construction and expansion continues apace in Slovenia, where the total number of highways have more than doubled since independence. Indeed, at the time of research some 160km of highways (and an uncountable number of roundabouts) were under construction causing inevitable delays on road journeys. Slovenia may look fantastic now, but just imagine what it will look like when it's finished.

FAST FACTS

Population: 2.05 million

GDP per capita: €18,200 (93% of EU average)

Inflation: 6.4%

Unemployment: around 10%

Size: 20,273 sq km (0.2% of Europe's total land mass)

Average size of household: 2.8 people

Percentage of English speakers: 48.2%

Bear population: 450-500

23 December 1990: 88.5% of the Slovenian electorate vote for an independent republic

Slovenia's national anthem: *Zdravljica* (A Toast to Freedom), written by poet France Prešeren in 1844

Getting Started

Slovenia is a dream destination for many reasons, but among the most obvi ous is that it requires so little advance planning. Tourist literature abounds maps are excellent and readily available, and the staff at tourist offices, trave agencies, hotels, train stations and so on are almost universally helpful an efficient and speak English very well. Slovenia is so well developed an organised that you don't have to plan much of anything before your trip almost everything can be arranged on the spot.

But this is fine only if your budget is unlimited, you don't have an interes in any particular activity, period of architecture or type of music, and you' eat or drink anything put down in front of you. Those who have a limit a to the amount they can spend while travelling, or want better value for thei money will benefit immensely from a bit of prior knowledge and carefu planning. And if you have specific interests – from white-water rafting an mountaineering to bird-watching and folk music – you'll certainly want t make sure that the things you expect to see and do will be possible at th particular time of year when you intend to travel.

WHEN TO GO

Every season has its attractions in Slovenia. Snow can linger in the mountain until late June, but spring is a great time to be in the lowlands and flower carpeted valleys (though it can be pretty wet in May and June). At the sam time the days are getting longer, the theatres and other cultural venues ar in full swing and off-season rates still generally apply.

For more information about Slovenia's climate, see p284.

Summer (mid-June to sometime in September) is the ideal time for hik ing and camping, but it's also the peak season for visitors, making accom modation in Ljubljana and on the coast hard to come by without advanc booking. September can be an excellent month, with plentiful local fruit an vegetables, shoulder-season tariffs in effect again and the tourist masses bac at home. You can still swim comfortably in the Adriatic in September, bu by mid-October most of the camping grounds have closed down and th

DON'T LEAVE HOME WITHOUT...

Unless you plan to do some serious hiking or engage in some sport, you don't have to remember any particular items of clothing for Slovenia – a warm sweater or windbreaker (even in summer) for the mountains at night, perhaps, and an umbrella, especially in spring or autumn. In addition, don't forget:

- check the visa situation and your passport expiry date (p292)
- organise a health-insurance policy (p302)
- a swimsuit, plastic sandals and a towel
- a compass to help orient yourself in the mountains
- an adapter plug for electrical appliances (if not from Europe)
- tea bags (since Slovenes drink buckets of the herbal variety but not much of the black stuff)
- sunglasses and sun block, even in the cooler months (those rays in the mountains can be fierce)
- a penknife, with such 'essentials' as a bottle opener and strong corkscrew
- binoculars for when trekking or viewing detail on churches and other buildings

ays are growing shorter. Autumn is beautiful, particularly in the mountains f Gorenjska and Štajerska, and it's the best time for hiking and climbing though October and November can be rainy).

Winter (December to March) in Slovenia is for skiers. It can be very cold nd, away from the mountains, often quite bleak. At the same time, winter ees museums and other tourist sights closed or their hours sharply curtailed. kiers should bear in mind that Slovenian school kids have winter holidays or about 10 days between Christmas and the start of the New Year and again or a week in the second half of February.

OSTS & MONEY

lthough prices have increased sharply with the advent of the euro, Slovenia generally cheaper than neighbouring Italy and Austria. At the same time, verything costs at least a third to half as much more than in nearby Hungary. roatia has always been more expensive than Slovenia.

If you stay in private rooms or guesthouses, eat at midrange restaurants nd travel 2nd class by train or bus, you should just get by on under €60 a day. ravelling in greater style and comfort – restaurant splurges with bottles of ine, a fairly active nightlife, small hotels/guesthouses with 'character' – will ost about twice as much in the capital but an average of about €80 in the rovinces. Those putting up at hostels or college dormitories, eating *burek* meat- or cheese-filled pastries) for lunch and at self-service restaurants for inner could squeeze by on €35 to €40 a day.

HOW MUCH?

100km by train/bus
€6.03/9.20

Bicycle rental (per day)
€5-15

Bottle of ordinary/quality Slovenian wine
€3.50/9.50

Cup of coffee in a cafe
€1-2.50

Ski pass (per day)
€15.85-24.60

RAVELLING RESPONSIBLY

lovenia is one of the 'greenest' countries in the world, with more than half f the country under forest cover and more than 11% of the countryside nder some sort of protection. The vast majority of Slovenes are very aware f their impact on the surrounding environment; everyone takes their rubish home with them, for example, when hiking or trekking. As a traveller, is impossible not to have some effect on the environment, but there are a umber of ways to minimise the impact.

Getting to Slovenia by train or bus from most parts of Europe is a relavely easy exercise. Naturally it's more time consuming than air travel, ut your carbon footprint would be a fraction compared. If you do fly, onsider offsetting your carbon emissions (for example on www.jpmorgan limatecare.com).

Within Slovenia, the transport network is relatively useful and affordable. rains travel the length and breadth of the country, and where they don't o, buses generally do. And most sizable towns and cities have local publicansport options. Away from the highest of mountains of Gorenjska and tajerska, getting around by bicycle is a highly viable option; bicycles can lso be transported on some trains.

It's easy to avoid large, generic hotels and hotel chains in Slovenia and opt istead for smaller, family-run establishments, therefore ensuring your euros o directly to the local community. Additionally, farm-stays accommodation, rivate rooms, and pensions (p281) are further alternatives.

Fresh seasonal fruit and vegetables are readily available throughout lovenia, especially at markets. They are cornucopias offering a bounty of easonal goodness: from strawberries and raspberries and cherries through ll the stone fruits to apples and pears and nuts. Much of this produce is ocally grown and free of chemical sprays.

The number of organic farms in Slovenia has mushroomed over the ast decade – from a mere 41 in 1998 to 1780 (or 5% of the total) in 008. The farms raise and process everything from cereals, dairy products

TOP PICKS

FESTIVALS & EVENTS

Slovenia marks red-letter days with festivals and special events throughout the year, some of them exotic in the extreme and dating back hundreds of years while others are very much part of this century. Among the best/most colourful/liveliest are the following:

- Kurentovanje (p247) in Ptuj in February
- Lent Festival (p253) in Maribor in June
- Trnfest (p89) in Ljubljana in August
- Rock Otočec (p21) near Novo Mesto in July
- Cows' Ball (p138) in Bohinj in September
- Laufarija (p165) in Cerkno at the start of Lent (late February/early March)

NATURAL WONDERS

In a land of hundreds of natural wonders – from ice caves and disappearing lakes to virgin forests and cobalt-blue rivers – it's difficult to narrow the list down to five. It's certain, however, that most travellers won't soon forget any of the following:

- Vršič Pass (p145)
- Škocjan Caves (p167)
- Logarska Dolina (p265)
- Soča River (p148)
- Vintgar Gorge (p131)
- Velika Planina (p110)

OUTDOOR ACTIVITIES

Perhaps more than any other country in Europe outside Scandinavia, Slovenes are attached to the great outdoors (p63). We recommend:

- Skiing in the Maribor Pohorje (p255)
- Canyoning near Bled (p127)
- Hiking in Triglav National Park (p144)
- Kayaking on the Krka River (p208)
- Taking the waters at Dolenjske Toplice (p209)
- Mountain biking in Koroška (p272)

green-coloured Ekološki label or Biodar label of the Slovenian Organic Farmers' Association.

READING UP

There's no shortage of books on Slovenia, but travellers writing diary accounts of southeast Europe have usually treated Slovenia rather cursorily or not at all, as they made tracks for 'more exotic' destinations like Croatia, Bosnia or even Serbia. In *Black Lamb and Grey Falcon,* her classic (and, at over almost 1200 pages, rather longwinded) look at Yugoslavia between the wars, Rebecca West allows Slovenia and the Slovenes fewer than a dozen brief references. And the recently re-issued *Foreign Travellers in the Slovene Karst 1486-1900* by Trevor Shaw will be a bit esoteric for most readers.

We know that a few other great writers did make it here, and there's documentation to prove at least one did. In Ljubljana's train station, for example, a brass plaque installed in 2003 to the left of the staircase leading down from platform No 1 (Map pp72–3) tells us that no less than James Joyce, together with his new paramour Nora Barnacle, spent the night of 19 October 1904 in Ljubljana. What the inscription fails to mention is that he couple, who had met just four months earlier and were on their way teach English at Berlitz in Pula, had caught the wrong train.

More recently, the Irish novelist Colm Tóibin in his *The Sign of the ross: Travels in Catholic Europe* included a short chapter called 'Slovenian pring'. There's not much new here except for a rather curious comment fter a crawl through the cafes and bars of the Old Town. 'The atmosphere vas sexually alive,' he wrote. '... In the way they ordered a beer, or smiled, r found a table, people oozed sex.' Ljubljana might ooze a lot of things, ut sex really isn't one of them.

Having said all that Slovenia is not completely devoid of books to inspire eaders and get them excited about their trip. Recommended reading:

acts about Slovenia (Government Communication Office) A government publication but a acker and free from many tourist offices, this 100-page booklet is written and updated annually y experts in their field and is an easy introduction to Slovenian history, government, geography, ulture and so on.

orbidden Bread (Erica Johnson Debeljak) Slovenia's past and present through the eyes of a ve-struck young American woman who follows her poet-lover to his homeland and adjusts to a ew country, language and culture.

uestions about Slovenia (Matjaž Chvatal) This rather naff, 95-page book in an oversized est-pocket format will tell you the differences between Slovenia, Slovakia and Slavonia, what *oline* (pig-slaughters) are and just what makes Slovenes tick – and talk.

lovenia from the Air (Matjaž Kmecl et al) This trilingual coffee-table book has the standard vow-factor photographs of Slovenia's lakes, coast, towns and, of course, mountains from on high, nd may even have you considering the ascent of Triglav.

lovenia: My Country (Joco Žnidaršič) With Slovenia so diverse and physically attractive, here's no shortage of picture and art books on the country and this is the best: a heartfelt but ever cloying paean to the celebrated photographer's homeland.

NTERNET RESOURCES

-uprava (http://e-uprava.gov.si/e-uprava/en/portal.euprava) The State Portal of the Republic f Slovenia has information about and links to just about anything you could want to know about he country – from today's pollution indices to how to trace your Slovenian roots.

overnment Communication Office (www.ukom.gov.si/en) Full of facts and figures about lovenia's politics, economy, culture and environment.

onely Planet (www.lonelyplanet.com) Information on Slovenia; you can ask questions before ou depart or dispense advice when you get back via the Thorn Tree forum.

lat'Kurja (www.matkurja.com/eng) The 'Mother Hen' site is a vast directory of Slovenian web esources.

lajdi (www.najdi.si) The most popular search engine in Slovenia (mostly in Slovene).

lovenia Times (www.sloveniatimes.com) Website of the independent (and free) magazine that omes out every two weeks.

lovenian Landmarks (www.burger.si) General and detailed information along with some 60-degree tours of Slovenia's towns and cities, museums and galleries, castles and manors, caves nd waterfalls.

lovenian Tourist Board (www.slovenia.info) The Slovenian Tourist Board's ambitious site has nformation on every conceivable sight and activity in the republic.

TA (www.sta.si/en) News and views from the Slovenska Tiskovna Agencija (Slovene Press gency).

elephone Directory of Slovenia (http://tis.telekom.si) National telephone directory.

Events Calendar

Major cultural and sporting events are listed in the Festivals & Events section of individual towns and cities. The following abbreviated list gives you a taste of what to expect. For a more complete list look under 'Events' on the website of the Slovenian Tourist Board (www.slovenia.info) or in the STB's annual *Calendar of Major Events in Slovenia*.

JANUARY

WOMEN'S WORLD CUP SLALOM & GIANT SLALOM COMPETITION (GOLDEN FOX), POHORJE mid-Jan

One of the world's major international ski events held only for women is staged on the ski slopes of Pohorje southwest of Maribor (www.pohorje.org).

MEN'S SLALOM & GIANT SLALOM VITRANC CUP COMPETITION, KRANJSKA GORA late Jan

Number one downhill ski event of the year for men takes place in the Julian Alps (www.pokal-vitranc.com).

FEBRUARY

KURENTOVANJE, PTUJ late Feb/early Mar

A 'rite of spring' celebrated for 10 days up to Shrove Tuesday (February or early March) and the most popular Mardi Gras celebration in Slovenia (www.kurentovanje.net).

MARCH

SKI JUMPING WORLD CUP CHAMPIONSHIPS, PLANICA mid to late Mar

Three days of high flying on skis near Kranjska Gora (www.planica.info).

APRIL

SPRING FLOWER SHOW & GARDENING FAIR, VOLČJI POTOK mid-Apr

Slovenia's largest flower and gardening show takes place at this arboretum near Kamnik (www.arboretum-vp.si).

MAY

DRUGA GODBA, LJUBLJANA mid-May/early Ju

A festival of alternative and world music in the Križanke in the capital (http://festival.druga-godba.si).

JUNE

INTERNATIONAL ROWING REGATTA, BLED mid-Ju

One of the country's most exciting (and fastest sporting events is held over three days on the lake (www.veslaska-zveza.si).

INTERNATIONAL BIENNIAL OF GRAPHIC ARTS, LJUBLJANA Jun/Sep

Held at Ljubljana's International Centre o Graphic Arts and other venues over nine weeks in odd-numbered (ie 2011, 2013 etc) years (www.mglc-lj.si).

IDRIJA LACE-MAKING FESTIVAL late Jun

The red-letter annual event in Idrija in Primorska with a contest at the end of up to 10(competitors.

ANA DESETNICA INTERNATIONAL STREET THEATRE FESTIVAL, LJUBLJANA LATE Jun/early Ju

One of the largest outdoor theatre festivals in Europe, held over a week in summer (www.anadesetnica.org).

FESTIVAL LENT, MARIBOR late Jun/mid-Ju

A two-week extravaganza of folklore and culture in Maribor's Old Town (http://lent.slovenija.net)

SEVIQC BREŽICE late Jun/late Ju

Month-long series of ancient music concerts in southeast Slovenia (www.seviqc-brezice.si).

JULY

PRIMORSKA SUMMER FESTIVAL late Jul/early Aug

Concerts, theatre and dance events held in various venues in Ankaran, Izola, Koper, Pian and Portorož over four weeks (www.portoroz.si).

OCK OTOČEC, NEAR NOVO MESTO early Jul
hree-day rock concert held at Prečna airfield, km northwest of Novo Mesto, and Slovenia's iggest open-air rock concert (www.rock-otocec om).

KLUŽE FESTIVAL, NEAR BOVEC early Jul/mid-Aug
ncreasingly well-attended theatre festival held in 19th-century fortress in the Soča Valley (www exponto.net).

JUBLJANA FESTIVAL early Jul/late Aug
he nation's premier festival of classical entertainment (music, theatre and dance) held in the apital (www.ljubljanafestival.si).

RAZEM KNIGHTS' TOURNAMENT, REDJAMA mid-Jul
ousting and other medieval shenanigans below lovenia's most beguiling castle (www.turizem kras.si).

AUGUST

RNFEST, LJUBLJANA Aug
robably the most popular annual festival in the apital, this month-long party at the KUD France rešeren cultural centre in Trnovo showcases nusic, dance and theatre from around the world www.kud-fp.si).

KARINA ETNO FESTIVAL, BLED late Jul/early Aug
Veek-long international festival of folk and world nusic in various venues in Bled (www.okarina com).

ADOVLJICA FESTIVAL early to late Aug
Dne of the most important festivals of anient classical music in Europe is staged in this Gorenjska town over 10 days (www.festival radovljica.si).

SEPTEMBER

COWS' BALL, BOHINJ mid-Sep
Zany weekend of folk dance, music, eating and drinking to mark the return of the cows from their high pastures to the valleys (www.bohinj.si).

DORMOUSE NIGHT, CERKNICA late Sep
A celebration and feast during the very short dormouse-hunting season in the forests around Snežnik Castle (www.mice.si).

OCTOBER

SLOVENIAN FILM FESTIVAL, PORTOROŽ early Oct
Pivotal event in the Slovenian cinema world, this three-day festival sees screenings and awards (www.fsf.si).

CITY OF WOMEN, LJUBLJANA mid-Oct
Two-week international festival focusing on contemporary arts and culture created by women (www.cityofwomen.org).

LJUBLJANA MARATHON late Oct
First run in 1996, this marathon draws an increasingly international field (www.ljubljanskimaraton.si).

NOVEMBER

ST MARTIN'S DAY 11 Nov
Nationwide celebration to mark the day when must (fermenting grape juice) officially becomes new wine (www.slovenia.info).

DECEMBER

CHRISTMAS CONCERTS early to mid-Dec
Held throughout Slovenia, especially Ljubljana, but the most famous are in Postojna Cave (www .postojna-cave.com), where you can also attend the Live Christmas Crib, a re-enactment of the Nativity with Christmas carols.

ITINERARIES

CLASSIC ROUTES

MOUNTAINS MAJESTY

One day to a week / Gorenjska Round Tri

What Slovenia has in spades is mountains, and they are 'just up the roac from Ljubljana.

From **Ljubljana** (p69) head north on route 211. Just after Medvode, g west on route 413 through colourful **Škofja Loka** (p110). Head north alon route 210 to the historic town of **Kranj** (p114) and continue northwest, pass ing through 'bee town' **Radovljica** (p118). Spend the night in picturesqu **Bled** (p123).

From either place rejoin the highway, route E61, and make tracks for th ski centre **Kranjska Gora** (p140) and the **Vršič Pass** (p145) in Triglav Nationa Park. The road down will deposit you in Primorska's **Soča Valley** (p148) Following the Soča River will bring you to the activities centre of **Bovec** (p148 and the WWI battlegrounds around **Kobarid** (p152). From here follow rout 102 through Tolmin to **Idrija** (p159). Ljubljana, via Logatec and Vrhnik (route 409), is only 55km to the northeast.

This unbelievably scenic, 330km circuit takes in some of the most attractive scenery in Slovenia: lakes, historic towns, mountain villages and the very peaks themselves. Although safe except in very inclement weather (when it is closed to traffic), the Vršič Pass is not for the faint-hearted.

ARST & COAST

Two days to a week / Ljubljana to Primorska

'his itinerary combines the best of two worlds: the evocative and sunbaked egion of the Karst and the historic and fun-filled Slovenian coast.

From **Ljubljana** (p69), follow motorway A1 to **Postojna** (p191). If you're not o caved-out after a visit, continue on to **Divača** (p167) and the awesome **kocjan Caves** (p167). By then you'll need to take some R&R at the bucolic asis that is **Lipica** (p168).

The fastest way to get to the Slovenian coast from Lipica is through Italy, ıst south of Trieste. If you'd rather stay on Slovenian soil, return to Divača nd head south along the motorway to **Koper** (p172), a cheaper place to stay n the coast than the other Venetian towns. Follow the coastal road to **Izola** p176), **Piran** (p179), and eventually **Portorož** (p184), with all types of accommodation for different budgets. To the south along the coast is **Sečovlje** (p188) nd its famous salt pans, a relaxing and very peaceful antidote to sometimes rash Portorož. A spur road just before the Croatian border crosses the rnica River and links up to the east with route 11 heading back for Ljubljana. t the Rižana exit head south for the Karst village of **Hrastovlje** (p170) and its onderful church. Motorway A1, some 8km north of Hrastovlje, will take ou back to the capital.

This 310km itinerary takes you through the Karst region – stopping at Slovenia's two most famous caves – and carries on to the coast before looping back up through the Karst to the capital.

ROADS LESS TRAVELLED

This gentle 290km drive is for those not wanting anything too demanding or dramatic: just sit back and watch the castles fly by. If you drive straight through, you could cover everything in two days or even less. Those who want to stop, stare and maybe even sleep in one of the castle hotels could turn it into a tour lasting up to a week.

CASTLES IN THE SKY

Two to seven days / Ljubljana to Posavj

Wars and development over the centuries have taken care of most c Slovenia's 1000-odd castles, but a few remain, many in more remote (al though easily accessible) areas of Dolenjska province.

From **Ljubljana** (p69), which has its own hilltop castle, follow motorwa A2/E70 southeast to Ivančna Gorica and the Cistercian abbey at **Stičn** (p205). Although it may appear at first to be a castle too far, **Bogenšpe** (p206) is the secular twin to Stična and is well worth the 20km up an 20km back.

A gentle ride awaits, following the Krka River past **Žužemberk** (p208) an **Novo Mesto** (p211) to **Otočec ob Krki** (p215), home to Slovenia's most unusu (and now poshest) castle hotel. The castle at **Kostanjevica na Krki** (p218 now home to an excellent museum, is another 18km to the southeast vi route 419.

The castle at **Brežice** (p221) contains an excellent regional museur and one of the finest ceiling frescoes in the land. But for something tha screams 'castle' – with turrets, drawbridge, dry moat and central court yard (not to mention a ghost that walks and wails) – travel 10km to th southeast to **Mokrice** (p224). You can return to the capital in no time bac on the A2/E70.

TAILORED TRIPS

WINE & WATER MIX

If you're like us, you know that a sauna and/or a soak is the perfect treatment for a little too much of the good life. So why not combine the two – wine and water (thermal, that is) – and detox as you indulge?

The wine regions of **Posavje** and **Podravje** (p50), running almost the full length of eastern Slovenia, are delightful areas to visit from both scenic and wine-tasting points of view. They also happen to be as awash with thermal water.

A mere 18km beyond the charming **Bizeljsko-Sremič** (p225) wine region, which effectively ends at Bizeljsko and is noted for its medium-dry whites and reds and for *repnice* (caves for storing wine), is the thermal spa of **Terme Olimia** (p235). Its healing waters are full of magnesium and calcium, and its attractions lie in both its curative powers and its recreational appeal. However, if you prefer something a little less of-this-century, go the extra distance to **Rogaška Slatina** (p240). Located some 15km further north, it overflows with magical olde worlde charm, not to mention its very own 'drinking cure' (water this time).

The **Haloze** (p249) wine region, celebrated for its pinot blanc, sauvignon and riesling, begins a mere 18km southwest of **Ptuj** (p243), where you'll find **Terme Ptuj** (p246).

The **Jeruzalem-Ljutomer** (p249) wine district begins at Ormož, due east of Ptuj. Were you to travel some 25km northeast along routes 230 and 439, you'd come to **Terme Banovci** (p276), a spa with a camping ground partly reserved for naturists. But the shy and/or chilly may want to move on to the more reserved spa town of **Radenci** (p278), a very modest 15km up the road.

History

EARLY INHABITANTS

The area of present-day Slovenia has been settled since the Palaeolithic Age. Stone implements that date back to 250,000 BC have been found in a cave at near Orehek southwest of Postojna in Notranjska.

During the Bronze Age (around 2000 to 900 BC), marsh dwellers farmed and raised cattle in the area south of present-day Ljubljana – the Ljubljansko Barje – and at Lake Cerknica. They lived in round huts set on stilts and traded with other peoples along the so-called Amber Route linking the Balkans with Italy and northern Europe.

A primitive bone flute discovered in 1995 in a cave at Divje Babe near Cerknica in Primorska and dating back some 35,000 years is thought to be the world's oldest known musical instrument.

Around 700 BC the Ljubljana Marsh people were overwhelmed by the Illyrian tribes from the south who brought iron tools and weapons. They settled largely in Dolenjska, built hilltop forts and reached their peak between 650 and 550 BC, during what is called the Hallstatt period. Iron helmets, gold jewellery and *situlae* (embossed pails) with distinctive Hallstatt geometric motifs have been found in tombs near Stična and at Vače, near Litija; you'll see some excellent examples of these findings at both the National Museum of Slovenia (p83) in Ljubljana and the Dolenjska Museum (p213) in Novo Mesto.

In about 400 BC, Celtic tribes from what are now France, Germany and the Czech lands began pushing southward towards the Balkans. They mixed with the local population and established the Noric kingdom, the first 'state' on Slovenian soil.

THE ROMANS

In 181 BC the Romans established the colony of Aquileia (Oglej in Slovene) on the Gulf of Trieste in order to protect the empire from tribal incursions, and Julius Caesar, after whom the Julian Alps in the northwest are named, actually visited in the 1st century AD. In the next century, the Romans annexed the Celtic Noric kingdom and moved into the rest of Slovenia and Istria.

The Romans divided the area into the provinces of Noricum (today's southern Austria, Koroška and western Štajerska), Upper and Lower Pannonia (eastern Štajerska, Dolenjska and much of Gorenjska) and Histria (Primorska and Croatian Istria), later called Illyrium, and built roads connecting their new military settlements. From these bases developed the important towns of Emona (Ljubljana), Celeia (Celje) and Poetovio (Ptuj), where reminders of the Roman presence can still be seen. Some fine exam-

TIMELINE

2000–900BC

Bronze Age settlers build wooden huts on stilts, make coarse pottery, farm and raise cattle in the Ljubljana Barje, the marshy area south of present-day Ljubljana

400 BC

Celtic tribes led by the Norics establish a kingdom called Noricum on Slovenian soil near the present-day city of Celje (known as Celeia at the time)

1st century AD

The Romans move into Slovenia from Italy and annex the Noric kingdom, marking the beginning of Roman occupation of the territory that would last for almost half a millennium

THE TALE IN THE PAIL

Hallstatt is the name of a village in the Salzkammergut region of Austria where objects characteristic of the early Iron Age (from about 800 to 500 BC) were found in the 19th century. Today it's used generically for the late Bronze and early Iron Age cultures that developed in Central and Western Europe from about 1200 to 450 BC.

Many regions of Slovenia were settled during this period, particularly Dolenjska and Bela Krajina. Burial mounds – 27 in Novo Mesto alone – have yielded swords, helmets, jewellery and especially *situlae* – pails (or buckets) that are often richly decorated with battle and hunting scenes.

Hallstatt art is very geometric, and typical motifs include birds and figures arranged in pairs. It was not until the advent of the late Iron Age La Tène culture (450 to 390 BC) of the European Celts that S-shapes, spirals and round patterns developed.

ples are the Citizen of Emona statue (p82) in Ljubljana, the Roman necropolis at Šempeter (p263) and the Mithraic shrines (p246) near Ptuj.

THE GREAT MIGRATIONS

In the middle of the 5th century AD, the Huns, led by Attila, invaded Italy via Slovenia, attacking Poetovio, Celeia and Emona along the way. Aquileia fell to the Huns in 452. However, Attila's empire was short-lived and was soon eclipsed first by the Germanic Ostrogoths and then the Langobards, who occupied much of the Slovenian territory. In 568 the Langobards struck out for Italy, taking Aquileia and eventually conquering the Venetian mainland.

THE EARLY SLAVS

The ancestors of today's Slovenes arrived from the Carpathian Basin in the 6th century and settled in the Sava, Drava and Mura River valleys and the eastern Alps. Under pressure from the Avars, a powerful Mongol people with whom they had formed a tribal alliance, the early Slavs migrated farther west to the Friulian plain and the Adriatic Sea, north to the sources of the Drava and Mura Rivers and east as far as Lake Balaton in Hungary. Early Slavic burial grounds can be found at Kranj (p117), where Langobard artefacts have also been recently discovered.

At that time these people were called Sclavi or Sclaveni, as were most Slavs. Later these 'proto-Slovenes' would be identified by their region: Carniola, Styria, Carinthia. It wasn't until the late 18th century during a period of national consciousness that the name *Sloveni* or *Slovenci* (Slovenians) came into common use.

5th century

In the fifth decade of this century, the Huns, led by Attila, invade Italy via Slovenia, attacking Poetovio (Ptuj), Celeia (Celje) and Emona (Ljubljana) en route.

6th century

Early Slavic tribes, divided in to two distinct but related groups, the Slaveni and Antes, settle in the Sava, Drava and Mura River valleys and the eastern Alps

7th century

A loose confederation of Slavic tribes establishes the Duchy of Carantania, the first Slavic political entity, and place its centre somewhere near Celovec, today's Klagenfurt in Austria

In their original homelands the early Slavs were a peaceful people, living in forests or along rivers and lakes, breeding cattle and farming by slash-and-burn methods. They were a superstitious people who saw *vile* (both good and bad fairies or sprites) everywhere and paid homage to a pantheon of gods and goddesses. As a social group they made no class distinctions but chose a leader – a *župan* (now the word for 'mayor') or *vojvoda* (duke) – in times of great danger. During the migratory periods, however, they became more warlike and aggressive.

The early Magyars were such fierce fighters that a common Christian prayer during the Dark Ages was 'Save us, O Lord, from the arrows of the Hungarians.'

THE DUCHY OF CARANTANIA

When the Avars failed to take Byzantium in 626, the alpine Slavs united under their leader, the duke Valuk, and joined forces with the Frankish king Samo to fight them. The Slavic tribal union became the Duchy of Carantania (Karantanija), the first Slavic state, with its seat at Krn Castle (now Karnburg) near Klagenfurt (Celovec in Slovene) in Austria.

By the early 8th century, a new class of ennobled commoners called *kosez* had emerged, and it was they who publicly elected and crowned the new *knez* (grand duke) on the *knežni kamen* ('duke's rock') in the courtyard of Krn Castle. Such a democratic process was unique in the feudal Europe of the early Middle Ages and continued until 1414. The model was noted by the 16th-century French political theorist Jean Bodin, whose work is said to have been a key reference for Thomas Jefferson when he wrote the American Declaration of Independence in 1775–76.

EXPANSION OF THE FRANKS

In 748 the Frankish empire of the Carolingians incorporated Carantania as a vassal state called Carinthia and tried to convert the people to Christianity. The new religion was first resisted, but Irish monks under the auspices of the Diocese of Salzburg began to preach in the vernacular and were more successful.

By the early 9th century, religious authority on Slovenian territory was shared between Salzburg and the Patriarchate (or Bishopric) of Aquileia (opposite). The weakening Frankish authorities began replacing Slovenian nobles with German counts, reducing the local peasantry to serfdom. The German nobility was thus at the top of the feudal hierarchy for the first time in Slovenian lands. This would later become one of the key obstacles to Slovenian national and cultural development.

THE CARINTHIAN KINGDOM

With the total collapse of the Frankish state in the second half of the 9th century, a Carinthian prince named Kocelj established a short-lived (869–74) independent Slovenian 'kingdom' in Lower Pannonia, the area stretching

748

The Carolingian empire of the Franks incorporates Carantania as a vassal state called Carinthia; with the establishment of a formal church, the Christianisation of the Slovenes begins

869–74

Carinthian Prince Kocelj rules a Slovenian 'kingdom' in Lower Pannonia, the area that stretches southeast from Styria (Štajerska) to the Mura, Drava and Danube Rivers

955

The marauding Magyars, who had invaded in and settled in Slovenian Pannonia, are stopped in their tracks by German king Otto I at Augsburg

THE PATRIARCHATE OF AQUILEIA

You'd never guess from its present size (population 3330), but the Friulian town of Aquileia north of Grado on the Gulf of Trieste played a pivotal role in Slovenian history, and for many centuries its bishops (or 'patriarchs') ruled much of Carniola (Kranjska).

Founded as a Roman colony in the late 2nd century BC, Aquileia fell to a succession of tribes during the Great Migrations and had lost its political and economic importance by the end of the 6th century. But Aquileia had been made the metropolitan see for Venice, Istria and Carniola, and when the church declared some of Aquileia's teachings heretical, it broke from Rome. The schism lasted only a century and when it was resolved Aquileia was recognised as a separate patriarchate.

Aquileia's ecclesiastical importance grew during the mission of Paulinus II to the Avars and Slovenes in the late 8th century, and it acquired feudal estates and extensive political privileges (including the right to mint coins) from the Frankish and later the German kings. It remained a feudal principality until 1420 when the Venetian Republic conquered Friuli, and Venetians were appointed patriarchs for the first time. Aquileia retained some of its holdings in Slovenia and elsewhere for the next 300 years. But the final blow came in 1751 when Pope Benedict XIV created the archbishoprics of Udine and Gorizia. The once powerful Patriarchate of Aquileia had outlasted its usefulness and was dissolved. The archaeological area and the patriarchal basilica of Aquileia have been on the World Heritage List since 1998.

outheast from Styria (Štajerska) to the Mura, Drava and Danube Rivers. It was to Lower Pannonia that the Macedonian brothers Cyril and Methodius, he 'apostles of the southern Slavs', had first brought the translations of he Scriptures to the Slovenes in 867. And it was here that calls for a Slavic rchdiocese were first heard.

HE MAGYARS & GERMAN ASCENDANCY

n about 900, the fearsome Magyars, expert horsemen and archers, subjugated ower Pannonia and the Slovenian regions along the Sava, cutting them off rom Carinthia. It wasn't until 955 that they were stopped by forces under ing Otto I at Augsburg.

The Germans decided to re-establish Carinthia, dividing the area into a alf-dozen border regions *(krajina)* or marches. These developed into the lovenian provinces that would remain basically unchanged until 1918: arniola (Kranjska), Carinthia (Koroška), Styria (Štajerska), Gorica (Goriška) nd the so-called White March (Bela Krajina).

A drive for complete Germanisation of the Slovenian lands began in the 0th century. Land was divided between the nobility and various church ioceses (Brixen, Salzburg, Freising), and German gentry were settled on it.

Lake Balaton in Hungary, which the early Slavs reached in their roamings, takes its name from the Slovenian word *blato* (mud).

970

ppearance of the *Freising lanuscripts,* the earliest known ext written in Slovene (or any lavic language for that matter), which contain a sermon on in and penance and instructions for general confession

early 12th century

Slovenia's first chartered towns – among them Ljubljana, Ptuj, Škofja Loka, Piran and Kamnik – begin to develop, increasing to almost two dozen within 150 years

late 13th century

The first feudal holdings in Slovenian lands – the provinces of Carniola, Gorizia, Istria, Carinthia and Styria – fall under Habsburg rule and would remain so until WWI

The population remained essentially Slovenian, however, and it was largel due to intensive educational and pastoral work by the clergy that the Slovenia identity was preserved. The *Freising Manuscripts* (p43), the oldest exampl of written Slovene, date from this period.

Most of Slovenia's important castles were built and many importan Christian monasteries – for example, Stična (p205) and Kostanjevica (p218) established between the 10th and 13th centuries. Towns also began to develo as administrative, trade and social centres from the 11th century

EARLY HABSBURG RULE

Ivan Cankar's *Hlapec Jernej in Njegova Pravica* (The Bailiff Yerney and His Rights), a tale of the unequal relationship between servant and master, is read as a metaphor for Slovenia under Habsburg rule.

In the early Middle Ages, the Habsburgs were just one of many Germa aristocratic families struggling for hegemony on Slovenian soil. Others, suc as the Andechs, Spanheims and Žoneks (later the Counts of Celje), wer equally powerful at various times. But as dynasties intermarried or died ou the Habsburgs consolidated their power.

Between the late 13th century and the early 16th century, almost all th lands inhabited by Slovenes passed into Habsburg hands except for Istri and the Littoral, which were controlled by Venice until 1797, and parts o Prekmurje, which belonged to Hungarian crown. Until the 17th century, rul was not direct but administered by diets (parliaments) of 'resident princes' prelates, feudal lords and representatives from the towns, who dealt wit matters like taxation.

By this time Slovenian territory totalled about 24,000 sq km, about 15% larger than its present size. Not only did more towns and boroughs receiv charters and rights, but the country began to develop economically with th opening of ironworks (eg at Kropa, p122) and mines (eg Idrija, p159). Thi economic progress reduced the differences among the repressed peasant and they united against their feudal lords.

TURKSH RAIDS, PEASANT UPRISINGS & REFORMATION

Attacks by the Ottoman Turks on southeastern Europe began in 1408 an continued for more than two and a half centuries, reaching the gate of Vienn on several occasions. By the start of the 16th century, thousands of Slovene had been killed or taken prisoner. The assaults helped to radicalise landles peasants and labourers who were required to raise their own defences *an* continue to pay tribute and work for their feudal lords.

More than a hundred peasant uprisings and revolts occurred on Slovenia territory between the 14th and 19th centuries, but they reached their pea between 1478 and 1573. Together with the Protestant Reformation at th end of the 16th century, they are considered a watershed of the Slovenia national awakening.

1408

Ottoman Turks start their attacks on southeastern Europe, which continue for over two centuries and took them to the gates of Vienna several times

1478–1573

Peasant riots, which together with the Protestant Reformation at the end of the 16th century, are considered a watershed of the Slovenian national awakening, are at their peak

1540–80

Protestant Reformation; fi books in Slovene appear, cluding a catechism publi by Primož Trubar, a compl translation of the Bible by Dalmatin 1584, and a gra of Slovene in Latin

In most of the uprisings, peasant 'unions' demanded a reduction in feudal payments and the democratic election of parish priests. The three most violent uprisings took place in 1478 in Koroška, in 1515, encompassing almost the entire Slovenian territory, and in 1573, when Ambrož 'Matija' Gubec led 12,000 Slovenian and Croatian peasants in revolt. Castles were occupied and pulled down and lords executed but none of the revolts succeeded as such.

The Protestant Reformation in Slovenia was closely associated with the nobility from 1540 onward and was generally ignored by the rural population except for those who lived or worked on lands owned by the church (though of Ljubljana's 5000 residents in 1570, two-thirds were Protestant). The effects of this great reform movement cannot be underestimated. Though only 1% of the current population is Protestant, the Reformation gave Slovenia its first books in the vernacular – some [illegible]0 in all. Not only did this raise the educational level of Slovenes, but it also lifted the status of the language itself, the first real affirmation of Slovenian culture.

The seventh stanza of France Prešeren's popular poem *Zdravljica* (A Toast) forms the lyrics of Slovenia's national anthem.

COUNTER-REFORMATION & PROGRESS

The wealthy middle class had lost interest in the Reformation by the time it peaked in the 1580s because of the widening economic gap between it and the nobility. They turned to the Catholic resident princes, who quashed Protestantism among the peasants and banished noble families who persisted in the new belief.

In the 18th century Habsburg economic decline brought on by a series of wars was reversed, and Empress Maria Theresa (1740–80) introduced a series of reforms. These included the establishment of a new state administration with a type of provincial government; the abolition of customs duties between provinces of the empire; the building of new roads; and the introduction of obligatory elementary school in German and state-controlled secondary schools. Her son, Joseph II (1780–90), went several steps further. He abolished serfdom in 1782, paving the way for the formation of a Slovenian bourgeoisie, and allowed complete religious freedom for Calvinists, Lutherans and Jews. He also dissolved the all-powerful (and often corrupt) Catholic religious orders and made primary education in Slovene compulsory.

As a result of these reforms, agricultural output improved, manufacturing intensified and shipping from Austria's main seaport at Trieste increased. The reforms also produced a flowering of the arts and letters in Slovenia, with the playwright and historian Anton Tomaž Linhart (p47) and the poet and journalist Valentin Vodnik (p43) producing their finest and most influential

16th century

Counter-Reformation is in full swing throughout Slovenia; the systematic Germanisation of Slovenia's culture, education and administration begins under the Hapsburgs

1782

Habsburg Emperor Joseph II abolishes serfdom, making way for the formation of a Slovenian bourgeoisie, and allows complete religious freedom for Calvinists, Lutherans and Jews

1809

Ljubljana is named the capital of the French-ruled Illyrian Provinces (1809–13), created by Napoleon from the from Slovenian and Croatian regions in a bid to cut the Habsburgs off from the Adriatic works at this time. The first newspaper in Slovene – *Lublanske Novize* – wa launched by Vodnik in 1797.

NAPOLEON & THE ILLYRIAN PROVINCES

The French Revolution of 1789 convinced the Austrians that reforms shoul be nipped in the bud, and a period of reaction began that continued until th Revolution of 1848. In the meantime there was a brief interlude that woul have a profound effect on Slovenia and its future.

After defeating the Austrians at Wagram in 1809, Napoleon decide to cut the entire Habsburg Empire off from the Adriatic. To do this h created six 'Illyrian Provinces' from Slovenian and Croatian regions, in cluding Koroška, Kranjska, Gorica, Istria and Trieste, and made Ljubljan the capital.

Although the Illyrian Provinces lasted only from 1809 to 1813, Franc instituted a number of reforms, including equality before the law and th use of Slovene in primary and lower secondary schools and in public of fices. Most importantly, the progressive influence of the French Revolutio brought the issue of national awakening to the Slovenian political arena fo the first time.

ROMANTIC NATIONALISM & THE 1848 REVOLUTION

Austrian rule, restored in 1814, was now guided by the iron fist of Princ Clemens von Metternich. He immediately reinstituted the Austrian feud system and attempted to suppress every national movement from the tim of the Congress of Vienna (1815) to the Revolution of 1848. Indeed, in 182 members of the Holy Alliance (Austria, Prussia, Russia and Naples) met a the Congress of Laibach (Ljubljana) to discuss measures to suppress th democratic revolutionary and national movements in Italy. But on a differer level the process of change had already started in Slovenia.

The period of so-called Romantic Nationalism (1814–48), also known a the Vormärz (pre-March) period in reference to the revolution that brok out across central Europe in March 1848, was one of intensive literary an cultural activity and led to the promulgation of the first Slovenian politic program. Although many influential writers published at this time (Matij Čop, Bishop Anton Martin Slomšek, Andrej Smole), no one so dominated th period as the poet France Prešeren (p44). His bitter-sweet verse, progressiv ideas, demands for political freedom and longings for the unity of all Sloven caught the imagination of the nation then and have never let it go.

In April 1848 Slovenian intellectuals drew up their first national politic program under the banner Zedinjena Slovenija (United Slovenia). In es sence it called for the unification of all historic Slovenian regions within a

1821

Slovenia's capital makes it to the world conference map when members of the Holy Alliance meet at the Congress of Laibach (Ljubljana) to discuss measures to suppress the democratic revolutionary and national movements in Italy

1848

Slovenian intellectuals issue a national political program, United Slovenia, calling for the unification of all historic Slovenian regions within an autonomous unit under the Austrian monarchy

1867

A number of Slovenes are incorporated into Hungar with the Compromise of 1 an agreement creating th Dual Monarchy of Austria empire) and Hungary (the kingdom)

autonomous unit under the Austrian monarchy, the use of Slovene in all schools and public offices and the establishment of a local university. The demands were rejected, as they would have required the reorganisation of the empire along ethnic lines. It must be remembered that the Slovenes of the time were not contemplating total independence. Indeed, most looked upon the Habsburg Empire as a protective mantle for small nations against larger ones they considered as predators like Italy, Germany and Serbia.

Slovenia 1945: Memories of Death and Survival after World War II by John Corsellis & Marcus Ferrar is the harrowing story of the forced return to Slovenia and execution of thousands of members of the anti-Communist Domobranci (Home Guards) after WWII.

CONSTITUTIONAL PERIOD

The only tangible results for Slovenes in the 1848 Austrian Constitution were that laws would henceforth be published in Slovene and that the Carniolan (and thus Slovenian) flag should be three horizontal stripes of white, blue and red. But the United Slovenia program would remain the basis of all Slovenian political demands up to 1918, and political-cultural clubs and circles began to appear all over the territory.

The rest of the 19th and early 20th centuries were marked by economic development: the railway from Vienna to Ljubljana opened in 1849, industrial companies were formed at Kranj and Trbovlje, and a mill began operating at Ajdovščina. Despite this, material conditions declined for the peasantry, and between 1850 and 1910 more than 300,000 Slovenes – 56% of the population – emigrated.

Some advances were made on the political side. Out of the influential *čitalnice* (reading clubs) and *tabori,* camps in which Slovenes of many different beliefs rallied, grew political movements. Parties first appeared toward the end of the 19th century, and a new idea – a union with the other Slavs to the south – was propounded from the 1860s onward by the distinguished Croatian bishop Josip Strossmayer. The writer and socialist Ivan Cankar even called for an independent federal Yugoslav ('south Slav').

SLOVENIA'S NATIONAL ANTHEM

God's blessing on all nations,
Who long and work for that bright day,
When o'er earth's habitations
No war, no strife shall hold its sway;
Who long to see
That all men free
No more shall foes, but neighbours be.

France Prešeren (1800–49), A Toast

1918

Austria-Hungary loses WWI and the political system collapses with the Armistice of 11 November; the Serbia-dominated Kingdom of Serbs, Croats and Slovenes is declared

1929

King Alexander seizes absolute power, abolishes the constitution and proclaims the Kingdom of Yugoslavia only to be assassinated five years later in France

1937

The Communist Party of Slovenia (KPS) is formed under the tutelage of Josip Broz Tito and the Communist Party of Yugoslavia (KPJ)

WWI & THE KINGDOM OF SERBS, CROATS & SLOVENES

Josip Broz Tito was born in 1892 in Kumrovec, just over the Štajerska border in Croatia, to a Slovenian mother and a Croatian father.

Slovenian political parties generally tended to remain faithful to Austria-Hungary (as the empire was known from 1867). With the heavy loss of life and property destruction during WWI, however, especially along the Soča (or Isonzo) Front (p154), support grew for an autonomous democratic state within the Habsburg monarchy. With the defeat of Austria-Hungary and the dissolution of the Habsburg dynasty in 1918, Slovenes, Croats and Serbs banded together and declared the independent Kingdom of Serbs, Croats and Slovenes, under Serbian King Peter I. The Serbian statesman Stojan Protić became prime minister, and the conservative Slovene leader of the Clerical Party, Fr Anton Korošec, was named vice-premier.

The peace treaties after the war had given large amounts of Slovenian and Croatian territory to Italy (Primorska and Istria), Austria (Koroška) and Hungary (part of Prekmurje), and almost half a million Slovenes now lived outside the borders (some, like the Slovenes in Koroška, had voted to do so, however). The loss of more than a quarter of its population and a third of its land would remain the single most important issue facing Slovenia between the wars.

The kingdom was dominated by Serbian control, imperialistic pressure from Italy and the notion of Yugoslav unity. Slovenia was reduced to little more than a province in this centralist kingdom, although it did enjoy cultural and linguistic autonomy, and economic progress was rapid.

In 1929 Peter I's son King Alexander seized absolute power, abolished the constitution and proclaimed the Kingdom of Yugoslavia. But the king was assassinated five years later by a Macedonian terrorist in Marseilles during an official visit to France, and his cousin, Prince Paul, was named regent.

Neil Barnett's relatively slim (175 pages) biography *Tito*, an entertaining and timely read, offers a new assessment of the limits of holding a state like Yugoslavia together by sheer force of personality.

The political climate changed in Slovenia when the conservative Clerical Party joined the new centralist government of Milan Stojadinović in 1935, proving how hollow that party's calls for Slovenian autonomy had been. As a result, splinter groups began to seek closer contacts with the workers' movements. In 1937 the Communist Party of Slovenia (KPS) was formed under the tutelage of Josip Broz Tito (1892–1980) and the Communist Party of Yugoslavia (KPJ).

WWII & THE PARTISAN STRUGGLE

Yugoslavia managed to avoid getting involved in the war until March 1941 when Prince Paul, under pressure from Berlin and Rome, signed a treaty with the Axis powers. He was overthrown in a coup backed by the British, who installed King Paul II. Paul at first attempted neutrality, but German armies invaded and occupied Yugoslavia in April and the Yugoslav army capitulated in less than two weeks.

1945

Occupied Slovenia is liberated by the Partisans (May); 12,000 Domobranci and anti-communist civilians executed (June); Slovenia included in the Federal People's Republic of Yugoslavia (November)

1948

Yugoslavia distances itself from and then breaks with the Soviet union; isolation from the markets of the Soviet bloc force Tito to look to the West

1956

Tito, in association with other world leaders, notably India's first Prime Minister Jawaharlal Nehru and former president of Egypt Gamal Abdul Nasser, founds the Non-Aligned Movement

Slovenia was split up among Germany (Štajerska, Gorenjska and Koroška), Italy (Ljubljana, Primorska, Notranjska, Dolenjska and Bela Krajina) and Hungary (Prekmurje). To counter this, the Slovenian Communists and other left-wing groups formed a Liberation Front (Osvobodilne Fronte, or OF), and the people took up arms for the first time since the peasant uprisings. The OF, dedicated to the principles of a united Slovenia in a Yugoslav republic, joined the all-Yugoslav Partisan army of the KPJ and its secretary-general, Josip Tito. The Partisans received assistance from the Allies and were the most organised – and successful – of any resistance movement during WWII.

After Italy capitulated in 1943, the anti-OF Slovenian Domobranci (Home Guards) were active in Primorska and, in a bid to prevent the communists from gaining political control in liberated areas, began supporting the Germans.

Among the four dissidents arrested, tried by a military court and sentenced to prison in June 1988 was Janez Janša, Slovenia's prime minister from 2004 to 2008.

Despite this assistance and the support of the fascist Ustaša nationalists in Croatia and later the Četniks in Serbia, the Germans were forced to evacuate Belgrade in 1944. Slovenia was not totally liberated until May 1945.

The following month, as many as 12,000 Domobranci and anti-communist civilians were sent back to Slovenia from refugee camps in Austria by the British. Most of them were executed by the communists over the next two months, their bodies thrown into the caves at Kočevski Rog (p211) in Dolenjska.

POSTWAR DIVISION

Of immediate concern to Slovenia after the war was the status of the liberated areas along the Adriatic, especially Trieste. A peace treaty signed in Paris in 1947 put Trieste and its surrounds under Anglo-American administration (the so-called Zone A) and the Koper and Buje (Istria) areas under Yugoslav control in Zone B. In 1954 Zone A (with both its Italian and ethnic Slovenian populations) became the Italian province of Trieste. Koper and a 47km stretch of coast later went to Slovenia while the bulk of Istria went to Croatia. The Belvedere Treaty (1955) guaranteed Austria its 1938 borders, including most of Koroška.

TITO & SOCIALIST YUGOSLAVIA

Tito had been elected head of the assembly, providing for a federal republic in November 1943. He moved quickly after the war to consolidate his power under the communist banner. However, it soon became obvious that Slovenia's rights to self-determination and autonomy within the framework of a federal Yugoslavia would be limited beyond educational and cultural matters. Serbian domination from Belgrade would continue and in some respects be even more centralist than under the Kingdom of Yugoslavia.

1980

Josip Broz Tito, his direct involvement in domestic policy and governing somewhat diminished, dies at age 87, opening the floodgates that would lead to the dissolution of the federal republic in the next decade

1988

Arrest and sentencing of three journalists and a junior army officer for passing on 'military secrets' brings mass demonstrations throughout Slovenia; independent political parties are established for the first time in over four decades

1989

The May Declaration calls for a sovereign state for Slovenes based on democracy and respect for human rights; parliament amended the constitution to legalise management of its own resources and peacetime command of the armed forces

Tito distanced himself from the Soviet Union as early as 1948, but his efforts to create a communist state, with all the usual arrests, show trials, purges and gulags, continued into the mid-1950s. Industry was nationalised, private ownership of agricultural land limited to 20 hectares, and a planned central economy put in place.

But isolation from the markets of the Soviet bloc forced Tito to look to the West. Yugoslavia introduced features of a market economy, including workers' self-management. Economic reforms in the mid-1960s as well as relaxed police control and border controls brought greater prosperity and freedom of movement, but the Communist Party saw such democratisation as a threat to its power. A purge of the reformists in government was carried out in 1971–72, and many politicians and directors were pensioned off for their 'liberalism' and 'entrepreneurial thinking'. A new constitution in 1974 gave the Yugoslav republics more independence (and autonomy to the ethnic Albanian province of Kosovo in Serbia), but what were to become known as the 'leaden years' in Yugoslavia lasted throughout the 1970s until Tito's death in 1980. By that time, though, Slovenia was, economically, the most advanced republic in Yugoslavia.

CRISIS, RENEWAL & CHANGE

The recently updated *Slovenia and the Slovenes: A Small State and the New Europe* by James Gow and Cathie Carmichael offers excellent analysis not just of history and politics but of culture and the arts as well.

The economic decline in Yugoslavia in the early 1980s led to inter-ethnic conflict, especially between Serbs and ethnic Albanians in autonomous Kosovo. Serbia proposed scrapping elements of the 1974 constitution in favour of more state uniformity in economic and cultural areas. This, of course, was anathema to Slovenes, who felt threatened.

In 1987 the Ljubljana-based magazine *Nova Revija* published an article outlining a new Slovenian national program, which included political pluralism, democracy, a market economy and independence, possibly within a Yugoslav confederation. The new liberal leader of the Slovenian communists, Milan Kučan, did not oppose the demands, and opposition parties began to emerge. The de facto head of the central government in Belgrade, Serbian communist leader Slobodan Milošević, resolved to put pressure on Slovenia.

In June 1988 three Slovenian journalists, including the former prime minister, Janez Janša, working for the weekly *Mladina* (Youth) and a junior army officer who had given away 'military secrets' were tried by a military court and sentenced to prison. Mass demonstrations were held throughout the country in protest.

In the autumn, Serbia unilaterally scrapped the autonomy of Kosovo (where 80% of the population is ethnically Albanian). Slovenes were shocked by the move, fearing the same could happen to them. A rally organised jointly by the Slovenian government and the opposition in Ljubljana early in the new year condemned the move.

1990	June/July 1991	October 1991
Slovenian electorate overwhelmingly votes for an independent republic to go into effect within six months; Belgrade brands the action secessionist and anticonstitutional and raids the state coffers of US$2 billion	Fighting erupts when the Yugoslav army marches on Slovenia and meets resistance from the Territorial Defence Forces; the war lasts 10 days and leaves 66 people dead	Keeping its promise it would withdraw the federal army from Slovenia within three months, the last soldiers of the Yugoslav Army quit Slovenian territory

In the spring of 1989 the new opposition parties published the May Declaration, demanding a sovereign state for Slovenes based on democracy and respect for human rights. In September the Slovenian parliament amended the constitution to legalise management of its own resources and peacetime command of the armed forces. Serbia announced plans to hold a 'meeting of truth' in Ljubljana on its intentions. When Slovenia banned it, Serbia and all the other republics except Croatia announced an economic boycott of Slovenia, cutting off 25% of its exports. In January 1990, Slovenian delegates walked out on a congress of the Communist Party, thereby sounding the death knell of the party.

INDEPENDENCE

In April 1990, Slovenia became the first Yugoslav republic to hold free elections. Demos, a coalition of seven opposition parties, won 55% of the vote, and Kučan, head of what was now called the Party of Democratic Renewal, was elected 'president of the presidency'. The leader of the Christian Democrats, Lojze Peterle, became prime minister.

In the summer, after Serbia had rejected the Slovenian and Croatian proposals for a confederation and threatened to declare a state of emergency, the Slovenian parliament adopted a 'declaration on the sovereignty of the state of Slovenia'. Henceforth Slovenia's own constitution would direct its political, economic and judicial systems; federal laws would apply only if they were not in contradiction to it. A referendum on the question of independence was scheduled for just before Christmas.

France Štiglic's 1955 film *Dolina Miru* (Valley of Peace) is the bitter-sweet story of two children, an ethnic German boy and a Slovenian girl, trying to find a haven during the tumult of WWII.

On 23 December 1990, 88.5% of the Slovenian electorate voted for an independent republic – effective within six months. The presidency of the Yugoslav Federation in Belgrade labelled the move secessionist and anticonstitutional. Serbia then proceeded to raid the Yugoslav monetary system and misappropriated almost the entire monetary issue planned for Yugoslavia in 1991 – US$2 billion. Seeing the writing on the wall, the Slovenian government began stockpiling weapons, and on 25 June 1991 Slovenia pulled out of the Yugoslav Federation for good. 'This evening dreams are allowed', President Kučan told a jubilant crowd in Ljubljana's Kongresni trg the following evening. 'Tomorrow is a new day.'

Indeed it was. On 27 June the Yugoslav army began marching on Slovenia but met resistance from the Territorial Defence Forces, the police and the general population. Within several days, units of the federal army began disintegrating; Belgrade threatened aerial bombardment and Slovenia faced the prospect of total war.

The military action had not come totally unprovoked. To dramatise their bid for independence and to generate support from a less than sympathetic West, which wanted to see Yugoslavia continue to exist in some form or

1992

The EC formally recognises Slovenia; Slovenia is admitted into the United Nations as the 176th member-state while rump Yugoslavia's application for admission as the Federal Republic of Yugoslavia (Serbia and Montenegro) is rejected

1995

A primitive bone flute discovered in a cave at Divje Babe near Cerknica in Primorska and dating back some 35,000 years is thought to be the world's oldest known musical instrument

2004

Slovenia becomes the first transition country to graduate from borrower status to donor partner at the World Bank (Mar); Slovenia enters the EU as a full member along with nine other countries another, Slovenian leaders had baited Belgrade by attempting to take control of the border crossings first. Belgrade apparently never expected Slovenia to resist, believing that a show of force would be sufficient for it to back down.

As no territorial claims or minority issues were involved, the Yugoslav government agreed on 7 July to a truce brokered by leaders of what was then called the European Community (EC). Under the so-called Brioni Declaration, Slovenia would put further moves to assert its independence on hold for three months provided it was granted recognition by the EC after that time. The war had lasted just 10 days and taken the lives of 66 people.

THE ROAD TO EUROPE

Arguably the most comprehensive history of Slovenia is *The Land Between: A History of Slovenia* (ed Oto Luthar), the story of the nation from earliest times to entry into the EU in essays by nine noted historians.

To everyone's surprise, Belgrade announced that it would withdraw the federal army from Slovenian soil within three months, and did so on 25 October 1991, less than a month after Slovenia introduced scrip of its own new currency – the tolar. In late December, Slovenia got a new constitution that provided for a parliamentary system of government. The National Assembly (Državni Zbor), the highest legislative authority, today consists of 90 deputies elected for four years by proportional representation; two of the deputies represent the Italian and Hungarian ethnic communities. The 40 members of the National Council (Državni Svet), which performs an advisory role, are elected for five-year terms by social, economic, professional and special-interest groups. The head of state, the president, is elected directly for a maximum of two five-year terms. Milan Kučan, arguably the nation's most popular and respected politician to date, held that role from independence until 2002 when the late Janez Drnovšek (1950–2008), a former prime minister, was elected. Diplomat Danilo Türk has held the title since 2007. Executive power is vested in the prime minister and his ministers. The current premier is Borut Pahor, who was able to form a coalition with two centre-left minority parties following national elections in November 2008 that ousted incumbent Janez Janša. The judicial system consists of a supreme court, four high courts that serve as appeals courts, 11 circuit courts and 44 district courts.

The EC formally recognised Slovenia on 15 January 1992, and it was admitted to the UN four months later as the 176th member-state. Slovenia began negotiations for entry into the European Union (EU) in 1998 and, along with nine other countries, was invited to make preparations for joining four years later. In a referendum held in March 2003, 89.6% of the electorate voted in favour of Slovenia becoming a member of the EU, while 66% were in favour of joining NATO.

In March 2004, Slovenia became the first transition country to graduate from borrower status to donor partner at the World Bank and in May of that year entered the EU as a full member. In January 2007, Slovenia became the first of the 10 new EU states to adopt the euro, replacing the tolar as the national currency. In its most prestigious and high-profile role to date, Slovenia assumed the presidency of the EU Council in the first half of 2008.

January 2007

Slovenia becomes the first of the 10 new EU states to adopt the euro in place of the tolar; it is its fourth currency (Yugoslav dinar, tolar scrip, tolar, euro) since achieving independence

November 2007

Danilo Türk is elected Slovenia's third president, following in the footsteps of Milan Kučan (1991–2002) and Janez Drnovšek (2002–07), who dies of cancer just months after leaving office

2008

In its most prestigious and high-profile role to date, Slovenia assumes the presidency of the EU Council in the first half of 2008 and is followed by France

The Culture

THE NATIONAL PSYCHE

Slovenes are a sophisticated and well-educated people. They have a reputation for being sober-minded, hard-working, dependable and honest – perhaps a result of all those years under the yoke of the Germanic Habsburgs. But they retain something of their Slavic character, even if their spontaneity is a little more premeditated and their expressions of passion a little more muted than that of their Balkan neighbours. Think quietly conservative, deeply self-confident, broadminded and tolerant. And mostly happy. A Slovenian friend once said: 'We have everything here that we need.' He's right – in a myriad of ways.

If you really want to understand Slovenes and *Sloventsvo* ('Slovene-ness'), there are two Slovenian words that you should know. The first is the adjective *priden,* variously defined as 'diligent', 'industrious', 'hardworking' and – tellingly – 'wellbehaved'. Erica Johnson Debeljak (p40), in her seminal (though unpublished in English) *And the Distance Smells of Apples: A Story of Migration,* a precursor to her memoir *Forbidden Bread* (p18) claims that *priden* 'comes close to defining the essence of the Slovenian soul'. Doing a spot of DIY, neighbour? How *priden* of you! Expecting that second child, you two? Aren't we *pridni*!

An excellent source for all things cultural in Slovenia is the website of Slovenia Cultural Profile (www.culturalprofiles.net/slovenia) regularly updated by the Slovenian Ministry of Culture in association with the British Council.

The second word is the noun *hrepenenje,* which expresses a more complicated concept. The dictionary says it means 'longing' or 'yearning' but that's only half the story. In truth, it's the desire for something seemingly unattainable and the sorrow that accompanies it. '*Hrepenenje* is the exclusive property of the dispossessed,' writes Johnson Debeljak, citing 'the country's agonising history of border changes, emigration, alienation and powerlessness within a larger unit.' The medieval tale *Lepa Vida* (p43) can be seen as the very embodiment of this 'melancholy yearning'.

Slovenes are gifted polyglots, and almost everyone speaks some English, German and/or Italian. The fact that you will rarely have difficulty in making yourself understood and will probably never 'need' Slovene shouldn't stop you from learning a few phrases of this rich and wonderful language (which counts as many as three dozen dialects and boasts not just singular and plural but the 'dual' number in which things are counted in twos in all cases). Any effort on your part to speak the local tongue (p305) will be rewarded 100-fold. *Srečno* (Good luck)!

LIFESTYLE

The population of Slovenia is divided almost exactly in half, between those who live in towns and cities and those who live in the country. But in Slovenia, where most urban dwellers still have some connection with the countryside – whether it's a village house or a *zidanica,* a cottage in one of the wine-growing regions, the division is not all that great. And with the arrival of large malls on the outskirts of the biggest cities and a Mercator supermarket in virtually every village in the land, the city has come to the country in Slovenia.

The French novelist Charles Nodier (1780–1844), who lived and worked in Ljubljana from 1811 to 1813, called Slovenia 'an Academy of Arts and Sciences' because of the people's flair for speaking foreign languages.

Most Slovenes believe that the essence of their national character lies in nature's bounty. For them a life that is not in some way connected to the countryside is inconceivable. At weekends many seek the great outdoors for some walking in the hills or cross-country skiing (see p63). Or at least a spot of gardening, which is a favourite pastime.

With farmhouse stays (p281) a popular form of accommodation in Slovenia, it's relatively easy to take a peek inside a local home. What you'll see generally won't differ too much from what you'd see elsewhere in Central

ERICA JOHNSON DEBELJAK

Erica Johnson was working as a credit analyst on Wall St in 1991 when she met her future husband, the Slovenian poet Aleš Debeljak (p44). The couple moved to Ljubljana two years later where they started a family and Erica reinvented herself as a writer. Her memoir *Forbidden Bread* has just been published by North Atlantic Books. Visit her at www.ericajohnsondebeljak.com.

Slovenia in the early 1990s = terra incognita. Scary? I did have doubts about moving here, but it had nothing to do with the war in Yugoslavia. My big fear was not working as I was such a workaholic. And there were all these larger-than-life literary types and macho dissident writers who drank and womanised. I thought I'd be home with my tail between my legs in six months.

No room in the inn for a foreigner number cruncher in the Lj of 1993? I wasn't allowed to work, even after I married Aleš – it was that bureaucratic. I studied the language and one day the editor of (national daily newspaper) *Delo* suggested I write something so I began a series of commentaries on life here. I had never dreamed of becoming a writer before then.

And the pieces were well received locally? Slovenes are always interested in what you think of them and here I was, this exotic bird, commenting on their culture. But I did it in a quirky way that wasn't insulting or patronising, gently making fun of their idiosyncrasies like their habit of wearing only slippers indoors and their fear of drafts. The bumbling but big-hearted foreigner... *Delo* told me my articles were the most photocopied ever from its archives.

From mimeograph to memoir? My articles were collected as *Foreigner in the House of Natives* and published locally in Slovene in 1999. I then rewrote the manuscript almost immediately for the international market as *And the Distance Smells of Apples: A Story of Migration* (p39) but it was never published. In *Forbidden Bread* I dropped a lot of the cultural and anthropological details and approached the subject in a more novelistic and popular way.

You say 'forbidden bread' and I say 'forbidden fruit'. The title of the book comes from a Slovenian saying that 'you always eat the bread you've forbidden yourself.' Forbidden fruit is what the gods don't want you to eat. Forbidden bread is your own prohibition. Aleš said this about foreign girls.

To paraphrase American humorist Will Rogers, I've never met a Slovene I didn't like. Discuss. Slovenes are charming and helpful and anger, especially in public, is never a problem here. But there is a dark and somewhat negative self-regard that can be ponderous. 'We're too small, that's our problem' and so on gets tiresome. And I am dissatisfied with our politicians and government. I've just written a '15-years-on' article along these lines. It's a kind of condemnation.

So the thrill is gone, the love affair over? Whatever criticism I have of Slovenia I always say that it gave me everything I cherish – a husband and three children and a career I really love.

When I'm on the town, find me at... The open-air market (p95), Paninoteka (p95), the Opera Bar (p97), for the vibe (but not the incongruous Australian decor).

and Western Europe, though you may be surprised at the dearth of children Slovenes don't have many kids – the nation has one of Europe's lowest rates of natural population increase (8.97 live births per 1000 population, with a natural increase in the population of slightly over 0.1%) – and women usually give birth on the late side (average age: 28). Most families tend to have just one child and if they have a second one it's usually a decade later.

ECONOMY

A largely heterogeneous and highly adaptable economy and a very hard-working people have always been central to Slovenia's prosperity. The country's accession with nine other nations to the EU in 2004 also opened up a vast market for the country's goods. Slovenia was the first of these 10 nations to be able to adopt the euro as its national currency, when its average annual inflation rate had dropped to just 2.5%. That has now jumped to almost 6%, both as a result of pricing in the new euro and the effects of the so-called credit crunch of late 2009. Overall unemployment remains relatively high at 6.7%

While Slovenia has been a model of economic success and enjoys the highest standard of living among the former socialist countries of Eastern and Central Europe, the picture is not all rosy. Much of the economy remains in state hands, foreign direct investment in Slovenia is one of the lowest in the EU on a per-capita basis and taxes remain relatively high. Ljubljana is responsible for as much as a quarter of the country's GDP due to the industry (pharmaceuticals, petrochemicals and food-processing), retailing, transport, telecommunications, and financial and other business services based in and around the capital. Tourism contributes just under 4% to GDP while agriculture accounts for only 2.5%.

POPULATION & MULTICULTURALISM

According to the most recent national census figures (2002), just over 83% of the population claims to be ethnic Slovene, descendants of the South Slavs who settled in what is now Slovenia from the 6th century AD.

'Others' and 'unknown ethnic origin', accounting for almost 17% of the population, include (in descending order) ethnic Serbs, Croats, Bosnians, Albanians, those who identify themselves simply as 'Muslims' and many citizens of former Yugoslav republics who 'lost' their nationality after independence for fear that Slovenia would not grant them citizenship. The status of many as noncitizens in Slovenia – the so-called *izbrisani,* or 'erased' – remains extremely controversial, and many Slovenes have very racist feelings about them.

The Italians (0.11% of the population) and Hungarians (0.32%) are considered indigenous minorities with rights protected under the constitution, and each group has a special deputy looking after their interests in parliament. According to the 2002 census, 3246 persons, mostly living in Prekmurje, defined themselves as Roma, although unofficial estimates put the total at between 7000 and 10,000.

Cleveland, Ohio, in the USA is the largest 'Slovenian' city outside Slovenia.

Ethnic Slovenes living outside the national borders number as many as 400,000, with the vast majority (almost 75%) in the USA and Canada. In addition, 50,000 or more Slovenes live in the Italian regions of Gorizia (Gorica), Udine (Videm) and Trieste (Trst), another 15,000 in Austrian Carinthia (Kärnten in German, Koroška in Slovene) and 5000 in southwest Hungary.

SPORT

Slovenia – a land where *smučanje* (skiing) is king – has produced many world-class ski champions, including Roman Perko in cross-country racing, Mitja Dragšič in men's slalom and Špela Pretnar in women's slalom. But the national heroes in recent years have been Primož Peterka, the ski-jumping World Cup winner in 1996–97 and 1997–98, extreme skier Davo Karničar, who made the first uninterrupted descent of Mt Everest on skis in 2000, Rok Benkovič, who took gold at the Nordic Ski World Championship at Oberstdorf in Germany in 2005 and, most recently, Petra Majdič who in 2006 was the first Slovenian skier to win a medal in a World Cup cross-country race and has gone on to collect 14 more.

Until not so long ago Slovenia was one of the few countries in Europe where *nogomet* (football) was not a national passion, but interest in the sport increased following the national team's plucky performance in the 2000 European Championship, and again two years later when they qualified for the 2002 World Cup by defeating Romania in a playoff. In the 2006 FIFA World Cup qualifiers, Slovenia beat Moldova 3-0 at Sportni Park stadium in Celje, and a shock 1-0 success against favourites Italy propelled them to the top spot in their group. But they failed to qualify. In a qualifying match for the 2010 World Cup in November 2009,

For the latest on Union Olimpija and Slovenian basketball see the website Slovenian www.eurobasket.com/slo/slo.asp.

Slovenia beat Russia at home in Maribor 1-0 and the national team started packing its bag for South Africa, its second appearance at a World Cup since independence.

There are 10 teams in the First Division (Prva Liga), with Maribor, Domžale and HIT Gorica of Nova Gorica consistently at the top of the league.

In general *kosarka* (basketball) is the most popular team sport here, and the Union Olimpija team reigns supreme. Other popular spectator sports are *hokej na ledu* (ice hockey) and *odbojka* (volleyball).

Slovenia punches well above its weight when it comes to winning Olympic medals. At the 2008 Olympic Games in Beijing, Slovenia took gold in the men's hammer throw, two silver medals (women's 200m freestyle swimming and laser sailing) and a bronze each in women's judo and men's 50m rifle shooting. The Slovenian ski-jumping team took a bronze medal at the 2002 Winter Olympics in Salt Lake City, but no medals came back to Slovenia from the winter games in Turin in 2006

Some 3500 sport societies and clubs count a total membership of 400,000 – 20% of the population – across the nation.

MEDIA

Slovenia counts a half-dozen daily newspapers (total circulation 350,000), the most widely read being the tabloid *Slovenske Novice* (Slovenian News) followed by the more established *Delo* (Work), *Dnevnik* (Daily) and *Večer* (Evening). Some 45 weeklies, fortnightlies and monthlies cover topics as diverse as agriculture, finance and women's fashion. *Mladina* (Youth) is a liberal and very influential weekly covering political and social issues.

Radiotelevizija Slovenija (or RTV SLO for short) incorporates both radio and TV. Radio Slovenija has three national channels (Radio A, Val 202 Slovenija and Radio ARS), two regional ones in Maribor and Koper, and special programs for the Hungarian minority (Radio MMR) in Lendava the Italian one (Radio Koper-Capodistria) in Koper.

RTV SLO broadcasts on three channels: SLO 1, which has everything from children's programs to news and films; SLO 2, which shows mostly sporting events; and SLO 3, which mostly broadcasts parliamentary sessions. A subsidiary called TV Koper-Capodistria broadcasts in Italian on the coast, and there is a regional station in Maribor. The two largest commercial stations – Pop-TV and Kanal A – are American-owned and often show films and other programs in English with Slovene subtitles.

RELIGION

Although Protestantism gained a very strong foothold in Slovenia in the 16th century, the majority of Slovenes – just under 58% – identified themselves as Roman Catholic in the most recent (2002) census. The archbishop of Ljubljana and primate of Slovenia is Alojz Uran. Maribor is now also an archbishopric and there are bishoprics at Koper, Celje, Novo Mesto and Murska Sobota.

Other religious communities in Slovenia include Muslims (2.4%), Eastern Orthodox Christians (2.3%) and Protestants (1%). Most Protestants belong to the Evangelical (Lutheran) church based in Murska Sobota in Prekmurje. Slovenia's first mosque will be built in the Vič district of southwest Ljubljana.

Jews have played a very minor role in Slovenia since they were first banished from the territory in the 15th century. In 2003 the tiny Jewish community of Slovenia (www.jewishcommunity.si) received a Torah at a newly equipped temporary synagogue in Ljubljana, the first since before WWII. The chief rabbi of Slovenia is based in Trieste.

WOMEN IN SLOVENIA

Women enjoy equal status with men under Slovenian law but, despite all the work done to eliminate discrimination against them bias remains. The share of women in government is low: at present just 12% of MPs are women and only three government departments have a female at the helm. It's a little better in business, with about 20% of directorial posts filled by women.

ARTS

Literature

Slovenia is a highly educated society with a literacy rate of virtually 100% among those older than 15 years of age. Indeed, being able to read and write is ingrained in the culture. 'What is your surname?' in Slovene is '*Kako se pišete?*' or 'How do you write yourself?'

Maja Weiss's *Varuh Meje* (Guardians of the Frontier, 2002), the first Slovenian feature film directed by a woman, follows three young college women who take a perilous canoe journey down the Kolpa River, crossing national, political and sexual boundaries.

The oldest example of written Slovene (or any Slavic language for that matter) can be found in the three so-called *Freising Manuscripts* (Brižinski spomeniki) from around AD 970. They contain a sermon on sin and penance and instructions for general confession. Oral poetry, such as the seminal *Lepa Vida* (Fair Vida), a tale of longing, homesickness and nostalgia, flourished throughout the Middle Ages, but it was the Reformation that saw the first book in Slovene, a catechism published by Primož Trubar in 1550. A complete translation of the Bible by Jurij Dalmatin followed in 1584, and in the same year Adam Bohorič published a grammar of Slovene in Latin, with the evocative title *Spare Winter Hours*. Almost everything else published until the late 18th century was in Latin or German, including Janez Vajkard Valvasor's ambitious account of Slovenia, *The Glory of the Duchy of Carniola* (1689), from which most of our knowledge of Slovenian history, geography, culture and folklore before the 17th century comes. Not only did Valvasor (1641–93) map huge areas of Carniola and its towns for the first time, he also explained the mystery of disappearing karst lakes and rivers, discovered the unusual amphibian *Proteus anguinus*, introduced the world to Erazem Lueger, the 15th-century Robin Hood of Slovenia, and catalogued early Slovenian folk tales and dress. *Die Ehre des Herzogthums Crain* (as it was called in German) ran into four volumes, containing 3500 pages with 535 maps and copper engravings.

The Enlightenment and the reforms carried out under Habsburg rulers Maria Theresa and Joseph II raised the educational and general cultural level of the Slovenian nation. In large part due to the support and philanthropy of Baron Žiga Zois (1747–1819), Slovenia gained its first dramatist (Anton Tomaž Linhart), poet (Valentin Vodnik) and modern grammarian (Jernej Kopitar) at this time. But it was during the so-called National Romantic Period that Slovenian literature truly came of age and gained its greatest poet of all times: France Prešeren (p44). Although many influential writers published at this time, including his friends and associates Matija Čop and Andrej Smole, no one so dominated the period as Prešeren. His bittersweet verse, progressive ideas, demands for political freedom and longings for the unity of all Slovenes caught the imagination of the nation and simply has never let it go.

Valvasor's explanation of how the water system in Lake Cerknica worked earned him membership in 1688 in the Royal Society in London, the world's foremost scientific institution at the time.

In the latter half of the 19th century, Fran Levstik (1831–87) brought the writing and interpretation of oral folk tales to new heights with his *Martin Krpan*, legends about the eponymous, larger-than-life (literally) hero of the Bloke Plateau in Notranjska. But it was Josip Jurčič (1844–81) who published the first full-length novel in Slovene, *Deseti Brat* (The 10th Brother, 1866).

The period from the turn of the 20th century up to WWII is dominated by two men who single-handedly introduced modernism into Slovenian literature: the poet Oton Župančič (1878–1949) and the novelist and

FRANCE PREŠEREN: A POET FOR THE NATION

Slovenia's most beloved poet was born in Vrba near Bled in 1800 and educated in Ribnica, Ljubljana and Vienna, where he received a law degree in 1828. Most of his working life was spent as an articled clerk in the office of a Ljubljana lawyer. By the time he had opened his own practice in Kranj in 1846 he was already a sick and dispirited man. He died three years later.

Although Prešeren published only one volume of poetry in his lifetime (*Poezije*, 1848), which sold a mere 30 copies, he left behind a legacy of work printed in the literary magazines *Kranjska Čbelica* (Carniolan Bee) and the German-language *Illyrisches Blatt* (Illyrian Sheet). His verse set new standards for Slovenian poetry at a time when German was the literary *lingua franca*, and his lyric poems, such as the masterpiece 'Sonetni Venec' (A Garland of Sonnets, 1834), are among the most sensitive, original and eloquent works in Slovene. In later poems, such as his epic 'Krst pri Savici' (Baptism by the Savica Waterfall, 1836), he expressed a national consciousness that he tried to instil in his compatriots.

Prešeren's life was one of sorrow and disappointment, which he met with stoicism and resignation. The sudden death of his close friend and mentor, the literary historian Matija Čop, in 1835 and an unrequited love affair with an heiress called Julija Primic brought him close to suicide. But this was when he produced his best poems.

In reality, Prešeren was a drunkard, a philanderer, a social outcast and maybe even a tad vain. He refused to have his portrait done and any likeness you see of him was done from memory after his death. But Prešeren was the first to demonstrate the full literary potential of the Slovenian language, and his body of verse – lyric poems, epics, satire, narrative verse – has inspired Slovenes at home and abroad for generations.

playwright Ivan Cankar (1876–1918). The latter has been called 'the outstanding master of Slovenian prose'. His works, notably *Hiša Marije Pomočnice* (The Ward of Our Lady of Mercy, 1904) and *Hlapec Jernej in Njegova Pravica* (The Bailiff Yerney and His Rights, 1907), influenced a generation of young writers.

Slovenian literature immediately before and after WWII was influenced by socialist realism and the Partisan struggle as exemplified by the novels of Lovro Kuhar-Prežihov Voranc (1893–1950). Since then, however, Slovenia has tended to follow Western European trends: late expressionism, symbolism (poetry by Edvard Kocbek, 1904–81) and existentialism (novels by Vitomil Zupan, 1914–87, and the drama of Gregor Strniša 1930–87).

Slovenia is the third-smallest literature market in Europe (a fiction 'bestseller' means 500 to 800 copies sold) and only the Danes borrow more library books than the Slovenes (average 10 books per person per year).

The major figures of Slovenian post-modernism since 1980 are the novelist Drago Jančar (1948–) and the poet Tomaž Šalamun (1941–). Important writers born around 1960 include the poet Aleš Debeljak (1961–) and the writer Andrej Blatnik (1963–). A personal favourite is Boris Pahor (1913–), a member of the Slovenian minority in Trieste whose books – including *Nekropola* (Pilgrim among the Shadows), a harrowing memoir of time spent in the Natzweiler-Struthof concentration camp at the end of WWII – are now being translated into English.

Young talent to watch out for includes Andrej E Skubic (1967–), whose 2004 novel *Fužinski Bluz* (Fužine Blues) is set in one of Ljubljana's less salubrious neighbourhoods on 13 June 2002, the day of the very first football match between independent Slovenia and Yugoslavia.

Visit www.preseren.net/ang for English translations of the works of national poet France Prešeren.

The *cause célèbre* of Slovenian letters at the moment is Goran Vojnovič (1980-), who won the coveted Kresnik Prize, the highest literary award for a novel in Slovene, in 2009 for his satirical *Čefurji Raus!*, roughly *Foreigners Out!* but *čefur* is a particularly pejorative term for those from the other former Yugoslav republics living in Slovenia. In what could only have boosted book sales, Vojnovič was arrested and questioned by police for a time over the content.

Music

As elsewhere in Central and Eastern Europe, music – especially the classical variety – is very important in Slovenia. There is a network of music schools at secondary level across the nation and attendance at concerts and recitals is high in cities and towns.

The conversion of the Slavs to Christianity from the 8th century brought the development of choral singing in churches and monasteries; the oldest Slovenian spiritual song dates from 1440. The most important composer in the late 16th century was Jacobus Gallus Carniola (1550–91), christened as Jakob Petelin, who wrote madrigals and choral songs as well as 20 sung masses.

The bilingual *Slovenian Folk Songs/Slovenske Ljudske Pesmi* (ed Marko Terseglav) is a good introduction to what was (and sometimes still is) sung up in them thar hills.

Baroque music had gone out of fashion by the time the Filharmonija was founded in Ljubljana in 1701, and classical forms from Italy had become all the rage. *Belin,* the first Slovenian opera, was written by Jakob Francisek Zupan in 1780, and Janez Novak composed classical music for a comedy written by Slovenia's first playwright, Anton Tomaž Linhart. The 19th-century Romantics such as Benjamin Ipavec, Fran Gerbič and Anton Foerster incorporated traditional Slovenian elements into their music as a way of expressing their nationalism. Perhaps Slovenia's best-known composer at this time was Hugo Wolf (1860–1903), born in Slovenj Gradec and celebrated for his *lieder*.

Slovenian music between the wars is best represented by the expressionist Marij Kogoj and the modernist Slavko Osterc Ensemble. Contemporary composers whose reputations go well beyond the borders of Slovenia include Primož Ramovš, Marjan Kozina, Lojze Lebič and the ultramodernist Vinko Globokar, who was born in France. Aldo Kumar has received awards for his theatre and film compositions; Milko Lazar is one of the more interesting

ANDREJ BLATNIK

Andrej Blatnik (www.andrejblatnik.com), who started his artistic career in the early 1980s playing bass guitar in a punk rock band, has published three novels and five collections of short stories, including *Menjave Kož,* translated into English as *Skinswaps* and available from Amazon. Here are some of his views:

Art in the previous regime 'Art was viewed as something high-class and intellectual. Punk rock brought art to street level in Slovenia.'

Censorship before independence 'By the 1980s things were very open here, even local communist cells were lenient. They'd call you in and say "It's OK if you think that, but do you have to write it?" The state was more interested then in what we were doing!'

Literature in Slovenia 'Literature has always had other duties in Slovenia beyond just art. Writers drew up early nationalist programs, the nation's constitution, they were the first to open up parts of our hidden history, putting the torture and the trials after WWII subtly in their novels. In a small country everything has a bigger effect, a greater echo. [Today] Literature has become more a personal task than one of team work. Once we used it to foster our identity and feed our pride. Now we have other successes and can rely on things like football. No one can rely on the previous experience of literature today.'

Themes in Slovenian writing 'Hrepenenje (p39), the desire for something uncertain perhaps linked with the lack of independence over the centuries, is very prominent in the work of Prešeren and Cankar. Urban themes are few and far between as there is no real city life as such here. Most people in Ljubljana are only first or second generation. There are exceptions [for example, Andrej E Skubic's Fužine Blues], with some young writers focusing on what is an increasingly multi-ethnic society. But most urban novels have been traditionally written abroad and end with the protagonist coming back to Slovenia and the countryside – usually to their mother's burial in the mud and the rain.'

Being a writer in Slovenia 'Between 60 to 70 novels are published a year and 200 books of poetry. There is some funding from the state and also a certain amount of prestige. You can make a living as a writer in Slovenia. State grants help as do public readings but it is a very, very modest living.'

composer-musicians to emerge in recent years. Opera buffs won't want to miss out on the chance to hear Marjana Lipovšek and Bernarda Fink, the country's foremost mezzo-sopranos. There are a total of five professional orchestras and two operas in Slovenia.

> The leader of celebrated punk band Laibach, Tomaž Hostnik, died tragically in 1982 when he hanged himself from a *kozolec*, the traditional Slovenian hayrack.

Popular music runs the gamut from Slovenian *chanson* (eg Vita Mavrič) and folk to jazz and mainstream polka best exemplified by the Avsenik Brothers Ensemble. However, it was punk music in the late 1970s and early 1980s that put Slovenia on the world stage. The most celebrated groups were Pankrti, Borghesia and especially Laibach, and they were imitated throughout Eastern Europe. Equally successful was Niet from the late '80s, who has recently begun touring again. The most popular rock band in Slovenia today remains Siddharta, still going strong after almost 15 years. The most popular solo musician is Magnifico (aka Robert Pešut), who combines Balkan, funk, pop and electronic music, to reasonable degrees of success. New talent to watch out for is the versatile musician and singer Neisha, the trio Eroika and the feel-good Eva Hren & Sladcore. A relatively new arrival is so-called turbo folk music: super-charged Balkan-style music slightly toned down for Slovenian ears.

FOLK MUSIC

Ljudska glasba (folk music) in Slovenia has developed independently from other forms of music over the centuries, and the collection and classification of children's songs, wedding marches and fables set to music began only in the National Romantic Period of the 19th century. Traditional folk instruments include the *frajtonarica* (button accordion), *cimbalom* (a stringed instrument not unlike a dulcimer played with sticks), *bisernica* (lute), *zvegla* (wooden cross flute), *okarina* (clay flute), *šurle* (Istrian double flute), *trstenke* (reed pipes), Jew's harp, *lončeni bajs* (earthenware bass), *berdo* (contrabass) and *brač* (eight-string guitar).

Folk-music performances are usually local affairs and are very popular in Dolenjska and especially Bela Krajina. Črnomelj and especially Adlešiči in Bela Krajina are centres of Slovenian folk music, and as many as 50 bands are active in the area.

> For a taster of turbo folk music, its sounds and sights and aficionados, check out the Atomik Harmonik (www.atomikharmonik.com) site.

There's also a folk-music revival in recent years. Listen for the groups Katice and Katalena, who play traditional Slovenian music with a modern twist, and Brina, Slovenia's Joni Mitchell. Terra Folk is the quintessential world-music band. Čompe plays music with very funny (and often poetic) lyrics. The band's name comes from a popular potato dish served in the Bovec area.

Architecture

Examples of Romanesque architecture can be found in many parts of Slovenia, including the churches at Stična Abbey in Dolenjska, at Muta and Dravograd in Koroška, and at Podsreda Castle in Štajerska.

Much of the Gothic architecture in Slovenia is of the late period; the earthquake of 1511 took care of many buildings erected before then (although both the Venetian Gothic Loggia and Praetorian Palace in Koper date back a century before). Renaissance architecture is mostly limited to civil buildings (eg town houses in Škofja Loka and Kranj, Brdo Castle in Gorenjska).

Italian-influenced baroque of the 17th and 18th centuries abounds in Slovenia, particularly in Ljubljana (eg the Ursuline Church of the Holy Trinity and the cathedral). Classicism prevailed in architecture here in the first half of the 19th century; the Kazina building in Ljubljana's Kongresni trg and the Tempel pavilion in Rogaška Slatina in Štajerska are good examples.

The turn of the 20th century was when the Secessionist (or art nouveau) architects Maks Fabiani and Ivan Vurnik began changing the face of Ljubljana (Miklošičev Park, the Prešeren monument, the Cooperative ank on Miklošičeva cesta) after the devastating earthquake of 1895. But o architect has had a greater impact on his city or nation than Jože Plečnik p86), a man who defies easy definition.

Postwar architecture is generally forgettable – Edvard Ravnikar's Trg Republike in Ljubljana is a blight on the national capital – but among the nost interesting contemporary architects working today are the team Rok Oman and Špela Videčnik, two of the so-called Six Pack of Slovenian archiects to emerge after independence who designed the extraordinary extension 2004) to the City Museum in Ljubljana

Architectural Guide to Ljubljana by Janez Koželj and Andrej Hrausky is a richly illustrated guide to 101 buildings and other features in the capital, with much emphasis on architect extraordinaire Jože Plečnik.

ainting & Sculpture

here are three dozen permanent art museums and galleries in Slovenia and undreds more temporary exhibition spaces, which will give you a rough dea of the role that visual arts play in the lives of many Slovenes.

Examples of Romanesque fine art are rare in Slovenia, surviving only in luminated manuscripts. Gothic painting and sculpture is another matter, owever, with excellent works at Ptujska Gora (the carved altar in the Church f the Virgin Mary), Bohinj (frescoes in the Church of St John the Baptist), nd Hrastovlje (Dance of Death wall painting at the Church of the Holy rinity). Important painters of this time were Johannes de Laibaco (John of jubljana), who decorated the Church of the Assumption in Muljava; Jernej f Loka, who worked mostly around Škofja Loka; and Johannes Aquila of adgona, who did the frescoes in the magnificent church at Martjanci.

For baroque sculpture, look at Jožef Straub's plague pillar in Maribor, he golden altar in the Church of the Annunciation at Crngrob or the vork of Francesco Robba in Ljubljana (Carniolan Rivers fountain now in he National Gallery). Fortunat Bergant, who painted the Stations of the Cross in the church at Stična Abbey, was a master of baroque painting.

Classicism prevailed in Slovenian art in the first half of the 19th century n the works of the painter Franc Kavčič, and the Romantic portraits and andscapes of Josip Tominc and Matevž Langus. Realism arrived in the econd half of the century in the work of such artists as Ivana Kobilca, urij Šubic and Anton Ažbe. The most important painters of that time, owever, were the impressionists Rihard Jakopič, Matija Jama, Ivan Grohar nd Matej Sternen, who exhibited together in Ljubljana in 1900.

The colourful tome *Craft Treasures of Slovenia* by leading ethnographer Janez Bogataj takes a close look at Slovenia's rich tradition of folk craft, with everything from ceramics and lace to woodcarving and painted beehive panels.

In the 20th century, the expressionist school of Božidar Jakac and the brothrs France and Tone Kralj gave way to the so-called Club of Independents the painters Zoran Mušič, Maksim Sedej and France Mihelič) and later the culptors Alojzij Gangl, Franc Berneker, Jakob Savinšek and Lojze Dolinar. he last two would later create 'masterpieces' of socialist realism under Tito vithout losing their credibility or (sometimes) their artistic sensibilities. avourite artists to emerge after WWII include Janez Bernik, Rudi Španzel nd, from Slovenj Gradec, Jože Tisnikar.

Since the 1980s postmodernist painting and sculpture has been more or ess dominated by the artists' cooperative Irwin, part of the wider multimedia roup Neue Slowenische Kunst (NSK). Among notable names are that of he artist Tadej Pogačar, sculptor Marjetica Potrč and video artists Marko eljhan and Marina Gržinič.

heatre & Dance

lovenian attendance of theatre productions was 1.029 million in 2007, vidence that this art form is a vital and popular discipline.

The exact birth date of Slovenian theatre is considered to be 28 December 789, when Anton Tomaž Linhart (1756–95), Slovenia's first playwright, taged the inaugural performance of his comedy *Županova Micka* (Micka, the

Mayor's Daughter). In 1867 a Dramatics Society was established in Ljubljan and a national theatre founded in 1892. Today Ljubljana and Maribor enjo a vibrant theatre scene and there are smaller theatres in such provincial citie as Novo Mesto, Kranj and Piran and. Experimental theatre, best exemplifie by Grejpfrut, which cooperates with the Ana Monro Theatre in Ljubljan in staging the Ana Desetnica International Festival of Street Theatre in lat June/early July. Recent award-winning dramas have been *Hodnik* (Th Corridor; 2003) by Matjaz Zupančič, Boštjan Tadel's *Anywhere Out of Th World* (2005) and *Nora Nora* By Evald Flisar (2004).

Much of Slovenian dance finds its origins in folk culture, and *ljudski ple* (folk dance) has a long tradition in Slovenia, including polkas, circle dance and Hungarian-style czardas. The first ballet group was established in 191 as part of the Slovene National Theatre, and a ballet school was set up. Th Ljubljana Ballet now performs at the Opera House and there's another com pany in Maribor. Avant-garde dance is best exemplified by Betontanc, a danc company established by Matjaž Pogrejc, which mixes live music and theatric elements – called 'physical theatre' – with some sharp political commen Other dancer-choreographers are Iztok Kovač and Matjaž Farič.

Cinema

The website of the Slovenian Film Fund (www.film-sklad.si) will tell you everything you need to know about films and filming in Slovenia.

Slovenia was never on the cutting edge of film-making as were some of th former Yugoslav republics (eg Croatia). However, it still managed to produc about a dozen full-length features annually, some of which – like Jože Gale' *Kekec* (1951) and France Štiglic's *Dolina Miru* (Valley of Peace, 1955) won international awards. Today that number has dropped to between fou and six a year.

Only two films were produced in Slovenia between the wars. In th 1950s Slovenian film tended to focus on subjects like the Partisan struggle eg Štiglic's *Na Svoji Zemlji* (On Our Own Land, 1948) and *Akcija* (Actio 1960) by Jane Kavčič – and life among the Slovenian bourgeoisie unde the Austro-Hungarian empire (eg Bojan Stupica's *Jara Gospoda* c Parvenus, 1953). The 1960s brought a new wave of modernism, best ex emplified by the work of the late Boštjan Hladnik (*Ples v Dežju* or Danc in the Rain, 1961) and Matjaž Klopčič (*Na Papirnatih Avionih* or O Wings of Paper, 1967).

What is now touted as the 'Spring of Slovenian Film' in the late 1990 was heralded by two films: *Ekspres, Ekspres* (Express, Express, 1997) b Igor Šterk, an award-winning 'railroad' film and farce, and *Autsajde* (Outsider, 1997) by Andrej Košak, about the love between a Slovenia girl and Bosnian 'outsider'.

The first film shot in Slovenia was a documentary called *V Kraljestvu Zlatoroga* (In the Realm of the Goldenhorn) in 1931.

Subsequent successes were: *Kruh in Mleko* (Bread & Milk, 2001), th tragic story of dysfunctional small-town family by Jan Cvitkovič; Saš Podgoršek's *Sladke Sanje* (Sweet Dreams, 2001), a coming-of-age piece se in 1970s Yugoslavia; and Damjan Kozole's *Rezerni Deli* (Spare Parts, 200 about the trafficking of illegal immigrants through Slovenia from Croati to Italy by a couple of embittered misfits living in the southern town Krško, site of the nation's only nuclear power plant. More recent (an much lighter) fare is Cvitkovič's *Odgrobadogroba* (Grave Hopping, 2006 an Oscar-nominated tragicomedy about a professional funeral speaker, an *Petelinji Zajtrk* (Rooster's Breakfast, 2007), a romance by Marko Naberšni set in Gornja Radgona on the Austrian border in northeast Slovenia.

ood & Drink

ittle Slovenia can boast an incredibly diverse cuisine, with as many as wo dozen different regional styles of cooking. Unfortunately, except for a ·w national favourites such as *žlikrofi* (stuffed pasta) from Idrija and *jota* hearty bean soup) from Istria or the Karst, and incredibly rich desserts like *ibanica* from Prekmurje and *kremna rezina* from Bled, you're not likely ɔ encounter many of these regional specialities on restaurant menus. This ; homecooking at its finest, and you should do everything within your harm-the-socks-off-them power to wangle an invitation to a Slovenian ome, where food is paramount.

There are several truisms concerning Slovenian cuisine. In general, it is lain and simple, pretty heavy and fairly meaty. And it is heavily influenced y its neighbours' cuisines. From Austria, there's sausage *(klobasa),* strudel *zavitek)* filled with fruit, nuts and/or curd cheese (*skuta*), and Wiener schnitel *(dunajski zrezek).* The ravioli-like *žlikrofi, njoki* (potato dumplings) and *ižota* (risotto) obviously have Italian origins, and Hungary has contributed *olaž* (goulash), *paprikaš* (piquant chicken or beef 'stew') and *palačinke* (thin ancakes filled with jam or nuts and topped with chocolate). From Croatia nd the rest of the Balkans have come such popular grills as *čevapčiči* (spicy ıeatballs of beef or pork) and *pljeskavica* (meat patties)

An excellent source is the Slovenian Tourism Board's free pamphlet *'aste Slovenia.*

Slovenian Cookery: Over 100 Classic Dishes by Slavko Adamlje is a practical illustrated guide to Slovenian cuisine.

TAPLES & SPECIALITIES

oup

1ost Slovenian meals start with *juha* (soup) – of which there are said to e a hundred different varieties – year-round but especially in winter. As a tarter, this is usually chicken or beef broth with little egg noodles (*kokošja* r *goveja juha z rezanci*). More substantial varieties include *jesprenj* (barley ɔup); *jota,* a very thick potage of beans, sauerkraut or sour turnip, someimes potatoes and smoked pork or sausage; and *obara,* a stew, often made vith chicken or veal.

1eat & Fish

'or most Slovenes, a meal is incomplete without *meso* (meat). The pig is ing in Slovenia and *svinjina* (pork) rules, though *teletina* (veal), *govedina* beef) and, in season, *divjačina* (game), such as *srna* (deer) and *fazan* pheasant), are also eaten. Indeed, even *konj* (horse) finds its way to the lovenian table. *Piščanec* (chicken) is not as common on a Slovenian menu s *puran* (turkey), while *gos* (goose), *jagnjetina* (lamb) and *koza* (goat) re rarely seen.

Some excellent prepared meats are *pršut,* air-dried, thinly sliced ham rom the Karst region that is related to Italian *prosciutto,* and *divjačinska alama* (salami made from game) popular in Gorenjska. Slovenes are big aters of *riba* (fish) and *morski sadež* (shellfish) even far from the coast. *'ostrv* (trout), particularly the variety from the Soča River, is superb.

It's the fiercely cold northeast wind in the Karst region called the *burja* that gives *pršut* its distinctive taste.

iroats

)istinctively Slovenian dishes are often served with *žganci,* groats made rom barley or corn but usually *ajda* (buckwheat). A real rib-sticker is *jdovi žganci z ocvirki,* a kind of dense buckwheat porridge with the saoury addition of *ocvirki* (pork crackling or scratchings).

TASTY TRAVEL

Slovenes eat something nobody else does: *polh* (dormouse or loir), a tree-dwelling nocturnal rodent not unlike a squirrel that grows to about 30cm long and sleeps through several months of the year. But unless you are in Notranjska, where it was once a staple, during the loir-hunting season (p21) in late September and have friends there, it's unlikely you'll get to taste this incredible edible varmint.

Like the French, Slovenes have a taste for horse flesh – literally – and are especially fond of *žrebe* (colt). They like the taste (it's sweeter than beef or mutton), the low fat and the deep, almost ruby-red colour. You can try it most easily as a burger at a fast-food outlet called Hot Horse (p95) in Ljubljana's Park Tivoli.

Dessert

Slovenian cuisine boasts several calorific desserts. *Potica*, a national institu tion, is a kind of nut roll (although it's often made with savoury fillings toc eaten after a meal or at teatime. *Prekmurska gibanica*, from Slovenia's easter most province, is a calorific concoction of pastry filled with poppy seed walnuts, apples and/or sultanas and cheese and topped with cream. *Blejsk kremna rezina* is a layer of vanilla custard topped with whipped cream an sandwiched neatly between two layers of flaky pastry.

DRINKS

Nonalcoholic Drinks

Taste Slovenia by Janez Bogataj is a richly illustrated tome that divides Slovenia into two-dozen culinary regions – from Haloze and Koroška to Soča and the Karst – and takes the reader along.

Most international brands of soft drinks are available in Slovenia, but *mir eralna voda* (mineral water) is the most popular libation for teetotallers i pubs and bars. *Sok* (juice) is more often than not boxed fruit drink wit added sugar.

Italian espresso is the type of *kava* (coffee) most commonly served and Illy the ubiquitous brand – but thick, sweet Turkish-style coffee i also popular, especially at home. If you don't want it too sweet, say: 'N *sladko, prosim*'.

Local people drink lots of *čaj* (tea) made from herbs, berries, blossom or leaves but seldom what they call 'Russian' (ie black) tea. It is still difficu to find black tea in the shops, so bring your own supply of tea bags if yo need that morning cuppa.

Alcoholic Drinks

You'll find more than 275 recipes from around Slovenia at www.kulinarika.net/english/cook.asp.

WINE

Vino (wine) has been made in what is now Slovenia since the arrival of th Celts in the 5th century BC, and many of the country's wines are of a ver high quality indeed. Unfortunately, most foreigners remember Slovenia wine – if at all – from the cheap bottles of unmemorable and dull white Lašl Rizling served at college parties; a trip to Slovenia will convince travellers tha the best wines stay at home. Be warned, though, that cheaper 'open win *(odprto vino)* sold by the decilitre (0.1L) in bars and restaurants are usuall rot-gut. For more detailed information, contact the **Wine Association of Sloveni** (Vinska Družba Slovenije; ☎ 01-244 18 00; www.vinskadruzba.si; Kongresni trg 14; 1000 Ljubljana).

Slovenia counts nine distinct wine-growing districts, though there a really just three major regions. Podravje (literally 'on the Drava'), encom passing the Prekmurje and Štajerska Slovenija (Slovenian Styria) district extends from northeast Štajerska into Prekmurje and produces whites almos exclusively, including Laški Rizling (welschriesling) and Renski Rizling (true German riesling), Beli Pinot (pinot blanc), Traminec (gewürtztraminer and Šipon (furmint).

Posavje is the region running from eastern Štajerska across the Sava River into Dolenjska and Bela Krajina and includes the Bizeljsko-Sremič, Dolenjska and Bela Krajina districts. This region produces both whites and reds, but its most famous wine is Cviček, a distinctly Slovenian dry light red – almost rosé – wine with a low (8.5% to 10%) alcohol content. Reds include ruby-red Metliška Črnina (Metlika black) and whites such as the sweet Rumeni Muškat (yellow muscatel).

The oldest vine in the world, planted more than four centuries ago and still producing grapes and wine, is in Maribor.

The Primorska wine region, which encompasses the districts of Slovenska Istra (Slovenia Istria), Kras (Karst), Vipavska Dolina (Vipava Valley) and the celebrated Goriška Brda (Gorica Hills), excels at reds, the most famous being teran, a ruby-red, peppery wine with high acidity made from Slovenian Refošk (Refosco) grapes in the Karst region. Other wines from this region are Malvazija (malvasia), a yellowish white from Slovenian Istria that is light and dry, and red merlots, especially the ones from the Vipava Valley and Goriška Brda.

On a Slovenian wine label, the first word usually identifies where the wine is from and the second the grape varietal: Vipavski merlot, Mariborski traminec etc. But this is not always the case, and some wines bear names according to their place of origin, such as Jeruzalemčan, Bizeljčan or Haložan.

You'll learn lots more about Slovenian viticulture, regions and wine labelling by visiting www.matkurja.com/projects/wine.

There is no *appellation contrôlée* as such in Slovenia; *zaščiteno geografsko poreklo* is a trademark protection that usually – although not in every instance – suggests a certain standard and guarantees provenance. Some 9% is designated *vrhunsko vino* (premium wine), 54% is *kakovostno vino* (quality wine) and 37% is *deželno vino* (regional wine), not dissimilar to French *vin du pays*. They can be red, white or rosé and dry, semidry, semisweet or sweet. Very roughly, anything costing more than about €6 in the shops is a serious bottle of Slovenian wine; pay more than €10 and you'll be getting something very fine indeed.

One excellent Slovenian sparkling wine that employs the demanding *méthode classique* is Zlata Radgonska Penina from Gornja Radgona in Slovenian Styria, which is based on chardonnay and Beli pinot. Another is Prestige Brut Nature from Janez Istenič's winery in Bizeljsko-Sremič is another. Kraška Penina, a sparkling Teran, is unique. Late-harvest dessert wines include Rumeni Muškat from Bela Krajina and Slovenian Istria.

A total of 22,500 hectares is under vine cultivation, producing an annual 80 to 100 million litres of wine of which 30% is red and 70% white.

Slovenes usually drink wine with meals or socially at home; it's not very common to see people sit down to a bottle at a café or pub. As elsewhere in Central Europe, a bottle or glass of mineral water is ordered along with the wine when eating. It's a different story in summer, when *brizganec* or *špricar* (spritzers or wine coolers) of red or white wine mixed with mineral water are consumed in vast quantities. Wine comes in 0.75L bottles or is ordered by the *deci* (decilitre, 0.1L). A normal glass of wine is about *dva deci* (0.2L), but no-one is going to blink an eye if you order three or more.

Most of the wine-producing districts have a *vinska cesta* (wine route) or two that you can follow in a car or on a bicycle. Many are outlined in the *Next*

A MATCH MADE IN HEAVEN

The pairing of food with wine is as great an obsession in Slovenia as it is in other wine-producing countries. Most people know that *pršut* with black olives and a glass of Teran is a match made in heaven, but what is less appreciated is the wonderful synergy other wines from the Karst – red Rebula, even white Malvazija – enjoy with these two foodstuffs. With heavier and/or spicier meat dishes such as goulash and salami, try Cviček. Malvazija, a yellowish white from the coast, is also good with fish, as is Laški Rizling. And with sweet food such as strudel and *potica,* it's got to be a glass of late-harvest Rumeni Muškat.

DUŠAN BREJC

Dušan Brejc, who has been studying, making, marketing and, of course, tasting wine for more than three decades and has been referred to as Mr Slovenian Wine, is director of the Ljubljana-based Wine Association of Slovenia (Vinska Družba Slovenije; www.vinskadruzba.si).

Whither Slovenian wine? When Slovenia joined the EU, imports outweighed exports for the first time. By 2006 imports were up by 1 million litres. Slovenes would still say their wines are the best in the world but they've responded to much cheaper mainly Italian, Spanish and French bottles available at hard-discount shops like Lidl and Aldi.

So much for the loyalty card at home. What can Slovenian wine do to get on the supermarket shelves abroad? In the wine world, we're a no-name country. I believe we have to start presenting ourselves in a different way, emphasising the generic. More Slovenia, less vineyards. Slovenia did have its glory days in the 1970s when Laški Rizling from Ljutomer accounted for 5% of white wine sales in the UK. Wine would be shipped from Štajerska, loaded at Koper and shipped directly to Ljutomer House in the Docklands.

What does a wine taster need beside indulgent taste buds? I take the aesthetic approach when it comes to most things and especially wine – pure intuition tells me what is good and what is not. Of course smells can get in the way. A bad smell for me is *really* bad and my nose was twitching on a recent trip to Corsica with all the *marquis* (scented herbal ground cover) in bloom. The first thing I realise I've missed about Slovenia when I step off the plane at Brnik is the deep smell of the forest.

How did it all start? Passed on from father to son? No, my father was a politician who was banished for organising trade unions in the Yugoslav kingdom, joined the Partisans during WWII and served as minister of culture and education under Tito. But wine was always served at Sunday lunch and even at the age of eight or nine I was allowed to taste it. Wine clearly had status at our family table.

So the moment we've been waiting for… What's your favourite Slovenian wine? I'm an insider, not a consumer. I'm too critical and could never name just one bottle of wine. I like red, I like white; I drink sparkling wine, I drink sweet white. I like beer and water but I never – *ever* – have soft drinks. If it's a *vin complet* I take the same approach whether it's a €2 bottle or one costing €200.

Aw, come on, don't let us copycats down. Name some houses. In Goriška Brda, Simčič has been around for several generations and is one of the best. Also very good is Ščurek known for some two decades and very consistent. But it's not just Primorska reds. In the last three years there's been much interest in the whites of the northeast – riesling from Marof, for example, and sauvignon blanc from Verus. In fact, sauvignon blanc has raised the profile of Slovenian wines in recent years and is now being compared to New Zealand's very best.

Exit series of six itineraries on maps produced by the STB and available free from tourist offices everywhere in Slovenia. Along the way, you can stop at the occasional *klet* (cellar) that offers wine tastings or at a *vinoteka* in wine towns. See individual chapters for details.

BEER

Pivo beer is very popular in Slovenia, especially outside the home and with younger people. Štajerska *hmelj* (hops) grown in the Savinja Valley are used locally, and are also widely sought by brewers from around the world. They have been described as having the flavour of lemon grass.

Slovenia has two major breweries: Union in Ljubljana, and Laško in the town of that name south of Celje. Union is lighter-tasting and sweeter than Zlatorog, the excellent and ubiquitous beer brewed by Laško, which also makes Laško Club. Union produces a nameless alcohol-free beer *(brezalkoholno pivo)*, a decent stout *(temno pivo)* and a low-alcohol (2.5%) shandy called Radler. Smile, also produced by Union, is usually consumed with a slice of lemon like Corona.

Laško also makes a light beer called Laško Light and a dark lager called, ppropriately enough, Laško Dark and Export pils. Its Bandidos throws in ther alcohols, including tequila and rum.

In a *pivnica* (pub), *točeno pivo* (draught beer) is ordered as a *veliko pivo* 'large beer'; 0.5L) or *malo pivo* ('small beer'; 0.3L). Both locally brewed and mported beers are also available at pubs, shops and supermarkets in 0.5L ottles or 0.3L cans.

The Wines of Slovenia by Julij Nemanič, which focuses on the top 60 producers in the country, is an excellent single source viticulture and wine in Slovenia.

PIRITS

n alcoholic drink as Slovenian as wine is *žganje*, a strong brandy or *eau le vie* distilled from a variety of fruits. Common types are *slivovka* (made vith plums), *češnjevec* (with cherries), *sadjevec* (with mixed fruit) and *brinevec* (with juniper). A favourite type is *medeno žganje* (or *medica*), which s fruit brandy flavoured with honey. One of the most unusual (if not the est) is Pleterska Hruška, a pear brandy (also called *viljamovka*) made by he Carthusian monks at the Pleterje monastery near Kostanjevica na Krki p220) in Dolenjska.

Some Slovenes enjoy a *špička* – slang for a little glass of schnapps – during he day as a pick-me-up. You'll probably receive the invitation '*Pridite na upico*' ('Come and have a drop') more than once.

ELEBRATIONS

t Easter there's always decorated Easter eggs and a ham cooked with erbs. And a Slovenian Christmas wouldn't be Christmas without a *potica* nut roll).

Although it's not a public holiday, St Martin's Day (11 November) is mportant, as on this day, the winemakers' *mošt* (must), which is essentially ermenting grape juice, officially becomes wine and can be sold as such. In he evening families traditionally dine on goose – the story goes that Martin id himself in a flock of geese when the faithful were looking for him to tell im he'd just been made a bishop – with *mlinci* (thin dried flatbread) and rink new wine, and some restaurants offer a special Martinovanje dinner ccompanied by folk music.

Štajerska's distinctive *bučno olje* (pumpkinseed oil) is not just an excellent condiment on salads but can also be poured over ice creams and sprinkled with green pumpkinseeds or cracked walnuts.

VHERE TO EAT & DRINK

Restaurants go by many names in Slovenia, but the distinctions are not ery clear. At the top of the heap, a *restavracija* is a restaurant where ou sit down and are served by a waiter. A *gostilna* or *gostišče* has waitrs too, but it's more like an inn, with rustic decor and usually (but not lways) traditional Slovenian dishes. A *samopostrežna restavracija* is a elf-service establishment where you order from a counter and carry our food on a tray. An *okrepčevalnica* and a *bife* serve simple fast food uch as grilled meats and sausages. A *krčma* may have snacks, but the mphasis here is on drinking (usually alcohol). A *slaščičarna* sells sweets nd ice cream whereas a *kavarna* provides coffee and pastries. A *mlečna estavracija* (milk bar) sells yogurt and other dairy products as well as *rofi* (jam-filled doughnuts).

Almost every sit-down restaurant in Slovenia has a menu with dishes transated into English, Italian, German and sometimes French and Russian. It's mportant to note the difference between *pripravljene jedi* or *gotova jedilna* ready-made dishes) such as goulash or stew that are just heated up and *jedi o naročilu* (dishes made to order). Lists of *danes priporočamo* or *nudimo* daily recommendations or suggestions) are frequently in Slovene only.

Many restaurants and inns have an inexpensive *dnevno kosilo* (set-lunch nenu). Three courses can cost as little as €6.

Of those polled, some 92.5% of Slovenes said that Slovenian wine is the best in the world (though the industry has lost a major share of the market to cheap EU imports over the last five years).

It's important to know that not many Slovenes eat in city-centre restau- rants, unless they have to because of work or because they happen to b entertaining after office hours. At the weekend, most will head 5km or 10kr out of town to a *gostilna* or *gostišče* that they know will serve them gooc home-cooked food and local wine at affordable prices.

Quick Eats

Mushroom picking is almost a national pastime in the hills and forests of Slovenia in summer and autumn.

The most popular street food in Slovenia is a Balkan import called *burek* flaky pastry sometimes stuffed with meat but more often cheese or even apple that is a cousin of Turkish *börek*. It's sold at outdoor stalls or kiosks and i very cheap and filling. Other cheap *malice* (snacks) available on the hoof ar *čevapčiči, pljeskavica* (spicy meat patties), *ražnjiči* (shish kebab) and pizz (which sometimes appears spelled in Slovene as *pica*).

VEGETARIANS & VEGANS

Slovenia is hardly a paradise for vegetarians, but there are a couple of meat free eateries in Ljubljana and you're sure to find a few meatless dishes o any menu. *Štruklji*, dumplings made with cheese and often flavoured wit chives or tarragon, are widely available, as are dishes like *gobova rižot* (mushroom risotto) and *ocvrti sir* (deep-fried cheese). Slovenes love fres *solata* (salad) – a most un-Slavic partiality – and you can get one anywher even in a countryside *gostilna*. In season (usually late summer and autumn the whole country indulges in *jurčki* (wild cep or Portobello mushrooms) in soups or salads or grilled.

EATING WITH KIDS

Although Slovenia has one of the lowest birth rates in the world and the vas majority of Slovenian families number just three people, Slovenes love childre and it is a very child-friendly country. The family goes everywhere together, an even the most sophisticated restaurants here welcome pint-sized diners.

HABITS & CUSTOMS

On the whole, Slovenians are not big eaters of breakfast *(zajtrk)*, preferring cup of coffee at home or on the way to work. Instead, many people eat a ligh meal *(malica)* at around 10.30am. Lunch *(kosilo)* is traditionally the mai meal in the countryside, and it's eaten at noon if *malica* has been skipped o much later – sometimes in the middle of the afternoon. Dinner *(večerja)* a supper, really – is less substantial when eaten at home, often just slice meats, cheese and salad.

SLOVENIA'S TOP SIX RESTAURANTS

Gostilna Lectar (p121) Arguably Gorenjska's best restaurant, the 'Gingerbread' serves enlightened Slovenian dishes amid authentic farmhouse decor.

Gostilna Lovenjak (p277) This *gostilna* and hotel just outside Murska Sobota serves Prekmurje specialities in traditional surrounds.

Gostilna Ribič (p248) The 'Angler' faces the Drava River in Ptuj and the speciality here is – not surprisingly – fish, especially trout.

Oštarija Debeluh (p224) We love 'Fatty's Inn' in Brevžice for the well-prepared exotica (colt carpaccio, anyone?) and the admirable all-Slovenian wine list.

Špajza (p92) The 'Pantry' is an oasis in Ljubljana's touristy Old Town, with wooden floors, frescoed ceilings, nostalgic bits and pieces and such excellent traditional dishes as oven-roasted kid.

Topli Val (p155) Our favourite 'destination' eatery in Primorska, the 'Warm Wave' in Kobarid serves superb Adriatic fish and seafood dishes and boasts an enviable wine card.

ORGANIC GROWTH

The number of organic farms in Slovenia has mushroomed over the past decade – from a mere 41 in 1998 to 1780 (or 5% of the total) in 2008. The farms raise and process everything from cereals, dairy products and meat to fruits and vegetables, oils, nuts and wine but the largest category remains grassland. Only products inspected and certified by the Ministry of Agriculture, Forestry and Food may bear the government's green-coloured *Ekološki* label or Biodar label of the Slovenian Organic Farmers' Association.

AT YOUR WORDS

'or pronunciation guidelines see p305.

ood Glossary

ASICS

elikatesa	de·lee·ka·*te*·sa	delicatessen
rana	*hra*·na	food
jca	*yai*·tsa	eggs
edilni list	ye·*deel*·nee list	menu
osilo	ko·*see*·lo	lunch
ozarec	ko·*za*·rets	glass
rožnik	*krozh*·neek	plate
ruh	krooh	bread
naslo	*mas*·lo	butter
nenu	me·*nee*	set menu
atakar/natakarica	na·*ta*·kar/na·*ta*·ka·ree·tsa	waiter/waitress
ož	nozh	knife
oper	*po*·per	pepper
estavracija	res·tav·*ra*·tsee·ya	restaurant
amopostrežna trgovina	sa·mo·pos·*trezh*·na tr·go·*vee*·na	grocery store
ir	seer	cheese
ladkor	*slad*·kor	sugar
ol	soh	salt
teklenica	stek·le·*nee*·tsa	bottle
opel/hladen	*to*·pel/*hla*·den	hot/cold
ržnica	*tuhrzh*·nee·tsa	market
ečerja	ve·*cher*·ya	dinner, supper
ilica	*vee*·lee·tsa	fork
inska karta	*veen*·ska *kar*·ta	wine list
/brez	z/brez	with/without
ajtrk	*zai*·tuhrk	breakfast
lica	*zhlee*·tsa	spoon

Diners at the same table wish one another *'Dober tek!'* (Bon appetit!) before starting a meal.

UHE (SOUPS)

ista juha	*chees*·ta *yoo*·ha	clear soup, bouillon
nevna juha	*dnev*·na *yoo*·ha	soup of the day
obova kremna juha	*go*·bo·va *krem*·na *yoo*·ha	creamed mushroom soup
oveja juha z rezanci	go·*ve*·dya *yoo*·ha s *re*·zan·tsee	beef broth with little egg noodles
rahova juha	*gra*·ho·va *yoo*·ha	pea soup
aradižnikova juha	pa·ra·*deezh*·nee·ko·va *yoo*·ha	tomato soup
režganka	prezh·*gan*·ka	toasted rye-flour soup thickened with cream
elenjavna juha	ze·le·*nyav*·na *yoo*·ha	vegetable soup

HLADNE ZAČETNE JEDI/HLADNE PREDJEDE (COLD STARTERS)

domača salama	do·*ma*·cha sa·*la*·ma	home-style salami
francoska solata	fran·*tzos*·ka so·*la*·ta	diced potatoes and vegetables with mayonnaise
kraški pršut z olivami	*krash*·kee puhr·*shoot* s o·*lee*·va·mee	air-dried Karst ham (prosciutt with salted black olives
narezek	na·*re*·zek	smoked cold meats
prekajena gnjat	pre·ka·*ye*·na gnyat	smoked ham
riba v marinadi	*ree*·ba v ma·ree·*na*·dee	marinated fish
šunka z hrenom	*shoon*·ka s *hre*·nom	smoked/boiled ham with horseradish

TOPLE ZAČETNE JEDI/TOPLE PREDJEDI (WARM STARTERS)

drobnjakovi štruklji	drob·*nya*·ko·vee *shtrook*·lyee	dumplings of cottage cheese and chives
ocvrti sir s tartarsko omako	ots·*vuhr*·tee seer s tar·*tar*·sko o·*ma*·ko	deep-fried cheese with tartar sauce
omlet z sirom/šunko	om·*let* s *see*·rom/*shoon*·ko	omelette with cheese/ham
rižoto z gobami	ree·*zho*·to s *go*·ba·mee	risotto with mushrooms
špageti po bolonjsko	shpa·*ge*·tee po bo·*lon'*·sko	spaghetti Bolognese
žlikrofi	*zhlee*·kro·fee	'ravioli' of cheese, bacon and chives

PRIPRAVLJENE JEDI/GOTOVA JEDILNA (READY-MADE DISHES)

bograč golaš	*bog*·rach *go*·lash	beef goulash served in a pot
jota	*yo*·ta	beans, sauerkraut and potatoes or barley cooked with pork in a pot
kuhana govedina z hrenom	*koo*·ha·na go·*ve*·dee·na s *hre*·nom	boiled beef with horseradish
kurja obara z ajdovimi žganci	*koor*·ya o·*ba*·ra s *ai*·do·vee·mee *zhgan*·tsee	chicken stew or 'gumbo' wit buckwheat groats
pečen piščanec	pe·*chen* peesh·*cha*·nets	roast chicken
prekajena svinjska rebrca z kislim zeljem	pre·ka·*ye*·na *sveen'*·ska *re*·buhr·tsa s *kees*·leem *ze*·lyem	smoked pork ribs with sauerkraut
ričet	*ree*·chet	barley stew with smoked por ribs
svinjska pečenka	*sveen'*·ska pe·*chen*·ka	roast pork

JEDI PO NAROČILU (DISHES MADE TO ORDER)

ciganska jetra	tsee·*gan*·ska *yet*·ra	liver Gypsy-style
čebulna bržola	che·*bool*·na buhr·*zho*·la	braised beef with onions
dunajski zrezek	*doo*·nai·skee *zre*·zek	Wiener schnitzel (breaded cutlet of veal or pork)
kmečka pojedina	*kmech*·ka po·*ye*·dee·na	'farmer's feast' of smoked meats and sauerkraut
kranjska klobasa z gorčico	*kran'*·ska klo·*ba*·sa s gor·*chee*·tso	Carniolan sausage with mustard
ljubljanski zrezek	lyoob·*lyan*·skee *zre*·zek	breaded cutlet with cheese
mešano meso na žaru	*me*·sha·no me·*so* na *zha*·roo	mixed grill
ocvrti piščanec	ots·*vuhr*·tee peesh·*cha*·nets	fried chicken
pariški zrezek	pa·*reesh*·kee *zre*·zek	veal cutlet fried in egg batter
puranov zrezek z šampinjoni	poo·*ra*·noh *zre*·zek s sham·pee·*nyo*·nee	turkey cutlet with white mushrooms

IBE (FISH)

rancin z maslom	*bran*·*tseen* s *mas*·lom	sea bass in butter
uhana/pečena postrv	*koo*·ha·na/pe·*che*·na pos·*tuhrv*	boiled/grilled trout
gnji/kalamari na žaru	*leeg*·nyee/ka·la·*ma*·ree na·*zha*·roo	grilled squid
orski sadež	*mor*·skee *sa*·dezh	shellfish
orski list v belem vinu	*mor*·skee leest v *be*·lem *vee*·noo	sole in white wine
cvrti oslič	ots·*vuhr*·tee *os*·leech	fried cod
rada na žaru	o·*ra*·da na *zha*·roo	grilled sea bream
ečene sardele	pe·*che*·ne sar·*de*·le	grilled sardines
bja plošča	*reeb*·ya *plosh*·cha	seafood plate
kampi na žaru	*shkam*·pee na *zha*·roo	grilled scampi (prawns)
koljke	*shkol'*·ke	clams

OLATE (SALADS)

učno olje	*booch*·no *o*·lye	pumpkinseed oil
žolova solata	fee·*zho*·lo·va so·*la*·ta	bean salad
isla rdeča pesa	*kees*·la *rde*·cha *pe*·sa	pickled beetroot (beets)
isle kumarice	*kees*·le *koo*·ma·ree·tse	pickled gherkins
umarična solata	*koo*·ma·reech·na so·*la*·ta	cucumber salad
aradižnikova solata	pa·ra·*deezh*·nee·ko·va so·*la*·ta	tomato salad
ezonska/mešana solata	se·*zon*·ska/*me*·sha·na so·*la*·ta	seasonal/mixed salad
rbska solata	*suhrb*·ska so·*la*·ta	'Serbian salad' of tomatoes and green peppers
elena solata	ze·*le*·na so·*la*·ta	lettuce salad
eljnata solata	*zel'*·na·ta so·*la*·ta	coleslaw

LADICE/SIRI (DESSERTS/CHEESES)

bolčni zavitek	*ya*·bol·chnee *zvee*·tek	apple strudel
rofi	*kro*·fee	jam-filled doughnuts
rehova potica	o·*re*·ho·va po·*tee*·tsa	Slovenian nut roll
alačinke z marmelado /orehi/čokolado	pa·la·*cheen*·ke z mar·me·*la*·do /o·*re*·hee/cho·ko·*la*·do	thin pancakes with marmalade/nuts/chocolate
rekmurska gibanica	*prek*·moor·ska *gee*·ba·nee·tsa	layered pastry with fruit, nut, cheese and poppyseed filling and cream
adna kupa	*sad*·na *koo*·pa	fruit salad with whipped cream
irova plošča	*see*·ro·va *plosh*·cha	cheese plate
ladoled	sla·do·*led*	ice cream
rta	*tor*·ta	cake

ALICE (SNACKS)

urek	*boo*·rek	pastry filled with meat, cheese or apple
evapčiči	che·*vap*·chee·chee	spicy meatballs of beef or pork
ica	*pee*·tsa	pizza
ljeskavica	*plyes*·ka·vee·tsa	spicy meat patties
omfrit	*pom*·freet	chips (french fries)
ažnjiči	*razh*·nyee·chee	shish kebab
roča hrenovka	*vro*·cha *hre*·nov·ka	hot dog

ESO & RIBA (MEAT & FISH)

ovedina	go·*ve*·dee·na	beef
iščanec	*peesh*·cha·nets	chicken

puran	poo·*ran*	turkey
svinjina	svee·*nyee*·na	pork
teletina	te·*le*·tee·na	veal

ZELENJAVA & PRILOGE (VEGETABLES & SIDE DISHES)

ajdovi/koruzni žganci	*ai*·do·vee/ko·*rooz*·nee *zhgan*·tsee	buckwheat/corn groats
bučke	*booch*·ke	squash or pumpkin
cvetača/karfijola	tsve·*ta*·cha/kar·fee·*yo*·la	cauliflower
grah	grah	peas
korenje	ko·*re*·nye	carrots
kruhovi cmoki	*kroo*·ho·vee *tsmo*·kee	bread dumplings
mlinci	*mleen*·tsee	pancakes
pire krompir	pee·*re* krom·*peer*	mashed potatoes
pražen krompir	*pra*·zhen krom·*peer*	fried potatoes
riž	reezh	rice
stročji fižol	*stroch*·yee fee·*zhoh*	string beans
špinača	shpee·*na*·cha	spinach
testenine	tes·te·*nee*·ne	pasta

SADJE (FRUIT)

ananas	*a*·na·nas	pineapple
breskev	*bres*·kev	peach
češnje	*chesh*·nye	cherries
češplja	*chesh*·plya	plum
grozdje	*groz*·dye	grapes
hruška	*hroosh*·ka	pear
jabolko	*ya*·bol·ko	apple
jagode	*ya*·go·de	strawberries
kompot	kom·*pot*	stewed fruit (many types)
lešniki	*lesh*·nee·kee	hazelnuts
maline	ma·*lee*·ne	raspberries
marelica	ma·*re*·lee·tsa	apricot
orehi	o·*re*·hee	walnuts
pomaranča	po·ma·*ran*·cha	orange
višnje	*veesh*·nye	sour cherries (morellos)

BREZALKOHOLNE PIJAČE (NONALCHOLIC DRINKS)

čaj	chai	tea
kapučino	ka·poo·*chee*·no	cappuccino
kava	*ka*·va	coffee
kava z smetano	*ka*·va z *sme*·ta·no	coffee with whipped crear
limonada	lee·mo·*na*·da	lemonade
pomarančni sok	po·ma·*ranch*·nee sok	orange juice
sok	sok	juice
tonik z ledom	*to*·neek z *le*·dom	tonic water with ice
zeliščni čaj	ze·*leesh*·chnee chai	herbal tea

VINA (WINES)

belo vino	*be*·lo *vee*·no	white wine
brizganec (špricar)	*breez*·ga·nets (*shpree*·tsar)	wine cooler (spritzer)
črno vino	*chuhr*·no *vee*·no	red (literally black) wine
peneče vino	pe·*ne*·che *vee*·no	sparkling wine
rose	ro·*ze*	rosé wine
sladko (desertno) vino	*slad*·ko (de·*zert*·no) *vee*·no	sweet (dessert) wine

IVA & ŽGANE PIJAČE (BEER & SPIRITS)

rinjevec	*bree*·nye·vets	juniper-flavoured brandy
ešnjevec	*chesh*·nye·vets	cherry brandy (kirsch)
ruškovec	*hroosh*·ko·vets	pear brandy
bolčnik	ya·*bolch*·neek	apple cider
edica	me·*dee*·tsa	honey-flavoured brandy
ivovka	*slee*·vov·ka	plum brandy
adjevec	*sad*·ye·vets	fruit brandy
vetlo pivo	*svet*·lo *pee*·vo	lager
emno pivo	*tem*·no *pee*·vo	dark beer/stout
ljamovka	*vee*·lya·mov·ka	pear brandy
ganje	*zhga*·nye	fruit brandy

Environment

THE LAND

Slovenia is a Central European country with a surface area of only 20,273 s km – about the size of Wales, Israel or the American state of New Jersey. borders Austria for 318km to the north and Croatia for 670km to the sout and southeast. Shorter frontiers are shared with Italy (280km) to the we and Hungary (102km) to the northeast.

Slovenia ranks 153rd in size – just between El Salvador and French-ruled New Caledonia – out of a total 233 nations and dependencies on earth.

The terrain is predominantly hilly or mountainous: just over 88% the surface lies more than 300m above sea level at an average elevation 557m. Forest, some of it virgin, and woodland cover 58% of the countr the figure jumps to 66% if you include reverting to natural vegetation an agricultural plots areas that have not been used for more than 20 years. Lan under agricultural use is rapidly diminishing and now accounts for abo a quarter of the total.

Geographers divide the country into as many as a dozen different areas, b there are basically four topographical regions. The Alps, including the Julia Alps, the Kamnik-Savinja Alps, the Karavanke chain and the Pohorje Massi are to the north and northeast. Spreading across their entire southern side a the pre-Alpine hills of Idrija, Cerkno, Škofja Loka and Posavje. The Dinari karst lies below the hills and encompasses the 'true' or 'original' Karst platea between Ljubljana and the Italian border. The Slovenian 'Mediterranean' litto ral follows a short (47km) coastline along the Adriatic Sea, and the essentiall flat Pannonian plain spreads to the east and northeast of the country.

The most ambitious mapping of settlements throughout Slovenia is *The Atlas of Slovenian Towns* (€23) from Geodesic Institute of Slovenia with 120 maps of cities and town at 1:12 500 and one of *Ljubljana* at 1:20 000.

Much of the interior of Slovenia is drained by two rivers – the Sava (221km and Drava (144km) – both of which flow southeastward and empty into th Danube. Other important rivers in Slovenia are: the Kolpa (118km), whic forms part of the southeastern border with Croatia; the Mura (98km) in th northeast; the Soča (96km) to the west, which flows into the Adriatic; an the Krka (94km) to the southeast. In addition there are many 'intermitten rivers (eg the Unica, Pivka and Reka), which disappear into karst caves an potholes, only to resurface elsewhere under different names. Slovenia's large natural lakes are Cerknica in Notranjska, which is dry for part of the yea (usually July to September or later), and Bohinj in Gorenjska.

Main Regions

The topographical divisions do not accurately reflect Slovenia's cultural an historical differences nor do the 210 *občine* (municipalities or administra tive communes) help the traveller much. Instead, Slovenia is best viewed a a country with a capital city (Ljubljana) and eight traditional *regije* (region or provinces): Gorenjska, Primorska, Notranjska, Dolenjska, Bela Krajina Štajerska, Koroška and Prekmurje.

Because the Karst region, a limestone plateau in Primorska, was the first such area to be described, it is also called the 'classic', 'real', 'true' or 'original' Karst and always spelled with an upper-case 'k'.

Greater Ljubljana, by far the nation's largest city, is pinched between hills t the west, east and southeast and the nonarable Ljubljana Marsh (Ljubljansk Barje) to the south. It is not in the centre of the country but close to it.

Gorenjska, to the north and northwest of the capital, is Slovenia's mos mountainous province and contains a dozen of the country's highest peak including Triglav (2864m). The landscape is Alpine and the provincia centre is Kranj.

Primorska, a very diverse region of hills, valleys, karst and a short coast line on the northwestern part of the Istrian peninsula, forms the country' western border, and the countryside feels Mediterranean on the whole. I has two 'capitals', Nova Gorica and Koper.

Notranjska, to the south and southeast of Ljubljana, is an underdevel-ped area of forests and karst – Slovenia's 'last frontier'. Its main towns are ;erknica and Postojna.

Dolenjska lies south of the Sava River and has several distinct areas, in-luding the Krka Valley, the hilly Kočevje region and remote Posavje. Novo Aesto is the main city here. Bela Krajina, a gentle land of rolling hills, birch tands and folk culture below Dolenjska, is washed by the Kolpa River. Its nost important towns are Metlika and Črnomelj.

Štajerska, by far Slovenia's largest *regija,* stretches to the east and northeast nd is a land of mountains, rivers, valleys, vineyards and ancient towns. Aaribor and Celje are the centres (and Slovenia's second- and third-largest ities respectively). Sitting atop Štajerska, is little Koroška, all that is left f the once great historical province of Carinthia. Its cultural heart is lovenj Gradec.

There are more Parisians (2.184 million) in central Paris than Slovenes (2.05 million) in all of Slovenia.

Prekmurje is basically a flat plain in Slovenia's extreme northeast, al-hough there are hills to the north. The capital and administrative centre s Murska Sobota.

VILDLIFE

lovenia, a small republic in the heart of Central Europe, is not the obvi-us place to view wildlife. However, common European animals abound nd its forests, marsh areas and short coast attract a tremendous amount f birdlife. There are upwards of six dozen types of plants that you'll find nly in Slovenia.

nimals

Vhile Slovenia counts some 15,000 animal species, most are common ;uropean varieties such as deer, boar, chamois, marmots, wolves and lynx, ll of which live here in abundance, especially in the Alpine areas and under orest cover in the Kočevje region of Dolenjska. The latter is also home to ;urope's largest population of brown bears *(Ursus arctos),* which currently umber between 450 and 500 and is culled annually by about 15%. There re also much rarer species such as the moor tortoise, cave hedgehog, scarab eetle and various types of dormouse. Two species unique to Slovenia are he marbled trout *(Salmo marmoratus)* from the Soča River and *Proteus nguinus,* a blind salamander that lives in karst cave pools (p193) and is the nly exclusively cave-dwelling vertebrate in the world.

Domesticated animals with a unique Slovenian pedigree include the Karst shepherd dog, the Lipizzaner horse (p169) and the Carniolan honeybee (p119).

'lants

lovenia is home to 3200 plant species, and about 70 of them – many in the lps – are unique to Slovenia or were first classified here. Triglav National 'ark is especially rich in endemic flowering plants, including the Triglav 'rose' actually a pink cinquefoil), various blue gentians, yellow hawk's beard, Julian oppy, Carniola lily, tufted rampion and the purple Zois bellflower.

IATIONAL PARKS

ust less than 12% of the countryside is protected under law at present. Further tatutes have already been approved by parliament, and eventually more than quarter of the territory will be conservation land of some kind.

There is one national park – the 838 sq km Triglav National Park p144), which encompasses almost all of the Julian Alps – although roposals have been made to set aside others in the Kamnik Alps, the 'ohorje Massif, the Karst and the Kočevje-Kolpa regions. Regional parks ow number three: in the Kozjansko region (p235) of southeast Štajerska, he area around the Škocjan Caves (p167) in Primorska and in Notranjska

The geographic centre of the Slovenia at Litija east of Ljubljana is a marked stone memorial including a variant of Prešeren's *A Toast* ending with 'As far as the sun may shine'.

RESPONSIBLE TOURISM

The rules and regulations in most protected parks and nature reserves are fairly obvious: no littering, no picking flowers, no setting fires, camping or parking except in designated areas and so on. But also remember that certain landscapes, Triglav National Park in particular, are very fragile, and there is no wild camping and mountain bikes are banned from trails. Please do your bit:

- Minimise the waste you must carry out by taking minimal packaging and bringing no more food than you will need.
- Don't use detergents or toothpaste in or near watercourses, even if they are biodegradable.
- Bear in mind that sensitive biospheres, for both flora and fauna, may be seriously damaged if you depart from designated paths in protected areas.
- Resist the temptation to drive your own or a rental car in fragile areas, like the Logarska Dolina and Robanov Kot in Štajerska, and go instead by bicycle or on foot.
- Use the recycling banks on the streets of larger towns or the litter bins at the very least.

To learn more about what the Environmental Agency of Slovenia is up to visit www.arso.gov.si.

(p196) – and 44 areas designated as country (literally 'landscape') park These can range in size from the Sečovlje salt pans (7.2 sq km; p188) sout of Portorož in Primorska and the pristine Logar Valley (24.3 sq km; p26 in Štajerska to the enormous Goričko Country Park (462 sq km; p273) i northern Prekmurje. There are also about 50 protected nature reserves, in cluding 200 hectares of primeval forest in the Kočevski Rog region (p21 of Dolenjska, and more than 600 natural heritage sites, such as tiny Wil Lake (Divje Jezero; p162) at Idrija in Primorska.

ENVIRONMENTAL ISSUES

Although Slovenia is a very green country, pollution is a problem bein tackled by the National Environmental Action Program (NEAP), a seven year plan approved by parliament in 2005, and the Environmental Agenc (Agencija za Okolje), a branch of the Ministry of the Environment an Spatial Planning.

Over the past two decades the biggest concern has been air pollutior Climatic change is particularly worrying in a country that calls itself 'th garden of Europe', and the reduction of greenhouse gas emissions is primary objective.

In particular, nitrous oxides emitted by cars on the highway connect ing Gorenjska with the coast are hurting the pine forests of Notranjsk and damaging buildings, outdoor sculptures and other artwork i many historical cities; many treasures, including the Carniolan River Fountain by Francesco Robba in Ljubljana, have had to be taken indoor for protection.

Sulphur dioxide levels are especially high in cities and towns – Ljubljan Šoštanj, Trbovlje – where coal fuels boilers and thermal power plants. Th nation's sole nuclear power plant (at Krško in Dolenjska) provides abou 40% of electric power, but half of it is owned by Croatia. Another (an bigger) Krško unit is under consideration, possibly finished by 2017.

In the past several years Slovenia has also introduced a series of en vironmental taxes, including a waste-disposal and water-pollution ta in a bid to hit the biggest abusers in the pocket. The Sava, Mura an lower Savinja Rivers are especially vulnerable, though the quality of wate in most Slovenian rivers is acceptable. Even so, rain has washed under ground all sorts of rubbish dumped in the Karst region, and waste car ried by the 'disappearing' Unica and Ljubljanica Rivers could threaten th Ljubljana Marsh.

›lovenia Outdoors

lovenes are very enthusiastic about outdoor activities and it won't be long efore you're invited to join in the fun. Indeed, these are the people who ıvented skiing almost four centuries ago, and hiking and climbing clubs cross the country count almost 60,000 paid-up members. And according ɔ local tradition, people here can't even call themselves Slovene until they ave reached the top of Mt Triglav (p144). It is a tradition in Slovenia to reet everyone you pass while hiking or climbing. Generally a simple '*Dober 'an*' (Hello) and/or a smile will suffice.

As a result of all this enthusiasm, the choice of activities and range of facili-ies available are endless. From skiing and climbing to caving and cycling, it's ll on offer and very affordable compared with other parts of Europe. The **lovenian Tourist Board** (www.slovenia.info) publishes specialist (and comprehensive) rochures and maps on skiing, hiking, cycling, golfing and fly fishing as well s one on the nation's top spas and heath resorts.

Attracting bathers for almost three centuries, Rogaška Slatina in Štajerska is Slovenia's oldest health resort.

You'll find these activities available throughout the country, and most escribed below are cross-referenced to the appropriate sections under ıdividual towns. You can always go it alone, but if you really want to be ı safe, experienced hands, engage the services of any of the travel agen-ies specialising in adventure sport. These are usually found in this book's nformation section of each town or city.

·KIING

kiing is by far the most popular recreational pursuit in Slovenia, and why ot? On the basis of written references that go back to the 17th century, ıany people believe that skiing was born on the slopes of the Bloke Plateau ı Notranjska. Today an estimated 300,000 people – some 15% of the popu-ıtion – ski regularly. Just about everyone takes to the slopes or trails in eason (mainly December to March), and you can too on the more than wo dozen ski grounds and resorts of varying sizes listed in the Slovenian 'ourist Board's useful *Ski Centers of Slovenia*. They're most crowded over ne Christmas holidays and in early February.

All but one of the Category I mountain huts in Slovenia – the one below Veliki Snežnik in Notranjska – are in the Alps.

Most of Slovenia's ski areas are small and relatively unchallenging com-ared to the Alpine resorts of France, Switzerland and Italy, but they do have ne attraction of lower prices and easy access. The latest weather and snow eports are available on the website of the **Snow Telephone** (Snežni Telefon; ☎ 041 82 500, 031 182 500; www.snezni-telefon.si) though only (and oddly) in Slovene.

The biggest downhill skiing area in Slovenia is Maribor Pohorje (p255) t altitudes of 325m to 1347m in the hills immediately south of Maribor in tajerska, with 40km of linked pistes and 36km of cross-country trails suit-ble for skiers of all levels. It offers a ski and snowboard school, equipment ental and floodlit night skiing, as well as being a good starting point for ski ɔuring through the forested hills of the Pohorje.

Kranjska Gora (p141), at 810m to 1291m in Gorenjska, has 20km of pistes, ut the skiing here is fairly dull and suited mostly for beginners and interme-iates. Nevertheless, for foreign visitors, it is probably Slovenia's best-known nd most popular ski resort, being easily accessible from Austria and Italy.

Website www.slo-skiing.net, from the people who run the tows and ropeways, is the best single source for information on Slovenian skiing grounds and centres.

Krvavec (p118), at between 1450m and 1971m in the hills northeast of ːranj in Gorenjska, is one of the best-equipped ski areas in the country; here are 20km of pistes and 40k of trails. In addition you'll find a number of ki (alpine and telemark) and snowboard schools, equipment rental, a good ariety of piste and off-piste skiing, a freestyle mogul course, a speed-skiing track, a half-pipe and snowboard cross trail, a ski shop and some good res taurants and bars. However, as it's only an hour's drive from Ljubljana, it best avoided at the weekends unless you like long queues.

Many Slovenian skiers think that the ski centre at Cerkno (p165), a between 900m and 1300m north of Idrija in Primorska, offers some of th best downhill skiing (and shortest tow queues) in the country. There are onl 18km of marked pistes and 5km of cross-country trails served by six moder (and covered) chairlifts and two tows, but all are covered by snow cannon which guarantees adequate snow cover throughout the season.

For spectacular scenery, you can't beat Kanin (p150), which perches abov Bovec in Primorska and can have snow until May, and at 1600m to 2300m i by far Slovenia's highest ski resort, and Vogel (p138), some 570m to 1800r above shimmering Lake Bohinj in Gorenjska. Both resorts enjoy stunnin views north to Triglav and the Julian Alps, and from the top station at Kani you can even glimpse the Adriatic. Vogel is more suited to experienced skie and has great opportunities for off-piste and ski-touring.

Snowboarders can find fun parks at Krvavec (p118) and Stari Vrh (p113 at 580m to 1216m near Škofja Loka in Gorenjska, and there are also half-pipe at Vogel and Rogla (p257), at 1517m near Zreče, north of Celje in Štajerska

There are marked cross-country ski trails at most Slovenian resorts, bu the major ones are at Kranjska Gora (40km), Maribor Pohorje (36km), Rogl (18km) and Logarska Dolina (15km).

HIKING & WALKING

Slovenia has an excellent system of trails – some 10,000km of them, in fac 8250km of which are mountain trails – and most are marked by a red circl with a white centre. At crossings, there are signs indicating distances an walking times. The Julian Alps, the Kamnik-Savinja Alps and the Pohorj Massif are the most popular places for hiking, but there are some wonderfu trails in the lower hills and valleys as well.

The 350km **E6 European Hiking Trail** running from the Baltic to the Adriati Seas enters Slovenia at Radlje ob Dravi in Koroška and continues to a poin south of Snežnik in Notranjska. The 600km **E7 European Hiking Trail**, whic connects the Atlantic with the Black Sea, crosses into Slovenia at Robi in Primorska, runs along the Soča Valley and then continues through th southern part of the country eastward to Bistrica ob Sotli in Štajerska befor exiting into Croatia. Both are marked by a red circle with a yellow centre.

For more on the E6 and E7 European Hiking Trails, see www.wandertheglobe.com/trekking/europe.shtml.

The **Slovenian Mountain Trail** (Slovenska Planinska Pot), which opened i 1953 and was the first such trail in Europe, runs for 500km from Maribo to Ankaran on the coast via the Pohorje Massif, the Kamnik-Savinja Alp the Julian Alps and the Cerkno and Idrija hills. It too is marked with a re circle with a white centre.

Slovenia has joined Austria, Germany, Liechtenstein, Switzerland, Italy, Franc and Monaco to develop the **Via Alpina** (www.via-alpina.com), a 342-stage long-distanc trail about 5000km long that follows the entire arc of the Alps from Trieste t Monaco. Some 24 stages pass through Slovenia: the 14-stage Red Trail (220km and the 10-stage Purple Trail (120km). The 470km-long **Sub-Alpine Trail** cove Slovenia's hill country – from Cerkno and Idrija to Posavje via Notranjska and is for less-ambitious, but equally keen, walkers and hikers.

The Ljubljana-based **Alpine Association of Slovenia** (Planinska Zveza Slovenij PZS; Map pp72-3; ☎ 01-434 56 80; www.pzs.si, in Slovene; Dvoržakova ulica 9; 🕑 8am-5pm Mo 8am-3pm Wed, 8am-2pm Fri), the umbrella organisation of 265 local hiking an climbing clubs, which has 58,250 fully paid members, is the fount of a information and can also organise mountain guides (of which they hav registered almost 1500). It publishes hiking maps and a very useful an

BEDDING DOWN ON HIGH

A *bivak* (bivouac) is the most basic hut in the mountains of Slovenia, providing shelter only, whereas a *zavetišče* (refuge) has refreshments, and sometimes accommodation, but usually no running water. A *koča* (hut) or *dom* (house) can be a simple cottage or a fairly grand establishment like some of those close to Triglav.

A bed for the night runs from €18 to €27 in a Category I hut, depending on the number of beds in the room, and from €12 to €20 in a Category II. Members of the PZS as well as visitors holding a UIAA-affiliated club membership card, get a 50% discount. Category III huts are allowed to set their own prices but usually cost less than Category I huts.

A hut is Category I if it is at a height of over 1000m and is more than one hour from motorised transport. A Category II hut is within one hour's walking distance from motorised transport. A Category III hut can be reached by car or cable car directly. Ten of the highest huts, including most of those around Triglav, are Category I huts.

Food prices at PZS huts are regulated as well. A simple meal should cost between €4.70 and €6.20 in a Category I hut and €3.50 and €5 in a Category II hut. Tea is €1.30 to €1.80 and 1.5L of mineral water is €2 and €3.50.

There are 58 mountain huts (41 of them Category I) in the Julian Alps, most of them open at least between June and September; some huts at lower altitudes are open all year. Huts are never more than five hours' walk apart. You'll never be turned away if the weather looks bad, but some huts on Triglav can be unbearably crowded at weekends – especially in August and September. Try to plan your hikes for midweek if possible, and phone or even email ahead – many huts now take bookings.

ual 'calendar' that lists mountain huts, refuges and bivouacs throughout lovenia. This association provides information about specific trails in riglav National Park and elsewhere as well as huts.

Of the 174 mountain huts and other accommodation maintained by the ZS across the country, some are very basic indeed whereas others come lose to hotel-style accommodation (above).

The Slovenian Tourist Board publishes the excellent (and free) *Hiking ı Slovenia* pamphlet with suggested itineraries. More comprehensive ources books and guides include the vinyl-bound *The Julian Alps of lovenia* (Cicerone) by Justi Carey and Roy Clark, with 50 walking routes nd short treks, and the same pair's brand-new *Trekking in Slovenia: The lovene High Level Route* (Cicerone), which includes 500km of mountain and upland trail walking. Mike Newbury's *A Guide to Walks and crambles in the Julian Alps* (Zlatorog Publications) includes routes out f Kranjska Gora.

MOUNTAINEERING & ROCK CLIMBING

Slovenia set up its first mountain association back in 1893, one of the first in the world.

'he principal rock- and ice-climbing areas in Slovenia include Triglav's nagnificent north face – where routes range from the classic Slovene Route Slovenski Pot; Grade II/III; 750m) to the modern Sphinx Face (Obraz finge; Grade IX+/X-; 140m), with a crux 6m roof – as well as the impressive northern buttresses of Prisank overlooking the Vršič Pass. The best nountaineering guidebook readily available is *Mountaineering in Slovenia* Sidarta) by the late Tine Mihelič, which describes some 85 tours in the ulian Alps as well as the Kamnik-Savinja Alps and the Karavanke.

Športno plezanje (sport climbing) is very popular here too. The revised *lovenija Športnoplezalni Vodnik* (Sport Climbing Guide to Slovenia; Sidarta) y climber Janez Skok et al covers 85 crags, with good topos and descriptions n English, German and Italian as well as Slovene.

THERMAL SPAS & HEALTH RESORTS

Taking the waters is one of the most enjoyable ways to relax in Sloveni especially after a day on the slopes or mountain trails. Slovenia has a scor of thermal spa resorts – two on the coast at Portorož and Strunjan and th rest in the eastern half of the country in Štajerska, Dolenjska and Prekmurj They are excellent places not only for 'taking the cure' but also for relaxin and meeting people. Many resorts use the Italian *terme* for 'spa' instead of th Slovene words *toplice* (thermal spring) or *zdravilišče* (health resort).

The hottest thermal water in Slovenia is at Moravske Toplice, with an egg-boiling temperature of 72°C at source.

Only two – Dolenjske Toplice (p208) in Dolenjska and Rogaška Slatin (p240) in Štajerska – are really spa towns as such, with that distinctive *fin-de siècle* feel about them. Others, such as Terme Ptuj in Štajerska and Term Čatež in Dolenjska, are loud, brash places dedicated to all the hedonisti pursuits you care to imagine, complete with swimming pools, waterslides tennis courts, saunas, massage services and wellness centres.

The Slovenian Tourist Board publishes a useful brochure entitled *Slovenia' Natural Health Spas,* which describes the country's top 15 spas. Another goo source of information is **Slovenia Spas** (www.spa-slovenia.com).

CYCLING & MOUNTAIN BIKING

Slovenia is a wonderful country for cycling and mountain biking; the Slovenia Tourist Board publishes a cycling brochure called *Cycling in Slovenia* tha introduces dozens of road- and mountain-bike trails. Places where you ca rent bicycles and/or mountains bikes are listed in the Activities or Gettin Around sections of each town.

The uncrowded roads around Bled and Bohinj are a joy to cycle on. Othe excellent areas for cycling are the Upper Savinja Valley in Štajerska, the Soč Valley in Primorska, the Drava Valley in Koroška and especially the Krk Valley in Dolenjska, which has become something of a cycling centre.

Mountain-bike enthusiasts should make tracks for Notranjska Regiona Park (p194), southwest Koroška (p272), the Maribor Pohorje (p255) and/o the Pohorje Central Pohorje Region (p257) in Štajerska. Please note tha mountain bikes are banned from all trails in Triglav National Park.

Two excellent sources of information (but in Slovene only) are th website of the Alpine Association of Slovenia's **Commission for Mountai Biking** (Komisija za Turno Kolesarstvo; http://ktk.pzs.si) and *Veliki Kolesarski Vodnik p Sloveniji* (Great Cycling Guide to Slovenia) by Igor Maher, with 72 circuit covering 3200km.

KAYAKING, CANOEING, RAFTING & CANYONING

River sports are hugely popular and practised anywhere there's running water in Slovenia, particularly on the Krka River in Dolenjska (for example at Žužemberk and Krka, p208), the Kolpa in Bela Krajina, especially at Vinica (p232), the Sava River at Bohinj (p136) in Gorenjska, the Savinja River at Logarska Dolina (p263) in Štajerska, the Drava River near Dravograd (p268) in Koroška but especially the Soča River at Bovec (p151) in Primorska.

The Soča is famed as one of the best white-water rafting and kayaking rivers in Europe, and it is one of only half a dozen rivers in the European Alps whose upper waters are still unspoiled. Agencies offering rafting and canoeing trips are detailed in the relevant regional chapters, especially under the Bovec section of the Primorska chapter.

Canyoning, a relatively new sport that has grown by leaps and bounds in recent years (p132), will have you descending through gorges, jumping over and sliding down waterfalls, swimming in rock pools and abseiling. It's been described as like being in one huge (and natural) water park.

AVING

t is hardly surprising that the country that gave the world the word 'karst' is iddled with caves – around 7500 have been recorded and described. There re about 20 'show caves' open to visitors, most of which – Škocjan (p167), ostojna (p191), Križna (p199), Planina (p193), Pivka (p193) and Predjama p195) – are in the karst areas of Primorska and Notranjska.

The main potholing regions in Slovenia are the Notranjska karst, centred round Postojna, and the Julian Alps of Gorenjska and Primorska. For nore information, club contacts and expeditions, contact the **Speleological ssociation of Slovenia** (Jamarska Zveza Slovenije; ☎ 01-429 34 44; www.jamarska-zveza.si; Lepi ot 6) in Ljubljana.

The deepest cave in Slovenia – Čehi II on Jelenk peak northwest of Bovec – goes down 1502m.

AILING

ailing is big on the Adriatic, but most yachties prefer the delights of Croatia's sland-studded Dalmatian coast to the strictly limited attractions of Slovenia's 7km littoral. The country's main marinas are at Izola and Portorož (p186), vhere you can charter yachts and powerboats.

ISHING

lovenia's mountain streams are teeming with brown and rainbow trout and rayling, and its lakes and more-sluggish rivers are home to pike, perch, carp, hub and other coarse fish. The best rivers for angling are the Soča, the Krka, he Kolpa, the Sava Bohinjka near Bohinj and the Unica in Notranjska. As lsewhere, angling is not a cheap sport in Slovenia – a permit at the more opular rivers will cost from €49 (Krka) to €99 (Unica) a day. Catch-and-elease permits are cheaper.

For information on licences and seasons, contact the **Slovenian Fishing nstitute** (Zavod za Ribištvo Slovenije; ☎ 01-244 34 00; www.zzrs.si; Župančičeva ulica 9) n Ljubljana.

The cobalt-blue Soča River in Primorska is recognised as offering some of the finest trout fishing in all of Europe.

ORSE RIDING

lovenia is a nation of horse riders. The world's most famous horse – the ipizzaner of the Spanish Riding School in Vienna – was first bred at Lipica n Primorska. About a dozen riding centres registered with the Ljubljana-ased **Equestrian Association of Slovenia** (Konjeniška Zveza Slovenije; ☎ 01-434 72 65; www onj-zveza.si, in Slovene; Celovška cesta 25) rent horses and offer lessons but finding maller stables and ranches renting privately is increasingly difficult due to he implementation of strict EU safety measures.

Among the best and most professional places to learn to ride in Slovenia re the Lipica Stud Farm (p170) in Primorska and, in Dolenjska, the Novo Aesto Sport Equestrian Centre (p213) and the Hosta Stud Farm at Sela pri entjerneju near Kostanjevica na Krki.

The Lipizzaner horse is so iconic in Slovenia that a pair of the beasts are shown prancing together on the verso of the Slovenian €0.20 coin.

ARAGLIDING, BALLOONING & FLYING

aragliding has taken off in Slovenia, especially in Gorenjska around Bohinj p136) and at Bovec (p150), where you can take a tandem flight from the upper able-car station on Kanin peak and descend 2000m into the Bovec Valley.

The tourist information centre in Ljubljana organises hot-air balloon p86) flights year-round.

Every self-respecting town in Slovenia seems to have an airstrip or aero-rome, complete with an *aeroklub* whose enthusiastic members will take you light-seeing'. The Ljubljana-based **Aeronautical Association of Slovenia** (Letalska Zveza lovenije; ☎ 01-422 33 33; www.lzs-zveza.si, in Slovene; Tržaška cesta 2) has a complete list.

If you're keen to learn to fly, why not go with the experts? The **Adria Airways lying School** (Letalska Šola Adrie Airways; ☎ 259 42 54; www.adria-airways.com; Kuzmičeva ulica 7) in Ljubljana offers instruction both in the air and on the ground in a stat of-the-art simulator (€49 per half-hour).

GOLF

There are 18-hole golf courses at Bled (King's Course) and Volčji Poto (both Gorenjska), Otočec and Mokrice Castle (Dolenjska), Ptuj (Štajersk and Moravske Toplice (Prekmurje). Nine-hole courses can be found at Ble (Lake Course) and Brdo near Kranj (both Gorenjska), Lipica (Primorska) an Podčetrtek and Slovenske Konjice, southeast of Zreče (both Štajerska).

The best links in Slovenia are the par 73 King's Course in Bled at Bled Go & Country Club (p128), which opened in 1937, the par 71 Golf Course Pt (p246) and the newly expanded 72-par 18-hole Golf Grad Otočec (p216).

For information, contact the **Slovenian Golf Association** (Golf Zveza Slovenije; ☎ 01 430 32 00; www.golfportal.info, in Slovene; Dunajska cesta 22) in Ljubljana. The Slovenia Tourist Board publishes the useful *Golf Courses in Slovenia* brochure.

BIRD-WATCHING

Although many Slovenes don't know it, Slovenia has some of the best bird watching in Central Europe. Some 376 species have been sighted here, 21 of which are breeders and 11 of which are under threat. The Ljubljana Mars (Ljubljansko Barje), south of the capital, Lake Cerknica (p196) in Notranjsk and the Sečovlje saltpans (p188) in Primorska are especially good for sightin water birds and waders, as is the Drava River and its reservoirs in northeas Slovenia. An especially wonderful (though messy) sight is the arrival of th white storks in Prekmurje (p278) in March/April. Other important habitat are the Julian and Savinja Alps, the Karst area and the Krakovski forest nort of Kostanjevica na Krki in Dolenjska.

See www.fatbirder.com/links_geo/europe/slovenia.html for more information on bird-watching in Slovenia.

For more information, contact the Ljubljana-based **Bird Watching & Stud Association of Slovenia** (Društvo za Opazovanje in Proučevanje Ptic Slovenije; DOPPS; ☎ 01-426 5 75; www.ptice.si, in Slovene; Tržaška cesta 2), a member of Bird Life International.

There's no guidebook devoted specifically to the birds of Slovenia bu Gerard Gorman's *Birding in Eastern Europe* published by **Wildsounds** (www.wil sounds.com) contains a section on the country, and Gorman's company **Probirde** (www.probirder.com), organises birding tours of Slovenia.

DIVING

You can dive in all Slovenian rivers, lakes and of course the sea, with the exceptions of the fish hatchery in Lake Bohinj and the shipping lanes and harbour areas. The sport is popular in Lake Bled, in the Kolpa River in Bela Krajina and at Ankaran, Portorož and Piran (p182) on the coast, where you can take lessons and even qualify. For more information, contact the **Slovenian Diving Federation** (Slovenska Potapljaška Zveza; ☎ 01-433 93 08; www.spz.si, in Slovene; 25 Celovška cesta) in Ljubljana.

Cave diving is a popular sport in Slovenia but is permitted only under the supervision of a professional guide. Cave diving has been done at Postojna, Škocjan and in the tunnel at Wild Lake (Divje Jezero) near Idrija.

HUNTING

Hunting is big business in Slovenia, and many Europeans (especially Italians) will pay big – um – bucks to bag a deer, a brace of grouse, a boar or even a bear, which now number between 400 and 500 in Slovenia (p61) and are culled regularly. The **Slovenian Hunting Association** (Lovska Zveza Slovenije; ☎ 01-241 09 10; www.lovska-zveza.si, in Slovene; Župančičeva ulica 9) in Ljubljana can provide information.

jubljana

Vith a dazzling hilltop castle as her crown and the emerald-green Ljubljanica River at her eet, Ljubljana is a princess in size petite. But her pint size conceals a wealth of culture, sights, ctivities and good old-fashioned fun that would be the envy of a city twice the size. And est of all, everything is within such easy reach – a mere stroll or cycle away.

The princess, whose name *almost* means 'beloved' *(ljubljena)* in Slovene, is also a hard vorker. As the country's largest city and its political, economic and cultural capital, this is vhere virtually everything of national importance begins, ends or is taking place. Of course hat might not be immediately apparent in spring and summer, when cafe tables spill into he narrow streets of the Old Town and street musicians and actors entertain passers-by n Prešernov trg and on the little bridges spanning the Ljubljanica River. Then it feels like a mall, self-contented town with responsibilities only to itself and its citizens.

Ljubljana's buzzing student community – there are more than 64,000 students attending jubljana University's 22 faculties, three art academies and one university college – and alternative-ifestyle centre at Metelkova are added bonuses. Admittedly, the city may lack the grandeur or ig-ticket attractions of, say, Prague or Budapest, but the great museums and galleries, parks and gardens and atmospheric bars and varied, accessible nightlife make it a wonderful, relaxed lace to visit and stay a while – almost certainly longer than you had planned.

HIGHLIGHTS

- Enjoy a flight up on the funicular to **Ljubljana Castle** (p80) for an overview of the city past, present and to come
- Follow in the footsteps of history by walking all or part of the **Trail of Remembrance** (p87) around the city
- Learn how it was, not so very long ago, in the workplace, the kitchen and even the bedroom at the **Slovenian Ethnographic Museum** (p81)
- Spend an evening at an outside table at the **Kavarna Tromostovje** (p96) and spot half the people you've met in Slovenia to date
- While away a lazy summer's afternoon at the **Laguna** (p87) water park north of Centre
- Crawl through the waterfront cafes and pubs of the Old Town and end up at any of the alternative clubs in **Metelkova Mesto** (p97)

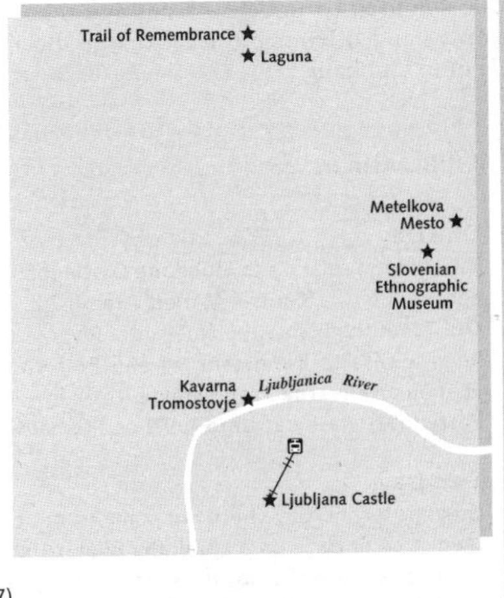

TELEPHONE CODE: 01	POPULATION: 216,200	ELEVATION: 295M

HISTORY

If Ljubljana really was founded by Jason and the Golden Fleece–seeking Argonauts (as local lore would have you believe), they left no proof. But legacies of the Roman city of Emona dating to the 1st century AD, a thriving town of 5000 inhabitants and a strategic crossroad on the routes linking Upper Pannonia in the south with the Roman colonies at Noricum and Aquileia to the north and west, remain. Remnants of walls, dwellings and early churches can still be seen throughout Ljubljana.

Emona was sacked and destroyed by the Huns, Ostrogoths and Langobards (Lombards) from the mid-5th century; by the end of the next century tribes of early Slavs began to settle here.

First mentioned in writing as 'Laibach' in 1144, Ljubljana changed hands frequently in the Middle Ages. The last and most momentous change came in 1335, when the Habsburgs became the town's new rulers, a position they would retain almost without interruption until the end of WWI in 1918.

The town and its hilltop castle were able to repel the Turks in the late 15th century, but a devastating earthquake in 1511 reduced much of the medieval Ljubljana to a pile of rubble. This led to a period of frantic construction in the 17th and 18th centuries that provided Ljubljana with many of its pale-coloured baroque churches and mansions – and of course the nickname 'Bela (White) Ljubljana'.

When Napoleon established his Illyrian Provinces in 1809 in a bid to cut Habsburg Austria's access to the Adriatic, he made Ljubljana the capital (though Austrian rule was restored just four years later). In 1821 Ljubljana walked onto the world stage when the four members of the Holy Alliance (Austria, Prussia, Russia and Naples) met at the Congress of Laibach to discuss measures to suppress the democratic revolutionary and national movements in Italy.

Railways linked Ljubljana with Vienna and Trieste in 1849 and 1857, stimulating economic development of the town. But in 1895 another, more powerful earthquake struck, forcing the city to rebuild once again. To Ljubljana's great benefit, the Secessionist and art nouveau styles were all the rage in Central Europe at the time, and many of the wonderful buildings erected then still stand.

During WWII Ljubljana was occupied by the Italians and then the Germans, who encircled the city with a barbed-wire fence creating, in effect, an urban concentration camp. Ljubljana became the capital of the Socialist Republic of Slovenia within Yugoslavia in 1945 and remained the capital after Slovenia's independence in 1991.

ORIENTATION

Ljubljana lies within the Ljubljana Basin (Ljubljanska Kotlina), which extends 25km to the north and northwest along the Sava River to Kranj. The basin has two distinct parts: the Ljubljana Marsh (Ljubljansko Barje)

LJUBLJANA IN...

One Day

Take the funicular up to **Ljubljana Castle** (p80) to get an idea of the lay of the land. Come down and explore the **Central Market Area** (p76). After a seafood lunch at **Ribca** (p95), explore the **Old Town** then cross the Ljubljanica River via St James Bridge and walk north along bust-lined Vegova ulica to **Kongresni trg** and **Prešernov trg** (p76). Plan your evening over a fortifying libation at **Kavarna Tromostovje** (p96): low key at **Jazz Club Gajo** (p99), chichi at **Top: Eat & Party** (p97), trashy at **Ultra** (p97) or alternative at **Metelkova Mesto** (p98).

Two Days

On your second day check out some of the city's excellent **museums** and **galleries** (p76), and then stroll or cycle on a **Ljubljana Bike** (p102) through **Park Tivoli** (p84), stopping for a oh-so-local horse burger at **Hot Horse** (p95) along the way. At this point, you might need a session at **Zlati Klub** (p87) after all that exercise. In the evening take in a performance at the Križanke or **Cankarjev Dom** (p99) and then visit one of the **clubs** (p97) you missed last night.

to the south and the fertile Ljubljana Plain (Ljubljansko Polje) to the north and east. The city is wedged between two sets of hills to the west, east and southeast.

Only a handful of Ljubljana's two dozen districts are of any importance to travellers. Center is the commercial area on the left bank of the Ljubljanica River, to the west and north of Castle Hill and the bite-sized Old Town. Tabor and Poljane are the easternmost parts of Centre, and Bežigrad, where the bulk of the university buildings are, lies to the north. Krakovo and Trnovo, two old suburbs with a lot of traditional charm, are to the south of Center.

Certain streets and squares (eg Čopova ulica, Prešernov trg, most of Trubarjeva cesta), much of the Old Town and also all of the riverfront areas are pedestrianised. The Ljubljanica is crossed by more than a dozen bridges though just three of them – historical Cobbler Bridge (Čevljarski Most), Triple Bridge (Tromostovje) and Dragon Bridge (Zmajski Most) – are really useful to travellers.

Ljubljana's Jože Pučnik Airport at Brnik, 27km north of the city, is easily accessible by bus and taxi (p102). The train and bus stations are opposite one another on Trg Osvobodilne Fronte (abbreviated Trg OF) at the northern end of Center.

Maps

Excellent free maps, some of which show the city's bus network and have a street index, are available from the tourist offices For extended stays, you might want to pick up the 1:20,000-scale commercial *Mestni Načrt Ljubljana* (Ljubljana City Map; €7.70) published by GZS and available from Kod & Kam (right), which has an enlarged 1:7000 plan of the centre and a 1:75,000 map of the surrounding areas on the reverse. The 1:15,000 *Atlas Mesta Ljubljana in Okolica* (€14.10) is a street atlas of the capital and its suburbs. The town centre appears on a scale of 1:6600.

INFORMATION

Bookshops

Geonavtik (Map p78; ☎ 252 70 27; www.geonavtik.com, in Slovene; Kongresni trg 1; 🕑 8.30am-8.30pm Mon-Fri, 8.30am-4pm Sat) Superb shop with travel and nautical guides, maps, books about Slovenia in English and a popular cafe/bar.

Knjigarna Behemot (Map p78; ☎ 251 13 92; www.behemot.si; Židovska steza 3; 🕑 10am-8pm Mon-Fri, 10am-3pm Sat) Pint-size independent English-language bookshop for bibliophiles.

Kod & Kam (Map pp72-3; ☎ 600 50 80; www.gzs-dd.si/kod&kam; Miklošičeva cesta 34; 🕑 8am-8pm Mon-Fri, 8am-1pm Sat) 'Whence & Whither', run by GZS, the national cartographic unit, stocks local city, regional and hiking maps as well as imported maps and guides.

Mladinska Knjiga Slovenska cesta (Map p78; ☎ 241 06 55; 1st fl, Slovenska cesta 29; 🕑 9am-7.30pm Mon-Fri, 9am-2pm Sat); Miklošičeva cesta (Map pp72-3; ☎ 234 27 80; Miklošičeva cesta 40; 🕑 8.30am-7pm Mon-Fri, 9am-noon Sat) 'MK ' is the city's biggest and best-stocked bookshop, with lots of guidebooks, maps, pictorials, fiction and newspapers and periodicals in English.

Discount Cards

The **Ljubljana Card** (www.ljubljana-tourism.si; €12.50), valid for three days (72 hours) and available from the tourist offices, offers free admission to many museums, unlimited city bus travel and discounts on organised tours, accommodation and restaurants, hire cars etc.

Internet Access

Web connection is available at virtually all hostels and hotels and there's free wi-fi along the banks of the Ljubljanica River. The Slovenian Tourist Information Centre (p75) offers access for €1 per half-hour and the STA Travel Café (p75) has a rate of €1 per 20 minutes). At ŠOU (p75) access is free on its two terminals. Other options include:

Cyber Café Xplorer (Map p78; ☎ 430 19 91; Petkovškovo nabrežje 23; per 30min/hr/5hr €2.50/4/12; 🕑 10am-10pm Mon-Fri, 2-10pm Sat & Sun) Ljubljana's best internet cafe, with 10 super-fast computers, wi-fi (per hour €2.40) and international phone calls at €0.10 per minute.

DrogArt (Map pp72-3; ☎ 439 72 70; Kolodvorska ulica 20; first 15min free, then per 30min/hr €1/1.80; 🕑 10am-4pm Mon-Fri) Opposite the train station.

Knižnica Župančiča (Župančic Library; Map pp72-3; ☎ 600 13 02, 291 23 96; Trg OF 100; per 30min/hr €1/2; 🕑 8am-8pm Mon-Fri) Enter via Vilharjev podhod, the pedestrian underpass/subway at the eastern end of the train station.

Portal.si Internet (Map pp72-3; ☎ 234 46 00; Trg OF 4; per hr €3.80; ☎ 5.30am-10.30pm Sun-Fri, 5am-10pm Sat) In the bus station (get code from window No 4).

Internet Resources

In addition to the websites of the Slovenian Tourist Information Centre and Ljubljana Tourist Information Centre (p75), the following sites might be useful:

LJUBLJANA

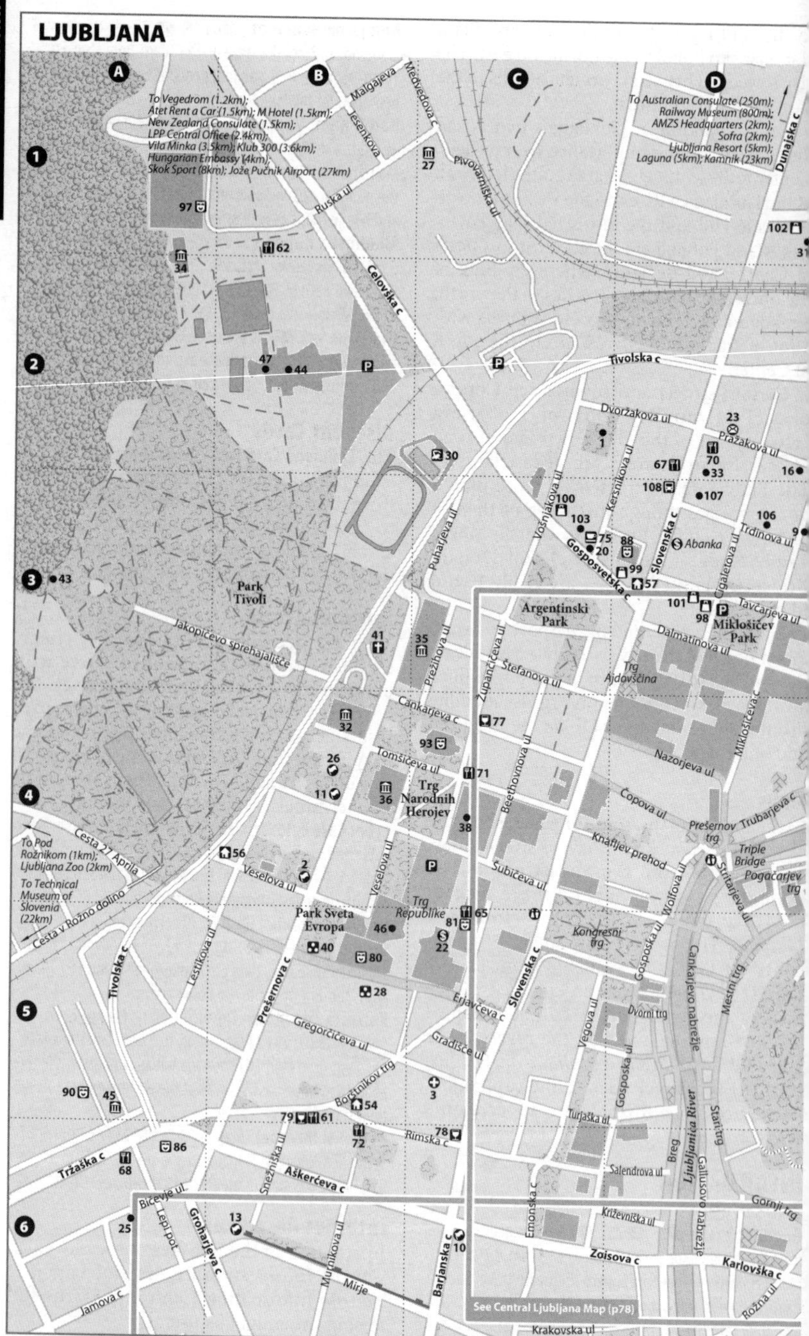
To Vegedrom (1.2km); Atet Rent a Car (1.5km); M Hotel (1.5km); New Zealand Consulate (1.5km); LPP Central Office (2.4km); Vila Minka (3.5km); Klub 300 (3.6km); Hungarian Embassy (4km); Skok Sport (8km); Jože Pučnik Airport (27km)
To Australian Consulate (250m); Railway Museum (800m); AMZS Headquarters (2km); Sofra (2km); Ljubljana Resort (5km); Laguna (5km); Kamnik (23km)
To Pod Rožnikom (1km); Ljubljana Zoo (2km)
To Technical Museum of Slovenia (22km)
Park Tivoli
Jakopičevo sprehajališče
Argentinski Park
Miklošičev Park
Trg Ajdovščina
Trg Narodnih Herojev
Park Sveta Evropa
Trg Republike
Kongresni trg
Prešernov trg
Triple Bridge
Pogačarjev trg
Dvorni trg
Ljubljanica River
Abanka
See Central Ljubljana Map (p78)

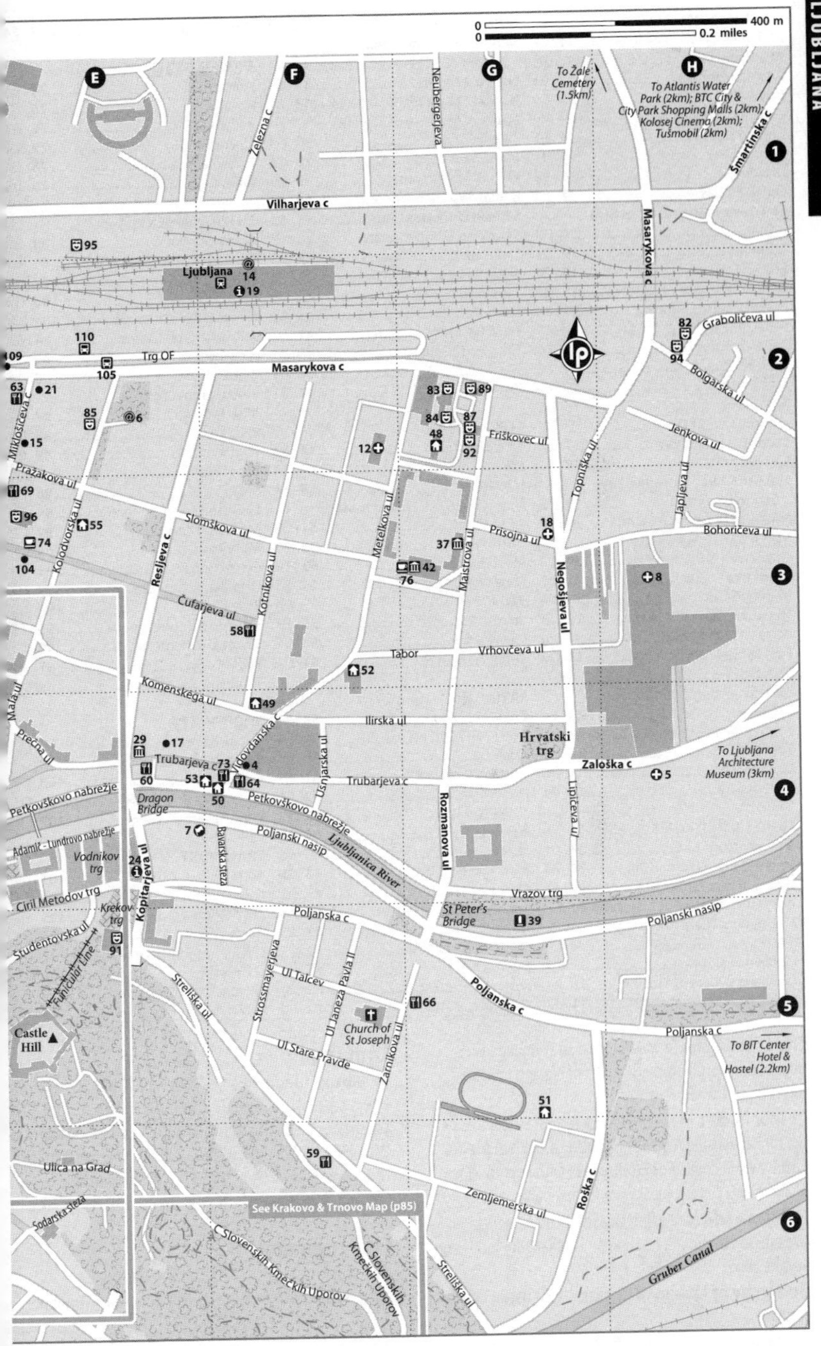
0 400 m
0 0.2 miles
To Žale Cemetery (1.5km)
To Atlantis Water Park (2km); BTC City & City Park Shopping Malls (2km); Kolosej Cinema (2km); Tušmobil (2km)
Šmartinska c
Železna c
Neubergerjeva
Vilharjeva c
Masarykova c
Ljubljana
Graboličeva ul
Trg OF
Masarykova c
Bolgarska ul
Jenkova ul
Miklošičeva c
Friškovec ul
Pražakova ul
Topniška ul
Japljeva ul
Kolodvorska ul
Slomškova ul
Metelkova ul
Maistrova ul
Prisojna ul
Bohoričeva ul
Resljeva c
Kotnikova ul
Negošjeva ul
Čufarjeva ul
Tabor
Vrhovčeva ul
Komenskega ul
Vidovdanska c
Ilirska ul
Hrvatski trg
Mala ul
Prečna ul
Trubarjeva c
Zaloška c
To Ljubljana Architecture Museum (3km)
Trubarjeva c
Dragon Bridge
Petkovškovo nabrežje
Usnjarska ul
Rozmanova ul
Lipičeva ul
Poljanski nasip
Ljubljanica River
Bavarska steza
Adamič - Lundrovo nabrežje
Vodnikov trg
Kopitarjeva ul
Ciril Metodov trg
Vrazov trg
Krekov trg
Poljanska c
St Peter's Bridge
Poljanski nasip
Študentovska ul
Funicular Line
Ul Talcev
Strossmayerjeva
Ul Janeza Pavla II
Poljanska c
Streliška ul
Church of St Joseph
Zarnikova ul
Poljanska c
Castle Hill
Ul Stare Pravde
To BIT Center Hotel & Hostel (2.2km)
Ulica na Grad
Zemljemerska ul
Roška c
Sodarska steza
See Krakovo & Trnovo Map (p85)
C Slovenskih Kmečkih Uporov
Streliška ul
Gruber Canal
E
F
G
H
1
2
3
4
5
6
95
14
19
110
105
109
63
21
85
6
15
83
89
84
87
92
48
12
69
96
55
74
104
18
37
42
76
8
58
52
49
29
17
73
4
60
53
50
64
5
7
24
39
91
66
51
59

INFORMATION

Alpine Association of Slovenia **1** C2
Atlas Express ...... (see 107)
Austrian Embassy **2** B4
Barsos-MC **3** C5
Canadian Consulate ...... (see 46)
Chemo Express **4** F4
Dental Clinic **5** H4
DrogArt **6** E2
Dutch Embassy **7** E4
Emergency Medical Assistance Clinic **8** H3
Erazem **9** D3
French Embassy **10** C6
German Embassy **11** B4
Health Centre Ljubljana **12** F2
Irish Embassy ...... (see 7)
Italian Embassy **13** B6
Knižnica Župančiča **14** F2
Kod & Kam **15** E2
Kompas **16** D2
Kulturni Center Q ...... (see 89)
Label **17** E4
Ljubljana Pharmacy **18** G3
Ljubljana Tourist Information Centre Branch **19** F2
Miklošič Educational Centre ...... (see 9)
Mint International House Ljubljana **20** C3
Mladinska Knjiga **21** E2
Mobitel Branch ...... (see 60)
Nova Ljubljanska Banka **22** C5
Portal.si Internet ...... (see 105)
Post Office Branch **23** D2
SiMobil ...... (see 57)
Slovenian Tourist Information Centre **24** E4
South African Consulate ...... (see 16)
Trek Trek **25** A6
UK Embassy ...... (see 46)
US Embassy **26** B4

SIGHTS & ACTIVITIES

Brewery Museum **27** C1
Ferant Garden (Roman Ruins) **28** B5
House of Experiments **29** E4
Ilirija Swimming Pool **30** C2
International Centre of Graphic Arts ...... (see 43)
Ljubljana Fairgrounds **31** D1
Ljubljana Gallery of Modern Art **32** B4
Ljubljana Stock Exchange **33** D2
Mala Galerija ...... (see 83)
Museum of Contemporary History of Slovenia **34** A2
National Gallery **35** C3
National Museum of Slovenia **36** B4
National Museum of Slovenia Collection **37** G3
Parliament Building **38** C4
Plečnik Monumental Lock **39** G5
Roman Wall Remains **40** B5
Serbian Orthodox Church **41** B3
Slovenian Ethnographic Museum **42** G3
Slovenian Museum of Natural History ...... (see 36)
Tivoli Mansion **43** A3
Tivoli Recreation Centre **44** B2
Tobacco Museum **45** A5
TR3 ...... **46** B5
Zlati Klub **47** B2

SLEEPING

Celica Hostel **48** G2
Dijaški Dom Tabor **49** F4
H2O Hostel **50** F4
Hostel DIC (Dijaški Dom Ivana Cankarja) **51** G5
Hotel Park **52** F3
Most Hostel **53** F4
Penzion Pod Lipo **54** B5
Slamič B&B ...... (see 75)
Stari Tišler **55** E3
Vila Veselova **56** B4
Zeppelin Hostel **57** D3

EATING

China Fast Food **58** F3
Don Felipe **59** F6
Falafel **60** E4
Gostilna Rimska XXI **61** B5
Hot Horse **62** B1
JB Restavracija **63** E2
Kavalino **64** F4
Maximarket **65** C5
Mencigar Nobile **66** G5
Mercator **67** D2
Mirje **68** A6
Nobel Burek **69** E3
Olimpije Burek Stand **70** D2
Operna Klet **71** C4
Restavracija 2000 ...... (see 65)
Thai Inn **72** B6
Zhong Hua **73** F4

DRINKING

Ambient **74** E3
KavaČaj **75** C3
Kavarna SEM **76** G3
Opera Bar **77** C4
Pr' Semaforju **78** C6
Žmavc **79** B5

ENTERTAINMENT

Cankarjev Dom **80** B5
Cankarjev Dom (Ticket Office) **81** C5
Escape **82** H2
Gala Hala **83** G2
Galerija Mizzart ...... (see 83)
Jalla Jalla Club **84** G2
Kino Dvor **85** E2
Kinoklub Vič **86** A6
Klub Channel Zero ...... (see 83)
Klub Gromka **87** G2
Klub K4 ...... **88** D3
Klub Monokel **89** G2
Klub Tiffany ...... (see 89)
KMŠ **90** A5
Ljubljana Puppet Theatre **91** E5
Menza pri Koritu **92** G2
Monokel ...... (see 89)
Opera House **93** C4
Orto Bar **94** H2
Roza Klub ...... (see 88)
Slovenian Youth Theatre **95** E1
Slovenska Kinoteka **96** E3
SubSub **97** A1
Tiffany ...... (see 89)

SHOPPING

Almira Sadar **98** D3
Darila Rokus **99** D3
Lovec **100** C3
Torbice Marjeta Grošelj **101** D3
Wine Cellars of Slovenia **102** D1

TRANSPORT

Adria Airlines Office **103** C3
Avis **104** E3
Bus Station **105** E2
Hertz **106** D3
LPP Information Centre **107** D3
LPP Kiosk **108** D3
Private Airport Van Stop **109** E2
Public Airport Bus Stop **110** E2

City of Ljubljana (www.ljubljana.si) Comprehensive information portal on every aspect of life and tourism direct from city hall.

In Your Pocket (www.inyourpocket.com) Insider info on the capital updated regularly. **Ljubljana Digital Media Lab** (www.ljudmila.org) Excellent site with links to all forms of alternative culture, music, venues and publications.

Ljubljana Life (www.ljubljana.info) Locally generated site offering useful information on Ljubljana for locals and visitors alike.

University of Ljubljana (www.uni-lj.si) Useful info for students.

Laundry

Washing machines (€7 per load) are available, even to nonguests, at the Celica Hostel (p90). Commercial laundries, including **Chemo Express** (Map p78; ☎ 251 44 04; Wolfova ulica 12; 🕑 7am-6pm Mon-Fri); Tabor (Map pp72-3; ☎ 231 07 82; Vidovdanska ulica 2; 🕑 7am-7pm Mon-Fri), charge from €4.20 per kg.

Left Luggage

Bus station (Map pp72-3; Trg OF 4; per day €2; ☎ 5.30am-10.30pm Sun-Fri, 5am-10pm Sat) Window No 3.

ain station (Map pp72-3; Trg OF 6; per day €2-3; ☎ 24hr) Coin lockers on platform 1.

ledical Services

arsos-MC (Map pp72-3; ☎ 242 07 00; info@barsos et; Gregorčičeva ulica 11; ⏰ 8am-3pm Mon, Wed & i; 8am-2pm Tue & Thu) Private clinic charging €30 per nsultation.

entral Pharmacy (Centralna Lekarna; Map p78; ☎ 244 23 60; Prešernov trg 5; ⏰ 7.30am-7.30pm Mon-i, 8am-1pm Sat)

ental Clinic (Stomotološka Klinika; Map pp72-3; ☎ 431 31 13; Zaloška cesta 2; ⏰ 8am-noon Mon-Sat)

mergency Medical Assistance Clinic (Klinični enter Urgenca; Map pp72-3; ☎ 522 84 28; info@kclj i; Bohoričeva ulica 4; ☎ 24hr) East of the Hotel Park Tabor.

ealth Centre Ljubljana (Zdravstveni Dom Ljubljana; ap pp72-3; ☎ 472 37 00; www.zd-lj.si; Metelkova ulica ; ⏰ 7am-7pm) For nonemergencies.

jubljana Pharmacy (Lekarna Ljubljana; Map pp72-3; ☎ 230 62 30; Prisojna ulica 7; ⏰ 24hr) All-night harmacy near the Emergency Medical Assistance Clinic.

loney

There are ATMs at every turn, including a row of them outside the main Ljubljana tourist nformation centre (TIC) office. At the train tation you'll find a **bureau de change** (☎ 7am-pm) changing cash for no commission but not ravellers cheques.

Some of the best exchange rates in Ljubljana are available at **Nova Ljubljanska Banka** (Map pp72-3; Trg Republike 2; ⏰ 8am-6pm Mon-ri) and **Ljubljana City Savings Bank** Center (Mestna Hranilnica Ljubljanska; Map p78; Čopova ulica 3; ⏰ 8.30am-pm & 3-5pm Mon-Fri); Old Town (Map p78; Mestni trg 16; ⏰ 8.30am-3.30pm Mon-Fri).

For information on getting cash advances and reporting a lost or stolen credit card, see p289.

Post

Main post office (Map p78; Slovenska cesta 32; ⏰ 8am-7pm Mon-Fri, 8am-1pm Sat) Holds *poštno ležeče* (poste restante) for 30 days and changes money.

Post office branch (Map pp72-3; Pražakova ulica 3; ⏰ 8am-7pm Mon-Fri, 8am-noon Sat) Southwest of the bus and train stations.

Toilets

Two convenient public toilets (€0.17) are in the Plečnikov podhod, the underpass (subway) below Slovenska cesta linking Kongresni trg with Plečnikov trg, and on Hribarjevo nabrežje below Kavarna Tromostovje (p96) on Prešernov trg.

Tourist Information

Ljubljana Tourist Information Centre (TIC; Map p78; ☎ 306 12 15; www.ljubljana-tourism.si; Kresija Bldg, Stritarjeva ulica; ⏰ 8am-9pm Jun-Sep, 8am-7pm Oct-May); train station (Map pp72-3; ☎ 433 94 75; Trg OF 6; ⏰ 8am-10pm Jun-Sep, 10am-7pm Mon-Fri, 8am-3pm Sat Oct-May) Run by the innovative Ljubljana Tourist Board (Zavod za Turizem Ljubljana), these two outlets are excellent sources of information on Ljubljana. Knowledgeable, enthusiastic staff dispense information and useful literature (*Ljubljana City Map, Where? Tourist Guide, Ljubljana from A to Z* booklet etc) and can help with accommodation.

Slovenian Tourist Information Centre (STIC; Map pp72-3; ☎ 306 45 75; www.slovenia.info; Krekov trg 10; ⏰ 8am-9pm Jun-Sep, 8am-7pm Mon-Fri, 8am-3pm Sat Oct-May) Good source of information for the rest of Slovenia, with internet and bicycle rental also available.

Škuc Culture Centre (Študentski Kulturni Center; ŠKUC; Map p78; ☎ 421 31 42; www.skuc.org; Stari trg 21; ⏰ noon-8pm) Information on cultural happenings, student life etc.

ŠOU Information Centre (Študentska Organizacija Univerze Ljubljani; ŠOU; Map p78; ☎ 438 03 20, 051 373 999; www.sou-lj.si; Trubarjeva cesta 7; ⏰ 9am-6pm Mon-Thu, 9am-3pm Fri) Information and free internet.

Travel Agencies

Erazem (Map pp72-3; ☎ 430 55 37; www.erazem.net; basement, Miklošičeva cesta 26; ⏰ 10am-5pm Mon-Fri) Staff make plane and train bookings and sell student, youth and hostel cards.

Kompas Slovenska cesta (Map p78; ☎ 200 62 22; www.kompas.net; Slovenska cesta 36; ⏰ 9am-7pm Mon-Fri, 9am-12.30pm Sat); Pražakova ulica (Map pp72-3; ☎ 200 63 33; Pražakova ulica 4; ⏰ 9am-6pm Mon-Fri, 9am-12.30pm Sat)

Label (Map pp72-3; ☎ 051 200 743; www.label.si; Trubarjeva cesta 47; ⏰ 10am-1pm & 4-8pm Mon-Fri, 10am-1pm & 6-8pm Sat) Organises adventure-sport excursions around Slovenia.

STA Ljubljana (Map p78; ☎ 439 16 90, 041 612 711; www.staljubljana.com, in Slovene; 1st fl, Trg Ajdovščina 1; ⏰ agency 10am-5pm Mon-Fri, internet cafe 8am-midnight Mon-Sat) Discount air fares for students and its cafe has internet access.

Trek Trek (Map pp72-3; ☎ 425 13 92, 041 521 655; www.trektrek.si; Bičevje ulica 5; ⏰ 10am-5pm Mon-Fri) Specialising in adventure travel in Slovenia, with emphasis on trekking and cycling holidays.

SIGHTS

The easiest way to see Ljubljana is on foot. The oldest part of town, with the most important historical buildings and sights (including Ljubljana Castle) lies on the right (east) bank of the Ljubljanica River. Center, which has the lion's share of the city's museums and galleries, is on the left (west) side of the river.

Prešernov Trg

This central and very beautiful square (Map p78) forms the link between Center and the Old Town. Taking pride of place is the **Prešeren monument** (1905) designed by Maks Fabiani and Ivan Zajc, and erected in honour of Slovenia's greatest poet, France Prešeren (1800–49). On the plinth are motifs from his poems. Just south of the monument is the **Triple Bridge** (Tromostovje), called the Špital (Hospital) Bridge when it was built as a single span in 1842, which leads to the Old Town. The prolific architect Jože Plečnik added the two sides in 1931.

To the east of the monument at No 5 is the Italianate **Central Pharmacy** (Centralna Lekarna), an erstwhile cafe frequented by intellectuals in the 19th century. To the north, on the corner of Trubarjeva cesta and Miklošičeva cesta, is the delightful Secessionist **Palača Urbanc** (Urbanc Palace) building from 1903, now being turn into a posh shopping mall. Diagonally across the square at No 1 is another Secessionist gem: the **Hauptman House**. Two doors down Wolfova ulica at No 4 you'll see a terracotta figure peeking out from a window. It's Julija Primič looking at the monument to her lifelong admirer France Prešeren.

The 17th-century salmon-pink **Franciscan Church of the Annunciation** (Frančiškanska Cerkev Marijinega Oznanjanja; ☎ 242 93 00; Prešernov trg 4; 🕑 6.40am-noon & 3-8pm) stands on the northern side of the square. The interior is not so interesting with its six side altars and enormous choir stall, though the main altar was designed by the Italian sculptor Francesco Robba (1698-1757). To the left of the main altar is a glass-fronted coffin with the spooky remains of St Deodatus.

Miklošičeva Cesta

This 650m-long thoroughfare links Prešernov trg with Trg OF and the train and bus stations; the southern end boasts a splendid array of fine Secessionist buildings. The cream-coloured former **People's Loan Bank** (Map p78; 1908) at No 4 is topped with blue tiles and the figures of two women holding symbols of industry (a beehive) and wealth (a purse). The one-time **Cooperative Bank** (Map p78) at No 5 was designed by Ivan Vurnik, and the red, yellow and blue geometric patterns were painted by his wife Helena in 1922. Just opposite is the **Grand Hotel Union** (Map p78), the *grande dame* of Ljubljana hotels built in 1905. About 150m to the north is **Miklošičev Park** (Map p78), laid out by Fabiani in 1902. All the buildings facing it are art nouveau masterpieces, with the exception of the unspeakable one housing offices, trade unions and a bank to the south.

Central Market Area

The **Central Market** (Centralna Tržnica; Map p78) lies across Triple Bridge to the southeast of Prešernov trg. The elegant covered walkway along the river, the **Plečnik Colonnade** (Plečnikov Arkada), forms part of the market to the north.

Walk through **Pogačarjev trg** and on to **Vodnikov trg**, with their wonderful open-air market stalls selling everything from wild mushrooms and forest berries to honey and homemade cheeses. Just north of Vodnikov trg is the iconic **Dragon Bridge** (Zmajski Most; Map pp72-3). See also p77.

The curious **cone** at the entrance to Pogačarjev trg was erected in honour of Plečnik in 1993. It represents a similarly shaped parliament building he designed (but never built) for the top of Castle Hill. The building on the southern side of the square

SLOVENIAN HERITAGE

If you are searching for your Slovenian roots, check first with the *mestna občina* (municipal government office) or *občina* (county office); they usually have birth and death certificates going back a century. Vital records beyond the 100-year limit are kept at the **Archives of the Republic of Slovenia** (Arhiv Republike Slovenije; Map p85; ☎ 241 42 00; www.arhiv.gov.si; Gruber Palace, Zvezdarska ulica 1; 🕑 8am-2pm Mon-Fri). Ethnic Slovenes living abroad might be interested in contacting the **Slovenian Emigrants Centre** (Slovenska Izseljenska Matica; Map p78; ☎ 241 02 80; www.zdruzenje-sim.si, in Slovene; 2nd fl, Cankarjeva cesta 1; 🕑 by appointment).

s the Renaissance **Bishop's Palace** (Škofijski Dvorec; iril Metodov trg 4), with a lovely arcaded central ourtyard. To the east the **Seminary** (Semenišče; olničarjeva ulica 4), its entrance framed by a pair of Atlas figures sculpted by Andrea Pozzo, ontains ornate baroque furnishings and a library with priceless incunabula, 16th-century nanuscripts and frescoes. The interior can be isited by appointment only; contact the TIC. There's a covered market with meat, fish and lairy products on the ground floor (p95).

Dominating Pogačarjev trg is the **Cathedral of St Nicholas** (Stolna Cerkev Sv Nikolaja; Map p78; ☎ 234 26 90; Dolničarjeva ulica 1; 🕑 10am-noon & 3-6pm). A church has stood here since the 13th century, but the existing twin-towered building dates from the start of the 18th century. Inside it's a vision of pink marble, white stucco and gilt and contains a panoply of baroque frescoes. Have a look at the magnificent carved choir stalls, the organ and the angels on the main altar – another Robba creation. Two stunning bronze doors were added in 1996 to commemorate the late Pope John Paul II's visit – the (main) west door facing the Bishop's Palace symbolises 1250 years of Christianity in Slovenia; the six bishops on the south door fronting Ciril Metodov trg depict the history of the Ljubljana diocese.

Old Town

Ljubljana's Old Town (Staro Mesto; Map p78) is its oldest and most important historical quarter. A large portion of the buildings here are baroque, although some houses along Stari trg and Gornji trg have retained their medieval layout.

MESTNI TRG

The first of the Old Town's three 'squares' (the next two are more like narrow cobbled streets), Mestni trg (Town Square) is dominated by the **town hall** (mestna hiša; ☎ 306 30 00; 🕑 7.30am-4pm Mon-Fri), the seat of the city government and sometimes referred to as the Magistrat or Rotovž. It was erected in the late 15th century and rebuilt in 1718. The Gothic courtyard inside, arcaded on three levels, is where theatrical performances once took place and contains some lovely sgraffiti. If you look above the south portal leading to a second courtyard you'll see a relief map of Ljubljana as it appeared in the second half of the 17th century.

In front of the town hall stands the **Robba Fountain** (1751); the three titans with their gushing urns represent the three rivers of Carniola: the Sava, Krka and Ljubljanica but are modern copies. The originals, worn down by time and eaten away by urban pollution, are now housed in the National Gallery (p83).

STARI TRG

The Old Square is the true heart of the Old Town. It is lined with 19th-century wooden shop fronts, quiet courtyards and cobblestone passageways. From behind the medieval houses on the eastern side, paths once led to Castle Hill, which was a source of water. The buildings fronting the river had large passageways built to allow drainage in case of flooding. Where No 2 is today a prison called **Tranča** stood until the 18th century, and those condemned to death were executed at a spot nearby. The great polymath Janez Vajkard Valvasor (p207) was born in house No 4 in 1641.

A small street to the north called Pod Trančo (Below Tranča) leads to **Cobbler Bridge** (Čevljarski Most). During the Middle Ages this was a place of trade, and a tolled gateway led to the town. Craftsmen worked and lived on bridges (in this case 16 shoemakers) to catch the traffic and avoid paying town taxes – a medieval version of duty-free.

Between Stari trg 11 and No 15 – the house that *should* bear the number 13 – there's a lovely rococo building called **Schweiger House**

WAGGIN' DRAGONS

Ljubljana's town hall is topped with a golden dragon, a symbol of Ljubljana but not an ancient one as many people assume. Just before the turn of the 20th century a wily mayor named Ivan Hribar apparently persuaded the authorities in Vienna that Ljubljana needed a new crossing over the Ljubljanica, and he submitted plans for a 'Jubilee Bridge' to mark 50 years of the reign of Franz Joseph. The result, the much-loved Dragon Bridge (Zmajski Most) was built to the northeast of Vodnikov trg, and renamed in 1919. City folk say the winged bronze dragons wag their tails whenever a virgin crosses the bridge. We don't believe in such old wives' tales as we've never seen it happen.

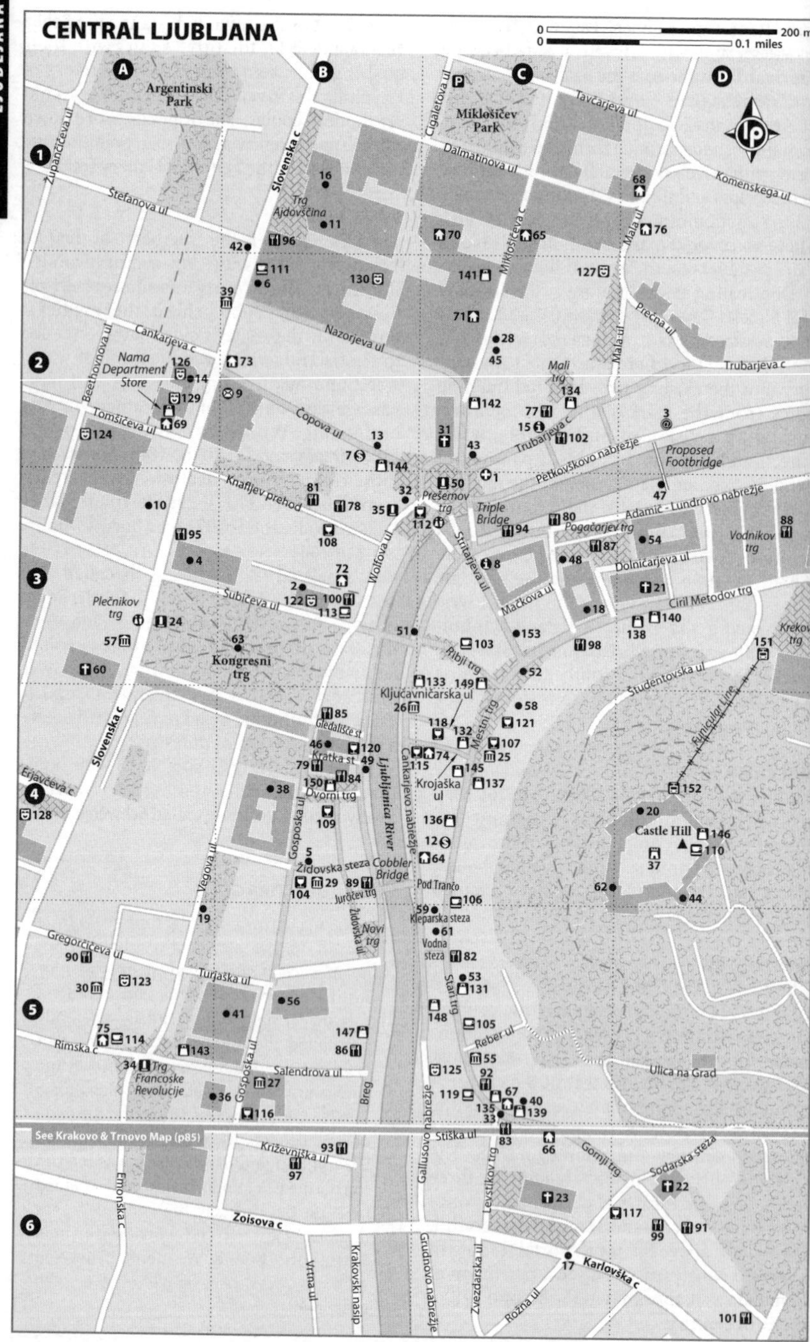
CENTRAL LJUBLJANA
200 m
0.1 miles
Argentinski Park
Miklošičev Park
Tavčarjeva ul
Dalmatinova ul
Komenskega ul
Županičičeva ul
Štefanova ul
Slovenska c
Trg Ajdovščina
Cigaletova ul
Miklošičeva c
Mala ul
Prečna ul
Nazorjeva ul
Cankarjeva c
Beethovnova ul
Nama Department Store
Tomšičeva ul
Čopova ul
Trubarjeva c
Mali trg
Petkovškovo nabrežje
Proposed Footbridge
Knafljev prehod
Prešernov trg
Triple Bridge
Adamič - Lundrovo nabrežje
Pogačarjev trg
Vodnikov trg
Wolfova ul
Stritarjeva ul
Dolničarjeva ul
Mačkova ul
Ciril Metodov trg
Plečnikov trg
Šubičeva ul
Kongresni trg
Ribji trg
Krekov trg
Študentovska ul
Funicular Line
Ključavničarska ul
Mestni trg
Gledališče st
Kratka st
Ljubljanica River
Cankarjevo nabrežje
Krojaška ul
Erjavčeva c
Dvorni trg
Castle Hill
Gosposka ul
Vegova ul
Židovska steza
Cobbler Bridge
Pod Trančo
Jurčičev trg
Židovska ul
Novi trg
Kleparska steza
Vodna steza
Gregorčičeva ul
Stari trg
Turjaška ul
Reber ul
Rimska c
Trg Francoske Revolucije
Salendrova ul
Breg
Ulica na Grad
See Krakovo & Trnovo Map (p85)
Stiška ul
Križevniška ul
Gornji trg
Sodarska steza
Emonska c
Gallusovo nabrežje
Levstikov trg
Zoisova c
Karlovška c
Vrtna ul
Krakovski nasip
Grudnovo nabrežje
Zvezdarska ul
Rožna ul

INFORMATION

Central Pharmacy **1** C3
Centre for Slovene as a Second/Foreign Language (see 38)
Chemo Express **2** B3
Cyber Café Xplorer **3** D2
Geonavtik **4** A3
Knjigarna Behemot **5** B4
Kompas **6** B2
Ljubljana City Savings Bank Building **7** B2
Ljubljana Tourist Information Centre **8** C3
Main Post Office **9** B2
Mladinska Knjiga **10** A3
Mobitel **11** B1
Nova Ljubljanska Banka **12** C4
SiMobil Branch **13** B2
Škuc Cultural Centre (see 55)
Slovenian Emigrants Centre **14** A2
ŠOU Information Centre **15** C2
STA Ljubljana **16** B1

SIGHTS & ACTIVITIES

Balkan Gate **17** C6
Bishop's Palace **18** C3
Busts & Plaques of Celebrated Slovenes **19** A5
Casemates **20** D4
Cathedral of St Nicholas **21** D3
Chapel of St George (see 62)
Church of St Florian **22** D6
Church of St James **23** C6
Citizen of Emona **24** A3
City Gallery **25** C4
City Gallery Branch **26** B4
City Museum of Ljubljana **27** B5
Cooperative Bank **28** C2
DESSA Architectural Gallery **29** B4
Equrna Gallery **30** A5
Franciscan Church of the Annunciation **31** C2
Grand Hotel Union (see 71)
Hauptman House **32** B3
Hercules Fountain **33** C5
Ilirija Column **34** A5
Julija Pimič Statue **35** B3
Križanke **36** B5
Ljubljana Castle **37** D4
Ljubljana University **38** B4
Mala Galerija **39** B2
Medieval Houses **40** C5
National and University Library **41** B5
Nebotičnik **42** B1
Palača Urbanc **43** C2
Pentagonal Tower **44** D4
People's Loan Bank **45** C2
Philharmonic Hall **46** B4
Plečnik Colonnade **47** D3
Plečnik Cone **48** C3
Plovila Iza (Boat Tours) **49** B4
Prešeren Monument **50** C3
Ribji Trg Pier (Boat Tours) **51** B3
Robba Fountain **52** C3
Schweiger House **53** C5
Seminary **54** D3
Škuc Gallery **55** C5
Slovenian Academy of Arts and Sciences **56** B5
Slovenian School Museum **57** A3
Town Hall **58** C4
Tranča **59** C5
Ursuline Church of the Holy Trinity **60** A3
Valvasor's Birthplace **61** C5
Virtual Museum (see 62)
Watchtower **62** C4
Zvezda Park **63** B3

SLEEPING

Alibi Hostel **64** C4
Alibi M14 Hostel **65** C1
Allegro Hotel **66** C6
Antiq Hotel **67** C5
City Hotel Ljubljana **68** D1
Fluxus Hostel **69** A2
Grand Hotel Union Business **70** C1
Grand Hotel Union Executive **71** C2
Hotel Emonec **72** B3
Hotel Slon Best Western Premier **73** B2
Maček Rooms **74** C4
Pri Mraku **75** A5
Tour As **76** D1

EATING

Ajdovo Zrno **77** C2
Cantina Mexicana **78** B3
Covered Market (see 54)
Delikatesa Ljubljanski Dvor **79** B4
Fish Market **80** C3
Gostilna As **81** B3
Julija **82** C5
Le Coq Blanc **83** C6
Ljubljanski Dvor **84** B4
Mercator Supermarket **85** B4
Namasté **86** B5
Open-air Market **87** C3
Open-air Market **88** D3
Paninoteka **89** B4
Pizzeria Foculus **90** A5
Pizzicato **91** D6
Pr' Potic **92** C5
Pri Vitezu **93** B6
Ribca **94** C3
Rio-Momo **95** A3
Šestica **96** B1
Shambala **97** B6
Sokol **98** C3
Špajza **99** D6
Sushimama **100** B3
Taverna Tatjana **101** D6
Zrno do Zrna **102** C2

DRINKING

Abecedarium Cafe **103** C3
BiKoFe **104** B4
Café Antico **105** C5
Cha **106** C4
Čuperterija **107** C4
Cutty Sark **108** B3
Dvorni Bar **109** B4
Grajska Kavarna **110** D4
Juice Box **111** B2
Kavarna Tromostovje **112** C3
Kavarna Zvezda **113** B3
Le Petit Café **114** A5
Maček **115** C4
Pod Skalco **116** B5
Pri Zelenem Zajcu **117** D6
Pr'Skelet **118** C4
Slaščičarna Pri Vodnjaku **119** C5
Solist **120** B4
Vinoteka Movia **121** C4

ENTERTAINMENT

As Lounge (see 81)
As Pub (see 81)
Bacchus Center **122** B3
Glej Theatre **123** A5
Jazz Club Gajo **124** A2
Kafeterija Lan **125** C5
Kino Komuna **126** A2
Križanke (see 36)
Philharmonic Hall (see 46)
Roxly **127** C2
Slovenian National Drama Theatre **128** A4
Top: Eat & Party **129** A2
Ultra **130** B2

SHOPPING

Akultura **131** C5
Antika Ferjan **132** C4
Antiques & Flea Market **133** C3
Carniola Antiqua **134** C2
Devetka **135** C5
Galerija Fortuna (see 135)
Galerija Idrijske Čipke **136** C4
Honey House **137** C4
Ika za Piko na I **138** D3
Katarina Silk **139** C5
Kraševka **140** D3
Ljubljanček **141** C2
MCD Shop **142** C2
Muzikalije **143** A5
Peko **144** B2
Piranske Soline **145** C4
Rustika **146** D4
Skrina **147** B5
Spin Vinyl **148** C5
Trubarjev Antikvariat **149** C3
Vinoteka Dvor Koželj **150** B4

TRANSPORT

ABC Rent a Car (see 68)
Budget (see 70)
Europcar (see 68)
Funicular Lower Station **151** D3
Funicular Upper Station **152** D4
Tourist Train **153** C3

with a large Atlas supporting the upper balcony. The figure has his finger raised to his lips as if asking passers-by to be quiet (the owner's name means 'Silent One' in German). In this part of the world, bordellos were traditionally located at house No 13 of a street, and he probably got quite a few unsolicited calls.

In Levstikov trg, the southern extension of Stari trg, the **Hercules Fountain** is a recent copy of the 17th-century original now in the town hall. To the southeast is the **Church of St James** (Cerkev Sv Jakoba; Map p78; ☎ 252 17 27; Gornji trg 18; 🕑 7am-8pm) built in 1615. More interesting than Robba's main altar (1732) is the altar in the church's **Chapel of St Francis Xavier** to the left, with statues of a 'White Queen' and a 'Black King' from the early 18th century.

Across Karlovška cesta is **Gruber Palace** (Gruberjeva Palača; Map p85; Zvezdarska ulica 1). Gabriel Gruber, the Jesuit who built the Gruber Canal (Gruberjev Prekop) that regulates the Ljubljanica, lived here until 1784. The palace is in Zopf style, a transitional art style between late baroque and neoclassicism, and now contains the national archives. If you look eastward down Karlovška cesta, you'll see what was once the **Balkan Gate** (Map p78), the southernmost point of the Old Town. From here the town walls ran up Castle Hill.

GORNJI TRG

Upper Square is the eastern extension of Stari trg. The five **medieval houses** at Nos 7 to 15 (Map p78) have narrow side passages (some with doors) where rubbish was once deposited so that it could be washed down into the river. The most important building on this elongated square is the **Church of St Florian** (Cerkev Sv Florijana). It was built in 1672 and dedicated to the patron saint of fires after a serious blaze destroyed much of the Old Town. Plečnik renovated it in 1934.

The footpath **Ulica na Grad**, leading up from the church, is an easy way to reach the castle.

Botanical Garden

About 800m southeast of the Old Town along Karlovška cesta and over the Ljubljanica River, this 2.5-hectare **botanical garden** (Botanični Vrt; Map p85; ☎ 427 12 80; Ižanska cesta 15; admission free; 🕑 7am-8pm Jul & Aug, 7am-7pm Apr-Jun, Sep & Oct, 7am-5pm Nov-Mar) was founded in 1810 as a sanctuary of native flora. It contains 4500 species of plants and trees, about a third of which are indigenous, and is overseen by the University of Ljubljana.

You can reach here on bus 3 from Slovensk cesta (stop: Strelišče). Alternatively take bus to the terminus (Trnovo) on Opekarska ces and walk across the new footbridge (Map p8 at the southern end of Prule.

Ljubljana Castle

There have been fortifications of one kind c another on Castle Hill (Grajska Planota), th city's focal point, since at least Celtic times, bu the existing **Ljubljana Castle** (Ljubljanski Grad; Map p7 ☎ 232 99 94; www.ljubljanafestival.si; admission free; 🕑 9am 11pm May-Sep, 10am-9pm Oct-Apr) mostly dates fror a 16th-century rebuilding following the 151 earthquake. It was a royal residence in the 17t and 18th centuries and a prison and barrack in the 19th and first half of the 20th centurie About 80% of the castle has been renovated i recent years, but remains an architectural mish mash, including fortified walls dating from th early 16th century, a late 15th-century chape and a 1970s concrete cafe. It is now frequentl used as a venue for concerts and other cultura activities, as well as a wedding hall.

The **Watchtower** (Razgledni Stolp; adult/senior & student/family €3.50/2/4.50; ☎ 9am-9pm May-Sep, 10am-6pr Oct-Apr), which is the tower on the southwester side of the castle courtyard, contains the **Virtua Museum** (Virtualni Muzej), a 23-minute 3D video tour of Ljubljana and its history in fou languages. The climb up to the top of the tower via a double wrought-iron staircase (95 step from the museum level) of the 19th-centur tower and a walk along the ramparts, is wortl the effort for the views down into the Olc Town and across the river to Center.

Attached to the tower, the **Chapel of St George** (Kapela Sv Jurija; 1489) is covered in frescoe and the coats of arms of the Dukes of Carniola In the castle's southern wing, the **Pentagonal Tower** (Peterokotni Stolp) hosts changing exhibitions, smaller concerts and theatrical performances. You can see remnants from the Middle Ages (Latin inscriptions, coats-of-arms) in the **casemates** *(kazemate)* of the northern wing.

Castle tours (adult/child/student €5/2.50/3.50; 🕑 10am, 11.30am, 2pm & 4pm Jul & Aug, 10am & 4pm Jun & 1st half of Sep) depart from the bridge at the castle's main entrance and include admission to the tower and museum.

The fastest (and easiest) way to reach the castle is via the 70m-long **funicular** (vzpenjača; ☎ 306 42 00; one-way up €1.80, down €1.50 return adult/senior, senior & child/family €3/2/7; 🕑 9am-11pm May-Sep, 10am-9pm Oct-Apr), which ascends from Krekov g every 10 minutes. There's also the hourly **urist train** (Stritarjeva ul; adult/child €3/2; up m-9pm, down 9.20am-9.20pm daily) from south of e TIC.

It takes about 15 minutes to walk to the astle from the Old Town. There are three outes: Študentovska ulica, which runs south om Ciril Metodov trg; steep Reber ulica from tari trg; and Ulica na Grad from Gornji trg.

abor

Iorth of Castle Hill across the Ljubljanica iver, this neighbourhood (Map pp72–3) leafy, residential, and home to the pulating Metelkova district of alternative ulture (p97). It also contains a couple of nportant museums.

The **Slovenian Ethnographic Museum** (Slovenski tnografski Muzej; ☎ 300 87 45; www.etno-muzej.si; etelkova ulica 2; adult/student & senior €4.50/2.50, admison free last Sun of month; 10am-6pm Tue-Sun), housed n the 1886 Belgian Barracks on the southern dge of Metelkova, has a permanent collection n the 3rd floor. There's traditional Slovenian rades and handicrafts – everything from beeeeping and blacksmithing to glass-painting nd pottery making – and some excellent xhibits directed at children. Temporary exibits are on the 1st and 2nd floors. There's n excellent cafe here.

The modern building across the courtyard o the northeast contains the **National Museum f Slovenia Collection** (Zbirka Narodnega Muzeja Slovenije; ☎ 230 70 30; www.nms.si; Maistrova ulica 1; adult/student senior/family €3/2.50/6, admission free 1st Sun of month; 10am-6pm Tue-Sun), a bizarre assortment of nostly applied art and *objets d'art* (furniture, eligious items, paintings etc) that are tenuously linked through themes. Surely this is a home away from home for these goodies until the main museum site is sorted.

Žale

This suburb about 2km northeast of Tabor contains Plečnik's largest masterpiece, the monumental **Žale Cemetery** (Pokopališče Žale; off Map pp72-3; ☎ 420 17 00; Med Hmeljniki 2; 6am-8pm Apr-Sep, 7am-6pm Oct-Mar), Ljubljana's very own Père Lachaise or Highgate and now on the European Heritage List. It has a series of chapels dedicated to the patron saints of Ljubljana's churches, the entrance is an enormous two-storey arcade and this peaceful and very green place is 'home' to a number of Slovenian actors, writers, painters and a certain distinguished architect – Gospod Plečnik himself. There are also the graves of Austrian, Italian and German soldiers from both World Wars and a small Jewish section too. You can reach Žale on bus 2, 7 or 22 (stop: Žale).

Center

This district on the left bank of the Ljubljanica is the nerve centre of modern Ljubljana. It is filled with shops, commercial offices, government departments and embassies. There are several areas of interest to travellers as well.

NOVI TRG

New Square (Map p78), south of Cobbler Bridge, was a walled settlement of fisherfolk outside the town administration in the Middle Ages, but it became more aristocratic from the 16th century. It suffered extensive damage in the 1895 earthquake, but medieval remnants include the very narrow street to the north called **Židovska ulica** (Jewish Street) and its offshoot Židovska steza (Jewish Lane), once the site of a synagogue and the centre of Jewish life here in the Middle Ages. **Breg**, the city's port when the Ljubljanica River was still navigable this far inland, runs south from the square and is now almost entirely pedestrianised. At Novi trg's western end is the **Slovenian Academy of Arts and Sciences** (Slovenska Akademija Znanosti in Umetnosti; Map p78; ☎ 470 61 00; Novi trg 3), housed in a 16th-century building that was the seat of the provincial diet under the Habsburgs. The **National and University Library** (Narodna in Univerzitetna Knjižnica; Map p78; ☎ 200 11 88; www.nuk.uni-lj.si; Turjaška ulica 1), Plečnik's masterpiece completed in 1941, is just opposite. To appreciate more of this great man's philosophy, enter through the main door (note the horsehead doorknobs) on Turjaška ulica – you'll find yourself in near darkness, entombed in black marble. But as you ascend the steps, you'll emerge into a colonnade suffused with light – the light of knowledge, according to the architect's plans. The **Main Reading Room** (Velika Čitalnica; adult/child €2/1; tours 2-6pm Mon, Tue & Thu-Sat, noon-6pm Sun Jul–mid-Aug), now open to nonstudents only by group tour in summer, has huge glass walls and some stunning lamps, also designed by Plečnik.

TRG FRANCOSKE REVOLUCIJE

French Revolution Sq was for centuries the headquarters of the Teutonic Knights of the Cross *(Križniki)*. They built a commandery here in the early 13th century, which was transformed into the **Križanke** (Map p78; ☎ 241 60 00; Trg Francoske Revolucije 1-2) monastery complex in the early 18th century. Today it serves as the headquarters of the Ljubljana Summer Festival (p88), with an open-air theatre seating 1400 people, and hosts other concerts at other times of the year. The **Ilirija Column** in the centre of the square recalls Napoleon's Illyrian Provinces (1809–13), when Slovene was taught in schools for the first time.

At the eastern end of Trg Francoske Revolucije, the excellent (and architecturally important) **City Museum of Ljubljana** (Mestni Muzej Ljubljana; Map p78; ☎ 241 25 35, 051 234 582; www.mestnimuzej.si; Gosposka ulica 15; adult/child/family €4/2.50/8; ☎ 10am-6pm Tue-Sun) focuses on Ljubljana's history, culture and politics via imaginative multimedia and interactive displays. The reconstructed Roman street that linked the eastern gates of Emona to the Ljubljanica and the collection of well-preserved classical artefacts in the basement are worth a visit in themselves, and the permanent Faces of Ljubljana exhibit of celebrated and lesser-known *žabarji* ('froggers', as natives of the capital are known) is memorable. They host some cracker special exhibits too.

KONGRESNI TRG

This lovely square, with leafy Park Zvevda (Star Park) – currently being dug up to shoehorn in an underground car park – in its centre, can be reached from Trg Francoske Revolucije by walking north along Vegova ulica, a pleasant street lined with trees and busts of Slovenian writers, scientists and musicians. Named in honour of the Congress of the Holy Alliance, convened by Austria, Prussia, Russia and Naples in 1821 and hosted by Ljubljana, Congress Sq contains several important buildings. To the south at No 12 is the central building of **Ljubljana University** (Univerza v Ljubljani; Map p78; ☎ 241 85 00; Kongresni trg 12), erected as a ducal palace in 1902. The **Philharmonic Hall** (Filharmonija; Map p78; ☎ 241 08 00; Kongresni trg 10) situated in the southeast corner is home to the Slovenian Philharmonic Orchestra, which was founded in 1701 and is one of the oldest in the world. Haydn, Beethoven and Brahms were honorary members, and Gustav Mahler was resident conductor for a season (1881–82).

The **Ursuline Church of the Holy Trinity** (Uršulins Cerkev Sv Trojice; Map p78; ☎ 252 48 64; Slovenska ce 21; ⏰ 6-7.30am, 9-11am & 4-7pm), which faces tl square from across Slovenska cesta and dat from 1726, is the most beautiful baroqu building in the city. It contains a multico oured altar by Robba made of African marbl To reach the church use the Plečnik unde pass (Plečnikov podhod) at the western en of Kongresni trg. Depending on what stag the excavations are at on the western edge the square, you may spot a small gilded statu on top of a column. It's a copy (the original in the National Museum) of the Roman-er **Citizen of Emona**, dating from the 4th centur and unearthed nearby in 1836.

At the other end of the underpass is th entrance to the rather esoteric **Slovenia School Museum** (Slovenski Šolski Muzej; Map p78; ☎ 25 30 24; www.ssolski-muzej.si; Plečnikov trg 1; adult/chi €2/1; ⏰ 9am-1pm Mon-Fri), which explores ho Slovenian kids learned the three Rs in th 19th century.

TRG REPUBLIKE

Republic Sq is Center's main plaza Unfortunately, it is basically a car park dominated by a pair of glowering, grey tower blocks – **TR3** (Map pp72-3; Trg Republike 3), housing office and embassies, and the headquarters of **Nov Ljubljanska Banka** (Map pp72-3; Trg Republike 2) – an a couple of garish revolutionary monuments The renovated **Parliament Building** (Map pp72-3 ☎ 478 97 87; www.dz-rs.si; Šubičeva ulica 4; admission free ⏰ tours 9am, 10am & 11am every 2nd Sat mid-Sep–Jul) built between 1954 and 1959 at the northeas corner of the square, is no beauty-pagean winner on the outside but the mammoth portal festooned with bronze sculptures is noteworthy. If you can time it right, it's worth joining one of the guided tours to see the inside, especially the period-piece mural by Slavko Pengov in the vestibule of the **Large Hall** (Velika Dvorana) depicting the history of Slovenia.

Cankarjev Dom (Map pp72-3; ☎ 241 71 00), the city's premier cultural and conference centre (p99), squats behind the TR3 building to the southwest.

Behind Cankarjev Dom is **Ferant Garden** (Map pp72-3; ☎ 241 25 06; Erjavčeva cesta 18; ⏰ by appointment Apr-Oct), with the remains of an early Christian church porch and baptistery with mosaics from the 4th century visible from the locked gate. To visit you must rst contact the City Museum (opposite). pposite and to the west of the Cankarjev om are the remains of a **Roman wall** dating om 14–15 AD.

luseum Area

our of Ljubljana's most important museums re located in this area, which is only a short istance to the northwest of Trg Republike.

ATIONAL MUSEUM OF SLOVENIA

)n the western side of parklike Trg Jarodnih Herojev, this **museum** (Narodni luzej Slovenije; Map pp72-3; ☎ 241 44 00; www nms.si; Prešernova cesta 20; adult/student & senior/family 3/2.50/6, incl Natural History Museum €5/4/10, admission ree 1st Sun of month; 10am-6pm Fri-Wed, 10am-8pm hu) occupies an elegant 1888 building. It as a large collection, but at the time of vriting, only highlights from the coin and ich archaeological collections, including a Roman lapidarium and Egyptian artefacts, vere on display. The Roman glass and the ewellery found in 6th-century Slavic graves s pretty standard fare, but treasures include he highly embossed Vače *situla*, a Celtic pail from the late 6th century BC unearthed in a town east of Ljubljana, and a Stone Age bone flute discovered near Cerkno in western Slovenia in 1995. Make sure you check out the ceiling fresco in the foyer, which features an allegorical Carniola surrounded by important Slovenes from the past and the statues of the Muses and Fates relaxing on the stairway banisters. Enter the museum from Muzejska ulica 1.

SLOVENIAN MUSEUM OF NATURAL HISTORY

Housed in 16 rooms and hallways of the same impressive building as the National Museum, the **Natural History Museum** (Prirodoslovni Muzej Slovenije; Map pp72-3; ☎ 241 09 40; www2.pms -lj.si; Prešernova cesta 20; adult/student & senior/family €3/2.50/6, incl National Museum €5/4/10, admission free 1st Sun of month; 10am-6pm Fri-Wed, 10am-8pm Thu) contains the usual reassembled mammoth and whale skeletons, stuffed birds, reptiles and mammals. However, the mineral collections amassed by the philanthropic Baron Žiga Zois in the early 19th century and the display on Slovenia's unique salamander *Proteus anguinus* are worth a visit. Enter the museum from Muzejska ulica 1.

NATIONAL GALLERY OF SLOVENIA

Slovenia's foremost collection of fine art is at the **National Gallery** (Narodna Galerija Slovenije; Map pp72-3; ☎ 241 54 18; www.ng-slo.si; Prešernova cesta 24 & Cankarjeva cesta 20; adult/student & senior €7/5, admission free 1st Sun of month, temporary exhibits €5/3; 10am-6pm Tue-Sun). It offers portraits and Slovenian landscapes from the 17th to 19th centuries (check out works by national Romantic painters Pavel Künl, Marko Pernhart and Anton Karinger), copies of medieval frescoes and a wonderful Gothic statuary (1896) in its old south wing. Although the subjects of the earlier paintings are the usual foppish nobles and lemon-lipped clergymen, some of the later works are remarkable and provide a good introduction to Slovenian art. Take a close look at the works of the impressionists Jurij Šubic *(Before the Hunt)* and Rihard Jakopič *(Birches in Autumn)*, the pointillist Ivan Grohar *(Škofja Loka in the Snow)* and Slovenia's most-celebrated female painter Ivana Kobilca *(Summer)*. The bronzes by Franc Berneker and Anton Gangl are truly exceptional. The gallery's modern north wing facing Puharjeva ulica has a permanent collection of European paintings from the Middle Ages to the 20th century on the 1st floor and is also used for temporary exhibits. In the vestibule of the Prešernova cesta entrance stands the original Robba Fountain, which was moved here from Mestni trg in the Old Town in 2008.

LJUBLJANA GALLERY OF MODERN ART

Housed in an ugly modern building (1939–51) designed by Edvard Ravnikar, this inwardly vibrant **gallery** (Moderna Galerija Ljubljana; Map pp72-3; ☎ 241 68 00; www.mg-lj.si; Cankarjeva cesta 15) was undergoing extensive renovation at the time of research though parts of its permanent collection were being shown in other galleries and venues around town, including its galleries in Center and Metelkova (p84). Keep an eye out for works by painters Tone Kralj *(Peasant Wedding)*, the expressionist France Mihelič *(The Quintet)* and the surrealist Štefan Planinc *(Primeval World series)* as well as sculptors such as Jakob Savinšek *(Protest)*. The museum also owns works by the influential 1980s and 1990s multimedia group Neue Slowenische Kunst (NSK; *Suitcase for Spiritual Use: Baptism under Triglav)* and the artists' cooperative Irwin *(Kapital)*.

A GALLERY OF GALLERIES

Ljubljana is awash in galleries both public and commercial. The following are among the best:

City Gallery (Mestna Galerija; Map p78; ☎ 241 17 70; www.mestna-galerija.si; Mestni trg 5; admission free; 10am-6pm Tue-Sat, 10am-1pm Sun); Cankarjevo nabrežje (Map p78; ☎ 241 17 90; Cankarjevo nabrežje 11; 10am-6pm Tue-Sat, 10am-1pm Sun) Rotating displays of modern and contemporary painting, sculpture, graphic art and photography.

DESSA Architectural Gallery (Map p78; ☎ 251 40 74; www.dessa.si; Židovska steza 4; admission free; 10am-3pm Mon-Fri) Small gallery spotlighting contemporary Slovenian and international architecture and architects.

Equrna Gallery (Galerija Equrna; Map p78; ☎ 252 71 23; www.equrna.si; Gregorčičeva ulica 3; admission free; 10am-7pm Mon-Fri, 10am-1pm Sat) Among the most innovative modern galleries in town.

Mala Galerija (Little Gallery; Map p78; ☎ 241 68 00; www.mg-lj.si; Slovenska cesta 35; admission free; 10am-6pm Tue-Sun) Metelkova (☎ 241 68 00; Metelkova ulica 22; 10am-6pm Tue-Sun) Rotating exhibits from Ljubljana Gallery of Modern Art.

Škuc Gallery (Galerija Škuc; Map p78; ☎ 251 65 40, 421 31 41; www.skuc.si; Stari trg 21; admission free; noon-8pm Tue-Sun) Cutting-edge with a studenty vibe in the heart of the Old Town.

OTHER BUILDINGS

The graceful **Opera House** (Map pp72-3; ☎ 241 17 40; www.opera.si; Župančičeva ulica 1), northeast of the National Museum, opened in 1892 as the Provincial Theatre, and plays in German and Slovene were performed here. After WWI it was renamed the Opera House and is now home to the Slovenian National Opera and Ballet (p99) companies though it too was closed during research as a new (and rather obtrusive) modern multistorey extension was being stapled on.

Along busy Slovenska cesta is the impressive art deco **Nebotičnik** (Skyscraper; Map p78; Štefanova ulica 1), designed by Vladimir Šubič (1933). At nine storeys, this was Ljubljana's tallest building for decades after it was built and, though it's in pretty sad shape, it still looks like it could be part of a set for a King Kong film.

The interior of the **Serbian Orthodox Church** (Srbska Pravoslavna Cerkev; Map pp72-3; ☎ 252 40 02, 041 744 402; Prešernova cesta; 9am-noon & 2-6pm Tue-Sun), built in 1936 and dedicated to Sts Cyril and Methodius, is covered from floor to ceiling with colourful modern frescoes. There is a richly carved iconostasis separating the nave from the sanctuary. Divine liturgy is sung at 10am Sunday.

Park Tivoli

You can reach Tivoli, the city's leafy playground laid out in 1813 and measuring 510 hectares, via an underpass from Cankarjeva cesta. Straight ahead, at the end of **Jakopičevo sprehajališče**, the monumental 'Jakopič Promenade' designed by Plečnik in the 1920s and 30s, is the 17th-century **Tivoli Mansion** (Grad Tivoli), which contains the **International Centre of Graphic Arts** (Mednarodni Grafični Likovni Center; Map pp72-3; ☎ 241 38 00; www.mglc-lj.si; Pod Turnom 3; adult/senior & student €3.40/1.70, at biennial €6/3; 11am-6pm Tue-Sun). The centre has new exhibitions every three months and hosts the International Biennial of Graphic Arts (p89) every odd-numbered year. There's a delightful terrace cafe here with views over the park.

The fascinating **Museum of Contemporary History of Slovenia** (Muzej Novejše Zgodovine Slovenije; Map pp72-3; ☎ 300 96 10; www.muzej-nz.si; Celovška cesta 23; adult/student €3.50/2.50; 10am-6pm Tue-Sat), housed in the 18th-century Cekin Mansion (Grad Cekinov) just northeast of the Tivoli Recreation Centre (p87), traces the history of Slovenia and Slovenians in the 20th century through multimedia and artefacts. Note the contrast between the sober earnestness of the communist-era rooms and the exuberant, logo-mad commercialism of the neighbouring industrial exhibits. The sections focusing on Ljubljana under occupation during WWII and the birth of independent Slovenia are very effective. The gloriously baroque Ceremonial Hall (Viteška Dvorana) on the 1st floor is how the whole mansion once looked.

The 20-hectare **Ljubljana Zoo** (Živalski Vrt Ljubljana; off Map pp72-3; ☎ 244 21 88; www.zoo-ljubljana.si; Večna pot 70; adult/child/senior & student

›/4.50/5; ⌚ 9am-7pm May-Aug, 9am-6pm Apr & Sep, m-5pm Mar & Oct, 9am-4pm Nov-Feb), on the south-rn slope of **Rožnik Hill** (394m), contains some)0 animals representing almost 120 species nd is an upbeat and well-landscaped menag-rie. There's a petting zoo and lots of other ctivities for children; consult the website for eding schedules.

rakovo & Trnovo

'hese two attractive districts south of Center re Ljubljana's oldest suburbs, and they have number of interesting buildings and historic ites. The neighbourhood around Krakovska lica, with all its two-storey cottages, was once alled the Montmartre of Ljubljana because f all the artists living there. There are many narket gardeners here who sell their pro-luce (notably a type of iceberg lettuce called *edena*) at Ljubljana's market.

The **Roman wall** running along Mirje from Barjanska cesta dates from about AD 15; he archway topped with a pyramid is a lečnik addition. Within the **Jakopič Garden** Jakopičev Vrt; Map p85; ☎ 241 25 06; Mirje 4; ⌚ by ppointment Apr-Oct) to the southeast, where the impressionist painter once worked in his summerhouse, there are more Roman ruins, including **Emona House** (Emonska Hiša), dating to the 1st century AD, with household artefacts, mosaics and the remains of sophisticated heating and sewage systems. Contact the City Museum (p82) if you want to visit.

Spanning the picturesque canal called Gradaščica to the south is little **Trnovo Bridge**, designed in 1932 by Plečnik, who added five of his trademark pyramids. On the south side is the **Church of St John the Baptist** (Cerkev Sv Janeza Krstnika; Map p85; ☎ 283 50 60; Kolezijska ulica 1), where the poet Prešeren met the love of his life, Julija Primic, and Plečnik worshipped.

A short distance south is the house where Jože Plečnik lived and worked for almost 40 years. Today it houses the Ljubljana Architectural Museum's **Plečnik Collection** (Map p85; ☎ 280 16 00; www.aml.si; Karunova ulica 4-6; adult/child €4/2; ⌚ 10am-6pm Tue-Thu, 9am-3pm Sat, by appointment Mon & Fri). There's an excellent introduction by guided tour to this almost ascetically religious man's life, inspiration and work.

Other Museums

Ljubljana contains many more interesting museums, some of them a bit further out from the centre.

Brewery Museum (Pivovarski Muzej; Map pp72-3; ☎ 471 73 40; www.pivo-union.si; Union Brewery, Pivovarniška ulica 2; admission free; 8am-1pm every 1st Tue) Beer-making displays, film, a tour of the brewery and a tasting (bus 1, 3 or 5 to Tivoli).

Ljubljana Architectural Museum (Arhitekturni Muzej Ljubljana; off Map pp72-3; ☎ 540 97 98; www.aml.si; Fužine Castle, Pot na Fužine 2, Studenec; adult/senior, student & child 6-16 €3.30/1.50; 9am-3pm Mon-Fri, 10am-6pm Sat, 10am-3pm Sun) Much emphasis on Plečnik, focusing on his work at home and abroad, and some stunning unrealised projects (bus 20 or 22 to Fužine).

Railway Museum (Železniški Muzej; off Map pp72-3; ☎ 291 26 41, 031 338 216; http://eng.slo-zeleznice.si/en/about_us/railway_museum; Parmova ulica 35; adult/senior, student & child €3.50/2.50; 10am-6pm Tue-Sun) A boiler room full of locomotives (one going back to 1861), carriages, uniforms and signalling equipment north of Center (bus 14 to Parmova).

Technical Museum of Slovenia (Tehniški Muzej Slovenije; Map pp72-3; ☎ 750 66 70; www.tms.si; Bistra Castle, Bistra pri Vrhniki; adult/student & child/family €4/3/11; 10am-6pm Tue-Fri, 8am-5pm Sat, 10am-6pm Sun Jul & Aug, 8am-4pm Tue-Fri, 8am-5pm Sat, 10am-6pm Sun Mar-Jun & Sep-Nov) Huge collection of antique motor vehicles and bicycles, water-driven and horse-powered mills, and implements used in agriculture, weaving, forestry, smithing, fishing and hunting. A geek's pleasure drome! It's 22km southwest of Ljubljana (bus to Vrhnika or train to Verd).

Tobacco Museum (Tobačni Muzej; Map pp72-3; ☎ 47 72 26; www.tobacna.si; Tobacco Factory, Tobačna ulica 5; admission free; 10am-6pm 1st Wed & 3rd Thu of month) Fascinating exhibits on the killer weed in Ljubljana's first factory founded in 1871 and employing 2500 people (bus 1 or 6 to Tobačna).

ACTIVITIES

Adventure Sports

Agencies like Label and Trek Trek (p75), and the excellent **Adrenaline-Check** (☎ 041 383 66; 051 266 812; www.adrenaline-check.com) at the Celica Hostel (p90), can organise a wide range of outdoor activities around Ljubljana and the rest of Slovenia between May and October, including trekking, mountaineering, rock climbing, ski touring, cross-country skiing, mountain biking, rafting, kayaking, canyoning, caving and paragliding.

Ballooning

The Ljubljana TIC (p75) organises **hot-air balloon rides** (adult/child €80/40; 6am & 8pm Apr-Aug, 8am & 5pm Sep-Mar) year-round lasting three to four hours (one to 1½ hours actually in the air) departing from the Slovenian Tourist Information Centre (p75).

JOŽE PLEČNIK, ARCHITECT EXTRAORDINAIRE

Few architects anywhere in the world have had as great an impact on the city of their birth as Jože Plečnik. His work is eclectic, inspired, unique – and found everywhere in the capital.

Born in Ljubljana in 1872, Plečnik was educated at the College of Arts in Graz and studied under the architect Otto Wagner in Vienna. From 1911 he spent a decade in Prague teaching and later helping to renovate Prague Castle.

Plečnik's work in his hometown began in 1921. Almost single-handedly he transformed the city, adding elements of classical Greek and Roman architecture with Byzantine, Islamic, ancient Egyptian and folkloric motifs to its baroque and Secessionist faces. The list of his creations and renovations is endless – from the National and University Library and the colonnaded Central Market to the magnificent cemetery at Žale.

Plečnik was also a city planner and designer. Not only did he redesign the banks of the Ljubljanica River (including Triple Bridge and the monumental lock downstream), entire streets (Zoisova ulica) and Park Tivoli, but he also set his sights elsewhere: on monumental stairways (Kranj), public buildings (Kamnik), chapels (Kamnik) and outdoor shrines (Bled). An intensely religious man, Plečnik designed many furnishings and liturgical objects – chalices, candlesticks, lanterns – for churches throughout the land (eg Škofja Loka's Church of St James, p112). One of Plečnik's designs that was never realised was an extravagant parliament, complete with an enormous cone-shaped structure, to be built on Castle Hill after WWII.

Plečnik's eclecticism and individuality alienated him from the mainstream of modern architecture during his lifetime, and he was relatively unknown (much less appreciated) outside Eastern and Central Europe when he died in 1957. Today he is hailed as a prophet of postmodernism.

oating & Rafting

he **Ljubljana Rowing Club** (Veslaški Klub Ljubljana; ap p85; ☎ 283 87 12; www.vesl-klub-ljubljanica , in Slovene; Velika Čolnarska ulica 20; per hr from €4; 11am-10pm mid-May–Sep) in Trnovo has din-ies and larger rowing boats for hire on the ubljanica River.

Skok Sport (off Map pp72-3; ☎ 512 44 02, 040 217 000; ww.skok-sport.si; Marinovševa cesta 8) in Šentvid, 8km orthwest of Center, organises rafting trips on e nearby Sava, from Medvode to Brod (1.5 ours) for €24 and from Boka to Trnovo (two ours) for €40. It can also arrange kayak and anoe excursions on the Ljubljanica and runs kayaking school (10-hour beginner's course 165). Take bus 8 to Brod.

owling & Billiards

lub 300 (off Map pp72-3; ☎ 510 39 40; www.klub300 om; Regentova cesta 35; game €2.60-3.45, rental shoes €1.50; 2pm-midnight Mon, Tue & Thu, noon-midnight Wed, 2pm-am Fri, 11am-2am Sat & Sun) is a super-modern 16-ane bowling centre with five billiard and pool ables. It's located northwest of Center (bus to Plešičeva stop). For a drugless high, try **osmic bowling** (per hr €28; 8pm-2am Sat), with pecial lighting effects and music.

wimming & Sauna

ivoli Recreation Centre (Map pp72-3; ☎ 431 51 55; elovška cesta 25) in Park Tivoli has an indoor wimming pool (open mid-September to une), a fitness centre, clay tennis courts and roller-skating rink, which becomes an ice ink in winter. It also has a popular sauna alled **Zlati Klub** (Gold Club; adult/student & senior morn-ng €12/10, afternoon €15.50/13; mixed 10am-8pm Mon, Ved, Thu, Sat & Sun, 10am-11pm Fri, women only 10am-8pm ue) with saunas, steam room, splash pools and outside swimming pool surrounded by high walls so you can sunbathe *au naturel*. Towels are an extra €2.20. Opening hours may be extended in summer.

Southeast of the Tivoli Centre is the **Ilirija swimming pool** (Map pp72-3; ☎ 231 02 33, 439 75 80; Celovška cesta 3; adult/child 6-10/child 11-14 Mon-Fri €6/2/4.50, Sat & Sun €7/2.50/5; 10am-7pm Mon-Fri, 9am-8pm Sat & Sun Jun-Aug). The most modern outdoor pool in Yugoslavia when built in 1929, it's now a bit rough around the edges.

Ljubljana boasts two enormous water parks. **Atlantis** (off Map pp72-3; ☎ 585 21 00; www.atlantis -vodnomesto.si; BTC City, Šmartinska cesta 152; day pass adult/child Mon-Fri €13.60/13.40, Sat & Sun €15.60/11.50; 9am-11pm) is the larger (15,000 sq metres) and more swish, with separate theme areas: Adventure World for kids, with a half-dozen pools and water slides; Thermal Temple with indoor and outdoor thermal pools; and Land of Saunas with a dozen different types of saunas. Get there on bus 27 (Stop: BTC Emporium).

Laguna (off Map pp72-3; ☎ 568 39 13; www.laguna.si; Dunjaska cesta 270; day pass adult/child/student & senior Mon-Fri €14/10/12, Sat & Sun €16/12/14; 9am-8pm May-Sep) at the Ljubljana Resort (p89) is more traditional, with several outdoor swimming pools and sunbathing areas, as well as fitness studio with sauna, badminton and volleyball courts. Take bus 6, 8 or 11 to the Ježica stop.

Walking & Hiking

Popular with walkers and joggers, the marked **Trail of Remembrance** (Pot Spominov) runs for 34km around Ljubljana where German barbed wire once completely enclosed the city during WWII. The easiest places to reach the trail are from the **AMZS headquarters** (off Map pp72-3; Dunajska cesta 128); take bus 6, 8 or 11 to the AMZS stop, or from Trg Komandanta Staneta just northwest of the central office of the public transport authority **LPP** (off Map pp72-3; Celovška cesta 160); take bus 1 to the Remiza stop. You can also join it from the northwestern side of Žale Cemetery (off Map pp72–3); take bus 19 to the Nove Žale stop, or south of Trnovo (Map p85); take bus 9 to the Veliki Štradon stop.

An easy and very popular hiking destination from Ljubljana is **Šmarna Gora**, a 669m-high hill above the Sava River, 12km northwest of Ljubljana. Take bus 25 from Slovenska cesta or Gosposvetska cesta to the Medno stop or bus 8 to Brod and begin walking. Another way to go is via the Smlednik bus from the main station and then follow the marked path from the 12th-century Smlednik Castle.

WALKING TOUR

This is a short and straightforward walk that will give you a taste of the Old Town, the banks of the Ljubljanica and the traditional suburb of Krakovo. Start the tour on **Prešernov trg** (p76) in the very heart of Ljubljana. Cross the celebrated **Triple Bridge** and head north (left) at the TIC for a stroll through the **Central Market** (p76), with its colourful stalls and Plečnik's elegant colonnades. Turn west (right) onto Ciril Metodov trg and walk towards the Old Town, Ljubljana's historical centre. Make a brief visit to the **Cathedral of**

WALK FACTS

Start Prešernov trg
End Krakovo (Vrtna ulica)
Distance 2km
Duration 1½ to two hours
Fuel Stop Čajna Hiša or Harambaša

St Nicholas (p79) before crossing into cobbled Mestni trg. Go past the impressive **town hall** (p79) and shiny new **Robba Fountain** (p79), exploring the narrow lanes that lead down to the river from the square before continuing on to Stari trg, where you might take a tea break at **Cha** (p96) and ruminate over some contemporary art at the **Škuc Gallery** (p84). Walk to the end of the Levstikov trg and head east (right) onto Karlovška cesta in front of the **Church of St James** (p80), crossing the Ljubljanica via the foot and vehicular bridge. Walk south along the riverbank for a short while and turn west (right) into Krakovska ulica. You're in the heart of Krakovo, an 'inner suburb' that often feels more like the countryside (just check out all those vegetable patches). Peek through the gates of the atmospheric courtyards before finishing off with a bite at **Harambaša** (p92) on Vrtna ulica.

COURSES

A free 1½-hour mini course in Slovene organised by the Centre for Slovene as a Second/Foreign Language (p285) is held at the Slovenian Tourist Information Centre (p75) at 5pm on Wednesday from May to September. Those more serious about learning the language should see p285.

LJUBLJANA FOR CHILDREN

The Ljubljana Tourist Board's website lists activities for children. Visit www.visitljubljana.si/en/expe riences/childrens_experiences.

Park Tivoli (p84), with a couple of children's playgrounds, swimming pools and a zoo, is an excellent place to take children as are the two water parks, Laguna (p87) and especially Atlantis (p87).

Kids love moving conveyances of any kind and they'll get a special kick out of both the funicular and the tourist train that transports the young, the old, the infirm and the lazy (and that would be just about all of us) to Castle Hill (p80). And they're just as good stationery when they're this big check out the locomotives at the Railw Museum (p86).

In the warmer months the **Mini Summer f Children International Festival** (☎ 434 36 20; wv .mini-teater.si; Grajska planota 1; 🕑 11am & 6.30pm Sun la Jun–Aug) stages puppet shows from around th world for kids at Ljubljana Castle. At oth times of the year, check out the program the Ljubljana Puppet Theatre (p99).

A super place for kids is the **House Experiments** (Hiša Eksperimentov; Map pp72-3; ☎ 300 88; www.h-e.si; Trubarjeva cesta 39; admission €5; 🕑 11ar 7pm Sat & Sun), a hands-on science centre wit almost four-dozen inventive and challengin exhibits that successfully mixes learning wi humour. There's a science adventure sho at 5pm.

TOURS

The Ljubljana TIC (p75) organises a numbe of guided tours of the city and even has **digital tour guide** (€10)) taking in 17 sights an lasting about two hours.

A two-hour guided **walking tour** (adult/chi €10/5; 🕑 10am & 5pm daily early Apr–early Oct) i English that takes in Ljubljana Castle (trans port via funicular or tourist train) depart from the town hall on Mestni trg.

During the same period a glass-enclose vessel offers guided one-hour English language **boat tours** (adult/child €10/5; 🕑 noo & 4pm) on the Ljubljanica River, departin from the little Ribji trg Pier (Map p78) alon Cankarjevo nabrežje. Without commentar costs €8/4 with more-frequent sailings a 10am, 11am and 1pm and hourly from 5pn to 8pm. A boat called the **Plovila Iza** (Map p78 ☎ 031 489 261; adult/child €8/4; 🕑 10am-8pm Jun-Sep departs hourly from the opposite side of th river along Hribarjevo Nabrežje.

For tours from Ljubljana to other parts o Slovenia, see p300.

FESTIVALS & EVENTS

The number one event on Ljubljana's socia calendar is the **Ljubljana Festival** (www.ljubljana festival.si), a celebration from early July to lat August of music, opera, theatre and dance held at venues throughout the city, but principally in the open-air theatre at the Križanke.

Druga Godba (http://festival.drugagodba.si), a festival of alternative and world music, takes place in the Križanke from late May to early June. The **Ljubljana Jazz Festival** (www.cd-cc.si) at both ie Križanke and the Cankarjev Dom in late ıne and early July has been taking place for ıore than a half century.

Vino Ljubljana is an international wine fair nd competition held in early June at the **iubljana Fairgrounds** (Ljubljanski Sejem; Map pp72-3; ttp://en.gr-sejem.si; Dunajska cesta 10) northwest of ıe train station.

Ljubljana is at its most vibrant in July and ugust during the so-called **Summer in the Old own** season when there are four or five free ultural events a week in the city's historic quares, courtyards and bridges.

The **Ana Desetnica International Street Theatre estival** (www.anadesetnica.org) organised by the na Monro Theatre in late June/early July s not to be missed. **Trnfest** (www.kud-fp.si), an nternational festival of alternative arts and ulture and many Ljubljančans' favourite anıual event, takes place at the KUD France rešeren (p99) in Trnovo and at other venues rom late July to late August.

City of Women (www.cityofwomen.org), held in the irst half of October in venues throughout jubljana, showcases all forms of artistic exression by women. The **International Ljubljana Marathon** (www.ljubljanskimaraton.si) takes off on the ast Saturday in October.

The **International Biennial of Graphic Arts** www.mglc-lj.si) at the International Centre of Graphic Arts in Park Tivoli, the Museum of Modern Art and several other venues, s held from mid-June to September every odd-numbered year.

SLEEPING

Ljubljana is not overly endowed with accommodation choices at the midrange level but hostels have been sprouting up here in recent years like mushrooms after rain. The TIC website has comprehensive details of hotels further out in the suburbs and of the half-dozen top-end hotels such as the **Austria Trend Hotel Ljubljana** (www.austria-trend.at/lju) north of Center and the world-class **Hotel Mons** (www.mons.si) in a wooded track on the fringe of the city to the southwest.

Budget

The TIC has a list of some two dozen **private rooms** (s/d from €25/40), but only a few are in Center and most require a bus trip north to Bežigrad or beyond. **Tour As** (Map p78; ☎ 434 26 60; www.apartmaji.si; Mala ulica 8; reception 8.30am-6pm Mon-Fri, 8.30am-1pm Sat) has 40 very comfortable apartments and studios – half of which are central – with one to three bedrooms for €65 to €139 a night.

Ljubljana Resort (off Map pp72-3; ☎ 568 39 13; www.ljubljanaresort.si; Dunajska cesta 270; adult €8-17, child €6-13; campsite mid-May–mid-Sep; P) It's got a pretty grandiose name, but wait till you see the facilities at this attractive 6-hectare camping ground-cum-resort 4km north of the city centre. Along with a 62-room hotel (singles €74 to €116, doubles €116 to €156) and five stationery mobile homes (€84 to €158) accommodating up to five people, there's the Laguna water park (p87) next door, which is free for guests. Take bus 6, 8 or 11 to the Ježica stop.

Hostel DIC (Map pp72-3; ☎ 474 86 00; www.hosteldic.com; Bldg B, Poljanska cesta 26; dm €9, s €21-24, d €28-34, tr €39-45; late Jun–late Aug; P) This summertime hostel, whose day job during the school year is the student dorm Dijaški Dom Ivana Cankarja (thus the ill-chosen name) has 480 beds that are the cheapest in town. It's about 1.2km east of Center in Poljane (bus 5 or 13 to the Roška stop).

Dijaški Dom Tabor (Map pp72-3; ☎ 234 88 40; www.d-tabor.lj.edus.si; Vidovdanska cesta 7; dm/s/d €11/26/38; late Jun–late Aug; P) In summer five colleges in Ljubljana open their halls of residence *(dijaški dom)* to visitors, and this 300-bed one is the most central. It's a 10-minute walk southeast of the bus and train stations. Eight dorm rooms have 10 beds. Enter from Kotnikova ulica.

Simbol Hostel (off Map p85; ☎ 041 720 825; www.simbol.si; Gerbičeva ulica 46; dm €15-17, d €45; P) It might seem a long way from Center but purpose-built Simbol, with its 15 brightly painted rooms over four floors, is Ljubljana's party hostel and it's within easy stumbling distance of the hot spots of Trnovo and Krakovo. The garden with barbecue is a plus, bikes are free for the first 24 hours (then €3 per day) and there's a swimming pool on the way. Bus 1 to Gerbičeva will do the trick from Center, though they'll pick you up from the bus or train station if you call.

Alibi Hostel (Map p78; ☎ 251 12 44; www.alibi.si; Cankarjevo nabrežje 27; dm €15-18, d €40-50) This very well-situated 106-bed hostel on the Ljubljanica has brightly painted, airy dorms with four to eight wooden bunks and a dozen doubles. There's a private suite at the top for six people.

Alibi M14 Hostel (Map p78; 232 27 70; www.alibi .si; 3 fl, Miklošičeva cesta 14; dm €18-20, d €50-60;) In the heart of Center is this pint-sized sister property to Alibi Hostel, which has six rooms, including a 10-bed dormitory, just south of Miklošičev Park.

H20 Hostel (Map pp72-3; 041 662 266, 051 303 300; info@simbol.si; Petkovškovo nabrežje 47; dm/d/tr/q €16/50/57/68;) One of our favourite newer hostels in Ljubljana, this six-room place wraps around a tiny courtyard bordering the Ljubljanica and one room has views of the castle. Rooms, with two to six beds, have their own kitchens.

our pick **Celica Hostel** (Map pp72-3; 230 97 00, 051 373 993; www.hostelcelica.com; Metelkova ulica 8; dm €18-22, s/d/tr cell €46/54/66, 4- to 5-bed per person €20-28, 6- to 7-bed per person €18-22; P) Still our favourite hostel in Ljubljana, this stylishly revamped former prison (1882) in Metelkova has 20 'cells', designed by 18 different artists and architects and complete with original bars. There are nine rooms and apartments with three to seven beds and a packed, popular 12-bed dorm. The ground floor is home to three cafes (set lunch €4.40 to €6.50, open 7.30am to midnight) and the hostel boasts its own gallery where everyone can show their work. Laundry is €7.

Most Hostel (Map pp72-3; 031 363 600, 051 303 300; Petkovškovo nabrežje 47;) Sister property of the H20 Hostel, the Most, whose name refers to the nearby bridge *(most)*, is a few doors to the west and even more fabulous, with nine rooms of between two and six beds and three kitchens in an old town house that feels almost like a B&B. Rates are about a euro or two cheaper here.

Zeppelin Hostel (Map pp72-3; 051 637 436; www .zeppelinhostel.com; 2nd fl, Slovenska cesta 47; dm €18-24, d €49-55;) Located in the historic Evropa building on the corner of Gosposvetska cesta, this hostel with three large and bright dorm rooms (four to eight beds) and one double is run by an affable Slovenian-Spanish couple who keep their guests informed with a 'parties & events' board.

Fluxus Hostel (Map p78; 251 57 60; www.fluxus -hostel.com; 2nd fl, Tomšičeva ulica 4; dm/d €28/60;) This little place with a mere three rooms – two dorms of six and eight beds and an en-suite double – is colourful and friendly and in a lovely old 19th-century building in the heart of Center. You really will feel like you're staying with friends (and you prob ably are). Note: there is no elevator.

Stari Tišler (Map pp72-3; 430 33 70; ww .stari-tisler.com; Kolodvorska ulica 8; d/tr €44/66) The fiv rooms on the 2nd floor above a popular coac house restaurant (open 9am to 9pm Monda to Friday, 11am to 7pm Saturday and Sunday that dates back to 1905 are basic and shar facilities in the hallway. But they're clean an bright and look onto a charming 'we're i the country!' courtyard. The winding iro staircase and ceiling mural at the top ar period pieces.

Midrange

Vila Veselova (Map pp72-3; 059 926 721; ww .v-v.si; Veselova ulica 14; dm/d/q €21/68/100; P) This very attractive bright yellow villa, wit its own garden and 42 beds in the centre o the museum district, offers mostly hostel ac commodation in five colourful rooms wit four to eight beds. A double and two apart ments with attached facilities and access to kitchen make it an attractive midrange optio however. Some rooms face Park Tivoli acros busy Tivolska c.

BIT Center Hotel (off Map pp72-3; 548 00 55; ww .bit-center.net; Litijska cesta 57; s/d/tr €38/53/58; P) The BIT Center offers one of the best-valu deals in Ljubljana although, at 3km east o the centre (bus 5, 9 or 13 to Emona stop) it's a bit far from the action. Its 39 room are spartan but bright and comfortable an there's a 30-bed hostel (dorm for HI member/nonmember €17/18.50) should you fee less than flush. A boon is the attached spor centre (open 7am to 11pm), with gym, sauna, squash and badminton courts, where guests get a 50% discount.

Maček Rooms (Map p78; 425 37 91; www.sobe -macek.si; Krojaška ulica 5; s/d/apt €55/96/120;) In a building that once took the overflow from the Alibi Hostel just downriver, these four gorgeous rooms and one apartment (all but one of which overlook the river) are owned by the city's most popular riverfront cafe-bar and will soon be among the most sought-after in town (and you read about them here first).

Vila Minka (Map pp72-3; 583 00 80; www.vila minka.si; Kogovškova ulica 10; s €50-60, d €65-80, apt for 2/3/4 from €80/90/120; P) This welcoming pension, some 4km northwest of Center in Koseze, has about a dozen rooms and apartments. It's a good choice for families or small groups with their own wheels (though can be reached on bus 5 in just 20 minutes). partments are positively huge, very bright nd well equipped. The glassed-in atrium, xcellent art on the walls and tranquil surounds are bonuses.

Penzion Pod Lipo (Map pp72-3; ☎ 031 809 893; ww.penzion-podlipo.com; Borštnikov trg 3; d/tr/q/ste 58/69/92/115; 🖳) Sitting atop one of Ljubljana's ldest *gostilna* (innlike restaurant) and a 400-ear-old linden tree, this 10-room inn offers xcellent value in a part of the city that is lling up with bars and restaurants. We love ne communal kitchen, the original hardwood loors and the east-facing terrace with deck hairs that catches the morning sun.

our pick Antiq Hotel (Map p78; ☎ 421 35 60; www ntiqhotel.si; Gornji trg 3; s €61-133, d €77-168, apt €123-204; ✲ 🖳) Ljubljana's first boutique hotel, cobled together from a series of town houses in he heart of the Old Town, has 16 rooms and partments, most of which are very spacious, nd multi-tiered back garden. The decor is itsch with a smirk and there are fabulous ittle nooks and touches everywhere but it's eginning to show a bit of wear and tear. Among our favourite rooms are enormous No on the 2nd floor, with views of the Hercules Fountain, and No 13 on the top floor with terrace and glimpses of Ljubljana Castle. The two cheapest rooms have their own bathrooms but they're on the corridor.

Hotel Emonec (Map p78; ☎ 200 15 20; www.hotel emonec.com; Wolfova ulica 12; s €64, d €69-77, tr/q €96/111; Ⓟ 🖳) The decor is simple and functionally modern at this 41-room hotel and the staff always less than welcoming, but everything is spotless and you can't beat the central location.

Slamič B&B (Map pp72-3; ☎ 433 82 33; www .slamic.si; Kersnikova ulica 1; s €65-80, d €95-107, ste from €135; Ⓟ ✲ 🖳) It's a titch away from the action but Slamič, a B&B above a famous cafe and teahouse, offers 11 bright rooms with antique(ish) furnishings and parquet floors. Choice rooms include the ones looking on to a back garden and the one just off an enormous terrace used by the cafe and made for smokers.

Hotel Park (Map pp72-3; ☎ 300 25 00; www.hotel park.si; Tabor 9; s €65-110, d €80-150; Ⓟ ✲ 🖳) A recladding outside and a face-lift within has turned this 243-room tower-block hotel into an even better-value midrange choice in central Ljubljana. The 200 pleasant, well-renovated 'standard' and 'comfort' (air-conditioned) rooms are bright and unpretentiously well equipped. Cheaper 'hostel' rooms on the 7th and 12th floors, some of which have shared facilities (but always a toilet) and others en suite shower, cost €23 to €29 per person in a double and €19 to €23 in a quad. Students with ISIC cards get a 10% discount.

Top End

City Hotel Ljubljana (Map p78; ☎ 239 00 00; www.cityhotel .si; Dalmatinova ulica 15; s €69-99, d €89-139, tr €96-159, ste from €200; Ⓟ ✲ 🖳 ♿) A top-to-tail refit has given this rather unprepossessing, six-storey hotel a new name and 202 fresher, quieter and more up-to-date guestrooms. It's an odd place – primary colours splashed hither and yon, a kind of circus makeup feel, trees and books and an 'ethno centre' (that would be Slovenian roots) in the lobby, but it all works and, frankly, we love it here. Ask to see the top floor in-the-round suite with dazzling views of the castle.

Pri Mraku (Map p78; ☎ 421 96 00; www.daj-dam .si; Rimska cesta 4; s €69-80, d €106-116, tr €126-135; Ⓟ ✲ 🖳) Although it calls itself a *gostilna*, At Twilight is really just a smallish hotel with 36 rooms in an old building with no lift and a garden. Rooms on the 1st and 4th floors have air-con. Almost opposite the Križanke on Trg Francoske Revolucije, it's ideally located for culture vultures but if you spot any of the staff smiling, write home.

Hotel Slon Best Western Premier (Map p78; ☎ 470 11 00; www.hotelslon.com; Slovenska cesta 34; s €98-135, d €125-180, ste from €210; Ⓟ ✲ 🖳 ♿) In the thick of things is the 171-room Hotel Elephant, with a history going back more than four centuries. It is said that this was the spot where a pachyderm presented to the Habsburg emperor by an African king tarried on its way to Vienna, although the present hotel dates from the 20th century and has a certain Eastern Bloc elegance. There are several categories of rooms, some with a Jacuzzi in the bathroom. We're told they do wonderful customised pillows here.

Allegro Hotel (Map p78; ☎ 059-119 620; www .allegrohotels.si; Gornji trg 6; s €95-115, d €130-150, tr €185; Ⓟ ✲ 🖳) The Old Town's second (but certainly not last) boutique hotel, the 12-room Allegro is a symphony of restrained designer chic with rooms that give on to Gornji trg and a charming back courtyard. Room No 3 has a balcony and No 12 at the top sleeps four (€210). The front lounge – a parlour, really – is on two levels and we love the original wood staircase.

The 187-room **Grand Hotel Union Executive** (Map p78; ☎ 308 12 70; www.gh-union.si; Miklošičeva cesta 1; s €99-194, d €109-224, ste €150-455; P), the art nouveau southern wing of a two-part hostelry, was built in 1905 and remains the most desirable address for visitors to Ljubljana. It has glorious public areas and guests get to use the indoor swimming pool, sauna and fitness centre on the 8th floor of the adjacent 133-room **Grand Hotel Union Business** (Map p78; ☎ 308 11 70; www.gh-union.si; Miklošičeva cesta 3; s €85-178, d €99-208, ste €150-372; P), the Grand Union's renovated modern wing with 133 rooms to the north. It caters to the business (not romantic) minded.

EATING

Although there are many quality top-end restaurants, it is still possible to eat well in Ljubljana at moderate cost; even the more-expensive restaurants offer an excellent-value three-course *dnevno kosilo* (set lunch) for as little as €6.50. The Old Town has a fair number of appealing restaurants, but the majority of the venues here are cafes. For cheaper options, try the dull but functional snack bars around the bus and train stations and both on and in the shopping mall below Trg Ajdovščina.

Restaurants

SLOVENIAN

Pizzicato (Map p78; ☎ 251 11 18; Gornji trg 33; dishes €5-9; noon-midnight Mon-Sat) An erstwhile pizzeria and Italian in the Old Town has metamorphosed into a lovingly restored traditional town house with affordable local dishes and charming staff. A wonderful addition to a very touristy part of town.

Sokol (Falcon; Map p78; ☎ 439 68 55; Ciril Metodov trg 18; mains €7-20; 7am-11pm Mon-Sat, 10am-11pm Sun) In an old vaulted house near the Central Market, traditional Slovenian food is served on heavy tables by costumed wait staff. Along with the traditional dishes like *obara* (veal stew; €7) and Krvavica sausage with cabbage and turnips (€8.50), there are the more esoteric deep-fried bull's testicles with tartare sauce (€9.50) and grilled stallion steak (€16).

Šestica (Sixth; Map p78; ☎ 242 08 55; Slovenska cesta 40; starters €6.20-9.80, set lunch €7-8.50, mains €7.50-16.90; 10am-11pm Mon-Fri, noon-11pm Sat) Šestica has been around since 1776, and it serves up plates of *goveji golaž s pečeno polento* (beef goulash with baked polenta; €7.70) and *svinjska pečenka* (roast pork; €9.30) to devoted patrons. The back courtyard is pleasant i summer, and the staff try hard to pleas There's a weekly Slovenian Night (Slovensk Večer; €35; from 8pm to 11pm Friday) c music and dance that includes a three-cours meal and unlimited wine.

Pri Škofju (At the Bishop's; Map p85; ☎ 426 45 0 Rečna ulica 8; starters €6.50-8, mains €8-17; 8am-midnig Mon-Fri, noon-midnight Sat & Sun) This wonderful littl place in tranquil Krakovo south of the centr serves some of the best prepared local dishe and salads in Ljubljana, with an ever-changin menu. Weekday set lunches are good valu at €6.50 to €8.

Pr' Potic (Map p78; ☎ 425 43 37; Stari trg 21; starte €6-9, mains €9-14; 10am-11pm Mon-Fr, noon-11pm Sat Sun) A wonderful replacement and much-love holdover from the socialist era, At the Potic is a very red (as in colour) eatery renowned fo its set lunch on weekdays (€8) and its excellen *potica* (Slovenian nut-roll; €3). The wines ar Slovenian only and excellent. The staff an service are same-same.

Mencigar Nobile (Map pp72-3; ☎ 439 70 40; Zarnikov ulica 3; starters €9-13, mains €9.50-23; noon-10pm Mon-Sa A rare breed indeed, this is a regional Slovenia restaurant serving dishes from Prekmurje Slovenian's flat-as a-pancake province in th far northeast. By all means try the, well, wal nut pancakes (*orehoje palačinke;* €4) but star off with Hungarian-inspired savouries such a *bograč* (beef goulash; €9), the Gypsy-style cutle (*kotlet po ciganjsko;* €10) or anything with *kaša* (groats). The menu is in English, Slovene and Prekmurje dialect; those who know *magyaru* will recognise a word or three.

our pick **Špajza** (Map p78; ☎ 425 30 94; Gornji trg 28; mains €14.60-22; 11am-10pm Mon-Fri, noon-10pm Sat & Sun) A welcome return to the Old Town is the Pantry, nicely decorated with its rough-hewn tables and chairs, wooden floors, frescoed ceilings and nostalgic bits and pieces. We come here for the 'Špajza filet' (€21), which is actually horseflesh, or a bit of *kozliček iz pečiče* (oven-roasted kid; €14.50) and wines from a dozen different Slovenian producers. A three-course set lunch is only €10.

SOUTH SLAV

Harambaša (Map p85; ☎ 041 843 106; Vrtna ulica 8; dishes €3.50-6; 10am-10pm Mon-Fri, noon-10pm Sat, noon-6pm Sun) At this small place in Krakovo you'll find authentic Bosnian – Sarajevan to be precise – dishes like *čevapčiči* (spicy meatballs of beef or pork) and *pljeskavica* (spicy meat patties) erved at low tables in a charming cottage ith a fireplace.

Pod Rožnikom (Under Mt Rožnik; off Map pp72-3; 251 34 46; Cesta na Rožnik 18; mains €5-15; 10am-pm Mon-Fri, 11am-11pm Sat & Sun) This place nder Mt Rožnik (sort of), just downwind om the zoo in Park Tivoli and known loally as Čad, serves southern Slav-style grills, ke *pljeskavica* (spicy meat patties) with *ajvar* roasted red peppers, tomatoes and eggplant ooked into a purée) and starters such as *preranac* (onions and beans cooked in an earthnware pot). Definitely worth the trip.

Sofra (off Map pp72-3; 565 68 00; Dunajska cesta 45; mains €7-12; 11am-11pm Mon-Fri, noon-11pm Sat) Often touted as the most authentic Bosnian estaurant in town, there's also live music very night from September to June, when our fellow diners are likely to provide as nuch entertainment as those performing.

Rio-Momo (Map p78; 031 751 751; Slovenska cesta 8; starters €4.40-6.50, mains €7.20-19; 11am-11pm) A ew arrival in the heart of town, this place erves excellent Serbian dishes (especially rills) in an attractive restaurant done up to ook like an old farmhouse. Try the spinach ie (€5) and the roasted peppers (€3.50).

NTERNATIONAL

Manna (Map p85; 283 52 94; Eipprova ulica 1a; starters 6.50-13, mains €12.20-35; noon-10pm Mon-Fri, 6-11pm at) Festooned across the front of this canal-side estaurant in Trnovo is the slogan '*Manna – Božanske Jedi na Zemlji*' (Manna – Heavenly Food on Earth). A Chaine de Rôtissiers establishment, it has very stylish decor, there's a wonderful covered inner courtyard for dining almost al fresco and the setting is pretty nice. There are various menus from €22 to €38.

Gostilna As (Map p78; 425 88 22; Čopova ulica 5/a; starters €7.50-20, mains €16.70-32; noon-midnight) The Ace Inn, in the passage linking Wolfova ulica and Slovenska cesta, is the place for a special occasion, with an embarrassment of caviar and truffles, a good wine list, and a few classic Slovene dishes to balance the menu. You can also enter from Slovenska cesta 30. The As Lounge in both the cellar and garden is much more informal, with sandwiches (€7.90 to €9.90), salads (€6.50 to €10.50), and a few less-elaborate main courses (€12 to €20). Enter Gostilna As from Knafljev prehod.

Pri Vitezu (Map p78; 426 60 58; Breg 18-20; mains €18-30; noon-11pm Mon-Sat) Located directly on the left bank of the Ljubljanica, At the Knight is the place for a special meal (Mediterranean-style grills and Adriatic fish dishes), whether in the brasserie, the salon or the very cosy Knight's Room.

JB Restavracija (Map pp72-3; 433 13 58, 430 70 70; Miklošičeva cesta 17; starters €10.50-14.50, mains €20-26.50; 11am-11pm Mon-Fri, 6-11pm Sat) Old-world charm, a hybrid international menu, a top-notch wine list and very stylish decor have made this restaurant one of the most popular in town for a fancy meal.

ITALIAN & MEDITERRANEAN

Kavalino (Map pp72-3; 232 09 90; Trubarjeva cesta 52; starters €5.20-9, mains €8.50-12; 8am-10pm Mon-Thu, 9am-11pm Fri & Sat) Our favourite Italian (they say Tuscan) place at the moment, Kavalino serves pizza (€5.80 to €6.80) like everybody does but it excels with its pasta (€6.60 to €8.50) especially its four types of ravioli. Excellent seating in the courtyard and upstairs gallery.

Gostilna Rimska XXI (Map pp72-3; 425 20 29; Rimska cesta 21; mains €10-24; 12.30pm-1am Mon-Fri) This sleek new *gostilna* that changes its menu daily serves Mediterranean-inspired dishes till late. Set lunch is €16 and a four-course tasting menu at dinner is €38.

Julija (Map p78; 425 64 63; Stari trg 9; starters €6.90-11.90, mains €10.90-18.90; noon-10pm) Julija serves up decent risottos (€8.90 to €11.90) and pastas (€8.90) either outside on the pavement terrace or in a Delft-tiled backroom behind a cafe decorated with 1920s prints. Set lunch is €8.

Like most European capitals nowadays, Ljubljana is awash in pizzerias, but the pick of the crop include the following:

Ljubljanski Dvor (Ljubljana Court; Map p78; 251 65 55; Dvorni trg 1; pizza €5-15; 10am-midnight Mon-Sat, noon-10pm Sun) Overlooks the Ljubljanica.

Mirje (Map pp72-3; 426 60 15; Tržaška cesta 5; pizza €6.50-8.50; 10am-10pm Mon-Fri, noon-10pm Sat) Southwest of the centre.

Pizzeria Foculus (Map p78; 251 56 43; Gregorčičeva ulica 3; pizza €4.70-8.50; 11am-midnight Mon-Fri, noon-midnight Sat & Sun) Boasts a vaulted ceiling painted with spring and autumn leaves.

Trta (Grapevine; Map p85; 426 50 66; Grudnovo nabrežje 21; pizza €5.20-8.10; 11am-10.30pm Mon-Fri, noon-10.30pm Sat) On the right bank of the Ljubljanica opposite Trnovo.

FRENCH

Le Coq Blanc (Map p78; 030 353 848; Gornji trg 4; starters €4.50-6.50, mains €9.70-16; 7am-midnight) Ljubljana's only French(ish) restaurant since the departure of Chez Eric from Mestni trg, the White Rooster occupies what was once a zany Bosnian restaurant and has retained its eccentric decor, furnishing and (we suspect) cook – there are lots of grills here and only a few dishes from southern France. Still the set lunch (€6/9.70 for two/four courses) is affordable.

MEXICAN & SPANISH

Cantina Mexicana (Map p78; 426 93 25; Wolfova ulica 4; starters €2.90-6.80, mains €7.90-18.80; 11am-midnight Sun-Thu, 11am-1am Fri & Sat) The capital's most stylish Mexican restaurant has an eye-catching red-and-blue exterior and hacienda-like decor inside. The fajitas (€8.70 to €14.30) are great. Enter from Knafljev prehod.

Don Felipe (Map pp72-3; 434 38 62; Streliška ulica 22; tapas €3.30-9, mains €12-22.50; noon-midnight) Southeast of Krekov trg, Don Felipe was Ljubljana's first Spanish restaurant and it remains the best. It specialises in tapas, has four different types of paella (€14.60 to €15.40) for two on offer and boasts some strikingly colourful decor.

MIDDLE EASTERN

Yildiz Han (Map p85; 426 57 17; Karlovška cesta 19; mains €8.50-15; noon-midnight Mon-Sat) If Turkish is your thing, head for authentic (trust us) Star House, which features belly dancing on Friday night.

ASIAN

Kitajska Zvezda (Map p85; 425 88 24; Hrenova ulica 19; starters €1.70-2.90, mains €4.50-7.90; 11am-11pm) If you're looking for your fix of rice or noodles, try the Chinese Star, which has a big open front on the river just south of the Old Town. Szechuan dishes, including the *mapo doufu* (tofu with garlic and chilli) are good, though it also does Cantonese and Shanghainese.

Zhong Hua (Map pp72-3; 230 16 65; Trubarjeva cesta 50; mains €5.90-10.10; 11am-10.30pm) Specialising in Shanghai cuisine – a style of cooking not easy to find even in world-class cities outside the Middle Kingdom – the sexily named 'China' hole-in-the-wall, just up from the Ljublanica, is just about the most authentic Chinese restaurant in town. Name a dish and they'll make it – and pretty authentically too. The less adventurous will stick with rice and noodle dishes (€4.40 to €5.90).

Thai Inn (Map pp72-3; 421 03 77; Rimska cesta 1 all dishes €6; 11am-10pm Mon-Fri, noon-10pm Sat) Th cooks are said to be Thai, the *tuk-tuk* (mc torised trishaw) has a Bangkok license pla and that certainly is King Bhumibol on th wall. And the food? Let's say it's on its way t Thailand – and very slowly.

Namasté (Map p78; 425 01 59; Breg 8; mair €7.90-20.60; 11am-midnight Mon-Sat, 11am-10pm Su Should you fancy a bit of Indian, head for thi place on the left bank of the Ljubljanica. Yo won't get high-street-quality curry but th thalis (€7.50 to €8.50) and tandoori dishe (from €9.80) are good. The choice of veg etarian dishes is better than average and se lunch is €8.

Shambala (Map p78; 031 843 833; Križevniška ulic 12; starters €4.50-18, mains €9-23; 11am-midnight Mor Sat) One of those hybrid Asian places that ca be found from Bondi to Boston, Shambal is a cut above with excellently prepared – i drowning in fusion-confusion – dishes lik Vietnamese pho (noodle soup; €12.50) Japanese tempura (€8) and beef with lemon grass. Cooler-than-cool tropical decor.

Sushimama (Map p78; 040 702 070; Wolfova ulic 12; starters €5-10, mains €15-20; 11am-11pm Mon-Sat Ljubljana's only Japanese restaurant has simple, restful decor and the full range of Japanes dishes – from miso soups to rice and noodl dishes (€6.50 to €13) but with fish this fresh i would be a shame not to indulge in the mixe sushi (€10 to €17) or sashimi (€13).

SEAFOOD

Operna Klet (Opera Cellar; Map pp72-3; 252 70 03 Župančičeva ulica 2; starters €3.50-15, mains €7.20-25 11am-11pm Mon-Fri, 11am-6pm Sat) This old-style restaurant near the Opera (enter from Tomšičeva ulica) concentrates on seafood and has a pleasant inner courtyard for alfresco dining in the warmer months. It packs them in at lunchtime.

Taverna Tatjana (Map p78; 421 00 87, 041 707 900; Gornji trg 38; mains €8.50-25; 3pm-midnight Mon-Sat) A wooden-beamed cottage pub with a nautical theme (think nets and seascapes), this is actually a rather exclusive fish restaurant with a lovely (and protected) back courtyard for the warmer months.

VEGETARIAN

Ajdovo Zrno (Map p78; 041 690 478; Trubarjeva cesta 7; soups & sandwiches €1.80-3, set lunch €3.75-6.30; 9am-8pm Mon-Fri, 11am-4pm Sat) Buckwheat Grain serves

›ups, sandwiches, fried vegetables and lots ‹ different salads (self-service: €3 to €4.80). nd it has terrific, freshly squeezed juices, ıcluding the unusual rose-petal juice with mon. Enter from Mali trg.

Vegedrom (Map pp72-3; ☎ 513 26 42; Vodnikova cesta ›; soups & salads €2.90-3.50, dishes €4.50-12.80; 9am- ›pm Mon-Fri, noon-10pm Sat) This appealing, if ›mewhat pricey, vegan restaurant in a lovely ld villa at the northeastern edge of Park ivoli also dibble-dabbles (or is that nibble- abbles?) in Indian food (€6 to €12.80). The enerous platters for two (€30) are reason- ble value and there's a salad bar (€5.50 › €6.50).

uick Eats

elikatesa Ljubljanski Dvor (Map p78; ☎ 426 93 27; ›ngresni trg 11; pizza slices €1.70-2.20; 10am-midnight on-Sat) Locals queue for huge, bargain slices ‹ pizzas, salads, and grilled vegetables sold by eight to take away or eat on the spot.

Restavracija 2000 (Map pp72-3; ☎ 476 69 80; Trg publike 1; dishes €2-3.50, set lunch €6.50; 9am-7pm on-Fri, 9am-3pm Sat) In the basement of the laximarket department store, this glass and ırome self-service eatery is surprisingly up- eat, and just the ticket if you want something uick while visiting the main museums.

Paninoteka (Map p78; ☎ 041 529 824; Jurčičev trg 3; ups & toasted sandwiches €2.80-6.30; 8am-1am Mon-Sat, m-11pm Sun) Healthy sandwich creations and ılads on a lovely little square by the river.

Hot Horse (Map pp72-3; ☎ 031 709 716; Park Tivoli; acks & burgers €2.80-6; 10am-6am Mon, 9am-6am e-Sun) This little place in the city's biggest ark supplies *Ljubljančani* (local people) ith their favourite treat: horse burgers (€4). 's just down the hill from the Museum of ontemporary History (p84).

Falafel (Map pp72-3; ☎ 041 640 166; Trubarjeva cesta ›; dishes €2.90-4.20, daily menu €4.50; 11am-midnight on-Fri, noon-midnight Sat, 1-10pm Sun) Sandwiches, ılads and the eponymous falafel – ideal for egies on the hoof.

Ribca (Map p78; ☎ 425 15 44; Adamič-Lundrovo nabrežje dishes €3-7.50; 8am-4pm Mon-Fri, 8am-2pm Sat) This asement seafood bar below the Plečnik olonnade in Pogačarjev trg serves tasty ied squid, sardines and herrings to hun- ry market-goers. Set lunch on weekdays is 7.50. It stays open to 10pm at the weekend summer.

China Fast Food (Map pp72-3; ☎ 031 568 278; Ledina nter, Kotnikova ulica 5; dishes €3.50-6.50; 10am-9pm Mon-Fri, 11am-9pm Sat) This tiny place tucked way in an overlooked shopping centre has but eight tables but boy can this guy cook!

There are a couple of stands selling cheese, meat and apple *burek* round the clock, including **Olimpije** (Map pp72-3; Pražakova ulica 2; burek €2; 24hr) southwest of the train and bus stations, and **Nobel Burek** (Map pp72-3; Miklošičeva cesta 30; burek €2, pizza €1.60; 24hr).

Markets & Self-Catering

Convenient supermarkets include a large **Mercator** (Map pp72-3; Slovenska cesta 55; 7am-9pm) southwest of the stations and a much smaller (but more central) branch of **Mercator** (Map p78; Kongresni trg 9; 7am-8pm Mon-Fri, 8am-3pm Sat & Sun) just up from the river.

The supermarket below the **Maximarket** (Map pp72-3; basement, Trg Republike 1; 9am-9pm Mon-Fri, 8am-5pm Sat) department store has the largest selection of food and wine in the city centre as well as a bakery.

Ljubljana's **open-air market** (Map p78; Pogačarjev trg & Vodnikov trg; 6am-6pm Mon-Fri, 6am-4pm Sat Jun-Sep, 6am-4pm Mon-Sat Oct-May) east and northeast of the cathedral sell mostly fresh fruit and vegetables, though some stands also sell seasonal goods such as wild mushrooms, honey, chestnuts, beeswax and fresh herbs.

To the west the **covered market** (Map p78; Pogačarjev trg 1; 7am-2pm Mon-Wed & Sat, 7am-4pm Thu & Fri) on the ground floor of the Seminary has a superb range of meats, charcuterie and dairy products. The nearby **fish market** (Map p78; Adamič-Lundrovo nabrežje 1; 7am-4pm Mon-Fri, 7am-2pm Sat) is on the lower level of the Plečnik Colonnade overlooking the river.

Vegetarian self-caterers might try **Zrno do Zrna** (Grain to Grain; Map p78; ☎ 430 55 55; Trubarjeva cesta 8; 6.30am-7.30pm Mon-Fri, 8am-3pm Sat), a bio shop selling vegetarian and vegan sandwiches and snacks along with organic produce and packaged goods.

DRINKING

Few European cities of comparable size to Ljubljana offer such a dizzying array of drinking options, whether your tipple is beer, wine and spirits or tea and coffee. In Ljubljana there's a fine line between cafes, most of which serve food as well as drinks, and pubs and bars, particularly in the warmer months, when tables of both line the pavements.

Cafes & Teahouses

Kavarna Zvezda (Map p78; ☎ 421 90 90; Wolfova ulica 14; 🕑 7am-11pm Mon-Sat, 10am-8pm Sun) The Star Cafe is celebrated for its shop-made cakes, especially *skutina pečena* (€2.70), an eggy cheesecake. There's now a branch in the Hotel Slon (p91).

Café Antico (Map p78; ☎ 426 40 88; Stari trg 17; 🕑 9am-midnight Mon-Thu, 9am-1am Fri, 10am-10pm Sat, 11am-10pm Sun) With frescoed walls, painted ceiling and retro-style furniture, this pretty place is perfect for a quiet tête-à-tête over a cup of coffee or glass of wine.

Cha (Map p78; ☎ 252 70 10, 421 24 44; Stari trg 3; 🕑 9am-10.30pm Mon-Fri, 9am-3pm & 6-10pm Sat) If you take your cuppa seriously, come here; the appropriately named Tea offers a wide range of green and black teas and fruit tisanes for €1.80 to €3.40 a pot.

Le Petit Café (Map p78; ☎ 251 25 75; Trg Francoske Revolucije 4; 🕑 7.30am-1am) Just opposite the Križanke, this pleasant, boho place offers great coffee and a wide range of breakfast goodies (€2.20 to €6.50), lunches and light meals (sandwiches €2.90 to €4.50).

Slaščičarna Pri Vodnjaku (Map p78; ☎ 425 07 12; Stari trg 30; 🕑 8am-midnight) For all kinds of chocolate (of the ice cream and drinking kind), the Confectionery by the Fountain will surely satisfy – there are almost three dozen different flavours (€1.20 per scoop) as well as teas (€2) and fresh juices (from €1.40).

Grajska Kavarna (Map p78; ☎ 439 41 40; Ljubljana Castle, Grajska planota 1; 🕑 9am-midnight May-Sep, 9am-11pm Oct-Apr) Some minimalist magician has waved their magic wand over what was a dreadful 1970s concrete Cinderella of a cafe within Ljubljana Castle and transformed it into, well, a five-star hotel princess. There's glass, there's steel, there's terracotta. It's nice(r).

Abecedarium Cafe (Map p78; ☎ 426 95 14; Ribji trg 2; 🕑 7am-1am) Ensconced in the oldest house (1528) in Ljubljana and one-time residence of the writer Primož Trubar (p43) who wrote *Abecedarium*, this place – as much a restaurant as a cafe these days – oozes atmosphere.

KavaČaj (Map pp72-3; ☎ 433 82 33; Kersnikova ulica 1; 🕑 7.30am-10pm Mon-Thu, 7.30am-9pm Fri, 9am-2pm Sat) This gem of a place, though a bit off the beaten track, serves excellent tea and coffee, and sells the stuff (and accoutrements) as well. There's a smokers' area upstairs on the terrace.

Ambient (Map pp72-3; ☎ 430 27 56; Čufarjeva ulica 5; 🕑 7am-1am Mon-Fri, 9am-1am Sat, 6pm-1am Sun) This stylish cafe-cum-bistro, hidden dow a narrow side street just east of Miklošičev cesta, caters to a diverse crowd, but especiall radio and TV people from the nearby studio throughout the day.

Juice Box (Map p78; ☎ 051 614 545; Slovenska ces 38; juices & smoothies €3.60-4.90; 🕑 7am-8pm Mon-Fr 8am-3pm Sat) Of the crop of juice bars that hav sprouted up in Ljubljana, this is the most cen tral and the best, with some excellent fruit an vegetable combinations.

Kavarna SEM (Map pp72-3; ☎ 300 87 45; Metelkov ulica 2; 🕑 8am-midnight Sat-Thu, 8am-2am Fri) Thi wonderful cafe in the Slovenian Ethnographi Museum (p81) is all glass and modern art wit views of the attached pottery workshop an live ethno music on Tuesday and Friday. Coo new hangout – in a museum (blimey).

Čuperterija (Map p78; ☎ 051 340 225; Mestni trg 4 🕑 9am-1am) This long narrow cafe with it funky wrought iron furnishings, pictur frames on the ceiling and raisin biscuits tha come with the coffee is the perfect (and mos central) place to while away part of an after noon in the Old Town.

Pubs & Bars

Kavarna Tromostovje (Map p78; ☎ 430 12 18; Prešerno trg 1; 🕑 8am-1am) This roped-off cafe-bar on the southern side of Prešernov trg changes its name more often than we shake hands, bu remains one of the most popular places for a drink if you just want to sit outside and watch the passing parade. Heat lamps in winter.

Maček (Map p78; ☎ 425 37 91; Krojaška ul 5; 🕑 9am-12.30am) The place to be seen on a sunny summer afternoon, the Cat is Kavarna Tromostovje's rival on the right bank of the Ljubljanica. Happy hour is between 4pm and 7pm weekdays.

Cutty Sark (Map p78; ☎ 425 14 77; Knafljev prehod 1, 🕑 9am-1am Mon-Sat, noon-1am Sun) A pleasant and well-stocked pub with colourful windows in the courtyard behind Wolfova ulica 6, the Cutty Sark is a congenial place for a *pivo* (beer) or glass of *vino* (wine). Happy hour is from 5pm to 7pm.

Dvorni Bar (Map p78; ☎ 251 12 57; Dvorni trg 2; 🕑 8am-1am Mon-Sat, 9am-midnight Sun) This wine bar is an excellent place to taste Slovenian vintages; it stocks more than 100 varieties and has wine tastings every month (usually the 2nd Wednesday).

Pr' Skelet (Map p78; ☎ 252 77 99; Ključavničarska ulica 5; 🕑 10am-3am) It might sound like a one-joke wonder and it kinda is, but you'll shake, rattle and roll at this skeleton-themed basement bar, where cocktails are two for one throughout the day.

Žmavc (Map pp72-3; ☎ 251 03 24; Rimska cesta 21; 🕑 7.30am-1am Mon-Fri, 10am-1am Sat, 6pm-1am Sun) A super-popular student hang-out west of Slovenska cesta, with *manga* comic-strip scenes and figures running halfway up the walls.

Šank Pub (Map p85; Eipprova ulica 19; 🕑 7am-1am) Down in studenty Trnovo, this raggedy little place with brick ceiling and wooden floor is a relaxed alternative to the Sax (p99).

Vinoteka Movia (Map p78; ☎ 452 54 48; Mestni trg 2; 🕑 noon-midnight Mon-Sat) If you're more interested in the grape than the grain, hop over to this excellent wine bar where, with due ceremony and ritual, you can taste your way through some award-winning Slovenian wines (€2.50 to €10 for 0.1L). It does retail as well.

BiKoFe (Map p78; ☎ 425 93 93; Židovska steza 2; 🕑 7am-1am Mon-Fri, 10am-1pm Sat & Sun) A favourite with the hipster crowd, this cupboard of a bar has mosaic tables, studenty art on the walls, soul and jazz on the stereo, and a giant water pipe on the menu for that long, lingering smoke (€4) outside. There's a shady outdoor patio too.

Pod Skalco (Under the Rock; Map p78; ☎ 426 58 20; Gosposka ulica 19; 🕑 6.30am-3am Mon-Thu, 5pm-3am Fri-Sun) The only thing this dive due south of the City Museum has going for it, is that it keeps late hours when you need them most. Enjoy.

Pr' Semaforju (Map pp72-3; ☎ 040 893 664; Slovenska cesta 5; 🕑 7am-midnight Mon-Fri) Student (and we're talking spotty teens here) hangout par excellence, At the Traffic Light (the name is translated into a dozen languages outside) is a slightly grotty cafe-bar that rocks over two floors later in the evening.

Pri Zelenem Zajcu (Map p78; Rožna ulica 3; 🕑 9am-midnight Mon-Wed, 9am-1am Thu-Sat) The Green Rabbit is Ljubljana's first (and last?) absinthe bar, with its own label and studenty vibe. It's a bit of a warren of a place (as it would be) but we're sure you'll feel comfortably frisky here. Otherwise you can just have a sip of Fukoff Vodke, the bar's own vodka.

Solist (Map p78; ☎ 040 206 400; Kongresni trg 10; 🕑 8.30am-1am) Nowhere near as pretentious as it sounds, this stylish bar attached to the rear of the Filharmonija (p99), and facing the Ljublanica, plays only classical music. Makes for a nice change.

Opera Bar (Map pp72-3; ☎ 421 03 90, Cankarjeva ulica 12; 🕑 7am-12.30am Mon-Wed, 7am-2am Thu & Fri, 9am-3am Sat, 10am-6pm Sun) A favourite of culture-vultures (the Opera *is* just across the road) this boozer done up in Aboriginal art – there's an Aussie connection – attracts a well-heeled clientele.

ENTERTAINMENT

Though it will cost you, **Ljubljana in Your Pocket** (www.inyourpocket.com; €2.90), which comes out every two months, is the best single source of information for what's on in the capital. The freebie **partyson** (www.partyson.com) is good for clubs and events. You might also check the **Ljubljana Life** (www.ljubljana.info) website, which is locally generated.

Nightclubs

Top: Eat & Party (Map p78; ☎ 040 177 775; www.klubtop.si; Tomšičeva ulica 2; 🕑 8.30am-10pm Mon-Wed, 8.30am-5pm Thu & Fri, 11am-5am Sat) This retro restaurant and cocktail bar on the 6th floor of the Nama department store with the fabulous views becomes a popular dance venue nightly and attracts a very chi-chi crowd. Take the glass-bubble lift from along Slovenska cesta or the lift in the passageway linking Cankarjeva ulica and Tomšičeva ulica.

InBox (off Map p85; ☎ 600 50 86; 040 477 961; www.inbox-club.si; Jurčkova cesta 224; 🕑 9pm-dawn Thu-Sat) Ljubljana's biggest club is hidden in a shopping centre opposite the Leclerc Hypermarket (take bus 27 to NS Rudnik, the last stop) in the far southeastern suburbs. It attracts the best DJs in Slovenia.

Klub K4 (Map pp72-3; ☎ 438 02 61; www.klubk4.org; Kersnikova ul 4; 🕑 10pm-2am Tue, 11pm-4am Wed & Thu, 11pm-6am Fri & Sat, 10pm-4am Sun) This evergreen venue in the basement of the Student Organisation of Ljubljana University (ŠOU) headquarters features rave-electronic music Friday and Saturday, with other styles of music on weeknights, and a popular gay and lesbian night on Sunday. It closes in July and August.

SubSub (Map pp72-3; ☎ 430 42 08; http://subsub.si; Hala Tivoli, Celovška cesta 25; 🕑 10pm-5am Fri & Sat) The city's oldest club (but not by this name), SubSub is below the Hala Tivoli in Park Tivoli and doesn't really kick off until about 1am. It is frequented (according to one wag) by Ljubljana's 'troubled youth' so it might be fun.

Ultra (Map p78; ☎ 051 210 000, 031 560 713; www.ultra-club.si; Nazorjeva ulica 6; 🕑 10pm-6am Wed-Sat) Ultra is a popular dance venue with four different theme nights and a switched-on raucous crowd. This might be the place where you'll catch some turbo folk, super-charged Balkan music.

Bacchus Center (Map p78; ☎ 241 82 44; www.bachus-center.com; Kongresni trg 3; ⏲ 9pm-5am Mon-Sat) This place has something for everyone, including a restaurant and bar-lounge, and attracts a pretty tame, pretty mainstream crowd.

As Lounge (Map p78; ☎ 425 88 22; www.gostilnaas.si; Čopova 5/a; ⏲ 11pm-3am Wed-Sat) DJs transform this candlelit basement bar into a pumping, crowd-pulling nightclub four nights a week. The way the name sounds in Slovene might have you thinking you're going to get lucky, but it just means 'ace'. Enter from Knafljev prehod.

KMŠ (Map pp72-3; ☎ 425 74 80; www.klubkms.si; Tržaška ulica 2; ⏲ 8am-10pm Mon-Fri, 9pm-5am Sat) Located in the deep recesses of a former tobacco factory complex, the Maribor Student Club stays comatose till Saturday when it turns into a raucous place with music and dancers all over the shop.

For an evening of alternative entertainment and partying, try **Metelkova Mesto** (Metelkova Town; Map pp72-3; www.metelkova.org; Masarykova cesta 24), an ex-army garrison taken over by squatters after independence, it's now a free-living commune – a miniature version of Copenhagen's Christiania. In this two-courtyard block, a dozen idiosyncratic venues hide behind brightly tagged doorways, coming to life generally after midnight daily in summer and on Friday and Saturday the rest of the year. Entering the main 'city gate' from Masarykova c, the building to the right houses **Gala Hala** (www.galahala.com), with live bands and club nights, and **Klub Channel Zero** (www.ch0.org), with punk and hardcore. Above it on the 1st floor is **Galerija Mizzart** (www.mizzart.net) with a great exhibition space (the name is no comment on the quality of the creations – promise!) and cafe. Easy to miss in the first building to the left is the **Kulturni Center Q** (Q Cultural Centre) including **Klub Tiffany** (www.ljudmila.org/siqrd/tiffany) for gay men and **Klub Monokel** (www.klubmonokel.com) for lesbians. Due south is the ever-popular **Jalla Jalla Club** (www.myspace.com/jallajallaclub), a congenial pub with concerts. Beyond the first courtyard to the southwest, **Klub Gromka** (www.klubgromka.org) in the building with the conical roof has folk, live concerts, theatre and lectures. Next door is **Menza pri Koritu** (www.menzaprikoritu.org), under the strange ET-like figures, with performance and concerts.

Cinemas

Slovenska Kinoteka (Slovenian Cinematheque; Map pp72-3; ☎ 434 25 20; www.kinoteka.org; Miklošičeva cesta 28) shows archival art and classic films, whereas its sister cinema **Kino Dvor** (Court Cinema; Map pp72-3; ☎ 239 22 13; www.kinodvor.org; Kolodvorska ulica 13) nearby screens more contemporary films.

Foreign films are never dubbed into Slovene but are shown in their original language with subtitles. For the latest films (€3.80 to €4.50) head for any of the cinemas listed below:

Kino Komuna (Map p78; ☎ 421 84 00; Cankarjeva cesta 1) In the passageway linking Cankarjeva ulica & Tomšičeva ulica.

Kinoklub Vič (Map pp72-3; ☎ 241 84 11; Trg Mladinskih Delovnih Brigad 6) Southwest of Center and recently renovated.

Kolosej (off Map pp72-3; ☎ 520 55 00; www.kolosej.si; Šmartinska cesta 152) Multiplex with a dozen screens in BTC City shopping centre 3.5km northeast of Center.

Gay & Lesbian Venues

Ljubljana may not be the most gay-friendly city in Central Europe, but there are a few decent options. For general information and advice, ring **Roza Klub** (Map pp72-3; ☎ 430 47 40; Kersnikova ulica 4), which is made up of the gay and lesbian branches of Škuc (Študentski Kulturni Center or Student Cultural Centre), or the Škuc Information Centre (p75).

Open Café (Map p85; ☎ 041 391 371; www.open.si; Hrenova ulica 19; ⏲ 9am-midnight Mon-Sat, 4-10pm Sun) This very stylish gay-owned and run cafe south of the Old Town has become the meeting point for Ljubljana's burgeoning queer culture. In June 2009 it was attacked by fascist homophobics who attempted to torch the place and some patrons fought back.

Kafeterija Lan (Map p78; ☎ 486 50 53; Gallusovo nabrežje 27; ⏲ 9am-midnight Mon-Thu, 9am-1am Fri & Sat, 10am-1am Sun) This little greener-than-green cafe-bar on the river below Cobbler Bridge is something of a hipster/gay magnet and has a nice terrace under a spreading chestnut tree (but no mighty smith, alas).

K4 Roza (☎ 430 47 40; Kersnikova ulica 4; ⏲ 10pm-6am Sun Sep-Jun) A popular spot for both gays and lesbians alike is this Sunday – (and very occasionally Saturday) night disco at Klub K4 (p97). The music takes no risks, but the crowd is lively and frisky. See the website for dates and details.

Tiffany (Map pp72-3; www.kulturnicenterq.org/tiffany/klub; Metelkova Mesto, Masarykova cesta 24; ⏲ vary). This on-again, off-again gay cafe-bar is in the mall building to the left (east) as you enter Metelkova Mesto. Dates and times for events nd parties vary; see the website.

Monokel (Map pp72-3; www.klubmonokel.com; Metelkova Mesto, Masarykova cesta 24; 9pm-1am Fri or at) For lesbians, Monokel is in the same build-ng as Tiffany.

heatre

jubljana has half a dozen theatres so there hould be something on stage for everyone. lovenian theatre is usually quite visual with lot of mixed media, so you don't always ave to speak the lingo to enjoy the produc-ion. In addition to concerts and other musi-al events, Cankarjev Dom (right) regularly tages theatrical productions.

Slovenian National Drama Theatre (Slovensko arodno Gledališče Drama; Map p78; 252 14 62, box ffice 252 15 11; www.drama.si; Erjavčeva cesta 1; box ffice 2-5pm & 6-8pm Mon-Fri, 6pm-showtime Sat) Built s a German-language theatre in 1911, this vonderful art nouveau building is home to he national theatre company.

Slovenian Youth Theatre (Slovensko Mladinsko ledališče; Map pp72-3; 300 49 00, box office 300 49 02; www.mladinsko.si; Festivalna Dvorana, Vilharjeva cesta 11; box office 10am-noon & 3.30-5.30 Mon-Fri, 10am-noon at) Established in 1955 as the first professional heatre for children and youth in Slovenia, this company has staged some highly acclaimed contemporary productions in the Festival Hall north of the train station.

KUD France Prešeren (Map p85; 283 22 88; www .kud-fp.si; Karunova ulica 14; box office 3pm to perform-ance daily) This 'noninstitutional culture and arts society' in Trnovo stages concerts as well as performances, literary events, exhibitions, workshops etc on most nights.

Glej Theatre (Gledališče Glej; Map p78; 421 92 40, 251 66 79; glej@siol.net; Gregorčičeva ulica 3) Glej (Look) has been Ljubljana's foremost experimental theatre since the 1950s and '60s, working with companies that include Betontanc (dance) and Grejpfrut (drama). It stages about five productions – theatre, mime, puppetry, multimedia – a year.

Ljubljana Puppet Theatre (Lutkovno Gledališče Ljubljana; Map pp72-3; 300 09 70, box office 300 09 82; www.lgl .si; Krekov trg 2; box office 4-6pm Mon-Fri, 10am-noon Sat & 1hr before performance) The Ljubljana Puppet Theatre stages its own shows throughout the year and hosts Lutke, the International Puppet Festival (Mednarodni Lutkovni Festival), every other even year in September.

Live Music

ROCK, POP & JAZZ

Orto Bar (Map pp72-3; 232 16 74; www.orto-bar.com; Grabolićeva ulica 1; 9pm-4am Mon-Wed, 9pm-5am Thu-Sat) A popular bar-club for late-night drinking and dancing with occasional live music, Orto is just five minutes' walk from Metelkova. Don't confuse it (unless you're keen) with the venue called Escape downstairs, which is a lap-dance club.

Jazz Club Gajo (Map p78; 425 32 06; www.jazz clubgajo.com; Beethovnova ulica 8; 7pm-2am Mon-Sat) Now in its 15th year, Gajo is the city's premier venue for live jazz and attracts both local and international talent. Jam sessions are at 8.30pm Monday.

Sax Pub (Map p85; 283 14 57; Eipprova ulica 7; noon-1am Mon, 10am-1am Tue-Sat, 4-10pm Sun) Two decades in Trnovo and decorated with colourful murals and graffiti inside and out, the Sax has live jazz at 9pm or 9.30pm on Thursday from late August to December and February to June. Canned stuff rules at other times.

Roxly (Map p78; 430 10 21, 041 399 599; www .roxly.si; Mala ulica 5; 7am-2am Mon-Wed, 7am-3am Thu & Fri, 10am-3am Sat) This cafe, bar and restaurant, kitted out like a hooker's boudoir (red flush, gilt frames etc) north of the Ljubljanica features live rock music from 10pm two or three nights a week.

Classical Music, Opera & Dance

Cankarjev Dom (Map pp72-3; 241 71 00; www .cd-cc.si; Prešernova cesta 10) Ljubljana's premier cultural and conference centre has two large auditoriums (the Gallus Hall is said to have perfect acoustics) and a dozen smaller performance spaces offering a remarkable smorgasbord of performance arts. The box office (241 72 99, open 11am to 1pm and 3pm to 8pm Monday to Friday; and 11am to 1pm Saturday, and one hour before performance) is in the subway below Maximarket supermarket on the opposite side of Trg Republike.

Philharmonic Hall (Filharmonija; Map p78; 241 08 00; www.filharmonija.si; Kongresni trg 10; box office 4-6pm Mon-Sat) Home to the Slovenian Philharmonic Orchestra, this smaller but more atmospheric venue also stages concerts and hosts performances of the Slovenian Chamber Choir (Slovenski Komorni Zbor), which was founded in 1991.

Opera House (Slovensko Narodno Gledališče Opera in Balet; Map pp72-3; 241 17 40, box office 241 17 64, 031 696 600; www.opera.si; Župančičeva ulica 1; 1-5pm Mon-Fri, 11am-1pm Sat & 1hr before performance) Home to the Slovenian National Opera and Ballet companies, this historic theatre was under renovation at the time of research.

Križanke (Map p78; ☎ 241 60 00, box office 241 60 26; www.festival-lj.si; Trg Francoske Revolucije 1-2; ⏲ 10am-8pm Mon-Fri, 10am-1pm Sat & 1hr before performance May-Sep, 10am-5pm Mon-Fri & 1hr before performance Oct-Apr) The open-air theatre at this sprawling 18th-century monastery hosts the events of the Ljubljana Summer Festival (p88). The smaller Knights Hall (Viteška Dvorana) is the venue for chamber concerts.

SHOPPING

Ljubljana has plenty on offer in the way of folk art, antiques, music, wine, food and, increasingly, fashion. If you want everything under one roof, head for **BTC City** (off Map pp72-3; ☎ 585 11 00; www.btc-city.com; Šmartinska cesta 152) or **City Park** (off Map pp72-3; ☎ 587 30 50; www.citypark.si; Šmartinska cesta 152/b), sprawling malls side by side with hundreds of shops open from 9am to 8pm Monday to Saturday in Moste, northeast of Center. They can be reached on bus 2, 7 and 27.

Art & Antiques

Worth checking out is the weekly **antiques & flea market** (Map p78; Cankarjevo nabrežje; ⏲ 8am-2pm Sun) held year-round on the embankment between Triple and Cobbler Bridges.

Antika Ferjan (Map p78; ☎ 426 18 15; 1st fl, Mestni trg 21; ⏲ 9am-7pm Mon-Fri, 10am-2pm Sat) Ferjan is a large shop with Slovenian and other European art and antique glass, furniture and clocks.

Carniola Antiqua (Map p78; ☎ 231 63 97; Trubarjeva cesta 9; ⏲ 4-7pm Mon, 10am-1pm & 4-7pm Tue-Fri, 10am-1pm Sat) Newly expanded, with a large selection of items from the 1950s and '60s, this is among the best and most helpful antique galleries in town.

Galerija Fortuna (Map p78; ☎ 425 01 87; Gornji trg 1; ⏲ 10am-1pm & 4-8pm Mon-Fri, 10am-1pm Sat) Packed into this shop in the Old Town are some really beautiful antiques, especially glassware from the 1920s and other art nouveau treasures.

Trubarjev Antikvariat (Map p78; ☎ 244 26 83; Mestni trg 25; ⏲ 8.30am-1.30pm & 3.30-7.30pm Mon-Fri, 8.30am-1.30pm Sat) Come here for antiquarian and secondhand books. There's a good selection of antique maps upstairs.

Clothing & Fashion

Almira Sadar (Map pp72-3; ☎ 430 13 29; Tavčarjeva ulica 6; ⏲ 10am-7pm Mon-Fri, 10am-2pm Sat) On offer here are uniquely patterned women's foundation pieces and accessories in natural materials from one of Slovenia's leading designers.

Torbice Marjeta Grošelj (Marjeta Grošelj Bags; Map pp72-3; ☎ 231 89 84; Tavčarjeva ulica 4; ⏲ 8.30am-12.30pm & 3.30-7pm Mon-Fri, 8.30am-noon Sat) This shop just next door to Almira Sadar sells handbags by designer Marjeta Grošelj in top-quality leather.

Peko (Map p78; ☎ 059 089 068; www.peko.si; Čopova ulica 1; ⏲ 9am-8pm Mon-Sat) Once the provenance of good solid socialist shoes manufactured in the good solid socialist town of Tržič, northwest of Ljubljana, Peko has gone all trendy and its shoes vie only in quality with its new line of handbags.

The southern reaches of the Old Town are an oasis of high-quality fashion boutiques including the following:

Akultura (Map p78; ☎ 425 17 00; Stari trg 11/a; ⏲ 10am-7pm Mon-Fri, 10am-1pm Sat) Skirts, jackets and gloves in multicoloured, butter-soft leathers. In summer, silk makes an appearance.

Devetka (Map p78; ☎ 426 95 90; Gornji trg 1; ⏲ 10am-1pm & 4-7pm Mon-Fri, 10am-1pm Sat) Women's foundation pieces as well as bed linens in bold geometrical prints.

Katarina Silk (Map p78; ☎ 425 00 10; Gornji trg 5; ⏲ 10am-7pm Mon-Fri, 10am-2pm Sat May-Sep, noon-7pm Mon-Fri, 10am-2pm Sat Oct-Apr) Silk scarves so fine they'll pass through a ring, and unique costume jewellery.

Folk Art & Gifts

Darila Rokus (Rokus Gifts; Map pp72-3; ☎ 234 97 27; Gosposvetska cesta 2; ⏲ 9am-7pm Mon-Fri, 9am-1pm Sat) This stunning shop is the main outlet for a company manufacturing high-end glassware and crockery designed by the likes of Oskar Kagoj, Zora Stančič and Mateja Horvat; reproductions of Plečnik's sketches and lanterns and Trubar's original catechism, fine folk art and vintage wines.

Skrina (Trousseau; Map p78; ☎ 425 51 61; Breg 8; ⏲ 9am-7pm Mon-Fri, 9am-1pm Sat) This is a good shop for distinctly Slovenian (and affordable) folk craft, like Prekmurje black pottery, Idrija lace, beehive panels with folk motifs, decorated heart-shaped honey cakes, painted Easter eggs, Rogaška glassware, colourful bridal chests and colourful stepped stools.

Galerija Idrijske Čipke (Idrija Lace Gallery; Map p78; ☎ 425 00 51; Mestni trg 17; ⏲ 10am-1pm & 3-7pm Mon-Fri, 10am-2pm Sat) If Idrija (p159) in Primorska is not on your itinerary but you hanker for some of the fine lace for which that town is renowned, visit this shop. It has the stuff in spades.

Ljubljanček (Map p78; ☎ 059 025 727, 041 711 070; iklošičeva cesta 1; ⏰ 8am-2pm & 3-7.30pm Mon-Fri, 8am-pm & 2-6pm Sat, 8am-noon Sun) This small souvenir hop in the Grand Hotel Union Executive pecialises in products and souvenirs with Ljubljana band, so expect lots of dragon notifs and idylls along the Ljubljanica.

Piranske Soline (Piran Saltpans; Map p78; ☎ 425 01 90; estni trg 19; ⏰ 9am-8pm Mon-Fri, 9am-3pm Sat & Sun) A ranch of the shop in Piran (p184), this place n the Old Town sells bath sea salts and other roducts from Sečovlje.

Rustika (Map p78; ☎ 427 62 03, 041 859 666; ⏰ 9am-pm Jun-Sep, 10am-7pm Oct-May) This attractive allery and shop, with wooden floors and a eally 'rustic' feel, is conveniently located in jubljana Castle and is good for folk art.

Ika za Piko na I (Map p78; ☎ 512 30 23; Mestni trg 3; ⏰ 10am-7.30pm Mon-Fri, 10am-2pm Sat) This cute hop opposite the cathedral and market with he odd name about 'putting a dot on the ' sells handmade items that put a modern pin on traditional forms and motifs. More han 100 designers have clothing, jewellery, orcelain etc on sale here.

ood & Wine

/inoteka Movia (p97) is the most central lace in Ljubljana to buy (and taste) quality lovenian wine.

Kraševka (Map p78; ☎ 232 14 45; Ciril Metodov trg 0; ⏰ 9am-7pm Mon-Fri, 8am-2pm Sat) This fantastic lelicatessen with stuff from farms (mostly) n the Karst stocks *pršut* (dry, cured ham) n all its variations and cheeses, as well as wines and spirits, oils and vinegars and hon-eys and marmalades.

Honey House (Map p78; ☎ 030 395 773; Mestni trg 7; ⏰ 9am-7pm) Slovenia is one of the largest pro-ducers of honey and honey-related products in Europe and this place stocks enough varie-ties of the sweet sticky stuff to satisfy any taste. Mead, propolis and royal jelly available too.

Wine Cellars of Slovenia (Vinske Kleti Slovenije; Map pp72-3; ☎ 431 50 15; Jurček Pavilion, Ljubljana Fairgrounds, Dunajska cesta 18; ⏰ 10am-7pm Mon-Fri, 9am-1pm Sat) If you're serious about wine, this enormous wine cellar and restaurant (open 10am to 11pm Monday to Saturday) north of Center is for you. It has a selec-tion of more than 800 wines, most of which are Slovenian.

Vinoteka Dvor Koželj (Map p78; ☎ 251 36 44; www.kozelj.si; Dvorni trg 1; ⏰ 11am-8pm Mon-Fri, 9am-2pm Sat) This small shop conveniently located a stumble away from the Dvorni Bar (p96) has an excellent (and very central) selection of wines for sale, and the owner is knowledge-able and helpful.

Music

MCD Shop (Map p78; ☎ 425 17 06, 040 450 509; Miklošičeva cesta 2; ⏰ 9am-8pm Mon-Fri, 9am-2pm Sat) This is Ljubljana's best music shop, with informed and very helpful staff.

Muzikalije (Map p78; ☎ 426 70 36, 241 82 80; Trg Francoske Revolucije 6; ⏰ 9am-6pm Mon-Fri, 9am-1pm Sat) This atmospheric shop near the Križanke is the place in Ljubljana for classical music, musical scores and instruments.

Spin Vinyl (Map p78; ☎ 251 10 18; Gallusovo nabrežje 13; ⏰ 10.30am-7pm Mon-Fri, 10.30am-2pm Sat, 10.30am-1pm Sun) A sizeable collection of secondhand vinyl and CDs complements the newer stuff, which is overwhelmingly alternative rock, both local and foreign.

Sporting Goods

Annapurna (Map p85; ☎ 426 34 28; Krakovski nasip 4; ⏰ 9am-7pm Mon-Fri, 9am-1pm Sat) If you've for-gotten your sleeping bag, ski poles, hiking boots, climbing gear or rucksack, this shop in Krakovo can supply you with all of it – and more.

Lovec (Map pp72-3; ☎ 231 73 87; Gosposvetska cesta 12; ⏰ 8am-7pm Mon-Fri, 8am-1pm Sat) For those into ridin', fishin' and shootin', Hunter has all the kit and equipment you'll need.

GETTING THERE & AWAY

Air

For details of flights to and from Ljubljana, see p293.

Bus

Buses to destinations both within Slovenia and abroad leave from the same shedlike **bus station** (Map pp72-3; ☎ 234 46 00, information 090-93 42 30; www.ap-ljubljana.si; Trg OF 4; ⏰ 6am-9pm Mon-Sat, 8am-8pm Sun) opposite the train station. Next to the ticket windows are multilingual information phones and a touch-screen computer. There's another touch-screen computer outside too.

You do not usually have to buy your ticket in advance; just pay as you board the bus. But for long-distance trips on Friday, just before the school break and public holidays, you are running the risk of not getting a seat – book one the day before and reserve a seat (€1.20/3.70 domestic/international).

You can reach virtually anywhere in the country by bus – as close as Kamnik (€3.10, 50 minutes, 25km, every half-hour) or as far away as Brežice (€10.70, 2¼ hours, 117km, four a day). Here are some sample one-way fares (return fares are usually double), travel times, distances and frequencies from the capital: Bled (€6.30, 1½ hours, 57km, hourly), Bohinj (€8.70, two hours, 91km, hourly), Koper (€11.20, 2½ hours, 122km, five daily with more in season), Maribor (€12.40, three hours, 141km, between two and four daily), Murska Sobota (€16.80, 4¼ hours, 199km, one or two a day), Novo Mesto (€7.20, one hour, 72km, up to seven a day), Piran (€12, three hours, 140km, up to seven daily) and Postojna (€6, one hour, 53km, up to 24 daily).

For details of international bus services from Ljubljana, see p295.

Car & Motorcycle

All the big international car-rental firms have offices in Ljubljana, including **Avis** (Map pp72-3; ☎ 430 80 10; www.avis.si; Čufarjeva ulica 2; ⏲ 7am-7pm Mon-Fri, 7am-1pm Sat, 8am-noon Sun), **Budget** (Map p78; ☎ 421 73 40; www.budget.si; Grand Hotel Union Business, Miklošičeva cesta 3; ⏲ 8am-4pm Mon-Fri, 9am-noon Sat & Sun) and **Hertz** (Map pp72-3; ☎ 434 01 47; www.hertz.si; Trdinova ulica 9; ⏲ 7am-7pm Mon-Fri, 8am-1pm Sat, 8am-noon Sun).

However, you should get a better deal at either one of the local firms listed below.

Atet Rent a Car (off Map pp72-3; ☎ 513 70 17, 031 639 697; www.atet.si; M Hotel, Derčeva ulica 4; ⏲ 8am-8pm Mon-Fri, 8am-3pm Sat) In the M Hotel, very much with the old-fashioned 'we try harder' mentality.

ABC Rent a Car City Hotel Ljubljana (Map p78; ☎ 059 070 500, 031 382 052; infoabc@siol.net; City Hotel Ljubljana, Dalmatinova ulica 15; ⏲ 8am-6pm Mon-Fri, 8-11am Sat, 8am-noon Sun); airport (☎ 031 382 051; Jože Pučnik Airport; ⏲ 8am-9pm) Has its own fleet and acts as an agent for Europcar (www.europcar.si). It levies a drop-off charge, even within the same city, if you do not drop it off where you picked it up.

For sample hire car rates and information on conditions, see p299.

Train

Domestic and international trains arrive at and depart from central Ljubljana's lone **train station** (Map pp72-3; ☎ 291 33 32; www.slo-zeleznice.si; Trg OF 6; ⏲ 5am-10pm) where you'll find a separate Info Center next to the Ljubljana TIC office. Buy domestic tickets from window Nos 1 to 8 and international ones from either window No 9 or the Info Center.

The following are some one-way 2nd-clas domestic fares, travel times, distances an frequencies from Ljubljana: Bled (€4.30 t €5.80, 55 minutes, 51km, up to 21 a day, Koper (€8 to €9.60, 2½ hours, 153km, u to four times a day, with more in summer, Maribor (€8 to €13.60, 1¾ hours, 156km, u to 25 a day), Murska Sobota (€11 to €16, 4½ hours, 216km, up to five a day) and Nov Mesto (€5.50, 1½ hours, 75km, up to 14 daily). Return fares are double the price, and there's surcharge of €1.55 on domestic InterCity (IC and EuroCity (EC) train tickets.

For more information on internationa trains leaving Ljubljana, see p295.

GETTING AROUND

To/From the Airport

The cheapest way to Ljubljana's Jože Pučnik Airport is by public bus (Map pp72–3; €4.10 50 minutes, 27km) from stop No 28 at the bu station. These run at 5.20am and hourly from 6.10am to 8.10pm Monday to Friday; at the weekend there's a bus at 6.10am and then one every two hours from 9.10am to 7.10pm.

A **private airport van** (Map pp72-3; ☎ 04-252 6 19, 041 792 865) also links Trg OF, near the bus station, with the airport (€8) up to 11 time daily between 5.20am and 10.30pm, and is a 30-minute trip. It goes from the airpor to Ljubljana 10 times a day between 5.45am and 11pm.

A taxi from the airport to Ljubljana wil cost from €40.

Bicycle

Ljubljana is a pleasure for cyclists, and there are bike lanes and special traffic lights everywhere.

Ljubljana Bike (☎ 306 45 75; 2hr/1 day €1/5; ⏲ 8am-9pm Jun-Sep, 8am-7pm Apr, May & Oct) has two-wheelers available from 10 locations around the city, including the train station, the STIC office (p75), the Celica Hostel (p90) and the Antiq Hotel (p91).

Lots of hostels and bars, including the Cutty Sark (p96), rent bicycles from €1.20/6 per hour/day.

Car & Motorcycle

You can street park (per hour €0.30 to €0.60, from 8am to 6pm Monday to Friday, and 8am to 1pm Saturday) in Ljubljana, though not always very easily, especially in the museum area and close to the Old Town. There are nclosed car parks throughout the city, and heir locations are indicated on most maps. The one below Miklošičev Park (Map p78), or example, charges €1.70 per hour for hours one to six and €1.50 per hour for the next six between 7am and 7pm. Between 7pm and 7am it's €1.50 per hour for the first two hours, and then €0.50 per hour. A 24-hour stretch costs €27.20.

Public Transport

Ljubljana's public transport system, run by **LPP** (Ljubljanski Potniški Promet; ☎ 582 24 20; www.lpp.si; Celovška cesta 160; 7am-7pm Mon-Fri, 7am-1pm Sat), is very user-friendly. There are a total of 21 lines numbered 1 to 27 (No 4, 10, 15, 16, 17 and 26 don't exist), and five of them are 'night' buses, with an 'N' prefixed to the route number. These start at 3.15am or 4am and finish at midnight; the rest begin their runs at 5.15am or 5.30am and stop any time between 9pm and 10.30pm. Buses on the main routes run about every five to 15 minutes; service is less frequent on other lines and on Sunday and public holidays.

You can pay the flat fare (€1) on board with exact change or use a tiny metal *žeton* (token; €0.80) available at many newsstands, kiosks and post offices. A stored-value magnetic card called **Urbana** (www.jh-lj.si/urbana) was being introduced at the time of research with the cap set at €50 but it is unlikely most travellers will need to use one of these.

Bus passes (as well as tokens, of course) can be purchased from three LPP locations, including the company's head office. More central is the **LPP Information Centre** (Map pp72-3; ☎ 430 51 75; Slovenska cesta 56; 7am-7pm Mon-Fri, 6am-1pm Sat) near the Borza (Ljubljana Stock Exchange); and the **LPP kiosk** (Map pp72-3; Slovenska cesta 55; 6am-7pm Mon-Fri, 7am-1pm Sat) at the system's central stop (Bavarski Dvor). Passes are available for a day (*dnevna vozovnica*, €4) or a week (*tedenska vozovnica*, €15).

From the bus or train stations, bus 2 will take you down Slovenska cesta to Mestni trg (Magistrat stop) in the Old Town. To reach Trnovo, catch bus 9 to the terminus (Trnovo stop). In general the central area of Ljubljana is perfectly walkable, so buses are really only necessary if you're staying out of town

Kavalir (Gallant; ☎ 031 666 333, 031 666 332; 10am-6pm) is a city-run transport service that will pick you up and drop you off anywhere in the pedestrianised Old Town free of charge. All you have to do is call (and wait – there are at the moment only two golf cart-like vehicles available).

Taxi

Metered taxis can be hailed on the street or hired from ranks near the train station, at the Ljubljana TIC on Stritarjeva ulica, in front of the Grand Union Hotel, or on Mestni trg. Flagfall is €1 to €1.50 and the per-kilometre charge is €1, depending on whether you call ahead or hail a taxi on the street. You can call a taxi on any of the following numbers: ☎ 031 311 311, 041 272 288, 041 540 593 or 041 752 751.

Gorenjska

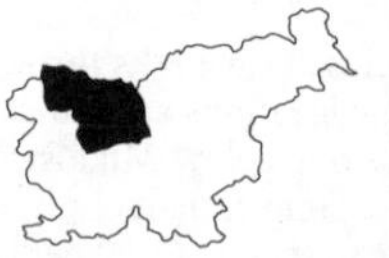

Mountains and lakes are the big draws in Gorenjska (Upper Carniola), and if you're int adventure sport, this is the province to head for. The Kamnik-Savinja Alps and its ski field begin just a short drive away from Ljubljana, and Triglav National Park, with hiking an biking trails galore as well as Slovenia's share of the Julian Alps, is just around the corne The lakes at Bled and Bohinj are popular centres for any number of outdoor activities. A mountain trek is an excellent way to meet other Slovenes in a relaxed environment so take advantage of this opportunity if you're in Gorenjska during the hiking season.

But Gorenjska is not just about shimmering lakes and mountain majesties; it also contains some of the country's most attractive and important historical towns. Škofja Loka, Kamnik Kranj and Radovljica – to name just a few – are treasure-troves of Gothic, Renaissance and baroque art and architecture, and they are wonderful bases from which to explore this diverse and visually spectacular province.

HIGHLIGHTS

- Climb to the top of **Mt Triglav** (p144), Slovenia's tallest peak, and proclaim yourself Slovene
- Drive or bike over the hair-raising (and spine-tingling) **Vršič Pass** (p144) in the Julian Alps
- Commune with nature *au naturel* at the naturist beach on the northern shore of **Lake Bohinj** (p138)
- Discover new things about the boards and bees at the fabulous **Beekeeping Museum** (p119) in Radovljica
- Hammer away in the delightful iron-mongering village of **Kropa** (p122)
- Take a 'flight' back in time via cable car to **Velika Planina** (p110) and its shepherds near Kamnik

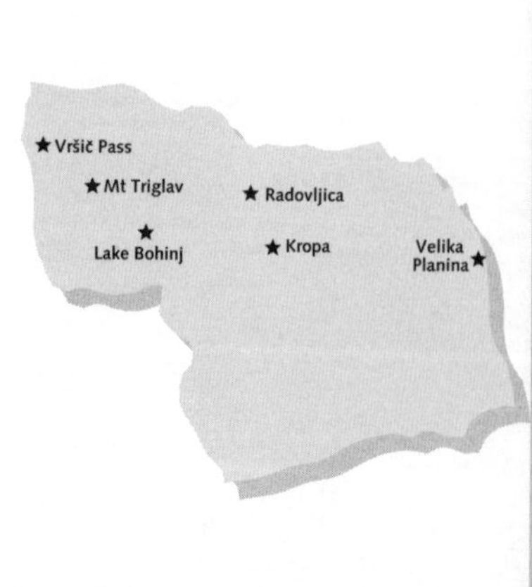

ITINERARY

BOHINJ ON THE TRADITIONAL SIDE

One Day / Gorenjska

As you cannot make a circular trip by car or by bike at Bohinj – the northern shore is bounded by footpaths only – an alternative is to follow the loop that captures several picturesque villages to the east of the lake. A bonus is that you'll catch a glimpse of Bohinj from its eastern shore. A bonus is that you'll catch a glimpse of Bohinj from its eastern shore and see some of the last remaining aspects of traditional lifestyles extant in this part of Slovenia.

Start the tour at **Bohinjska Bistrica** (**1**; p133), where the trains to and from Bled and the Soča Valley arrive and depart. You'll find an ambitious water park (p138) at Bohinjska Bistrica, but those more cerebral-minded might want to check out the **Tomaž Godec Museum** (Muzej Tomaža Godca; 04-577 01 42; Zoisova ulica 15; adult/child €2.50/2; 10am-noon & 5-8pm Tue-Sun Jun-Aug, 10am-noon & 4-6pm Tue-Sun Jan-May, Sept & Oct), in a reconstructed tannery that traces the history of iron forging in the valley, the long process of making leather and it also looks at the Isonzo/Soča Front.

It's an easy 6km to **Ribčev Laz** (**2**; p133), on the eastern edge of the lake, to a stunning 15th-century church dedicated to St John the Baptist. But several paintings on the outside southern wall depict not Christ's baptiser but St Christopher. In the Middle Ages people believed they would not die on the day they gazed upon an icon of the patron saint of travellers. No fools, our ancestors – they painted them on churches – but apparently forgot to look at least once in their lives as they're all dead now.

About 1.5km northeast is **Stara Fužina** (**3**; p134), once known for its cheese dairy, which now houses a museum focusing on Alpine dairy farming in the Bohinj Valley. From here head east for a couple of kilometres to the village of **Studor** (**4**; p136) to have a look at the fine examples of hayracks dating back as far as the 18th century. The next village is **Srednja Vas** (**5**; p139), with some decent *gostilne* (inn-like restaurants). From here head east for 2km and just before Jereka head south for the same distance back to Bohinjska Bistrica.

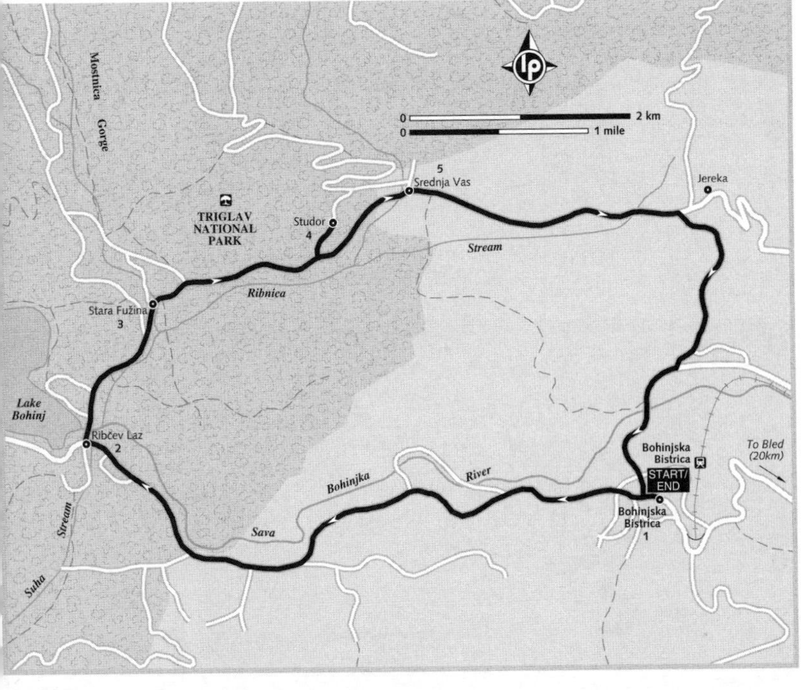

KAMNIK

☎ 01 / pop 13,670 / elev 382m

A historical town in the bosom of the mountains just 23km northeast of Ljubljana, Kamnik is often given a miss by travellers en route to 'sexier' Bled or Bohinj. But the town's tidy and attractive medieval core, with its houses and portals of hewn stone, balconies and arcades, is well worth a visit, as is the nearby arboretum and thermal spa. And Kamnik is the gateway to the incomparably beautiful mountain pastures of the Velika Planina.

Orientation

Kamnik lies on the west bank of the Kamniška Bistrica River and to the south of the Kamnik Alps. The Old Town consists of medieval Glavni trg and its souther extension, Šutna.

Kamnik's bus station lies beside the river ea of Glavni trg and at the end of Prešernova ulic The town has three train stations. The mai station is on Kranjska cesta, southwest of Šutn Kamnik-Mesto, which is convenient for the Ol Town and its sights, is on Kolodvorska ulic west of the Little Castle. Kamnik-Graben sta tion, the terminus of the Ljubljana–Kamnik lin is northwest of Glavni trg on Tunjiška cesta.

Information

Kamnik Alpine Society (Planinsko Društvo Kamnik; ☎ 839 13 45; www.drustvo-pdkamnik.si; Šutna 42; 9am-noon Mon & Fri, 1-5pm Wed) Advice and guides for walking in the Kamnik Alps.

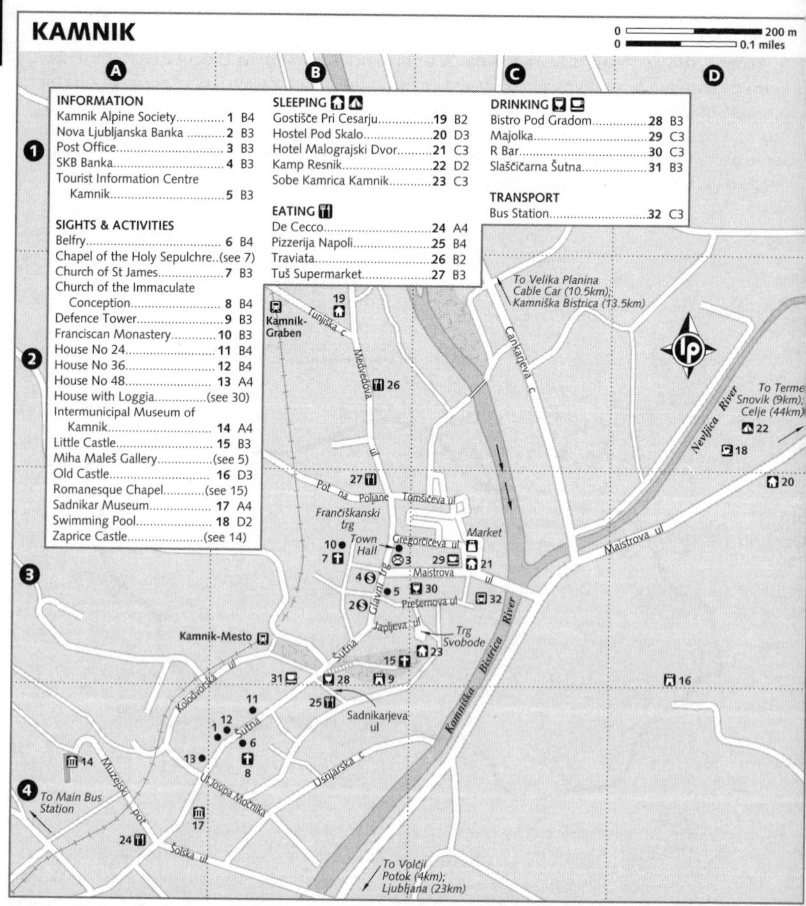

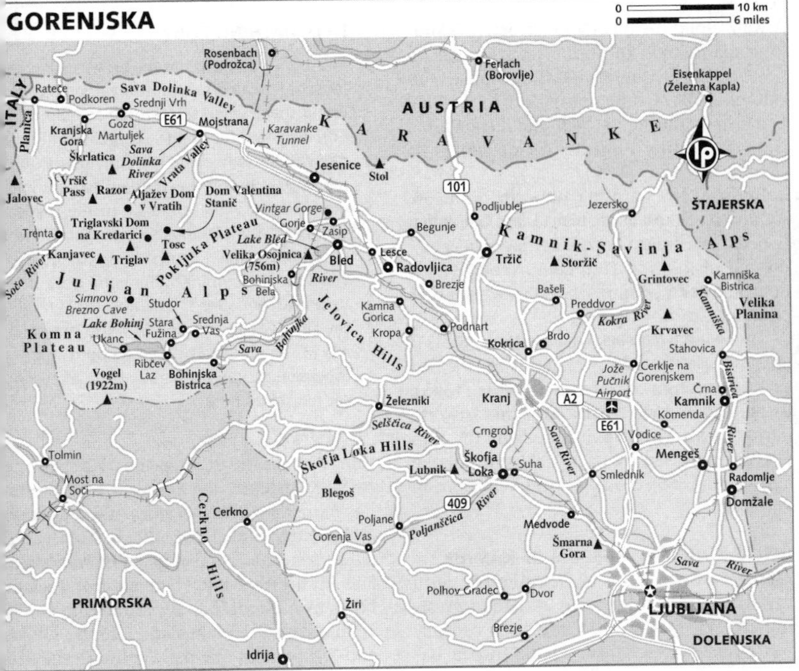

Nova Ljubljanska Banka (Glavni trg 10)
Post office (Glavni trg 27)
SKB Banka (Glavni trg 13)
Tourist Information Centre Kamnik (TIC; ☎ 831 82 50; www.kamnik-tourism.si; Glavni trg 2; ⌚ 9am-8pm Jul & Aug, 10am-6pm Mon-Sat, 10am-2pm Sun Jun & Sep, 8am-4pm Mon-Fri, 8am-noon Sat Oct-May) Free internet access and city tours (adult/child €5/3; 10am and 9pm Sat, 10am Sun).

Sights

GLAVNI TRG & SURROUNDS

The **Franciscan monastery** (Frančiškanski samostan; ☎ 831 80 37; http://franciskani-kamnik.rkc.si; Frančiškanski trg 2; ⌚ by appointment), a short distance to the west of Glavni trg, was built in 1492. It has a rich 10,000-volume library of theological, philosophical and scientific manuscripts and incunabula dating from the 15th to 18th centuries (including an original copy of the Bible translated by Jurij Dalmatin in 1584). Next door is the **Church of St James** (Cerkev Sv Jakoba; Frančiškanski trg) and just off the main altar is the tent-like **Chapel of the Holy Sepulchre** (Kapela Božjega Groba), which was designed by Jože Plečnik in 1952 and is full of symbols relating to Christ and Christianity. Plečnik also did the attractive beige-and-orange **house with loggia** on the eastern side of the square; it's now the R Bar (p109).

The **Little Castle** (Mali Grad), on a low hill above the southern end of Glavni trg, has foundations going back to the 11th century and this is where the town mint once stood. Kamnik's most important historical monument is the unique two-storey **Romanesque chapel** (adult/child €3/2; ⌚ 9am-7pm mid-Jun–mid-Sep), which has 15th-century frescoes in its lower nave, wall paintings by Janez Potočnik (1749–1834) in the presbytery and a Gothic stone relief of a cross flanked by two angels above the main entrance. There are some excellent views of the Old Town and the surrounding countryside from here. To the southwest you'll find the square **Defence Tower** (Obrambni Stolp).

The **Miha Maleš Gallery** (Galerija Mihe Maleša; ☎ 839 16 16, 831 75 04; www.muzej-kamnik-on.net; Glavni trg 2; adult/child €2.50/1.50, with Intermunicipal Museum of Kamnik €3/2.10; ⌚ 9am-1pm & 4-7pm Tue-Sat) contains some 2600 works by the eponymous painter and graphic artist Miha Maleš (1903–87), who was born in Kamnik. Enter from the north side of the TIC.

ŠUTNA

A walk along the quiet and attractive 500m-long main street of Šutna is a trip back in time: check the fine neoclassical house with columns at **No 24**, the stone relief of the Paschal Lamb above the door at **No 36** and the medieval fresco indicating a butcher's shop sign at **No 48** (now a grocery store).

In the centre of Šutna, opposite Šutna 36, stands the **Church of the Immaculate Conception** (Cerkev Marijinega Brezmadežnega Spočetja), erected in the mid-18th century but with a detached **belfry** (zvonik) that shows an earlier church's Gothic origins.

The **Sadnikar Museum** (Sadnikarjev Muzej; ☎ 839 13 62; Šutna 33; admission €2.50; ⏲ by appointment), the first private museum to open in Slovenia (1893), exhibits some 1500 articles of Gothic artwork, period furniture and paintings from the 18th century amassed by pack-rat Josip Nikolaj Sadnikar (1863–1952), a local veterinarian and painter.

INTERMUNICIPAL MUSEUM OF KAMNIK

Zaprice Castle (Grad Zaprice; Muzejski pot 3), with towers, ancient stone walls and an interesting chapel, was built in the 16th century but converted a century later into a baroque manor house. Today it houses the **Intermunicipal Museum of Kamnik** (Medobčinski Muzej Kamnik; ☎ 831 76 47; www.muzej-kamnik-on.net; adult/child €2.50/1.50, with Miha Maleš Gallery €3/2.10; ⏲ 8am-1pm & 4-7pm Tue-Fri, 10am-1pm & 4-6pm Sat, 10am-1pm Sun), with dullish exhibits connected with Kamnik's glory days and 18th-century furniture by German designer Michael Thonet (1796–1871). More interesting are the **granaries** outside, from the 18th and 19th centuries, which have been brought here from the Tuhinj Valley, and the **lapidarium** in the courtyard with stone bits and bobs from the 15th to 18th centuries.

OTHER SIGHTS

The **Old Castle** (Stari Grad), a 13th-century ruin on Bergantov Hill (585m) east of the centre, can be reached on foot from the end of Maistrova ulica in about 20 minutes. The trail is marked on the free Kamnik map available from the TIC.

About 4km south of Kamnik is **Volčji Potok** (☎ 831 23 45; www.arboretum-vp.si; Volčji Potok 3; adult/child/senior & student/family €5.50/3.30/4.50/13.50; ⏲ 8am-8pm Apr-Aug, 8am-7pm Sep, 8am-6pm Mar & Oct), Slovenia's largest and most beautiful arboretum. With the heart-shaped park of a forme castle as its core, the 80-hectare arboretu has more than 2500 varieties of trees, shrub and flowers from all over the world. The red letter event here is the **Spring Flower Show** i late April/early May. There are five weekda buses from Kamnik to the arboretum (€1.30 10 minutes) at 5.55am, 8am, 1.15pm, 2.45pm and 7.10pm and one daily at the weekend a 4.50pm on Saturday, 4pm on Sunday. More buses go to Radomlje, which is 1.5km sout of the arboretum.

HELL HATH NO FURY

The Little Castle is home to Veronika, a legendary countess who was turned partly into a snake when she refused to help the Christian faithful build a church. The old gal was not only mean but spiteful, too. In her rage at having been asked to contribute, she struck the entrance to the castle with her fist. If you look to the right of the portal to the main courtyard as you go in, you'll see the imprint of her hand (sort of). Veronika continues to rule the treasure of the Little Castle and, in a way, the community of Kamnik too. She appears both on the town seal and on the license plate of every car registered here.

Activities

There's an outdoor **swimming pool** (☎ 83 12 92, 031 278 568; Maistrova ulica 15; day pass adult child Mon-Fri €3.40/2, Sat & Sun €4.30/2; ⏲ 10am-6pm Mon-Fri, 10am-7pm Sat & Sun mid-Jun–Aug) near the camping ground.

On a warm day you might be tempted by **Terme Snovik** (☎ 834 41 00; www.terme-snovik.si; adult/child/student Mon-Fri from €8/5.50/6.50, Sat & Sun from €9/7/8; ⏲ indoor pools 9am-8pm Sun-Tue & Thu, 9am-10pm Wed, Fri & Sat, outside pools late Apr–Sep), a spa and water park with enormous covered and open-air pools and a gaggle of saunas in Potok, 9km northeast of Kamnik. Buses from Kamnik (€1.80, 15 minutes) go to the spa at 8.30am, 10.30am and 12.30pm weekdays and at 10.30am on Saturday and Sunday.

Festivals & Events

Major events in Kamnik (www.kamnik-tourism.si for information) are the **Medieval Days** (Srednjeveški Dnevi) in mid-June and the **National Costumes Festival** (Dnevi Narodnih ɿoš) held on the second weekend in ·eptember. But the biggest event by far is **ˌamfest** (www.kamfest.org), the so-called Festival ·ith a View, held in the Little Castle in ·ugust with two-dozen cultural events over ·wo weeks.

·leeping

ˌamp Resnik (☎ 831 73 14, 041 435 380; www.hostel camp-podskalo.com; Nevlje1/a; per person/car/tent/caravan ·2/2/2/4; ⏰ May-Sep; Ⓟ) This tiny 1-hectare ·amping ground with 100 sites for 200 ·uests is northeast of the Old Town on the ·Ievljica River. There's a tennis court, and ·he public swimming pool is next door.

Hostel Pod Skalo (☎ 839 12 33, 041 707 425; ·www.hi-kamnik.com; Maistrova ulica 32; s/d/tr from ·30.50/45/67.50; Ⓟ) This HI-affiliated hos·el opposite the camping ground has just 10 ·ooms with two and three beds. It's a pretty ·asic but serviceable place.

Sobe Kamrica Kamnik (☎ 831 77 07, 041 222 ·00; www.kamrica-kamnik.com; Trg Svobode 2; per person ·32; Ⓟ) The Kamrica is central but small, ·ounting just five rooms. It's a cosy, flower·edecked place; ask for the charming room in ·the back with views (just) of the Little Castle and use of the kitchen.

Gostišče Pri Cesarju (☎ 839 29 17, 041 629 846; www .cesarski-dvor.si; Tunjiška cesta 1; s/d/tr €40/66/88; Ⓟ) This 12-room guest house 500m north of Glavni trg is an excellent choice, but the mansard rooms on the 2nd floor are rather cramped.

Hotel Malograjski Dvor (☎ 830 31 00; www.hotel kamnik.si; Maistrova ulica 13; s/d €68/96; Ⓟ) This family-run three-star hotel with 21 rooms and an apartment for four people is Kamnik's finest caravanserai. Glavni trg is due west and there's a back garden.

Eating

Pizzerija Napoli (☎ 839 27 44, 051 898 150; Sadnikarjeva ulica 5; pizza & pasta €4.50-7.50; ⏰ 11am-11pm Mon-Thu, 11am-midnight Fri & Sat, noon-10pm Sun) South of the Little Castle in Šutna, this homey pizzeria, one of the few places for a meal in central Kamnik, has a great terrace and does takeaway as well.

Traviata (☎ 831 79 44, 059 920 758; Medvedova ulica 24; pizza & pasta €6-8; ⏰ 8am-10pm Mon-Thu, 8am-11pm Fri & Sat, 10am-8pm Sun) This popular inn 200m north of Glavni trg has turned away from traditional Slovene fare in favour of – you guessed it – pizza and pasta. There's outside seating in the back courtyard.

De Cecco (☎ 031 667 139; Šutna 68; meals from €10; ⏰ 10am-midnight Mon-Thu, 10am-1am Fri & Sat) South of the museum at the end of Muzejski pot, this pasta and pizza place is housed in a rather poshly done-up villa.

There's a **Tuš** (Trg Talcev 8; ⏰ 7.30am-8pm Mon-Fri, 7.30am-5pm Sat, 7.30am-noon Sun) supermarket just off Medvedova ulica north of Glavni trg.

Drinking

Majolka (☎ 839 10 81, 081 602 638; Maistrova ulica 11; ⏰ 7am-10pm Mon-Thu, 7am-11pm Fri & Sat, 9am-6pm Sun) This delightful cafe just west of the Hotel Malograjski Dvor is the nicest place in town for a cup of coffee and a slice of something sweet. The attached gallery has a lovely range of antiques, paintings, porcelain and souvenirs.

Slaščičarna Šutna (☎ 831 97 30; Šutna 4; ⏰ 7am-10pm Mon-Sat, 8am-10pm Sun) A pleasant cafe-bar on the old main street, this place has good cakes and ice cream.

R Bar (Maistrova ulica 2; ⏰ 7am-9pm Mon-Fri, 7am-2pm Sat, 8am-1pm Sun) This bar in the house that Plečnik built keeps early-bird hours but has big plate-glass windows from which to observe the action on Glavni trg. The wisteria is coming on nicely as well. This is Kamnik's longest-established pizzeria; go with the tried and the true.

Bistro Pod Gradom (Sadnikarjeva ulica 1a; ⏰ 8am-11pm) This cafe-bar just below the castle attracts the young bloods of Kamnik day and night.

Entertainment

Slovenia's first choir, **Lira** (www.lira-kamnik.si), was founded in 1882 and is still going strong, occasionally giving local concerts. Ask the tourist-office (p105) staff for information.

Getting There & Around

Buses from Ljubljana (€3.10, 50 minutes, 25km) run almost every 20 minutes on weekdays and half-hourly on Saturday and hourly on Sunday. You can also reach Gornji Grad (€3.60, one hour, 27km) on five buses a day (one to three at weekends) and Kamniška Bistrica (€2.30, 30 minutes, 15km) on three (two daily at weekends). To Kranj (€4.10, 50 minutes, 33km) count on four weekday buses. In July and August there's a bus leaving for Logarska Dolina (€7.60, two hours, 81km) in Štajerska at 6.55am on Sunday, returning at 4.25pm from the Rinka Waterfall.

Kamnik is on a direct rail line to/from Ljubljana (€2.20, 45 minutes, 23km, up to 17 a day) via Domžale.

You can book a taxi on ☎ 031 713 421 or 041 694 230.

The TIC rents **bicycles** (per 2/4/8hr €2/3.50/6)

VELIKA PLANINA

☎ 01 / elev to 1666m

The Velika Planina, loosely translated as 'Great Highlands', is a wonderful place to explore and is accessible to 1418m by cable car from the lower station just 11km north of Kamnik.

Velika Planina is where traditional dairy farmers graze their cattle between June and September. If you follow the road from the upper station up the hill for about 2km, you'll reach a highland plain filled with more than 50 shepherds' huts and the tiny **Church of Our Lady of the Snows** (Cerkev Sv Marije Snežne) modelled after traditional local dairies. The low-lying rounded buildings with conical roofs are unique to Velika Planina, but they are replicas. The originals dating from the early 20th century were all burned to the ground by the Germans in WWII except for the tiny two-room **Preskar's Hut** (Preskarjeva Bajta; ☎ 831 82 50; admission €2.50; 10am-5pm Sat & Sun late Jun–early Sep), which has been converted into a museum.

Velika Planina is also an excellent spot for **hiking** and **mountain biking**. Ask the TIC in Kamnik for their brochure *Velika Planina*, which outlines six biking trails of up to 30km and three hiking ones of up to 3½ hours. A circular walk of the plain and **Mala Planina** (1569m) to the south, for example, will take about three hours. In summer, the friendly shepherds in their big black hats will sell you curd, sour milk and white cheese.

The popular **Velika Planina ski grounds** (☎ 832 72 58; www.velikaplanina.si; day pass adult/child/student €20/16/18) have 6km of ski slopes and 10km of cross-country trails. When the slopes are skiable, a chairlift ferries skiers up to Gradišče from the upper cable-car station daily between December and April, where four T-bar tows should be running.

Sleeping & Eating

Domžalski Dom na Mali Planini (☎ 051 340 730, 031 264 740; year-round) This Category II lodge at 1534m, with 13 rooms of three to eight beds, is one of a handful of mountain huts an lodges with accommodation in the area.

Gostišče Zeleni Rob na Veliki Planini (☎ 832 7 58, 051 341 406; 8am-8pm Jun-Sep, 8am-8pm Fri-Su Oct-May) The snack bar and pub at Zeleni Ro (Green Edge) is about 1km up the hill fron the upper cable-car station.

Getting There & Around

The **cable car** (žičnica; ☎ 839 71 77, 832 55 66; ww .velikaplanina.si; adult/child/senior & student return €11/8/1C hourly 8am-6pm Mon-Thu, 8am-8pm Fri-Sun mid-Jun mid-Sep, 8am, noon & 4pm Mon-Thu, 8am & hourly noon-6pr Fri, hourly 8am-6pm Sat & Sun mid-Sep–mid-Dec & Apr–mid Jun, hourly 8am-6pm daily mid-Dec–Mar), which can b reached on any bus bound for Kamnišk Bistrica, runs year-round.

KAMNIŠKA BISTRICA

☎ 01 / pop 18 / elev up to 600m

This pretty little settlement in a valley nea the source of the Kamniška Bistrica River is 15km north of Kamnik, and the Categor II **Dom v Kamniški Bistrici** (☎ 832 55 44, 231 26 45 kambistrica@volja.net; year-round) offers hostel like accommodation in 13 rooms of two to five beds with a total of 36.

Kamniška Bistrica is the springboard for some of the more ambitious and rewarding Kamnik Alps treks, such as the ones to **Grintovec** (2559m; 11 hours return), **Brana** (2252m; eight hours) and **Planjava** (2394m; 10 hours). Information is available from the TIC in Kamnik.

The most-popular hikes, however, are the easier, 3½-hour hikes northwest to the mountain pass at **Kokra Saddle** (Kokrsko Sedlo; 1793m), with accommodation at the Category I **Cojzova Koča na Kokrskem Sedlu** (☎ 051 241 639, 051 635 549; pdkamnik@siol.net; daily mid-Jun–mid-Oct), with 135 beds; and north to **Kamnik Saddle** (Kamniško Sedlo; 1903m), where you'll find the Category I **Koča na Kamniškem Sedlu** (☎ 051 241 639, 051 611 367; daily mid-Jun–mid-Oct) mountain lodge with 142 beds.

Kamniška Bistrica can be reached from Kamnik (€2.30, 30 minutes, 15km) on three weekday buses a day, leaving at 7am, 11.30am and 4.52pm Monday to Friday, at 7.20am and 4.45pm on Saturday, and at 7.50am and 4.55pm on Sunday.

ŠKOFJA LOKA

☎ 04 / pop 12,275 / elev 354m

Among the most beautiful and oldest (in the late 10th century German Emperor Otto II

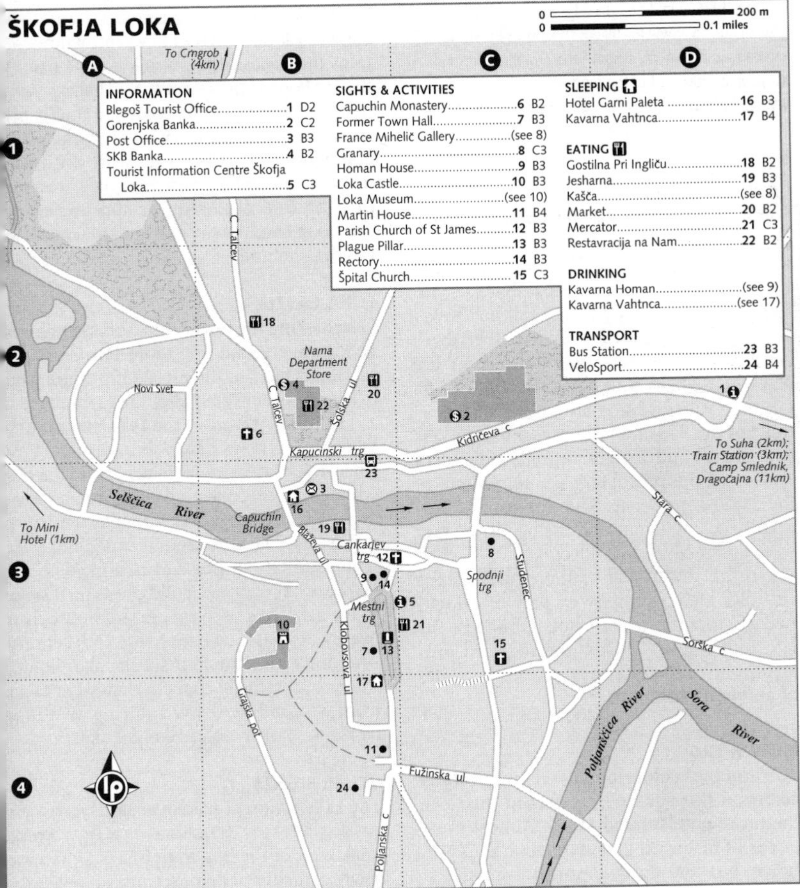

presented the Bavarian Bishops of Freising with the valleys along the two rivers here) settlements in Slovenia, Škofja Loka (Bishop's Meadow) has an Old Town protected as a historical and cultural monument since 1987. When the castle and other old buildings are illuminated on weekend nights, Škofja Loka takes on the appearance of a fairy-tale village. It's also an excellent springboard for walking in the Škofja Loka Hills to the west.

Orientation

The newer part of Škofja Loka and central Kapucinski trg lie to the north of the Selščica River. The Old Town on the opposite bank consists of two long squares, Mestni trg, which runs south from Cankarjev trg and the river, and to the east the rat-run that is busy Spodnji trg.

Škofja Loka's bus station is on Kapucinski trg. The train station is 3km to the northeast at the end of Kidričeva cesta in the suburb of Trata.

Information

Gorenjska Banka (Kapucinski trg 7) Diagonally opposite the bus station.

Post office (Kapucinski trg 14)

SKB Banka (Kapucinski trg 4) Next to Nama department store.

Tourist Information Centre Škofja Loka (TIC; ☎ 512 02 68; www.skofjaloka.info; Mestni trg 7; 🕒 8.30am-7pm Mon-Fri, 8.30am-2pm Sat & Sun mid-Jun–mid-Sep, 8.30am-7pm Mon-Fri, 8.30am-12.30pm &

5-7pm Sat & Sun mid-Sep–mid-Jun) Blegoš tourist office (☎ 517 06 00; www.lto-blegos.si; Kidričeva cesta 1a; 8am-6pm Mon-Fri, 4-6pm Sat & Sun mid-Jun–mid-Sep) Some 150m east of the centre.

www.skofjaloka.si Useful website courtesy of city hall.

Sights

CANKARJEV TRG

Some parts of the **Parish Church of St James** (Župnijska Cerkev Sv Jakoba; Cankarjev trg) date back to the 13th century, but its most important elements – the nave, the presbytery with star vaulting (1524) and the tall bell tower (1532) – were added over the next three centuries. On either side of the choir are black marble altars designed in about 1700. On the vaulted ceiling are bosses with portraits of the Freising bishops, saints, workers with shears and a blacksmith; two crescent moons in the presbytery are reminders of the Turkish presence. The dozen or so distinctive ceiling lamps and the baptismal font were designed by Jože Plečnik.

On the south side of the church is the church's **rectory** *(župnišče)*, part of a fortified aristocratic manor house built in the late 16th century. Below the rounded projection on the corner are curious consoles of animal heads.

MESTNI TRG

The group of colourful 16th-century **burgher houses** on this square have earned the town the nickname 'Painted Loka'. Almost every one is of historical and architectural importance, but among the more impressive is **Homan House** (Homanova Hiša; Mestni trg 2), dating from 1511 with graffiti and bits of frescoes of St Christopher and of a soldier. The **former town hall** (stari rotovž; Mestni trg 35) is remarkable for its stunning three-storey Gothic courtyard and the 17th-century frescoes on its facade. Further south, 17th-century **Martin House** (Martinova Hiša; Mestni trg 26) leans on part of the old **town wall**. It has a wooden 1st floor, a late Gothic portal and a vaulted entrance hall. The **plague pillar** in the centre of Mestni trg was erected in 1751.

SPODNJI TRG

This square to the east of Mestni trg was where the poorer folk lived in the Middle Ages; today it is a busy thoroughfare. The 16th-century **granary** (kašča; Spodnji trg 1) at the northern end is where the town's grain store collected as taxes, were once kept. It now con tains the Kašča restaurant and wine bar. O the 1st floor is the **France Mihelič Gallery** (Galeri Franceta Miheliča; ☎ 517 04 00; adult/child €1.50/1; b appointment), which displays the works of th eponymous artist born in nearby Virmaš in 1907. The **Špital Church** (Spodnji trg 9) was buil in 1720 around the town's almshouse, an the poor lived in the cells of the courtyar building behind.

LOKA CASTLE

Overlooking the town from a grassy hill wes of Mestni trg, the fine **castle** (Loški Grad; Grajsk pot 13) was built in the early 13th century bu extensively renovated after the earthquake in 1511. Today it houses the **Loka Museum** (Lošk Muzej; ☎ 517 04 00; www.loski-muzej.si; adult/child €4/2.5C 10am-6pm Tue-Sun), which has one of the bes ethnographical collections in Slovenia spreac over two-dozen galleries that extend ove two floors. The area around Škofja Loka wa famous for its smiths and lace-makers, anc there are lots of ornate guild chests on display In the garden is a typical peasant house from nearby Pušta dating back to the 16th century And don't miss the four spectacular Golden Altars in the castle chapel. They were taken from a church destroyed during WWII in Dražgoše, northwest of Škofja Loka.

OTHER SIGHTS

The 18th-century **Capuchin monastery** (Kapucinski samostan; ☎ 512 09 70; Kapucinski trg 2; by appointment), west of the bus station, has a priceless **library** of medieval manuscripts, as well as the *Škofja Loka Passion,* a processional with dramatic elements, from around 1720.

The stone **Capuchin Bridge** (Kapucinski Most) leading from the monastery originally dated from the 14th century and is an excellent vantage point for the Old Town and castle as well as the river with its deep gorge, dams, abandoned mills and 18th-century barracks.

Activities

The Škofja Loka Hills to the west, a region of steep slopes, deep valleys and ravines, is an excellent area for **walks** or **hikes**, and there are several huts with accommodation in the area. Before you set out, buy a copy of the 1:50,000 hiking map *Škofjeloško in Cerkljansko Hribovje* (Škofja Loka and Cerkno Hills; €8.10) and ask the TIC for the pamphlet *Škofja Loka Walk* *ound the Town and Surroundings,* which ill direct you to both Suha and Crngrob on ot (p114).

One of the easiest trips in the brochure is **Lubnik**, a 1025m peak northwest of the Old own, which can be reached on foot in two ours via Vincarje or the castle ruins near abrovo. Start the walk from Klobovsova lica in Mestni trg. A mountain hut near the ummit, Category II **Dom na Lubniku** (☎ 512 05 , 031 727 046; info@pd-skofjaloka.com; ⏲ daily Mar-Dec, t & Sun Jan & Feb), has seven triple rooms.

A hike to 1562m **Blegoš** further west would e much more demanding, but it takes only bout three hours from Hotavlje, a village bout 2km from Gorenja Vas and accessible y bus from Škofja Loka. There are two huts the area. Category II **Koča na Blegošu** (☎ 512 5 67, 051 614 587; info@pd-skofjaloka.com; ⏲ daily late pr–late Oct, Sat & Sun late Oct–late Apr), at 1391m, has 1 beds. **Zavetišče GS na Jelencih** (☎ 518 11 28, 041 41 997; pd.gorvas@volja.net; ⏲ Sat & Sun Nov–early May), bout 2km to the southwest and at 1185m, has 0 dorm beds.

The **Stari Vrh ski centre** (☎ 518 81 36, 041 650 49; www.starivrh.si; day pass adult/child/student €26/17/21), 2km west of Škofja Loka, is situated at altiudes of 580m to 1216m and covers 12km of ki slopes and trails. There are five T-bar tows nd a chairlift.

Festivals & Events

The staging of the **Škofja Loka Passion play** http://pasijon.skofjaloka.si) throughout the Old Town in the three weeks up to Easter (late March/April) and involving as many as 800 actors and 80 horses is Škofja Loka's biggest annual event. **Venerina Pot** (Path of Venus; http://ven era.skofjaloka.si) is a medieval-inspired festival held on the last weekend in June. A music festival called **Pod Homanovo Lipo** takes place under the big linden tree in front of Homan House on Mestni trg on certain nights in July and August.

Sleeping

Camp Smlednik (☎ 01-362 70 02; www.dm-camp smlednik.si; Dragočajna 14a; per adult €7-8, child €3.50-4, 2-/3-/4-person bungalows €40/50/60; ⏲ May–mid-Oct; P) This 4-hectare camping ground for 400 guests in Dragočajna, 11km to the east, is the closest one to Škofja Loka. It is situated on the left bank of the Sava River and beside Lake Zbilje. There is also a beach with separate facilities set aside for naturists.

Kavarna Vahtnca (☎ 512 14 79; www.vahtnca.si; Mestni trg 31; s/d €30/45) This attractive new cafe in the heart of Škofja Loka's Old Town has two very modern rooms upstairs that will put you in the centre of the action.

Hotel Garni Paleta (☎ 512 64 00, 041 874 427; www .paleta-skofjaloka.si; Kapucinski trg 17; s/d/tr/q €41/62/88/110; P) This colourful and upbeat place next door to an art-supplies shop (thus the name) just over Capuchin Bridge has six Ikea-standard, but nonetheless, comfortable rooms with exceptional bathrooms. Room 1, 3, 5 and 6 have views of the river *and* the castle.

Mini Hotel (☎ 515 05 40; www.minihotel.si; Vincarje 47; s/d/tr/q €43/65/82/99; P) This guest house is in the suburb of Vincarje, about 1km west of the bus station, and has eight sparkling rooms, squash and tennis courts, a sauna and a gym.

Eating

Jesharna (☎ 512 25 61; Blaževa ulica 10; pizza & pasta €4.50-8.20; ⏲ 9am-11pm Mon-Fri, 10am-11pm Sat, 11.30am-10pm Sun) This very friendly, very upbeat *picerija in špageterija* (pizzeria and spaghetti house) overlooking the river has free internet access. It's more or less opposite the post office.

Restavracija na Nam' (☎ 512 50 19; Kapucinski trg 4; set lunch €5, pizza from €5; ⏲ 9am-8pm Mon-Sat) This self-service restaurant is on the 2nd floor of the Nama department store (enter from Cesta Talcev).It's pretty basic cafeteria food.

Gostilna Pri Ingliču (☎ 512 66 30, 041 686 768; Cesta Talcev 4a; starters €4.50-6.30, mains €7-12; ⏲ 9am-11pm Thu-Sat, Mon & Tue, 9am-6pm Sun) This popular *gostilna* (innlikw restaurant) just a wee bit out of the centre serves standard Slovenian dishes as well as pizza and has both a big courtyard and an inviting terrace

Kašča (☎ 512 43 00, 41 355 959; Spodnji trg 1; starters €5-7.50, mains €7-14; ⏲ noon-midnight) This attractive (and huge) pub and wine bar in the cellar of the town's 16th-century granary also serves good Slovenian dishes, including ones peculiar to the Škofja Loka area, as well as pizza.

The **market** (Šolska ulica; ⏲ 7am-1pm Thu & Sat) is northeast of the Nama department store. You'll find a **Mercator** (Mestni trg 9; ⏲ 8am-7pm Mon-Fri, 7am-1pm Sat, 8am-noon Sun) supermarket in the centre of the Old Town.

Drinking

Kavarna Homan (☎ 512 30 47; Mestni trg 2; ⏲ 8am-11pm Mon-Thu, 8am-midnight Fri & Sat, 8am-10pm Sun) This ground-floor cafe in historical Homan House is always busy, especially in the warm weather when tables are set out on Mestni trg under the giant linden tree.

Kavarna Vahtnca (Mestni trg 31; 11am-midnight Mon-Fri, 8am-11pm Sat & Sun) With a tiered back terrace in the heart of Škofja Loka's Old Town peeking up at the castle, and tables on the main square, this attractive new place with rooms above it in the heart of the Old Town should be your first port of call.

Getting There & Away

Count on at least hourly buses weekdays between 7.10am and just after 11.30pm to Kranj (€2.30, 30 minutes, 13km) and between 4.35am and 9.10pm to Ljubljana (€3.10, 40 minutes, 25km). But there are far fewer departures at the weekend.

Škofja Loka can be reached by up to 15 trains a day from Ljubljana (€1.60, 25 minutes, 20km) via Medvode. Almost 20 go to Jesenice (€3.60 to €5.20, 50 minutes, 44km) via Kranj, Radovljica and Lesce-Bled. Up to eight of these cross the border for Villach, 87km to the north in Austria.

Getting Around

Local buses make the run between the train station in Trata and the bus station on Kapucinski trg. You can order a taxi on ☎ 041 625 875. The Blegoš tourist office (p111) rents bicycles for €5/8 per four hours/day. **Velosport** (☎ 512 32 00; Poljanska cesta 4; 9am-1pm & 3-7pm Mon-Fri, 9am-noon Sat) rents mountain bikes.

AROUND ŠKOFJA LOKA

Suha

☎ 04 / pop 160 / elev 338m

The 15th-century **Church of St John the Baptist** (Cerkev Sv Janeza Krstnika) at Suha, about 2.5km east of Škofja Loka, is unexceptional except for the presbytery, which has an interior completely covered with amazing frescoes painted by Bartholomew of Loka in the 16th century. The paintings on the vaults and walls show various Apostles, the coronation of Mary and scenes from the life of Christ. The panels below depict the five wise and five foolish virgins (the latter forgot to put oil in their lamps, according to the Gospel of St Matthew). Inside the arch facing the altar is a frightening scene from the Last Judgment. The gold baroque altar dates from 1672.

If the church is locked, request the key from the presbytery at No 32, the first building on the left as you enter Suha village and abo 150m beyond the church.

Crngrob

☎ 04 / pop 35 / elev 450m

The **Church of the Annunciation** (Cerkev Marijine Oznanenja; by appointment) at Crngrob, abo 4km north of Škofja Loka, has one of the mo treasured frescoes in Slovenia. Look for it o the outside wall under a 19th-century portic near the church entrance. Called Holy Sunda (Sveta Nedelja) and produced in the worksho of Johannes de Laibaco (John of Ljubljana in 1460, it explains in pictures what goo Christians do on Sunday (pray, go to Mas help the sick) and what they do not do (gambl drink, play bowls or fight). The consequence o doing any of the latter is damnation – vividl illustrated with souls being swallowed whol by a demon. On the south wall there's a larg 19th-century fresco of St Christopher.

The interior of the church, which was buil and modified between the 14th and 17th cen turies, contains more medieval frescoes o the north wall as well as a huge gilded ba roque altar (1652), the largest in Slovenia The colourful star vaulting of the presbyter has a number of bosses portraying the Virgi Mary, the Bishops of Freising, and a man o horseback, probably a church benefactor. Th people at house No 10 nearest the churc hold the keys.

Crngrob is easily accessible on foot or by bicycle (left) from Škofja Loka via Groharjevo naselje, which runs north from the Capuchin monastery and Cesta Talcev. An alternative is to take the bus bound for Kranj, get off at the village of Dorfarje (€1.30, 10 minutes, 4km) and walk northwest for about 1.5km.

KRANJ

☎ 04 / pop 34,950 / elev 386m

Backed by a battalion of mountain peaks, including snow-capped Storžič (2132m), Kranj is Slovenia's fourth-largest and most industrialised city. But the Old Town, perched on an escarpment above the confluence of the Sava and Kokra Rivers, looks pretty picturesque when seen from across the Sava, looking to the northeast and contains some of the most important architectural wealth of Gorenjska. This is a view you'll enjoy briefly from the right-hand window of the bus from Ljubljana to Bled or Kranjska Gora, between gaps in the light-industrial foreground.

istory

secondary Roman road linking Emona Ljubljana) and Virunum (near today's lagenfurt in Austria) ran through Kranj ntil about the 5th century; a hundred years ter the marauding Langobards established base here. They were followed by tribes of arly Slavs, whose large burial grounds can be partly seen below the floor of the Gorenjska Museum in the old town hall.

In the 11th century, Kranj was an important border stronghold of the Frankish counts in their battles with the Hungarians, and the town gave its name to the entire region – Kranjska (Carniola in English). It was also an important market and ecclesiastical centre in

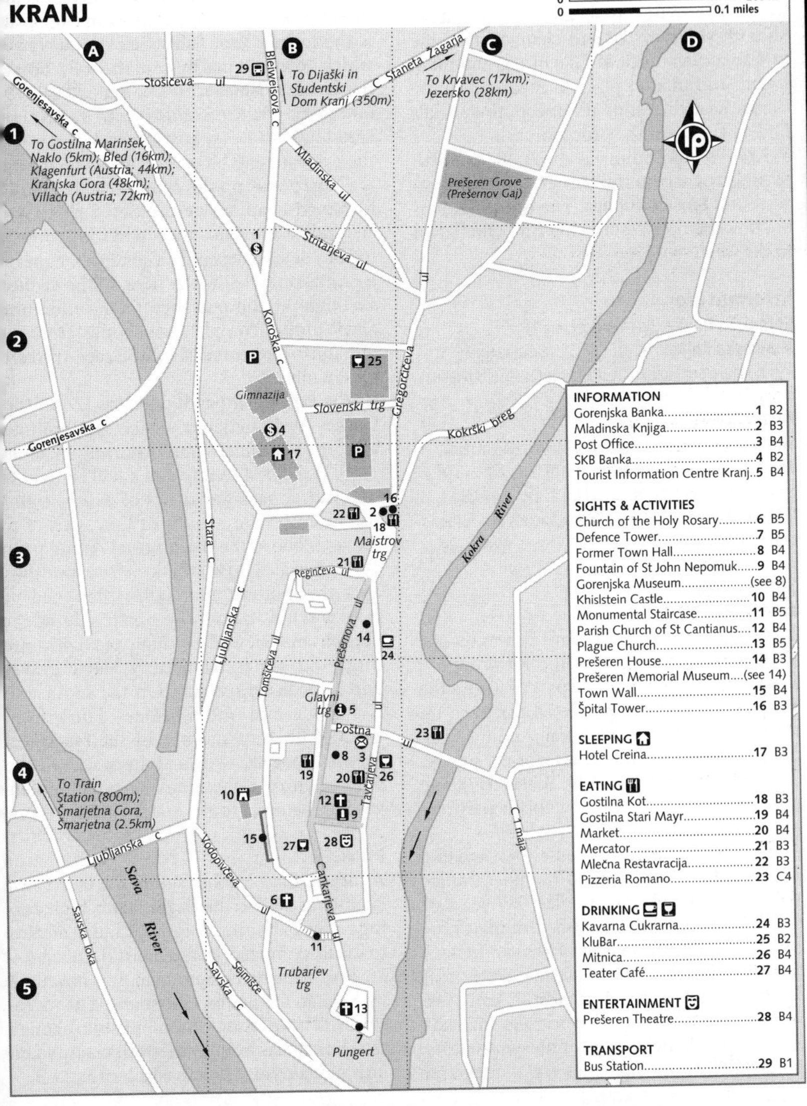

the Middle Ages and when the progressive Protestant movement reached Gorenjska, it was centred in Kranj. The city grew faster after the arrival of the railway in 1870.

Orientation

The attractive Old Town, barely measuring 1km by 250m, contains everything of interest in Kranj. It is essentially composed of three pedestrian streets running north to south. The main one begins as Prešernova ulica at Maistrov trg and changes its name to Cankarjeva ulica at Glavni trg, the main square and market place in medieval times. Cankarjeva ulica ends at Pungert, the 'Land's End' at the tip of the promontory.

Kranj's bus station is about 600m north of Maistrov trg on the corner of Bleiweisova cesta and Stošičeva ulica. The train station is on Kolodvorska cesta below the Old Town to the west.

Information

Gorenjska Banka (Bleiweisova cesta 1)
Mladinska Knjiga (☎ 201 58 35; Maistrov trg 1; 🕑 8.30am-7pm Mon-Fri, 8.30am-1pm Sat) Sells regional maps.
Post office (Poštna ulica 4)
SKB Banka (Koroška cesta 5) Next to the Hotel Creina.
Tourist Information Centre Kranj (TIC; ☎ 238 04 54; www.tourism-kranj.si; Glavni trg 2; 🕑 8am-7pm Mon-Sat, 9am-6pm Sun) Free internet access in a 16th-century town house.

Sights

MAISTROV TRG

The gateway to the Old Town, this was the site of the upper town gates in the 15th century. It was the most vulnerable part of Kranj; the steep Kokra Canyon protected the town on the eastern side and thick walls did the trick on the west from Pungert as far as the square. The **Špital Tower** (Špitalski Stolp; Maistrov trg 3), one of seven along the wall, now forms part of a butcher shop.

The restored **Prešeren House** (Prešernova Hiša; Prešernova ulica 7) was home to the poet France Prešeren (1800–49) for the last 2½ years of his life; he died in the front bedroom. It now contains the **Prešeren Memorial Museum** (Prešernov Spominski Muzej; ☎ 201 39 83; adult/child/student & senior/family €2.30/1.50/1.70/4.20; 🕑 10am-6pm Tue-Sun) in five rooms, two of them with original furnishings. Unfortunately, most of the explanatory notes next to the poet's letters, diaries and manuscripts are in Slovene only. Prešeren is buried in the parish cemetery, now called **Prešeren Grove** (Prešernov Gaj), about 500m to the north.

GLAVNI TRG

A beautiful plaza, Main Square is lined with Gothic and Renaissance buildings; the ones on the western side with their painted facades, vaulted hallways and arched courtyards are masterpieces. The 16th-century one opposite is the former **town hall** (mestna hiša; Glavni trg 4), which now contains most of the collection of the **Gorenjska Museum** (Gorenjski Muzej; ☎ 201 39 8[illegible]; www.gorenjski-muzej.si; adult/child/student & senior/family €2.30/1.50/1.70/4.20; 🕑 10am-6pm Tue-Sun). Among the eye-catching bits and bobs lying around is a large porcelain stove topped with a Turk's turbaned head, an embroidered sheepskin coat called a *kožuh* and a child's toy consisting of a devil sharpening a gossip's tongue on a grindstone. Below the floor of the vaulted vestibule at the entrance to the museum Slavic tombs (complete with bones) from the 9th and 10th centuries can be seen through glass panels.

The **Parish Church of St Cantianus** (Župnijska Cerkev Sv Kancijana), which was built on to part of an older church starting in about 1400, is the best example of a hall church (ie one with a nave and aisles of equal height) in Slovenia. The Mount of Olives relief in the arch above the main portal dating from 1450 is well worth a look before entering, as is the modern altar (1934) designed by Ivan Vurnik. Below the north side of the church and viewed through plexiglass are more old bones from early Slavic graves and a medieval ossuary. On the south wall is a lapidarium of tombstones dating from the Middle Ages and nearby the **Fountain of St John Nepomuk**, with a stone statue of the 14th-century Bohemian martyr complete with an octopus in the water.

PUNGERT

Another 300m uarther south, the Old Town dead-ends behind the **Plague Church**, built during a time of pestilence in 1470 and dedicated to the three 'intercessors against the plague' – Sts Rok, Fabian and Sebastian. It is now used by Serbian Orthodox Christians. The three-storey **defence tower** (obrambni stolp) beside the church was built in the 16th century and now contains an attractive gallery and cafe.

THER SIGHTS

ne of the most exciting 'new' attractions here e the **Kranj tunnels** (Kranjski Rovi; ☎ 238 04 54; adult/ ild €3/2.50; 🕑 5pm Tue & Fri, 10am Sat & Sun) under the ld Town, which can be visited on a guided our organised by the TIC (opposite). Built s air-raid shelters during WWII, the 1.3km ng tunnels were used to grow mushrooms the 1980s and 1990s and then abandoned to ave bats, crickets and spiders. You'll also see ascent 'straw' stalactites and ice stalagmites. ours of the tunnels depart from TIC.

At the end of Tomšičeva ulica northwest f Pungert is the **Church of the Holy Rosary** Roženvenska Cerkev), built in the 16th cenury. It was a Protestant sanctuary during the eformation. Beside the church are arcades, a ountain and a **monumental staircase** designed n the late 1950s by Jože Plečnik to give Kranj dramatic entrance up from the Sava River.

To the north of here is a lengthy section f the restored **town wall** and **Khislstein Castle** Grad Khislstein; Tomšičeva ulica 44), part of which was uilt during the Turkish invasions of the 15th entury. Check out the lovely arcaded courtard if you can gain access; it was undergoing nassive renovations when we last visited.

ctivities

A very easy destination for a walk is **Šmarjetna ora**, a 643m hill 3km northwest of the Old Town, where a fort stood during the Hallstatt eriod. The reconstructed **Church of St Margaret** s atop the hill. The views from here of Kranj, he Alps and the Sava River are astonishing.

Another easy walk follows the left bank of the Kokra River north from the eastern end of Poštna ulica for 8km and then back again. Ask the TIC for the *Canyon of the River Kokra Learning Trail*.

Festivals & Events

If you're in Kranj on the second Sunday in August, follow the flocks to Jezersko, 28km northeast of Kranj on the Austrian border, for the annual **Shepherds' Ball** (Ovčarski Bal; www .jezersko.si). It's a day and evening of folk music, dancing and drinking *žganje* (brandy) – the ovine alternative to the bovine event in Bohinj (p138).

Sleeping

The TIC can find you a private room from €25 or, in summer, a bed in a student dormitory from €12.

Dijaški in Študentski Dom Kranj (☎ 201 04 30; www .dsd-kranj.si; Kidričeva ulica 53; s/d/tr €16/28/36) This student hostel some 350m north of the bus station has accommodation in rooms with three beds, available in July and August and at the weekend during the rest of the year.

Gostilna Marinšek (☎ 257 72 70, www.marinsek.net; Glavna cesta 2; s/d €28/56) This B&B in Naklo is above a popular restaurant and pub that sells its own homemade beer. Rooms are fairly standard but not unattractive.

Hotel Creina (☎ 281 75 00; www.hotel-creina.si; Koroška cesta 5; s €60-80, d €80-100; P ⛝ 💻) This central brick-and-timber hotel with 87 recently renovated rooms is the only game in town if you want to stay someplace central. It is popular with Austrian business people and tour groups headed for the Alps. The airport at Brnik is only 7km to the southeast.

Eating

Mlečna Restavracija (☎ 236 61 79; Maistrov trg 13; dishes €3.50-8.50; 🕑 9am-9pm Mon-Fri, 9am-1pm Sat) The uninspiringly named Milk Restaurant is a cheap *bife* (buffet) and vegetarian eatery house in an ornamental old iron and glass conservatory.

Gostilna Kot (☎ 202 61 05; Maistrov trg 4; starters €3-7.50, mains €4.50-15; 🕑 7am-10pm Mon-Thu, 7am-11pm Fri, 8am-6pm Sat) Squeezed right into the thick of things in Maistrov trg, the Corner Inn is justly famed for its affordable and quite good daily specialities for under €5.

Pizzeria Romano (☎ 236 39 00; Tavčarjeva ulica 31a; pizza €5-7.50, grills €5.50-8; 🕑 8am-11pm Mon-Thu, 8am-midnight Fri & Sat, 4-11pm Sun) This simple place northeast of the post office and perched precariously above the Kokra River Gorge has pizza, pasta and great grilled dishes.

Gostilna Stari Mayr (☎ 280 00 20; Glavni trg 16; starters €6-9.50, mains €7-15; 🕑 8am-10pm) This old-style eatery has received a good scrubdown both inside and out and, while it still serves stick-to-the-ribs Slovenian dishes that will keep you going for longer than you'd think, it has a more enlightened menu as well. Fabulous back terrace.

The large **market** (Tavčarjeva ulica; 🕑 6am-6pm mid-Mar–mid-Oct, 7am-3pm mid-Oct–mid-Mar) northeast of the Parish Church of St Cantianus sells mostly fruit and vegetables. You'll find a branch of **Mercator** (Maistrov trg 11; 🕑 7am-7pm Mon-Fri, 7am-1pm Sat) supermarket in the Old Town

Drinking

Kavarna Cukrarna (☎ 281 82 90; Tavčarjeva ulica 9; 🕑 8am-11pm Mon-Thu, 8am-midnight Fri & Sat, 5-10pm Sun) This cafe with a balcony overlooking the dramatic Kokra River Gorge is a great place for a drink and a slice of something sweet.

Mitnica (☎ 040 678 778; Tavčarjeva ulica 35; 7am-11pm Mon-Wed, 7am-1am Thu, 7am-2am Fri & Sat, 3-11pm Sun) This very welcoming cafe-bar in the basement of a 16th-century toll house with a huge terrace backing on to the river is just the place to relax in Kranj on a warm afternoon.

Teater Café (☎ 202 44 41; Glavni trg 8; 8am-midnight Mon-Thu, 8am-2am Fri & Sat, 9am-midnight Sun) This cafe attracts an artsy crowd even when there's nothing on at the Prešeren Theatre (below) just opposite. Check out the bar with the brass trim in the form of lion's heads.

KluBar (☎ 236 41 21; www.klubar.si; Slovenski trg 7; 6.30am-midnight Mon-Wed, 6.30am-3am Thu & Fri, 9am-3am Sat, 3pm-midnight Sun) This enormous pub, next to the Storžič cinema, is popular with a very young crowd and is about the only place worth mentioning in 'new' Kranj.

Entertainment

Prešeren Theatre (☎ 280 49 11; Glavni trg 6; box office 10am-noon Mon-Fri & 1hr before performance) This provincial theatre is very active, staging four plays and up to 200 performances a year. Note the rather dashing statue of Prešeren out front.

Getting There & Away

Buses depart from Kranj at least half-hourly for Ljubljana (€3.60, 40 minutes, 28km) and Radovljica (€3.10, 30 minutes, 22km); and hourly for Bled (€4.10, 50 minutes, 31km), Bohinjska Bistrica (€6, 1¼ hours, 51km) and Škofja Loka (€2.30, 25 minutes, 13km). A bus goes to Brezje (€2.70, 30 minutes, 18km) at 5.05am weekdays year-round and at 7.40am on Sunday from May to September. You can also reach Bovec via Kranjska Gora (€9.90, 3½ hours, 109km) and the Vršič Pass on a daily bus at 7.10am in July and August.

Up to 20 trains a day pass through Kranj from Ljubljana (€2.20 to €4.80, 30 minutes, 29km) via Medvode and Škofja Loka. They continue to Radovljica, Lesce-Bled and Jesenice (€4.50 to €5.90, 40 minutes, 35km), where up to eight cross the border for Villach, 72km to the north in Austria.

Getting Around

Local buses make the run from the train station to the bus terminus on Stošičeva ulica. You can ring a local taxi on ☎ 233 52 40 or 041 542 040.

KRVAVEC

☎ 04 / elev to 1971m

Krvavec ski centre (☎ 252 59 30; www.rtc-krvav .si; day pass adult/child/senior & student €28/18/25 17km northeast of Kranj and easily dor as a day trip from Ljubljana, is one of th most popular (and crowded) in Slovenia. gondola transports you up to the centre a 1450m, and eight chairlifts and three T-ba tows serve the 33km of slopes and 3km c cross-country runs. Krvavec is also an ex cellent starting point for hikes in summe to **Kriška Planina** or **Jezerca**, about an hour walk from the cable car's upper statio Something new here is **Igloo Village** (Eskimsk Vas; ☎ 300 38 45; www.eskimska-vas.si), which i rebuilt of ice and snow every year durin the skiing season in 18 days. It's a bar, res taurant and – believe it or not – a hote where you sleep on (and under) sheepskin in rooms of 5°C. An evening package o snowshoeing, dinner and a party with D costs €45; with an overnight and breakfas it's €89 (children €35 to €65 dependin on age).

RADOVLJICA

☎ 04 / pop 6020 / elev 491m

A charming town full of historic buildings Radovljica enjoys an enviable position ato an outcrop 75m above a wide plain calle the Dežela, literally 'Country' in Slovene Views of the Alps, including Triglav, fron the Old Town are astonishing. Radovljic is an easy day trip from Bled, just 7km tc the northwest.

Radovljica was settled by the early Slavs and grew into an important market towr by the early 14th century. With increasec trade on the river and the iron forgeries a nearby Kropa and Kamna Gorica, Radovljica expanded. The town was built around a large rectangular square fortified with a wall and defence towers. Radovljica's affluence in the Middle Ages can be seen in the lovely buildings still lining Linhartov trg.

Orientation

The centre of old Radovljica is Linhartov trg; the new town extends primarily north and northwest along Gorenjska cesta towards Lesce. Radovljica's bus station is 400m northwest of Linhartov trg on Kranjska cesta. The train station is 100m below the Old Town on Cesta Svobode.

formation

renjska Banka (Gorenjska cesta 16)
st office (Kranjska cesta 1)
B Banka (Gorenjska cesta 10)
urist Information Centre Radovljica (TIC; ☎ 531
00; tdradovljica@siol.net; www.radovljica.si; Gorenjska
sta 1; ⌚ 8am-6pm Mon-Fri, 8am-noon Sat May-Sep,
m-4pm Mon-Fri, 9am-1pm Sat Oct-Apr)

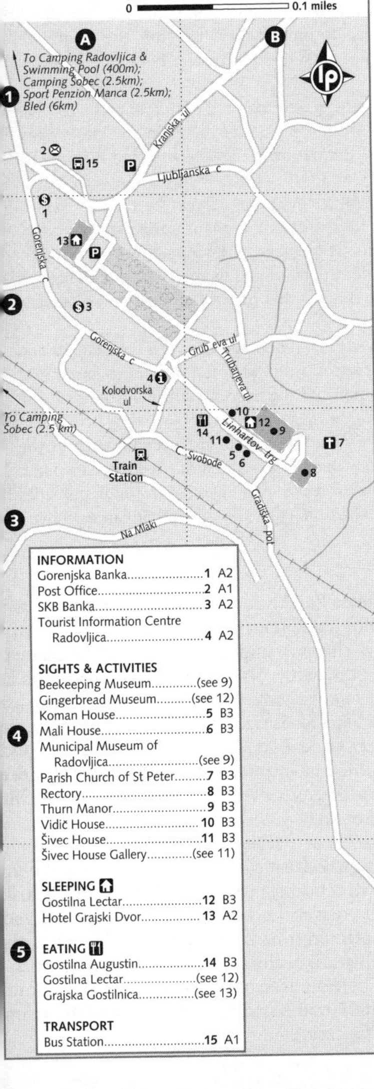

Sights

THURN MANOR

This baroque **palace** (Linhartov trg 1) began life as Ortenburg Castle in the early Middle Ages but was rebuilt with a large hall on the ground floor after the earthquake of 1511. The cream-and-white structure has interesting reliefs and stucco work on its facade and now contains two museums.

Although it might not sound like a crowd-pleaser the **Beekeeping Museum** (Čebelarski Muzej; ☎ 532 05 20; www.muzeji-radovljica.si; adult/child/family €2.50/2/7, with Municipal Museum of Radovljica €4/3/11; ⌚ 10am-6pm Tue-Sun May-Oct, 8am-3pm Tue, Thu & Fri, 10am-noon & 3-5pm Wed, Sat & Sun Mar, Apr, Nov & Dec, 8am-3pm Tue-Fri Jan & Feb) is one of the most interesting in the country, and there's not a whole lot you won't know about things apiarian after buzzing around it for an hour or so.

The museum's exhibits take a close look at the history of beekeeping in Slovenia (which was at its most intense in the 18th and 19th centuries), the country's unique contribution to the industry with the development of the Carniolan honeybee *(Apis mellifera carnica)* and the research of men such as Anton Janša (1734–73), who set up a research station in the Karavanke and is considered around the world as the 'father of modern beekeeping'. And the museum doesn't fail to pass on a few fun facts to know and tell. Did you realise that bees cannot see the colour red but go gaga over yellow? The museum's collection of illustrated beehive panels *(panjske končnice;* p120) from the 18th and 19th centuries, a folk art unique to Slovenia, is the largest in the country.

Bees are still kept in Slovenia for their honey and wax but much more lucrative are such by-products as pollen, propolis and royal jelly used as elixirs and in homoeopathic medicine. Propolis is a brownish, waxy substance collected from certain trees by bees and used to cement or caulk their hives. Royal jelly, so beloved by the European aristocracy of the 1920s and 1930s and by the Chinese today, is the substance fed to the queen bee by the workers.

The rather esoteric permanent collection at the **Municipal Museum of Radovljica** (Mestni Muzej Radovljica; ☎ 532 05 20; www.muzeji-radovljica.si; adult/child/family €2.50/2/7, with Beekeeping Museum €4/3/11), which shares the building with and keeps the same hours as the Beekeeping Museum, is devoted to the life and work of

THE BOARDS & THE BEES

The keeping of honeybees (species *Apis*) has been an integral part of Slovenian agriculture since the 16th century when *ajda* (buckwheat) was first planted on fallow ground to allow the more intensive use of farm land. Bees favour buckwheat, so Slovenia, especially the Alpine regions of Carniola (Kranjska), was soon awash in honey for cooking and beeswax for candles.

Originally bees were kept in hollow logs or woven baskets, but the entire hive was damaged when the honeycomb was removed. The invention of the *kranjič* hive, with removable boxes that resembled a chest of drawers, solved the problem by creating individual hives. It also led to the development of Slovenia's most important form of folk art.

Kranjič hives have *panjske končnice* (front boards) above the entrance, and painting and decorating these panels with religious motifs soon became all the rage. Ethnographers are still out to lunch over whether the illustrations were appeals to protect the hives from fire or disease, meant to guide the bees (they can distinguish colour) back home or to help beekeepers identify their hives.

The first panels, dating back to the mid-18th century, were painted in a 'folk baroque' style and the subjects were taken from the Old and New Testaments (Adam and Eve, the Virgin Mary, Sts Florian and George, and especially patient Job, the patron of beekeepers) and history (the Turkish invasions, Napoleon, the Illyrian Provinces and the Counter-Reformation with Martin Luther being driven to hell by a devil). The most interesting panels show the foibles, rivalries and humour of the human condition. A devil may be sharpening a gossip's tongue on a grindstone or two women fighting over a man's trousers (ie his hand in marriage). A very common illustration shows the devil exchanging old wives for nubile young women – to the delight of the husbands. Another – in a 'world turned upside down' – has gun-toting deer and bears laying a hunter in his grave.

The painting of beehive panels in Slovenia enjoyed its golden age between about 1820 and 1880; after that the art form went into decline. The introduction of a new and much larger hive by Anton Žnidaršič at the end of the 19th century obviated the need for small illustrations, and the art form degenerated into kitsch.

Nowadays you'll see the best examples of painted beehive panels in museums, such as the ones at Radovljica and Maribor, but there are still a few traditional – and protected – ones around, such as those at Muljava in Dolenjska. Nowadays the most common hives are the large box ones painted bright yellow (a colour bees like) and the 'hives on wheels' – trucks that can be moved into the sun or to a promising meadow.

Anton Tomaž Linhart (1756–95), Slovenia's first dramatist and historian, who was born in Radovljica.

LINHARTOV TRG

Radovljica's main square is lined with houses mostly from the 16th century and has been described as 'the most homogeneous old town core in Slovenia'.

Lovely buildings across from Thurn Manor include **Koman House** (Komanova Hiša; Linhartov trg 23), which has a baroque painting on its facade of St Florian, the patron saint of fires (he douses, not sets, them) and **Mali House** (Malijeva Hiša; Linhartov trg 24), which has a barely visible picture of St George slaying the dragon. The 17th-century **Vidič House** (Vidičeva Hiša; Linhartov trg 3) has a corner projection and is colourfully painted in red, yellow, green and blue, while **house No 17** has a fresco of Martin of Tou sharing his cloak with a beggar.

The most important house on the square 16th-century **Šivec House** (Šivčeva Hiša; ☎ 532 05 Linhartov trg 22; adult/child/family €2/1.50/7; 10am-1 & 5-8pm Tue-Sun Jul & Aug, 10am-1pm & 4-7pm Tue-S May, Jun, Sep & Oct, 10am-noon & 4-6pm Tue-Sun Nov-Ap which is an interesting hybrid: Renaissan on the outside and Gothic within. On t ground floor there is a vaulted hall, which no serves as a **gallery**, and on the 1st floor the is a wood-panelled late-Gothic drawing roo with a beamed ceiling used as a wedding ha There is also a chimneyless 'black kitchen' a an interesting collection of children's boo illustrations by celebrated Slovenian artis There's a fresco on the exterior that sho the Good Samaritan performing his wo of mercy.

Opposite Šivec House in the cellar of the ostilna Lectar (below) is a small **Gingerbread useum** (Lectarski Museum; ☎ 537 48 00; admission €1; oon-10pm Wed-Mon), which exhibits and demnstrates in living colour the particularly lovenian art of *lectarstvo*, the making and haping of honey dough into hearts, figures nd so on. It's well worth a look after a visit the Beekeeping Museum.

At the end of the square is the Gothic **arish Church of St Peter** (Župnijska Cerkev Sv etra), a hall church modelled after the one Kranj. The three portals are flamboyant othic, and the sculptures inside were done y Angelo Pozzo in 1713. The building with he arcaded courtyard south of the church is ne **rectory** *(župnišče)*, where exhibitions are ometimes held.

ctivities

sk the TIC for a copy of the guide *Radovljica nd Its Surroundings*, which outlines **hiking trails** and **cycling tracks** and suggests tineraries.

There is a public **swimming pool** (☎ 531 57 70; opališka cesta; day pass adult/child €5.30/3.70; 9am-pm Jun–mid-Sep) near the Radovljica campng ground, open in summer, with tennis ourts nearby.

estivals & Events

The biggest event of the year is the two-week **estival Radovljica** (www.festival-radovljica.si), one of he most important festivals of ancient clasical music in Europe, held in August.

Sleeping

Camping Radovljica (☎ 531 24 57, 531 57 70; www plavalniklub-radovljica.si; Kopališka cesta 9; adult/child €10.50/5.25; Jun–mid-Sep; P) The town's smallish camping ground (1.5 hectares) is next to the public swimming pool, and the daily rate includes use of it.

Camping Šobec (☎ 535 37 00; www.sobec.si; Šobčeva cesta 25; camping per adult €10.70-12.80, child €8-9.60, bungalows for 2 €75-120, for 3-6 €94-150; late Apr–Sep; P) The largest (15 hectares with 500 sites) and arguably the best-equipped camping ground in Slovenia is in Lesce, about 2.5km northwest of Radovljica. Situated on a small lake near a bend of the Sava Dolinka River, the camping ground can accommodate up to 1500 people in tents and bungalows.

Gostilna Lectar (☎ 537 48 00; www.lectar.com; Linhartov trg 2; s €45, d €50-80, tr €70-100;) One of our favourite places to stay in Slovenia, this delightful B&B in the heart of the Old Town has nine individually decorated rooms done up in folk motif – painted headboards, rooms signs (each is named differently) made of *lect* (gingerbread) – that could have ended up kitsch but instead feel like those in a village farmhouse from the 19th century. Room No 1 – Pri Fotografu (At the Photographer's), with its terrace and million euro views of the square, should be your first choice.

Hotel Grajski Dvor (☎ 531 55 85; www.hotel-grajski-dvor.si; Kranjska ulica 2; s/d €35/65; P) Radovljica's only hotel, the five-floor, 55-room Castle Courtyard is central but certainly not luxurious. The attached Grajska Gostilnica restaurant (below) is worth a visit.

Sport Penzion Manca (☎ 531 40 51; www.manca-sp.si; Gradnikova cesta 2; s €43-60, d €68-76, tr €88-98; P) This excellent-value pension about 2.5km north of Linhartov trg has 17 spic-and-span modern rooms and all sorts of sports facilities – from swimming pool and sauna to bicycles. Some rooms have views of the Karavanke range, others of Mt Triglav itself.

Eating

Grajska Gostilnica (☎ 531 44 45; Kranjska ulica 2; starters €4.60-7.50, mains €8.70-12; 11am-11pm) The restaurant at the Hotel Grajski Dvor has become popular for its pasta (€5 to €6.70) dishes, a great wine list and an atmospheric cellar below. All the metalwork was produced by UKO in Kropa (p123).

our pick **Gostilna Lectar** (Linhartov trg 2; starters €6.40-8.50, mains €8.80-12; noon-11pm) Some people say this is the best restaurant in Gorenjska and we're inclined to agree – though even if the food (enlightened Slovenian mostly) wasn't so good we'd come for the farmhouse decor, roaring fire in winter and fantastic back terrace with views of the mountains in summer.

Gostilna Augustin (☎ 531 41 63; Linhartov trg 15; starters €5-8, mains €10-15; 10am-10pm) This delightful restaurant with a bar open daily between 10pm and midnight is one of the most welcoming in Gorenjska. It serves excellent Slovenian dishes to order and bans pizzas altogether. Set lunch is a snip at €7 (€9 at the weekend). Don't miss the cellar dining room, which was once part of a prison (and may have seen an execution or two), and the wonderful back terrace with stunning views of – wait for it – Mt Triglav itself.

Getting There & Away

Buses depart for Bled (€1.80, 15 minutes, 7km) almost every 30 minutes between just before 5.30am and 10.40pm and for Ljubljana (€5.60, 70 minutes, 50km) via Kranj between 5.14am and 9.14pm. There are also buses to Kranjska Gora (€5.20, 50 minutes, 41km, up to eight a day) and Kropa (€2.30, 20 minutes, 13km, seven to 12 a day).

Radovljica is on the rail line linking Ljubljana (€3.60, one hour, 48km) with Jesenice (€1.60, 20 minutes, 16km) via Škofja Loka, Kranj and Lesce-Bled. Up to a dozen trains a day pass through the town in each direction. About eight of the northbound ones carry on to Villach, 54km to the north in Austria.

BREZJE

04 / pop 493 / elev 488m

The **Basilica of Our Lady of Perpetual Help, Queen of the Slovenes** (Bazilika Marije Pomojaj, Kralijici Slovencev; ☎ 537 07 00; www.marija.si; Brezje 72) in this village about 6km southeast of Radovljica has been a centre of pilgrimage since the time of the Illyrian Provinces and today attracts upwards of half a million of the Catholic faithful each year. It is to Slovenia what Lourdes is to France, Knock is to Ireland and Częstochowa is to Poland; indeed, this was Pope John Paul II's first port of call when he first visited Slovenia in 1988 and again in 1996. Still, apart from Janez Vurnik's stunning main altar, the altar painting of Our Lady of Perpetual Help by Leopold Layer and some works by Ivan Grohar, the neo-Moorish basilica dating from 1900 is unexceptional. Brezje can be reached by bus from Bled (€2.30, 25 minutes, 13km, three daily) via Radovljica (€1.80, 10 minutes, 6km).

KROPA

☎ 04 / pop 850 / elev 531m

While in Radovljica, don't miss the chance for an easy half-day trip to visit Kropa, a delightful little village tucked away in a narrow valley below the Jelovica Plateau 13km to the southeast. Kropa has been a 'workhorse' for centuries, mining iron ore and hammering out the nails and decorative wrought iron that can still be seen in many parts of Slovenia. Today Kropa has turned its attention to screws – the German-owned Novi Plamen factory is based here – but artisans continue their work, clanging away in the workshop on the village's single street. Th[e] work of their forebears is evident in weath[er] vanes, shutters and ornamental street lamp[s] shaped like birds and dragons.

Sights

BLACKSMITH MUSEUM

The fascinating collection at this **museu[m]** (Kovaški Muzej; ☎ 533 72 00; www.muzeji-radovljica.si; Krop[a] 10; adult/child/family €2.50/2/7, with forge display adult/chi[ld] €3/2.50; 🕑 10am-6pm Tue-Sun May-Oct, 8am-3pm Tue, Th[u] & Fri, 10am-noon & 3-5pm Wed, Sat & Sun Mar, Apr, Nov [&] Dec, 8am-3pm Tue-Fri Jan & Feb) traces the history [of] iron mining and forging in Kropa and nearb[y] Kamna Gorica from the 14th to the early 20t[h] centuries. Nail and spike manufacturing wa[s] the town's main industry for most of tha[t] period; from giant ones that held the pylon[s] below Venice together to little studs for sno[w] boots, Kropa produced more than 100 varieties in huge quantities. You did not becom[e] a master blacksmith here until you could fi[t] a horseshoe around an egg – without cracking the shell.

The museum has working models of forge[s], a couple of rooms showing how workers an[d] their families lived in very cramped quarters (up to 45 people in one house) and [a] special exhibit devoted to the work of Jož[e] Bertoncelj (1901–76), who turned out exquisite wrought-iron gratings, candlesticks[,] chandeliers and even masks. The museum shows two films, one on nail production an[d] one on local customs.

The house itself was owned by a 17th-century iron baron called Klinar, and it contains some valuable furniture and paintings[.] Among the most interesting pieces is a 19th-century wind-up 'jukebox' from Bohemia[.] Ask the curator to insert one of the large perforated rolls and watch the piano, drums[,] triangle and cymbals make music.

OTHER SIGHTS

An 18th-century furnace called **Vice Forge** (Vigenj Vice; admission €2, with museum adult/child €3/2.50) lies a short distance north of the museum behind **house No 56**, birthplace of the Slovenian painter Janez Krstnik Potočnik (1749–1834), whose work can be seen in the baroque **Church of St Leonard** (Cerkev Sv Lenarta) on the hill to the east, and in Kamnik. Below it is the **Kroparica**, a fast-flowing mountain stream that once turned the 50 water wheels that powered the fur-aces for the forges. Kropa has many other vely old houses, including several around g **Kropa**, the main square, which also has n interesting old wayside shrine. The cary-looking neo-Gothic pile up on the ill to the west is the **Church of the Mother of od** (Cerkev Matere Božje). Opening hours f the Vice Forge are the same as for the lacksmith Museum.

estivals & Events

'he most important day of the year in ropa is **Smith's Day** (Kovaški Dan; www.uko.si) elebrated with all manner of sporting and ultural events on 2 July.

leeping & Eating

ostilna Pr' Kovač (At the Smith's; ☎ 533 63 20, 041 59 273; Kropa 30; per person €25) This convivial and ery popular *gostilna* (starters €4.50 to €8, nains €7.50 to €12, open 10am to 11pm 'uesday to Sunday) in a lovely 400-year-old ouse with outside seating just north of the lacksmith Museum, has three rooms available for between two and six people.

Gostilna Pri Jarmu (☎ 533 67 50; Kropa 2; starters 2.50-8, mains €5.50-10; 🕑 10am-midnight daily Mayep, Fri-Tue Oct-Jun) This humble *gostilna* called t the Yoke at the southern end of Kropa erves hearty Slovenian favourites, as well as decent range of vegetarian dishes (€5 to 7) and pizza (€2.80 to €6).

There's a **Mercator** (Kropa 3a; 🕑 8am-6pm Monri, 7am-1pm Sat) supermarket branch between Gostilna Pri Jarmu and the post office.

Shopping

JKO Kropa forgers' workshop (☎ 533 73 00; www uko.si; Kropa 7a; 🕑 7am-6pm Mon-Fri, 9am-noon Sat ul & Aug, 7am-3pm Mon-Fri, 9am-noon Sat Sep-Jun) Across from the museum, this place has a shop selling all manner of articles made of wrought iron – from lamps and doorknobs to garden gates.

Getting There & Away

Between seven and 12 buses a day run to Radovljica (€2.30, 20 minutes, 13km). They stop in front of the Mercator supermarket.

BLED

☎ 04 / pop 10,900 / elev 501m

With its emerald-green lake, picture-postcard church on an islet, a medieval castle clinging to a rocky cliff and some of the highest peaks of the Julian Alps and the Karavanke as backdrops, Bled is Slovenia's most popular resort and its biggest tourist money spinner. Not surprisingly, it can be overpriced and swarming with tourists.

But as is the case with many popular destinations around the world, people come in droves – and will continue to do so – because the place *is* special. On a clear day you can make out Mt Stol (2236m) and Slovenia's highest peak, Mt Triglav (2864m), in the distance and then the bells start ringing from the belfry of the little island church. You should visit Bled at least once. It really is magical.

History

Bled was the site of a Hallstatt settlement in the early Iron Age, but as it was far from the main trade routes, the Romans gave it short shrift. More importantly, from the 7th century the early Slavs came in waves, establishing themselves at Pristava below the castle, on the tiny island and at a dozen other sites around the lake.

Around the turn of the first millennium, the German Emperor Henry II presented Bled Castle and its lands to the Bishops of Brixen in South Tyrol, who retained secular control of the area until the early 19th century when the Habsburgs took it over.

Bled's beauty and its warm waters were well known to medieval pilgrims who came to pray at the island church; the place made it into print in 1689 when Janez Vajkard Valvasor described the lake's thermal springs in *The Glory of the Duchy of Carniola*. But Bled's wealth was not fully appreciated at that time, and in the late 18th century the keeper of the castle seriously considered draining Lake Bled and using the clay to make bricks.

Fortunately, along came a Swiss doctor named Arnold Rikli, who saw the lake's full potential. In 1855 he opened baths where the casino now stands, taking advantage of the springs, the clean air and the mountain light. With the opening of the railway from Ljubljana to Tarvisio (Trbiž) in 1870, more and more guests came to Bled and the resort was a favourite of wealthy Europeans from the turn of the century right up to WWII. In fact, under the Kingdom of Serbs, Croats and Slovenes, Bled was the summer residence of the Yugoslav royal family.

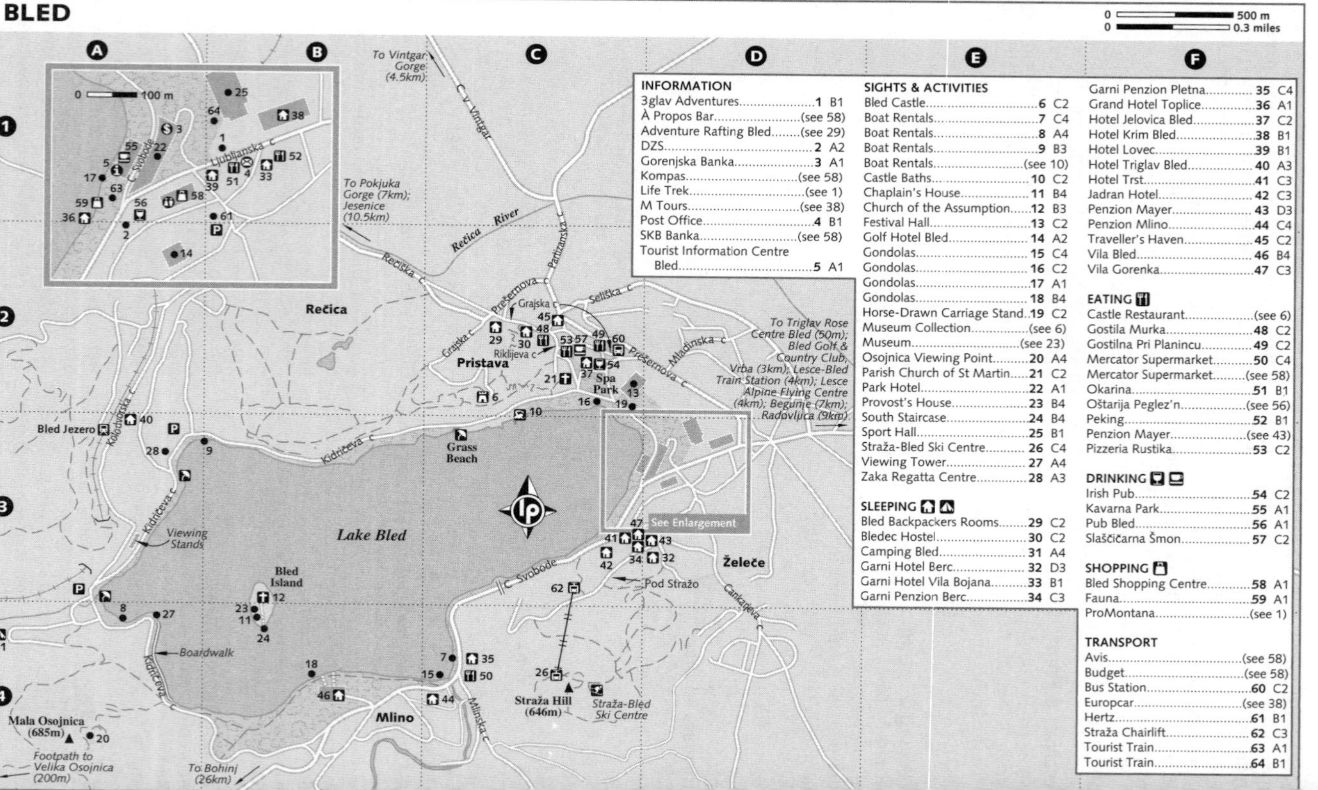
BLED
0 500 m
0 0.3 miles
INFORMATION
3glav Adventures 1 B1
À Propos Bar (see 58)
Adventure Rafting Bled (see 29)
DZS 2 A2
Gorenjska Banka 3 A1
Kompas (see 58)
Life Trek (see 1)
M Tours (see 38)
Post Office 4 B1
SKB Banka (see 58)
Tourist Information Centre Bled 5 A1
SIGHTS & ACTIVITIES
Bled Castle 6 C2
Boat Rentals 7 C4
Boat Rentals 8 A4
Boat Rentals 9 B3
Boat Rentals (see 10)
Castle Baths 10 C2
Chaplain's House 11 B4
Church of the Assumption 12 B3
Festival Hall 13 C2
Golf Hotel Bled 14 A2
Gondolas 15 C4
Gondolas 16 C2
Gondolas 17 A1
Gondolas 18 B4
Horse-Drawn Carriage Stand 19 C2
Museum Collection (see 6)
Museum (see 23)
Osojnica Viewing Point 20 A4
Parish Church of St Martin 21 C2
Park Hotel 22 A1
Provost's House 23 B4
South Staircase 24 B4
Sport Hall 25 B1
Straža-Bled Ski Centre 26 C4
Viewing Tower 27 A4
Zaka Regatta Centre 28 A3
SLEEPING
Bled Backpackers Rooms 29 C2
Bledec Hostel 30 C2
Camping Bled 31 A4
Garni Hotel Berc 32 D3
Garni Hotel Vila Bojana 33 B1
Garni Penzion Berc 34 C3
Garni Penzion Pletna 35 C4
Grand Hotel Toplice 36 A1
Hotel Jelovica Bled 37 C2
Hotel Krim Bled 38 B1
Hotel Lovec 39 B1
Hotel Triglav Bled 40 A3
Hotel Trst 41 C3
Jadran Hotel 42 C3
Penzion Mayer 43 D3
Penzion Mlino 44 C4
Traveller's Haven 45 C2
Vila Bled 46 B4
Vila Gorenka 47 C3
EATING
Castle Restaurant (see 6)
Gostila Murka 48 C2
Gostilna Pri Planincu 49 C2
Mercator Supermarket 50 C4
Mercator Supermarket (see 58)
Okarina 51 B1
Oštarija Peglez'n (see 56)
Peking 52 B1
Penzion Mayer (see 43)
Pizzeria Rustika 53 C2
DRINKING
Irish Pub 54 C2
Kavarna Park 55 A1
Pub Bled 56 A1
Slaščičarna Šmon 57 C2
SHOPPING
Bled Shopping Centre 58 A1
Fauna 59 A1
ProMontana (see 1)
TRANSPORT
Avis (see 58)
Budget (see 58)
Bus Station 60 C2
Europcar (see 38)
Hertz 61 B1
Straža Chairlift 62 C3
Tourist Train 63 A1
Tourist Train 64 B1
0 100 m
Ljubljanska c
C Svobode
To Vintgar Gorge (4.5km)
C v Vintgar
To Pokjuka Gorge (7km); Jesenice (10.5km)
Rečica River
Rečiška c
Partizanska c
Prešernova c
Grajska c
Seliška c
Riklijeva c
Mladinska c
To Triglav Rose Centre Bled (50m); Bled Golf & Country Club; Vrba (3km); Lesce-Bled Train Station (4km); Lesce Alpine Flying Centre (4km); Begunje (7km); Radovljica (9km)
Rečica
Pristava
Spa Park
Bled Jezero
Kolodvorska c
Kidričeva c
Grass Beach
See Enlargement
Viewing Stands
Lake Bled
Bled Island
Svobode c
Pod Stražo
Želeče
Cankarjeva c
Boardwalk
Straža Hill (646m)
Straža-Bled Ski Centre
Mlinska c
Mlino
Mala Osojnica (685m)
Footpath to Velika Osojnica (200m)
To Bohinj (26km)

rientation

Bled' refers both to the lake and to the set-ements around it, particularly the built-up rea to the northeast where most of the ho-ls are located. This development is domi-ated by a modern shopping complex called ne Bled Shopping Centre (Trgovski Center led). Bled's main road, Ljubljanska cesta, uns eastward from here. Footpaths and a oad called Cesta Svobode (when south of ne lake), Kidričeva cesta (to the southwest) nd Veslaška promenada (to the north) circle ne lake.

Bled's bus station is at the junction of Cesta Svobode and Grajska cesta, just up rom the Hotel Jelovica. There are two train tations. Lesce-Bled is 4km to the southeast n the road to Radovljica and on the line inking Ljubljana with Jesenice and Austria. Bled Jezero station, on Kolodvorska cesta orthwest of the lake, connects Jesenice to he north with Nova Gorica, Sežana and taly to the southwest.

nformation

BOOKSHOP

DZS (☎ 574 56 51; Cesta Svobode 19; ⌚ 8.30am-7pm Mon-Fri, 8.30am-1pm Sat) Has some regional maps and uides in English.

NTERNET ACCESS

Most of the hostels in Bled offer free inter-net access. Access at the Tourist Information Centre Bled (below) is free for the first 15 minutes and then €2.50/4 for 30/60 minutes.

À Propos Bar (☎ 574 40 44; Ljubljanska cesta 4; per 15/30/60 min €1.30/2.10/4.20; ⌚ 8am-midnight Sun-Thu, 8am-1am Fri & Sat) In Bled Shopping Centre; wireless connection as well.

MONEY

Gorenjska Banka (C Svobode 15) Just north of the Park Hotel.

SKB Banka (Ljubljanska cesta 4) In the Bled Shopping Centre.

POST

Post office (Ljubljanska cesta 10)

TOURIST INFORMATION

Tourist Information Centre Bled (TIC; ☎ 574 11 22; www.bled.si; Cesta Svobode 10; ⌚ 8am-9pm Mon-Sat, 9am-5pm Sun Jul & Aug, 8am-7pm Mon-Sat, 11am-5pm Sun Mar-Jun, Sep & Oct; 9am-6pm Mon-Sat, noon-4pm Sun Nov, 9am-6pm Mon-Fri, 8am-1pm Sun Dec-Feb)

TRAVEL AGENCIES

3glav Adventures (☎ 041 683 184; www.3glav-adventures.com; Ljubljanska cesta 1; ⌚ 9am-7pm Apr-Oct) The number one adventure-sport specialists in Bled.

Adventure Rafting Bled (☎ 574 40 41, 051 676 008; www.adventure-rafting.si; Grajska cesta 21; ⌚ Apr-Oct) Based at the Bled Backpackers Rooms hostel.

Kompas (☎ 572 75 00; www.kompas-bled.si; Bled Shopping Centre, Ljubljanska cesta 4; ⌚ 8am-7pm Mon-Sat, 8am-noon & 4-7pm Sun Jul & Aug, 8am-7pm Mon-Sat Sep-Jun)

Life Trek (☎ 578 06 62; www.lifetrek.si; Ljubljanska cesta 1; ⌚ 8am-8pm Jun–mid-Sep, 9am-4pm mid-Sep–May)

M Tours (☎ 575 13 00; www.mtours.net; Ljubljanska cesta 7; ⌚ 8am-8pm Mon-Sat, 8am-noon & 4-8pm Sun Jun-Sep, 10am-4pm Mon-Sat Oct-May) In the eastern wing of the Hotel Krim Bled.

Triglav Rose Centre Bled (☎ 578 02 00; www.tnp.si; Ljubljanska cesta 27; ⌚ 10am-6pm Tue-Sun May-Sep, noon-4pm Tue-Fri Oct & Dec-Apr) Information on Triglav National Park.

Sights

BLED CASTLE

Perched atop a steep cliff more than 100m above the lake, **Bled Castle** (Blejski Grad; ☎ 572 97 80; www.blejski-grad.si; Grajska c 25; adult/child/student €7/3.50/6; ⌚ 8am-8pm Apr-Oct, 8am-6pm Nov-Mar) is how most people imagine a medieval fortress to be – with towers, ramparts, moats and a terrace offering magnificent views on a clear day. The castle, which is built on two levels, dates back to the early 11th century although most of what stands here now is from the 16th century and for 800 years it was the seat of the Bishops of Brixen.

The baroque southern wing houses the **museum collection** that traces the history of Lake Bled and its settlements from earliest times in eight thematic sections – from the formation of the lake and natural environment and arrival of early settlers to the development of Bled as a resort in the 19th century. There's a large collection of armour and weapons (swords, halberds and firearms from the 16th to 18th centuries), jewellery found at the early Slav burial pits at Pristava, and a few interesting carvings, including a 16th-century one of the overworked St Florian dousing yet another conflagration, as well as tapestries and ancient tiled stoves. But most of it is pretty forgettable stuff. The smallish 16th-century Gothic **chapel** contains paintings of castle donor Henry II and his wife Kunigunda on either side of the main altar.

Admission to the castle includes entry to the rather touristy **Castle Printworks** (Grajska Tiskarna) as well as the **Castle Wine Cellar** (Grajska Klet) and **Herbal Gallery** (Zeliščna Galerija), both of which are essentially shops. The terrace of the castle restaurant affords wonderful views of the lake and surrounding mountains.

You can reach the castle on foot via one of three trails signposted 'Grad'. The first trail starts from the car park behind the Bledec Hostel; the second is a tortuous path up from the Castle Baths; and the third starts just north of the neo-Gothic **Parish Church of St Martin** (Farna Cerkev Sv Martina; Riklijeva cesta) designed by Friedrich von Schmidt in 1905.

BLED ISLAND

Tiny, tear-shaped **Bled Island** (Blejski Otok; ww .blejskiotok.si), the only true island in Sloveni has been the site of a Christian church sinc the 9th century. But excavations have show that the early Slavs worshipped at a paga temple here at least a century before that.

Getting to the island by a piloted **gondo** (pletna; ☎ 041 427 155; per person return €12) is the a chetypal tourist experience; there are jetti below the TIC, below Spa Park (Zdravilišl Park) to the north, in Mlino on the sout shore and near Zaka Regatta Centre. You g about half an hour to explore the island. In a the trip takes about 1¼ hours. Alternativel you can rent a rowing boat at the Castle Bath

ZLATOROG & HIS GOLDEN HORNS

The oft-told tale of Zlatorog, the mythical chamois (*gams* in Slovene) with the golden horns who lived on Mt Triglav and guarded its treasure, almost always involves some superhuman (or, in this case, superantelopine) feat that drastically changed the face of the mountain. But don't let Slovenes convince you that their ancient ancestors passed on the tale. The Zlatorog story first appeared in the *Laibacher Zeitung* (Ljubljana Gazette) in 1868 during a period of Romanticism and national awakening. This one tells of how the chamois created the Triglav Lakes Valley, a wilderness of tumbled rock almost in the centre of Triglav National Park.

Zlatorog roamed the valley (at that time a beautiful garden) with the White Ladies, good fairies who kept the mountain pastures green and helped humans whenever they found them in need.

Meanwhile, down in the Soča Valley near Trenta, a plot was being hatched. It seemed that an innkeeper's daughter had been given jewels by a wealthy merchant from Venice. The girl's mother demanded that her daughter's suitor, a poor but skilled hunter, match the treasure with Zlatorog's gold hidden under Mt Bogatin and guarded by a multiheaded serpent. If not, he was at least to bring back a bunch of Triglav roses to prove his fidelity. This being mid-winter, it was an impossible task.

The young hunter, seething with jealousy, climbed the mountain in search of the chamois, figuring that if he were to get even a piece of the golden horns, the treasure of Bogatin – and his beloved – would be his. At last the young man spotted Zlatorog, took aim and fired. It was a direct hit.

The blood gushing from Zlatorog's wound melted the snow, and up sprang a magical Triglav rose. The chamois nibbled on a few petals and – presto! – was instantly back on his feet. As the chamois leapt away, roses sprang up from under his hooves, luring the hunter onto higher and higher ground. But as they climbed, the sun caught Zlatorog's golden horns. The glint blinded the hunter, he lost his footing and plunged into a gorge.

The once kind and trusting Zlatorog was enraged that a mere mortal would treat him in such a manner. In his fury he gored his way through the Triglav Lakes Valley, leaving it much as it looks today. He left the area with the White Ladies, never to return.

And the fate of the others? The innkeeper's daughter waited in vain for her lover to return home. As spring approached, the snow began to melt, swelling the Soča River. One day it brought her a sad gift: the body of her young swain, his lifeless hand still clutching a Triglav rose. As for the innkeeper's rapacious wife, we know nothing. Perhaps she learned Italian and moved to Venice with the merchant.

Observant (and thirsty) travellers will see the face of Zlatorog everywhere they go in Slovenia. It's on the label of the country's most popular beer (p52).

Mlino or at the large beach at the southwest d of the lake and do it yourself.

The boat sets you down on the island's uth side at a monumental **South Staircase** užno Stopnišče) built in 1655. As you walk p you'll pass the **Chaplain's House** (Meznarija) d the **Provost's House** (Stavba Proštije) from e 17th and 18th centuries, with the Brixen ishops' coat of arms on the facade. The tter now contains a small **museum** (admission l church €3; 9am-7pm May-Sep, 9am-6pm Apr & Oct, m-4pm Nov-Mar) with an interesting display of aditional costumes across the country.

The baroque **Church of the Assumption** (Cerkev arijinega Vnebovzetja; admission with museum €3), open e same hours as the museum and dating om the 17th century, contains some fresco agments from the 14th century, a large old altar and, under the floor of the nave, art of the apse of a **pre-Romanesque chapel**, e only one in Slovenia. The 15th-century **elfry** contains a 'wishing bell' that visitors n ring if they want to ask a special favour. aturally everyone and their grandmother oes it – again and again and again.

AKE BLED

his lake is not a very large body of water – measures only 2km by 1380m – and the econd-best way to see it is from the shore. walk around the lake (6km) shouldn't take ut a couple of hours at the most, including e short (but steep) climb to the brilliant **ojnica viewing point**. Along the way, you'll ass linden, chestnut and willow trees hang-g over the water, boat slips, wooden walk-ays, anglers, the start of several hikes and couple of interesting sights.

On the south shore you'll pass through the amlet of Mlino, then leave the main road for path that passes beneath the grand edifice f the Hotel Vila Bled. Around the far end of e lake, beyond a 300m stretch of boardwalk ver the lake and past the camping ground, is e **Zaka Regatta Centre**, where an international owing competition is staged in late June and Slovenia-wide one in September. The **Castle aths** are a bit further on.

You can jump aboard the **tourist train** (adult/ ild €3/2; 9am-9pm Jun-Oct, 9am-7pm Nov-May) for e 45-minute twirl around the lake, which eparts from in front of the **Sport Hall** (Športna vorana; Ljubljanska cesta 5) and, more centrally, om just south of the TIC up to 20 times a ay in season. Romantics will prefer one of the **horse-drawn carriages** (fijaker; ☎ 041 710 970; www.fijaker-bled.si, in Slovene) from the stand near the **Festival Hall** (Festivalna Dvorana; Cesta Svobode 11). A spin around the lake for five people costs €30, and it's the same price for two people to the castle; an extra 30 minutes inside costs €40. You can even get a carriage for four to Vintgar; the two-hour return trip costs €70.

Activities

ADVENTURE SPORTS

Travel agencies (p125) organise a wide range of outdoor activities in and around Bled, including trekking, mountaineering, rock climbing, ski touring, cross-country skiing, mountain biking, rafting, kayaking, canyoning, caving, horse riding and paragliding.

The 3glav agency's most popular trip is the Emerald River Adventure (€55), an 11-hour **hiking** and **swimming** foray into Triglav National Park and along the Soča River. A two-day guided ascent of Triglav from Pokljuka, the Vrata Valley or Kot Valley costs €188. If you don't fancy scaling mountains, a day-long trek through the Alpine meadows of the Triglav Lakes Valley costs €69.

A 2½-hour **rafting** trip down the Sava Bohinjka/Soča River costs €25/30, and a three-hour **canyoning** descent is €50. **Kayak** trips lasting three hours cost €44. **Paragliding** is €85 and **skydiving** €190. **Horse riding** starts at €44 for a two-hour outing.

BOATING

You can rent **rowing boats** (per hr up to 4/6 people €10/15) for getting to the island or just pottering about (motor boats are banned on the lake) from the Castle Baths (p128). Boats for up to four people are also available from the Garni Penzion Pletna (p129) in Mlino, or further west near the entrance to the camping ground for €14/17 for three/four people.

FISHING

Fauna (p131) sells fishing permits valid for a day on the lake (€23), the Radovna River (€50) and the Sava Bohinjka River (€59 to €69, depending on location and catch).

FLYING

The **Lesce Alpine Flying Centre** (Alpski Letalski Center Lesce; ☎ 532 01 00; www.alc-lesce.si; Begunjska cesta 10) 4km to the southeast has panoramic flights in Cessna 172s over Bled (€75 for three people),

Bohinj (€135) and even Triglav (€195), or anywhere you want for €240 an hour.

GOLF

The 18-hole, par-73 King's Course at the **Bled Golf & Country Club** (☎ 537 77 11; www.golfbled.com; Mon-Fri €59, Sat & Sun €69; 🕑 8am-7pm Apr-Oct), about 3km to the east of the lake near Lesce, is Slovenia's best golf course and, with its dramatic mountain backdrop, one of the most beautiful in Europe. This club also has the nine-hole, par-36 **Lake Course** (€30) open the same hours. You can rent a set of clubs for €20, and there's a PGA pro who gives lessons from €30.

HIKING

There are many short and easy signposted hikes around Bled (numbered signs correspond to numbered routes on the local hiking maps, such as the 1:30,000 GZS map *Bled* which costs €7.70). One of the best is trail No 6 from the southwest corner of the lake to the summit of Velika Osojnica (756m). The view from the top – over the lake, island and castle, with the peaks of the Karavanke in the background – is stunning, especially towards sunset. The climb to the first summit is steep, but the round trip, returning via Ojstrica (610m), takes only three hours or so. For details of longer treks see p127.

SKIING

Beginners will be content with the tiny (6-hectare) **Straža-Bled ski centre** (☎ 578 05 30; www.bled.si; Rečiška cesta 2; day pass adult/child/student & senior €14/7/11), southwest of the Grand Hotel Toplice. A chairlift takes you 634m up the hill in three minutes; you'll be down the short slope in no time. Rental skis and poles are available from Life Trek (p125) and Kompas (p125). In summer the slope becomes a **summer tobogganing track** (poletno sankanje; ☎ 031 182 514; 1/2/3 rides adult €6/10/13, child €4/6/8; 🕑 11am-8pm mid-Jun–Aug, 11am-6pm Sat & Sun May, early-Jun & Sep, 11am-4.30pm Sat & Sun Apr & Oct), where you wend your way down a metal chute sitting on a mini 'bobsled'.

SWIMMING

Bled's warm (23°C at source) and crystal-clear water – it rates a Blue Flag (a voluntary and independent eco-label awarded to beaches around the world for their cleanliness and water quality) – makes it suitable for swimming well into the autumn, and there a decent beaches around the lake, including big gravel one near the camping ground ar a lovely grass one on the northern side. Ju east of the latter is the large **Castle Baths** (Graj Kopališče; ☎ 578 05 28; Veslaška promenada 11; day pa adult/child/student €6.50/3/4.50; 🕑 7am-8pm Jul & Au 7am-7pm Jun & Sep), with an indoor pool and pro tected enclosures in the lake itself with hug water slides. You can rent deck chairs, chaise longues and umbrellas (€3) here.

Hotels with indoor swimming pools fille with thermal water and saunas that are ope to nonguests include the **Grand Hotel Toplic** (☎ 579 10 00; www.hotel-toplice.com; Cesta Svobode 1 adult/child €6.50/3.50), **Park Hotel** (☎ 579 18 00; Ces Svobode 15; admission €5-7), **Hotel Jelovica Bled** (☎ 57 60 00; www.hotel-jelovica.si; Cesta Svobode 8; adult/chi €6/3), **Hotel Krim Bled** (opposite; admission €10) an **Hotel Lovec** (p130; admission €12).

Tours

The so-called **Old Timer Train** (Muzejski Vlak; adult/chi return €37/22, with lunch & side trips €68/35; 🕑 Sat Apr-No offers excursions in vintage carriages haule by a steam locomotive between one and thre times a month. Trains usually depart from Jesenice, 13km to the northwest, and Mos na Soči, stopping at Bled Jezero station an Bohinjska Bistrica before carrying on to Nov Gorica. Ask the TIC about departure times You can buy tickets from most travel agencie in Bled, including Kompas (p125).

Festivals & Events

A number of special events take place during the summer in Bled, including the **International Rowing Regatta** (www.veslaska-zveza.si) in mid-June; the **International Music Festiva** (www.festivalbled.com) of violinists in early July **Bled Days** (www.bled.si) in late July, a multimedia festival where there are fireworks and the entire lake is illuminated by candlelight; and the **Okarina Etno Festival** (www.okarina.com), a two-day international festival of folk and world music in late July/early August. For information visit www.bl ed.si.

Summertime concerts take place at the Festival Hall (Cesta Svobode 11) and the Parish Church of St Martin (p126), which houses one of the finest organs in Slovenia. In December, the Pokljuka Plateau west of Bled is the venue for the **Biathlon World Cup** (www.biathlon-pokljuka.com) championship of cross-country skiing and rifle shooting.

ꞁeeping

ꞁefitting a resort of such popularity, Bled ꞁas a wide range of accommodation – from ꞁlovenia's original hostel to a five-star hotel in ꞁ villa that was once Tito's summer retreat.

ꞁUDGET

ꞁrivate rooms are offered by dozens of homes ꞁn the area. Both Kompas and M Tours (p125) ꞁave lists, with prices for singles at €16 to ꞁ33 and doubles €24 to €50. Apartments for ꞁwo cost from €36 to €63 and for four €62 ꞁo €110.

Camping Bled (☎ 575 20 00; www.camping-bled ꞁcom; Kidričeva cesta 10\c cesta; adult €8.50-12.50, child ꞁ5.95-8.75; Apr–mid-Oct; P 🖳) This popular ꞁ.5-hectare site fills a rural valley behind a ꞁwaterside restaurant at the western end of ꞁhe lake about 2.5km from the bus station. ꞁThere's space for 920 campers. It is strictly ꞁorbidden to camp elsewhere on the lake, and ꞁhe law is enforced.

Bledec Hostel (☎ 574 52 50; www.mlino.si; Grajska ꞁesta 17; HI members/nonmembers dm high season €17.50/20, ꞁow season €15.50/18, d high season €23.50/26, low season ꞁ21.50/24; P 🖳) This well-organised HI-ꞁaffiliated hostel in the shadow of the castle ꞁhas 13 rooms of three to five beds with at-ꞁtached bathrooms. It also has a bar, an inex-ꞁpensive restaurant and a laundry room (per ꞁload €8.50). Internet access and use of their ꞁbikes is free.

Bled Backpackers Rooms (☎ 574 40 41, 051 678 ꞁ008; www.bled-backpackersrooms.com; Grajska cesta 21; dm ꞁper person €16-17; 🖳) With the attached George Best Bar open to at least midnight daily, this five-room place with 20 beds is Bled's party hostel. We love the room with the huge balcony and the storage lockers that open from the top.

Vila Gorenka (☎ 051 369 070; http://freeweb.siol.net/mz2; Železka cesta 9; per person €18.50-25; P 🖳) This budget establishment has 10 double rooms with washbasins in a charming old two-story villa, just next to the Mayer Penzion. Toilets and showers are shared and internet access is free. Some rooms on the 2nd floor have small balconies overlooking the lake.

Traveller's Haven (☎ 031 704 455, 041 396 545; www.travellers-haven.si; Riklijeva cesta 1; dm/d €19/48; 🖳) This stunning new facility in a converted old villa (c 1910) has six rooms with between two and six beds, a great kitchen, free internet and laundry, and a chilled vibe.

MIDRANGE

Penzion Mlino (☎ 574 14 04; www.mlino.si; Cesta Svobode 45; per person €25-35; P) This 13-room pension, as well known for its restaurant as its accommodation, is just about as close as you'll get to the lake at this price. The same owners operate the Bledec Hostel.

Garni Penzion Pletna (☎ 574 37 02; www.sloveniaholidays.com/sobe-pletna; Cesta Svobode 37; s €40-45, d €50-65, tr €70-85; P) This friendly pension with attached shop has five pleasant rooms facing the lake.

Garni Hotel Vila Bojana (☎ 576 81 70; www.bled-hotel.com.si; Ljubljanska cesta 12; s €45-70, d €59-109; P 🖳) This welcoming 11-room hotel purpose-built in the 1930s may not be lakeside but is central to everything. Be warned, though – there's no lift.

Hotel Jelovica Bled (☎ 579 60 00; www.hotel-jelovica.si; Cesta Svobode 8; s €47-65, d €60-122; P 🖳) It's one of the better-value hotels in this price category in Bled. Close to the bus station, the 100-room Jelovica fronts Spa Park above the lake and has a fully equipped health and spa centre.

Garni Hotel Berc (☎ 576 56 58; www.berc-sp.si; Pod Stražo 13; s €40-50, d €70-80; P 🖳) This purpose-built place, reminiscent of a Swiss chalet, has 15 rooms on two floors in a quiet location above the lake.

Garni Penzion Berc (☎ 574 18 38; Želeška cesta 15; s €35-40, d €60-55) Just opposite Garni Hotel Berc is this place, with 11 more-simple rooms than the hotel.

Penzion Mayer (☎ 574 10 58, 576 57 40; www.mayer-sp.si; Želeška cesta 7; s €55, d €75-80, apt for 2/4 €120/150; P 🖳) This flower-bedecked 12-room inn in a renovated 19th-century house is in a quiet location above the lake. The larger apartment is in a delightful wooden cabin and the in-house restaurant is excellent.

Hotel Krim Bled (☎ 579 70 00; www.hotel-krim.si; Ljubljanska cesta 7; s €49-69, d €76-104; P 🖳) This sprawling 115-room hotel charges a lot less than most for its singles and doubles, but its location – up from the lake along busy Ljubljanska cesta – is not the best. The wellness centre with three saunas and whirlpool is a draw though.

TOP END

Hotel Triglav Bled (☎ 575 26 10; www.hoteltriglavbled.si; Kolodvorska cesta 33; s €89-159, d €119-179, ste €139-209; P 🖳 ♿) This bijoux of a 22-room boutique hotel in a painstakingly restored caravanserai that opened in 1906 opposite Bled Jezero train station raises the bar of accommodation standards in Bled. The rooms (hardwood floors, Oriental carpets) are furnished with antiques, there's an enormous sloped garden that grows the vegetables served in the terrace restaurants and the views of the lake, its island and slopes to the south from here, there and everywhere (including the indoor pool) are breathtaking.

Hotel Lovec (☎ 576 86 15; www.lovechotel.com; Ljubljanska cesta 6; s €110-148, d €133-225, ste from €185; P) A new favourite, the Lovec boasts 60 of some of the most attractive rooms in Bled. We love the rooms (eg 402 and 403) with blond wood walls, red carpet and bath with Jacuzzi in front of a massive window facing the lake.

Grand Hotel Toplice (☎ 579 10 00; www.hotel-toplice.com; Cesta Svobode 12; s €140-180, d €158-220, ste €212-280; P) With a history that goes back to the mid-19th century, the 87-room Toplice is Bled's 'olde worlde' hotel, with attractive public areas and superb views of the lake on its northern side. Its two extensions – the 29-room Hotel Trst (Cesta Svobode 19, s €61 to €71, d €76 to €86) just opposite and the more ivy-bedecked Jadran Hotel (Cesta Svobode 23, s €71 to €91, d €84 to €116) with 45 rooms up on the hill – are half the price.

Vila Bled (☎ 575 37 10; www.vila-bled.com; Cesta Svobode 26; s €180-200, d €210-230, ste lake view €260-290, park view €230-250; P) This 30-room hotel is where Tito and his foreign guests once put their feet up and their heads down. The 10 rooms and 20 suites (one with Jacuzzi) are furnished in retro-style 1950s decor. The hotel is surrounded by a large park with a tennis court, and it has its own covered lido and private boat dock.

Eating

Pizzeria Rustika (☎ 576 89 00; Riklijeva cesta 13; pizza €5.70-9.50; 3-11pm Mon, noon-11pm Tue-Sun) A marble-roll down the hill from Bled's hostels, this place has its own wood-burning oven and seating on two levels plus outside terrace.

Peking (☎ 574 17 16; Ulica Narodnih Herojev 3; rice & noodles €4.50-6, mains €6.90-15.50; noon-11pm) This Chinese eatery opposite the Hotel Krim Bled has such favourites as *hui guo rou* (twice-cooked pork) and *ma po doufu* (spicy bean curd). They ain't exactly what you'd get in Chengdu, but this is Slovenia, after all.

Gostilna Pri Planincu (☎ 574 16 13; Grajska cesta 8; starters €5.30-6.10, mains €7.50-22; noon-10pm) In situ since 1903, At the Mountaineer's is a homey pub-restaurant just down the hill from all of Bled's hostels. It offers Slovenian mains as well as grilled Balkan specialities like *čevapčiči* (spicy meatballs of beef or pork; €7.50) and *pljeskavica z kajmakom* (Serbian-style meat patties with mascarpone-like cream cheese; €8.50).

Oštarija Peglez'n (☎ 574 42 18; Cesta Svobode 19/a; starters €7.50-9.50, mains €8-22; noon-midnight) One of the better restaurants in Bled, the Iron Inn is just opposite the landmark Grand Hotel Toplice. It has fascinating retro decor with lots of old household antiques and curios (including the eponymous iron) and serves some of the best fish dishes in town.

Gostila Murka (☎ 574 33 40; Riklijeva cesta 9; starters €7-8, mains €8-13; 10am-10pm Mon-Fri, noon-11pm Sat & Sun) This rather colourful and very traditional Slovenian eatery set within a generous-sized and very leafy garden may at first appear a bit theme park-ish. But the food is authentic and the welcome very warm.

Penzion Mayer (Želeška cesta 7; starters €6-9, mains €9.80-19.80; 6pm-midnight Tue-Sun) The restaurant at this delightful inn (p129) serves such tasty Slovenian fare as sausage, trout, roast pork and *skutini štruklji* (cheese curd pastries). The list of Slovenian wines (only) is a cut above.

Okarina (☎ 574 14 58; Ljubljanska cesta 8; starters €3.60-14.80, mains €9.80-24; 6-11pm Mon-Fri, noon-midnight Sat & Sun) This very upmarket restaurant has lots of colourful art spread over a modern dining room and serves both international favourites and decent Indian dishes like chicken masala (€16.50) and rogan josh (€17.80). There's a good choice of vegetarian dishes and a little annexe behind serves Balkan grills (€6.90 to €9.90).

Castle Restaurant (☎ 579 44 24; Grajska cesta 61; starters €6.50-11, mains €12-21; 11am-10pm) The fabulous views are 'free' from the superbly situated terrace of the restaurant in the castle. It's run by Bled's catering and tourism school that and staffed by its charming students.

You'll find a **Mercator** (Ljubljanska cesta 4; 7am-8pm Mon-Sat, 8am-noon Sun) supermarket at the eastern end of Bled Shopping Centre and a smaller **Mercator** (Mlinska cesta 1; ☎ 7am-7pm Mon-Sat, 7am-3pm Sun) branch on the south side of the lake.

Drinking

Pub Bled (☎ 574 26 22, 041 755 265; Cesta Svobode 19/a; 9am-2am Sun-Thu, 9am-3am Fri & Sat) This friendly pub above the Oštarija Peglez'n restaurant has great cocktails and, on some nights, a DJ.

Irish Pub (☎ 041 672 069; Cesta Svobode 8/a; 7am-2am Mon-Fri, 9am-2am Sat & Sun) This raucous boozer ext to the Hotel Jelovica is the pub of choice mong locals and visitors alike.

Slaščičarna Šmon (☎ 574 16 16; Grajska cesta 3; 7.30am-10pm) Bled's culinary speciality is *remna rezina* (€2.20), a layer of vanilla ustard topped with whipped cream and andwiched between two layers of flaky pas-ry, and while Šmon may not be its place f birth, it remains the best place in which o try it.

Kavarna Park (☎ 579 18 00; Cesta Svobode 10; 9am-11pm) Opposite the Hotel Park, this cafe as a commanding position over the lake's astern end and is said to be the birthplace of led's famous cream cake (€2.70).

hopping

roMontana (☎ 578 06 60; www.promontana.si; ubljanska cesta 1; 8am-7pm Mon-Fri, 8am-1pm & -7pm Sat & Sun Jun-Sep, 8am-7pm Mon-Fri, 8am-1pm 3-7pm Sat & Sun Oct-May) This shop behind glav sells all kinds of sporting equipment ncluding skis.

Fauna (☎ 574 26 31, 041 633 147; www.faunabled.com; esta Svobode 12; 8am-noon & 3-7pm Mon-Fri, 8am-noon at, 8-10am Sun) This shop sells fishing licenses nd all equipment and has a gillie service.

ietting There & Away

3US

There are buses every 30 minutes or so to Radovljica (€1.80, 15 minutes, 7km) via both Lesce and Begunje and at least one an hour to Bohinjska Bistrica (€3.10, 30 minutes, 22km) and on to Lake Bohinj (€3.60, one hour, 26km), and hourly for Kranj (€4.10, 50 minutes, 31km) and Ljubljana (€6.30, 1½ hours, 57km). Other destinations served from Bled include Bovec (€7.20, three hours, 74km) via Kranjska Gora and the Vršič Pass. A bus leaves daily at 7.50am in July and August and on Saturday and Sunday only in June and September.

CAR

All the big rental-car agencies have offices in Bled, including the following:

Avis (☎ 576 87 00; Grajska cesta 4; 9am-5pm Mon-Fri, 8am-noon Sat & Sun) Near the bus station.

Budget (☎ 578 03 20; Ljubljanska cesta 4; 8am-noon & 5-7pm Mon-Fri, 8am-noon Sat) In the Bled Shopping Centre.

Europcar (☎ 579 70 03, 031 382 055; Ljubljanska cesta 7; 8am-2pm Mon-Fri, 8am-noon Sat) In the Hotel Krim Bled.

Hertz (☎ 574 55 88; Cankarjeva cesta 2; 8am-7pm Mon-Fri, 8am-1pm Sat) In the Hotel Kompas Best Western.

TRAIN

Bled has no central train station. Trains to Bohinjska Bistrica (€1.60, 20 minutes, 18km, eight daily) and Nova Gorica (€5.60, 1½ hours, 79km, seven daily) use little Bled Jezero train station, which is 2km west of central Bled – handy for the camping ground and the Hotel Triglav Bled but little else. From there you can make connections for Sežana, 40km to the southeast, and Italy. This mountain railway is one of the most picturesque in Slovenia. If you are headed southwest to Nova Gorica, sit on the right-hand side of the train to view the valley of the cobalt-blue Soča River.

Trains for Ljubljana (€4.30 to €5.80, 55 minutes to one hour, 51km, up to 21 daily) via Škofja Loka, Kranj and Radovljica use Lesce-Bled station, 4km to the east of town.

Getting Around

You can order a local taxi on ☎ 031 705 343 or 051 646 365. Bicycles and mountain bikes can be rented from Kompas (p125) for €3.50/6/8/11 per hour/three hours/six hours/day. See 3glav (p125) for mountain bikes (€5/10/15 per two hours/half-day/full day).

AROUND BLED

Vintgar Gorge

One of the easiest and most satisfying day trips from Bled is to **Vintgar Gorge** (Soteska Vintgar; adult/child/student €4/2/3; 8am-7pm late Apr–Oct), some 4km to the northwest. The highlight is the 1600m wooden walkway, built in 1893 and continually rebuilt since. It criss-crosses the swirling Radovna River four times over rapids, waterfalls and pools before reaching 13m-high **Šum Waterfall**. The entire walk is spectacular, although it can get pretty wet and slippery. There are little snack bars at the beginning and the end of the walkway and picnic tables at several locations along the way.

It's an easy walk to the gorge from Bled. Head northwest on Prešernova cesta then north on Partizanska cesta to Cesta v Vintgar. This will take you to Podhom, where signs show the way to the gorge entrance. To return, you can either retrace your steps or, from Šum Waterfall, walk eastward over Hom (834m) to the ancient pilgrimage **Church of St Catherine**, which retains some 15th-century fortifications. From there it's due

ROBERT 'BOB' ŽEROVEC

Robert 'Bob' Žerovec has spent the last half-dozen years leading canyoning trips from Bled (p127).

Forgive a canyoning virgin but what's it all about, Alfie? You simply walk up to some point into a canyon and follow the water course down. You encounter pools and other obstacles that you can't avoid on the way, of course, so you use various canyoning techniques, like sliding, swimming, jumping and repelling. Think of it as one big natural water park.

Hmmm.... Sounds scary. Am I going to crack open my skull – or worse? No, you'll be wearing a neoprene suit and helmet. Canyoning can be dangerous if you don't know what you are doing but that's where an experienced guide comes in. We know the weather conditions and water levels and when you can and cannot go in. Timing is often crucial. But overall nothing is extreme in canyoning. We take it step by step.

So I'm not, errr, too advanced for the sport? In age, no! There's no age limit in canyoning. If you're fit, you can do it at any age. We've had people from 12 to 80 joining tours.

When did it all this start? Did I miss that day at school? The sport first became popular in the US as 'canyoneering' in the late 1970s and early '80s. People got more interested in it here than walking and hiking about six years ago and now it's our fastest-growing adventure sport. It's fun but never extreme.

So thrills without the spills? You might say that. From a business point of view canyoning is better for us now than hiking and climbing. We used to go to the hostels regularly and ask people who wanted to climb Triglav and we'd get a client every few days. But then there was a dispute about fees among guides and the rate was set at €180 per person per day. Triglav got very expensive.

You don't miss being on top of the world? I'm still part of the mountain rescue team and I'll guide as a climber but you just don't get the same sort of thrills. And canyoning does involve climbing and rope techniques. I haven't left it altogether.

So Triglav remains paramount? For Slovenes, yes – I think we're the only country with a mountain on our flag. Climbing Triglav is considered a very Slovenian thing and those who haven't been to the top usually feel guilty. It's almost religious. Let's just say every Slovene sleeps more soundly after climbing Triglav. Maybe it's because they've been that much closer to heaven.

Robert 'Bob' Žerovec (www.3glav-adventures.com) has been a qualified mountain guide for two decades.

south through Zasip to Bled. Count on about three hours all in.

From May to September, a **tourist bus** (☎ 578 04 20; www.alpetour.si, in Slovene; 1-way €3.50) leaves Bled bus station daily at 10am and heads for Vintgar, stopping at the Krim and Grand Toplice Hotels, Mlino, the far end of the lake and Bled Castle, arriving at 10.30am. It returns from Vintgar at 12.30pm.

Pokljuka Plateau

The area around Bled offers endless possibilities for excursions, notably the forests and meadows of the Pokljuka Plateau below Triglav to the west. Here you can go exploring in the 2km-long Pokljuka Gorge (Pokljuška Soteška), some 7km west of Bled and 2km from Gorje (€1.30, 10 minutes, 5km), which is served by up to two dozen buses a day from Bled on weekdays and up to nine at the weekend. Well-marked trails criss-cross the plateau from town and are outlined on the 1:30,000 GZS map *Bled* (€7.70) and the 1:50,000-scale *Triglavski Narodni Park* (Triglav National Park; €8.10) PZS map, both available from the TIC in Bled. You can also begin an ascent of Triglav from Pokljuka (p134).

BOHINJ

☎ 04 / pop 5225 / elev 525m

Bohinj, a larger and less-developed glacial lake 26km to the southwest, is a world apart from Bled. Though it may not have a romantic little island or a castle looming high on a rocky cliff, it does have Triglav in view when the weather clears, and it lies entirely within the borders of Triglav National Park. The area's handful of museums and historical churches will keep culture vultures busy during their visit, and for action types there are activities galore – from ayaking and mountain biking to trekking up riglav via one of the southern approaches.

istory

ohinj was densely settled during the Iallstatt period due to the large amounts f iron ore in the area, and a trade route nked the lake with the Soča Valley and the .driatic Sea via a pass at Vrh Bače southeast f Bohinjska Bistrica. During the Middle ges, when the area fell under the jurisiction of the Bishops of Brixen at Bled, ohinj was known for its markets and fairs, hich were held near the Church of St John he Baptist. Here peasants from the Friuli egion around Trieste traded salt, wine and oodstuffs with their Slovenian counterarts for iron ore, livestock and butter. As he population grew, herders went higher nto the Julian Alps in search of pasture and while charcoal burners cleared the pper forests for timber to fuel the forges. 'riglav was 'conquered' from Bohinj for the irst time in the late 18th century. Most of he events in France Prešeren's epic poem *aptism at the Savica Waterfall* take place round Bohinj.

rientation

ake Bohinj, 4.5km long, 1200m wide and p to 45m deep, lies in a valley basin on the outhern edge of Triglav National Park. The avica River flows into the lake from the west nd the Sava Bohinjka flows out from the outheastern corner.

There is no town called Bohinj; the name refers to the entire valley, its settlements and the lake. The largest town in the area is Bohinjska Bistrica (population 1800), 6km to the east of the lake. Small villages on or near the southern and eastern shores include Ukanc; Ribčev Laz, where you can find everything of a practical nature; Stara Fužina at the mouth of the Mostnica Gorge; Studor, a veritable village of hayracks; and Srednja Vas. There are no settlements on the northern side.

In Ribčev Laz, buses stop near the TIC and in Bohinjska Bistrica at the combination town hall *(občina)* on Triglavska cesta and at the train station, 700m northeast of the town at Triglavska cesta 1.

Information

Alpinsport (☎ 572 34 86; www.alpinsport.si; Ribčev Laz 53; 9am-8pm Jul-Sep, 9am-7pm Oct-Jun) In a kiosk at the stone bridge over the Sava Bohinjka.

Bohinjska Bistrica post office (Trg Svobode 2)

Gorenjska Banka (Trg Svobode 2/b; 9-11.30am & 2-5pm Mon-Fri, 8-11am Sat) In Bohinjska Bistrica next to the post office.

PAC Sports Hostel Pod Voglom (☎ 572 34 61, 040 864 202; www.pac-sports.com; Hostel Pod Voglom, Ribčev Laz 50; 7am-11pm Jul & Aug, 10am-6pm Sep-Jun); Penzion Rožič kiosk branch (☎ 041 365 521; Ribčev Laz 42; 3-8pm Mon-Fri, 9am-8pm Sat & Sun)

Ribčev Laz post office (Ribčev Laz 47; 8-9.30am, 10am-3.30pm & 4-6pm Mon-Fri, 8am-noon Sat) With an ATM.

Tourist Information Centre Bohinj (☎ 574 60 10; www.bohinj.si; Ribčev Laz 48; 8am-8pm Mon-Sat,

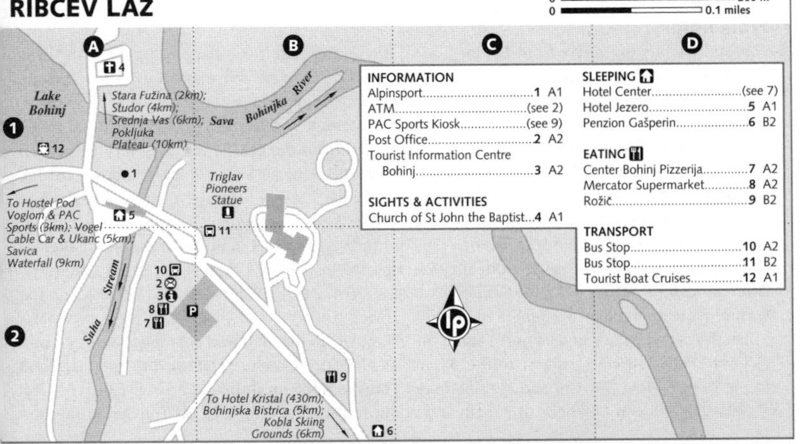

8am-6pm Sun Jul & Aug, 8am-6pm Mon-Sat, 9am-3pm Sun Sep-Jun) Tourist Information Centre Bohinjska Bistrica (☎ 574 75 90; Triglavska cesta 30, Bohinjska Bistrica; 🕑 7am-8pm Mon-Fri, 8am-6pm Sat, 8am-1pm Sun Jun-Aug, Dec & Jan, 7am-3pm Mon-Fri, 9am-1pm Sat Sep, Oct, Feb-May) Free Internet. Sells Bohinj Guest Card (€13) with discounts to museums, activities, accommodation and restaurants and free parking.

Sights

CHURCH OF ST JOHN THE BAPTIST

This **church** (Cerkev Sv Janeza Krstnika; Ribčev Laz; 🕑 9an noon & 4-7pm mid-Jun–mid-Sep, by appointment other times on the northern side of the Sava Bohinjka jus across the stone bridge, is what every med eval church should be: small, on a reflectin body of water and full of exquisite frescoes.

FOUR ROUTES TO THE TOP

There are about 20 different ways to reach the top of Triglav, with the main approaches being to the south (Bohinj and Pokljuka) and the north (Mojstrana and the Vrata Valley). They offer varying degrees of difficulty and have their pluses and minuses. Experienced hikers tend to go for the more forbidding northern approaches, then descending via one of the gentle southern routes. Novices usually ascend and descend near Bohinj. The western route from Trenta in the Soča Valley is steep and less frequented due to its relatively remote start. Most treks require one or two overnight stays in the mountains.

Mojstrana is the easiest trailhead to get to from Ljubljana (€7.50, 1¾ hours, 77km) by public transport – hourly buses between Kranjska Gora and the capital stop here. The Savica Waterfall at Bohinj is also walkable from Ukanc, which is served by bus (p139). If you're driving, there are parking areas at Rudno Polje and at the head of the Vrata Valley near Aljažev Dom, though the latter can only be reached on an unsurfaced road with gradients up to 1:4.

From Pokljuka

The approach to Triglav from Rudno Polje (1347m) on the Pokljuka Plateau, 18km southwest of Bled, is the shortest way to reach the peak – a round trip of 25km, with 1500m of ascent. A very fit and experienced mountain walker could do this in around eight to 12 hours of hiking, but most mortals stay overnight at a hut. The route follows a well-marked trail under Viševnik (2050m) and over the Studor Saddle (1892m), before contouring around the slopes of Tosc (2275m) to the Category I **Vodnikov Dom na Velem Polju** (☎ 04-572 32 13, 051 607 211; planinsko-drustvo-srednja-vas@siol.net; 🕑 late Jun–Sep), with 58 beds at 1817m and reached in three hours. Another two hours' climbing leads to Category I **Dom Planika pod Triglavom** (☎ 04-574 40 69, 051 614 773; 🕑 Jul-Sep) with 123 beds at 2401m, from which a further hour or so of very steep climbing and scrambling along the summit ridge, grabbing hold of metal spikes and grips, takes you to the top of Old Mr Three Heads.

From Bohinj

The approaches to Triglav from Bohinj (525m) are longer and involve more ascent than those in the north and the west but are more gently graded. They are more often used for descent. However, the following route would make a good three-day loop.

From the Savica Waterfall a path zigzags up the steep Komarča Crag (1340m), with an excellent view of the lake. Three to four hours hike north from the falls is the Category I **Koča pri Triglavskih Jezerih** (☎ 01-231 26 45, 050-615 235; info.pdljmatica@siol.net; 🕑 mid-Jun–mid-Oct) at 1685m, a 200-bed hut at the southern end of the fantastic Triglav Lakes Valley where you spend the first night. If you want a good view over the valley and its seven permanent lakes (the others fill up in spring only), you can climb to Tičarica (2091m) to the northeast in about an hour. An alternative – although longer – route from the waterfall to the Triglav Lakes Valley is via Category I **Dom na Komni** (☎ 572 14 75, 040 695 783; info.pdljmatica@siol.net; 🕑 year-round), with 120 beds, and the Komna Plateau, a major battlefield in WWI.

On the second day you hike north along the valley, which the immortal chamois Zlatorog is said to have created, then northeast to the desert-like Hribarice Plateau (2358m). You then descend to the Dolič Saddle (2164m) and the Category I **Tržaška Koča na Doliču** (☎ 574 40 69, 051 614 780; 🕑 late Jun–Sep) with 144 beds at 2151m and about four hours from Koča pri Triglavskih Jezerih.

s the most beautiful and evocative church in ll of Slovenia, with the possible exception of ne Church of the Holy Trinity at Hrastovlje n Primorska.

The nave of the church is Romanesque, but he Gothic presbytery dates from about 1440. large portion of the latter's walls, ceilings nd arches are covered with 15th- and 16th-century frescoes. As you face the arch from the nave, look for the frescoes on either side gorily depicting the beheading of the church's patron saint. On the opposite side of the arch, to the left, is Abel making his offering to God and, to the right, Cain with his inferior one. Upon the shoulder of history's first murderer sits a white devil – a very rare symbol. Behind

You could well carry on to **Dom Planika pod Triglavom** at 2401m and about 1½ hours to the northeast, but this hut is often packed. It's better to stay where you're sure there's a bed unless you've booked ahead. From Dom Planika it's just over an hour to the summit of Triglav.

You could return the way you came, but it's far more interesting to go back to Bohinj via Stara Fužina. This way passes the **Vodnikov Dom na Velem Polju** at 1817m – less than two hours from Dom Planika – where there are two routes to choose from: down the steep Voje Valley, or along the Uskovnica ridge, a highland pasture to the east. The former takes about four hours; the route via Uskovnica is a little longer but affords better views. The trail to Rudno Polje and the road to Bled branches off from the Uskovnica route.

From Mojstrana

This approach, which is dominated by the stupendous northern face of Triglav, is popular with experienced climbers, and is often combined with a more leisurely descent along the Triglav Lakes Valley to Bohinj. From the village of Mojstrana, which has **Camping Kamne** (p142) and a **Mercator** (Triglavska cesta 28; 7am-7pm Mon-Fri, 7am-5pm Sat, 8am-noon Sun) supermarket, a mostly unsurfaced road leads 11km to the Category II **Aljažev Dom v Vratih** (☎ 04-589 51 00, 031 384 011; pd.dovje-mojstrana@siol.net; late Apr–mid-Oct) with 138 beds at 1015m. Walking here should take about three hours, including time for a look at Peričnik Waterfall on the way. You'll probably want to spend the night here, as it is among the most beautiful sites in the park, with a perfect view of Triglav's north face, the third largest rock wall in Europe. Nearby is a 10m boulder called Mali Triglav (Little Triglav), where you can practise your ascent of the Big One.

From here, the steep and exposed Tominšek Trail leads via the northwest flank of Cmir (2393m) and below Begunjski Vrh (2461m) to Begunjski Studenec, a spring with excellent drinking water at 2100m (three hours). Much of this trail is a *via ferrata* (iron way) protected with iron spikes and cables.

From the spring you can choose to walk to either Category I **Dom Valentina Staniča** (☎ 051 614 772; pd.jav.kor.bela@s5.net; late Jun–late Sep), 30 minutes to the southeast with 136 beds at 2332m, or to Category I **Triglavski Dom na Kredarici** (☎ 04-531 28 64, 01-231 26 45; info.pdljmatica@siol.net; mid-Jun–mid-Oct), an hour to the south. The latter is the main hut serving the northern routes and at 2515m is the highest accommodation in the land; the summit is two hours away. Although Triglavski Dom has 140 beds in 30 rooms and another 160 beds in eight dormitories, it is almost always full; the best idea is to spend the night at Dom Staniča and make the ascent in the morning (two hours from hut to summit).

From Trenta

Because Trenta is more difficult to reach from the population centres of Ljubljana and southern Austria, the western approach to Triglav is quieter than the other routes. It's a long climb, though, starting from an altitude of just over 600m.

From Trenta, an hour's hike eastward along the Zajdnica Valley leads to the foot of Triglav's massive western face, where you begin zigzagging monotonously up an easy but seemingly endless trail for four more hours to the Dolič Saddle and the **Tržaška Koča na Doliču** at 2151m. From here, you can follow the normal route to the summit via **Dom Planika pod Triglavom** at 2401m or take the slightly more difficult western ridge (2½ hours), passing the ruined Morbegna barracks built by the Italian army in WWII at 2500m.

you on the lower walls of the presbytery are rows of angels, some with vampire-like teeth; look for the three men above them singing. They have goitres, once a common affliction in mountainous regions due to the lack of iodine in the diet. The carved wooden head of St John the Baptist on the side altar to the right dates from 1380.

MUSEUMS

The **Alpine Dairy Museum** (Planšarski Muzej; ☎ 577 01 56; Stara Fužina 181; adult/child €2.50/2; ⌚ 11am-7pm Tue-Sun Jul & Aug, 10am-noon & 4-6pm Tue-Sun early Jan–Jun, Sep–late Oct) in Stara Fužina, about 1.5km north of Ribčev Laz, has a small collection related to Alpine dairy farming in the Bohinj Valley, once the most important such centre in Slovenia. Until the late 1950s large quantities of cheese were still being made on 28 highland pastures, but a modern dairy in nearby Srednja Vas does it all now. The four rooms of the museum – a cheese dairy itself once upon a time – contain a mock-up of a mid-19th-century herder's cottage, fascinating old photographs, cheese presses, wooden butter moulds, copper rennet vats, enormous snowshoes and sledges, and wonderful hand-carved crooks.

While you're in Stara Fužina, take a walk over to the village of **Studor**, just 2km to the east. **Oplen House** (Oplenova Hiša; ☎ 572 35 22; Studor 16; adult/child €2.50/2), which keeps the same hours as the Alpine Dairy Museum, is a typical old peasant's cottage with a chimneyless 'smoke kitchen' that has been turned into a museum focusing on the domestic life of peasants in the Bohinj area at the turn of the 20th century. But Studor's real claim to fame is its many *toplarji*, the double-linked hayracks with barns or storage areas at the top. Look for the ones at the entrance to the village; they date from the 18th and 19th centuries.

SAVICA WATERFALL

One of the reasons people come to Bohinj is to hike to the magnificent **Savica Waterfall** (Slap Savica; adult/child €2.40/1.30, parking €3; ⌚ 9am-6pm Jul & Aug, 9am-5pm Apr-Jun, Sep & Oct), which cuts deep into a gorge 60m below.

The waterfall, the source of Slovenia's longest and mightiest river, is 4km from the Hotel Zlatorog in Ukanc and can be reached by footpath from there. Cars (and the bus in summer) continue via a paved road to a car park beside the Savica restaurant, from which it's a 20-minute walk up more than 500 step and over rapids and streams to the falls.

The falls are among the most impressiv sights in the Julian Alps, especially after heav rain, but bring something waterproof or yo may be soaked by the spray. Two Categor I huts with accommodation and food to th west are **Dom na Komni** (☎ 040 695 783, 040 620 78 komna@siol.net; ⌚ year-round) with 108 beds a 1520m; and **Koča pod Bogatinom** (☎ 572 32 13, 04 645 865; www.pdsrednjavas.si, in Slovene; ⌚ late Jun–Sep with 53 beds at 1513m. Both can be reache from the waterfall in about 2½ hours.

Activities

ADVENTURE SPORTS

Alpinsport (p133) and PAC Sports (p133 offer a wide range of activities, includin **canyoning** (from €45-70), **rafting** (€25-33) on th lake and Sava Bohinjka River, and **tanden paraglider flights** (€85) – even from the top o Vogel (€120)! PAC Sports can arrange visit to **Bohinj Adrenalin Park** (Adrenalinski Park Bohin ☎ 572 34 61; adult/child/student €29/25/27; ⌚ 10an & 5pm Jul & Aug, by appointment Jun & Sep), featur ing high rope courses and walkways, gian swings and so on behind the Hostel Po Voglom (p138).

BOATING

PAC Sports and Alpinsport rent **kayaks** (1hr/3hr day €4/10/14) and **canoes** (1hr/3hr/day €6/16/27).

In season, the cunningly named **Tourist Boat** (Turistična Ladja; ☎ 041 434 986; 1-way adult/child/family €8.50/6/18, return €10/7/23; ⌚ half-hourly 10am-6pm Jun–mid-Sep, 10am, 11.30am, 1pm, 2.30pm, 4pm & 5.30pm early Apr–May; 11.30am, 1pm, 2.30pm & 4pm mid-Sep-Oct) sails between Ribčev Laz and Ukanc.

BOWLING

The five **bowling lanes** (€12.50-20; ⌚ 3-11pm Mon-Fri, 10am-2am Fri & Sat, 10am-8pm Sun) at the Bohinj Park Hotel (p139) in Bohinjska Bistrica are open to all. The differences in cost per string depends on when you bowl – the cheapest being all day Sunday and the most expensive between 8pm and 2am on Friday and Saturday.

FISHING

Lake Bohinj is home to lake trout and char, and the jade-coloured Sava Bohinjka River, which starts at the stone bridge in front of the church in Ribčev Laz, is rich in brown trout and grayling. You can buy

shing licences (lake €25, river as far as Bitnje catch/catch release €55/38) valid for a day from the TIC nd hotels. The season runs from March to te October.

IKING

. circular walk around the lake (12km) om Ribčev Laz should take between three nd four hours. Otherwise you could just do arts of it by following the hunters' trail in e forest above the south shore of the lake the Hotel Zlatorog and taking the bus ack, or walking along the more tranquil orthern shore under the cliffs of Pršivec 1761m). Much more strenuous is the hike p to **Vogel** (1922m) from the cable car's pper station. Take a map and compass, nd don't set out if it looks stormy; Vogel is prone to lightning strikes. The whole trip should take about four hours. Another excellent hike is the two-hour hike north from Stara Fužina through the Mostnica Gorge to the **Mostnica Waterfalls** (Mostniški Slapovci), which rival Savica Waterfall after heavy rain.

The 1:25,000 *Bohinjsko Jezero z Okolico* (Lake Bohinj & Surrounds; €7) map available at the TIC lists a dozen excellent walks. Also useful is the 1:15,000 *Bohinj* (€6) map with as many walks outlined.

HORSE RIDING

The **Mrcina Ranč** (☎ 041 790 297; www.ranc-mrcina.com; per hr €18) in Studor offers a range of guided tours lasting one hour to three days on sturdy Icelandic ponies.

JULIAN ALPS & TRIGLAV NATIONAL PARK

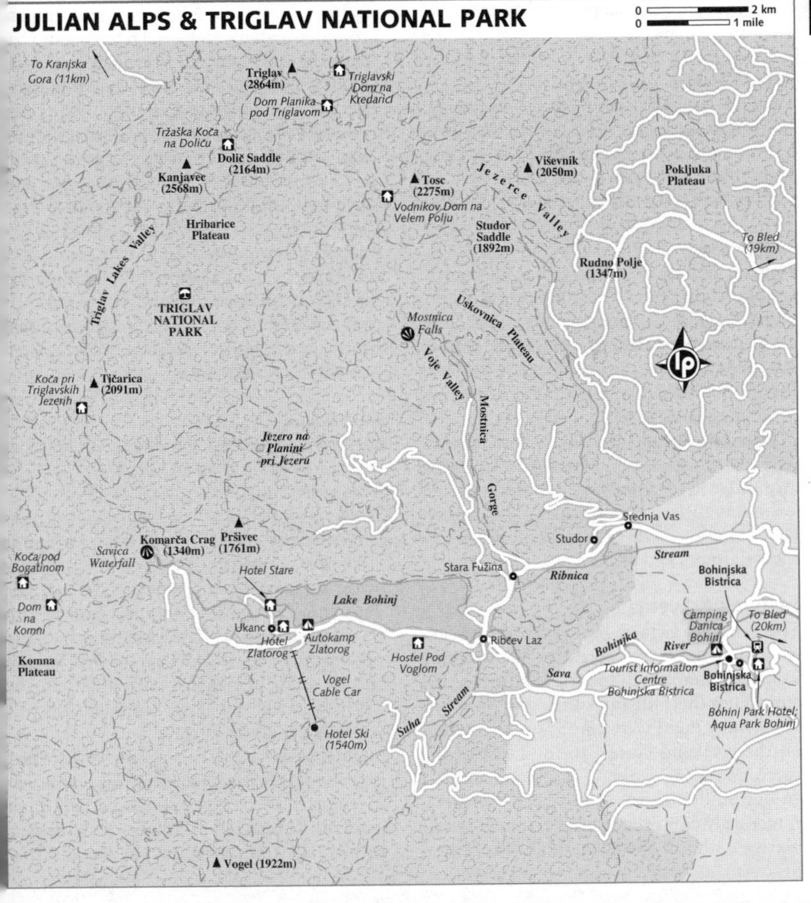

SKIING

The main station at Bohinj is **Vogel ski centre** (☎ 572 97 12; www.vogel.si; Ukanc 6; day pass adult/child €25/18), 1540m above the lake's southwestern corner and accessible by cable car. With skiing up to 1800m, the season can be long, sometimes from late November to late April or even early May. Vogel has 18km of ski slopes and 2.5km of cross-country runs served by four chairlifts and four T-bar tows.

The lower station of the **cable car** (adult/child 1-way €9/7 return €13/9; every 30min 8am-6pm) is about 250m uphill south of the Hotel Zlatorog in Ukanc, about 5km west of Ribčev Laz.

The lower (up to 1480m) **Kobla ski centre** (☎ 574 71 00; www.bohinj.si/kobla; day pass adult/child/student €20/15/17) is about 1km east of Bohinjska Bistrica. It has 23km of slopes and 13km of cross-country runs served by three chairlifts and three T-bars.

STEAM TRAIN

The Old Timer Train (p128) passes through Bohinjska Bistrica on its way to and from Jesenice and Most na Soči up to three times a month between April and November. Ask the TIC for its current schedule.

SWIMMING

Some of the beaches on Lake Bohinj's northern shore are reserved for naturists in summer. Nonguests can use the indoor swimming pool at the **Hotel Zlatorog** (☎ 572 33 81; Ukanc 65; pool/pool & sauna Mon-Fri €6/7, Sat & Sun €8/9; 4-10pm) should Bohinj's infamous early morning fog drive you inside.

Aqua Park Bohinj (☎ 577 02 10; www.vodni-park-bohinj.si; Triglavska cesta 17; adult/child 3hr €10.20/6.30, day €12.20/8.90; 9am-9pm), a water park in Bohinjska Bistrica, has 380 sq metres of pools with flume and slides as well as saunas, steam rooms, fitness and wellness centres.

Festivals & Events

The **Cows' Ball** (Kravji Bal) is a wacky weekend of folk dance, music, eating and drinking in mid-September to mark the return of the cows from their high pastures to the valleys. On **Bonfire Night** (Kresna Noč), celebrated on the weekend closest to the Feast of the Assumption (15 August), candle-lit flotillas go out on the lake, and there are fireworks. A relatively new event that is gaining in popularity is the **International Wildflower Festival** (Mednarodni Festival Alpskega Cvetja) ov two weeks in late May/early June that in cludes guided walks and tours, tradition craft markets and concerts. For details on a three events, go to www.boh inj.si.

Sleeping

BUDGET

The main TIC can arrange **private rooms** (p person €11-16.50) and **apartments** (apt for 2 €36.50-48.5 for 4 €53.50-77) in Ribčev Laz, Stara Fužina an neighbouring villages

Autokamp Zlatorog (☎ 572 34 82; www.aaturize.com; Ukanc 2; per person €7-12; May-Sep; P ♿) Th pine-shaded 2.5-hectare camping ground ac commodating 500 guests is at the lake's west ern end 4.5km from Ribčev Laz.

Camp Danica Bohinj (☎ 574 60 10, 572 17 02; ww.camp-danica.si; Triglavska cesta 60; per adult €7.60-11, chi €6.10-9; late Apr–Sep; P) The Danica campin ground, which measures 4.5 hectares and ha space for 700 campers, is located in a sma wood 200m west of the bus stop in Bohinjsk Bistrica on the road to the lake.

Hostel Pod Voglom (☎ 572 34 61; www.hostel-po voglom.com; Ribčev Laz 50; dm 17-19, r per person with bat €23-26, without bath €20-22; P 💻) This welcom addition to Bohinj's budget accommodatio scene some 3km west of the centre has 11 beds in 46 somewhat frayed rooms in tw buildings. The so-called Hostel Building ha doubles, triples and dormitory accommoda tion (up to four beds) with shared facilities rooms in the Rodica Annexe, with betwee one and four beds, are en suite.

MIDRANGE

Pension Planšar (☎ 572 30 95, 041 767 254; www.plansa.com; r per person €17-25, apt for 2 €40-45, apt for 4 €75-80 This welcoming place in Stara Fužina, bette known for its fabulous cheeses (opposite), ha two cosy rooms and an apartment for rent.

Penzion Gašperin (☎ 572 36 61; www.bohin.si/gasperin; Ribčev Laz 36/a; per person €25-35; P 💻) This spotless chalet-style guest house with 23 rooms (almost half of which are spanking new) is just 350m southeast of the TIC and run by a friendly British/Slovenian couple. Most rooms have balconies though we particularly like room Nos 1, 2 and 3.

Hotel Center (☎ 572 31 70; www.bohinj.si/center; Ribčev Laz 50; s €30-49, d €60-98; P 💻) This 15-room place above a popular pizzeria is more guest house than hotel with its standard-issue furnishings and views, but the name says it l and it's about as central as you're going to nd in Ribčev Laz.

Hotel Stare (☎ 574 64 00; www.impel-bohinj.si; Ukanc 8; s €45-55, d €70-90; P) This isolated 10-oom pension, north of the Hotel Zlatorog on e Sava Bohinjka River, is surrounded by 3.5 ectares of lovely garden. If you really want to et away from it all without having to climb ountains, this is your place.

Hotel Zlatorog (☎ 572 33 81; www.aaturizem.com; kanc 65; s €59-74, d €72-102; P) Out of the way nd pleasant for that reason, this lakeside hotel ist under 5km west of Ribčev Laz has 43 rooms its main hotel building and another 31 in a illa annexe. It's Slovenia's first official organic otel; no synthetic pesticides or fertilizers were sed to grow anything on offer here.

Hotel Kristal (☎ 577 82 00; www.hotel-kristal-slovenia om; Ribčev Laz 4/a; s €53-70, d €86-120; P) This xceedingly friendly, family-run hotel with 0 rooms and lots of activities available is bout 500m south of the Pension Rožič. Its estaurant is very popular.

OP END

Iotel Jezero (☎ 572 91 00; www.bohinj.si/alpinum/ zero; Ribčev Laz 51; s €60-80, d €100-140; P) urther renovations have raised the stand-rds (and added a lift) to this 76-room place ust across from the lake. It has a lovely in-loor swimming pool, two saunas and a itness centre.

Bohinj Park Hotel (☎ 577 02 11; www.bohinj-park hotel.si; Triglavska cesta 17; s €89-120, d €138-200, ste from 400; P) We might not have hosen this spanking new 109-room hotel t first glance – in Bohinjska Bistrica, a full km from our destination: Lake Bohinj. But t's a green and very energy-efficient oasis, it as an excellent and quite intimate in-house estaurant, there's bowling (p136) and the Aqua Park Bohinj (opposite) is at the back door and included in the price.

Eating

Center Bohinj Pizzerija (pizza €6-10, mains €8.50-11.50; 9am-10pm Dec-Oct) This jack-of-all-trades below the Hotel Center (opposite) just down from the TIC is the only eatery in the very centre of Ribčev Laz. It can satisfy all tastes (except very demanding ones).

Rožič (☎ 572 33 93; Ribčev Laz 42; starters €6-9, mains €9-13; 7am-midnight) The restaurant at a popular pension in Ribčev Laz has a lovely covered terrace, although the views of the main road are not very special. The traditional decor, ambiance and hearty dishes make up for that though. Set menus are a snip at €8 and €10.

Gostilna Mihovc (☎ 572 33 90; Stara Fužina 118; starters €4-5, mains €6.90-9; 10am-midnight) This place in Stara Fužina is popular – not least for its homemade brandy. Try the *pasulj* (bean soup) with sausage (€6) or the beef *golač* (goulash; €5.20).

Planšar (☎ 572 30 95; Stara Fužina 179; noon-8pm Tue-Sun Jul & Aug or by appointment) If you're craving for something light, but also incredibly tasty, head straight for the Herder, which is just opposite the Alpine Dairy Museum, which specialises in homemade dairy products: hard Bohinj cheese, a soft, strong-tasting cheese called *mohant*, cottage cheese, curd pie, sour milk and so on. You and a friend can taste a variety of them for €7 or make a meal of cheese and different types of grain dishes such as buckwheat (*žganci;* €7) and barley (*ješprenj;* €8). Other dishes you can sample include *štruklji* (cheese dumplings; €7) and *jota* (a thick soup of beans and salt pork; €8).

Gostilna Rupa (☎ 572 34 01; Srednja Vas 87; starters €6.60-11, mains €7-16; 10am-midnight Jul & Aug, 10am-midnight Tue-Sun Sep-Jun) If you're under your own steam, head for this country-style restaurant in the next village over from Studor and about 5km from Ribčev Laz. Among the excellent home-cooked dishes are *ajdova krapi*, crescent-shaped dumplings made from buckwheat and cheese, various types of local *klobasa* (sausage) and Bohinj trout.

There's a **Mercator** (Ribčev Laz 49; 7am-8pm Mon-Sat, 7am-5pm Sun) supermarket next to the TIC in Ribčev Laž and a much bigger **Mercator** (Trg Svobode 2; 7am-8pm Mon-Sat, 8am 1pm Sun) next to the post office and Gorenjska Banka in Bohinjska Bistrica.

Shopping

The traditional craft of Bohinj is the *gorjuška čedra,* a small hand-carved wooden pipe with a silver cover for smoking tobacco or whatever. The TIC sells the real thing and can tell you which masters are still making them in the area.

Getting There & Away

Buses run regularly from Ukanc – marked 'Bohinj Zlatorog' on most schedules – to Ljubljana (€8.70, two hours, 91km, hourly) via Ribčev Laz, Bohinjska Bistrica and Bled (€4.10, one hour, 34km), with up to six extra buses daily between Ukanc and Bohinjska Bistrica (€2.70, 25 minutes, 16km) via Stara Fužina, Studor and Srednja Vas.

The lake itself is not on a train line. From Bohinjska Bistrica, passenger trains to Novo Gorica (€4.90, 1½ hours, 61km, up to nine a day) make use of a century-old, 6.3km tunnel under the mountains that provides the only direct option for reaching the Soča Valley. In addition there are six daily auto trains *(avtovlaki)* to Podbrdo (€7.70, 10 minutes, 7km) and three that carry on to Most na Soči (€11.80, 35 minutes, 28km).

Getting Around

From late June to September, buses make the run daily from Bohinjska Bistrica train station to the Savica Waterfall car park (€2.30) via Hotel Jezero in Ribčev Laz. There are daily departures from the station at 9.05am, 10.26am, 2.52pm and 4.52pm and from the Hotel Jezero at 9.19am and 10.39am. On Saturday and Sunday there's an extra departure from the station/hotel at 7.05am and 7.19am respectively.

You can rent bicycles and mountain bikes from Alpinsport and PAC Sports for €4/9/13.50 per one hour/three hours/day.

KRANJSKA GORA

☎ 04 / pop 1510 / elev 803m

Nestling in the Sava Dolinka Valley some 40km northwest of Bled, Kranjska Gora (Carniolan Mountain) is Slovenia's largest and best-equipped ski resort. It's at its most perfect under a blanket of snow, but its surroundings are wonderful to explore at other times as well. There are endless possibilities for hiking and mountaineering in Triglav National Park, which is right on the town's doorstep to the south, and few travellers will be unimpressed by a trip over Vršič Pass (1611m), the gateway to the Soča Valley.

The Sava Dolinka Valley separates the Karavanke range from the Julian Alps. It has been an important commercial route between Gorenjska and Koroška for centuries; the 853m pass at Rateče is the lowest Alpine link between the Sava and Drava Valleys. The first railway in Gorenjska – from Ljubljana to Tarvisio (Trbiž) in Italy – made use of this pass when it opened in 1870.

Kranjska Gora was just a small valley village called Borovška Vas until the late 19th century, when skiing enthusiasts began to flock here. Planica (south of Rateče), the cradle of ski jumping, helped put the town on the world map earlier in the 20th century.

Orientation

Kranjska Gora sits at the foot of Vitranc (1631m) and in the shadow of two higher peaks (Razor and Prisojnik/Prisank) that rise above 2600m. Rateče and Planica, famous for ski-jumping championships, are 6km to the west, while Jasna Lake, the town's gateway to Triglav National Park, is 2km to the south.

Kranjska Gora is a very small town with some unattractive modern buildings around its periphery and a more atmospheric (and older) core along Borovška cesta. The chairlifts up to the ski slopes on Vitranc are at the western end of town off Smerinje ulica.

Buses stop along Koroška cesta about 250m west of the big TGC shopping centre at the main entrance to the town from the motorway.

Information

Gorenjska Banka (Borovška cesta 95)

Post office (Borovška cesta 92) Next to Mercator supermarket.

SKB Banka (Borovška cesta 99a) Beside the ski school.

Tourist Information Centre Kranjska Gora (TIC; ☎ 580 94 40; www.kranjska-gora.si; Tičarjeva cesta 2; 🕑 8am-8pm Mon-Sat, 9am-6pm Sun Jun-Sep & mid-Dec–Mar, 8am-3pm Mon-Fri, 8am-4pm Sat, 9am-1pm Sun May, 8am-3pm Mon-Fri, 9am-4pm Sat Apr & Oct–mid-Dec)

Sights

The endearing late-18th-century **Liznjek House** (Liznjekova Domačija; ☎ 588 19 99; Borovška cesta 63; adult/child €2.50/1.70; 🕑 10am-6pm Tue-Sat, 10am-5pm Sun May-Oct, 9.30am-4pm Tue-Fri, 10am-5pm Sat & Sun Dec-Mar) contains quite a good collection of household objects and furnishings peculiar to this area of Gorenjska. Among the various exhibits here are some excellent examples of trousseau chests covered in folk paintings, some 19th-century icons painted on glass and a collection of linen tablecloths (the valley was famed for its flax and its weaving).

Antique carriages and a sledge are kept in the massive 18th-century barn out the back, which once housed food stores as well as pigs

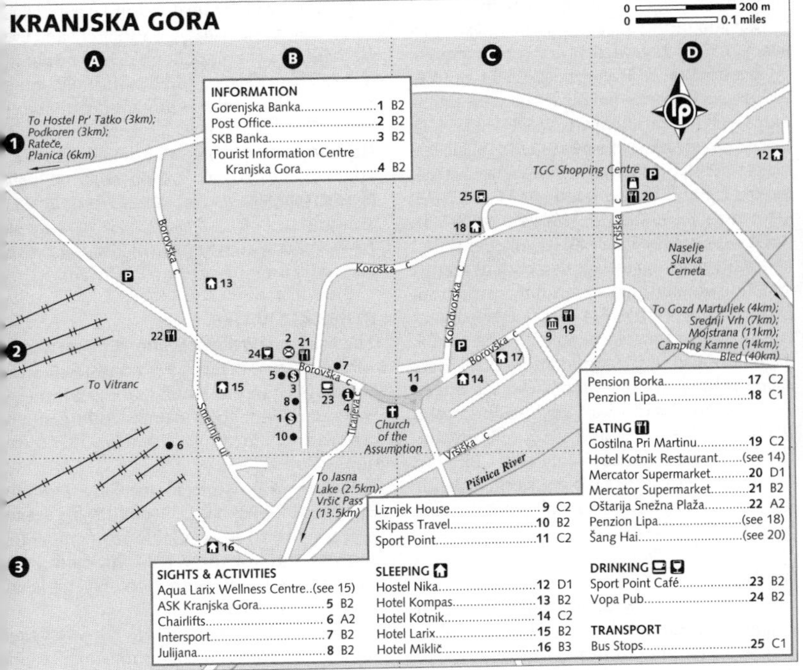

and sheep. The stable reserved for cows below the main building now contains a **memorial room** dedicated to the life and work of Josip Vandot (1884–1944). Vandot was a writer born in Kranjska Gora who penned the saga of Kekec, the do-gooder shepherd boy who, together with his little playmate Mojca and his trusty dog Volkec, battles the evil poacher and kidnapper Bedanec. It's still a favourite story among Slovenian kids and has been made into several popular films.

Activities

SKIING

Most of Slovenia's ski areas are small and relatively unchallenging compared to the Alpine resorts of France, Switzerland and Italy, but they do have the attraction of lower prices and easy access.

The snow-covered slopes of the Sava Dolinka Valley, running for almost 11km from Gozd Martuljek all the way to Rateče and Planica, are effectively one big piste. However, the main areas make up the **Kranjska Gora ski centre** (☎ 580 94 00; www.kr-gora.si; half-day pass adult/child/senior & student €24/15/20, day pass €28/16/24) and Podkoren, 3km to the west, with ski jumping concentrated at Planica. The season usually lasts from mid-December to early March.

Skiing in Kranjska Gora is on the eastern slopes of Vitranc, and some runs join up with those at Podkoren – site of the Men's World Cup Slalom and Giant Slalom Competition (Vitranc Cup) in late January – on Vitranc's northern face to an altitude of 1570m. Together Kranjska Gora and Podkoren have five chairlifts and 15 tows. Generally, skiing is easier at Kranjska Gora than at Podkoren, where two of the most difficult slopes – Ruteč (761m) and Zelenci (398m) – are located. In all, the two centres have 20km of pistes and 40km of cross-country courses.

The ski-jumping centre at **Planica** (www.planica.si), 6km to the west and across the motorway from Rateče, has six jumps with lengths of 25m, 120m and 180m. The short lift near the Dom Planica hut reaches an altitude of 900m. There are also some good possibilities at Planica for tobogganing and for cross-country skiing in the Tamar Valley. The Ski Jumping World Championships are held here every year in mid-March.

Kranjska Gora has lots of places offering ski tuition and hiring out equipment. **ASK Kranjska Gora** (☎ 588 53 02; www.ask-kg.com; Borovška cesta 99a; 🕑 9am-4pm Mon-Sat, 10am-6pm Sun mid-Dec–mid-Mar, 9am-3pm Mon-Fri mid-Mar–mid-Dec) in the same building as SKB Banka, **Intersport** (☎ 588 14 70, 588 47 70; www.intersport-bernik.com; Borovška cesta 88a; 🕑 8am-8pm mid-Dec–mid-Mar, 8am-8pm Mon-Sat, 8am-1pm Sun mid-Mar–mid-Dec) and **Skipass Travel** (☎ 582 10 00; www.skipasstravel.si; Borovška cesta 95; 🕑 8am-4pm mid-Dec–mid-Mar, 9am-3pm Mon-Fri mid-Mar–mid-Dec) all offer skiing and snowboarding instruction both in groups and individually. For one-on-one instruction, expect to pay from €26/41 for one/two hours (from €39/56 for two people). These establishments also rent equipment, as does **Sport Point** (☎ 588 48 83; www.sport-point.si; Borovška cesta 74; 🕑 7.30am-9pm Mon-Fri, 7.30am-10pm mid-Dec–mid-Mar, 9am-7pm mid-Mar–mid-Dec) diagonally opposite the church. Skis and poles should cost €13.50 to €21 a day or €67.50 to €105 per week, depending on the style and class. Snowboards cost from €15/75 a day/week.

HIKING

The area around Kranjska Gora and into Triglav National Park is excellent for hikes and walks ranging from the very easy to the difficult. One of the best references available is the vinyl-bound *The Julian Alps of Slovenia* (Cicerone) by Justi Carey and Roy Clark, with 50 walking routes and short treks. Mike Newbury's *A Guide to Walks and Scrambles in the Julian Alps* (Zlatorog Publications) uses Kranjska Gora as a base for its suggested itineraries.

Between Podkoren and Planica is an idyllic 15-hectare nature reserve called **Zelenci** (837m), with a turquoise-coloured lake that is the source of the Sava River. You can easily walk here in about two hours on a path from Kranjska Gora via Podkoren and on to **Rateče**. These attractive alpine villages are notable for their medieval churches, rustic wooden houses and traditional hayracks. Then, if you want to continue on your journey, there's a well-marked trail via Planica to the Category II 128-bed **Dom v Tamarju** (☎ 587 60 55, 041 448 830) at 1108m in the **Tamar Valley**, 6km to the south. The walk is spectacular, and lies in the shadow of **Mojstrovka** (2366m) to the east and **Jalovec** (2645m) to the south. From here, the **Vršič Pass** is less than three hours away on foot.

Another great walk from Kranjska Gora – and quite an easy one – takes you north and then east through meadows and pasture lan to the traditional village of **Srednji Vrh** and **Go Martuljek** in a couple of hours. The views of th Velika Pisnica Valley and the Martuljek rang of mountains to the south are breathtakin From Gozd Martuljek, it's only 9km east t **Mojstrana**, the starting point for the norther approaches to Triglav. In Mojstrana, the **Trigla Museum Collection** (Triglavska Muzejska Zbirka; ☎ 589 35; Triglavska cesta 50; adult/child €2.50/1.70; 🕑 10am-5p Tue-Sun May-Oct), housed in an old inn, shows th history of mountaineering in Slovenia.

OTHER ACTIVITIES

The **Aqua Larix Wellness Centre** (☎ 588 45 00; ww .hitholidays-kg.si; Borovška cesta 99; nonguests pool €8-9, pc & sauna €13-16) in the Hotel Larix is an indo water park with pools, saunas and treatme centres and a great place to relax after a da on the slopes.

Fishing is possible in the Sava Dolink River and Jasna Lake. A day **fishing licen** (€20) for the river, available from the TI allows a total of three fish, the daily lim from the Sava. A license to fish in Jasn Lake costs the same.

Julijana (☎ 588 13 25, 051 623 701; www.sednj .si), a small travel agency in a kiosk sou of SKB Banka, can organise **rafting trips** o the Sava and Soča for €35 (minimum fo people) between April and October.

Sleeping

Accommodation costs in Kranjska Go peak from December to March and in mi summer. April is the cheapest time to vis though some hotels close for renovatio and redecorating at this time.

BUDGET

The TIC has **private rooms** (per person €13-2 and **apartments** (apt for 2 €33-43, for 4 €63-92), wi prices depending on the category and th time of year. There are a lot of houses wi rooms available in the development call Naselje Slavka Černeta, south of the TG shopping centre.

Camping Kamne (☎ 589 11 05; http://campi kamne.com; Dovje 9; per person €6-7, bungalows for 2 €2 26, bungalows for 4 €44-50; 🕑 year-round; P) Th closest camping ground to Kranjska Gora this 1.2-hectare site for 120 guests at Dov near Mojstrana, 14km east of Kranjska Gor It has a small outdoor swimming pool i the grounds.

Hostel Nika (588 10 00, 031 644 209; nika@youth)stel.si; Bezje 16; dm €12, s €16, d €30-34;) This tmospheric old place on the Sava Dolinka ith 66 beds in Čičare is about 800m northast of the centre and just across the main oad from the TGC Shopping Centre. Do not onfuse with the institutional and depressing 'orentov Dom hostel.

Hostel Pr' Tatko (031 479 087; www.prtatko om; Podkoren 72; dm €13-17, q €56-76;) One f Slovenia's more unusual hostels is in 'odkoren, under a big linden tree just 3km o the northwest of Kranjska Gora. It's a hree-room affair in a traditional old farmouse with between four (one en suite) and ight beds. There's a decent-sized kitchen nd common room. It'll teach you how o collect mushrooms in season and build beehive.

MIDRANGE

Pension Borka (031 536 288; darinka2007@gmail com; Borovška cesta 71; per person €25) Not a patch or would that be plaster?) on the Tatko but lot more central, this very frayed property has some three-dozen rooms – mostly doubles and triples – crying out for a refit. There's a large cellar restaurant.

Penzion Lipa (582 00 00; www.penzion-lipa.si; Koroška cesta 14; s €25-35, d €50-70) This guest house with a very popular family-style restaurant and 13 attractive rooms and apartments has even more attractive rates. It's right by where the buses stop.

Hotel Kotnik (588 15 64; www.hotel-kotnik.si; Borovška cesta 75; s €54-60, d €72-80;) If you're not into big high-rise hotels with hundreds of rooms, choose this charming, bright yellow, low-rise property. It has 15 cosy rooms, a great restaurant and pizzeria, and it couldn't be more central.

TOP END

Hotel Miklič (588 16 35; www.hotelmiklic.com; Vitranška ulica 13; s €51-77, d €78-130;) This pristine 14-room small hotel south of the centre is surrounded by luxurious lawns and flowerbeds and boasts an excellent restaurant and a small fitness room with sauna. It's definitely a cut above most other accommodation in Kranjska Gora.

Hotel Kompas (589 21 00; www.hitholidays-kg.si; Borovška cesta 100; s €80-99, d €128-186;) With 149 rooms, the four-star Kompas is Kranjska Gora's biggest hotel. It's a pleasant enough place, with recently renovated public areas and is set back in its own grounds. It boasts an indoor pool (though you'll get free access to the Aqua Larix Wellness Centre) and the chairlifts to the slopes are just over the road.

Hotel Larix (588 41 00; www.hitholidays-kg.si; Borovška cesta 99; s €80-99, d €128-186;) Even closer to the lifts, and in the same stable as the Kompas, is the 118-room Larix. It boasts the wonderful Aqua Larix Wellness Centre (opposite), with sauna, steam and a pool that seems to go on forever.

Eating

Šang Hai (588 13 46; Naselje Slavka Černeta 34; starters €2.50-3.50, mains €6.40-12; noon-midnight) If you fancy a change from local fare and pizza, try this Chinese restaurant, on the ground floor of the TGC Shopping Centre and facing the car park on the north side.

Gostilna Pri Martinu (582 03 00; Borovška cesta 61; starters €4.70-8, mains €6.50-12.50; 10am-11pm) This atmospheric tavern-restaurant in an old house opposite the fire station is one of the best places in town to try local specialities, such as *ješprenj* (barley soup; €3.60, *telečja obara* (veal stew; €4) and *ričet* (barley stew with smoked pork ribs; €5.90).

Hotel Kotnik (588 15 64; Borovška cesta 75; starters €8-11, mains €6.60-17; 11am-10pm) One of Kranjska Gora's better eateries, the restaurant in this stylish inn, with bits of painted dowry chests on the walls, serves grilled meats – pepper steak is a speciality – that should keep you going for a while. The adjoining pizzeria (pizza €5.10 to €7.20, open noon to 10.30pm) with the wood-burning stove is a great choice for something quicker.

Penzion Lipa (Koroška cesta 14; starters €7-14, mains €8-20; 11am-11pm) This attractive, family-style restaurant below a popular guest house (left) also does decent pizzas and pasta dishes (€5.90 to €7).

Oštarija Snežna Plaža (588 48 36; Borovška cesta 99; dishes €5-9; 8.30am-10pm) This place with the seasonal name (Snow Beach Inn) that lasts all year offers punters cheap and cheerful Slovenian and Balkan dishes at the foot of the chairlifts.

There's a **Mercator** (Borovška cesta 92; 7am-8pm Mon-Sat, 7am-noon Sun) supermarket in the centre of the village; and another **Mercator** (Naselje Slavka Černeta 33; 7am-7pm Mon-Sat, 7am-noon Sun) branch on the 1st floor of the TGC shopping centre.

Drinking

Sport Point Café (☎ 588 48 83; Borovška cesta 93/a; 🕒 7.30am-9pm Mon-Fri, 7.30am-10pm Sat & Sun) This convenient spot next to the TIC is the place to see and be seen and almost contains a sporting goods shop in memorabilia.

Vopa Pub (☎ 041 840 806; Borovška cesta 92; 🕒 7am-1am Sat, 7am-2am Sun) This raucous place next to the post office is Kranjska Gora's most popular late-night and après-ski venue, with live music and DJs (sometimes till as late as 5am) at the weekend.

Getting There & Around

Buses run hourly to Ljubljana (€8.70, two hours, 91km) via Jesenice (€3.10, 30 minutes, 24km), where you should change for Bled (€2.70, 20 minutes, 19km). There's just one direct departure to Bled (€4.70, one hour, 40km) on weekdays at 9.15am and at 5am on Saturday. A service to Bovec (€6.70, two hours, 46km) via Vršič Pass departs four times daily (five at the weekend) from late June to August.

Intersport, Sport Point and Julijana (p141) all rent bicycles and mountain bikes for around €3.50/6.50/10 per hour/half-day/day. Juliana also rents motor scooters (half-day/day €19/27).

TRIGLAV NATIONAL PARK

☎ 04 & 05 / elev to 2864m

Triglav National Park (Triglavski Narodni Park), abbreviated TNP everywhere in Slovenia, with an area of 83,800 hectares (just over 4% of Slovenian territory), is one of the largest national reserves in Europe. It is a pristine, visually spectacular world of rocky mountains – the centrepiece of which is Triglav (2864m), the country's highest peak – as well as river gorges, ravines, canyons, caves, rivers, streams, forests and Alpine meadows. It is a popular weekend destination for all manner of activity, from hiking and mountain biking to fishing and rafting. And there are approaches from Bohinj, Kranjska Gora and, in Primorska, Trenta – to name just a few gateways.

Marked trails in the park lead to countless peaks and summits besides Triglav. Favourite climbs include **Mangart** (2679m) on the Italian border (the 12km road that descends to the Predel Pass is the highest road in Slovenia), the needlepoint of **Jalovec** (2645m) in the north, and the sharp ridge of **Razor** (2601m) southeast of Vršič. But Triglav National Park is not only about climbing mountains. There are easy hikes through beautiful valleys, forests and meadows, too. Two excellent maps for this purpose are the PZS 1:50,000-scale *Triglavski Narodni Park* (Triglav National Park; €8.10) and Freytag & Berndt's 1:50,000 *Julische Alpen* €7. The English-language *Triglav National Park: The Two-in-One Guide* (Založba Mladinska Knjiga; €17), which comes as a 104-page booklet with a map, is also worth consideration.

Although Slovenia counts three large regional parks and 44 much smaller country (or 'landscape') parks, this is the country's only gazetted national park, and it includes almost all of the Alps lying within Slovenia. The idea of a park was first mooted in 1908 and realised in 1924, when 1600 hectares of the Triglav Lakes Valley were put under temporary protection. The area was renamed Triglav National Park in 1961 and expanded 20 years later to include most of the eastern Julian Alps. Today the park stretches from Kranjska Gora in the north to Tolmin in the south and from the Italian border in the west almost to Bled in the east. The bulk of the park lies in Gorenjska, but once you've crossed the awesome Vršič Pass – at 1611m, Slovenia's highest – and begun the descent into the Soča Valley, you've entered Primorska.

Triglav National Park is rich in fauna and especially flora (p61). For details on responsible park behaviour see p62.

Kranjska Gora to Soča Valley

One of the most spectacular – and easy – trips in Triglav National Park is simply to follow the paved road, usually open from May to October only, from Kranjska Gora via the Vršič Pass to Bovec, about 50km to the southwest. Between late June and September, you can do the trip by bus. At other times, you'll need your own transport – be it a car, motorbike or mountain bike.

The first stop from Kranjska Gora is **Jasna Lake** (Jezero Jasna), about 2km south of town. It's a beautiful, almost too-blue glacial lake with white sand around its rim and the little Pivnica River flowing alongside. Standing guard is a bronze statue of that irascible old goat **Zlatorog** (p126) and a decent *gostišče* (inn with restaurant).

As you zigzag up to just over 1100m, you'll come to the **Russian Chapel** (Ruska Kapelica), a little wooden church erected on the site where

CLIMBING THE BIG ONE

The 2864m limestone peak called Triglav (Three Heads) has been a source of inspiration and an object of devotion for Slovenes for more than a millennium. The early Slavs believed the mountain to be the home of a three-headed deity who ruled the sky, the earth and the underworld. No one managed to reach the summit until 1778 when an Austrian mountaineer and his three Slovenian guides climbed it from Bohinj. For Slovenes under the Habsburgs in the 19th century, the 'pilgrimage' to Triglav became, in effect, a confirmation of one's ethnic identity, and this tradition continues to this day: a Slovene is expected to climb Triglav at least once in his or her life.

You can climb Slovenia's highest peak too, but despite the fact that on a good summer's day hundreds of people will reach the summit, Triglav is not for the unfit or faint-hearted. In fact, its popularity is one of the main sources of danger. On the final approach to the top, there are often scores of people clambering along a rocky, knife-edge ridge in both directions, trying to pass each other.

If you are fit and confident, and have a good head for heights, then by all means hire a guide and just go for it. Under *no* circumstances should you make the trek by yourself. Guides can be hired through 3glav (p125) in Bled, Alpinsport (p133) in Bohinj and Dom Trenta (p146) in Trenta, or book in advance through the Alpine Association of Slovenia (PZS; p64). Only experienced mountain walkers with full equipment – including good hiking boots, warm clothes, hat, gloves and waterproofs, map and compass, whistle, head torch, first-aid kit, and some emergency food and drink – should consider making the ascent without a guide. Take care – people die on Triglav every year and (ominously) you'll see plaques marking these tragedies as you approach the summit.

Triglav is usually inaccessible to hikers from middle to late October to early June. June and the first half of July are the rainiest (and sometimes snowiest) times in summer months, so late July, August and particularly September and early to mid-October are the best times to make the climb. Patches of snow and ice can linger in the higher gullies until late July, and the weather can be very unpredictable at altitudes above 1500m, with temperatures varying by as much as 20°C and violent storms appearing out of nowhere.

Before you attempt the climb, try to get hold of the dated but still useful *How to Climb Triglav* (Kako na Triglav; Planinska Založba; €13.35), a superb, 63-page booklet that describes a dozen of the best routes, which may be available in bookshops and tourist offices in Slovenia as well as online from the PZS. The most useful map for the ascent of Triglav is the PZS 1:25,000 *Triglav Planinska Karta* (€8.10), with all the trails and huts clearly marked. The PZS also publishes a two-sheet 1:50,000-scale map of the Julian Alps; for Triglav and the park you want the eastern part: *Julijske Alpe – Vzhodni Del* (€8.10).

It is park tradition in Slovenia to greet (or at least smile at) everyone you pass while climbing. And don't be surprised when you've reach the top and you find yourself being turned over and having your bottom spanked. It's a long-established tradition for Triglav 'virgins'. Once at the summit, you – like your humble author on his last visit (p4) – can proclaim with pride: *'Danes sem slovenec/slovenka'* (Today I am a Slovene).

more than 400 Russian prisoners of war were buried in an avalanche in March 1916 while building the road you are travelling on.

The climb then begins in earnest as the road meanders past a couple of huts and corkscrews up the next few kilometres to **Vršič Pass** (1611m), about 13km from Kranjska Gora. The area was the scene of fierce fighting during WWI, and a high percentage of the dead lay where they fell (at 1525m there's a **military cemetery** to the east of the road). The Tičarjev Dom mountain hut is also east of the road, just before it begins to drop down the far side. To the west is **Mojstrovka** (2366m), to the east **Prisojnik/Prisank** (2547m) and to the south the valley of the Soča River points the way to Primorska. A hair-raising descent of about 10km ends just short of a **monument to Dr Julius Kugy** (1858–1944), a pioneer climber and writer whose books eulogise the beauty of the Julian Alps.

From here you can take a side trip along the first part of the **Soča Trail** (Soška Pot) to the **source of the Soča River** (Izvir Soče), about

2.5km to the northwest. Fed by an underground lake, the infant river bursts from a dark cave before dropping 15m to the rocky bed from where it begins its long journey to the Adriatic. The trail then continues for another 18km in 16 stages along the cobalt Soča as far as Bovec.

Not long after joining the main road again, you'll pass the entrance to the **Alpinum Juliana** (admission free; 8.30am-6.30pm May-Sep), a 2.57-hectare botanical garden established in 1926 that showcases the flora of all of Slovenia's Alps (Julian, Kamnik-Savinja and Karavanke) as well as the Karst. The elongated mountain village of **Trenta** (population 115, elevation 620m) is just south.

Trenta has a long tradition of mountain guides. Shepherds and woodsmen made the first ascents of the Julian Alps possible in the 19th century, and their bravery and skill are commemorated in a plaque just below the botanical garden. Na Logu, in the upper part of Trenta, is the gateway to the western approach to Triglav, a much less frequented and steeper climb than most of the others (p134).

In Spodnja Trenta (Lower Trenta) the **Dom Trenta** (Trenta Lodge; ☎ 05-388 93 30; www.tnp.si; Trenta 31; 10am-6pm late Apr–Oct, 10am-2pm mid-Jan–late Apr) is an information centre for Triglav National Park and contains the **Trenta Museum** (Trentarski Muzej; adult/child/senior & student/family €4/2.50/3/10), which focuses on the park's geology and natural history as well as the Trenta guides and pioneers of Slovenian alpinism.

The equally long village of **Soča** (population 14, elevation 480m) is another 8.5km downstream. The **Church of St Joseph** (Cerkev Sv Joža) from the early 18th century has paintings by Tone Kralj (1900–75). Completed in 1944 as war still raged in central Europe, one of the frescoes depicts Michael the Archangel struggling with Satan and the foes of humanity, Hitler and Mussolini.

Bovec (p148), the recreational centre of the Upper Soča Valley (Gornje Posočje), is 12km west of Soča.

SLEEPING

The staff at Dom Trenta (above) in Trenta has seven **private rooms** (per person from €20) and nine **apartments** (for 4 from €75) in summer.

There are several mountain huts on or near the Vršič road, all of which offer basic dishes. Category II **Koča na Gozdu** (☎ 041 682 704, 050 626 641; info@prezlc.si; Vršiška cesta 86; daily late Apr–Sep, Thu-Sun Oct–late Apr) with 43 beds is at 1226r whereas **Erjačeva Koča na Vršiču** (☎ 04-586 60 7 051 399-226; plan.drustvo@siol.net; Vršiška cesta 90; S & Sun May-Dec), also Category II with 99 bed is at 1525m. Category II **Tičarjev Dom na Vrši** (☎ 04-586 60 70, 051 634 571; plan.drustvo@siol.net; Tren 85; May–mid-Oct) with 91 beds and berths si right on the pass.

Above Tičarjev Dom is Category II **Poštars Dom na Vršiču** ☎ 041 610 029; pd.telekom@siol.net; Vršiš cesta 91; mid-Jun–Sep) with 66 beds at 1688n Near the source of the Soča River at 886m the Category III **Koča pri Izviru Soče** (☎ 04-586 70, 041 603 190; plan.drustvo@siol.net; late Apr–ea Oct) with 34 beds.

Camping grounds abound in the park use them! In Trenta there's 45-site **Campin Trenta** (☎ 05-388 93 55, 041 615 966; www.sloven holidays.com/camping-trenta; Trenta 60a; per person € 9.60; Apr-Oct) and the smaller (but nicer **Kamp Triglav** (☎ 05-388 93 11; marija.kravanja@vol .net; Trenta 18; per person €8; Apr-Oct) with 40 sites Side by side in Soča at Soča 38 is **Kamp Korit** (☎ 05-388 93 22, 051 645 677; per person €8; Ma Oct) and the delightful **Eko Camp** (☎ 041 383 66 051 266 812; per person €9; May-Oct), where th Adrenaline-Check adventure-sports agenc (p86) is based. The former is a standard issue site with 25 pitches as well as accommodation in a dormitory (per person €12 and mobile-home apartments (per perso €20). The Eko Camp, a mecca for youn adventurous travellers hosted by three wel coming Slovenes, also has accommodatio tents in wooden frames (€15) as used by loca shepherds (who make cheese nearby) an hammocks (€10).

The lovely **Kekčeva Domačija** (Kekec Homestead ☎ 05-381 1088, 041 413 087; www.kekceva-domacij .si; Trenta 76; per person €59), about 2.5km off the main road heading for the source of the Soča has eight apartments named after characters in the Kekec tales (p140) as the eponymous movie (1951) was filmed nearby. Cute – or sc former Prime Minister Janez Janša seems tc think so when he held his wedding reception here in July 2009.

GETTING THERE & AWAY

One bus at 6.30am daily in July and August and on Saturday and Sunday only in June and September link Ljubljana with Bovec (€12, 4¼ hours, 137km) in Primorska via Kranj, Lesce-Bled, Kranjska Gora, the Vršič Pass and Trenta.

Primorska

may come as a surprise to many that Primorska, the long slender province that extends om Austria and Triglav National Park to Istria and the Adriatic Sea, means 'Littoral' in Slovene. Vith Slovenia's coastline measuring only 47km long, why such an extravagant name?

It all has to do with weather. Almost all of Primorska gets the warm winds from the coast at influence the valleys as far as Kobarid and Bovec and inland. As a result, the climate nd the flora here are distinctly Mediterranean right up to the foothills of the Alps. Yet the rovince has four distinct regions: the Soča Valley (partly covered in the Triglav National ark section of the Gorenjska chapter); central Primorska with its rolling Cerkno and Idrija ills; the unique Karst with its wonderful *pršut* (dry-cured ham), olives and wine; and the oast itself (sometimes called Slovenian Istria).

Primorska offers an endless list of activities and sights; it can claim to be 'Europe in miniature'. here are mountains to climb and rivers to raft in the Soča Valley, wines to taste in the vineyards f the Vipava Valley and Goriška Brda (Gorica Hills) hills near Nova Gorica, expansive caverns at kocjan and white stallions to ride at Lipica in the Karst and beaches on which to while away ne hours at Piran and Portorož. Most activities can be enjoyed on the same day.

At the same time, Primorska can claim some of the most important and historic places in the ountry. Koper, Piran and Izola – three erstwhile Venetian ports full of Gothic architecture and rt – will keep even the most indefatigable of sightseers busy, and there are hilltop churches, ncient monasteries and richly endowed museums sprinkled throughout the province.

HIGHLIGHTS

- Dare the devil himself by **canyoning** or **rafting** (p151) on the Soča River from Bovec
- Descend into the nether world that should be set to music from the film *Fantasia* with a tour of the **Škocjan Caves** (p167)
- Enjoy a fresher-than-fresh seafood meal along the coast at **Izola** (p178) or **Piran** (p183)
- Sample some of the world-class red wines from (or, even better, in) the picture-postcard wine-producing region of **Goriška Brda** (p159)
- Discover the inner you (and many of the 270 types of feathered friends passing through) in the still and very salty **Sečovlje Salina Nature Park** (p188)
- Be reminded of where you come from (and where you certainly are going to) at the **Church of the Holy Trinity** (p170) in Hrastovlje

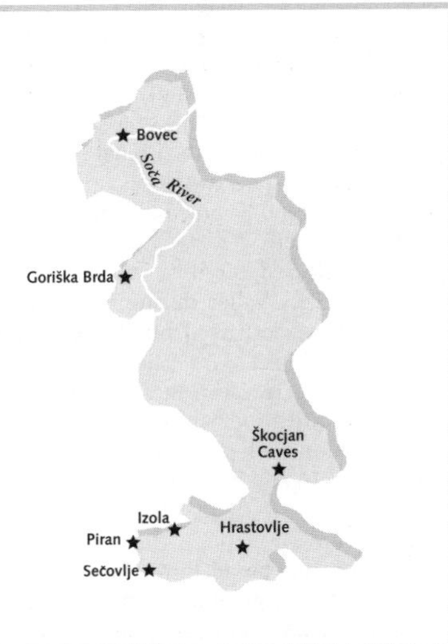

SOČA VALLEY

The Soča Valley region (Posočje) stretches from Triglav National Park to Nova Gorica, including Bovec, Kobarid, Tolmin and Most na Soči. Its most dominant feature is the 96km Soča River, which can widen to 500m and narrow to less than a metre but always stays that deep, almost unreal aquamarine colour. Most people come here for the rafting, hiking and skiing though the valley has more than its share of historical sights and locations. During WWI millions of troops were brought here to fight on the battle front stretching from the Karst to Mt Rombon. Between the wars, Primorska and the Soča Valley fell under Italian jurisdiction; many Italians were expelled or left the province voluntarily after WWII.

PRIMORSKA

BOVEC

☎ 05 / pop 1785 / elev 470m

Effectively the capital of the Soča Valley, Bovec has a great deal to offer adventure-sports enthusiasts. With the Julian Alps above, the Soča River below and Triglav National Park all around, you could spend a week here hiking, kayaking, mountain biking and, in winter, skiing at Mt Kanin, Slovenia's highest ski station, without ever doing the same thing twice.

History

The area around Bovec is first mentioned in documents dating back to the 11th century. At that time it was under the direct rule of the Patriarchs of Aquileia but was later transferred to the Counts of Gorica and, in about 1500, to the Habsburgs. The Turks passed through the area on their way to the Predel Pass in the 15th century, and on two occasions (in 1797 and again in 1809) Napoleon's army attacked Austria from here.

Bovec suffered terribly in the fighting around the Soča Valley during WWI. Much of the town was destroyed, but its reconstruction by the architect Maks Fabiani in the 1920s gave Bovec an interesting combination of traditional and modern buildings. Further reconstruction took place after severe earthquakes in 1976 and in 1998.

Orientation

Bovec lies in the broad Bovec Basin (Bovška Kotlina) at the meeting point of the Soča and Koritnica Valleys. Towering above are several peaks of more than 2000m, including Mt Rombon (2208m) to the north and Mt Kanin (2587m) to the northwest. The Soča River flows past Bovec 2km to the south at Čezsoča. The Italian border is 16km to the southwest via the pass at Učeja and 17km north at Predel Pass.

The centre is Trg Golobarskih Žrtev, one of the few named streets in town. Actually, 's a long square that forms the main east–'est drag and runs northward to the neo-omanesque church of St Urh. Buses stop own the side street just before Mercator in Iala Vas.

nformation

ar Kavarna (☎ 388 63 35; Trg Golobarskih Žrtev 25;) min €1.50; ⏲ 7am-11pm Mon-Thu, 7am-midnight Fri Sat, 8am-8pm Sun) Internet access.

ovec Kanin Ski Centre (☎ 389 60 03; www oveckanin.si; Trg Golobarskih Žrtev 47; ⏲ 7.30am-9pm ıl & Aug, 8am-noon & 1-4.30pm Sep-Jun) Next to the ova KMB Banka.

ova KBM Banka (Trg Golobarskih Žrtev 47)

ost office (Trg Golobarskih Žrtev 8; ⏲ 8-9.30am, 0am-3.30pm & 4-6pm Mon-Fri, 8am-noon Sat)

ourist Information Centre Bovec (TIC; ☎ 384 19 9, 389 64 44; www.bovec.si; Trg Golobarskih Žrtev 8; ⏲ 8am-8.30pm Jul & Aug, 9am-5pm Sep-Jun) With an TM next door.

ights

The **Kluže Fortress** (Trdnjava Kluže; ☎ 384 19 00; www kluze.net; adult/child/student €3/1/2; ⏲ 9am-8pm Jul & Aug, 10am-5pm Sun-Fri May & Oct, 10am-6pm Sat & Sun May & Sep), built by the Austrians in 1882 on the site of a 17th-century fortress and above a 70m ravine on the Koritnica River, is 4km northeast of Bovec and worth the trip just to see its location. Even more awesome is the upper fortress called **Fort Herman** built half-way up Mt Rombon to the west up in 1900 when Kluže proved to be obsolete. There's a permanent exhibition on the ecology of the region and the history of the fortress. You can reach the fortress on the main road from Bovec towards Log pod Mangrtom and the Predel Pass into Italy.

The ambitious and/or those looking for a breath of fresh air might walk the 2km along a marked trail eastward from Kluže through the magical Bavšica Valley to the hamlet of Zabrajda and the **Matija Komac Beehive** (Čebelnjak Matije Komaca), one of the best examples of a 19th-cenury *kranjič* hive, with removable boxes and painted front panels (p120).

The Bovec Basin abounds in family-run dairies such as the in-town **Ostan Cheese Dairy** (☎ 389 61 77; 041 589 877; Trg Golobarskih Žrtev 54) that produce traditional sheep's cheese. Ask the TIC for a copy of the pamphlet *Along the Bovška Ovca Sheep Trail* and track down your own favourite.

Activities

ADVENTURE SPORTS

There are almost a dozen adrenaline-raising adventure-sports companies in Bovec organising all kinds of activities. Among the better known and more reliable are: **Avantura** (☎ 041 718 317; www.avantura.org; Trg Golobarskih Žrtev 19; ⏲ 9am-7pm Jun-Aug); **Bovec Rafting Team** (☎ 388 61 28, 041 338 308; www.bovec-rafting-team.com; Mala Vas 106; ⏲ 9am-8pm May-Sep), in a kiosk opposite the Martinov Hram restaurant and just up from the bus stops; **Outdoor Freaks** (☎ 389 64 90, 041 553 675; www.outdoorfreaks.si; Trg Golobarskih Žrtev 38; ⏲ 9am-7pm May-Sep), in the

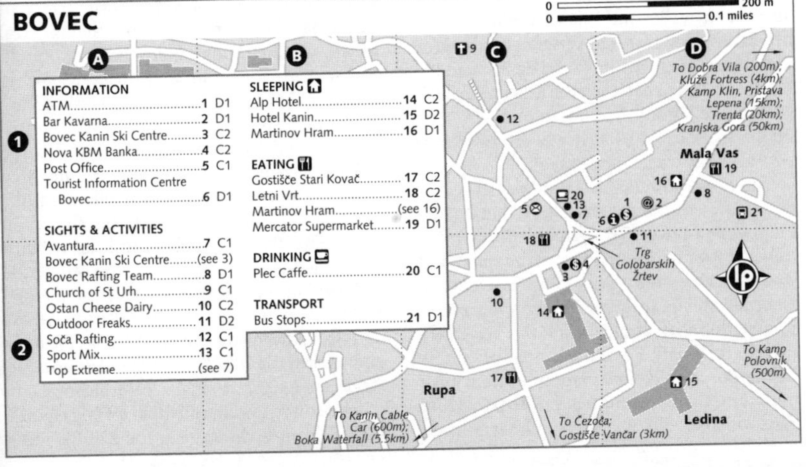

Rombon building on the main square; **Soča Rafting** (☎ 389 62 00, 041 724 472; www.socarafting.si; Trg Golobarskih Žrtev 14; ⏰ 9am-7pm Apr-Oct, 9am-noon & 4-8pm Nov-Mar), about 200m uphill from the TIC and the only agency open all year; **Sport Mix** (☎ 389 61 60, 031 871 991; www.sportmix.traftbovec.si; Trg Golobarskih Žrtev 18; ⏰ 8am-9pm Jul & Aug, 9am-7pm May-Jun & Sep); and **Top Extreme** (☎ 031 620 636; www.top.si; Trg Golobarskih Žrtev 19; ⏰ 9am-7pm Jun-Aug).

CYCLING

Ask the TIC for the *Biking Trails* pamphlet, which lists 16 trips of various degrees of difficulty.

The **Kanin Mountain Bike Park** (www.mtbparkkanin.com) is just 2km from the Bovec Kanin ski centre cable car's station B (oneway €5); its 4.5km trail is divided into three degrees of difficulty and is open all year.

Sport Mix, Soča Rafting and Outdoor Freaks all rent **bicycles** and **mountain bikes** (per hr/half-day/day/3 days/week €7.50/12/18/39/85).

PRIMORSKA

FISHING

Alp Hotel and Kamp Klin both sell fishing licences for hooking the famous Soča trout. There are two types of permit: one for the area east of Čezsoča, as well as the Lepenjica River (€69), and another for the Soča River below Bovec (€59), where there is a lot more kayaking and boating. The season lasts from April to October.

HIKING & WALKING

The 1:25,000-scale map called *Bovec z Okolico* (Bovec with Surroundings; €7.60) lists a number of walks and hikes ranging from a two-hour stroll south to **Čezsoča** and the protected luminously white gravel deposits in the Soča to an ascent of **Mt Rombon** (2208m), which would take a good five hours one way. The smaller-scaled 1:40,000 Bovec (€7.60) from GZS also has walks in the area.

The most popular do-it-yourself walk in the area is to **Boka Waterfall**, 5.5km to the southwest of Bovec. The waterfall drops 106m from the Kanin Mountains into the valley and is almost 30m wide – it's an impressive sight, especially in late spring when the snow melts. To get there on foot, follow the relatively easy marked path B2 or the more difficult S1 on the *Bovec z Okolico* map; mountain-bike track No 1 on the *Biking Trails* pamphlet map will also take you there. The trip up to the falls (850m) and back takes about 1 hours, but the path is steep in places and ca be very slippery.

From the uppermost stop (station D) of th cable car more ambitious walkers and hike could make the difficult three-hour clim of Kanin (2587m) or reach the **Prestreljeni Window** (2498m) in about an hour.

The adventure-sports agencies on p14 can organise **walks and hikes** with an experi ence guide (per two/four/eight hours fror €52/90/150) to such places as the **Mangrt Saddl** (2072m) along the highest road in Slovenia where you'll find accommodation at th Category I **Koča na Mangrtskem Sedlu** (☎ 388 6 32, 041 954 761; erikcuder@gmail.com; ⏰ daily mid-Jun–Sep Sat & Sun Oct) with 53 beds at 1906m, and to **Kr Lake**, 1340m above the Lepena Valley, wher you'll find the Category I **Planinski Dom p Krnskih Jezerih** (☎ 302 30 30, 051 328 928; planinsko.novagorica@siol.net; ⏰ Jun-Sep) with 170 bed at 1385m.

PARAGLIDING

In winter you can take a tandem paraglide flight (ie as a passenger accompanied by a qualified pilot) from the top of the Bovec Kanin cable car, 2000m above the valley floor The cost of a flight ranges from €110; ask the Avantura agency for details. Paragliding is at its best from the Mangrt Saddle (2072m) between June and September.

SKIING

The **Bovec Kanin Ski Centre** (☎ 389 60 03; www.boveckanin.si; day pass adult/child/senior & student €26/19/20) in the mountains northwest of Bovec has skiing up to 2300m – the only real altitude alpine skiing in Slovenia. As a result, the season can be long, with good spring skiing in April and even May. The ski area – 17km of pistes and 15km of cross-country runs served by three chairlifts and three T-bars – is reached by a cable car in three stages. The bottom station is 600m southwest of the centre of Bovec on the main road. The ski centre plans to link up with the Sella Nevea ski centre on the other side of Kanin in Italy, which will increase the pistes to 30km and lifts and tows to 14. There's an **information centre** (☎ 389 60 03; www.boveckanin.si; Trg Golobarskih Žrtev 47; ⏰ 7.30am-9pm Jul & Aug, 8am-noon & 1-4.30pm Jun-Sep) in central Bovec.

You can rent a complete ski kit (skis, poles, boots) from Soča Rafting for €22/55/110 a ay/three days/week. A snowboard will cost €16/40/89 for the same period. Individual ski lessons cost €30 per hour; it's €50 for six hours in a group.

The **Kanin cable car** (adult/child oneway €10/6, return €13/10) runs continuously during the ski season; in July and August it runs hourly from 7am to 4pm (last down at 5pm) and every hour from 8am to 3pm (last down at 4pm) at the weekend in June and September. Several walks lead from the upper station (opposite).

WATER SPORTS

Rafting, kayaking and canoeing on the beautiful Soča River (10% to 40% gradient; Grades I to VI) attract people to Bovec. The season lasts from April to October, when organised excursions are available daily.

Rafting trips of two to eight people on the Soča over a distance of 8km to 10km (1½ hours) cost from €36 to €46 and for 21km (2½ hours) from €48 to €55, including neoprene long johns, windcheater, life jacket, helmet and paddle. You should bring along a swimsuit, T-shirt and towel. A canoe for two is €45 for the day, and a single kayak is €30. A number of kayaking courses are also on offer (eg a one-/two-day course for beginners costs from €53/97). A guided 10km kayak trip costs from €42 to €45 per person.

A 3km **canyoning** trip near the Soča, in which you descend through gorges and jump over falls attached to a rope, lasting two/three hours costs €45/85. **Hydrospeed**, which is like riding down a river on a boogie board, costs from €46 to €52 for 7km to 10km (1½ to two hours).

Festivals & Events

The **Kluže Festival** (www.exponto.net) is an increasingly well-attended theatre event held at the nearby 19th-century fortress every year from early July to mid-August.

Sleeping

Private rooms (per person €15-30) are easy to come by in Bovec, and the TIC and other agencies have hundreds on their lists.

Kamp Polovnik (☎ 389 60 07, 031 344 417; www.kamp-polovnik.com; Ledina 8; adult €5-7, child €3.75-5.25; Apr–mid-Oct; P) About 500m southeast of the Hotel Kanin, this is the closest camping ground to Bovec. It is small (just over a hectare with 70 sites) but located in an attractive setting.

Kamp Klin (☎ 388 95 13; kampklin@siol.net; Lepena 1; per person €10-15; mid-Mar–Oct; P) This lovely 1 hectare site for 200 chilled campers is in Lepena on the idyllic Lepenjica River, about 15km southeast of Bovec. There's an eight-room pension here too.

Martinov Hram (☎ 388 62 14; sara.berginc@volja.net; Trg Golobarskih Žrtev 27; s/d €34/56; P) This lovely and very friendly guest house just 100m east of the centre has 14 beautifully furnished rooms and an excellent restaurant with an emphasis on specialities from the Bovec region.

Pristava Lepena (☎ 388 99 00, 041 671 981; www.pristava-lepena.com; Lepena 2; per person €53-69; mid-Apr–mid-Oct; P) This positively idyllic 'holiday village' is set in an Alpine meadow 15km southeast of Bovec. There are five rooms and eight apartments in six traditional houses, a lovely restaurant, and fishing and riding (€16 to €23 per hour) opportunities.

Alp Hotel (☎ 388 40 00; www.alp-chandler.si; Trg Golobarskih Žrtev 48; s €54-64, d €78-98; P) This 103-room hotel, with a bit of landscaped garden around it, is fairly good value and as central as you are going to find in Bovec. There are three saunas and guests get to use the swimming pool at the nearby Hotel Kanin.

Hotel Kanin (☎ 389 68 82; www.hoteli-kanin.com; Ledina 6; s €56-72, d €64-93; P) About 150m southeast of the Alp Hotel, this 124-room property is set in much quieter surrounds and has a large indoor swimming pool and a new wellness centre. The rooms are not as nice as those at the Alp Hotel, though some have been renovated and have balconies looking onto a quiet back garden.

our pick **Dobra Vila** (☎ 389 64 00; www.dobra-vila-bovec.com; Mala Vas 112; s €68-115, d €88-135, tr €137-168; P) This absolute stunner of a 10-room boutique hotel is housed in an erstwhile telephone-exchange building dating to 1932. It has its own small cinema, a library and wine cellar and a fabulous restaurant with winter garden and outdoor terrace. And it's peppered with interesting artefacts and objets d'art; we love the 1932 Bianchi Freccia d'Oro 175T motorcycle in one of the windows. Rates include dinner.

Eating & Drinking

Gostišče Vančar (☎ 389 60 76, 031 312 742; Čezsoča 43; starters €5-6, mains €6-8; 11am-10pm Jul & Aug, 11am-10pm Tue-Sun Sep-Jun) This inn 3km south of Bovec is where local people go to taste such Bovec specialities as *kalja* (a sweet-corn pudding) and *bovški krafni* ('raviolis' stuffed with dried pears, raisins and walnuts). Expect huge portions and warm service.

Martinov Hram (starters €5.90-9, mains €7.90-13.50, pizza €6.50-8.90; 10am-10pm Tue-Fri, 10am-midnight Sat & Sun) This traditional restaurant in an attractive inn (p151) specialises in game, Soča trout and mushroom dishes. During the winter pizza rears its ugly head. There is a lovely roadside terrace in front. Set lunch is €13.

Gostišče Stari Kovač (388 66 99; Rupa 3; starters €6.50-7, mains €8-11, pizza €5-7.50; noon-10pm Tue-Sun) The Old Blacksmith, just west of the Alp Hotel, is a good choice for pizza cooked in a wood-burning stove.

Letni Vrt (389 63 83, 041 775 127; Trg Golobarskih Žrtev 1; meals from €15; 11am-10pm Wed-Mon) Opposite the Alp Hotel, the Summer Garden has pizza, grilled dishes and trout at affordable prices. Its garden is lovely in summer – as it would be.

Plec Caffe (041 775 127; Trg Golobarskih Žrtev 18; 8am-1am Jul & Aug, 5pm-1am Sep-Jun) This pleasant cafe in the heart of town attracts punters till the wee (for Bovec) hours year-round.

Mercator (Mala Vas 6; 7am-8pm Mon-Wed, Fri & Sat, 7am-noon Thu, 8am-noon Sun) This large branch of the popular supermarket chain is just west of the bus stops.

Getting There & Away

Buses to Kobarid (€3.10, 30 minutes, 22km) and Tolmin (€4.70, one hour, 38km) depart up to six times a day, with fewer frequencies at the weekend. There are also a couple of buses to Ljubljana (€13.60, 3½ hours, 151km, three a day) via Kobarid, Tolmin and Idrija (€8.70, 2½ hours, 95km) and four to Nova Gorica (€7.50, two hours, 77km). From late June to August a service to Kranjska Gora (€6.70, two hours, 46km) via the Vršič Pass departs four times daily (five at the weekend).

KOBARID

05 / pop 1230 / elev 234m

The charming town of Kobarid is a lot quainter than Bovec, 22km to the northwest, and the woodland scenery somewhat tamer. Despite being surrounded by mountain peaks higher than 2200m, Kobarid feels more Mediterranean than Alpine and the architecture retains its Italianate look. The Italian border at Robič is only 9km to the west.

Indeed, on the surface not a whole l has changed in this sleepy hollow since th American writer Ernest Hemingway describ Kobarid (then Caporetto) in his groundbrea ing novel *A Farewell to Arms* (1929), depicti the horror and suffering of WWI. It was little white town with a campanile in a valley he wrote, 'a clean little town and there was fine fountain in the square'. The bell in th tower still rings on the hour, but the foun tain has disappeared (though you could sti hear the water rushing below the courtyar at Trg Svobode 15, behind the rather strikin statue of the poet and priest Simon Gregorči (1844–1906) until a decade ago.

Kobarid did have a history before WW and things have happened here since. It wa a military settlement during Roman time was hotly contested in the Middle Ages an was hit by a devastating earthquake in 197 which destroyed some historical buildings an farmhouses with folk frescoes. But the worl will always remember Kobarid as Caporetto the site of the decisive battle of 1917 in whic the combined forces of the Central Power defeated the Italian army.

Orientation

Kobarid lies in a broad valley on the west bank of the Soča River. The centre of town is Trg Svobode, dominated by the Gothic Church o the Assumption and that famous bell tower Buses stop in front of the Cinca Marinca bar cafe on the eastern side at Trg Svobode 10.

Information

Abanka (Markova ulica 16)

Nova KBM Banka (Trg Svobode 2)

Post office (Trg Svobode 2; 8-9.30am, 10am-3.30pm & 4-6pm Mon-Fri, 8am-noon Sat)

Tourist Information Centre Kobarid (TIC; 380 04 90; www.lto-sotocje.si; Gregorčičeva ulica 8; 9am-8pm Jul & Aug, 9am-12.30pm & 1.30-7pm Mon-Fri, 9am-1pm Sat Sep-Jun) Next door to the award-winning Kobarid Museum.

Sights & Activities

KOBARID MUSEUM

Located in 18th-century Mašera House, this **museum** (Kobariški Muzej; 389 00 00. 041 714 072; www.kobariski-muzej.si; Gregorčičeva ulica 10; adult/child/student & senior €5/2.5/4; 9am-7pm Jul-Sep, 9am-6pm Mon-Fri, 9am-7pm Sat & Sun Apr-Jun & Oct, 10am-5pm Mon-Fri, 10am-6pm Sat & Sun Nov-Mar) is devoted almost entirely to the Soča Front (p154) and deals with the tragedy of the 'war to end all wars'.

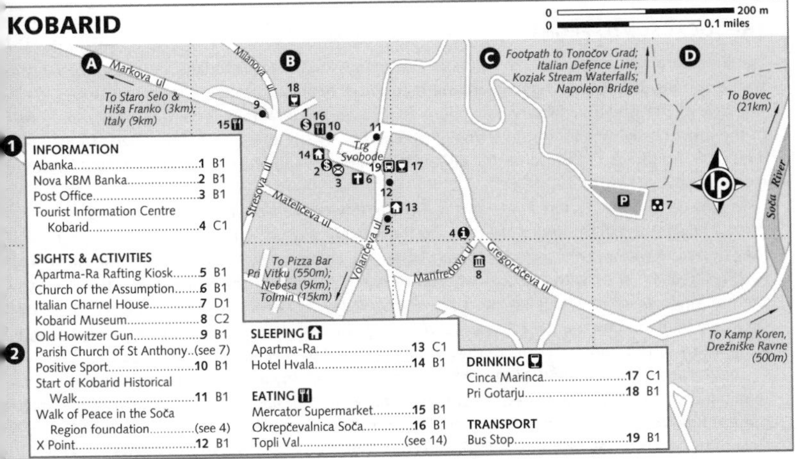

The museum is divided into about a dozen rooms on three floors. The rooms on the 1st and 2nd floors deal with the 29 months of fighting and have themes. The **Krn Room** looks at the initial assaults along the Soča River after Italy's entry into the war in May 1915. The **White Room** describes the particularly harsh conditions of waging war in the mountains in the snow and fog. The **Hinterland Room** explains what life was like for soldiers during pauses in the fighting and also for the civilian population that was uprooted by war and famine; the **Black Room** displays horrific photographs of the dead and dying. The **Kobarid Rooms** bring it all home.

On the 3rd floor the **Battle of Kobarid Room** deals with the events over three days – 24 to 27 October 1917 – when the combined Austrian and German forces met up near Kobarid and launched the offensive that defeated the Italian army.

Among the collection are photographs documenting the horrors of the front, military charts, diaries and maps, and two large relief displays showing the front lines and offensives through the Krn Mountains and the positions in the Upper Soča Valley the day before the decisive breakthrough. There's also a 20-minute multimedia presentation.

TOURS & WALKS

The **Walk of Peace in the Soča Region Foundation** (☎ 389 01 67; www.potimiruvposocju.si; Gregorčičeva ulica 8) based at the TIC office organises a number of guided walks along sections of the 100km-long Walk of Peace (Pot Miru), a trail following the Soča/Isonzo Front from Tolmin in the south to Log pod Mangrtom in the north. Most are for groups, but there's a three-hour undemanding walk to the **Kolovrat Outdoor Museum** (Kolovrat Muzej na Prostem) costing €10 and departing from the TIC at 10am on Wednesday and Sunday.

Do-it-yourself walkers should ask the TIC for the free brochure describing the 5km-long **Kobarid Historical Walk** (Kobariška Zgodovinska Pot). From the Kobarid Museum walk to the north side of Trg Svobode, a winding road lined with the Stations of the Cross climbs up a hill called Gradič to the **Italian Charnel House** (Italijanska Kostnica), which contains the bones of more than 7000 Italian soldiers killed on the Soča Front. Benito Mussolini attended the dedication in September 1938. The charnel house is topped with the 17th-century **Parish Church of St Anthony** (Župnijska Cerkev Sv Anton), which was moved here in 1935.

From the ossuary, a path leads north (take the left-hand fork after a minute's walk) for just over 1km to **Tonočov Grad**, an ancient fortified hill where an archaeological project has uncovered the remains of 20 houses and several churches dating from the 5th and 6th centuries.

The path then descends through the remains of the **Italian Defence Line** (Italijanska Obrambna Črta) built in 1915, past cleared trenches, gun emplacements and observation

THE SOČA/ISONZO FRONT

The breakthrough in the Soča Front (more commonly known to historians as the Isonzo Front) by the combined Austro-Hungarian and German forces near Caporetto (Kobarid) in October 1917 was one of the greatest military campaigns fought on mountainous terrain in history and one of the most costly ever fought in terms of human life. By the time the fighting had stopped 17 days later, hundreds of thousands of soldiers lay dead or wounded, gassed or mutilated beyond recognition.

In May 1915, Italy declared war on the Central Powers and their allies and moved its army across the southwestern border of Austria to the strategically important Soča Valley. From there, they hoped to move eastward to the heart of Austria-Hungary. By then, however, the Austrians had fortified the lines with trenches and bunkers for 80km from the Adriatic and the Karst to the mountain peaks overlooking the Upper Soča Valley as far north as Mt Rombon. The First Offensive launched by the Italians was successful in the first month, and they occupied Kobarid and Mt Krn to the northeast, where they would remain for some 29 months.

The Italians launched another 11 offensives over the next 2½ years, but the difficult mountain terrain meant a war of attrition between the two entrenched armies. Territorial gains were minimal, but the fighting in the mountains and the limestone plateau to the south was horrific. With the stalemate, much of the fighting shifted to Gorica (Gorizia) on the edge of the Karst.

On 24 October 1917 the stalemate was broken when the Austro-Hungarians and Germans formulated an unusual plan of attack based on surprise and moved hundreds of thousands of troops, arms and material (including seven German divisions) into the area between Bovec and Tolmin, with Kobarid as the first target. The 12th Offensive – the first by the Austrians – began with heavy bombardment.

What would become known as 'the miracle of Kobarid' routed the Italian army and pushed the fighting back to the Friulian Plain, where the war continued for another year. The sketches of the breakthrough by one Lieutenant Erwin Rommel, who would become known as the 'Desert Fox' while commanding Germany's North African offensive in WWII, are invaluable for understanding the battle. But no account is more vivid than the description of the Italian retreat in Hemingway's *A Farewell to Arms*. The novelist himself was wounded on the Gorica battlefield in the spring of 1917 while driving an Italian ambulance.

The 12th Offensive was the greatest breakthrough in WWI, and it employed some elements of what would later be called 'lightning war' (blitzkrieg). The Italians alone lost 500,000 soldiers, and another 300,000 were taken prisoner. Casualties on the Soča Front for the entire 1915–17 period, including soldiers on the battlefields and men, women and children behind the lines, number almost a million.

PRIMORSKA

posts, before crossing the Soča over a new 52m **footbridge**. A path leads up a side valley to a series of walkways that take you to the foot of the spectacular **Kozjak Stream Waterfalls** (Slapovi Potoka Kozjak). The return path leads to **Napoleon Bridge** (Napoleonov Most), a replica of a bridge built by the French in the early 19th century and destroyed in May 1915.

ADVENTURE SPORTS

Kobarid is beginning to give Bovec a run for its money in adventure sports, and you'll find several outfits on or off the town's main square that can organise rafting (€30 to €47), canyoning (€40 to €79), kayaking (€40) and paragliding (€110) between April and October. They include the long-established **X Point** (☎ 388 5 08, 041 692 290; www.xpoint.si; Trg Svobode 6); **Positive Sport** (☎ 040 654 475; www.positive-sport.com; Markov ulica 2); and Apartma-Ra (opposite).

The Hotel Hvala (opposite) sells **fishing permits** (per day €52-98) for the Soča River.

Sleeping

Kamp Koren (☎ 389 13 11; www.kamp-koren.si; Drežniške Ravne 33; per person €9-10.50; mid-Mar–Oct; P) The oldest (and, some would say, friendliest) camping ground in the valley, this 2-hectare site with 70 pitches is about 500m northeast of Kobarid on the left bank of the Soča River and just before the turn to Drežniške Ravne, a lovely village with traditional farmhouses. In full view is the Napoleon Bridge.

Apartma-Ra (☎ 041 641 899; apartma-ra@siol.net; 'egorčičeva ulica 6/c; per person €15-25; P) This elcoming little place between the museum nd Trg Svobode (enter via the driveway rom Volaričeva ulica) has five rooms and partments, some with terraces. Bicycles are vailable for rent to guests for around €10 er day.

Hiša Franko (☎ 389 41 20; www.hisafranko.com; Staro elo 1; s €68-115, d €80-135; P) This guest house n an old farmhouse 3km west of Kobarid in taro Selo, halfway to the Italian border, has 0 themed rooms – we love the Moja Afrika My Africa) and Soba Zelenega Čaja (Green 'ea Room) ones – some of which have terraces nd Jacuzzis.

Hotel Hvala (☎ 389 93 00; www.hotelhvala.si; rg Svobode 1; s €72-76, d €104-112; P) The est place to stay in Kobarid is the delightul Hotel Thanks (actually it's the family's ame), which has 31 rooms – some recently enovated to a level unseen in provincial lovenia. The snazzy new lift takes you on a ertical tour of Kobarid (don't miss both the oča trout and Papa Hemingway at work), here's a bar, a Mediterranean-style cafe n the garden and a superb restaurant (see elow).

Nebesa (☎ 384 46 21, 041 769 484; www.nebesa.si, Livek 9; d €210-250; P) The Paradise compound, vith its four two-person modern chalets and ts scenic location 900m up in the mountains bout 9km southeast of Kobarid on the road o Tolmin, is one of the few places to stay in Slovenia that is a 'destination' unto itself. Self-contained, with kitchen, fireplace and open terraces, the chalets measure more than 50 sq metres and are among the most dramatic (and romantic) places to stay in Slovenia. There's a swimming pool and whirlpool, and wine cellar with complimentary tipple and locally produced cheeses.

Eating

Okrepčevalnica Soča (☎ 389 05 00; Markova ulica 10; pizza €5-7.50; 11am-10pm) The simple Soča Snack Bar opposite the Hotel Hvala has snacks and pizza – though you can drink here a lot later (and earlier) than stated here.

Pizza Bar Pri Vitku (☎ 389 13 34; Pri Malnih ulica 41; pizza & pasta €5.50-7.50; 11am-midnight Mon-Fri, noon-midnight Sat & Sun) This upbeat little pub-restaurant is about 500m south of the town centre and serves decent pizza and pasta dishes as well as more ambitious grilled dishes.

our pick **Topli Val** (Trg Svobode 1; starters €8-10, mains €9.50-25; noon-10pm) With a name like Warm Wave and owners originally from Portorož, this excellent restaurant at the Hotel Hvala is bound to specialise in seafood. It's excellent – from the mixed shellfish starter (€16) and carpaccio of sea bass (€8) to the Soča trout and signature lobster with pasta (€28). Expect to pay about €30 to €60 per person with a decent bottle of wine, such as a Mavrič or Blažič from Goriška Brda (€15 to €20), although the house wine (with its collectors' 'Hemingway' label) is a snip at €9 a bottle. There's a lovely front terrace and back garden open in warmer months.

Hiša Franko (Staro Selo 1; starters €12-16, mains €20-24; noon-3pm & 6-11pm Tue-Sun) Kobarid's 'other' slow-food phenomenon is this gourmet restaurant in the guesthouse of the same name (left) in Staro Selo just west of town. Tasting menus, which change according to the season, cost €45/70 for five/nine courses. It closes on Tuesday in winter.

Mercator (Markova ulica 1; 8am-7pm Mon-Sat) This large branch of the popular supermarket chain is just west of Trg Svobode.

Drinking

Cinca Marinca (☎ 389 13 03; Trg Svobode 10; 7am-11pm Mon-Fri, 7am-late Sat & Sun) This cafe-bar is just the place to cool your heels and slake your thirst while waiting for the bus to stop outside. It's open late when the rest of Kobarid has gone to bed early.

Pri Gotarju (☎ 388 57 43; Krilanova ulica 3; 7am-11pm Sun-Thu, 7am-midnight Fri & Sat) This cafe-pub in a shady garden is a pleasant place for a drink – especially in the courtyard in summer. In the grassy area near the petrol station opposite there is a rusting 150mm howitzer that weighs more than 5000kg and was built by Krupp in 1911.

Getting There & Around

There are half a dozen buses a day to the northwest and Bovec (€3.10, 30 minutes, 22km) and to the southeast and Tolmin (€2.70, 30 minutes, 18km). Other destinations include Ljubljana (€11.40 three hours, 129km, two a day) via Most na Soči train station (good for Bled and Bohinj), Cerkno and Idrija (€7.20, two hours, 73km) and Nova Gorica (€6, 1¼ hours, 55km, four a day). Daily at 6.34am in July and August, a bus crosses over the spectacular Vršič Pass to Kranjska Gora (€6.70, three hours, 68km).

NOVA GORICA

☎ 05 / pop 12,400 / elev 92m

Nova Gorica is a university city straddling the Italian border – an easy entry and exit point from the rest of the EU to the west. It is surprisingly green, with tree-lined boulevards and a couple of lovely parks and gardens, and its immediate surrounds – the Franciscan monastery at Kostanjevica nad Gorico to the south and the ancient settlement of Solkan in the north with several baroque manor houses – offers some startling contrasts. Slovenian, Venetian, Friulian and Austrian influences can be felt everywhere in the hinterland.

Nova Gorica straddles two important wine-growing areas: Goriška Brda to the northwest and the wide Vipava Valley to the southeast. It's also an excellent springboard for some of Slovenia's most popular destinations: the Soča Valley, Bled and Bohinj in Gorenjska and the beautiful Karst region leading to the coast.

History

When the town of Gorica, capital of the former Slovenian province of Goriška, was awarded to the Italians under the Treaty of Paris in 1947 and became Gorizia, the ne socialist government in Yugoslavia set itse to building a model town on the eastern sid of the border 'following the principles of L Corbusier', the Swiss functionalist archite who has a lot to answer for. Appropriatel enough they called it 'New Gorica' an erected a chain-link barrier between th two towns.

This 'mini-Berlin Wall' was finally pulle down to great fanfare in 2004 after Sloveni joined the EU, leaving Piazza Transalpin (Trg z Mozaikom) straddling the now non existent border right behind Nova Goric train station. A museum now tries to explai this bizarre arrangement to those more in tent at trying their luck at one of the city' half-dozen casinos.

Orientation

Nova Gorica sits on a broad plain south o the Soča River. It is an unusually long town running about 5km from crossing with Ital at Rožna Dolina (Casa Rossa) in the south t Solkan in the north. The bus station is in th centre of town at Kidričeva ulica 22, 400n

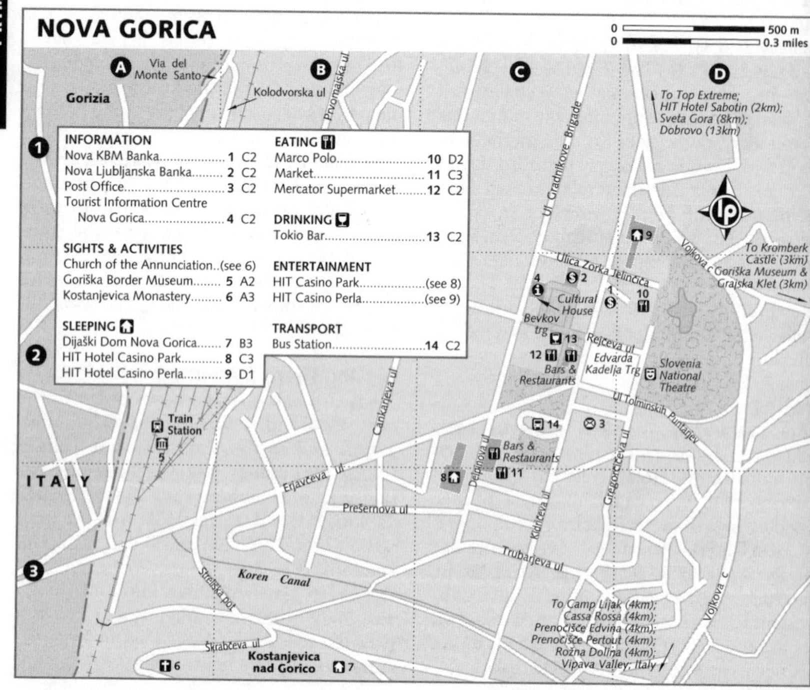

uthwest of the Hotel Casino Perla. The train ation is at Kolodvorska ulica 6, about 1.5km the west.

formation

ova KBM Banka (Kidričeva ulica 11) Just south of the otel Casino Perla.

ova Ljubljanska Banka (Bekov trg 3) In the central uare next to the TIC.

ost office (Kidričeva ulica 19) Opposite the bus station.

ourist Information Centre Nova Gorica (TIC; ☎ 333 5 00; www.novagorica-turizem.com; Bekov trg 4; 8am-8pm Mon-Fri, 9am-1pm Sat & Sun Jul & Aug, 8am-m Mon-Fri, 9am-1pm Sat & Sun Sep-Jun) In the lobby of e Kulturni Dom (Cultural House), with free internet access.

ights

n the train station, the rather esoteric **Goriška order Museum** (Muzej Državna Meja na Goriškem; ☎ 333 4 00; Kolodvorska ulica 8; admission free; 1-5pm Mon-i, 9am-7pm Sat, 10am-7pm Sun), which traces the tory of divided Gorica/Gorizia from 1945 to hat pivotal day in April 2004 when the walls ame a-tumblin' down, is not going to hold our attention for long. And the neo-baroque **asilica of Our Lady of the Assumption** (Bazilika Marije Venbovzete), built in 1927 on the site f a 16th-century apparition of Mary at the **ranciscan monastery** (Frančiškanski samostan; ☎ 330 40 0; www.svetagora.si; Skalniška 17) compound perched top 682m-high **Sveta Gora** (Monte Santo) 8km orth of Nova Gorica in Solkan, is not worth he trip. Frankly, you can see the church from nost of the town anyway.

The **Kostanjevica Monastery** (Samostan Kostanjevica; ☎ 330 77 50; Škrabčeva ulica 1; 9am-noon & 3-5pm Mon-at, 3-5pm Sun), on a 143m hill 800m south of the rain station, was founded by the Capuchin Franciscans in the early 17th century and has wonderful **library** (admission €1) with 10,000 volumes and 30 incunabula. The narrow, single-nave **Church of the Annunciation** (Cerkev Marijinega Oznanenja) nearby has interesting stuccos. In the spooky crypt is the **tomb of the Bourbons** (grobnica bourbonov; admission €1.50), which contains the mortal remains of the last members of the French house of Bourbon, including Charles X (1757–1836). After having been deposed in France's July Revolution of 1830, Charles when into exile, eventually find refuge with the Habsburgs in Austria. He died of cholera while on holiday on the coast in Gorizia and was buried here.

Three kilometres east of the town, fabulous **Kromberk Castle** (Grad Kromberk; Grajska ulica 1) dating from the 17th century houses the **Goriško Museum** (Goriški Muzej; ☎ 335 98 11; www.goriskimuzej.si; adult/child €2/1; 8am-7pm Mon-Fri, 1-7pm Sun Jun-Sep, 8am-3pm Mon-Fri, 1-5pm Sun). It features important archaeological, ethnological and fine-arts collections. You'll also find the fabulous Grajska Klet (p158) restaurant located here.

Activities

Top Extreme (☎ 031 620 636; www.top.si; Vojkova ulica 9) in Solkan, north of the centre, has **bungee jumping** (jump €45; 11am-4pm Sat or Sun May-Oct) from the 55m-high Solkan Bridge over the Soča. It's available at the weekend in season, but make sure you book ahead. It also organises rafting, kayaking and canyoning on the river (p149).

Ask the TIC for the pamphlet *Peš Poti na Goriškem* (Footpaths in Goriška), which outlines a dozen **hiking trails** of between 3km and 20km (1½ hours to six hours) around Nova Gorica, including Kostanjevica, Sveta Gora and Branik. Its *Kolesarimo po Novi Gorici* (Let's Cycle across Nova Gorica) map traces paths and trails for **cycling** though town and to places farther afield like Kromberk Castle.

Sleeping

Camp Lijak (☎ 308 85 57, 031 894 694; www.camplijak.com; Ozeljan 6; per person €7-8.50; mid-Mar–Oct) This 1 hectare camping ground some 4km southeast of Nova Gorica on the road to Ajdovščina has space for 100 campers and offers two mobile home for up to six tentless people for €85 to €95, depending on the season.

Dijaški Dom Nova Gorica (☎ 335 48 00; www.hostel-ng.si; Streliška pot 7; dm per person €17, s/d/tr €26/46/51; late Jun–Aug) This student dormitory at the southern end of Kidričeva ulica has 340 beds and accepts foreign guests in season only.

Prenočišče Pertout (☎ 330 75 50, 041 624 452; www.prenociscepertout.com; Ulica 25 Maja 23; s/d/tr €24/34/51; P) This five-room hostelry with singles, doubles and triples in Rožna Dolina, south of the centre, is scarcely 200m from the Italian crossing at Cassa Rossa.

Prenočišče Edvina (☎ 333 01 80, 031 885 656; prenocisca.edvina@siol.net; Vipavska cesta 134; s/d/tr €24/38/51; P) This two-room B&B is also in Rožna Dolina, a stone's throw from the more established Pertout.

HIT Hotel Sabotin (☎ 336 50 00; www.hit.si; Cesta IX Korpusa 35; s €50-81, d €76-118, tr €102-144; P) This 68-room hotel in an old baroque manor house in Solkan, about 2km north of the

PRIMORSKA

bus station, is the best-value (and most atmospheric) of the three HIT hotels in Nova Gorica. Rates depend on the season and whether you are in an old or room renovated in 2006.

HIT Hotel Casino Park (☎ 336 20 00; www.hit.si; Delpinova ulica 5; s €94-119, d 142-178; P) This flashy 82-room hotel, surrounded by lots of trees and lawn, is convenient to the bus station. Some of the rooms here have waterbeds.

HIT Hotel Casino Perla (☎ 336 30 00; www.hit.si; Kidričeva ulica 7; s €102-169, d €169-224; P) The larger and more expensive of the two central HIT hotels, the 249-room Perla is a favourite with Italians, who can't get enough of the casino. It's in a big glass and steel modern structure with a modern extension that could be anywhere – Hong Kong, Las Vegas, Disneyland.

Eating & Drinking

Both Delpinova ulica and the pedestrian walkway south of Bekov trg and opposite the shopping centre are chock-a-block with fast-food eateries and cafes. The Sabotin and Perla hotels both have several decent restaurants.

Marco Polo (☎ 302 97 29; Kidričeva ulica 13; mains €6-17; 11am-11pm Sun-Thu, 11am-midnight Fri & Sat, noon-midnight Sun) This Italian eatery with a delightful (though caged – as in behind bars) back terrace 250m east of the TIC, is one of the town's best places to eat, serving pizza (€5.60 to €7.60), pasta (€5 to €12) and more ambitious dishes.

Grajska Klet (☎ 302 71 60; Grajska ulica 1; per person from €35; noon-10pm Fri-Tue) If you've won big at the casino or just want to treat yourself, the place to go is the Castle Cellar on the ground floor of Kromberk Castle, one of the best restaurants in the region. It specialises in using fresh local produce, including Adriatic seafood and Soča trout, and will happily cater for vegetarians. Lovely terrace.

Tokio Bar (Bevkov trg 1; 8am-midnight Sun-Thu, 9am-2am Fri & Sat) This uber-decorated bar is very central and popular with students.

There's a large **Mercator** (Delpinova ulica 22; 7am-7pm Mon-Sat) in the shopping centre south of Bevkov trg. The outdoor **market** (Delpinova ulica; 7am-2pm Mon-Sat) is east of the Hotel Casino Park.

Entertainment

HIT Casino Perla (☎ 336 30 81; Kidričeva ulica 7; admissi free Mon-Fri, €5 Sat & Sun; 24hr) and **HIT Casino Pa** (☎ 336 26 38; Delpinova ulica 5; admission free Mon-F €5 Sat & Sun; 24hr) are the company store nothing makes more money in Nova Goric and it's all from the Italians across the bord who can't gamble at home. Both casinos off all the usual games – American and Frenc roulette, blackjack, several types of poker, ba carat (chemin de fer) – and there are almo 1500 slot machines between them.

Getting There & Away

BUS

From Nova Gorica you can expect buses eve two hours or so to Ljubljana (€10.70, 2½ hou 117km) via Postojna (€6.70, 1½ hours, 63km Other destinations include Bovec (€7.50, tw hours, 77km, four a day) via Kobarid (€6, 1 hours, 55km), Idrija (€6.30, 1½ hours, 60kr one or two) via Tolmin (€4.70, one hou 39km) or Ajdovščina and Piran (€10.70, thr hours, 117km, one daily at 5.30am and anoth at 7am in July and August) via Koper (€9.2 2½ hours, 99km). Daily in July and August ar at the weekend in June and September, a b crosses over the Vršič Pass to Kranjska Go (€10.70, three hours, 118km).

Nova Gorica is an easy way to get to/fro Italy; Italian bus 1 (€1) will whisk you fro Via G Caprin opposite the Nova Gorica tra station to its counterpart in Gorizia.

TRAIN

About a half-dozen trains head northeast ea day for Jesenice (€5.90, two hours, 89km) v Most na Soči, Bohinjska Bistrica (€4.90, 1 hours, 61km) and Bled Jezero (€5.50, 1 hours, 79km) on what is arguably Sloveni most beautiful train journey. In the oth direction, an equal number of trains go Sežana (€2.90, one hour, 40km), where yo can change for Ljubljana or Trieste in Italy

Nova Gorica is linked to Ajdovšči (€2.20, 40 minutes, 26km) to the southea by two trains a day (at 5.35am and 2.40pm throughout the year but on weekdays on from September to late June.

Getting Around

Local (and free of charge) buses ser Solkan, Rožna Dolina, Šempeter and Vrtoj from the main station. You can order a ta on ☎ 031 344 443 or 041 632 428.

ROUND NOVA GORICA

oriška Brda

☎ 05 / elev up to 800m

or a close look at the picture-postcard **Goriška rda**, the hilly wine region that stretches om Solkan west to the Italian border, start n **Dobrovo**, 13km to the northwest of Nova orica. The Renaissance-style **Dobrovo Castle** rad Dobrovo; ☎ 395 95 86; Grajska cesta 9; adult/child €2/1; 8am-4pm Tue-Fri, 10am-6pm Sat & Sun), dating from 606, has a dozen rooms spread over three oors filled with elegant period furnishings nd exhibits on the wine industry. In the cellar ere is a **vinoteka** (☎ 395 92 10; 11.30am-9pm e-Sun) where you can sample the local vinges (white rebula and chardonnay or the inot and merlot reds), which go nicely with e cheese, air-cured *pršut* (dry-cured ham) nd salami on offer. There's also an excellent **staurant** (☎ 395 95 06, 041 633 227; starters €5-12, mains -15; noon-11pm Tue-Sun) here. Just opposite the astle entrance is the **Tourist Information Centre rda** (☎ 395 95 94; www.brda.si; Grajska cesta 10; 8am-m Tue-Fri, 10am-6pm Sat & Sun Apr–mid-Nov).

More than 100 wineries offer tastings in oriška Brda, though you should call ahead. sually open to groups only is the enormous **inska Klet Goriška Brda** (☎ 331 01 02; www.klet-brda ; Zadružna cesta 9; tasting €10; 8am-7pm Mon-Fri, 8am-m Sat Apr–mid-Nov, 8am-5pm Mon-Fri, 8am-1pm Sat mid-v–Mar), the largest wine cellar in Slovenia., hich is just down the hill from the castle. ther highly recommended wineries within asy striking distance of Dobrovo are **Erzetič** ☎ 395 94 60; www.vina-erzetic.com; Višnjevik 25/a), km to the north, and the same distance to e northwest **Kabaj-Morel** (☎ 395 95 60; kabaj orel@email.com; Šlovrenc 4) and **Mavrič** (☎ 304 52 ; jozkomavric@siol.net; Šlovrenc 9). In addition to its rapes and wine, Goriška Brda is celebrated r its fabulous cherries usually available in arly June.

This area has been under the influence of orthern and central Italy since time immeorial, and you'll think you've crossed the order as you go through little towns with arrow streets, houses built of karst limestone nd the remains of feudal castles. One good xample is **Šmartno** (San Martino; population 20), a pretty little fortified village with stone alls and a 16th-century tower, which now ontains a **gallery** (☎ 031 715 861; Šmartno 13). Visit **rda House** (Briška Hiša; Šmartno 48; 10am-3pm Thu & , 2-6pm Sat & Sun) for an idea of what life was ke in medieval Brda.

Southeast from Nova Gorica is **Vipava Valley**, famous for its wines, especially red Teran. For details see p166.

CENTRAL PRIMORSKA

Central Primorska is a land of steep slopes, deep valleys and innumerable ravines with plenty of good hiking, the magical Idrijca River and a couple of interesting towns. The region is dominated by the Cerkno and Idrija Hills, foothills of the Julian Alps that eventually join the Škofja Loka Hills in Gorenjska to the east. It's an area often overlooked by travellers heading for the 'sexier' Alps, Karst or beaches – and is all the more attractive for that reason.

Nowhere else in Slovenia are fields found on such steep slopes and houses in such remote locations as in the regions around Idrija and Cerkno. The ravines and valleys were very useful to the Partisans during WWII, and the region is dotted with monuments testifying to their presence: the Franja hospital near Cerkno, the Slovenija Partisan printing house at Vojsko, 14km northwest of Idrija, and the Pavl hospital, 20km southeast of Idrija.

IDRIJA

☎ 05 / pop 5745 / elev 325m

When most Slovenes think of Idrija, three things spring to mind: *žlikrofi* ('ravioli' of cheese, bacon and chives), lace and mercury. The women of Idrija have been taking care of the first two for centuries, stuffing the crescent-shaped 'Slovenian ravioli' with a savoury mixture of bacon, potatoes and chives as fast as they spin their web-like lace *(čipka)*. The men, on the other hand, went underground to extract the 'quicksilver' *(živo srebro)* that made Idrija one of the richest towns in Europe in the Middle Ages.

History

The first mine opened at Idrija in 1500; within three centuries Idrija was producing 13% of the world's quality mercury. All that meant money – for both Idrija and the imperial court in Vienna. Idrija miners faced many health hazards, but the relatively high wages attracted workers from all over the Habsburg Empire And because of the toxic

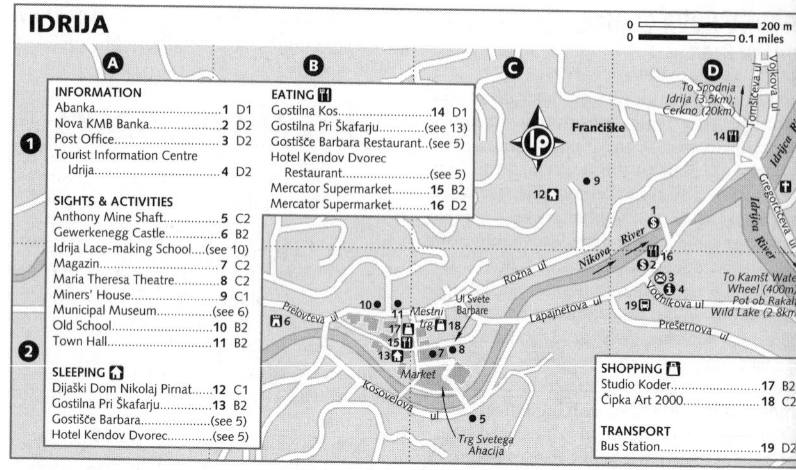

effects of mercury, doctors and lawyers flocked as well.

The mercury market bottomed out in the 1970s, and the production of this once precious element has ceased altogether in Idrija. Indeed, the European Commission has banned exports of mercury from the EU as of 2011. But the mine has left the town a difficult and expensive legacy. Idrija sits on something like 700km of shafts that go down 15 levels to 32m below sea level. The first four have now been filled with water and more have to be loaded with hard core and concrete to stabilise the place. Otherwise, they say, the town will sink.

Orientation

Idrija sits snugly in a deep basin surrounded by hills at the confluence of the Idrijca and Nikova Rivers. The centre of town is Mestni trg, but everything of a practical nature is to the southeast over the Nikova River on or just off Lapajnetova ulica, where you'll find the bus station wedged between Vodnikova ulica and Prešernova ulica.

Information

Abanka (Lapajnetova ulica 47)
Nova KBM Banka (Lapajnetova ulica 43)
Post office (Vodnikova ulica 1)
Tourist Information Centre Idrija (TIC; ☎ 374 39 16; www.idrija-turizem.si; Vodnikova ulica 3; ⏲ 9am-6pm Mon-Fri, 10am-4pm Sat & Sun Jul & Aug, 9am-4pm Mon-Fri, 10am-4pm Sep-Jun) On the 1st floor behind modern post office, with free internet access.

Sights

MUNICIPAL MUSEUM

This award-winning **museum** (Mestni Muzej; ☎ 37 66 00; www.muzej-idrija-cerkno.si; Prelovčeva ulica 9; adul child/student €3/1.70/2.50; ⏲ 9am-6pm) is housed i the enormous Gewerkenegg Castle on top o the hill to the west of Mestni trg. The collec tions, which deal with mercury, lace and loca history (but, sadly, not *žlikrofi*) are exhibite in three wings centred around a courtyard The **rococo frescoes** of plants, scrolls and col umns framing the windows and arcades dat from the 18th century.

Mercury (Hg on the periodic table) i the only metal that exists in a liquid stat at room temperature. The silvery metal i extracted from the mercury ore – a bright red mineral called cinnabar – by smelting at a high temperature. Mercury is a very heavy metal, much denser than iron, and in the castle's north wing, amid a jungle of minerals and fossils, is a large cauldron of mercury with an iron ball floating – yes, floating! – on the top.

Part of the **ethnographical collection** in this wing shows rooms in a typical miner's house at various times in history. A miner's job carried status, and they earned more than double the average wage in this part o Slovenia. The miners were well organised, and socialism was popular in the late 19th and early 20th centuries.

In the Rondel Tower of the east wing there's a mock-up of the 'call man', the unspeakable so-and-so who summoned miners

) work every day at 3.30am by hitting a hol-)w log with a mallet in the town centre. At ie bottom of the **Mercury Tower** at the start of ie south wing is a Plexiglas cube filled with rops of mercury and 15 halogen lights on acks, representing the number of levels in ie mercury mine here.

One large room in the south wing is given ver entirely to the **bobbin lace** *(klekljana čipka)* voven here in broad rings with distinctive atterns. Some 40 different motifs run the amut from the usual hearts and flowers to orseshoes, crescents and lizards. Check out he tablecloth that measures 3m by 1.80m. It vas designed for Madame Tito and took 5000 ours to make.

An exhibition on the 2nd floor of the south ving traces Idrija history in the 20th century – rom WWI and the Italian occupation to VWII and the birth of socialist Yugoslavia. 'ake a look at the enormous, bright-red ammer and sickle in the last room; it once dorned the entrance to the mercury mine.

ANTHONY MINE SHAFT

The **mine** (Antonijev Rov; ☎ 377 11 42, 031 810 194; www rzs-idrija.si; Kosovelova ulica 3; adult/child €6/4; tour 0am & 3pm Mon-Fri, 10am, 3pm & 4pm Sat & Sun), a 'liv-ng museum' in the Šelštev building south of Trg Svetega Ahacija, allows you to get a eeling for the working conditions of mer-ury miners in Idrija. The entrance is the Anthony Shaft, built in 1500, which led to he first mine: 1.5km long, 600m wide and 400m deep.

The tour, lasting about 1¼ hours, begins in the 'call room' of an 18th-century building where miners were selected each morning and assigned their duties by the *obergutman* (supervisor). There's an excellent 20-minute video in several languages (including English) describing the history of Idrija and the mine.

Before entering the shaft, which was sunk in 1500 and led to the first mine measuring 1.5km long, 600m wide and 400m deep, you must don green overcoats and helmets with the miners' insignia and wish each other '*Srečno!*' (Good luck!), the traditional miners' farewell.

As you follow the circular tour, you'll see samples of live mercury on the walls that the miners painstakingly scraped to a depth of about 5cm, as well as some cinnabar ore. The 18th-century **Chapel of the Holy Trinity** (Cerkev Sv Trojice) in the shaft contains statues of St Barbara, the patroness of miners, and St Ahacius, on whose feast day (22 June) rich deposits of cinnabar were discovered.

OTHER SIGHTS

There are several fine neoclassical buildings on Mestni trg, including the **town hall** (mestna hiša; Mestni trg 1), built in 1898. To the west of the square is the **Idrija Lace-Making School** (Čipkarska Šola Idrija; ☎ 373 45 70; Prelovčeva ulica 2; adult/student €2.50/2; 10am-1pm & 3-6pm Mon-Fri by appointment) in the Stara Šola (Old School), built in 1876. Lace-making is still a popular elective course of study in elementary schools in Idrija.

ON THE WINGS OF MERCURY

Medieval alchemists, who named mercury after the fast-footed winged messenger of the Roman gods because of its fluidity, were convinced that all metals originated from quicksilver and tried to use the metal to obtain gold from other metals. The biggest boon came in the 16th century, when it was discovered that mercury, which bonds as an alloy to many metals, could separate gold or silver from rock or ore.

Mercury was used as an early antidote to syphilis. The Venetians needed it to make their famous mirrors, and later milliners used it to lay felt for making hats. Mercury is a highly toxic substance and can affect behaviour; occupational mercurialism from vapours and absorption by the skin is a serious disorder. As a result, many milliners went crazy, and this was the inspiration for the Mad Hatter in *Alice's Adventures in Wonderland* by Lewis Carroll (1865). In modern times, mercury has been used in the drug, paper and electrical industries, in dentistry and in some detonators and bombs.

Mercury mining in Idrija came to an end both because the use of heavy metals had been largely abandoned by many industries in favour of more environmentally friendly substances and for economic reasons. A 2.5L flask (about 34kg) of mercury that went for US$800 in the 1970s was worth only US$100 a decade later.

In Trg Svetega Ahacija – the centre of town in the Middle Ages – the large 18th-century building on the north side is the **Magazin** (Trg Svetega Ahacija 4), a granary and warehouse where the miners, who were paid in food as well as in cash, kept their stores. To the east is the tiny circular **Maria Theresa Theatre** (Gledališče Marije Terezije; Trg Svetega Ahacija 5), built in 1770 and the oldest in the country.

Laid out across the slopes encircling the valley are Idrija's distinctive miners' houses. Large wooden A-frames with cladding and dozens of windows, they usually had four storeys with living quarters for three or four families. You can visit a traditional **miner's house** (Frančiška cesta; adult/child €1.70/1.30; 9am-4pm by appointment) above the centre of town accompanied by a guide from the museum.

One of the most interesting examples of mining technology that still exists is the **Kamšt** (372 66 00; Vodnikova ulica; adult/child €1.70/1.30; 9am-4pm by appointment), a 13.6m waterwheel made of wood that was used to pump the water out of flooded mines from 1790 until 1948. It is about 1.5km southeast of Mestni trg.

PRIMORSKA

Activities

An excellent 3km trail called **Pot ob Rakah** follows the Idrijca River Canal from the Kamšt (see above) to **Wild Lake** (Divje Jezero), a tiny, impossibly green lake fed by a karst spring more than 80m under the surface. After a heavy rainfall, water gushes up from the tunnel like a geyser and the lake appears to be boiling (although the surface temperature never exceeds 10°C).

The lake was declared a natural monument in 1967, and little signboards around the shore identify the plants and trees and point out the lake's unique features. The body of water flowing from Wild Lake into the Idrijca just happens to be the shortest river in Slovenia. The **Jezernica River** is a mere 47m long.

If you were to follow the canal for 15km to the southwest, you'd come to the first of the **barriers** *(klavže)* of stacked wood and stones that dammed the Idrijca and Belca Rivers to float timber in the 18th century. They were once called 'Slovenian pyramids' because of their appearance. Wood was an important resource here, both to support the 700km of mine shafts and because the heat needed to extract mercury from cinnabar required a lot of fuel. The dams continue for 12km down the Belca River. They have been declared '1 category technical monuments'.

The area of the Idrijca near the footbridg is good for **swimming** in summer, when th water averages about 20°C.

Festivals & Events

The big event in Idrija is the four-day **Lace Making Festival** (Festival Idrijske Čipke; www.idrija-turize .si) in late June, now in its third decade, whic includes a children's competition with up t a hundred taking part.

Sleeping

The TIC has a list of **private rooms** (per perso €21-30) available.

Dijaški Dom Nikolaj Pirnat (373 40 70; ww .ciu-np.si; Ulica IX Korpusa 17; dm €11-13; Jul & Au P) This student dormitory 300m north east of Mestni trg has 44 beds available i multibed rooms available in summer and limited number of doubles, triples and quad the rest of the year.

Gostilna Pri Škafarju (377 32 40, 041 698 09 www.skafar.si; Ulica Svete Barbare 9; per person €25; P) I addition to food (below), this popular *gostiln* (innlike restaurant) offers accommodatio in four smallish but well-appointed mansar rooms for between one and three people. Yo sure can't beat the location.

Gostišče Barbara (377 11 62, 041 716 701; ww .barbara-idrija.si; Kosovelova ulica 3; s/d/tr €45/55/7 P) A very centrally located place abov the Anthony Mine Shaft, this seven-room in has an excellent restaurant (opposite), wit rather limited opening hours.

Hotel Kendov Dvorec (372 51 00; www.kendo -dvorec.com; s €120-220, d €150-280, tr €177; P) I you're looking for somewhere romantic i the area, this 'castle hotel' in Spodnja Idrija 4km north of Idrija, has 11 rooms in a con verted mansion, the oldest part of which dates from the 14th century. It's fitted wit 19th-century antique furniture and enjoy stunning views along the Idrijca Valley. It restaurant (opposite) is said to be worth th journey in itself.

Eating

Gostilna Kos (372 20 30; Tomšičeva ulica 4; starters €3 7.50, mains €7-12; 7am-3pm Mon, 7am-10pm Tue-Sat Pri Škafarju does acceptable *žlikrofi*, but th best place to have this most Idrijan of spe cialities (€6 to €9.50), especially the mush room ones, is at the 'Blackbird'.

Gostišče Barbara Restaurant (Kosovelova ulica 3; ırters €4-7.10, mains €7.10-11.30; 4-10pm Mon-Fri) his restaurant in the inn of that name serves low food' and many consider it to be the est restaurant in town. There's a set menu r €12.

Gostilna Pri Škafarju (Ulica Svete Barbare 9; starters .20-7.20, mains €7.70-15.50; 11am-10pm Wed-Sun) izza (€5.20 to €7.60) baked in a beautiful ood-burning tile stove is why most people ome to this friendly *gostilna*, but there are lenty of other things on the menu such as *likrofi* (€6.90 to €11).

Hotel Kendov Dvorec (4-/7-course menu €35/70; noon-midnight) This excellent restaurant in the ery stylish Hotel Kendov Dvorec in Spodnja drija has an excellent list of Slovenian wines nd a lovely garden. Booking is essential.

There's a large **Mercator** (Lapajnetova ulica 45; 8am-7pm Mon-Fri, 8am-noon Sat) supermarket op-osite the bus station plus a smaller **Mercator** lica Svete Barbare 9; 7am-7pm Mon-Fri, 7am-noon Sat) n the heart of the old town.

hopping

drija lace is among the finest in the world, nd a small piece makes a great gift or sou-enir. There are two places almost side by ide in the main square worth a look, includ-ng **Čipka Art 2000** (372 25 73; www.comcom.si/cika ırt2000; Mestni trg 14; 9am-6pm Mon-Fri, 9am-6pm Sat Sun May-Sep, 8am-6pm Mon-Fri, 9am-noon Sat Oct-Apr), a varehouse-like place with a relatively small election of lace, and the far superior **Studio oder** (377 13 59; www.idrija-lace.si; Mestni trg 16; 10am-noon & 4-7pm Mon-Fri, 10am-noon Sat), a very stylish shop run by a helpful couple across from the town hall.

Getting There & Away

There are hourly buses to Cerkno (€3.10, 30 minutes, 21km) and Ljubljana (€6.30, 1½ hours, 53km), up to five to Tolmin (€5.60, one hour, 47km), one or two to Bovec (€9.20, 2½ hours, 99km) and one or two to Nova Gorica (€6.30, 1½ hours, 60km) via Ajdovščina.

CERKNO

05 / pop 1650 / elev 324m

Cerkno is a quiet town in the Cerknica River Valley with less than a third as many people as its neighbour 20km to the south, Idrija. Still, it has an important museum as well as the remains of a secret Partisan hospital from WWII. Just before Lent Cerkno becomes an important destinations for ethnologists and party-goers alike when the Laufarija, the ancient Shrovetide celebration (p165), takes place. And it is near Cerkno that what is thought to be the oldest known musical instrument on earth (below) was discovered in 1995.

Orientation & Information

Glavni trg, where the buses stop, is the main square and the centre of Cerkno.

Nova KMB Banka (Glavni trg 5)

Post office (Bevkova ulica 9) In the *občina hiša* (council house) diagonally opposite Cerkno Museum.

STONE AGE MUSIC

The image of our Neanderthal ancestors sitting around a campfire making beautiful music together is not an easy one to conjure up. But it's whole lot easier now following a major discovery made in a mountain cave near Cerkno.

Palaeontologists were messing around in the area in 1995 collecting Stone Age tools when a local pundit who happened to pass by told them he knew where they'd find lots more like that. He led them to Divje Babe, a cave some 200m above the main road linking Cerkno with the Tolmin–Idrija highway, and they began digging. Among the buried tools was a piece of cave bear femur measuring 10cm long and perforated with four aligned holes – two intact and two incomplete at either end. It looked exactly like, well, a flute.

Because objects of such antiquity cannot be dated by the usual radiocarbon techniques, the flute was sent to the City University of New York to undergo electron spin resonance, which measures the small amounts of radiation absorbed by objects from the time of their burial. And the verdict? According to researchers, the flute is anywhere between 45,000 and 82,000 years old, depending on how much moisture – which inhibits the absorption of radiation – the cave floor has been exposed to. One thing is certain, however: Slovenia can now claim the oldest known musical instrument on earth. And – just in case you were wondering – the flute still works.

Tourist Information Centre Cerkno (TIC; ☎ 373 46 45; www.cerkno.si/turizem; Močnikova ulica 2; 8am-4pm Mon-Fri, 8am-1pm Sat, 8am-noon Sun) Faces Glavni trg to the east, with free internet access.

Sights

CERKNO MUSEUM

The **museum** (Cerkljanski Muzej; ☎ 372 31 80; www.muzej-idrija-cerkno.si; Bevkova ulica 12; adult/child €2.10/1.30; 9am-3pm Mon-Fri, 10am-1pm & 2-6pm Sat & Sun) is about 150m southwest of Glavni trg. The permanent exhibit called 'Cerkljanska through the Centuries' traces the development of the region from earliest times up to the end of the 20th century. Most people, however, come to see the museum's collection of Laufarija masks contained in the exhibit 'The Pust Is to Blame' (see below).

FRANJA PARTISAN HOSPITAL

This **hospital** (Partizanska Bolnišnica Franja; ☎ 372 31 80; www.muzej-idrija-cerkno.si), hidden in a canyon near Dolenji Novaki about 5km northeast of Cerkno, treated wounded Partisan soldiers from Yugoslavia and other countries from late 1943 until the end of WWII. It was hit by a devastating flood in 2007 and should now have reopened after extensive rebuilding.

Franja Hospital has nothing to do wit political or economic systems; it is a me morial to humanity, courage and sel sacrifice. It is named after its chief phys cian, Dr Franja Bojc-Bidovec, and was bu in December 1943 for the needs of IX Corp which accounted for 10,000 soldiers. By Ma 1945 it had more than a dozen buildings, ir cluding treatment sheds, operating theatre X-ray rooms and bunkers for convalescenc More than 500 wounded were treated her and the mortality rate was only about 10%

The complex, hidden in a ravine by th Pasica Stream with steep walls riddled wit caves and recently shored up, had an abun dance of fresh water, which was also used t power a hydroelectric generator. Local farm ers and Partisan groups provided food, whic was lowered down the steep cliffs by rop medical supplies were diverted from hospi tals in occupied areas or later air-droppe by the Allies. The hospital came under at tack by the Germans twice – once in Apri 1944 and again in March 1945 – but it wa never taken.

DIVJE BABE ARCHAEOLOGICAL PARK

This **park** (Arheološki Park Divje Babe; ☎ 373 46 45; ww .cerkno.si/turizem; admission €10; 9am-5pm Apr-Sep b

PRIMORSKA

THE LAUFARIJA TRADITION

Ethnologists believe that the Laufarija tradition and its distinctive masks came from Austria's South Tyrol hundreds of years ago. *Lauferei* means 'running about' in German, and that's just what participants do as they nab their victim. The masks with the crazy, distorted faces on display here are originals bought from one of the Laufarji clubs.

Groups of boys and young men (and now a few girls and women) belonging to Laufarji societies (not unlike the Mardi Gras krewes in New Orleans) organise the event every year and about two dozen perform. Those aged 15 and over are allowed to enter, but they must prove themselves as worthy apprentices by sewing costumes. These outfits – though not ornate – must be made fresh every year because many of them are made out of leaves, pine branches, straw or moss stitched onto a burlap (hessian) backing and take quite a beating during the festivities.

The action takes place on the Sunday before Ash Wednesday and again on Shrove Tuesday (Pustni Torek). The main character is the Pust, whose mask is horned and who wears a moss costume weighing up to 100kg. He's the symbol of winter and the old year – and he *must* die.

The Pust is charged by people with a long list of grievances – a bad harvest, inclement weather, lousy roads – and, of course, is found guilty. Some of the other two dozen Laufarji characters represent crafts and trades – the Baker, the Thatcher, the Woodsman – while the rest have certain character traits or afflictions such as the Drunk and his Wife, the Bad Boy, Sneezy and the Sick Man, who always plays the accordion. The Old Man wearing Slovenian-style lederhosen and a wide-brimmed hat executes the Pust with a wooden mallet, and the body is rolled away on a caisson.

If you don't get a chance to come to Cerkno for Mardi Gras to see the famous show, you'll have to be content with looking at the masks in the Cerkno Museum (above).

pointment), at the site of the cave some 200m p in the Cerkno Hill 16km southwest of erkno where the Stone Age flute (p163) was ound, can now be visited with a guide from he TIC. Truth be told, there's not a whole ot to see here. But it's a peaceful, very idyllic pot, and was once – apparently – where our ncestors partied.

ctivities

'he English-language *Cerkno Map of Local Valks*, available from the TIC and the Hotel Cerkno, lists eight walks in the Cerkno Hills Cerkljansko Hribovje), most of them pretty asy and lasting between 1½ and five hours eturn. Walk No 7 goes to the **Franja Partisan Iospital** (3½ hours) and back. The highest eak in the area is **Porezen** (1632m) to the ortheast, which has a category II mountain ut called **Dom Andreja Žvana-Borisa na Poreznu** (☎ 051 615 245, 031 874 091; daily Jul–mid-Sep, at & Sun May, Jun & Oct) at 1590m with 66 beds nd berths.

The **Cerkno Ski Centre** (☎ 374 34 00; www ski-cerkno.com; day pass adult/child/senior/student 28/18/20/25.50), 10km northeast of Cerkno, s atop Črni Vrh (1291m) and covers 18km f ski slopes and 5km of trails. There are ix chairlifts and two tows and cannons for naking artificial snow. Many people say this s their favourite ski centre in Slovenia due o the ease of access and relatively short lift nd tow queues.

Festivals & Events

aufarija (www.laufarija-cerkno.si) the biggest annual event in these parts, unfolds in late February/early March in Glavni trg. For the background see the boxed text, opposite.

Sleeping & Eating

Gačnk v Logu (☎ 372 40 05, 041 753 524; www.cerkno com; per person €27-29) This B&B and restaurant in Dolenji Novaki (house No 1), not far from the Franja Partisan Hospital, has 10 rooms with between two and four beds. The restaurant (open 9am to 11pm) is very popular with local people, particularly for lunch at the weekend.

Želinc farmhouse (☎ 372 40 20, 374 40 98; www zelinc.com; Straža 8; s €30-37, d €52-64; P) This very ecofriendly farmhouse with 15 singles and doubles and two apartments for three is near Straža, 5km southwest of Cerkno on route No 102 to Idrija.

Hotel Cerkno (☎ 374 34 00; www.hotel-cerkno.si; Sedejev trg 8; s €52-59, d €76-92; P) This 75-room partially renovated hotel is in a modern building just south of Glavni trg. It's a comfortable enough place with a large indoor pool (nonresident adult/child €5.70/4.70), sauna, gym and three clay tennis courts (per hour €3).

Okrepčevalnica Pr' Padkejc (☎ 377 57 54; Platiševa ulica 70; dishes €6.50-12; 7.30am-10pm Mon-Thu, 7.30am-midnight Fri, 8am-1am Sat, 7am-mignight Sun) Unduly humble this 'snack bar' is actually more like a comfortable *gostilna* about 800m north of the centre. It's famed for its cold cuts and other prepared meets like *pršut* (air-dried ham) and horsemeat sausages.

There's a **Mercator** (Sedejev trg 8; 8am-7pm Mon-Fri, 7am-noon Sat, 8-11am Sun) supermarket next to the Hotel Cerkno.

Getting There & Away

There are hourly bus departures to Idrija (€3.10, 30 minutes, 21km) on weekdays, with between four and five at the weekend, up to four a day to Ljubljana (€7.50, 1¾ hours, 77km) and one or two to Bovec (€7.20, 1¾ hours, 74km) via Most na Soči, Tolmin and Kobarid. Another four (two on Saturday, one on Sunday) go just to Tolmin (€4.70, 50 minutes, 36km), where you can change for Nova Gorica and the coast.

KARST REGION

The Karst region (www.kras-carso.com) is a limestone plateau stretching from Nova Gorica southeast to the Croatian border, west to the Gulf of Trieste and east to the Vipava Valley. Because it was the first such area to be researched and described in the 19th century, it is called the Classic, Real, True or Original Karst and always written with an upper-case 'K'. Other karst areas (from the Slovene word *kras*) around the world only get a lower-case 'k'.

Rivers, ponds and lakes can disappear and then resurface in the Karst's porous limestone through sinkholes and funnels. Some rivers have created large underground caverns like the caves at Škocjan. Calcium carbonate in the water dripping from the roofs of caves creates stalactites (the ones that hang down) and stalagmites (the ones that shoot up). When these underground caverns collapse – and they do periodically – they form a depression *(polje)* that collects soil (mostly red clay, the *terra rossa* of the Karst) and then vegetation. These fertile hollows are cultivated by local farmers, but because of the proximity of underground rivers, they tend to flood quickly after heavy rain.

The Karst, with its olives, ruby-red Teran wine, *pršut*, old stone churches and red-tiled roofs, is some people's favourite region of Slovenia. But although the weather is very pleasant for most of the year, with lots of sun and low humidity, don't be fooled into thinking it's paradise. The bora *(burja)*, a fiercely cold northeast wind from the Adriatic, can do a lot of damage in winter, ripping off roofs, uprooting trees and blowing away topsoil. It does give the *pršut* its distinctive taste, though.

VIPAVA VALLEY

05 / elev up to 180m

This wide and fertile valley stretches southeast from Nova Gorica into the Karst. Some of the red wines produced here are world class, and Vipava merlot is among the best wines of Central Europe. It's an excellent place to tour by car or bike; ask the TIC in Nova Gorica for the brochure *Wine Road of the Lower Vipava Valley*. The valley's mild climate also encourages the cultivation of stone fruits such as peaches and apricots and in autumn, when the red sumac changes colour, the valley can look like it is in flames.

The Vipava Valley is where the Romans first launched their drive into the Danube region, and it was overrun by the Goths, Huns and Langobards from the 4th to 6th centuries before the arrival of the early Slavs. Along the way though the valley, about 22km southeast of Nova Gorica, is **Vipavski Križ** (Santa Croce), a walled medieval village atop a hill with a ruined castle, a Gothic church and a 17th-century monastery containing some wonderful illuminated medieval manuscripts.

Another 4km to the west is **Ajdovščina** (Aidussina). This was the site of Castra ad Fluvium Frigidum, a Roman fort on the River Frigidus (Vipava) and the first important station on the road from Aquileia to Emona (Ljubljana).

The town of **Vipava**, in the centre of the valley some 33km southeast of Nova Gorica, is full of stone churches below **Mt Nanos**, a karst plateau from which the Vipava River spring Be sure to make a side trip 2km north t Dornbeck and **Zemono Manor** (Dvorec Zemono; ww .zemono.si; Prešernova ulica 6), a summer mansio built in 1680 by one of the Counts of Goric as a hunting lodge; the main hall is covered i wonderful frescoes. Today the mansion, bui in the shape of a cross inside a square wit arcaded hallways and a raised central are houses the **Gostilna Pri Lojzetu** (☎ 368 70 07, 040 7 726; starters €7-13, mains €18-27, 2-/3-course menus €20/4 ⌚ 5-10pm Wed & Thu, noon-10pm Fri-Sun), a luxuriou restaurant in the manor's wine cellar. Have peek at the baroque murals near the entranc they portray a phoenix and a subterranea cave, symbols of fire and water. In Vipava winery worth visiting is **Vipava 1894** (☎ 367 1 00; www.vipava1894.si; Vinarska cesta 5), the largest i the valley.

In **Branik**, look up for a glimpse of **Rihembe Castle** (Cesta IX Korpusa 46), which dates back t the 13th century and has a dominant cy lindrical tower in the centre at Branik bu is not open to the public. Some 6km to th southeast is the walled village of **Štanjel,** wit its own castle containing a restaurant and gallery and magnificent Ferrari Gardens t the north and, just west of the centre, th **Tourist Information Centre Štanjel** (TIC; ☎ 769 0 56, 041 383 986; tic.stanjel@komen.si; ⌚ 10am-6pm Tue Sat, 2-5pm Sun May-Oct, 10am-4pm Tue-Sat Nov-Apr) bu the areas with the most to see and do are t the south.

About 10km southwest of Štanjel an 12.5km northwest of Sežana is the fabulou **our pick Mladinski Hotel Pliskovica** (☎ 764 02 50; 04 947 327; www.hostelkras.com; Pliskovica 11; dm €14-16, €36; 💻), a hostel with six rooms and 45 bed purpose-built into a 400-year-old Karst house It has a kitchen, laundry room, free use o bicycles and is open year-round.

Getting There & Away

Buses departing from Nova Gorica fo Postojna every two hours or so pass through Ajdovščina (€3.60, 40 minutes, 27km) and Vipava (€4.10, 50 minutes, 34km). Three buses a day at 10.40am, 2.18pm and 3.30pm link Sežana (€2.70, 30 minutes, 18km) with the hostel at Pliskovica.

Trains between Nova Gorica and Sežana serve Štanjel (€2.20, 40 minutes, 24km) and Dutovlje (€2.90, 50 minutes, 31km), 4.5km east of Pliskovica, six times a day on weekdays and twice at the weekend.

KOCJAN CAVES

05 / elev 424m

he immense system of karst caves at Škocjan, Unesco World Heritage site since 1986, are ar more captivating than the larger one at ostojna, 33km to the northeast in Notranjska, nd for many travellers, a visit here will be a ighlight of their trip to Slovenia – a page ight out of Jules Verne's *A Journey to the entre of the Earth.*

The Škocjan Caves (Škocjanske Jame), .8km long and 250m deep, were carved out y the Reka River, which originates in the oothills of Snežnik, a 1796m mountain to the outheast. The Reka enters the caves in a gorge elow the village of Škocjan and eventually ows into the Dead Lake, a sump at the end of he cave where it disappears. It surfaces again – his time as the Timavo River – at Duino in taly, 40km to the northwest, before emptying nto the Gulf of Trieste.

Unesco included the surrounding 401 ectare **Škocjan Caves Regional Park** (Regijski Park kocjanske Jame; 708 21 00; www.park-skocjanske-jame si; Škocjan 2) in its World Heritage Sites list in 996. Today, visitors can explore about 3km of these spectacular caves.

Orientation

The caves are situated approximately 1.5km east of the main Ljubljana–Koper highway. The closest town of any size is Divača (population 1325), about 5km to the northwest. Divača's train station, where buses also stop, is at Trg 15 Aprila 7, about 500m west of this highway.

Information

Banka Koper (Kolodvorska ulica 2/a) In Divača just west of the petrol station.

Post office (Kraška cesta 77; 8-9.30am, 10am-3.30pm, 4-6pm Mon-Fri, 8am-noon Sat) In Divača opposite the petrol station.

Sights

ŠKOCJAN CAVES

Visiting the **caves** (708 21 10; www.park-skocjanske-jame.si; Škocjan 2; adult/child/senior & student €14/6/10; tours hourly 10am-5pm Jun-Sep 10am, 1pm & 3.30pm Apr, May & Oct 10am & 1pm Mon-Sat, 10am, 1pm & 3pm Sun Nov-Mar) involves a shepherded 1½- to two-hour walking tour that includes hundreds of steps. It usually ends with ride on a funicular-like lift but on our last visit this was under reconstruction.

The **ticket office** (9am-last tour) and the shop opposite sell all kinds of literature, including the 1:6000 *Regijski Park Škocjanske Jame* (Škocjan Caves Regional Park; €3.50) map and *The Škocjan Caves* (€4.50) guide. If you have time before your tour, follow the path leading north and down some steps from the reception area for 200m to the lookout (signposted 'Razgledišče/Belvedere'). Extending before you is a superb vista of the Velika Dolina (Big Valley) and the gorge where the Reka starts its subterranean journey.

Visitors to the caves walk with the guide (or guides) from the ticket office for about 500m down a gravel path to the main entrance in the Globočak Valley. There visitors will be separated into groups according to language spoken. Through a 116m-long tunnel built in 1933, you soon reach the head of the so-called **Silent Cave** (Tiha Jama), a dry branch of the underground canyon that stretches for 500m. The first section, called **Paradise**, is filled with beautiful stalactites (the best in Slovenia) stalagmites and flow stones that look like snow drifts; the second part (called **Calvary**) was once the river bed. The Silent Cave ends at the **Great Hall** (Velika Dvorana), 120m wide and 30m high. It is a jungle of exotic dripstones and deposits; keep an eye out for the mighty stalagmites called the Giants (Orjaki) and the Organ (Orgle).

The sound of the Reka River, as it rushes through cascades and whirlpools below, heralds your entry into the **Murmuring Cave** (Šumeča Jama), with walls 100m high. To get over the Reka and into **Müller Hall**, where the so-called 'tourist walkway' dating back to the 19th century is now protected, and long, narrow **Svetina Hall**, you must cross **Cerkevnik Bridge,** some 45m high and surely the highlight of the trip. Only experienced speleologists are allowed to explore the 5km of caves and halls that extend to the northwest of the bridge ending at Dead Lake (Mrtvo Jezero).

From Svetina Hall you climb up a path hewn into the stone to **Bowls Hall** (Dvorana Ponvic), remarkable for its rare bowl-like potholes that were formed when water flooding the cave churned and swirled up to the ceiling. They look like troughs or even rice terraces.

Schmidl Hall, the final section, emerges into the Velika Dolina. From here you walk past **Tominč Cave**, where finds from a prehistoric settlement have been unearthed, and over a walkway near the **Natural Bridge**. Until the lift, which carries you 90m up the rock face, reopens you follow a marked trail up some 400 steps to the ticket office and reception area.

You might be surprised to learn that the Škocjan Caves are home to an incredible amount of flora and fauna: 250 varieties of plants and 15 different types of bats; your guide will point out mounds of bat guano. The temperature in the caves is constant at 12°C so you should bring along a light jacket or sweater. Good walking shoes (the path can get pretty wet and slippery in the high humidity) are recommended.

OTHER CAVES

The 803m-long **Vilenica Cave** (Jama Vilenica; ☎ 734 42 59, 051 648 711; www.vilenica.com; adult/child €5/3.35; 10am, 3pm & 5pm Sun May-Sep, 3pm Sun Oct-Apr) is 2km northwest of Lokev, halfway between Divača and Lipica. It was the first karst cave to open to the public in the early 19th century and still welcomes guests every Sunday year-round.

Divača Cave (Divaška Jama; ☎ 031 522 785, 041 498 103; www.divaska-jama.info; adult/child €5/3.35; 3pm Sun May-Oct), about 3km northeast on the road to Divača, is only 672m long but has excellent dripstones and rock formations.

Sleeping & Eating

our pick Pr' Vncki Tamara (☎ 763 30 73, 040 697 827; pr.vnck.tamarai@gmail.com; Matavun 10; per person €23-26) This welcoming spot in Matavun is just steps south of the entrance to the caves and as close as you are going to get. It has four traditionally styled rooms with a total of 10 beds in a charming old farmhouse. We love the old kitchen with the open fire.

Gostilna Malovec (☎ 763 12 25; www.sloveniaholidays.com/malovec; Kraška cesta 30/a; s/d/tr €25/40/60) The Malovec, in Divača, has a half-dozen basic, but comfortable, renovated rooms in a building beside its butcher's (!) and popular restaurant (starters €3 to €6, mains €5 to €15, open 8am to 10pm daily), which serves Slovenian favourites (including first-rate *gibanica* – a rich dessert) to an appreciative crowd.

Gostilna Pri Jami (☎ 763 29 61, 051 360 604; Matavun 12; starters €4-5.80, mains €5.70-12; 9am-8pm) By the Caves is just that – a restaurant next to the ticket office to the caves. Filling, predictable food – but the only game near the caves.

Orient Express (☎ 763 30 10, 041 616 868; Kraška cesta 67; starters €2.50-6, pizza €5-14, grills €7.20-9.50; 11am-11pm Sun-Fri, 11am-2am Sat) For somethin a bit more, well, 21st century, cross the roa from the Malovec for this large and livel pizzeria and pub with great salads (€2.90 t €4.20) and a large back terrace.

There's a large **Tuš** (Kolodvorska ulica 2; 7am-8pr Mon-Fri, 7am-5pm Sat, 7.30am-noon Sun) supermarke near the Banka Koper in Divača and a muc smaller **Fama** (Kraška cesta 32; 7am-7pm Mon-Sat, 8 11am Sun) supermarket near Gostilna Malovec

Getting There & Around

Buses from Ljubljana to Koper and the coas stop at Divača (€7.90, 1½ hours, 82km, half hourly). Other destinations include Sežan (€2.70, 20 minutes, 16, up to six a day) Postojna (€3.60, 30 minutes, 28km) an Murska Sobota (€23.20, six hours, 280km via Maribor and Celje. For Croatia, there ar buses to Poreč and Rovinj (€14.40, four hours 169km) at 3.08pm from June to September.

Divača is on the rail line linking Ljubljan (€6.50, 1½ hours, 104km, hourly) wit Sežana (€2.60, 10 minutes, 9km). Around 1 trains a day run in each direction. Divača i also the railhead for up to five trains a da to Koper (€3.60 to €7, 50 minutes, 49km via Hrpelje-Kozina.

The Škocjan Caves are about 5km by road southeast of the Divača train station. Staf at the train station ticket office will provide you with a photocopied route map for walking to the caves, and there's a copy posted outside. Alternatively, a courtesy van meets incoming trains at 10am, 11.04am, 2pm and 3.35pm, arriving at the caves about 12 minutes later. Anyone with a bus or train tickets can ride free.

LIPICA

☎ 05 / pop 100 / elev 403m

The impact of Lipica, some 9km southwest of Divača and 2km from the Italian border, on the world of sport has been far greater than its tiny size would suggest. This tiny village lives for and on and through one commodity only: horseflesh. In this case, it's the snow-white beauties called Lipizzaners, which were first bred here for the Spanish Riding School in Vienna in the late 16th century.

Although very much part of the region, Lipica feels like Eden after all that limestone. Indeed, the word '*lipica*' in Slovene means 'little linden', after the trees that grow in such abundance here.

istory

1 1580 Austrian Archduke Charles, son f Ferdinand I, founded a stud farm here) breed and train horses for the imperial ourt in Vienna. He was looking for a lighter, ıore elegant breed for parades and military urposes (which would later lead to the de-elopment of dressage). Andalusian horses om Spain were coupled with the local Karst reed that the Romans had once used to pull hariots – and the Lipizzaner was born. But ıey weren't quite the sparkling white beauties e know today. Those didn't come about for nother 200 years when white Arabian horses ot into the act.

The stud farm remained the property of he court in Vienna until the end of WWI vhen the Italians took control of Primorska nd the horses were moved to Hungary and hen Austria. In 1943, with WWII still raging, he Germans moved more than 200 horses to he Sudetenland in Bohemia (now the Czech Republic). When the area was liberated by American forces in 1945, most of the horses nd the stud farm's archives were shipped off o Italy. Sadly, only 11 horses returned when perations resumed at Lipica in 1947.

Today some 400 Lipizzaners remain at the riginal stud farm while Lipizzaners are also red in various locations around the world, including Piber, northeast of Graz in Austria, which breeds the horses for the Spanish Riding School. And of course everyone claims theirs is the genuine article. Indeed, in a bid to get its case across, Slovenia has a pair of Lipizzaners on the reverse side of its €0.20 coin.

Orientation & Information

The centre of everything in Lipica is the stud farm in the southwest corner of the village. You might try to elicit information from here but it's hard to imagine any place less helpful in all of Slovenia than this. Instead, try the front desk at either of the hotels nearby. You'll find an ATM at the Hotel Maestoso.

Sights

LIPICA STUD FARM

The 311-hectare **stud farm** (Kobilarna Lipica; ☎ 739 15 80; www.lipica.org; Lipica 5; 🕑 8.15am-6pm) can be visited on a **guided tour** (adult €9-10, child & student €4.50-5; 🕑 hourly 9-11am & 1-6pm daily Jul & Aug 9-11am & 1-5pm Mon-Fri, 9-11am & 1-6pm Sat & Sun Apr-Jun, Sep & Oct 10am, 11am & hourly 1-3pm Mon-Fri, 10am, 11am & hourly 1-4pm Sat & Sun Mar, 10am, 11am & hourly 1-3pm daily Nov-Feb). The tours begin opposite the information and ticket office; a visit covers the stables (the one called Velbanca dates back to 1703) and the riding halls to give you an idea of what

PRIMORSKA

DANCING HORSES OF LIPICA

Lipizzaners are the finest riding horses in the world, much sought after for *haute école* dressage. And with all the trouble that's put into producing them, it's not surprising. They are very intelligent, sociable horses, quite robust and graceful.

Breeding is paramount and it is carried out with all the precision of a well-organised crime. Just four equine families with 16 ancestors can be traced back to the early 18th century (another two lines date to the early 19th century), and their pedigrees read like those of medieval royalty. When you walk around the stables at Lipica you'll see charts on each horse stall with complicated figures, dates and names like 'Conversano' and 'Neapolitano'. It's all to do with the horse's lineage.

Lipizzaners foal between January and May, and the colts and fillies suckle for six or seven months. They remain in the herd for about three years. They are then separated for training, which takes another four years.

Lipizzaners are not white when they are born but grey, bay or even chestnut. The celebrated 'imperial white' does not come about until they are between five and 10 years old, when their hair loses its pigment. Their skin remains grey, however, so when they are ridden hard enough to sweat, they become mottled.

A fully mature Lipizzaner measures about 15 hands (about 153cm) and weighs between 500kg and 600kg. They have long backs, short, thick necks, silky manes and expressive eyes. They live for 25 to 30 years and are particularly resistant to disease. Like most horses they are somewhat short-sighted (near-sighted) and they will nuzzle you out of curiosity if you approach them while they graze.

it's like to learn dressage and control a very large animal.

The highlight of a visit (if you time it right) is the **exhibition performance** (adult €16-17, child & student €8-8.50 incl stud farm tour; 3pm Tue, Fri & Sun Apr-Oct) of these elegant horses as they go through their complicated paces with riders *en costume*. It's not as complete a show as the one at the Spanish Riding School in Vienna or in such ornate surroundings, but watching great white horses pirouetting and dancing to Viennese waltzes sort of makes up for it. You can also attend the more frequent **training performance** (adult €9-10, child & student €4.50-5 incl stud farm tour; 10am-noon Tue-Sun Apr-Oct).

If you miss the performances, try to be around when the horses are moved from the stables to pasture (usually between 9am and 10am) and again in the afternoon (around 5.30pm to 6pm).

PRIMORSKA

Activities

The only way you are going to get on a Lipizzaner at Lipica these days is to sign up for a **riding course**. These range from a week-long course for absolute beginners of six 30-minute lessons (€195) to a dressage program (12 lessons, €3600) for advanced riders. You can also have a jaunt in a horse-drawn, four-person **carriage** (30/60 min €20/40; 10am-2pm & 4-6pm Tue-Sun Apr-Oct).

The **Lipica Golf Course** (739 17 24; www.lipica.org; 9-/18-holes Mon-Fri €23/30, Sat & Sun €28/38, half-set clubs €10) behind the Maestoso has nine holes for a par 36, a driving range (€3) and a couple of putting greens. It's the only links in Slovenia open all year.

Near the Hotel Maestoso are five **tennis courts** (739 17 24; per hr €4-8, racquet €5) available for hire.

Nonguests can use the **swimming pool** (adult/child & student €6/4.20, with sauna for all €13) at the Hotel Maestoso.

Sleeping & Eating

There are just two hotels in Lipica, both managed by the **Lipica Stud Farm** (739 15 80; www.lipica.org). Rates depend on the season and are heavily discounted for stays of a week or more if you are taking a riding course. Note that there are no addresses as such in Lipica.

Hotel Klub (739 15 50; s/d from €32/49; P) The 75-roomer is generally for those staying for longer periods. It has a sauna and fitness centre and is slightly closer to the stud farm than the Maestoso.

Hotel Maestoso (739 17 90; s/d €80/120, ste for €165; P) This 65-room hotel has most of the amenities, including an indoor swimming pool, a sauna and nearby tennis courts.

Letni Vrt (739 15 80; dishes €5-15.50; 11am-7pm Apr-Oct) The Summer Garden is an open-air cafe with terrace east of the Maestoso serving simple meals and Balkan grills. It is open in the warmer months only.

Maestoso (starters €6-9.60, mains €7-17.50; 7am-10pm) This cafe-restaurant with a terrace is the better of the two places to eat in Lipica and is open year-round.

Getting There & Around

Most people visit Lipica as a day trip from Sežana, 4km to the north, or Divača, 13km to the northeast, both of which are on the Ljubljana–Koper rail line. There is no public transport from the train stations in Sežana and Divača to Lipica; a taxi from either will cost between €1 and €20. Bicycles are available for hire from the fitness centre at the Hotel Klub for €5/10/14 per hour/three hours/day.

HRASTOVLJE

05 / pop 145 / elev 164m

The Romanesque church in this tiny Karst village is the Istrian equivalent of St John the Baptist's Church in Bohinj. OK, so it's not on a lake. But it is small, surrounded by medieval walls with corner towers and covered inside with extraordinary 15th-century frescoes. This is the reason to make the trip here – as difficult as it can be.

Hrastovlje lies near the source of the Rižana River, whose valley effectively forms the boundary between the Karst and the coast. From here northward to the village of Črni Kal and on to Osp, a row of fortresses were built below the limestone plains during the Bronze Age, which the Illyrian tribe of Histrians later adapted to their needs. The valley and surrounding areas would prove to be safe havens for later inhabitants during the Great Migrations and the Turkish invasions.

Sights

The **Church of the Holy Trinity** (Cerkev Sv Trojica; 031 432 231; adult/student & child €2/1; 8am-noon & 1-5pm), which has a nave and two aisles, was built between the 12th and 14th centuries

the southern Romanesque style. The for-
fications were added in 1581 in advance of
e Ottomans.

The sombre exterior does not prepare
ou for what's inside. The interior of the
urch is completely festooned with **narra-
e frescoes** painted by Johannes de Castuo
ohn of Kastav) in around 1490. The paint-
gs are a *Biblia pauperum* – a 'Bible of the
oor' – to help the illiterate understand the
ld Testament stories, the Passion of Christ
d the lives of the saints. It is a unique and
ue way to see and understand how our
cestors viewed their lives, joys, hopes and
fferings some five centuries ago. Spare
e 20 minutes it takes to listen to the taped
mmentary (in four languages, including
nglish) that will guide you around the
tle church.

Facing you as you enter the church is
e main altar, carved in the 17th century,
d the central apse with scenes from the
rucifixion on the ceiling and portraits of
e Trinity and the Apostles. On the arch,
ary is being crowned Queen of Heaven.
o the right of the central aisle are episodes
om the seven days of Creation, and to
e left is the story of Adam and Eve, as
ell as the murder of Abel by Cain and
e latter's banishment – all easy stories
r an unlettered 15th-century peasant
comprehend.

On the ceilings of the north (left) and south
ight) aisles are scenes from daily life (sow-
g, hunting, fishing, making wine etc) as well
the liturgical year and its seasonal duties.
hrist's Passion is depicted at the top of the
uthernmost wall, including his descent
to hell, where devils are attacking him with
azing cannons.

Below the scenes of the Passion is what
tracts most people to this little church:
e famous **Dance of Death** (Mrtvaški Ples),
Danse Macabre, a fresco that shows 11
eletons leading the same number of people
rward to a freshly dug grave, a pick and
ovel at the ready. A twelfth skeleton is
olding open the lid of a coffin. The doomed
ne-up includes a child, a cripple, a young
an, a moneylender (who is attempting
bribe his skeletal escort with a purse), a
erchant, a monk, a bishop, a cardinal, a
ueen, a king and a pope. On the cardinal's
ssock you can still see graffiti left by a
sitor in 1640.

Ghoulish and strange though the Dance of Death may appear to be at first, it carries a simple message: we are all equal in the eyes of God no matter how important we (or others) think we are in this mortal life. Wake up and smell the coffee.

Getting There & Away

Hrastovlje is 24km southwest of Divača off the main highway to the coast; Koper is 18km to the northwest. Any bus travelling this road in either direction will drop you off just west of Črni Kal, where a massive flyover has cut travel time to the coast substantially, but it's still another 8km south to Hrastovlje. Without a car or bicycle the only sure way of making it to Hrastovlje is by a single daily train.

A train leaves Divača (€2.90) at 6.15am daily, arriving at Hrastovlje station at 6.48am; the church is about 1km to the northwest. The next train of any kind through this backwater is the 1.46pm from Monday to Friday from Koper (€1.60, 20 minutes, 18km), which then carries on to Divača, Postojna and Ljubljana, arriving there at 4.35pm. There's a daily train from Koper at 7.27pm that follows the same route.

THE COAST

Slovenia's very short coast (47km) on the Adriatic Sea (Jadransko Morje) is an area of both history and recreation. Three seaside towns – Koper, Piran and Izola – are full of important Venetian Gothic architecture and art, and there are clean beaches, boats for rent and rollicking clubs.

But the Slovenian coast is not everybody's cup of tea. It is overbuilt, jammed from May to September and the water is not especially inviting, though there are some decent beaches at Portorož. Many Slovenes give it a miss in favour of the unspoiled beaches of Istria or Dalmatia. If you want solitude, head for the hinterland to the south or east where 'Slovenian Istria' still goes about its daily life.

Many of the hotels, camping grounds, tourist offices and restaurants here close or severely curtail their opening times during the off-season, which is from November to March or April.

KOPER

☎ 05 / pop 24,725 / elev 11m

Coastal Slovenia's largest town, Koper (Capodistria in Italian) at first glance appears to be a workaday port city that scarcely gives tourism a second thought. Yet its central core is delightfully medieval and far less overrun than its ritzy cousin Piran, 17km down the coast. Its recreational area, the seaside resort of Ankaran, is to the north across Koper Bay.

History

Koper has been known by many names during its long and turbulent history. As an island separated from the mainland by a canal, it was called Aegida by ancient Greek sailors, Capris by the Romans (who found it being used to raise goats) and Justinopolis by the Byzantines. The Patriarchs of Aquileia (p29), who took over the town in the 13th century and made it the base for their estates on the Istrian peninsula, renamed it Caput Histriae – Capital of Istria – from which its Italian name Capodistria is derived. They fortified the town and erected some of Koper's most beautiful buildings, including its cathedral and palaces.

Koper's golden age arrived during the 15th and 16th centuries under the Venetian Republic. Trade increased and Koper became the administrative and judicial centre for much of Istria. It also had a monopoly on salt, which Austria desperately needed. But when Trieste, 20km to the northeast, was proclaimed a free port in the early 18th century, Koper then lost much of its importance.

Between the World Wars Koper was controlled by the Italians, who launched a program of Italianisation. After the defeat of Italy and Germany in WWII the disputed Adriatic coast area – the so-called Free Territory of Trieste – was divided into two zones. Under the so-called London Agreement of 1954, Zone B and its capital, Koper, went to Yugoslavia while Zone A, including Trieste, fell under Italian jurisdiction.

Up to 25,000 Italian-speaking Istrians fled to Trieste, but 3000 of them stayed on in Koper and other coastal settlements. Today Koper is the centre of the Italian ethnic community of Slovenia, Italian is widely spoken here and the street signs are in two languages.

Orientation

The centre of Koper's semicircular Ol Town is Titov trg, a marvellous Gothi Renaissance square with Venetian influence The marina and tiny city beach are to th northwest. The joint bus and train statio is 1.5km to the southeast on Kolodvorsk cesta. Be advised that massive road work have brought much of the traffic in Kope to a standstill of late.

Information

BOOKSHOP

Mladinska Knjiga (☎ 663 38 80; Pristaniška ulica 5; 8.30am-7.30pm Mon-Fri, 8am-1pm Sat)

INTERNET ACCESS

Internet access at the TIC (below) is free fo the first hour, then €1 per hour. Koper is free wireless zone; get tickets from Pina (se below).

Pina Internet Café (☎ 627 80 72; Kidričeva ulica 43; adult/student per hr €4.80/1.20; noon-10pm Tue-Fri, 4-10pm Sat & Sun) Internet cafe with 10 terminals; free wi-fi.

MONEY

Banka Koper (Kidričeva ulica 14)

Maki Exchange Bureau (☎ 627 25 44; Pristaniška ulic 11; 8.30am-6.30pm Mon-Fri, 8.30am-12.30pm Sat)

Nova Ljubljanska Banka (Pristaniška ulica 45; 8.30am-1pm & 3.30-5pm Mon-Fri)

POST

Post office (Muzejski trg 3)

TOURIST INFORMATION

Tourist Information Centre Koper (TIC; ☎ 664 64 03; www.koper-tourism.si; Titov trg 3; 9am-8pm Jul & Aug 9am-6pm May & Jun, 9am-5pm Sep-Apr) On the ground floor of the Praetorian Palace.

TRAVEL AGENCIES

Kompas (☎ 663 05 82; Pristaniška ulica 17; 8am-7.30pm Mon-Fri, 8am-1pm Sat)

Palma Travel Agency (☎ 663 36 60; Pristaniška ulica 21; 8am-7pm Mon-Fri, 9am-noon Sat)

Sights

The easiest way to see most everything of interest in Koper's Old Town is to walk from the marina on Ukmarjev trg east along Kidričeva ulica to Titov trg and then south down Čevljarska ulica, taking various detours along the way.

IDRIČEVA ULICA

ne of the most colourful streets in Koper, idričeva ulica starts at Carpacciov trg, where he **Column of St Justina** (Steber Sv Justine) com-nemorates Koper's contribution – a galley – the Battle of Lepanto in which Turkey was efeated by the European powers in 1571. Just orth is a large Roman covered basin that now serves as a fountain. At the western end of the square is the large arched **Taverna**, a onetime salt warehouse dating from the 15th century.

On the north side of Kidričeva ulica there are several churches from the 16th century, including the **Church of St Nicholas** (Cerkev Sv Nikolaja; Kidričeva ulica 30), some lovely restored **Venetian houses** (eg No 22) and the 18th-century

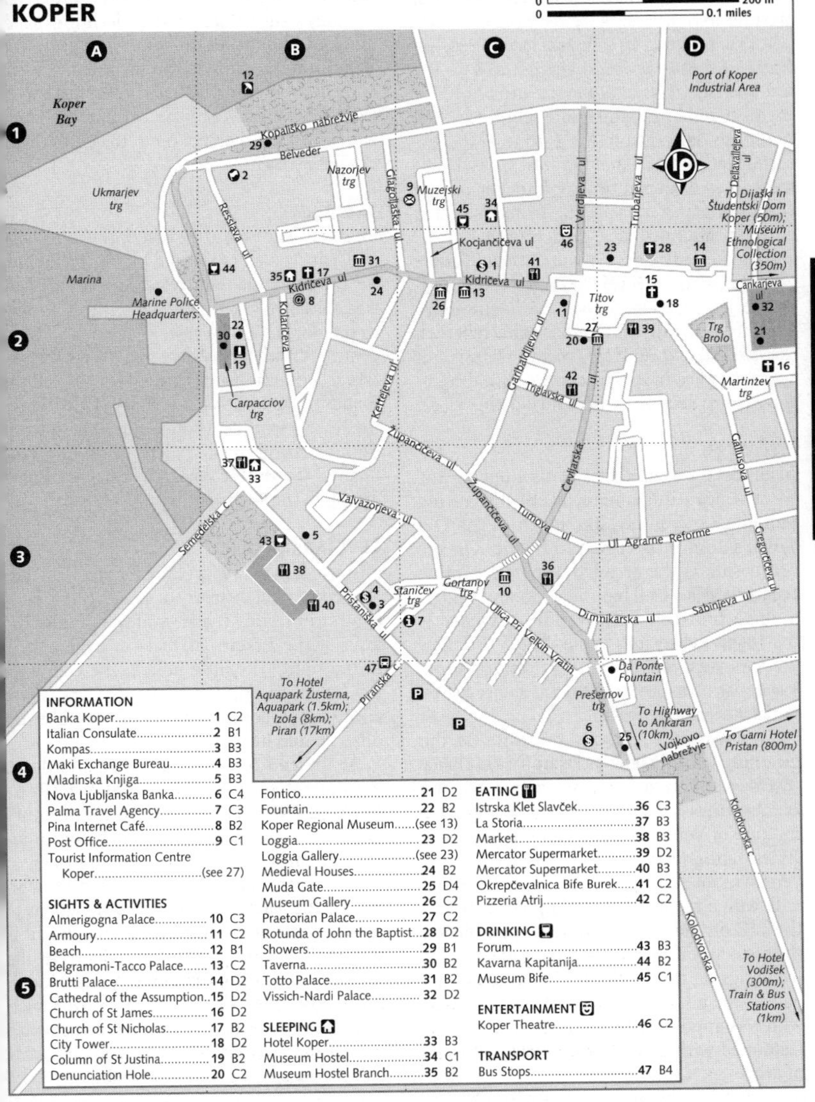

baroque **Totto Palace** (Palača Totto; Kidričeva ulica 22/a), with a relief of the winged lion of St Mark taken from Koper's medieval fortress. Opposite the palace are some wonderful old **medieval town houses** (Kidričeva ulica 33), with protruding upper storeys painted in a checked red, yellow and green pattern.

The **Belgramoni-Tacco Palace** (Palača Belgramoni-Tacco; Kidričeva ulica 19), dating from the early 17th century, houses the **Koper Regional Museum** (Pokrajinski Muzej Koper; ☎ 663 35 70; www.pmk-kp.si; adult/child €2/1; ⏰ 8am-1pm & 6-9pm Tue-Sun Jul & Aug, 8am-3pm Tue-Fri, 9am-1pm Sat & Sun Sep-Jun), with displays of old maps and photos of the port and coast, Italianate sculptures and paintings dating from the 16th to 18th centuries, and copies of medieval frescoes. Don't miss the wonderful bronze knocker on the front door of Venus arising from a seashell and the fabulous back garden with Roman remains. Next door is the **Museum Gallery** (Muzejska Galerija; ☎ 663 35 77; Kidričeva ulica 21; admission free; ⏰ same as Koper Regional), with temporary exhibits. The museum's **ethnological collection** (etnološka zbirka; ☎ 663 35 86; Gramšijev trg 4; ⏰ same as Koper Regional) is in a 17th-century building in the eastern section of the Old Town.

TITOV TRG

In almost the exact centre of old Koper, Titov trg is a beautiful square full of interesting buildings; mercifully, like much of the Old Town's core, it is closed to traffic. On the north side is the arcaded Venetian Gothic **Loggia** (Loža; Titov trg 1) built in 1463 and undergoing a protracted renovation. Attached is the **Loggia Gallery** (Loža Galerija; ☎ 627 41 71; www.obalne-galerije.si; adult/child €2/1; ⏰ 10am-1pm & 6pm-9pm Tue-Sat, 10am-noon Sun Jul & Aug, 10am-1pm & 4-7pm Tue-Sat, 10am-noon Sun Sep-Jun).

To the south, directly opposite, is the gleaming white **Praetorian Palace** (Pretorska Palača; ☎ 664 64 03; Titov trg 3; admission free; ⏰ 9am-8pm Jul & Aug 9am-6pm May & Jun, 9am-5pm Sun Sep-Apr), a mixture of Venetian Gothic and Renaissance styles dating from the 15th century and the very symbol of Koper. It contains the town hall, with a reconstructed old pharmacy and the TIC on the ground floor and exhibits on the history of Koper and a ceremonial hall for weddings on the 1st floor. The facade of the palace, once the residence of Koper's mayor who was appointed by the doge in Venice, is festooned with medallions, reliefs and coats of arms.

On the square's western side, the **Armou** (Armeria; Titov trg 4) was a munitions dump fou centuries ago. Opposite is the **Cathedral of th Assumption** (Stolnica Marijinega Vnebovzetja; ⏰ 7am-9pn and its 36m-tall belfry, now called the **Ci Tower** (Mestni Stolp; adult/child €2/1.50; ⏰ 10am-2p & 4-9pm Jul & Aug, 10am-7pm May & Jun, 10am-7pm Sat Sun Apr, Sep & Oct), with 204 climbable stairs. Th cathedral, partly Romanesque and Gothic bu mostly dating from the mid-18th century, ha a white classical interior with a feeling of spac and light that belies the sombre exterior.

Behind the cathedral to the north is a cir cular Romanesque **Rotunda of John the Baptis** (Rotunda Janeza Krstnika), a baptistery datin from the second half of the 12th century wit a ceiling fresco.

TRG BROLO

Linked to Titov trg to the east, **Trg Brolo** is a wid and leafy square of fine old buildings, includ ing the late-18th-century baroque **Brutti Palac** (Palača Brutti; Trg Brolo 1), now the central library to the north. On the eastern side is the 17th century **Vissich-Nardi Palace** (Palača Vissich-Nardi; Tr Brolo 3) containing government offices and th **Fontico** (Fontiko; Trg Brolo 4), a granary (1416) wher the town's wheat was once stored with won derful medallions and reliefs. Just south is th disused **Church of St James** (Cerkew Sv Jakoba) dating to the 14th century.

ČEVLJARSKA ULICA

Historic **Čevljarska ulica** (Cobbler Street), a narrow commercial street for pedestrians, runs south from Titov trg. As you walk under the arch of the Praetorian Palace, have a look to the right. The little hole in the wall with the Italian inscription *'Denontie'* was where anonymous denunciations of officials and others could be made.

At the end of Čevljarska ulica and down the stone steps is the **Almerigogna Palace** (Palača Almerigogna; Gortanov trg 13), a painted 15th-century Venetian Gothic palace (now a pub) and arguably the most beautiful building in Koper.

The 17th-century Italian family who erected the **fountain** in Prešernov trg, 200m to the southeast, was named Da Ponte; thus it is shaped like a bridge (*ponte* in Italian). At the southern end is the **Muda Gate** (Vrata Muda). Erected in 1516, it's the last of a dozen such entrances to remain standing. On the south side of the archway you'll see the city symbol: the face of a youth in a sunburst.

ctivities

:oper's tiny **beach** (Kopališko nabrežje 1; admission ee; 8am-7pm May-Sep), on the northwest edge f the Old Town, has a small bathhouse with oilets and showers, grassy areas for lying in ne sun and a bar and cafe. Frankly, you'd o better to visit the **Aquapark** (☎ 610 03 00; ww.terme-catez.si/en/obala/aquapark; day pass adult/child on-Fri €13/9, Sat & Sun €17/12; 8am-8pm), which as 1200 sq metres of open and covered wimming pools, at the Hotel Aquapark ;usterna (right).

estivals & Events

:oncerts, theatre and dance events take place uring the **Primorska Summer Festival** (www.porto oz.si) in Koper and Ankaran as well as Izola, ian and Portorož over four weeks in July and he first half of August.

leeping

UDGET

3oth Kompas and the Palma Travel Agency p172) can arrange **private rooms** (per person s €21-2) and **apartments** (apt for 2 €34-40, apt for 4 €59-70), nost of which are in the new town beyond he train station.

Camp Adria Ankaran (☎ 663 73 50; www.adria ankaran.si; Jadranska cesta 25; adult €11-13.50, child €5-.50; late Apr–mid-Oct;) This enormous camping ground in Ankaran 10km to he north (the closest site to Koper) with 400 sites for 1200 guests over 7 hectares on the eastern side of the Adria Ankaran oliday resort and down to the sea. There is any number of sporting facilities, and the camping charge includes use of the two seawater swimming pools (nonguests pay €15/10 per adult/child).

Museum Hostel (☎ 626 18 70, 041 504 466; doris boi77@gmail.com; Muzejski trg 6; per person €20-25;) This good-value place is more a series of bright apartments with modern kitchens and bathrooms than a hostel. Reception is at the little Museum Bife, a cafe-bar on Muzejski trg; the rooms are actually at Mladinska ulica 7 and Kidričeva ulica 34.

Dijaški in Študentski Dom Koper (☎ 662 62 50, 051 344 98; www.ddkoper.si, in Slovene; Cankarjeva ulica 5; s/d €28/50; late Jun–Aug) This modern five-storey dormitory about 150m east of Trg Brolo rents out some 50 beds in 18 double and triple rooms primarily in July and August though three rooms are available year-round.

MIDRANGE & TOP END

Hotel Vodišek (☎ 639 24 68; www.hotel-vodisek.com; Kolodvorska cesta 2; s €48-60, d €72-90, tr €89-110;) This small hotel with 35 reasonably priced rooms is in a shopping centre halfway between the Old Town and the train and bus stations. Guests get to use the hotel's bicycles for free.

Hotel Aquapark Žusterna (☎ 610 03 00; www .terme-catez.si; Istrska cesta 67; s €72-82, d €112-132;) This 117-room sister-hotel of the Koper, about 1.5km to the west on the main coastal road, is not convenient for touring the Old Town, but its Aquapark (left) is a major draw for those seeking recreation.

Garni Hotel Pristan (☎ 614 40 00; www.pristan -koper.si; Ferrarska ulica 30; s/d/tr €77/120/150;) This 16-room property in a modern boat-shaped building above a shopping mall about 700m east of Titov trg is close to many of the large Slovenian and international shipping companies based in Koper and is most suited for business travellers. Weekend stays are 20% cheaper.

Hotel Koper (☎ 610 05 00; www.terme-catez.si; Pristaniška ulica 3; s/d from €81/126;) This pleasant, 65-room property on the edge of the historic Old Town is the only really central hotel in town. Rates include entry to the Aquapark. Choose a harbour-facing room such as No 303.

Eating

Okrepčevalnica Bife Burek (☎ 271 347; Kidričeva ulica 8; snacks & light bites €1.80-2.50; 7am-10pm) This place serves good-value *burek,* which you can carry to Titov trg and eat there.

Istrska Klet Slavček (☎ 627 67 29, 041 345 776; Župančičeva ulica 39; dishes €3-14; 7am-10pm Sun-Fri) The Istrian Cellar, situated below the 18th-century Carli Palace, is one of the most colourful places for a meal in Koper's Old Town. Filling set lunches go for less than €8, and there's local Malvazija and Teran wine from the barrel.

Pizzerija Atrij (☎ 627 22 55; Čevljarska ulica 8m, enter from Triglavska ulica 2; pizza €3.50-6.70; 9am-9pm Mon-Thu, 9am-10pm Fri, 10am-10pm Sat) This popular pizzeria down an alleyway no wider than your average quarterback's shoulder spread has a small covered garden in back and a salad bar.

La Storia (☎ 626 20 18; Pristaniška ulica 3; starters €6.50-9.90, mains €8.90-24.90; 11am-11pm Mon-Fri, noon-11pm Sat & Sun) This Italian-style trattoria with sky-view ceiling frescoes focuses on salads, pasta and fish dishes and has outside seating in the warmer months.

There's an outdoor **market** (Pristaniška ulica; 7am-2pm Mon-Sat) in the open courtyard of the shopping centre. A short distance to the southeast is a huge **Mercator** (Pristaniška ulica 2; 7am-8pm Mon-Fri, 7am-1pm Sat) supermarket, with a smaller **Mercator** (Titov trg 2; 7am-8pm Mon-Fri, 7am-1pm Sat, 8am-noon Sun) in the Old Town.

Drinking

The Slovenian Istria (Slovenska Istra) wine-producing area is known for its white Malvazija and chardonnay and red Refošk.

Forum (☎ 627 20 94; Pristaniška ulica 2; 7am-11pm Mon-Sat, 9am-10pm Sun) This cafe-bar at the northern side of the market and facing a little park and the sea is a popular local hangout.

Kavarna Kapitanija (☎ 040 799 000; Ukmarjev trg 8; 7am-midnight, 8am-midnight Sat & Sun) This attractive space, with its wide-open terrace and comfortable wicker lounges, would be even more inviting if the tacky souvenir kiosks and parked cars across the grassy strip didn't block the harbour view.

Entertainment

Koper Theatre (Gledališče Koper; ☎ 663 13 81; Verdijeva ulica 3) Just north of Titov trg, the city's recently renovated theatre stages plays as well as concerts and dance performances.

Getting There & Away

BUS

Although train departures are limited, the bus service to and from Koper is generally good. Buses go to Izola, Strunjan, Piran (€2.70, 30 minutes hour, 18km) and Portorož every half-hour on weekdays and every 40 minutes at the weekend. The buses start at the train and bus station and stop at the market on Pristaniška ulica before continuing on to Izola. Some five daily buses daily make the run to Ljubljana (€11.10, 1¾ to 2½ hours, 122km).

Buses to Trieste (€3, one hour, 23km, up to 13 daily) run along the coast via Ankaran and Muggia Monday to Saturday between 6am and 7.30pm. Destinations in Croatia include Rijeka (€11.20, two hours, 84km, 10.10am Monday to Friday), Rovinj (€12, three hours, 129km, 3.50pm daily June to September) via Poreč (€10, two hours, 88km), plus one to three to Poreč only, including one at 7.30am Monday t Friday and another two at 3.55pm daily Jun to September.

TRAIN

Koper is on a minor rail line linking it wit Ljubljana (€8 to €9.60, 2½ hours, 153km via Postojna and Divača, with four loc trains and two faster IC services (€13.6 2¼ hours) at 5.25am and 2.45pm. To g to Buzet and Pula in Croatia from Kope you must change at Hrpelje-Kozina (€2.9 to €5.90, 30 minutes, 37km, five daily) fo any of three trains a day.

Getting Around

Local buses 1 and 2 link the bus and trai stations to the eastern edge of Cankarjev ulica in the Old Town, with a stop nea Muda Gate.

Parking in much of the Old Town is severely restricted – or banned altogether – between 6am and 3pm. Generally, you mus leave your vehicle in the pay car parks alon Pristaniška ulica.

To order a taxi in Koper ring ☎ 051 67 271, 040 222 272 or 041 737 083.

IZOLA

☎ 05 / pop 11,400 / elev 2m

Izola, a somewhat scruffy fishing port 7km southwest of Koper, is the poor relatior among the historical towns on the Slovenian coast, especially genteel Piran. As a result, it is often bypassed by foreign visitors. But Izola does have a certain Venetian charm, a few narrow old streets, and some nice waterfront bars and restaurants where you might tarry.

History

The Romans built a port called Haliaetum at Simon's Bay (Simonov Zaliv) southwest of the Old Town, and you can still see parts of the original landing when the tide is very low. While under the control of Venice in the Middle Ages, Izola – at that time an island (*isola* is Italian for 'island') – flourished, particularly in the trading of such commodities as olives, fish and wine. But a devastating plague in the 16th century and the ascendancy of Trieste as the premier port in the northern Adriatic destroyed the town's economic base. During the period of the Illyrian Provinces in the early 19th century, the French pulled down the town walls and used them to fill

PRIMORSKA

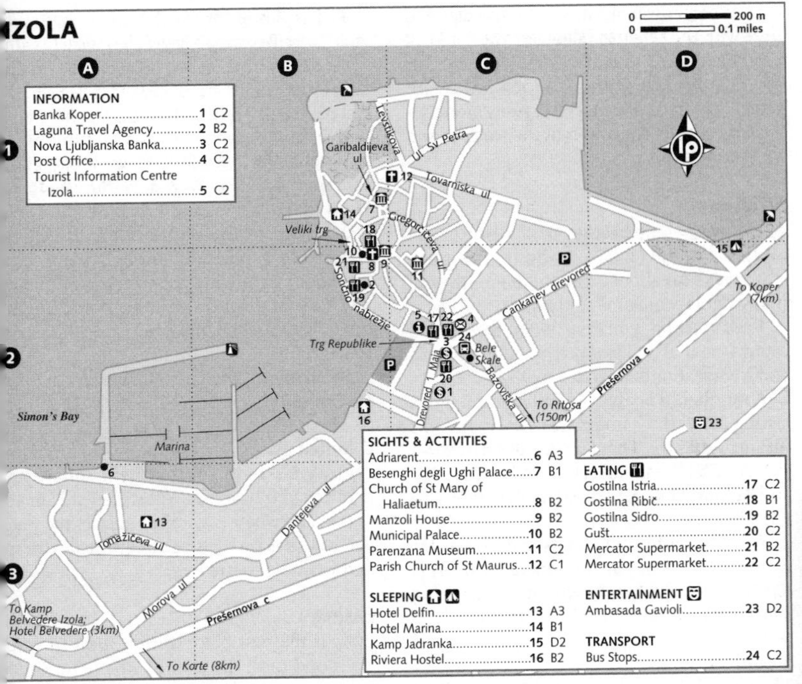

he channel separating the island from the nainland. Izola remains the country's fore- nost fishing port.

rientation

lmost everything of a practical nature s located around central Trg Republike. uses stop in front of the Bela Skale travel gency at Cankarjev drevored 2 on the quare's southeastern edge. To reach the Old Town and its main square, Veliki trg, valk north along Sončno nabrežje, the waterfront promenade.

nformation

Banka Koper (Drevored 1 Maja 5)
aguna Travel Agency (☎ 641 86 30, 041 412 611; strska vrata 7; 9am-1pm & 4-7pm Mon-Sat, 9am-noon Sun)
Nova Ljubljanska Banka (Trg Republike 3) Opposite he bus stops.
Post office (Cankarjev drevored 1)
Tourist Information Centre Izola (TIC; ☎ 640 10 50; www.izola.eu; Sončno nabrežje 4; 9am-9pm Mon-Sat, 10am-5pm Sun Jun-Sep, 9am-5pm Mon-Fri, 10am-5pm Sat Oct-May)

Sights

Izola isn't overly endowed with important historical sights; Napoleon and his lot took care of that. Those that survive include the renovated salmon-coloured 16th-century **Parish Church of St Maurus** (Župnijska Cerkev Sv Mavra; Garibaldijeva ulica) and its detached bell tower on the hill above the town, the **Municipal Palace** (Mestna Palača; Veliki trg), which now houses offices of the local council and, behind it, the lovingly restored **Church of St Mary of Haliaetum** (Cerkev Sv Marije Alietske; Veliki trg). Opposite the church is the renovated Venetian Gothic **Manzioli House** (Manziolijev trg) was built in 1470 and was the residence of an Istrian chronicler in the 16th century. Today it houses the bureau looking after the interests of the *communità italiana* (Italian community) in Izola.

Izola's most beautiful building, however, is the rococo **Besenghi degli Ughi Palace** (cnr Gregorčičeva ulica & Ulica Giordano Bruno) below the Parish Church of St Maurus. Built between 1775 and 1781, the mansion has windows and balconies adorned with stuccos and wonderful wrought-iron grilles painted light blue and is now a music school.

Izola can now make its superlative claim to fame with the **Parenzana Museum** (640 10 50; 1st fl, Ulica Alme Vivode 3; adult/child €2.10/1.50; 9am-3pm Mon-Fri), a branch of the Pomorski Museum Sergej Mašera in Piran. It has train models – the largest such collection in the world – and ship models too.

Activities

There are pebble **beaches** to the north and southeast of the Old Town, but the best one is at **Simon's Bay** about 1.5km to the southwest. It has a grassy area for sunbathing.

The *Prince of Venice* is a 39.6m high-speed catamaran that makes day trips between Izola and Venice. For details, see p297.

A number of boats offer sailing excursions lasting 2½ to three hours from the main port just off Veliki trg. They include **Delfin II** (641 45 38, 041 675 781; adult/child €12/8; 10am Tue & Thu) and **Meduza** (041 675 781; adult/child €12/8; 10am & 5pm daily).

You can rent sailing boats/speedboats for from €60/95 a day from **Adriarent** (663 24 60, 041 300 050; 8-10am & 6-8pm) at the marina a short distance from the Hotel Delfin.

Sleeping

The Laguna Travel Agency (p177) has **private rooms** (s €18-26, d €26-36) and **apartments** (apt for 2 €38-56, apt for 4 €51-82).

Kamp Jadranka (640 23 00; freetimedoo@siol.net; Polje cesta 8; camp sites per person €10; year-round; P) This small site on the waterfront 1km east of the Old Town is just off the busy coastal road and fills up quickly in summer.

Kamp Belvedere Izola (660 51 00; www.belvedere.si; Dobrava ulica 1/a; camp sites adult €9-12, child €6-9; Apr-Aug; P) This 2.5-hectare camping ground on a bluff 3km west of Izola has wonderful views of the town and the Adriatic, a large swimming pool and sites for 500 campers.

our pick Old Schoolhouse Korte (Stara Šola Korte; 642 11 14, 031 375 889; www.hostel-starasola.si; Korte 74; dm €17-19, s & d €20-24; P) This renovated old school in the idyllic hilltop Slovenian Istrian village of Korte, 8km south of Izola, opened its doors as a hostel in late 2006 and has become a winner among cognoscenti. It's got 17 modern rooms with between two and four beds and a couple of apartments with two bedrooms and a living room. You could do your own cooking but the food at the nearby **Gostilna Korte** (642 02 00, 041 607 863; Korte 44), celebrated far and wide, is hard to resist.

Riviera Hostel (662 17 45; www.s-sgtsi.kp.ed.si, in Slovene; Prekomorskih Brigad ulica 7; s/d/tr €28/52/ Jul & Aug) This 174-bed hostel in the Sredn Gostinska in Turistična Šola (Middle School Catering and Tourism) overlooks the mari and welcomes foreign guests in summer.

Hotel Delfin (660 70 00; www.hotel-delfin. Tomažičeva ulica 10; s €45-58, d €76-102; P Hard by Izola's marina complex, the Delfi is a bit out of the centre but still near th water. It's a pleasant enough place on hill about 1km southwest of Trg Republik and has its own swimming pool. But it huge, with 219 rooms, and caters largely tour groups.

Hotel Marina (660 41 00; www.hotelmarina.si; Veliki 11; s €53-126, d €71-156, ste €137-220; P) Th 52-room Hotel Marina, faced with chocolat coloured glazed brick, couldn't be any mo central: it's right on the main square an fronting the harbour. Rates depend on th season and whether your room faces the wat and has a balcony. There's a very attractive sp and wellness centre here.

Eating

Izola is the best place on the coast to enjo a seafood meal. Be careful when you orde however, and ask the exact price of the fish As seafood is sold by decagram (usually ab breviated as *dag* on menus), you might en up eating (and paying) a lot more than yo expected. And be sure to have a glass of low alcohol Malvazija, the pale-yellow local whit that is light and reasonably dry.

Gušt (041 650 333; Drevored 1 Maja 3; pizza & past €4.60-10.90; 10am-midnight) This *picerija* an *špageterija* opposite the Banka Koper ha decent pizza, pasta and salads (from €4.50).

Gostilna Istria (641 80 50, 031 384 243; Trg Republik 1; dishes €7.50-16, pizza €5.20-6.50; 7am-midnight Mon Sat, 8am-midnight Sun) An old favourite, this rela tively simple eatery on the main road into th Old Town has good-value set lunches (€7) an stays open throughout the day. Try the gnoc chi with *pršut* in a red Refošk wine sauce.

Gostilna Sidro (641 47 11; Sončno nabrežje 24 starters €4.50-9.50, mains €8-22; 8am-10pm) One o Izola's best restaurants, Sidro is an old standb on the waterfront just up from the TIC.

Gostilna Ribič (641 83 13; Veliki trg 3; starters €6-15, mains €9-25; noon-1am) Another of the town's top restaurants, this is eatery on the inner harbour is much loved by locals and specialises in turbot. Set lunch is €8.

There's a **Mercator** (Trg Republike 4; 7am-8pm on-Fri, 7am-5pm Sat, 8am-noon Sun) supermarket pposite the bus stops and a more central **ercator** (Veliki trg; 7am-8pm Mon-Sat, 8am-noon Sun) ear the inner port.

ntertainment

mbasada Gavioli (641 82 12, 041 353 722; Industrijska sta; midnight-6am Sat) In the industrial area outheast of the port, the Amabasada Gavioli ill holds the crown as queen of Slovenia's lectronic clubs, showcasing a procession of nternational and local DJs.

etting There & Away

requent buses between Koper (€1.80, 15 ninutes, 8km) and Piran (€1.80, 20 mintes, 10km) and Portorož go via Izola. Other estinations from Izola (via Koper) include jubljana (€11.40, 2½ hours, 130km, five a ay, with up to nine in July and August) and Nova Gorica (€9.60, 2½ hours, 103km, one r two a day).

International routes include six buses a day five on Saturday) to Trieste (€3.10, 40 minites, 23km) in Italy and up to five departures o Umag (€5.20, 1¼ hours, 45km) and Pula €8.70, 2½ hours, 94km) at 7.45am and 2.12pm laily and to Rovinj (€11.10, three hours, one laily) at 4.07pm June to September.

For getting to/from Italy by boat see p297.

Getting Around

From June to August a minibus does a coninuous loop from the Belvedere Izola holiday village west of the Old Town to Simon's Bay, Izola Marina, Trg Republike and the Jadranka camping ground and back.

Order a taxi in Izola on 040 602 602 or 041 706 777.

You can rent bicycles from **Ritosa** (641 53 37, 640 12 41; Kajuhova ulica 28; per day €15; 8am-7pm Mon-Fri, 8am-noon Sat). You can also rent them from the Hotel Marina (opposite) for €5/8/10 per two/five/12 hours.

STRUNJAN

05 / pop 610 / elev up to 116m

For centuries the people who lived at Strunjan, a peninsula halfway between Izola and Piran, were engaged in making salt; you'll see the disused pans spread out before you on the descent along the main road (route No 111) from the Belvedere tourist complex. Today the area is protected, and this is because of the expanded 429-hectare **Strunjan Country Park** (Krajinski Park Strunjan), which contains the saltpans and the contiguous **Stjuža Lagoon**, both classified as natural monuments.

Although there has been much development around Strunjan Bay to the southwest, much of the peninsula is remarkably unspoiled. It is bounded by a high cliff, **Cape Ronek** (Rtič Ronek; 116m), at its northernmost point; below it is Moon Bay (Mesečec Zaliv), the prettiest inlet on the coast, which can be seen from the footpath along the cape.

Frequent bus services link Strunjan with Izola (€1.30, seven minutes, 4km), Koper, Piran (€1.80, 12 minutes, 6km) and Portorož.

PIRAN

05 / pop 4470 / elev 23m

Picturesque Piran (Pirano in Italian), sitting at the tip of a narrow peninsula, is everyone's favourite town on the Slovenian coast. Its Old Town is a gem of Venetian Gothic architecture, but it can be a mob scene at the height of summer. In April or October, though, it's hard not to fall in love with the winding Venetian Gothic alleyways and tempting seafood restaurants.

History

Piran has been settled since ancient times, and it is thought that the town's name comes from the Greek word for fire *(pyr)*. In those days, fires were lit at Punta, the very tip of the peninsula, to guide ships to the port at Aegida (now Koper). The Romans established a settlement here called Piranum after their victory over the Illyrians and Celts. They in turn were followed by the early Slavs, the Byzantines, the Franks and the Patriarchs of Aquileia.

Venetian rule began in the late 13th century and lasted in one form or another for more than 500 years. Unlike Koper and Izola, whose citizens rose up against the Venetians time and time again, Piran threw its full support behind Venice in its struggles with Aquileia and Genoa. (The fact that Venice was Piran's biggest customer for the salt it produced was certainly an incentive.) The Venetian period was the town's most fruitful, and many of its beautiful buildings and its fortifications were erected then.

Today Piran is one of the best preserved historical towns anywhere on the Adriatic and is protected by the Slovenian government in its entirety as a cultural monument.

Orientation

Piran's Old Town rests on the westernmost point of Slovenian Istria. Strunjan Bay lies to the north; Piran Bay and Portorož, Slovenia's largest beach resort, are located to the south.

Tartinijev trg, north of Piran Harbour and the small marina, is the centre of the Old Town today, but in the Middle Ages the focal point was Trg 1 Maja (also written Prvomajski trg) to the northwest.

Buses from everywhere except Portorož arrive at the bus station, at Dantejeva ulica 6, a 300m stroll south along the portside Cankarjevo nabrežje from central Tartinijev trg.

Information

Banka Koper (Tartinijev trg 12)

Caffe Neptun (☎ 041 724 237; www.caffeneptun.com; Dantejeva ul 4; per 20min €1; 🕑 7am-1am Mon-Sat, 8am-10pm Sun) Modern cafe near the bus station with internet access; free with drink.

Maona Tourist Agency (☎ 673 45 20; www.maona.si; Cankarjevo nabrežje 7; 🕑 9am-8pm Mon-Sat, 10am-1pm & 5-7pm Sun Jul & Aug, 9am-8pm Mon-Fri, 10am-1pm & 5-7pm Sat, 9am-1pm Sun May & Sep) Unstintingly helpful travel agency organising everything from private rooms to activities and cruises.

Post office (Cankarjevo nabrežje 5)

Tourist Information Centre Piran (☎ 673 02 20, 673 44 40; www.portoroz.si; Tartinijev trg 2; 🕑 9am-8pm Jul & Aug, 9am-5pm Sep-Jun) In the impressive Municipal Hall; website includes Piran.

Turist Biro (☎ 673 25 09; www.turistbiro-ag.si; Tomažičeva ulica 3; 🕑 9am-1pm & 4-7pm Mon-Sat, 10am-1pm & 4-6pm Sun) Opposite the Hotel Piran.

PRIMORSKA

Sights

SERGEJ MAŠERA MARITIME MUSEUM

Located in the **Gabrielli Palace** (Palača Gabrielle; Cankarjevo nabrežje 3) on the waterfront, this **museum** (Pomorski Muzej Sergej Mašera; ☎ 671 00 40; www.pommuz-pi.si; adult/child/senior & student incl Saltworks Museum in Sečovlje €3.50/2.10/2.50; 🕑 9am-noon & 5-9pm Tue-Sun Jul & Aug, 9am-5pm Tue-Sun Sep-Jun) is named in honour of a Slovenian naval commander whose ship was blown up off the Croatian coast in WWI. The mid-19th-century palace, with its lovely moulded ceilings, parquet floors and marble staircase, is worth a visit in itself.

The museum's excellent exhibits focus on sea, sailing and salt-making – three things that have been crucial to Piran's development over the centuries. The salt pans at Sečovlj southeast of Portorož, get most of the atte tion on the ground floor. There are son old photographs showing salt workers goin about their duties in coolie-like straw hats, a well as a wind-powered salt pump and litt wooden weights in the form of circles an diamonds that were used to weigh salt du ing the Venetian Republic. The 2000-year-ol Roman amphorae beneath the glass floor he are impressive.

The antique model ships upstairs are ver fine (especially the 17th-century galleon an 18th-century corvette); other rooms are fille with old figureheads and weapons, includ ing some very lethal-looking blunderbusse The folk paintings are ex-voto offerings tha were placed by sailors on the altar of the pil grimage church at Strunjan for protectio against shipwreck.

A short distance to the south, the **Museum of Underwater Activities** (Muzej Podvodnih Dejavnost ☎ 041 685 379; www.muzejpodvodnihdejavnosti.s Župančičeva ul 24; adult/student & child €3/2; 🕑 9.30am 10pm Jun-Sep) makes much of Piran's clos association with the sea and diving.

TARTINIJEV TRG

The **statue** of the nattily dressed gentlema in Tartinijev trg, an oval-shaped, marble paved square that was the inner harbou until it was filled in 1894, is that of local boy-cum-composer and violinist Giuseppe Tartin (1692–1770). To the east is the **Church of St Peter** (Cerkev Sv Petra; 1818), which contains the wonderful 14th-century **Piran Crucifix**. Across from the church is **Tartini House** (Tartinijeva Hiša ☎ 663 35 70; Kajuhova ulica 12; adult/child €1.50/1; 🕑 9am-noon & 6-9pm Tue-Sun Jul & Aug, 11am-noon & 5-6pm Tue-Sun Sep-Jun), the composer's birthplace and a popular concert venue.

One of Piran's most eye-catching structures is the red 15th-century Gothic **Venetian House** (Benečanka; Tartinijev trg 4), with its tracery windows and balcony in the northeast of the square. There is a story attached to the stone relief between the two windows of a lion with a banner in its mouth and the Latin inscription *Lassa pur dir* above it. A wealthy merchant from Venice fell in love with a beautiful local girl, but she soon became the butt of local gossips. To shut them up (and keep his lover happy), the merchant built her this little palace complete with a reminder for his loose-lipped neighbours: 'Let them talk'.

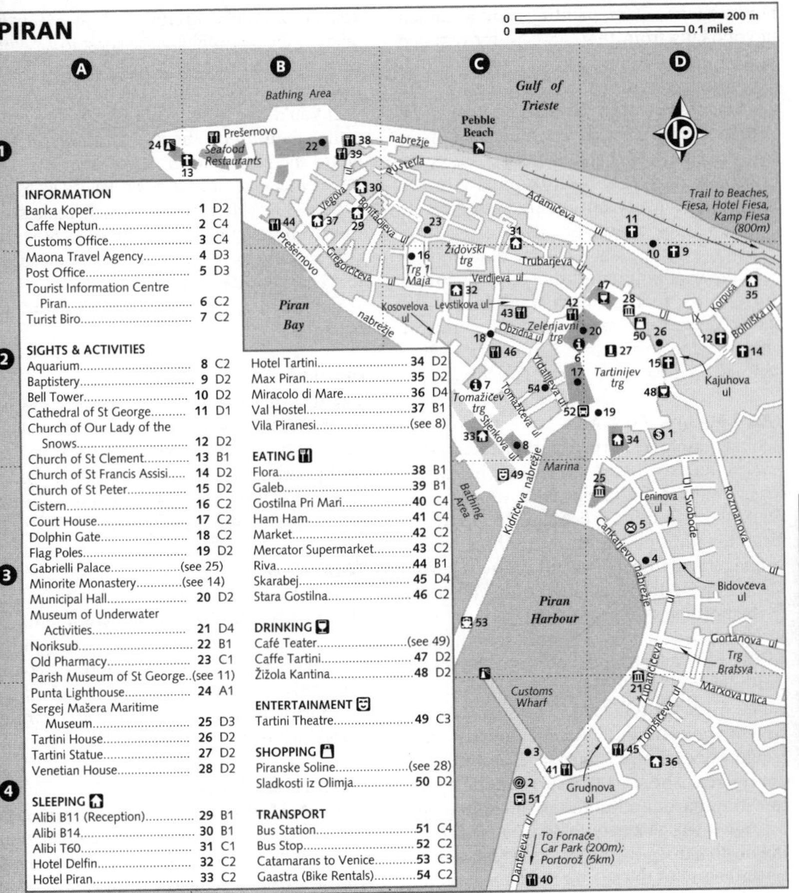

The **Court House** (Sodnijska Palača; Tartinijev trg 1), which has two 17th-century doors, and the porticoed 19th-century **Municipal Hall** (Občinska Palača; Tartinijev trg 2) with the TIC are to the south. The two 15th-century **flag poles** at the entrance to the square bear Latin inscriptions praising Piran, the town's coat of arms, a relief of St George, the patron, to the left and one of St Mark with the lion symbol on the right.

CATHEDRAL OF ST GEORGE & SURROUNDS

The Renaissance and baroque **Cathedral of St George** (Stolna Cerkev Sv Jurija; Adamičeva ulica 2) stands on a ridge north of Tartinijev trg above the sea. To the east runs a 200m stretch of the 15th-century **town walls** complete with loopholes. They once ran from the sea all the way to the harbour, and seven crenellated towers are still intact.

The church was founded in 1344 and was rebuilt in baroque style in 1637. If time weighs heavily on your hands, visit the attached **Parish Museum of St George** (Župnijski Muzej Sv Jurija; ☎ 673 34 40; admission €1; 🕑 11am-5pm), which contains church plate, paintings and a lapidary in the crypt.

The cathedral's freestanding 47m-high **bell tower** (zvonik; admission €1; 🕑 11am-2pm & 6-9pm), built in 1609, was clearly modelled on the campanile of San Marco in Venice and its 146 stairs can be climbed daily for excellent views of the town and harbour. Next to it, the octagonal **baptistery** (krstilnica) from

1650 contains altars, paintings and a Roman sarcophagus from the 2nd century recycled as a baptismal font.

On your way down to Tartinijev trg are the **Minorite Monastery** (Minoritski Samostan; ☎ 673 44 17; Bolniška ulica 20) with a wonderful cloister and the **Church of St Francis Assisi** (Cerkev Sv Frančiška Asiškega) built originally in the early 14th century but enlarged and renovated over the centuries. Inside are ceiling frescoes, a giant clam shell for donations, a baroque wall pulpit and the Tartini family's burial plot. In the **Church of Our Lady of the Snows** (Cerkev Marije Snežne; Bolniška ulica) almost opposite the monastery is a superb 15th-century arch painting of the Crucifixion.

TRG 1 MAJA & PUNTA

Behind the market north of Tartinijev trg, medieval homes have been built into an ancient defensive wall along Obzidna ulica, which passes under the 15th-century **Dolphin Gate** (Dolfinova Vrata), with a plaque showing three of our smiling friends. **Židovski trg**, the centre of Jewish life in Piran in the Middle Ages, is about 100m to the northwest of here.

Trg 1 Maja (1st May Sq) may sound like a socialist parade ground, but it was the centre of Piran until the Middle Ages, when it was called Stari trg (Old Sq). The surrounding streets are a maze of pastel-coloured overhanging houses, vaulted passages and arcaded courtyards. The square is surrounded by interesting baroque buildings, including the former town **pharmacy** (lekarna; Trg 1 Maja 2) on the north side (now the Fontana restaurant). In the centre of the square is a large baroque **cistern** *(vodnjak)* that was built in the late 18th century to store fresh water; rainwater from the surrounding roofs flowed into it through the fish borne by the stone *putti* cherubs in two corners.

Punta, the historical 'point' of Piran, still has a **lighthouse**, but today's is small and modern. Attached to it in back, however, the round, serrated tower of the **Church of St Clement**, originally built in the 13th century but altered 500 years later, evokes the ancient beacon from which Piran got its name. It has a lovely (though decrepit) stuccoed ceiling.

Activities

BOATING & CRUISES

The Maona Tourist Agency (p180) and several other agencies in Piran and Portorož can book you on any number of cruises – from a loop th takes in the towns along the coast to day-lor excursions to Brioni National Park and Rovi in Croatia, or Venice and Trieste in Italy.

If you'd like to see what's *below* the wat rather than on or above it and not get we board the glass-bottom **Subaquatic** (☎ 041 6 783; www.subaquatic.si; adult/child €13/8; 🕒 10am, 2p 4.14pm & 6.30pm daily Apr-Sep), which makes th run from the main pier in Piran to Strunja via Fiesa and back. Just don't count on seein Red Sea–style corals in these parts.

For day trips to Venice from Piran se p297.

DIVING

Noriksub (☎ 673 22 18, 041 746 153; www.norik-sub. Prešernovo nabrežje 24; shore/boat dive €30/45; 🕒 10am noon & 2-6pm Tue-Sun Jun–mid-Sep, 10am-4pm Sat & Su mid-Sep-May) organises shore and boat-guide dives, gives PADI open-water courses (begin ners €240) and hires equipment.

SWIMMING

Piran has several 'beaches' – rocky areas alon Prešernovo nabrežje – where you might ge your feet wet. They are a little better on th north side near Punta, but as long as you'v come this far keep walking eastward on th paved path for just under 1km to Fiesa, whic has a small but clean beach.

Festivals & Events

The **Tartini Festival** (www.tartinifestival.org) of classical music takes place in venues throughou Piran, including the vaulted cloister of th Minorite monastery, in from late Augus to mid-September.

Sleeping

BUDGET

Private rooms (s €16-30, d €23-42) and **apartments** (apt for 2 €38-50, for 4 €60-84) are available through the Maona Tourist Agency and Turist Biro (p180) throughout the year, but the biggest choice is available during summer.

Kamp Fiesa (☎ 674 62 30; www.kamp-fiesa.com; adult €9.50-11, child €4-4.50; 🕒 May-Sep; P) The closest camping ground to Piran is at Fiesa, 4km by road but less than 1km if you follow the coastal path *(obalna pešpot)* east from the Cathedral of St George. It's tiny and becomes very crowded in summer but it's in a quiet valley by two small, protected ponds and right by the beach.

Alibi B11 (☎ 031 363 666; www.alibi.si; Bonifacijeva :a 11; per person €20-25; 💻) The flagship of the libi stable is not its nicest property but ception for all three hostels is here. It has ve doubles and three rooms with three to ur beds over four floors in an ancient (and ather frayed) townhouse on a narrow street at has since been enlivened by Slovenia-emed wall murals. Diagonally opposite is **ibi B14** (Bonifacijeva ulica 14; per person €20-25; 💻), more upbeat four-floor party place with even rooms, each with two to four beds and ath. We love the wall paintings of Slovenian ties, Triglav and vineyards, and there's also washing machine. More subdued is **Alibi 50** (Trubarjeva ulica 60; per person €25; ❄) to the east ith a fully equipped doubles (TV, fridge and athroom) on each of five floors served by a intage wooden staircase. The view terrace of ie top room is priceless.

Val Hostel (☎ 673 25 55; www.hostel-val.com; 'egorčičeva ulica 38/a; per person €22-25; 💻) This cen-:al partially renovated hostel on the corner f Vegova ulica has 22 rooms (56 beds) with hared shower, free internet access, kitchen nd washing machine. It's a great favourite vith backpackers, but there's a surcharge of €2 or one night's stay in the high season.

MIDRANGE & TOP END

our pick Miracolo di Mare (☎ 921 76 60, 051 445 511; www.miracolodimare.si; Tomšičeva ulica 23; s €50-55, d €60-0; 💻) Our new favourite B&B on the coast, he Wonder of the Sea has a dozen charming though smallish) rooms, some of which (like No 3 and the breakfast room) give on to the nost charming raised back garden in Piran. Floors and stairs are wooden (and original) and beds metal framed.

Max Piran (☎ 673 34 36, 041 692 928; www.maxpiran com; Ulica IX Korpusa 26; s €35-40, d €60-70; 💻) Piran's nost romantic accommodation has just six rooms, each bearing a woman's name rather than number, in a delightful coral-coloured 18th-century townhouse. It's just down from the cathedral.

Hotel Fiesa (☎ 671 22 00; www.hotelfiesa.com; Fiesa 57; park view d €62-78, tr €74-85, sea view d €78-98, tr €88-115; P) Although not in Piran itself, this 22-room pink-coloured hotel overlooking the sea near the Kamp Fiesa camping ground is one of the most atmospheric places to stay in the area. Among the best sea-facing rooms are Nos 1, 2, 7, 8 and 9, all of which have balconies.

Hotel Tartini (☎ 671 10 00; www.hotel-tartini-piran.com; Tartinijev trg 15; s €62-88, d €84-118, tr €114-162, ste €140-192; P ❄ 💻) This attractive, 45-room property faces Tartinijev trg and manages to catch a few sea views from the upper floors. The staff are especially friendly and helpful. If you've got the dosh, splash out on suite No 40/a; we're suckers for eyrie-like round rooms with €1 million views.

Hotel Piran (☎ 676 21 00; www.hoteli-piran.si; Stjenkova ulica 1; s €72-102, d €84-144, ste €152-198; P ❄ 💻) One of Piran's only two central hotels, the Hotel Piran, with 80 renovated rooms and 10 suites, is right on the water. Its latest addition is the **Vila Piranesi** (☎ 676 21 00; www.hoteli-piran.si; Kidričevo nabrežje 4; apt for 2 €76-116, with harbour view €98-142), with 17 super-modern and large (24 sq metre to 42 sq metre) self-contained apartments above the renovating aquarium.

Eating

One of Piran's attractions is its plethora of fish restaurants, especially along Prešernovo nabrežje, though don't expect any bargains. Most cater to the tourist trade and are rather overpriced.

Flora (☎ 673 12 58; Prešernovo nabrežje 26; pizza €4-7.50; 🕑 10am-1am Jul & Aug, 10am-10pm Sep-Jun) The terrace of this simple pizzeria east of the Punta lighthouse has uninterrupted views of the Adriatic.

Skarabej (☎ 040 522 271; Župančičeva ulica 21; starters €5-9, mains €6-13.50; 🕑 9am-11pm) This very welcoming and attractive – note the fantastic mosaic of the namesake 'scarab' on the back wall – serves excellent pizza (€5.50 to €8) and pasta (€5 to €7.50) as well as more ambitious dishes.

Stara Gostilna (☎ 673 31 65, 040 640 240; Savudrijska ulica 2; starters €5-9, mains €7.50-17; 🕑 9am-11pm) This delightful bistro in the Old Town serves both meat and fish dishes and has some of the best service in town.

Galeb (☎ 673 32 25; Pusterla ulica 5; mains €8-11; 🕑 11am-4pm & 6pm-midnight Wed-Mon) This excellent family-run restaurant with seafront seating is east of the Punta lighthouse. The food is good but takes no risks.

our pick Golstilna Pri Mari (☎ 673 47 35, 041 616 488; Dantejeva ul 17; starters €5-10, mains €8.50-16; 🕑 10am-11pm Tue-Sun Jul & Aug, noon-10pm Tue-Sat, noon-6pm Sun Sep-Jun) This stylish Italian-owned restaurant south of the bus station serves the most inventive Mediterranean and Slovenian dishes in town. Try the fish paté and mussels in wine or *fritto misto*. Expect a warm, multilingual welcome.

Riva (☎ 673 22 25; Gregorčičeva ulica 46; starters €5-8.55, mains €8-24; 🕐 11.30am-midnight) The only seafood restaurant we patronise on Prešernovo nabrežje is this classy place with the fine decor and superb sea views.

There's an outdoor **market** (Zelenjavni trg; 🕐 7am-2pm Mon-Sat) in the small square behind the Municipal Hall. You'll also find a small **Mercator** (Levstikova ulica 5; 🕐 7am-8pm Mon-Sat, 8am-noon Sun) supermarket in the Old Town and a **Ham Ham** (Tomšičeva ulica 41; 🕐 7am-midnight) convenience store opposite the bus station.

Drinking & Entertainment

Caffe Tartini (☎ 051 694 100; Tartinijev trg 3; 🕐 7am-3am) This cafe in a classical building opposite the Venetian House is a wonderful place for a cup of something hot or a glass of wine.

Žižola Kantina (Tartinijev trg 10; 🕐 9am-3am) This simple, nautically themed bar named after the jujube (Chinese date) that grows prolifically along the Adriatic has tables right on the main square and serves 15 different flavours of *žganje* (Slovenian fruit brandy).

Café Teater (☎ 041 711 888; Stjenkova ulica 1; 🕐 7am-3am Mon-Fri, 9am-3am Sat & Sun) With a waterfront terrace and faux antique furnishings, this is where anyone who's anyone in Piran can be found.

Tartini Theatre (Gledališče Tartini; ☎ 676 67 00; www.avditorij.si; Kidričevo nabrežje) Built in 1910 and seating 300 spectators, this theatre hosts a program of classical concerts throughout the year.

Shopping

Piranske Soline (☎ 673 31 10; Tartinijev trg 4; 🕐 9am-1pm & 5-9pm Jul & Aug, 10am-5pm Sep-Jun) In the Venetian House, this place sells bath sea salts and other products from Sečovlje (p188).

Sladkosti iz Olimja (☎ 059-922 189; Tartinijev trg 6; 🕐 8am-noon & 5-10pm Jul & Aug, 9am-5pm Sep-Jun) This extravagant shop next door to the Venetian House sells 'sweets from Olimje', the chocolate capital of Slovenia in Štajerska.

Getting There & Away

From the bus station, buses run every 20 to 30 minutes to Koper (€2.70, 30 minutes, 18km) via Izola (€1.90, 20 minutes, 10km). Other destinations include Ljubljana (€12, three hours, 140km, five to eight daily) via Divača and Postojna, and Nova Gorica (€10.30, 2¾ hours, 113km, one at 2.40pm Monday to Friday year-round and another at 4.50pm daily in July a August). Sečovlje (€1.80, 15 minutes, 9.5k is served by up to eight a day and Strunj (€1.00, 10 minutes, 6km) by between four a seven. There's also a very long-distance b to Murska Sobota (€28, 7½ hours, 338km) v Maribor, Celje and Radenci.

Some five buses go to Trieste (€10, 1 hours, 36km) in Italy between 6.45am a 6.55pm Monday to Saturday. One bus a d heads south for Croatian Istria from June September, leaving at 4.25pm and stopping the coastal towns of Umag, Poreč and Rovi (€10.30, 2¾ hours, 111km).

From Tartinijev trg, minibuses (€1 o board, €0.40 in advance from newsagencie €6 for 20 rides) shuttle to Portorož and th camping grounds at Lucija every half-ho from 5.40am to 11pm (11.45pm on Frida Saturday and, in July and August, Sunda continuously year-round.

Piran despatches catamarans to Venic (p297) at least once a week.

Getting Around

CAR

Traffic is severely restricted here, and yo will almost certainly have to park your car a the **Fornače car park** (per hr/day/week €1.20/12/72) an walk or take a free shuttle bus into the centr You could take a ticket and try to drive int the centre (first hour €5, then €3.50 per hour but old Piran is so small, parking is so limite and its alleyways so narrow (mostly footpaths that you will regret it for sure.

TAXI

For a taxi in Piran call ☎ 051 607 333 or 03 730 700.

BICYCLE

Very cheap bikes are available from **Gaastr** (☎ 673 25 88, 040 255 400; Vidalijeva ulica 3; per day €1 🕐 9am-1pm & 5-8pm Jul & Aug, 9am-1pm & 4-5pm Mon Sat Sep-Jun), a shop in the Old Town selling sailing duds. The Maona Tourist Agency (p180) has better ones for €6/9/15/20 pe two-/five-/10-/24-hour period.

PORTOROŽ

☎ 05 / pop 2900 / elev 31m

Every country with a coast has got to have a honky-tonk beach resort – a Blackpool, a Bondi or an Atlantic City – and Portorož (Portorose in Italian) is Slovenia's very own. But the 'Port

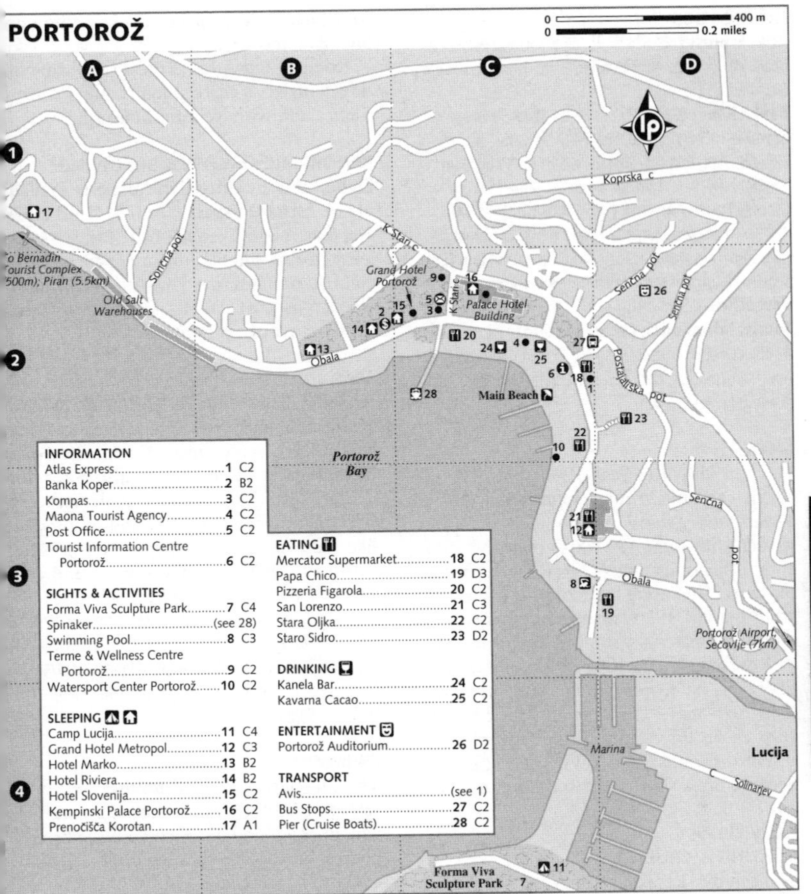

of Roses', which skirts a sandy bay about 5km southeast of Piran, is today actually quite classy for a seaside town, even along Obala, the main drag. And with the reopening of the landmark Palace, the art nouveau hotel that put Portorož on the map, it may even start to relive its glory days. Portorož's sandy beaches are relatively clean, and there are pleasant spas and wellness centres where you can take the waters or cover yourself in curative mud. The vast array of accommodation options makes Portorož a useful fall back if everything's full in Piran

History

Portorož may look as if it was born yesterday, but that's not the case. Though most of the development along Obala dates from the late 1960s and 1970s, the settlement was first mentioned in the 13th century, and its sheltered bay was fiercely contested over the next 200 years.

But Portorož didn't achieve real fame until the late 19th century when Austro-Hungarian officers came here to be treated with the mud collected from the salt pans at Sečovlje (p188). Word spread quickly and the Palace hotel (1912) was established.

Orientation

Portorož's main development looks on to the bay from Obala, but there are satellite resorts and hotel complexes to the northwest at Bernardin and south near the Portorož Marina at Lucija. Buses stop opposite the main beach on Postajališka pot.

Information

Atlas Express (☎ 674 67 72; atlas.portoroz@siol.net; Obala 55; ⌚ 9am-4pm Mon-Fri, 10am-1pm Sat) Local rep for American Express.
Banka Koper (Obala 33) Beside the Hotel Slovenija.
Kompas (☎ 617 80 00; Obala 41; ⌚ 9am-7pm Mon-Fri, 9am-1pm & 5-8pm Sat & Sun Jul & Aug, 9am-7pm Mon-Fri, 9am-1pm Sat & Sun Sep-Jun)
Maona Tourist Agency (☎ 674 03 63; Obala 14/b; ⌚ 9am-8pm Mon-Sat, 10am-1pm & 5-8pm Sun Jul & Aug, 9am-7pm Mon-Fri, 10am-7pm Sat, 10am-1pm Sun Sep-Jun) Branch of the excellent travel agency in Piran.
Post office (K Stari cesti 1)
Tourist Information Centre Portorož (TIC; ☎ 673 44 40; www.portoroz.si; Obala 16; ⌚ 9am-9pm Jul & Aug, 9am 7pm Apr, May, Sep & Oct, 9am-5pm Mon-Sat, 10am-2pm Sun Sep-Jun)

Sights

Perched atop the Seča Peninsula near the Lucija camping ground, **Forma Viva** (☎ 671 20 80; www.obalne-galerije.si) is an outdoor sculpture garden with some 130 works of art carved in stone. This is just one of several such parks in Slovenia. They were international exhibitions from the late 1950s where sculptors worked with local materials: stone at Portorož, wood at Kostanjevica na Krki in Dolenjska, iron at Ravne na Koroškem in Koroška and – God help us! – concrete in Maribor. The real reason for coming is the fantastic view of Portorož and Piran Bays. The salt pans at Sečovlje are a short walk to the south.

PRIMORSKA

Activities

BOATING & CRUISES

You can hire kayaks, pedal boats, wakeboards and various other seagoing paraphernalia at the **Watersport Centre Portorož** (Center Vodnih Športov Portorož; ☎ 041 617 999) on the grassy beach area west of the Grand Metropol Hotel.

Spinaker (☎ 041 281 133; www.spinaker.si; Obala 7; 2/3/4hr €79/113/139; ⌚ 10am-6pm May-Sep) can take five of you sailing along the coast to Piran and beyond from the main pier in Portorož. It also rents Zero 22 sailing boats (from €149 a day) and run day-long sailing courses (€50).

A couple of boats make the run between the main pier in Portorož and Izola in summer on trips lasting four hours. They include the **Meja** (☎ 041 664 132; adult/child €10/7; ⌚ 9.15am Tue & Fri) and the **Svetko** (☎ 041 623 191; adult/child €15/10.50; ⌚ 2.30pm daily). The **Solinarka** (☎ 031 653 682; www.solinarka.com; adult/child €12.50/6.25; ⌚ varies) tour boat sails from Portorož to Piran an Strunjan and back.

Kompas and Atlas Express (left) can boo day trips to Venice aboard the *Prince* *Venice* and with Venezia Lines (p297)

PANORAMIC FLIGHTS & SKYDIVING

Sightseeing by ultra-light plane is availab at the **Portorož airport** (☎ 617 51 40, 041 719 26 info@portoroz-airport.si; Sečovlje 19; ⌚ 8am-8pm Apr-Se 3-5pm Oct-Mar). Flights for three people lastin eight/15 minutes over Portorož and Piran/th whole coast cost €55/80. Skydiving costs fron €170 for a tandem jump.

SPAS

Terme & Wellness Centre Portorož (☎ 692 80 60; ww .lifeclass.net; Obala 43; ⌚ 8am-9pm Jun-Sep, 7am-7pm Oc May), a large spa connected with the Gran Hotel Portorož that you can also enter fron K Stari cesti, is famous for thalassotherap (treatment using sea water and by-product like mud from the salt flats). The spa offer various types of warm sea-water and brin baths (€36 to €44), Sečovlje mud baths (€23 massage (€30 for 20 minutes) and a host o other therapies and beauty treatments. Th palatial indoor **swimming pool** (nonguests 2/4hr pas Mon-Fri €8/12, Sat & Sun €10/15; ⌚ 1-8pm Mon-Wed & Fri-Sun, 2-8pm Thu).

SWIMMING

The lifeguard-patrolled **beaches** (⌚ 8am-8pm Apr-Sep) at Portorož, including the main one which accommodates 6000 fried and bronzed bodies, have water slides and outside showers, and beach chairs (€4.10) and umbrellas (€4.10) are available for rent. Beaches are off-limits between 11pm and 6am and camping is strictly forbidden.

The large outdoor **swimming pool** (adult/child €4/3; ⌚ 9am-7pm May-Sep), south of the Grand Hotel Metropol, is open in the warmer months.

Festivals & Events

An unusual local event involving a lot of pageantry is the **Baptism by Neptune** (Neptunov Krst) of new recruits to the naval school held in the first half of September.

Sleeping

BUDGET

The Maona Tourist Agency (left) has **private rooms** (s €18-21, d €26-40, tr €36-52) and **apartments** pt for 2 €40-50, apt for 4 €65-75), with prices varying idely and depending on both the category nd the season. Some of the cheapest rooms re up on the hillside, quite a walk from the each. Getting a room for fewer than three ights (for which you must pay a supplement f 30% to 50%) or a single any time can be ifficult, and in winter many owners don't ent at all.

Camp Lucija (☎ 690 60 00; www.metropol-hotels om; Seča 204; adult €10-16, child €6-7; early Apr–arly Oct) This 5.5-hectare camping ground is below the Seča Peninsula and outh of the marina about 2km from the bus tation. It offers all sorts of sporting facilities and can (and often does) accommodate 000 guests.

Prenočišča Korotan (☎ 674 5400; www.sd.upr.si/dp/prenocisca; Obala 11; s/d/tr/q €36/49.50/66/79; Jul Aug) Just off the main road between Piran nd the centre of Portorož, this unusually pmarket summer-only hostel in Korotan has n-suite rooms and computers for internet access. Be warned, though, that there is a 40/20% upplement for stays of just one/two nights.

MIDRANGE & TOP END

Portorož counts upwards of two dozen hotels, nd very few of them fit into the budget category. Rates at hotels in Portorož can be very igh during the summer months; many close for the winter in October or November and do not reopen until April or even May.

Hotel Marko (☎ 617 40 00; www.hotel-marko.com; Obala 28; s €64-96, d 80-120) Much of Portorož is high-rise city. For something on a more human scale, check out this lovely 48-room hotel with scenic gardens just opposite the main beach.

Hotel Riviera & Hotel Slovenija (☎ 692 00 00; www.lifeclass.net; Obala 33; s €142-185, d €184-250) These four-star sister properties are joined at the hip and are good choices if you want to stay someplace central. The Riviera has 160 rooms, three fabulous swimming pools and an excellent wellness centre. The Slovenija is somewhat bigger with 183 rooms. Both have four stars.

Kempinski Palace Portorož (☎ 692 70 00; www.kempinski-portoroz.com; Obala 45; s/d from €135/185, ste from €600) She was a long time coming but, boy, has the old gal come a long way. Now a 181-room five-star masterpiece in the Kempinski stable with a new and an old wing, the Palace has nevertheless been renovated to within an inch of her life; you'll look high and low for any original features (stone staircase, chandeliers in the Crystal Hall). Keep your eyes instead on things like the rose-themed rooms, the faux-baroque trendy furniture, the

PRIMORSKA

SALT OF THE SEA

Although salt-making went on for centuries along the Slovenian coast at places like Sečovlje and Strunjan, the technique changed very little right up to 40 years ago when harvesting on a large scale all but ended.

Sea water was channelled via in-flow canals – the 'salt roads' – into shallow ponds separated by dikes, which were then dammed with small wooden paddles. Wind-powered pumps removed some of the water, and the rest evaporated in the sun and the wind as the salt crystallised from the remaining brine. The salt was collected, drained, washed and, if necessary, ground and iodised. It was then loaded onto a heavy wooden barge called a *maona* and pulled to salt warehouses *(skladišča soli)*.

Salt harvesting was seasonal work, lasting from 24 April (St George's Day) to 24 August (St Bartholomew's Day), when the autumn rains came. During that time most of the workers lived with their families in rented houses lining the canals at Sečovlje. They paid the landlord with their 'salt funds' – the pans around each house.

The set-up of each house was pretty much the same. The large room downstairs served as a storehouse while upstairs there were two bedrooms and a combination living room and kitchen. All the windows and doors opened on both sides so that workers could observe changes in the weather – as crucial to them as to sailors. Rain and wind could wipe out the entire harvest if the salt was not collected in time.

In September the workers returned to their villages to tend their crops and vines. Because they lived both on the land and 'at sea', Slovenian salt workers were said to 'sit on two chairs'.

enormous front balconies with stunning sea views and the interconnecting indoor and outdoor pools.

Eating

Pizzeria Figarola (☎ 674 22 00; Obala 14a; pizza €5.50-10.50; ⏰ 10am-10pm) There must be a dozen pizzerias along Obala but Figarola, with a huge terrace just up from the main pier, is the place of choice.

Papa Chico (☎ 677 93 10; Obala 26; mains €5.90-16.30; ⏰ 10am-2am) This pleasant cantina serves 'Mexican fun food' (go figure), including hysterical fajitas (from €9.40).

Staro Sidro (☎ 674 50 74; Obala 55; mains €7-21; ⏰ noon-11pm Tue-Sun) A tried-and-true favourite in Portorož, the Old Anchor is next to the lovely (and landmark) Vila San Marco. It specialises in seafood and has both a garden and a lovely terrace overlooking Obala and Portorož Bay.

Stara Oljka (☎ 674 85 55; Obala 20; starters €5-9.60, mains €8.60-24; ⏰ 10am-midnight) The Old Olive Tree specialises in grills (Balkan, steaks etc), which you can watch being prepared in the open kitchen. There's a large and very enticing sea-facing terrace.

San Lorenzo (☎ 690 10 00; Obala 77; mains €9.50-25; ⏰ noon-11pm) Located on the ground floor of the Grand Hotel Metropol, this Italian/Mediterranean restaurant is very fancy schmancy and among the finest Portorož has to offer. The wine selection is superb.

You'll find a branch of the **Mercator** (Obala 53; ⏰ 7am-8pm Mon-Sat, 8am-noon Sun) supermarket chain next to the bus stops.

Drinking & Entertainment

Kavarna Cacao (☎ 674 10 35; Obala 14; ⏰ 8am-1am Sun-Thu, 8am-3am Fri & Sat) This place, now with a carbon-copy branch in Ljubljana, wins the award as the most stylish cafe-bar on the coast and boasts a fabulous waterfront terrace.

Kanela Bar (☎ 674 61 81; Obala 14; ⏰ 9am-3am) Secreted between the beach and the Cacao, the 'Cinnamon' is a workhorse of a rock 'n' roll bar up late (and early) with frequent live concerts.

Portorož Auditorium (Portorož Avditorij; ☎ 676 67 00; www.avditorij.si; Senčna pot 12; ⏰ box office 8am-2pm Mon-Fri) The main cultural venue in Portorož, with two main indoor theatres and a huge open-air amphitheatre, the auditorium is 200m behind where the buses stop. Some of the events of the **Primorska Summer Festival** (www.portoroz.si) in Ju[l] and part of August take place here.

Getting There & Away

BOAT

For information on the daily service fro[m] Portorož to Trieste from May to Septembe[r] see (p297).

BUS

Buses leave Portorož for Koper (€2.30, 2[0] minutes, 15km) and Izola (€1.80, 15 minute[s] 7km) about every 20 to 40 minutes through[-] out the year. Count on between four to seve[n] departures to Strunjan (€1.30, six minute[s] 3km). Other destinations from Portorož an[d] their daily frequencies are the same as thos[e] for Piran (p184).

Minibuses (p184) make the loop fro[m] the Lucija camping grounds through centra[l] Portorož to Piran throughout the year.

CAR

The main car-rental companies, includin[g] **Avis** (☎ 674 05 55) at Atlas Express (p186), ar[e] all represented in Portorož.

Getting Around

CAR

Parking space is tight in Portorož, and yo[u] must 'pay and display' to park in Portorož. One hour costs €1.20, a full day €12.

TAXI

For a local taxi in Portorož ring ☎ 040 58[8] 100 or ☎ 031 730 700.

BICYCLE

The Maona Tourist Agency (p186) rents bicycles for €6/9/15/20 per two-five-10-/24-hour period. The ones from Atlas Express (p186) costs a bit more.

AROUND PORTOROŽ

Sečovlje

☎ 05 / pop 630 / elev 2.5m

The disused salt pans at Sečovlje, covering an area of 721 hectares from Seča to the Dragonja River on the Croatian border, have been turned into **Sečovlje Salina Nature Park** (Krajinski Park Sečoveljske Soline; ☎ 672 13 30; www.kpss.soline.si; adult/child/family €5/3/10; ⏰ 9am-8pm Jun-Sep, 9am-5pm Oct-May), which attracts some 270 bird species (including 90 breeders). The area, criss-crossed with dikes, channels, pools and canals, was

PRIMORSKA

ıce a hive of activity and one of the biggest ıoney-spinners on the coast in the Middle ges. Today, it looks like a ghost town with s empty grey-stone houses and pans slowly eing taken over by hardy vegetation.

In the centre of the reserve is the wonder-ıl **Saltworks Museum** (Muzej Solinarstva; ☎ 671 00 ; www.pommuz-pi.si; adult/child/senior & student incl aritime Museum in Piran €3.50/2.10/2.50; 9am-8pm n-Aug, 9am-6pm Apr, May, Sep & Oct) housed in two uildings. The exhibits relate to all aspects f salt-making and the lives of salt workers nd their families: tools, weights, water jugs, raw hats, baking utensils and the seals sed to mark loaves of bread baked com-ıunally. Out among the pans south of the ıuseum is a **wind-powered pump** (just follow ıe earthen dikes to reach it) that still twirls ı the breeze. The museum staff make use f it and other tools to produce a quantity f salt – up to 2000 tonnes – every year in ne traditional way and will demonstrate he process.

The main entrance to the park is at Lera just south of Seča and off the main road from Portorož which is a couple of kilometres south of Lucija. The other entrance, which is at Fontanigge and leads to the museum, is not connected by land with the Lera section. It is right on the border with Croatia; to reach it you must pass through Slovenian immigration and customs first, so don't forget your passport. Just before you cross the Croatian checkpoint, however, you make a sharp turn to the east (right) and continue along a sealed road for just under 3km. The two museum buildings stand out along one of the canals.

Buses from Portorož stop at the town of Sečovlje, about 1.5km north of the border, so it's best to catch a bus heading into Istria if you can time it right and get off just before the Croatian frontier.

The ideal way to visit the salt pans in summer is on the Solinarka (p186) but times vary so check with the TIVC in Portorož or Piran to avoid disappointment.

Notranjska

More than half of all of Slovenia is covered in forest but not Notranjska. In fact, almost a of 'Inner Carniola' is wooded, making it one of the best places in the country for outdoc activities. Notranjska Regional Park encompasses a large portion of the province, and ther are country parks at Rakov Škocjan gorge and around isolated Snežnik Castle.

Transport through the forests of this isolated province has been difficult; when the railwa linking Trieste and Ljubljana opened in 1857, it sidestepped much of the province. Notranjsk was hit by massive emigration (especially around Cerknica) from the turn of the century up t WWII. Today, much of Notranjska is given over to logging and sometimes you'll see nothin for kilometres on the region's narrow back roads but trucks loaded with timber, especially o the Bloke Plateau – the birthplace of skiing, according to local lore – and in the Lož Valley.

But woodlands are not the only distinguishing physical characteristic of the province Slovenia counts more than 7500 karst caves and sinkholes created by *ponor* (or 'disappearing rivers and some 20 of these caverns, most of them in Notranjska, are open to visitors.

Notranjska is the most typical Dinaric region of Slovenia, but its karst is different fron Primorska. Abundant rain and snow fall here, but the ground is like a great Swiss cheese the water vanishes and resurfaces on the fringes of karst fields called *polje*. Notranjska is als known for its underground rivers and 'intermittent' lakes at Cerknica and Planina.

Notranjska's isolated setting has spawned some of Slovenia's most cherished myths an legends, notably that of the Turk-slayer Martin Krpan, made famous in Fran Levstik's boo of the same name.

HIGHLIGHTS

- Follow Gospod Lueger's lead and throw cherries from **Erazem's Nook** (p195) in Predjama Castle
- Visit the renovated period rooms in back-of-beyond **Snežnik Castle** (p198)
- Get forked with Uršula at Cerknica's **Pustni Karneval** (p197)
- Spot the difference while examining a 'human fish' *(Proteus anguinus)* in the **Proteus Vivarium** (p193) at Postojna Cave
- Slide or skate (if you're so lucky) across the frozen surface of the reappeared **Lake Cerknica** (p196)

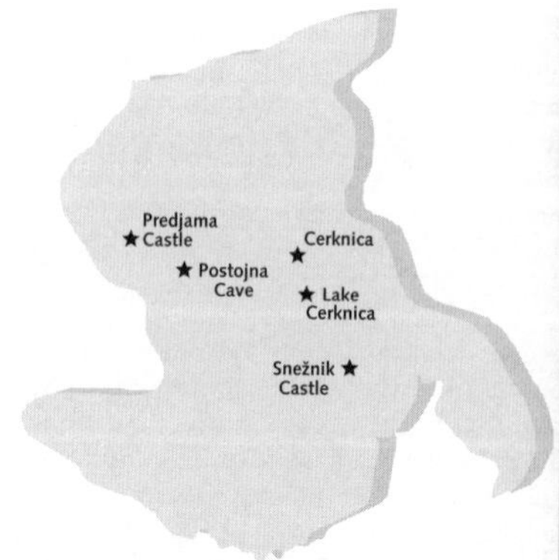

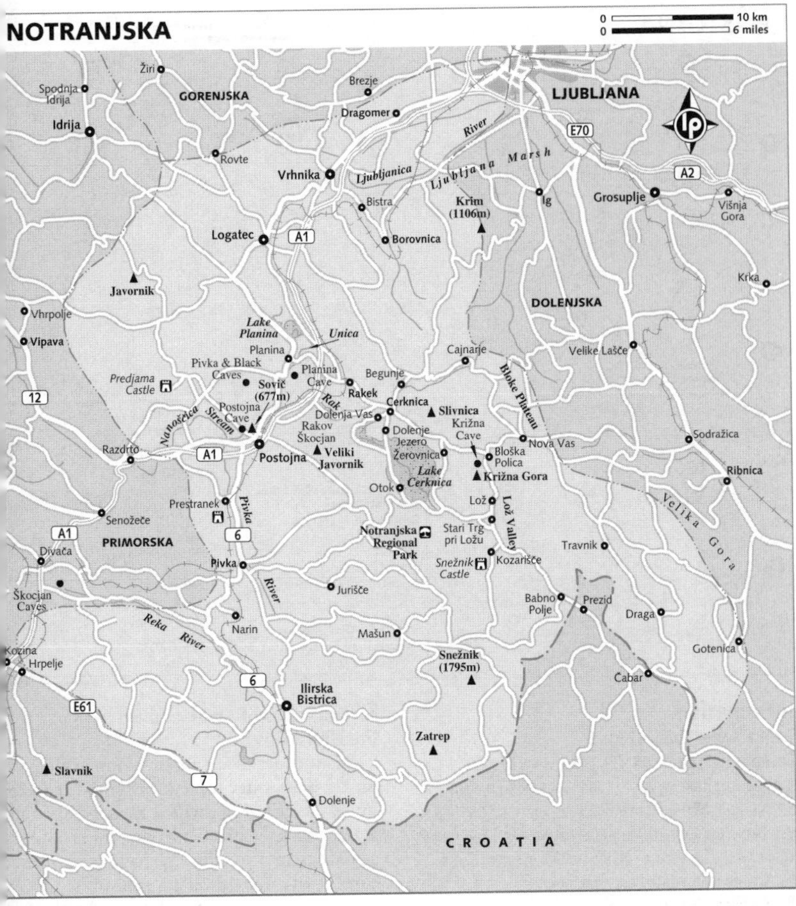

POSTOJNA

☎ 05 / pop 8870 / elev 555m

The karst cave at Postojna, one of the largest in the world, is among Slovenia's most popular attractions and its stalagmite and stalactite formations are unequalled anywhere. A visit is a 'must' on the 'to do' list of most arrivals in Slovenia so expect a scrum of tour groups throughout most of the year.

The cave has been known – and visited – by residents of the area for centuries; you need only look at the graffiti dating back seven centuries in the Gallery of Old Signatures by the entrance. But people in the Middle Ages knew only the entrances; the inner parts were not explored until April 1818, just days before Habsburg Emperor Franz I (r 1792–1835) came to visit. The following year the Cave Commission accepted its first organised tour group, including Archduke Ferdinand, and Postojna's future as a tourist destination was sealed. Since then more than 32 million people have visited the cave.

Orientation

The town of Postojna lies in the Pivka Valley at the foot of Sovič Hill (677m). The Pivka River and the entrance to the cave are about 1.5km northwest of Titov trg in the town centre.

Postojna's bus station is at Titova cesta 36, about 250m southwest of Titov trg. The train station is on Kolodvorska cesta about 600m southeast of the square.

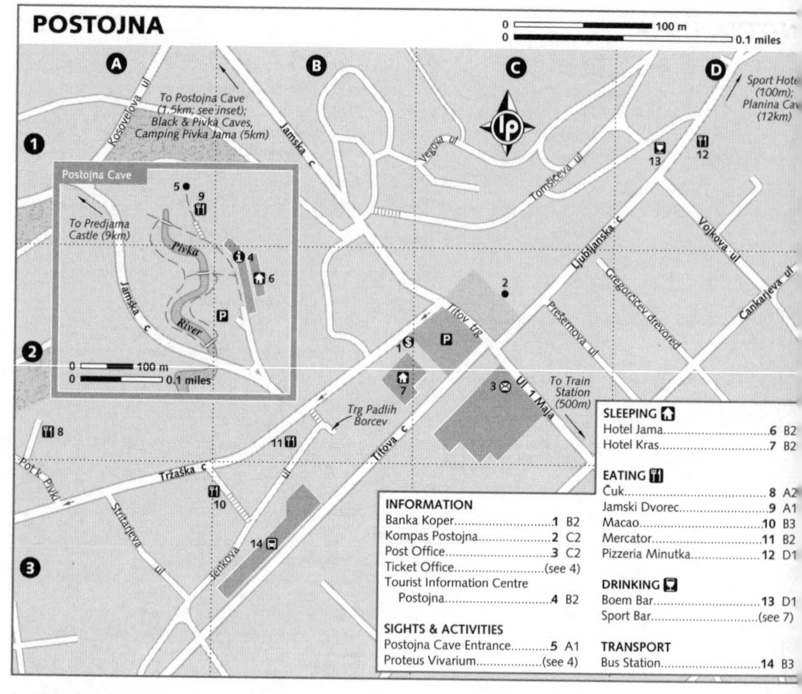

Information

Banka Koper (Tržaška cesta 1)

Kompas Postojna (☎ 721 14 80; www.kompas-postojna.si; Titov trg 2a; 🕑 8am-7pm Mon-Fri, 9am-1pm Sat Jun-Aug, 8am-6pm Mon-Fri, 9am-1pm Sat May, Sep & Oct, 8am-5pm Mon-Fri, 9am-1pm Sat Nov-Apr) This travel agency is the best source of information in town. It also has private rooms and changes money.

Post office (Ulica 1 Maja 2a)

Tourist Information Centre Postojna (TIC; ☎ 720 16 10; www.tdpostojna.si, in Slovene; Jamska cesta 28) In a kiosk just south of the cave entrance. Opening hours are the same as Postojna Cave.

Sights & Activities

POSTOJNA CAVE

The **Postojna Cave** (Postojnska Jama; ☎ 700 01 00; www.postojnska-jama.si; adult/child/student €20/13/16, parking €3.50; 🕑 tours hourly 9am-6pm Jul & Aug, to 5pm May, Jun & Sep, 10am, noon, 2pm & 4pm Apr & Oct, 10am, noon & 3pm Nov-Mar) system, a series of caverns, halls and passages some 20.6km long and two million years old, was hollowed out by the Pivka River, which enters a subterranean tunnel near the cave's entrance. The river continues its deep passage underground, carving out several series of caves, and emerges again a the Unica River.

Visitors get to see about 5.7km of the cav on 1½-hour tours; some 4km of this is covere by an electric train, which runs as far as th **Big Mountain** (Velika Gora) cavern. From her a guide escorts you through halls, galleries an caverns in one of five languages.

These are dry galleries, decorated with a vas array of white stalactites shaped like needles enormous icicles and even fragile spaghett The stalagmites take familiar shapes – pears cauliflower and sand castles – but there ar also bizarre columns, pillars and translucen curtains that look like rashers of bacon.

From the Velika Gora cavern you continu across the **Russian Bridge**, built by prisoners o war in 1916, through the 500m-long **Beautifu Caves** (Lepe Jame) that are filled with wonderful ribbon-shaped stalactites and stalagmites two million years old (it takes 30 year to produce 1mm of stalactite). The halls o the Beautiful Caves are the farthest poin you'll reach; from here a tunnel stretches to the Black Cave (Črna Jama) and Pivka Cave (opposite).

The tour continues south through the Winter Hall (Zimska Dvorana), past the Diamond Stalagmite and the Pillar Column, which have become symbols of the cave. You then enter the Conference Hall (Kongresna Dvorana), which is the largest in the cave system and can accommodate 10,000 people for musical performances. In the week between Christmas and New Year, the Live Christmas Crib (Jaslice) – the Nativity performed by miming actors – also takes place in the cave. Visitors reboard the train by the Conference Hall and return to the entrance.

Postojna Cave has a constant temperature of 8°C to 10°C with a humidity of 95%, so a waterproof jacket is essential. Green felt capes can be hired at the entrance for around €2.50. Check the website for package deals, including combination tickets that include Black and Pivka Caves and Predjama Castle.

Some 200 species of fauna, including cave beetles, bats, hedgehogs and, most famous of all, *Proteus anguinus*, the unique 'human fish' first described by Janez Vajkard Valvasor (see below), are studied at **Proteus Vivarium** (adult/child/student €7/4/6, with Postojna Cave €25/15/20; 9.30am-5.30pm May-Sep, 9.30am-4.30pm Apr & Oct, 9.30am-2.30pm Nov-Mar), part of a speleobiological research station located in the cave. It is open to visitors and has a video introduction to underground zoology. A 45-minute tour then leads you into a small, darkened cave – the so-called Gallery of New Signatures – to peep at some of the shy creatures you've just learned about.

OTHER CAVES

For more information about other caves north of Postojna, ask at the TIC at Postojna Cave or at Kompas Postojna (opposite) in town.

Pivka Cave (Pivka Jama) and **Black Cave** (Črna Jama; adult/child/student €7/4/6; 9am & 3pm Jun-Aug), the most popular caves in the area after Postojna, are about 5km to the north, with the entrance in the Pivka Jama camping ground. You reach the 4km-long system by descending more than 300 steps. A walkway has been cut into the wall of a canyon in Pivka Cave, with its two siphon lakes and a tunnel, and a bridge leads to Black Cave. This is a dry cavern and, as the name implies, its dripstones are not white. A tour of both caves takes about two hours.

Planina Cave (Planinska Jama; ☎ 756 52 42, 041 338 696; www.planina.si; adult/child €6.50/3.50; tours 5pm Mon-Fri Jun-Aug, 3pm & 5pm Sat, 11am, 3pm & 5pm Sun Apr-Sep), 12km to the north-east near the unpredictable Lake Planina, is the largest water cave in Slovenia and a treasure-trove of fauna (including

THE HUMAN FISH

Proteus anguinus is one of the most mysterious creatures in the world. A kind of salamander, but related to no other amphibian, it is the largest known vertebrate permanently living in caves. The blind little fellow lives hidden in the pitch black for up to a century and can go for years without food.

The chronicler Valvasor wrote about the fear and astonishment of local people when an immature 'dragon' was found in a karst spring near Vrhnika in the late 17th century, but he judged it to be 'an underground worm'. Several other reports about this four-legged 'human fish' (*človeška ribica* as it's called in Slovene) were made before a doctor in Vienna realised its uniqueness in 1768. In announcing its existence to the scientific world, he called it *'Proteus anguinus'*, after the protector of Poseidon's sea creatures in Greek mythology and the Latin word for 'snake'.

Proteus anguinus is 25cm to 30cm long and a bundle of contradictions. It has a long tail fin that it uses for swimming, but can also propel itself with its four legs (the front pair have three small 'fingers' and the back have two 'toes'). Although blind, with atrophied, almost invisible eyes, *Proteus anguinus* has an excellent sense of smell and is sensitive to weak electric fields in the water. It uses these to move around in the dark, locate prey and communicate. It breathes through frilly, bright-red gills at the base of its head when submerged, but also has rudimentary lungs for breathing when outside the water. The humanlike skin has no pigmentation whatsoever, but looks pink in the light due to blood circulation.

The question that scientists have asked themselves for three centuries is: how do the beasties reproduce? The process has never been witnessed in a natural state, and they haven't been very cooperative in captivity. It is almost certain that they hatch their young from eggs and don't reach sexual maturity until the (almost human) age of 16 or 18.

Proteus anguinus). The cave's entrance is at the foot of a 100m rock wall. It's 6.5km long, and you are able to visit about 900m of it in an hour. There are no lights so take a torch.

More ambitious **caving treks** (€30 to €60) to Planina and other caves in the area and lasting between three and six hours can be organised through the Sport Hotel (below).

MOUNTAIN BIKING

The Sport Hotel (below) can arrange all sorts of activities, including weekend packages with mountain-biking trips (€80) in nearby Notranjska Regional Park, including accommodation.

Sleeping

Kompas Postojna (p192) organises private rooms (per person from €18) in town and farmhouse stays (per person from €20) further afield in Narin (15km southwest) and Razdrto (11km west). The most central rooms are at Jamska cesta 21 and Kajuhova ulica 20.

Camping Pivka Jama (☎ 720 39 93; www.venus-trade.si; Veliki Otok 50; camping adult €9.90-11.40, child €7.90-8.90, 4-bed bungalow €74-84, 4-bed bungalow with kitchen €89-99; Apr-Oct; P) This 7-hectare site is hidden in a deep pine forest near the entrance to Pivka and Black Caves. Some of the little stone-and-wood bungalows have kitchens, and there's a swimming pool.

Sport Hotel (☎ 720 22 44; www.sport-hotel.si; Kolodvorska cesta 1; dm €25-35, s €55-75, d €70-80, tr €96-101; P) A hotel of some sort or another since 1880, the Sport offers reasonable value for money, with 32 spic-and-span and very comfortable rooms, including five with nine hostel beds each. There's a kitchen with small eating area and a restaurant with set menus from €8 to €20 and laundry costs €10. It's just 300m north of the centre of Postojna.

Hotel Jama (☎ 728 24 00; www.turizem-kras.si; Jamska cesta 30; s €51-56, d €82-92, tr €113-128; P) This 156-room property 200m southeast of the entrance to Postojna Cave has had something of a facelift in recent years, but there is little reason to stay out here unless you want to be the first person in the cave in the morning as the area is dead after nightfall.

Hotel Kras (☎ 700 23 00; www.hotel-kras.si; Tržaška cesta 1; s €68-74, d €84-96, apt €100-120; P) This rather flash garni hotel has risen, phoenix-like, from the ashes of a decrepit old caravanserai in the heart of town, and now boasts 27 comfortable rooms with all the mod-cons. If you've got the dosh, choos one of the apartments on the top (5th) floc with enormous terraces.

Eating

Macao (☎ 757 28 88; Tržaška cesta 11a; starters €1.6 3.20, mains €4-9.20) Don't expect the real McCo at this hole-in-the-wall Chinese eatery jus north of the bus station but it's there if yo need a fix of rice or noodles.

Čuk (☎ 720 13 00; Pot k Pivki 4; starters €5-7.5 pizza & pasta €6-9.50; 10am-11pm Mon-Fri, 11an midnight Sat, noon-11pm Sun) Excellent and larg restaurant southwest of Titov trg just o Tržaška cesta, Čuk takes its pizza seriously but offers a wide range of Slovenia mains too.

Pizzeria Minutka (☎ 720 36 25; Ljubljanska cesta 1 starters €4.65-7.50, pizza €5.60-7.20, mains €7.50-13.50) pizzeria with a terrace, Minutka is a favourite with locals and also does more ambitiou main courses. It's rolling distance from th Sport Hotel.

Jamski Dvorec (☎ 700 01 81; starters €6.50-10, main €13.50-22; 9am-6pm) Housed in a stunnin 1920s-style building next to the entrance t the cave, the Cave Manor has fairly averag international dishes but its set menus at €1 and €12 are a big attraction.

There is a **Mercator** (Tržaška cesta 9; 7am-7pr Mon-Fri, 7am-1pm Sat) a short distance southwes of Titov trg.

Drinking

Two places worth heading for if the whistle i dry include the **Boem Bar** (☎ 726 13 11; Ljubljansk cesta 11; 7am-11pm Mon-Thu, 7am-midnight Fri & Sat 10am-11pm Sun), a comfortable place near th Sport Hotel, and the lively **Sport Bar** (☎ 700 2 00; Tržaška cesta 1; 8am-11pm Sun-Thu, 8am-2am Fri & Sat) at the Hotel Kras.

Getting There & Away

Buses from Ljubljana to the coast as well a Ajdovščina stop in Postojna (€6, one hour 53km, hourly). Other destinations include Cerknica (€3.10, 30 minutes, 24km, six on weekdays), Koper (€6.90, 1¼ hours, 68km four to seven daily), Nova Gorica (€6.70, 1½ hours, 63km, five to eight a day) and Piran (€8.30, 1½ hours, 86km, three or four a day), and Snežnik and Stari Trg pri Ložu (€8, two hours, 88km, one on weekdays at 2.10pm).

International bus destinations include Trieste (€5.70, 1¼ hours, 52km, 6.50am Monday to riday and 7.40am Monday to Saturday) in orthern Italy, Rijeka (€11, 1½ hours, 82km) nd Split (€37.50, 9½ hours, 474km) in Croatia t 8.35pm daily, and Banja Luka (€29.90, six ours, 378km, 3.04pm Tuesday & Thursday) n Bosnia-Hercegovina.

Postojna is on the main train line linkng Ljubljana (€4.90, one hour, 67km) with ežana and Trieste via Divača (€2.90 to €4.45, 0 minutes, 37km), and is an easy day trip om the capital. As many as 20 trains a day nake the run from Ljubljana to Postojna and ack. You can also reach here from Koper €5.90 to €10.30, 1½ hours, 86km) on one of p to seven trains a day.

Getting Around

Buses bound for Postojna Cave and Predjama Castle leave Postojna's train station at 0.30am, noon, 2.30pm and 4.10pm. The bus is free but those with train tickets take precedent. The last bus from the castle is at 4.40pm and from the cave at 5.05pm.

If you need a taxi in Postojna, call ☎ 031 777 974 or 041 752 751.

The Sport Hotel (opposite) rents mountain bikes (€9/15 per half-/full day).

PREDJAMA CASTLE

☎ 05 / pop 85 / elev 490m

Situated in the gaping mouth of a cavern halfway up a 123m cliff just 9km northwest of Postojna, **Predjama Castle** (Predjamski Grad; ☎ 751 50 15; www.turizem-kras.si; adult/child/student €8/5.50/7; 9am-7pm Jul & Aug, 9am-6pm May, Jun & Sep, 10am-5pm Apr & Oct, 10am-4pm Nov-Mar) has one of the most dramatic settings of any castle in the world. Although a castle has stood on the site since 1202, the one you see today dates from the 16th century. Then – as now – the four-storey fortress looked unconquerable.

The castle's eight rooms spread over four floors contain little of interest – oil paintings, weapons, a 15th-century pietà, costumed wax mannequins, one of which dangles from the dripping rock-roofed torture chamber. But it does have a drawbridge over a raging river, holes in the ceiling of the entrance tower for pouring boiling oil on intruders, a very dank dungeon, and an eyrie-like hiding place at the top called Erazem's Nook.

The **cave** (Jama pod Predjamskim Gradom; adult/child/student €7/4/6, with castle €13/8/11; tours 11am, 1pm, 3pm & 5pm May-Sep) below Predjama Castle is a 6km network of galleries spread over four levels. Much of it is open only to speleologists, however casual visitors can see about 900m of it. Longer tours that go to the end of the cave's **Eastern Passage** (€60, five hours) or **Erazem's Gallery** (Erazmov Rov, €30, one hour) are available by prior arrangement only.

The red-letter day in these parts is the **Erazem Knights' Tournament** (www.turizem-kras.si), a day of duelling, jousting and archery with authentic weapons on the castle grounds in mid-July.

Gostilna Požar (☎ 751 52 52; Predjama 2; meals from €15; 10am-10pm Thu-Tue, daily Aug) is a simple restaurant conveniently located next to the ticket kiosk and in full heart-stopping view of the castle, specialising in grilled and game dishes.

Free buses link Postojna's railway station with Predjama Castle daily at 10.30am, noon, 2.30pm and 4.10pm, and leave from the castle at 11am, 12.30pm, 3pm and 4.40pm.

A taxi from Postojna, including an hour's wait at Predjama Castle, will cost €30, which staff at Kompas Postojna (p192) can arrange.

CERKNICA

☎ 01 / pop 3890 / elev 559m

Cerknica is the largest town on a lake that isn't always a lake – one of Slovenia's most unusual natural phenomena. It's an excellent springboard for both the gorge at Rakov Škocjan and Notranjska Regional Park as a whole.

The area around Lake Cerknica has been settled since prehistoric times, and a trade route once ran over the Bloke Plateau to the east, linking Slovenia and Croatia. During the Roman period, Cerknica was a stopover on the road leading from Emona (Ljubljana) to the coast. Cerknica was given town status in the 11th century.

But Cerknica is a good example of how important communication lines are for the development of a town. The railway linking Trieste and Ljubljana opened in 1857, but it dodged Cerknica in favour of Rakek, 5km to the northwest. The highway from Ljubljana towards the coast follows the same route, and Cerknica remains something of a backwater to this day.

Orientation

Cerknica lies about 3km north of Lake Cerknica. Cesta 4 Maja is the main street in the centre of town. The bus station is on Čabranska ulica about 100m to the southwest and behind the post office.

DEATH ON THE THRONE

Erazem Lueger was a 15th-century robber-baron who, like Robin Hood, waylaid wagons in the deep forest, stole the loot and handed it over to the poor (or so he said). During the wars between the Hungarians (under 'good' King Matthias Corvinus) and the Austrians (behind 'wicked' Frederick III), Lueger (naturally) supported the former. He holed up in Predjama Castle and continued his daring deeds with the help of a secret passage that led out from behind the rock wall.

In the autumn of 1484 the Austrian army under Gašpar Ravbar, the governor of Trieste, attacked the castle, but it proved impregnable for months. All the while Erazem mocked Ravbar and his soldiers, even showering them with fresh cherries to prove that he came and went as he pleased.

But Erazem proved to be too big for his britches and met an ignoble fate. Having gone 'to where even the sultan must go on foot' (as Valvasor put it), Erazem was hit by a cannon ball as he sat on the toilet. It seems a turncoat servant had betrayed him by marking the location of the water closet with a little flag for Ravbar and his men.

Information

Notranjska Regional Park (Notranjski Regijski Park; ☎ 059 091 612; www.notranjski-park.si; Tabor 42; 🕑 by appointment) Headquarters of the new 22,282-hectare regional park 100m north of the TIC.

Nova Ljubljanska Banka (Cesta 4 Maja 64) In the Imam shopping centre.

Post office (Cesta 4 Maja 52) Next door to the TIC.

SKB Banka (Partizanska cesta 1) Next door to Valvasor Hram.

Tourist Information Centre Cerknica (☎ 709 36 36, 031 465 707; tdrustvo@volja.net; Cesta 4 Maja 51; 🕑 8am-3.30pm Mon-Fri, 8.30am-1pm Sat)

Sights

LAKE CERKNICA

Since ancient times periodic Lake Cerknica (Cerniško Jezero) has baffled and perplexed people, including the Greek geographer and historian Strabo (63 BC–AD 24), who called the mysterious body of water Lacus Lugeus (Mourning Lake). It wasn't until Valvasor explained how the water system worked at the end of the 17th century that it was fully understood.

Cerknica is a *polje*, a field above a collapsed karst cavern full of sinkholes, potholes, siphons and underground tunnels, which can stay dry for much of the year but then floods. From the south, the *polje* is fed by a disappearing river, the Stržen, and to the east and west it collects water underground from the Bloke Plateau and the Javornik Mountains. During rainy periods, usually in the autumn and spring, all this water comes rushing into the *polje*. Springs emerge and the water begins to percolate between the rocks. The sinkholes and siphons cannot handle the outflow underground, and the polje becomes Lake Cerknica – sometimes in less than a day.

The surface area of Lake Cerknica can reach 29 sq km, but it is never more than a few metres deep. At that time it is an important wetland, attracting some 250 species of birds each year. During dry periods (usually July to September or later), farmers drive cattle down to the *polje* to graze.

The lake really begins at the village of Dolenje Jezero (population about 225), 2.5km south of Cerknica, where you will find the **Lake House Museum** (Muzej Jezerski Hram; ☎ 709 40 53, 041 561 870; www.jezerski-hram.si; Dolenje Jezero 1e; adult/child €3.50/1.50; 🕑 demonstration 3pm Sat Apr-Oct), with a 5m by 3m 1:2500-scale working model of Lake Cerknica. It shows how the underground hydrological system actually works in a 45-minute-long demonstration and a 24-minute video about the lake in the four seasons. There's also an ethnological collection, focusing on the fishing industry and boat-building.

RAKOV ŠKOCJAN

Protected Rakov Škocjan is a 6km-long gorge lying some 5km west of Cerknica. The Rak River, en route to join the Pivka River at Planina Cave, has sculpted 2.5km of hollows, caves, springs and **Veliki** and **Mali Naravni Most**, the Big and Little Natural Bridges. There are lots of hiking and biking trails through and around the gorge and it is surrounded by Notranjska Regional Park. To the south lies the Snežnik-Javornik Massif, including its tallest peak, **Veliki Javornik** (1268m).

From Rakek train station (p198), you can reach the gorge on foot in about an hour.

ctivities

he TIC sells **fishing licences** (fly-fishing per day lake/ ık River/Unica River €16/10/99).

The **Kontrabantar farmhouse** (☎ 709 22 53; Dolenja ıs 72; per hr €10; ⏰ noon-10pm Thu-Sun) in Dolenja as, 2km southwest of Cerknica, has horses, ding lessons and riding gear for rent. It also ffers tours by coach (€40) around the lake.

The staff at the excellent Hotel Rakov Škocjan ɔ198) can organise any number of activities, om guided **hiking** (from €20 per person) and **ving** (from €23) to **cycling** and **fly-fishing** in the urrounding park. They offer packages such as ne that includes accommodation, half-board, bicycle and a trip to Križna Cave (p199) for 38 per person per day in a double. Ask them or the free English-language booklet *Rakov kocjan and the Nature Trail.*

The **Cerknica Mountain Trail** heads southwest rom Cerknica to thickly forested **Veliki Javornik** 1268m). From here you can take a side trip of bout two hours to the gorge at Rakov Škocjan opposite). Otherwise the trail skirts the southrn shore of Lake Cerknica and carries on ortheast to **Križna Gora** (857m) and its nearby **ave** (p199). It continues northwest to **Slivnica** 1114m), home of the witch Uršula (see the ollowing) and other sorcerers, where you will ind the Dom na Slivnici (right) mountaintop uest house. The next day you walk northnorthwest to **Stražišče** (955m) and then south along the main road for 3km to Cerknica.

Festivals & Events

Cerknica is famous for its pre-Lenten carnival called **Pustni Karneval** (www.cerknica.net/pust), which takes place for four days over the weekend before Ash Wednesday (late February/early March). Merrymakers wearing masks of Uršula, who makes her home on Mt Slivnica, and other legendary characters parade up and down Cesta 4 Maja while being provoked by upstarts with pitchforks.

Sleeping & Eating

Dom na Slivnici (☎ 709 41 40, 041 518 108; s/d €28.60/44; ⏰ daily May-Sep, Sat & Sun Oct-Apr; P) This splendidly positioned five-room guest house with 12 beds at 1075m, just below Mt Slivnica, is accessible by foot or by road about 8km east of Cerknica. There's a popular restaurant here too.

TeliCo (☎ 709 70 90, 041 711 088; www.telico.info; Brestova ulica 9; s €23-30, d €36-46; P) This small seven-bed B&B on the eastern edge of town, with two double rooms with bathroom and WC, has stunning views and its own swimming pool.

Logar farmhouse (☎ 709 20 71, 031 784 232; www.slovenia.info/logar; Žerovnica 16; s/d €45/60; P) This farmhouse in Žerovnica, an idyllic village

TALES FROM A DARK PROVINCE

Slovenian folk tales are rife with fairies, witches and things that go bump in the night, but among the most common stories are those describing the derring-do of 'super heroes', whose strong wills and unusual strength enabled them to overcome evil and conquer their brutish enemies.

The legends are not limited to one geographical area. Peter Klepec, who swept away his enemies using trees uprooted with his bare hands, lived on the Kolpa River and is associated with Bela Krajina. Another hero called Kumprej ruled the Upper Savinja Valley in Štajerska with his mighty voice and fearsome blade. His shoes were five times larger than those of the average person and when he disappeared shoeless a poor couple made footwear for their entire family from the clodhoppers.

But perhaps the most popular stories revolve around the feats of one Martin Krpan, the hero of the Bloke Plateau in Notranjska. Krpan's traits and characteristics are familiar. He was an outlaw with a big heart hunted by the imperial guard for smuggling salt. When he was arrested, Martin Krpan proved his super-human strength to the emperor in Vienna by picking up and carrying his own horse. (Portrayed in a statue of this *silen človek,* or 'powerful man', in the centre of Cerknica.)

Realising his fortune at having such a powerful giant under his control, the emperor set Martin Krpan on Berdavs, the local scourge and personification of the marauding Turk. Martin Krpan defeated Berdavs and chopped off his head with a magic axe – complete with a handle made of Slovenian linden wood. For his pains the imperial court allowed him to freely transport and sell salt.

The tales of Martin Krpan are traditional but reached a wider audience when the writer Fran Levstik collected and published them under the title *Martin Krpan* in 1858.

some 6km southeast of Cerknica on the lake's eastern shore (when full), has doubles as well as a four-person apartment. You'll need your own transport.

our pick Hotel Rakov Škocjan (☎ 709 74 70, 051 310 477; www.h-rakovskocjan.com; Rakov Škocjan 1; s/d/tr €45/76/106; P) In the heart of Notranjska Regional Park and surrounded by deep forest ribboned with hiking and cycling trails, this 13-room guest house 7km west of Cerknica is the ideal spot for a no-holds-barred active holiday. It has a sauna and an excellent restaurant (starters €4 to €7, mains €7.70 to €15; open 7am to 10pm) specialising in game dishes like venison and boar, that is open to nonguests as well, with outdoor grill and terrace seating in the warmer months.

Pizzeria Glaž'k (☎ 709 33 44; Partizanska cesta 17; pizzas €4.90-6.50; 7am-11pm Mon-Fri, 7am-midnight Sat & Sun) This basic pizzeria is up a gentle slope 200m north of Cesta 4 Maja and across from the landmark 16th-century Parish Church of Our Lady. Set lunch is a bargain at €4.50.

Valvasorjev Hram (☎ 709 37 88; Partizanska cesta 1; mains €6-10; 8am-11pm Mon-Sat, 3-10pm Sun) This simple eatery opposite the TIC serves hearty dishes like *jota* (bean soup) and *klobasa* (sausage) as well as pizza. It has its own wine cellar and outside seating in summer.

You'll find a small **Mercator** (Cesta 4 Maja 50; 7.30am-9pm Mon-Sat, 8am-noon Sun) diagonally opposite the TIC.

Getting There & Around

Buses run between Cerknica and Ljubljana (€6, 1¼ hours, 52km, six to eight a day) and Postojna (€2.70, 30 minutes, 17km, five on weekdays). Up to half a dozen go to the train station in Rakek (€1.80, 10 minutes, 6km) and to Stari Trg pri Ložu (€2.70, 30 minutes, 18km). Two buses a day cross the Croatian border to Prezid (€4.10, one hour, 35km) at 1.30pm and 4.55pm Monday to Friday).

Rakek, about 8km northwest of Cerknica, is on the rail line that connects Ljubljana with Sežana. About 10 trains a day to and from the capital stop at Rakek (€4.30 to €8, one hour, 55km). Heading south, all stop at Postojna (€1.60 to €3.90, 15 minutes, 12km) and Pivka, but only about half continue on to Divača (€3.60 to €7, 50 minutes, 49km) and Sežana.

The Hotel Rakov Škocjan (above) rents bicycles and mountain bikes for €3/15 per hour/day.

SNEŽNIK CASTLE & AROUND

☎ 01 / elev 593m

Just south of the village of Kozarišče (population 240), in the secluded Lož Valley (Loška Dolina) some 21km southeast of Cerknica stands 16th-century Renaissance **Snežnik Castle** (Grad Snežnik; ☎ 705 78 14; www.nms.si; Kozarišče 67; adult/child & concession/family €4/3/8; tours hourly 10am-6pm Tue-Sun Apr-Sep, 10am-4pm Tue-Sun Oct-Mar), part of the National Museum of Slovenia. Surrounded by a large and shaded garden, Snežnik has just undergone a complete renovation and is one of the loveliest and best-situated fortresses in Slovenia. The entrance to the castle is through a double barbican with a drawbridge over a moat. The exhibits over four floors in the main building are essentially the entire household inventory of the Schönburg-Waldenburg family, who bought the castle in 1853 and used it as a summer residence and hunting lodge until WWII. The castle is crammed with tasteful period furniture and portraits; one room is done up in Egyptian gifts, handicrafts presented to Herman Schönburg-Waldenburg by a friend early in the 20th century. Temporary exhibits are held in the bailey.

The 19th-century dairy building adjacent to the castle is the rather esoteric **Hunting Museum & Dormouse Collection** (Lovski Muzej in Polharska Zbirka; ☎ 705 75 16, 031 288 470; Kozarišče 70; adult/child €3/1; 10am-noon & 3-7pm Wed-Fri, 10am-1pm & 2-7pm Sat & Sun mid-May–Oct). The dormouse (p50) or loir *(polh)* is a traditional food in Notranjska and the hunting and eating of said rodent is tied up with a lot of tradition, which the museum explores. The fur is used to make a *polhovka*, the distinctive fur cap worn by Božiček, Slovenia's version of Santa Claus, and dormouse *mast* (fat) is a much-prized machine oil. According to popular belief, the dormouse is shepherded by Lucifer himself and thus deserves its fate in the cooking pot. The hunting museum is a nightmare of stuffed animals, antlers and other 'trophies' from the Snežnik-Javornik Massif and Cerknica Lake areas.

The big occasion in these parts of Notranjska is **Dormouse Night** (Polharska Noč) when it's open season for trapping the incredible edible *polh*. It's held on the first Saturday after 25 September.

Snežnik Castle's isolation makes it tough to reach by public transport. Without a car, bicycle or horse, you'll have to take a bus from Cerknica to Stari Trg pri Ložu (€2.70, 30 minutes, 18km) and walk 4km. Staff at he Hotel Rakov Škocjan (opposite), in the egional park some 30km to the northwest, an arrange transport to and from the castle or €25 per car.

Križna Cave (☎ 041 632 153; www.krizna-jama.si; dult/child €6/4; ⏰ tours 11am, 1pm, 3pm & 5pm Jul Aug, 11am, 1pm & 3pm Sep, 3pm Sat & Sun Apr-Jun), bout 7km north of Snežnik Castle and a ilometre or so after you turn off the main oad from Cerknica, is one of the most nagnificent water caves in the world. It is .2km long and counts almost two dozen nderground lakes filled with green and lue water as well as a unique 'forest' of ce stalagmites near the entrance. The dry art of the cave, which includes a short boat ride at the end, can be seen on a one-hour tour without advance booking. To go as far as the Kalvarija (Calvary) chamber by rubber raft via 13 lakes (€26 to €38, depending on group size), you must book in advance. It's a 3½- to four-hour tour if you elect to do the entire cave, and the price includes all equipment.

A stage of the E6 European Hiking Trail (p64) leads south from near Snežnik Castle for about 15km to **Velika Snežnik** (1796m), the highest non-Alpine mountain in Slovenia, whose peak remains covered in snow until well into the spring. There is accommodation at the Category I PZS-maintained hut **Koča Draga Karolina na Velikem Snežniku** (☎ 051 615 356, 041 595 879; pd.sneznik@email.si; Sat & Sun May-Jul, Sep & Oct, daily Aug).

Dolenjska & Bela Krajina

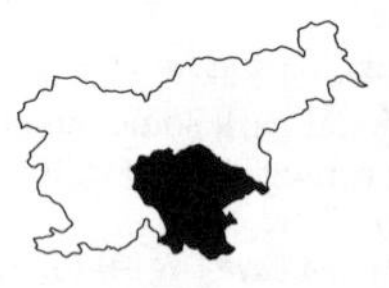

'Lower Carniola' is a gentle area of rolling hills, vineyards, forests and the Krka River flowing southeast into Croatia. Those white, hilltop churches with their red-tile roofs that you'll see everywhere once protected the people from the marauding Turks and other invaders; the ones on the flat lands are newer – built in the baroque style and painted the mustard colour ('Maria Theresa yellow') so common in Central Europe.

The E6 and E7 European Hiking trails pass through Dolenjska, and there are lots of chances to do some kayaking or canoeing on the Krka. The province is also the cycling centre of Slovenia and famous for its thermal spas. And if you're here to practise your Slovene, this is the region to do it: many people say that the 'purest' Slovene is around the village of Rašica, south of the town of Krka.

Bela Krajina, the 'White March', is separated from Dolenjska by the scenic Gorjanci Mountains. The province, which takes its name from the countless stands of birch trees here, is a treasure trove of Slovenian folklore, and, you'll see more traditional dance and hear more music here than anywhere else in the country.

HIGHLIGHTS

- Cycle the back roads of the picturesque **Krka River valley** (p207)
- Visit the haunt of the Partisans at Baza 20 in the virgin forests of **Kočevski Rog** (p211)
- Walk back in time at **Bogenšperk Castle** (p206), especially in the late great Janez Vajkard Valvasor's study
- Make a pilgrimage to the **Three Parishes** (p229) churches in Rosalnice near Metlika
- Enjoy the almost medieval merrymaking of the **Jurjevanje** (p231) festival in Črnomelj in mid-June
- Kayak the rapid-water run on the **Kolpa River** (p232) from Stari Trg to Vinica
- Cock your ear to Bela Krajina folk music, especially around **Adlešiči** (p232)

ITINERARY

KRKA CRUISING

One to two days / Dolenjska

If you are continuing on to other towns in Dolenjska or even destinations in Bela Krajina from say, Bogenšperk Castle (p206) or the abbey at Stična (p205) and have your own transport – car, bicycle or four-legged beastie – the ideal way to go is to follow route No 216 along the Krka River, which cuts a deep and picturesque valley along its upper course. Along the way you'll chance upon historical churches, mighty castles and even a couple of caves worth visiting. A few buses from Ljubljana to Novo Mesto via Dolenjske Toplice follow this route but they are very infrequent.

The journey really begins about 5km south of **Ivančna Gorica** (**1**), in **Muljava** (**2**; p207), a picturesque town of double hayracks and beehives, which will keep both religious and literary pilgrims busy. Near the village of **Krka** (**3**), about 4km to the southwest, are a pair of **caves** (p208), one of which is the source of the 94km-long Krka River. Carry on for another 13km or so and you'll reach **Žužemberk** (**4**; p208), a town dominated at street level by a multi-turreted caste but watched from on high by the mammoth **Parish Church of Sts Mohor and Fortunat** (Župnijska Cerkev Sv Mohorja in Fortunata), built over six decades in the 18th century and dedicated in 1769. Nine kilometres to the south of Žužemberk at **Soteska** (**5**) are the ruins of **Soteska Castle**, a fortress admired by Valvasor but more or less razed during WWII. Nearby is the irresistibly sweet **Garden Pavilion**, a cylindrical structure from the late 17th century with *trompe l'œil* frescoes.

At Soteska you can elect to carry on south on the No 216 to the spa town of **Dolenjske Toplice** (**6**; p208) or turn east on to route No 419 and continue following the Krka River. If you choose the latter, within 6km you'll reach **Straža** (**7**), which boasts the massive **Church of the Assumption of Mary** (Cerkev Marije Vnebovzete), built at the very end of the 18th century and featuring some impressive illusionist paintings. Then it's onto Dolenjska's main city, **Novo Mesto** (**8**; p211).

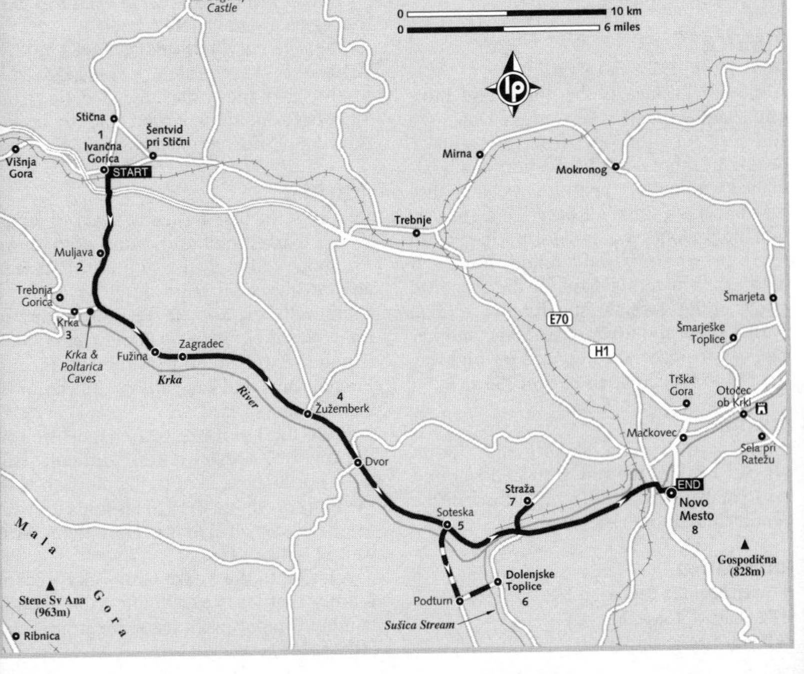

DOLENJSKA

The castles along the Krka River in Dolenjska are some of the best preserved in Slovenia, as are the many monasteries and abbeys. And you can't miss Dolenjska's distinctive *toplarji* (double hayracks); they're here in spades.

Dolenjska was settled early on and is well known for its Hallstatt (early Iron Age) ruins (p27), especially near Stična, Šmarjeta and Novo Mesto. The Romans made the area part of the province of Upper Pannonia (Pannonia Superior) and built roads connecting Emona (Ljubljana) with smaller settlements at Praetorium Latobicorum (Trebnje), Acervo (Stična) and Neviodonum (Drnovo).

In the Middle Ages, the people of Dolenjska clustered around the many castles along the river (eg at Žužemberk and Otočec) and at parish centres like Šentvid. Monasteries sprung up at Stična, Kostanjevica na Krki and near Šentjernej. But Dolenjska declined after the Middle Ages and progress only came in the late 19th century when a railway line linked Novo Mesto with Ljubljana.

RIBNICA

☎ 01 / pop 3395 / elev 492m

Although Ribnica is the oldest and most important settlement of western Dolenjska and just over the hills from Notranjska, people in this region have traditionally affiliated with neither province. As far as they are concerned, this is Kočevsko, a sparsely inhabited wooded area with underground rivers, brown bears and a unique history. It is an excellent springboard for the unspoiled forests of the Kočevski Rog. Ribnica is 16km northwest of the town of Kočevje, another gateway to Kočevski Rog and on highway No 106 to the Croatian port of Rijeka.

Orientation

Ribnica's main street, Škrabčev trg, lies on the east bank of the tiny Bistrica River and runs parallel to it. Buses stop in front of the Parish Church of St Stephen.

Information

Nova Ljubljanska Banka (Škrabčev trg 11) Southeast of the Church of St Stephen.

Post office (Kolodvorska ulica 2)

Tourist Information Centre Ribnica (TIC; ☎ 836 93 35, 051 415 429; www.miklovahisa.si/tic; Škrabčev trg 23; 9am-7pm Mon-Fri, 8am-noon Sat, 10am-2pm Su Jul & Aug only)

Sights

On the west bank of the Bistrica, **Ribnica Cast** (Ribniški Grad; Gallusovo nabrežje 1) was originally bui in the 11th century but was transformed an expanded over the centuries. Only a sma section – a Renaissance wall and two towers survived bombings during WWII. Today th castle houses a small **ethnographic collectio** (☎ 835 03 76, 041 390 057; www.miklovahisa.si/muze adult/child & student/senior €2.50/1.70/2.10; 10am 1pm & 4-7pm Tue-Sun) showcasing the tradition woodcrafts and pottery made in the area.

The **Parish Church of St Stephen** (Župnijska Cerke Sv Štefana; Škrabčev trg), built in 1868 on the sit of earlier churches, would not be of muc interest were it not for the two striking tow ers added by Jože Plečnik in the form of hi signature pyramids in 1960 to replace the one toppled during WWII.

Opposite the church is **Štekliček Hous** (Šteklíčkova Hiša; Škrabčev trg 16), where the 19th century poet and patriot France Prešere spent two years (1810–12) in what was the the region's best-known school.

The gallery at **Mikel House** (Miklova Hiša; ☎ 835 0 76; Škrabčev trg 21; admission free; 8am-4pm Mon-Fri), lovely cream-and-white building dating fro 1858, has exhibitions of contemporary art an does double duty as the town's library.

Activities

Ribnica is the base for many excellent walks A well-marked trail leads north of the towr for about 4.5km to the summit of **Stene Sv Ana** (963m), with fantastic views over the Ribnica Valley; ask the TIC for a copy o the *Natural Heritage of Ribnica* pamphlet Along the way you'll pass the entrance tc France Cave and the hilltop Church of S Anne (930m).

From the Jasnica recreational centre (on the way to Kočevje) a more difficult path leads north about 6km to the junction with the Ribnica Alpine Trail. This joins up with the E7 European Hiking Trail about 5km west of Velike Lašče.

A trail into the Velika Gora ridge west of Ribnica that leads to a comfortable mountain hut is more easily accessible from Nova Štifta (p205).

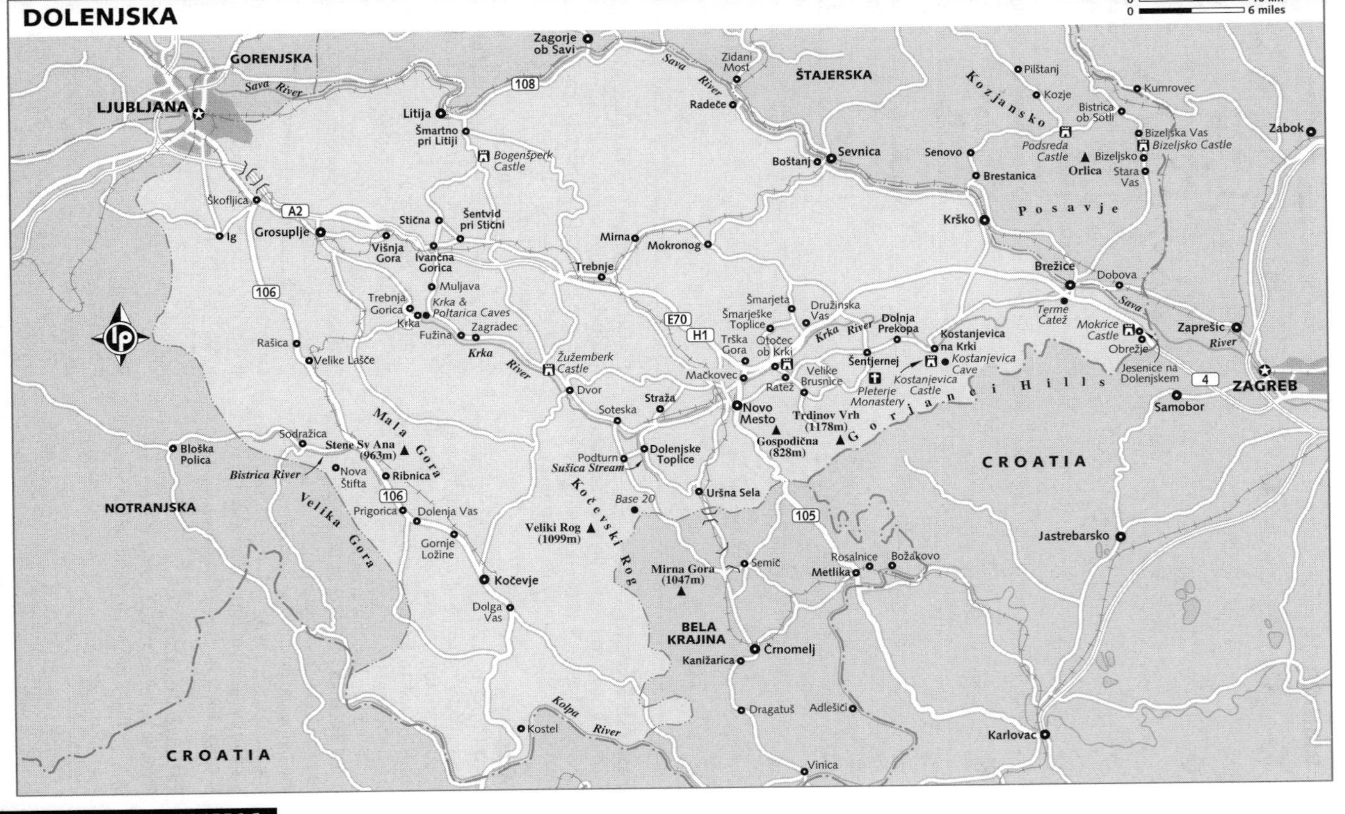
DOLENJSKA
0 6 miles
LJUBLJANA
GORENJSKA
Sava River
Škofljica
Ig
Grosuplje
A2
106
Rašica
Velike Lašče
Sodražica
Bloška Polica
NOTRANJSKA
Bistrica River
Stene Sv Ana (963m)
Nova Štifta
Mala Gora
Velika Gora
Ribnica
Prigorica
Dolenja Vas
Gornje Ložine
Kočevje
Dolga Vas
Kostel
Kolpa River
CROATIA
Litija
Šmartno pri Litiji
Bogenšperk Castle
Zagorje ob Savi
108
Šentvid pri Stični
Stična
Ivančna Gorica
Višnja Gora
Muljava
Krka & Poltarica Caves
Trebnja Gorica
Krka
Fužina
Zagradec
Krka River
Žužemberk Castle
Dvor
Soteska
Podturn
Sušica Stream
Base 20
Kočevski Rog
Veliki Rog (1099m)
Mirna Gora (1047m)
BELA KRAJINA
Kanižarica
Črnomelj
Dragatuš
Adlešiči
Vinica
Semič
Metlika
Rosalnice
Božakovo
105
Uršna Sela
Dolenjske Toplice
Straža
Novo Mesto
Mačkovec
Gospodična (828m)
Trdinov Vrh (1178m)
Trebnje
Mirna
Mokronog
E70
H1
Trška Gora
Otočec ob Krki
Šmarješke Toplice
Šmarjeta
Ratež
Velike Brusnice
Družinska Vas
Šentjernej
Pleterje Monastery
Dolnja Prekopa
Kostanjevica na Krki
Kostanjevica Castle
Kostanjevica Cave
Gorjanci Hills
CROATIA
Jastrebarsko
Karlovac
Samobor
ZAGREB
4
Zaprešic
River
Jesenice na Dolenjskem
Obrežje
Mokrice Castle
Terme Čatež
Brežice
Dobova
Sava
Posavje
Krško
Brestanica
Senovo
Sevnica
Boštanj
ŠTAJERSKA
Radeče
Zidani Most
Sava River
Kozjansko
Pilštanj
Kozje
Podsreda Castle
Orlica
Bistrica ob Sotli
Bizeljsko
Bizeljska Vas
Bizeljsko Castle
Stara Vas
Kumrovec
Zabok

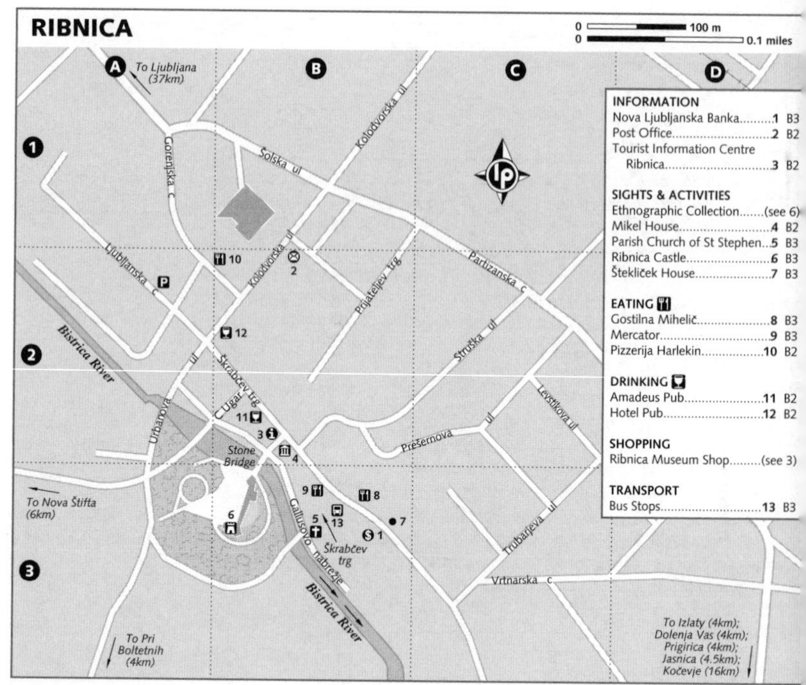

Festivals & Events

Ribnica's main event is the **Dry Goods and Pottery Fair** (Ribniški Semenj Suhe Robe in Lončarstva; www.ribnica.si) held on the first Sunday in September.

Sleeping

Izlaty (☎ 836 45 15, 041 373 550; lauryka_1@gmail.com; Prigorica 115; s/d from €20/30; P) This small *gostilna* (innlike restaurant), 4km southeast of Ribnica on the road to Kočevje and less than 1km from the pottery village of Dolenja Vas, has basic but comfortable accommodation.

Pri Boltetnih (☎ 836 02 08, 041 898 034; bernarda .arko@gmail.com; Dane 9; per person €24; P 💻) This engaging farmhouse at Dane, an 'end-of-the-line' village 4km west of Ribnica, offers accommodation in three rooms and is about the best place to stay in the area.

Eating & Drinking

Pizzerija Harlekin (☎ 836 15 32; Gorenjska cesta 4; pizzas €4-6; 🕑 10am-11am Mon-Sat, 10am-10pm Sun) North of the centre, this convenient place serves pizzas and salads.

Gostilna Mihelič (☎ 836 31 31; Škrabčev trg 22; starters €4.50-8.50, mains €7.50-16.50; 🕑 9am-10pm Tue-Fri, 9am-11pm Sat, 8am-5pm Sun) This old place with brick vaulted ceilings opposite the Church of St Stephen is one of the very few central places for a proper meal in Ribnica. It serves excellent Balkan-style grills (€5 to €7.50).

There's a central **Mercator** (Škrabčev trg 19; 🕑 7am-7.30pm Mon-Fri, 7am-1pm Sat, 7-11am Sun) with extended hours just up from the Church of St Stephen.

Amadeus Pub (☎ 051 341 042; Škrabčev trg 25; 🕑 7am-11pm Mon-Thu, 7am-midnight Fri & Sat, 9am-11pm Sun) This convivial cafe-pub next door to the TIC is a popular hang-out for young Ribničani.

Hotel Pub (Škrabčev trg 52; 🕑 6am-11pm Mon-Thu, 6am-midnight Fri & Sat, 7am-11pm Sun) Don't get your hopes up at this large, modern joint with the huge back terrace around the corner from the main drag. Here you'll get pints but not pillows.

Shopping

Ribnica Museum Shop (Muzejska Trgovina Ribnica; ☎ 041 786 935; Škrabčev trg 23; 🕑 9am-7pm Mon-Fri, 8am-noon Sat, 10am-2pm Sun Jul & Aug only) This shop, sharing space with the TIC, sells all manner of *suha roba* wooden products) produced in the area, as ell as clay pottery and whistles from nearby Dolenja Vas. The TIC can help you arrange isits to master crafts-people in the area.

etting There & Around

uses run at least hourly north to Ljubljana €5.60, one hour, 47km), and south to Kočevje €2.70, 30 minutes, 17km). The infrequent us to Sodražica (€1.80, 15 minutes, 10km) s good for stopping in Nova Štifta.

NOVA ŠTIFTA

☎ 01 / elev 625m

The **Church of the Assumption of Mary** (Cerkev Marije nebovzete; ☎ 836 99 43, 041 747 188; Nova Štifta 3; 10am-noon & 2-6pm) at Nova Štifta, in the foothills of the Velika Gora 6km west of Ribnica, s one of the most important pilgrimage sites n Slovenia and has been since the 17th century. Completed in 1671, the baroque church s unusual for its shape – both the nave and he presbytery are in the form of an octagon. The arcade on the west side fronting he entrance accommodated extra pilgrims n important holy days. The church proved o popular that the enclosed (and decorated) tairway on the north side was added in 1780 o allow even more of the faithful to reach the lerestory, the upper storey of the nave.

The interior of the church, with its main nd two side golden altars and pulpit carved y Jurij Skarnos, is blindingly ornate. Look for he painting of an aristocratic couple on the orth side of the presbytery. The organ (1904) with almost 900 pipes is noteworthy. In the ourtyard opposite the Franciscan monastery where the church key is kept) stands a wonerful old Dolenjska *toplarji* (double hayrack) nd a linden tree, planted in the mid-17th entury, complete with a tree house that has een there for over a century.

Dom na Travni Gori (☎ 836 63 33; travna.gora@gmail.com; Ravni Dol 43; per person €18), a guest house 905m up, with restaurant and 19 beds, can be reached in less than an hour on a marked trail heading southwest from just opposite the monastery.

STIČNA

☎ 01 / pop 780 / elev 357m

The abbey at Stična is the oldest monastery in Slovenia and one of the country's most important religious and cultural monuments. At only 35km from Ljubljana, Stična can be visited on a day trip from the capital or en route to Novo Mesto, the valley of the lower Krka or Bela Krajina.

Orientation

The village of Stična is about 2.5km north of Ivančna Gorica (population 1720), where you'll find the train station (Sokolska ulica 1). Long-distance buses stop in front of the station.

Sights

Stična Cistercian Abbey (Cistercijanska Opatija Stična; ☎ 787 78 63, 041 689 994; www.mks-sticna.si; Stična 17; adult/student/senior/family €4.50/2/3/7; tours 8.30am, 10am, 2pm & 4pm Tue-Sat, 2pm & 4pm Sun) was established in 1136 by the Cistercians, a branch of the Benedictines who worked as farmers and observed a vow of silence. It became the most important religious, economic, educational and cultural centre in Dolenjska, but it was finally abandoned in 1784 when Emperor Joseph II decided to dissolve all religious orders in the Habsburg Empire.

German Cistercians returned in 1898, and today almost the entire complex is again in use. There are currently some 15 priests and monks in residence.

DRY & SELL

Among the inhabitants of the Kočevsko region, up until the early days of WWII, were some 2500 German speakers who had been brought there by feudal lords as early as the 15th century. Because the karst soil was too poor to make an adequate living from farming year-round, these Kočevarji were allowed to supplement their income with wooden products (*suha roba,* literally 'dry goods') that they produced at home: pails, sifters, baskets, mangles and kitchen utensils. The men sold these products throughout the Habsburg Empire, and even the advent of the railway in 1893 did not put an immediate end to this itinerant way of life. Until well into the 20th century the sight of the *suha roba* pedlar – his products piled high on his *krošnja* (wooden backpack) and staff in hand – was as Slovenian as a *kozolec* (hayrack).

The entrance to the walled monastery, an incredible combination of Romanesque, Gothic, Renaissance and baroque architecture, is on the east side across a small stream. On the north side of the central courtyard is the Old Prelature, a 17th-century Renaissance building, which contains the **Museum of Christianity in Slovenia** (Muzej Krščanstva na Slovenskem), a hotchpotch of antique clocks, paintings, furniture and farm implements, mixed with chalices, monstrances and icons. There are a few 16th-century missals and medical texts in Latin and German, but all the medieval documents are facsimiles of the originals carted off to libraries in Vienna and Ljubljana when the order was disbanded.

On the west side of the courtyard, the **Abbey Church** (1156) was built as a buttressed, three-nave Romanesque cathedral, but it was rebuilt in the baroque style in the 17th and 18th centuries. Look inside for the Renaissance red-marble tombstone of Abbot Jakob Reinprecht in the north transept and the blue organ cupboard with eight angels (1747) in the choir loft. The greatest treasures here are the Stations of the Cross painted in 1766 by Fortunat Bergant.

South of the church is Stična's vaulted cloister, mixing Romanesque and early Gothic styles. The cloister was an ambulatory for monks in prayer and connected the church with the monastery's other wings. The arches and vaults are adorned with frescoes of the prophets and Old Testament stories and allegorical subjects such as the Virtues and the Four Winds. The carved stone faces on the west side that were meant to show human emotions and vices – upon which the clergy were expected to reflect as they said their office.

On the south side of the cloister is a typically baroque monastic refectory, with an 18th-century pink ceiling and decorative swirls and loops made of white stucco. **Neff's Abbey**, built in the mid-16th century by Abbot Volbenk Neff, runs to the west. The arches in the vestibule on the ground floor are painted with a dense network of leaves, blossoms, berries and birds.

The Cistercians sell their own products (honey, wine, herbal teas, liqueurs) in a small shop at the abbey entrance.

Sleeping & Eating

Grofija (☎ 787 81 41; www.grofija.com; Vir pri Stični 30; per person €28-32; P) This 19th-century farmhouse called County has four rooms and is 2km along a circuitous route southeast of th abbey. Of historical note: a Hallstatt settle ment (p27) dating from 800 BC once stoo near the farmhouse's tennis court.

Krjavel (☎ 787 71 10, 051 367 330; Ljubljanska ces 38; pizza €5.60-6.40, mains €4.80-12; ⏰ 10am-11pm Ju Sep, 9am-10pm Mon-Sat, 11am-9pm Sun Oct-May) Th little place in Ivančna Gorica, about 150 northeast of the train station and just off th road to the abbey, serves local favourites an quite decent pizza.

You'll find a small **Tuš** (Stična 27a; ⏰ 7am-7p Mon-Fri, 7am-3pm Sat, 8am-noon Sun) supermarket jus up the hill from the abbey. There's a muc larger **Mercator** (Trg OF 1; ⏰ 7am-7pm Mon-Fri, 7am 1pm Sat) in Ivančna Gorica just east of th train station.

Getting There & Away

Stična is served by up to a dozen buses a da from Ljubljana (€4.70, one hour, 36km) o weekdays, reducing to five on Saturday.

Ivančna Gorica is on the rail line linkin Ljubljana with Novo Mesto, Črnomelj an Metlika. Up to 14 trains a day arrive fro the capital (€2.90, one hour, 37km) with a many heading for Novo Mesto (€2.90, 5 minutes, 38km).

BOGENŠPERK CASTLE

☎ 01 / elev 412m

About 20km to the northeast is 16th-centur **Bogenšperk Castle** (Grad Bogenšperk; ☎ 898 76 64, 04 703 992; www.bogensperk.si; Bogenšperk 5; adult/child & student/senior €3.50/2.50/2.70; ⏰ tours hourly 10am-6p Tue-Sat, 10am-7pm Sun Jul & Aug, 10am-5pm Tue-Sat, 10am 6pm Sun Sep-Jun, 10am-5pm Sat & Sun Mar & Nov), which in many respects is the secular equivalen of the abbey at Stična. Here the celebrated polymath Janez Vajkard Valvasor (opposite) spent the most productive two decades of his life, writing and eventually publishing *The Glory of the Duchy of Carniola* (1689), his encyclopaedic work on Slovenian history, geography and culture.

Valvasor bought the Renaissance-style castle from the aristocratic Wagen family in 1672 and installed his printing press, engraving workshop and extensive library here. But due to the enormous debts incurred in getting his *magnum opus* published, he was forced to sell up 20 years later.

The castle, with its rectangular courtyard and three towers (the fourth was struck by lightning and burned down in the 19th entury), houses a museum devoted to the reat man, his work and Slovenian culture. alvasor's library is now used as a wedding all (complete with a cradle, as is traditional a Slovenia), but his study, with its beautiul parquetry, black limestone columns and ainted ceiling, is pretty much the way he left when he performed his last alchemy experiments here. Other rooms contain examples f Valvasor's original cartography and etchng, an original four-volume set of his famous ork, a working printing press like the one e used himself and a collection of hunting ophies, including a 360kg brown bear shot t Banjaloka in Kočevski Rog in 1978. The nost interesting exhibits, however, are the nes that deal with folk dress, superstition nd folk medicine.

Bogenšperk is accessible from Ivančna Gorica only by car or bicycle. Trains link jubljana with Litija (€2.90 to €4.50, 30 mintes, 31km, up to two dozen a day), but it's till another 7km south to Bogenšperk – much f it uphill.

KRKA VALLEY

The Krka River springs from a karst cave outhwest of Stična, near the village of Trebnja Gorica, and runs to the southeast and east intil it joins the mightier Sava River near Brežice. At 94km it is Dolenjska's longest and most important waterway and one of the cleanest rivers in Slovenia. For details on going it on your own, see p203.

Muljava

☎ 01 / pop 280 / elev 320m

Muljava's claim to fame is twofold: home to a wonderful Gothic church with 15th-century frescoes and the birthplace of the writer Josip Jurčič (1844–81), whose *The 10th Brother* is considered the first novel in Slovene.

The **Church of the Assumption** (Cerkev Marijinega Vnebovzetja; ☎ 780 60 32) lies east of the main road at the start of the village; seek the key from the vicarage to the north (left) at No 39. Not all the frescoes (1456) by Johannes de Laibaco (John of Ljubljana) in the presbytery and on the vaulted arches (Cain and Abel making their sacrifices, symbols of the Apostles and St Margaret) are very clear, but the one depicting the death of the Virgin Mary on the south wall is still vibrant.

The **Josip Jurčič Museum** (Muzej Josipa Jurčiča; ☎ 787 65 00; www.jurcic.si, in Slovene; Muljava 11; adult/child/student €2.70/2.30/2.50; 9am-noon & 2-5pm Tue-Sat, 2-5pm Sun Mar-Dec) is housed in the author's birthplace, a small cottage typical of the region 250m west of the main road. As it is devoted to a noted Slovenian writer it is of limited interest to foreigners though the cottage itself, frozen in time, gives a good idea of rural living conditions

VALVASOR, SLOVENIA'S RENAISSANCE MAN

Most of our knowledge of Slovenian history, geography, culture and folklore before the 17th century comes from the writings of one man, Janez Vajkard Valvasor, and more specifically his book *The Glory of the Duchy of Carniola*.

Valvasor, whose name comes from the *valvassores* (the burghers who lived in the towns of the Holy Roman Empire in the early Middle Ages), was born to a noble family from Bergamo in 1641, in Ljubljana's Old Town – a plaque marks the spot in Stari trg. After a Jesuit education there and in Germany, he joined Miklós Zrínyi, the Hungarian count and poet, in the wars against the Turks and travelled widely, visiting Germany, Italy, North Africa, France and Switzerland. He collected data on natural phenomena and local customs as well as books, drawings, mineral specimens and coins.

In 1672 Valvasor installed himself, his books and his precious collections at Bogenšperk Castle (opposite), where he conducted scientific experiments (including alchemy) and wrote. In 1689 he completed his most important work. Published in German at Nuremburg under the title *Die Ehre des Herzogthums Crain* it ran to four volumes, comprising 3500 pages with 535 maps and copper engravings. *The Glory of the Duchy of Carniola* remains one of the most comprehensive works published in Europe before the Enlightenment, a wealth of information on the Slovenian patrimony that is still explored and studied to this day.

Valvasor did not live to enjoy the success of his labour. Publishing such a large work at his own expense ruined him financially and he was forced to leave Bogenšperk in 1692. Valvasor died a year later at Krško, 65km to the east on the Sava River.

in 19th-century Dolenjska. South of the house is a well-preserved *kozolec* (hayrack), and a beehive with 28 still-vibrant (and rare) painted *panjske končnice* (front panels) from the 19th century.

Gostilna Pri Obrščaku (☎ 787 63 81; Muljava 22; meals from €15; 7am-9pm Mon, Tue & Thu-Sat, 8am-8pm Sun), named after one of the central characters in Jurčič's novel, is a roadside *gostilna* with a covered terrace that serves up hearty Slovenian fare.

There's a **Mercator** (Muljava 21; 7am-6pm Mon-Fri, 7am-1pm Sat) supermarket in the heart of Muljava.

Krka River Caves

☎ 01 / elev 268m

Two kilometres from the main road and just southeast of the village of Trebnja Gorica, **Krka Cave** (Krška Jama; ☎ 041 276 252; www.tdkrka.si, in Slovene; ticket office Krka 4; adult/child €2.50/1.60; tours hourly 2-5pm Sat & Sun Apr-Sep) isn't in the same league as Postojna or Škocjan Caves, but along the 1.9km route (a bit more than half the total length) you get to see some stalactites shaped like ribbons and fragile-looking 'spaghetti', a century-old specimen of *Proteus anguinus* (see p193) and a siphon lake that is the source of the Krka River. The usual depth of the lake is 17m, but in winter – depending on the rain and the snowfall – the lake can rise almost as high as the ceiling. The cave temperature is 8°C to 9°C. **Poltarica Cave** (Jama Poltarica; ☎ 031 766 555; by appointment) is a newly opened cave 400m before the entrance to Krka Cave.

One of the most popular places in Slovenia for **fishing** is the 9km stretch of the Krka from its mouth to Zagradec, about halfway to Žužemberk. The best time for fly-fishing is March to June when rainbow and brown trout abound. Permits (€49 to €60 a day) are available at Gostilna Pri Gradu (right).

Žužemberk

☎ 07 / pop 1065 / elev 240m

About 17km from Muljava, this is the site of mighty **Žužemberk Castle** (☎ 388 51 80, 041 324 710; www.zuzemberk.si, in Slovene; Grajski trg 1; by arrangement), which is perched on a cliff overlooking the Krka River. First mentioned in 1295, the castle was completely rebuilt and the old walls fortified with round towers in the 16th century, only to be all but flattened during air raids in WWII. Five squat towers have been rebuilt or partially reconstructed, and renovations continue apace. Annual events at th castle include the **Summer Castle Performanc** (Poletne Grajske Prireditve), a series concerts held from June to September, an **Medieval Day** (Srednjeveški dan) in early Jul

ACTIVITIES

The fast-flowing Krka offers excellent **kayakin** and **canoeing**, and Žužemberk is a good spo from which to set out. Any of the followin outfits can oblige for €20 to €25 for adults an €15 to €20 for children.

Carpe Diem (☎ 780 60 11, 041 739 771; www.kayak.si; Krka 27) In Krka.

Rafting Klub Gimpex Straža (☎ 031 340 422; www.rafting-gimpex.si, in Slovene; Stara Cesta 1) In Straža, 12km to the southeast of Žužemberk.

Žužemberk Kayak & Raft Club (☎ 308 70 55, 031 556 641; Prapreče 1) About 1km northwest of Žužemberk.

SLEEPING & EATING

Koren (☎ 308 72 60; www.turizem-koren.si; Dolga Vas 5 per person €20, apt €40-50) This farmhouse in Dolg Vas near Žužemberk has accommodation fo 13 people in five rooms and one apartment.

Gostilna Pri Gradu (☎ 308 72 90; Grajski trg 4 starters €5.80-6.50, mains €6.90-18; 6am-11pm Sun Thu, 2pm-midnight Fri & Sat) This old-style eater under a linden in front of the castle has terrace open in the warmer months. It offers pretty standard fare but is just about the only game in town.

There's a **Mercator** (Grajski trg 3; 7am-7pm Mon Fri, 7am-2pm Sat, 8-11.30am Sun) wedged between the Gostilna Pri Gradu and the castle.

GETTING THERE & AWAY

The bus stop is in front of the post office a Grajski trg 28. Up to four buses a day go to Ljubljana (€6, one hour, 5km) on weekdays with just one on Saturday and Sunday. From Monday to Friday one bus a day departs at 8.14am for Novo Mesto (€4.10, 45 minutes, 31km) via Dolenjske Toplice.

DOLENJSKE TOPLICE

☎ 07 / pop 795 / elev 179m

Within striking distance of Novo Mesto (13km to the northeast), this thermal resort is the oldest and one of the few real spa towns in Slovenia. Located in the karst valley of the Krka River below the wooded slopes of Kočevski Rog, Dolenjske Toplice is an excellent place in which to hike, cycle, fish or simply relax.

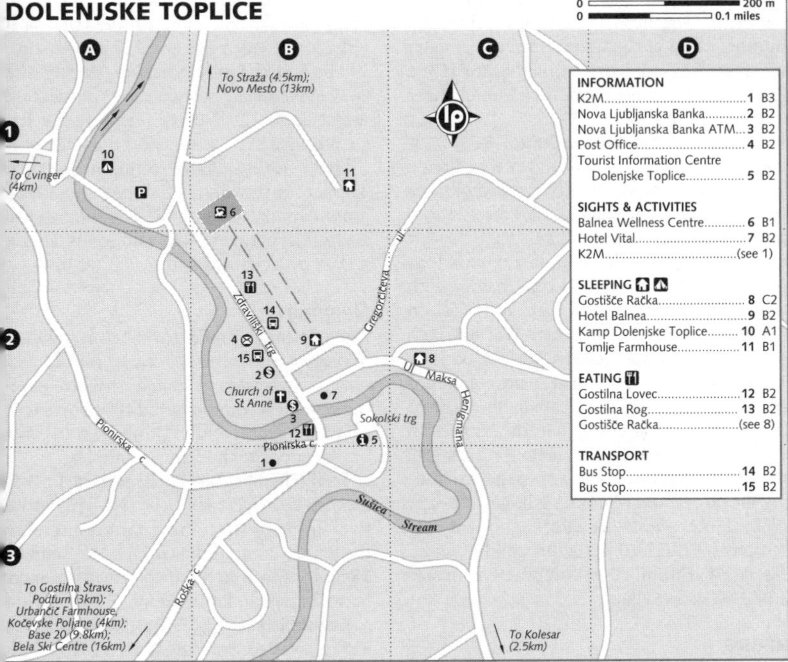

History

Although the curative powers of the thermal springs were known as early as the 14th century, the first spa was not built here until 1658. The Kopališki Dom (Bathers' House), complete with three pools, was raised in the late 18th century when the first chemical analysis of the thermal waters was done. Within a century, Dolenjske Toplice had almost 30 rooms, basic medical facilities and its very own guidebook, but tourism did not really take off until 1899, with the opening of the Zdraviliški Dom (Health Resort House). Strascha Töplitz as it was then called (after the nearby town of Straža) was a great favourite of Austrians from around the turn of the century up to WWI.

Orientation

Dolenjske Toplice lies about 1.5km south of the Krka River on an undulating stream called the Sušica. Virtually everything – including the three hotels of the thermal resort – are on or just off the main street, Zdraviliški trg. Buses stop here just south of and opposite the post office.

Information

K2M (☎ 306 68 30, 041 887 362; www.k2m.si; Pionirska cesta 3; 9am-6pm Mon-Fri, 9am-noon Sat) Travel agency with private rooms, guides, excursions and bike rentals.

Nova Ljubljanska Banka (Zdraviliški trg 8) Opposite the Hotel Kristal, with an ATM at Zdraviliški trg 10a, south of the Church of St Anne.

Post office (Zdraviliški trg 3)

Terme Krka Dolenjske Toplice (☎ 391 94 00; www.terme-krka.si) Central contact for bookings at the three main hotels and camping ground, beauty and medical treatments etc.

Tourist Information Centre Dolenjske Toplice (TIC; ☎ 384 51 88; www.kkc-dolenjske.si; Sokolski trg 4; 9am-6pm Mon-Fri, 9am-3pm Sat, 9am-noon Sun May-Sep, 9am-4pm Mon-Fri, 9am-noon Sat & Sun Oct-Apr)

Activities

THERMAL SPA

Taking the waters is the *sine qua non* of Dolenjske Toplice: the 36°C warm mineral water gushing from 1000m below the three covered thermal pools at the **Hotel Vital** (Zdraviliški trg 11; adult €9-12, child €7.50-9.50; 7am-8pm), which include the Cave and Prince pools, is ideal for such ailments as rheumatism, and can avert backache. The health resort also offers any number of other therapies, from underwater massage (€23) to detox aromatherapy (€38). Guests at the three Terme Krka hotels have free use of the pools.

The large **Balnea Wellness Centre** (☎ 391 97 50), 200m north of the hotels and reached via a lovely park or walkway, is composed of three parts. The park-like **Laguna** (Lagoon; day pass Mon-Fri adult/child €9.20/7.20, Sat & Sun €12.20/10.20; 9am-9pm Sun-Thu, 9am-11pm Fri & Sat) complex counts four pools (three outdoor and one inside) with thermal water of between 27°C and 32°C. In the **Oaza** (Oasis; day pass Mon-Fri/Sat & Sun €16.20/18.20; 11am-9pm Mon, Wed & Thu, 9am-9pm Tue & Sun, 11am-11pm Fri, 9am-11pm Sat) section are a host of indoor and outdoor saunas and steam baths over two floors, including a rooftop naturist sauna with excellent, err, views. The **Aura** (11am-9pm) section has treatments and massages, including the rather sticky-sounding honey massage (€60). Hotel guests get into Laguna for free but pay €9.20/11.20 per adult/child at Oaza. There are a number of combination tickets and packages available.

HIKING

A number of walks and bike paths of less than 5km can be accessed from Dolenjske Toplice, or you might consider hiking in the virgin forests of Kočevski Rog (see opposite).

Marked paths listed on the free *Dolenjske Toplice Municipal Tourist Trails* include four hiking and six cycling trails. In addition the TIC distributes some two dozen separate sheets with themed hikes, walks and cycle routes. One is a 2.5km **archaeological walk** west to Cvinger (263m), where Hallstatt tombs and iron foundries have been unearthed. Nature lovers may be interested in the 8km **herbalist trail**, a loop south to Sela and Podturn and back via forest roads, which takes in a herbalist farm and the 15th-century Church of the Holy Trinity at Cerovec. Further afield is the 2km **Dormouse Trail**, which makes a loop from Kočevske Poljane about 4.5km southwest of Dolenjske Toplice and could be combined with a hike to Base 20 (opposite).

OTHER ACTIVITIES

Horse riding is available at the **Urbančič farmhouse** (☎ 306 53 36, 040 608 969; Kočevske Poljane 13; per hr €10-15) in Kočevske Poljane, 4km to the southwest but be sure to book ahead.

A travel agency called K2M (p209) can organise kayak, canoe and rafting trips on the Krka for between €14 and €20 per person.

The **Bela Ski Centre** (Smučarski Center Bela; ☎ 38 94 35; nada.frankovic@iskra-semic.si; day pass adult/child student & senior €22/17/18.70), formerly the Rog Črmošnjice ski centre, is on the edge of the Kočevje forest 16km south of Dolenjske Toplice. It has 6km of slopes and 7km of cross-country trails on the slopes of Mt Gač at altitudes between 700m and 965m. They are served by a chairlift and five T-bar tows.

Sleeping

Kamp Dolenjske Toplice (☎ 391 94 00; www.terme-krka.si; per person €2.90-9.60, incl 3hr pool pass €9.40-16.40; year-round; P) This 3-hectare camping ground accommodating 100 people is just off the northern end of Zdraviliški trg, more or less opposite the Balnea complex.

Tomlje farmhouse (☎ 306 50 23, 031 643 345; Zdraviliški trg 24; s/d/tr €19/32/48; P) This attractive and very welcoming farmhouse above the Balnea complex has rooms with a total of 15 beds as well as three apartments sleeping between two and four people.

Gostišče Račka (☎ 306 55 10, 041 210 486; www.gostisce-racka.si; Ulica Maksa Henigmana 15; s/d €30/56; P) This modernised and attractive village house to the east of the centre has six rooms as well as apartments for up to six people that are 10% cheaper after two nights' stay.

our pick **Hotel Balnea** (☎ 391 94 00; www.terme-krka.si; Zdraviliški trg 11; s/d €86/142; P) Terme Krka's original accommodation duo, the Hotel Vital and the Hotel Kristal, facing one another across the spa town's central square, may have more history and be cheaper but few newly-built hotels in Slovenia can compare with this 63-room four-star (plus) palace in terms of design and facilities. The child-like drawings in the public areas are fetching, the aphorisms etched into the walls of the lift infectious and we love the back-facing rooms with balconies looking on to a restful park. Stroll to the wellness centre in your robe via covered (and heated) walkway.

Eating

Gostišče Račka (Ulica Maksa Henigmana 15; pizza & pasta €3-6; 8am-11pm Sun-Thu, 8am-midnight Fri & Sat Jul & Aug, 8am-10pm Sun-Thu, 8am-11pm Fri & Sat Sep-Jun) This guest house does double duty as a restaurant and is a popular place for pizza and pasta.

Gostilna Lovec (☎ 040 225 135; Pionirska cesta 2; arters €4.50-6, mains €6-12; ⏰ 7am-11pm Mon-Thu, m-midnight Fri & Sat, 8am-11pm Sun) About as cen-al as you'll find, this lively *gostilna* with an utside terrace along the narrow Sušica of-rs Slovenian favourites like grilled *klobasa* sausage; €5) and some decent fish dishes, cluding trout (about €5.50).

Gostilna Rog (☎ 391 94 12; Zdraviliški trg 22; meals from 0; ⏰ 9am-10pm Sun-Thu, 9am-11pm Fri, 9am-midnight at) On the edge of the park, the Horn serves raditional Slovenian dishes and has folk music from 8pm on Friday and Saturday.

Two *gostilne* a short distance out of town vith main courses from €8 to €20 and defi-itely worth the distance are **Gostilna Štravs** ☎ 306 53 90; www.stravs.si; Podturn 28; ⏰ 8am-11pm), km southwest in Podturn and specialising in reshwater fish and game; and the favourite f locals, **Kolesar** (☎ 306 50 03; www.gostisce-kolesar om; Dolenje Sušice 22; ⏰ 10am-11pm Tue-Sun), 2.5km o the southeast.

Getting There & Around

There are frequent weekday buses to Novo Mesto (€2.20, 20 minutes, 13km) but few at the weekend. Two weekday buses go o Ljubljana (€7.20, 1½ hours, 73km) via Žužemberk (€2.70, 30 minutes, 18km) at 5.35am and 10.29am.

You can hire bicycles from the K2M tourist agency for €5/14 per hour/day.

KOČEVSKI ROG

☎ 07 / elev to 1098m

One of the most pristine areas in Slovenia, Kočevski Rog has been a protected nature area for more than a century, and six virgin forests, covering an area of more than 200 hectares, are preserved here. Brown bears, as many as 500 of them, are believed to live here and constitute the largest such population in Europe.

The region was – and still is – so remote and filled with limestone caves that during the early days of WWII the Partisans, under the command of Marshal Tito, headquartered here, building bunkers, workshops, hospitals, schools and even printing presses. The nerve centre was the so-called **Base 20** (Baza 20; ☎ 306 60 25; www.dolmuzej.com/en/muzej/baza20), about 10km southwest of Dolenjske Toplice at 711m, which was reconstructed and turned into a national monument after the war.

Once a favourite 'pilgrimage' spot for many Slovenes and Yugoslavs, Base 20 is unfortunately now just a shadow of its former self, its 26 wooden buildings slowly being consumed by the forest, though two barracks (Nos 16 and 22) and their weather exhibits are open to the public. A plaque erected near the site in 1995 diplomatically pays homage to everyone involved in the 'national liberation war', presumably including the thousands of Domobranci (Home Guards) executed here by the Partisans in 1945. The site is always open, but a tourist guide at **Lukov Dom** (☎ 041 315 165; 1½hr tour adult/child & student €4.50/2.50, film €1; ⏰ 8am-4pm Mon-Fri Apr-Oct), the building at the start of the trail, is on hand in season. **Okrepčevalnica Pri Bazi 20** (☎ 041 959 109; ⏰ 10am-9pm Tue-Fri, 9am-9pm Sat & Sun) is a simple eatery near the main car park.

There is no scheduled bus service, but Base 20 is easily reached by sealed road on foot or bicycle from Podturn, 7km to the north.

NOVO MESTO

☎ 07 / pop 22,940 / elev 189m

Situated on a sharp bend of the Krka River, the inappropriately named New Town – it's actually pretty old – is the political, economic and cultural capital of Dolenjska and one of its prettiest towns. It is an important gateway to the historical towns and castles along the lower Krka, the karst forests of the Gorjanci Hills to the southeast, Bela Krajina and Croatia. Indeed, Zagreb is a mere 74km east of Novo Mesto via route A21 (E70).

Today's Novo Mesto shows two faces to the world: the Old Town perched high up on a rocky promontory above the left bank of the Krka; and a new town to the north and south, which thrives on the business of Krka, a large pharmaceutical and chemical company, and Revoz, which produces Renault cars.

History

Novo Mesto was settled during the late Bronze Age around 1000 BC, and helmets and decorated burial urns unearthed in surrounding areas suggest that Marof Hill, northwest of the Old Town, was the seat of Hallstatt princes during the early Iron Age. The Illyrians and Celts came later, and the Romans maintained a settlement here until the 4th century AD.

During the early Middle Ages, Novo Mesto flourished as a market because of its location and later became the centre of the estates owned by the Cistercian abbey at Stična. By the 16th century some 15,000 loads of freight passed through Novo Mesto each year. But plague, fires, and raids by the Turks on their way to Vienna took a toll on the city and, within a hundred years, Novo Mesto's main square had become grazing land for cattle.

Prosperity returned in the 18th and 19th centuries: a college was established in 1746, Slovenia's first National Hall (Narodni Dom) opened here in 1875 and a railway line linked the city with Ljubljana in the 1890s. Heavy bombardments during Word War II, particularly in 1941 and 1943, se verely damaged the city.

Orientation

The centre of the toe-shaped Old Tow is Glavni trg, a large, cobbled squar lined with arcaded shops, bars, cafes an public buildings.

The bus station is southwest of the Ol Town across the Krka River on Topliška cest Novo Mesto has two train stations: the mai one on Kolodvorska ulica about 2km northwe of the Old Town and little Novo Mesto-Cent on Ljubljanska cesta at the western edge of th Old Town. From here it is a five-minute wal eastward to Novi trg, which has been converte into a pedestrian mall and business centre.

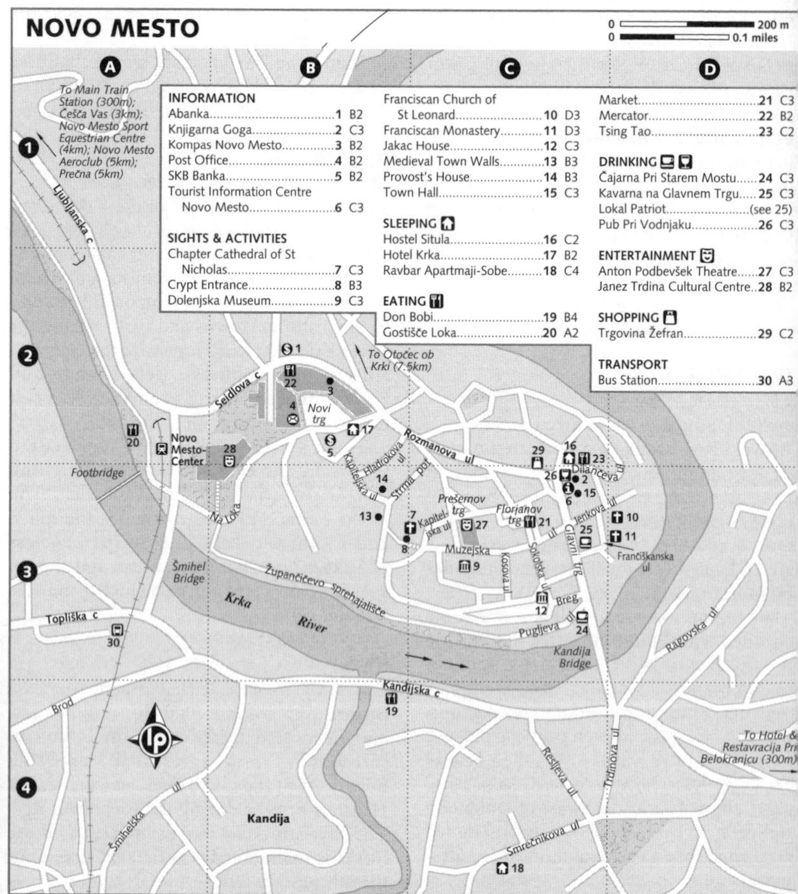

nformation

anka (Rozmanova ulica 40)

njigarna Goga (☎ 393 08 01; Glavni trg 6; 9am-m Mon-Fri, 9am-1pm Sat) Lovely arcade bookshop with gional maps, guides and cafe.

ompas Novo Mesto (☎ 393 15 20; www.robinson.si; Novi trg 10; 8am-6pm Mon-Thu, 8am-4pm Fri, m-noon Sat) Organises excursions and adventure sports Dolenjska.

ost office (Novi trg 7)

KB Banka (Novi trg 3)

ourist Information Centre Novo Mesto (TIC; 393 92 63; www.novomesto.si; Glavni trg 6; 9am-pm Mon-Fri, 9am-4pm Sat, 9am-noon Sun Apr-Oct, m-6pm Mon-Fri, 9am-2pm Sat Nov-Mar) Next door to e town hall.

ights

HAPTER CATHEDRAL OF ST NICHOLAS

erched above the Old Town, this Gothic **athedral** (Stolna Cerkev Sv Nikolaja; Kapiteljska ulica) is ovo Mesto's most visible historical monument. And, with a 15th-century vaulted (and ery floral) presbytery and crypt (entrance n the south side), frescoes on the walls, a elfry that had once been a medieval defence ower, and an altar painting of the church's ponymous saint supposedly painted by the enetian master Jacopo Tintoretto (1518–94), t is also the city's most important.

If the church is locked, you'll find the ey at the **Provost's House** (Proštija; Kapiteljska lica 1), the yellow building to the northwest uilt in 1623. Just south of this is a secion of the **medieval town walls** erected in the 4th century.

DOLENJSKA MUSEUM

Below the cathedral about 100m to the southeast is the enormous **Dolenjska Museum** (Dolenjski Muzej; ☎ 373 11 30; www.dolmuzej.com; Muzejska ulica 7; incl Jakac House adult/student & child €5/3; 9am-5pm Tue-Sat, 9am-1pm Sun). The oldest building, which once belonged to the Knights of the Teutonic Order, houses a valuable collection of archaeological finds unearthed in the southern suburb of Kandija in the late 1960s. Don't miss the Hallstatt helmet dating from the 4th century BC with two enormous axe blows on top, the fine bronze *situla* (or pail) from the 3rd or 4th century BC embossed with battle and hunting scenes, and the Celtic ceramics and jewellery (particularly the bangles of turquoise and dark-blue glass).

Other collections in the complex include one devoted to recent history and an excellent ethnographic collection with farm implements, commemorative jugs presented at weddings, decorated heart-shaped honey cakes, and icons painted on glass.

The museum also administers **Jakac House** (Jakčev Dom; ☎ 373 11 31; Sokolska ulica 1; adult/child €2.50/1.80; 9am-5pm Tue-Sat, 9am-1pm last Sun of month), which exhibits some of its 830-odd works by the prolific painter and local boy Božidar Jakac (1899–1989). The artist visited dozens of countries in the 1920s and 1930s, painting and sketching such diverse subjects as Parisian dance halls, Scandinavian port towns, African villages and American city skylines. But his best works are of Novo Mesto's markets, people, churches and rumble-tumble wooden riverside houses. The Dolenjska Museum's permanent art collection of paintings from the 17th to 20th centuries is now also exhibited here.

GLAVNI TRG

The neo-Renaissance **town hall** (rotovž; Glavni trg 7), out of step with the square's other arcaded buildings, ostentatiously calls attention to itself at all hours with its bells and unusual facade. The coat of arms on the front is that of Archduke Rudolf IV, the town's 14th-century founder.

Southeast of the town hall is the bright yellow **Franciscan Church of St Leonard** (Frančiškanska Cerkev Sv Lenarta; Frančiškanska ulica), which was originally built by monks fleeing the Turks in Bosnia in 1472, and the attached **Franciscan monastery** (Frančiškanski samostan; Frančiškanska ulica 1), whose library contains some 12,000 volumes, including 12th-century incunabula.

Activities

The Hostel Situla (p214) rents **kayaks** and **canoes** (per hr €7 Mon-Fri, per hr €9 Sat & Sun) for use on the Krka.

The **Novo Mesto Aeroclub** (☎ 334 82 22, 041 987 123; www.aeroklub-nm.si; Prečna 46; 9am-7pm), 5km northwest of Novo Mesto and served by bus, has sightseeing flights over Novo Mesto and the Krka Valley in Cessna 172s. A 15-minute flight over Novo Mesto costs €75 for up to three passengers; 90 minutes down to the coast is €290.

About 3km south of Prečna, the **Novo Mesto Sport Equestrian Centre** (☎ 337 30 40, 041 554 265; www.konji-cescavas.si; Češča Vas 55; per hr €10-15; by appointment) has Holsteiners and Arabians for riders of all levels. You can ride on any day, but should book first.

Sleeping

The TIC has a list of private rooms (from €25 per person). The closest camping grounds are at Otočec ob Krki, 7.5km to the northeast, and Dolenjske Toplice, 12km to the southwest.

our pick **Hostel Situla** (☎ 394 20 00; www.situla.si; Dilančeva ulica 1; dm €13.50-19, s €25, d €35-60, tr/q €57/76; P) This positive stunner of a property gets our vote as the most beautiful hostel in Slovenia and should be a destination in itself. Partially built within the walls of an 18th-century town house and partly new, the Situla has 82 beds in 16 rooms deposited willy-nilly over five 'I'm-lost-again' floors. Creative types were let loose here and the Iron Age is very much apparent, with artwork taken from *situlae* (p27) on each floor, representing different themes (eg rituals and hunting and fishing, trade). The theme continues in the 'Hallstatt Prince and Princess' rooms. There's a great bar and cafe and, while each floor counts a kitchen, the excellent restaurant has set lunch from €4 daily and a la carte dinner at the weekend. Dorms have five to eight beds but the cheapest accommodation is 'under the stars' – six mattresses on the floor of a mansard attic room. We'll be back.

Ravbar Apartmaji-Sobe (☎ 373 06 80, 041 738 309; www.ravbar.net; Smrečnikova ulica 15-17; s €20-30, d €30-40, apt for 2 €40-60, apt for 4 €65-75; P) This family-run guest house has seven rooms and nine modern, spotlessly clean apartments in a leafy and quiet suburban area south of the river. The owners are great travellers having recently toured the world by car for two years. Read more at www.rav bar.org.

Hotel Pri Belokranjcu (☎ 302 84 44; www.hotel.pribelokranjcu.si; Kandijska cesta 63; s/d/tr €38/55/72; P) About 1.5km from the Old Town, this rather boxy place behind a popular restaurant on a busy road has 19 comfortable rooms with some restful countryside views in the back. There's a branch in Metlika (p228).

Hotel Krka (☎ 394 21 00; www.terme-krka.si; Novi trg 1; s €77-82, d €114-124, ste from €157; P) The only four-star place to stay in the centre of town is this business hotel, with 53 modern, comfortable rooms, some of which are adapted for the disabled. Guests get to use the thermal pools at Šmarješke Toplice (p217) for free.

Eating

Don Bobi (☎ 338 24 00; Kandijska cesta 14; pizza €4.9 8.20; 10am-11pm Mon-Fri, noon-midnight Sat) Th simple eatery on the 'other' (ie south) sid of the river is said to serve the best pizza an pasta in town.

Tsing Tao (☎ 332 43 88; Dilančeva ulica 7; starters €. 3, mains €4.90-8.90; 10am-10pm Mon-Thu, 10am-11p Fri, 11am-11pm Sat, 11am-10pm Sun) Tucked away i a cellar north of Glavni trg and next to th Hostel Situla, this convivial restaurant name after China's largest-selling beer has mai courses like chicken with chilli and peanu (€6.40) and lots of rice and noodle dishe (€4.90 to €6.20).

Restavracija Pri Belokranjcu (Kandijska cesta 63; start ers €4.50-9, mains €7-17; 8am-11pm Mon-Sat) Thi popular restaurant in an inn a short distanc from the Old Town serves hearty Slovenia favourites and has good-value set menu (€11 and €12), including a very un-Slovenia vegetarian one.

Gostišče Loka (☎ 332 11 08; Župančičevo sprehajališče 2 starters €5-6.40, mains €6.60-19.80; 9am-10pm Mon-Thu 11am-midnight Fri & Sat, 11am-10pm Sun) Located righ on the Krka River, just beyond the small foot bridge linking the two banks, the Meadow In serves decent fish dishes and pizza and past (€4.90 to €10.20) and is the place to try Cviček the uniquely Slovenian light (10% alcohol) red wine from Dolenjska. There's riverbank seating available in the warmer months.

There is an outdoor **market** (Florjanov trg 6am-5pm Mon, Wed & Fri) selling fruit and vegetables in the centre of the Old Town. Enter the large **Mercator** (Novi trg 5; 7am-7pm Mon-Fri 7am-1pm Sat) supermarket from Seidlova cesta.

Drinking

Lokal Patriot (☎ 337 45 10; www.lokalpatriot.si; Glavni trg 11; 7am-11pm Mon-Wed, 7am-midnight Thu, 9am-2am Fri & Sat, 11am-10pm Sun) The venue of choice among Novo Mesto's movers and boppers at the moment, this bar and club below a large cafe has programs throughout the week and DJs (and sometimes live music) at the weekend.

Pub Pri Vodnjaku (☎ 041 616 882; Glavni trg 3; 6.30am-midnight Sun-Thu, 6.30am-2am Fri & Sat) Novo Mesto's favourite boozer is as central as you'll find – just 'by the fountain' at the northern end of Glavni trg.

Čajarna Pri Starem Mostu (☎ 337 01 60; Glavni trg 17; 7am-10pm Mon-Thu, 7am-midnight Fri, 9am-midnight Sat, 9am-9pm Sun) The Teahouse by the Old Bridge

– consequently – on the picturesque Krka ıd does tea in spades (with a nice line of apots and assorted paraphernalia for sale) s well as drinks, snacks and cakes.

Kavarna na Glavnem Trgu (☎ 051 809 752; Glavni g 11; 7am-midnight Mon-Thu, 7am-2am Fri & Sat, 7am-pm Sun) Punters will be excused for thinking ey've stepped into a New Orleans cathouse at ıe ingeniously named 'Cafe' on Main Square'; 's done up boudoir-style in red, green and lue plush, with gold trim and extravagant handeliers. Keeps late hours for a cafe.

ntertainment

'he **Anton Podbevšek Theatre** (Anton Podbevšek Teater; ☎ 391 78 16; www.antonpodbevsekteater.si; Prešernov trg 3) ıas a studio cinema with screenings, usually t 8.30pm, and stages theatrical and musi-al performances, sometimes in conjunction vith the **Janez Trdina Cultural Centre** (Kulturni Center ıneza Trdine; ☎ 393 03 90; www.kcjt.si; Novi trg 5). Ask he staff about concerts held in the courtyard f the Provost's House and elsewhere during he **Novo Mesto Summer Nights** (Novomeški Poletni ečeri; http://veceri.novomesto.si) festival held from une to August.

hopping

'rgovina Žefran (☎ 041 350 424; Glavni trg 1; 8am-ıoon & 3.30-7pm Mon-Fri, 9am-noon Sat) This hole-in-he-wall in the back of a courtyard at the start of Glavni trg does a lovely line of local sou-venirs and handicrafts, including comestibles ike local honey and Cviček.

Getting There & Away

BUS

There are frequent departures to Dolenjske Toplice Mesto (€2.20, 20 minutes, 13km) as well as Otočec ob Krki (€1.80, 10 minutes, 7km, five a day), Šentjernej (€2.70, 30 minutes, 17km, four to eight daily) and Šmarješke Toplice (€2.30, 20 minutes, 12km, seven daily). Some seven to 10 buses a day go to Brežice (€5.20, 70 minutes, 45km) and Kostanjevica na Krki (€3.10, 40 minutes, 25km), and four to Ljubljana (€7.20, one hour, 72km) via Trebnje or Žužemberk. One or two daily buses go to Črnomelj (€5.20, one hour, 43km).

TRAIN

Up to 14 trains a day serve Novo Mesto from Ljubljana (€5.50, 1½ hours, 75km) via Ivančna Gorica and Trebnje Gorica. Ten of these continue on to Črnomelj (€2.90, 45 minutes, 32km) and Metlika (€3.60, one hour, 47km), where there are connections to Karlovac in Croatia.

Getting Around

You can call a taxi in Novo Mesto on ☎ 332 57 77 or 041 625 108. The TIC rents bicycles (per hour/day/weekend €2/7/15).

OTOČEC OB KRKI

☎ 07 / pop 700 / elev 173m

The castle at Otočec, on a tiny island in the middle of the Krka River, 7.5km northeast of Novo Mesto, is one of Slovenia's loveliest and most complete fortresses. The first castle here stood on the right bank of the river, but during the Mongol onslaught in the mid-13th century, a canal was dug on the south side, creating an artificial island. The present castle, which dates from the 16th century, now houses a five-star hotel. The area around Otočec, the gateway to the lower Krka and the Posavje region, has become something of a recreational (especially cycling) centre.

Orientation & Information

The castle (and hotel) is 1km east of Otočec village on a secondary road running parallel to the river. You reach the castle via a wooden bridge. The cheaper Hotel Šport, owned by the same group, is up the hill a few steps north of the bridge. The independent camping ground is southwest of the island on the south bank.

You can change money at the reception of the Hotel Šport or at the post office in Otočec village. There's an ATM at the petrol station next to the Hotel Šport and outside a bungalow, outside the Tango restaurant.

Sights

Even if you're not staying at the hotel, there's no harm in having a look around **Otočec Castle** (Otoški Grad) and, if the weather is warm, enjoying a drink or a coffee at the terrace cafe in the courtyard. The castle, with elements of late Gothic and Renaissance architecture, consists of two wings and entrance block connected by a pentagonal wall. There are four squat, rounded towers with very thick walls, narrow windows and conical roofs at each end.

Activities

The **sport centre** just east of the Hotel Šport can organise **horse riding** and **hot-air ballooning**. The **tennis centre** has three indoor courts (per hour

€20 to €24, for guests €18 to €20, open 8am to 11pm) and six outdoor courts (per hour €6 to €8, for guests €5 to €7, open 8am to 11pm). There's also a sauna and steam room (€8 to €10), and fitness centre (per hour €6), which guests get to use for free.

Rent canoes from **Kamp Otočec** (☎ 040 466 589; per hr €2); the best areas for boating on the Krka are downstream from Struga.

The Krka River around Otočec is a popular **fishing spot** for pike, perch and carp, and fishing permits (per day €15) are available from the castle hotel.

Golf Grad Otočec (☎ 307 56 27, 041 304 444; www.terme-krka.si; 9/18 holes Mon-Fri €25/45, Sat & Sun €30/50 Mar-Oct), along the Krka about 800m from the castle hotel, has now doubled in size and is Slovenia's newest 18-hole golf course (par 72). Hiring a set of clubs costs €10 and a pull car/electric cart is €4/25.

Sleeping

Kamp Otočec (☎ 040 466 589; www.sloveniaholidays.com/camp-otocec; adult €7-8.50, child €3.50-4.25; Apr–mid-Oct; P) This camping ground, with 40 sites accommodating 160 guests, is on a 2-hectare strip of land running along the south bank of the Krka with its own grassy 'beach'. To reach it from the castle, cross the second bridge, turn left (east) and walk for 300m.

Šeruga farmhouse (☎ 334 69 00; turist.kmetija.seruga@siol.net; s/d €32/54) If your budget won't extend to accommodation at the Hotel Grad Otočec and you want something a bit more rural, this farmhouse in an idyllic valley in Sela pri Ratežu (house No 15), a hamlet about 4km south of Otočec village, has nine double rooms (some with kitchen), a self-catering apartment for four and a recommended restaurant open for lunch and dinner and specialising in trout and *štruklji* (dumplings made with cheese) of various types.

Hotel Šport (☎ 384 86 00; www.terme-krka.si; s €62-66, d €84-96; P) This hotel, housed in a concrete-and-glass box opposite the island and the castle, has 88 rooms as well as 38 rooms in attractive detached bungalows (singles €33 to €36, doubles €50 to €56) in the adjacent holiday centre.

Hotel Grad Otočec (☎ 384 89 00; www.terme-krka.si; s/d €180/260, ste from €300; P) The five-star Otočec Castle Hotel is one of the most atmospheric places to stay in Slovenia, but having just emerged from a year-long renovation (in which they grafted an unsight lift onto a castle tower) is now off-limi to all but the very well-heeled and glove The 10 rooms, with polished parquet floor Oriental carpets, marble-topped tables an large baths, are now of a uniform siz though you could lose yourself in one of th half-dozen suites. There are lots of theme packages (golf, cycling, wellness) on offe and guests get to use the thermal pools Šmarješke Toplice and Dolenjske Toplic free of charge.

Eating

Tango (☎ 384 86 00; meals from €10; noon-11pm Sur Thu, noon-1am Fri & Sat) Diagonally opposite th Hotel Šport building, the Tango should be distant second choice to the Grad, but give how fast the Grad fills up with nonguests an wedding parties, you may have no choice.

Gostilna Vovko (☎ 308 56 03; www.gostilna-vovkoi.s Ratež 48; starters €3.50-6, mains €7-16.50; 11am-10p Tue-Sat, 11am-4pm Sun) If you happen to be unde your own steam (of two or four wheels) hea south from Otočec for a couple of kilometre to the village of Ratež, and try this excellen local gostilna serving barbecued meats an such local specialities as pumpkin gnocch and Dolenjska's own take on *žlikrofi* ('ravio lis' stuffed with millet porridge and toppe with crackling).

Grad (☎ 384 87 00; starters €6-23, mains €14-25 6am-11pm) At the Hotel Grad Otočec, this restaurant seats 45 people while the smalle Hunter's Room accommodates another 16 With ancient stone walls, stained glass and locally made artisan furniture, it's loaded with atmosphere (check out the plexiglass 'trophies' in the Hunter's Room). Specialities are game and fish; try the unusual beech leaf soup followed by the red trout with a glass of Dolenjska Cviček and blueberry strudel. The four-course set menus, one of them for vegetarians, are excellent value at €35.

Getting There & Away

The buses linking Novo Mesto (€1.70, 15 minutes, 7.5km, five a day to 5pm) and Šmarješke Toplice (€1.80, 15 minutes, 7km, 11 a day to 10.15pm) stop at the bridge leading to the castle.

The sport centre rents bicycles and mountain bikes (per hour/four hours €6/10).

You can book a taxi on ☎ 041 708 733 or 041 466 330.

ROUND OTOČEC OB KRKI

he vineyards of **Trška Gora** (428m) can be :ached by road and trail from Mačkovec, out 5km southwest of Otočec. From there llow the road north for 1km to Sevno and ien continue along the winding track for km until you reach Trška Gora and the **Church St Mary**. From here there are wonderful views the Gorjanci Hills, Kočevski Rog and the rka Valley.

Approximately 13km southeast of Otočec, the shadow of **Trdinov Vrh** (1178m), the ighest peak in the Gorjanci and right on ie Croatian border, is **Gospodična** (828m) nd **Planinski Dom pri Gospodični na Gorjancih** (☎ 041 682 469, 051 661 903; 🕑 Wed-Sun mid-Apr–id-Oct, Sat & Sun mid-Oct–mid-Apr), a Category II mountain lodge containing a restaurant nd 49 beds. The route from Otočec goes or 5km southeast to Velike Brusnice, famous for its cherries (and cherry festival in nid-June), then to Gabrje (4.5km) and to Gospodična (3.5km).

MARJEŠKE TOPLICE

☎ 07 / pop 505 / elev 258m

f all that Cviček wine is taking its toll on you, onsider taking a break at Šmarješke Toplice, spa town in a small, lush valley about 5km ortheast of Otočec. While it doesn't have nything close to the history or atmosphere of Dolenjske Toplice, 25km to the southwest, t has lovely grounds and more than enough acilities to keep you busy and help recharge hose batteries.

The three natural pools that once stood n the site of the spa were used by local people as far back as the 18th century and were collectively known as the Lake Spa. Development did not come until 1950, when the first hotel was built, but even that remained a rather exclusive facility reserved for communist bigwigs. Today the spa is well known as a serious therapy centre for those with cardiovascular problems and increasingly as a haven for relaxation and wellness.

Orientation & Information

The spa complex and its hotels are northeast of the tiny village of Šmarješke Toplice. Buses stop in front of, and opposite, the Tuš supermarket next to the **post office** (🕑 8-9.30am & 10am-5pm Mon-Fri, 8am-noon Sat), where you can change money.

Activities

The spa counts six thermal pools fed by 32°C spring water rich in carbon dioxide and minerals. The two **indoor pools** (nonguests Mon-Fri €9, Sat & Sun €10) are in the hotel complex and used for therapy.

Within the complex is the **Vitarium Centre** (☎ 384 34 83; www.terme-krka.si/en/smarjeske/wellness/vitarium), a health spa and 'clinique' with detox and slimming treatments and fitness centre; **Vitarium Aqua**, a renovated complex of saunas and baths; and the **Centre for Nordic Walking**, which can provide you with walking sticks (€6) not unlike cross-country ski poles and a guide or brochure with 15 self-led walks of between 3.4km and 51km around Šmarješke Toplice.

The largest of the four **outdoor pools** (nonguests Mon-Fri €8, Sat & Sun €8.50) is below the sports centre; there's a children's pool nearby. The basin of an older (and smaller) pool directly above the hot spring is made of wood. As a result the water temperature is always 2°C warmer. In summer take a short detour 200m to the west of the pools to see the lovely (and highly unusual at this latitude) **Lotus Pool** in full bloom.

The **sports centre** has four clay tennis courts (one illuminated at night) for hire, and racquets are available. There are also facilities for table tennis, minigolf and lawn bowls.

Sleeping & Eating

Domen farmhouse (☎ 07-384 30 10, 041 890 901; domen.zorko@email.si; Družinska Vas 1; s/d €18/30; P 💻) A budget alternative to staying at the spa is this 18-room pension in Družinska Vas, about 1.5km east of Šmarješke Toplice. It has a tennis court and a decent *gostilna* (see p218) attached.

Aparthotel Vila Toplice (☎ 384 41 00, 051 664 776; www.vilatoplice.si; Šmarješke Toplice 240; apt for 2/4/6 €79/89/119; P 💻 ♿) This villa, about 1km east of the main complex on the road to Bela Cerkev, has 15 luxury apartments for two to six people, with kitchens. It has its own steam bath, sauna, solarium, massage pool and small fitness centre.

Terme Krka Šmarješke Toplice (☎ 384 34 00; www.terme-krka.si; P ✕ 💻 ♿) The complex counts three hotels. Šmarjeta (singles €64 to €69, doubles €112 to €122) has 100 freshened-up rooms (all with showers, some with balconies) and is the largest hotel in the complex. Toplice (singles €76 to €81, doubles €126 to €136), in the middle section of the complex, counts 47 rooms with small balconies and views of the nearby hills and forests. Vitarium (singles €88 to €93, doubles €132 to €142), with 72 rooms, is the newest of the trio, offering the best (and most expensive) accommodation in Šmarješke Toplice.

Gostilna Pri Jovotu (starters €4-7, mains €7-20; 10am-10pm Mon-Thu, 10am-midnight Fri & Sat, 10am-7pm Sun) This popular *gostilna* at the Domen farmhouse (see p217) serves tasty Balkan grills and Slovenian home-style dishes, including suckling pig roasted over a spit at the weekend.

There's a **Tuš** (Šmarješke Toplice 116; 7.30am-7pm Mon-Fri, 7.30am-5pm Sat, 8am-noon Sun) supermarket next to the post office in Šmarješke Toplice village.

Getting There & Around

There are up to seven buses a day to Novo Mesto (€2.30, 20 minutes, 12km) and Otočec (€1.80, 15 minutes, 7km) from the village of Šmarješke Toplice.

The sports centre rents bicycles (per hour/four hours/day €4/6/16).

You can book a taxi in Šmarješke Toplice on ☎ 041 625 108.

KOSTANJEVICA NA KRKI

☎ 07 / pop 720 / elev 50m

Situated on an islet just 500m long and 200m wide in a loop of the Krka River, Kostanjevica is Slovenia's smallest town. And with a charter that dates back to 1252, it is also one of its oldest. But the glory days of Kostanjevica have long since passed, and today the town is so sleepy it is almost comatose. Though it is dubbed 'the Venice of Dolenjska' by the tourist industry, as well as being under full protecti as a cultural monument, many of its buildin are in poor condition with the exception of t former Cistercian monastery 1 km south town. Still, it remains an important art cent and its location is magical. It's best seen fro on high but if you can't afford a ride in a hot-a balloon (p220), have a look at the photograp of the town in *Slovenia from the Air* (p19).

Orientation

Although most of Kostanjevica's historic sights are on the island, some other interes ing places as well as things of a more practic nature are on the mainland to the northwe or southeast, reached by two small bridge Buses stop along Ljubljanska cesta.

Information

Nova Ljubljanska Banka (Ljubljanska cesta 6) Southwest of the bus stops on the main road into town.

Post office (Kambičev trg 5; 8-9.30am & 10am-5pm Mon-Fri, 8am-noon Sat)

Tourist Information Centre Kostanjevica (TIC; ☎ 498 81 50; tic-gbj@galerija-bj.si; Grajska cesta 45; 9am-6pm Tue-Sun Apr-Oct, 9am-4pm Tue-Sun Nov-Mar) On the ground floor of an old mill just beyond the entrance to Kostanjevica Castle.

Sights

OLD TOWN

No one is going to get lost or tired touring Kostanjevica – walk 400m up Oražnova ulic and 400m down Talcev ulica and you've see the lot.

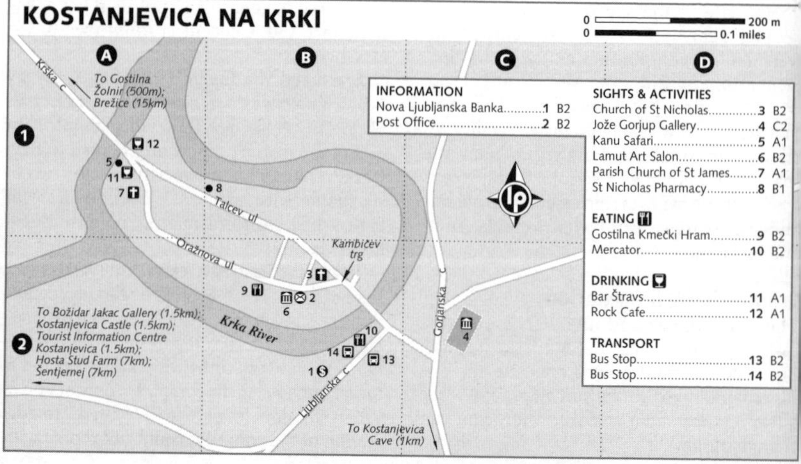

On Kambičev trg, across the small bridge om the bus stop (but enter from Oražnova ica), stands the **Church of St Nicholas** (Cerkev v Miklavža), a tiny late-Gothic structure datg from the late 16th century. In the presby-ry the brightly coloured frescoes (1931) of enes from the Old and New Testaments were ainted by Jože Gorjup (1907–32). You can e more of this expressionist's work, includg the wonderful *Bathers* series, at the **Jože orjup Gallery** (☎ 486 60 13; www.galerija-bj.si/agorjup; orjanska cesta 2; admission €2; 8am-2pm Mon-Fri) in the rimary school back over the same bridge.

If you walk northwest along Oražnova lica for about 200m, you'll reach a 15th-entury manor house that now contains the **amut Art Salon** (Lamutov Likovni Salon; ☎ 498 81 52; ww.galerija-bj.si/arazstav; Oražnova ulica 5; admission €2; 9am-6pm Tue-Sun), a branch of the Božidar akac Gallery.

Continue along Oražnova ulica, passing decrepit *fin-de-siècle* house (No 24), to the **arish Church of St James** (Župnijska Cerkev Sv akoba), a 13th-century Romanesque building vith a mostly baroque interior, at the island's orthwestern tip. Above the carved stone poral on the western side are geometric designs nd decorative plants and trees. On the south ide is a 15th-century depiction of Jesus rising rom the tomb, as well as ancient grave markrs embedded in the wall.

Talcev ulica, the island's other street, is ined with attractive 'folk baroque' houses, ncluding the 200-year-old **St Nicholas Pharmacy** vith five gables at No 20.

KOSTANJEVICA CASTLE

About 1.5km southwest of town, this former Cistercian monastery, which most people call **Kostanjevica Castle** (Kostanjeviški Grad; ☎ 498 70 8, 498 61 20; www.galerija-bj.si; Grajska cesta 45; adult/tudent & child/family €3/1.50/5; 9am-6pm Tue-Sun Apr-ct, 9am-4pm Tue-Sun Nov-Mar), was established in he mid-13th century and remained a very wealthy institution in the Middle Ages. It was abandoned in 1785 when monastic orders were dissolved. Today it houses a large and important art collection.

The beautifully painted main entrance through two squat painted towers leads to an enormous courtyard enclosed by a cloister with 230 arcades across three floors. To the west stands the disused **Church of the Virgin Mary** containing elements from the 13th to 18th centuries; it is now used as exhibition space.

FORMA VIVA

The castle grounds are used to exhibit more than a hundred large wooden sculptures from Forma Viva, an international exhibition that was held in several places in Slovenia from 1961 to 1988, whereby sculptors worked with materials associated with the area. Here it was oak, in Portorož stone, iron at Ravne in Koroška and (shudder) concrete in Maribor. In 1998 Forma Viva was revived at Kostanjevica and it is once again a biennial event at the castle in July.

The **Božidar Jakac Gallery** upstairs in the castle contains 16th-century frescoes taken from the church, and also works by such Slovenian artists as the impressionist Božidar Jakac (1899–1989) and brothers France (1895–1960) and Tone Kralj (1900–75). There is also a permanent collection of Old Masters from the Carthusian monastery at Pleterje (see p220). Jakac's oils and pastels (eg *Before the Storm* and *Midnight on Hradčani*), are outstanding. The expressionist France Kralj was versatile and prolific, turning out hundreds of works in oil, ink, bronze and wood; don't miss his sculptures *The Reapers, Mother and Child* and *Stallion*. Some of Tone Kralj's early work such as *Veined Sunset* and *Evening of Life* is almost surreal, but his later move to a kind of socialist realism obliterates all traces of it. The collection from Pleterje features works by French, German, Italian and Flemish artists of the 16th to 18th centuries and is sombre stuff.

Also in the castle is the **Cviček Wine Cellar** (Vinska Klet Cviček; admission with tasting €7.50), a true cellar if there ever was one with ancient casks and mould a-blooming in the vaulted ceiling. Ask the TIC for its useful brochure *The Land of Cviček: Podgorjanska Wine Tourist Road*.

KOSTANJEVICA CAVE

This tiny **cave** (Kostanjeviška Jama; ☎ 498 70 88, 041 97 001; www.kostanjeviska-jama.com, in Slovene; adult/child/student €6/3/4; tours 10am, noon, 2pm, 4pm & 6pm daily Jul & Aug, Sat & Sun mid-Apr–Jun, Sep & Oct), on a partly unsealed road about 1.5km southeast of town, has half-hour tours in spring, summer and autumn. The guide will lead you 300m in (only 750m of the cave has been fully explored), past a small lake and several galleries full of stalactites and stalagmites. The temperature is a constant 12°C. The cave is home to several species of bat.

Activities

Kanu Safari (☎ 031 531 069; www.kanusafari.com; ⌚ 8am-8pm mid-Apr–mid-Oct) based at the grassy 'beach' along the Krka in front of Bar Štravs, rents canoes for €10 per hour and can drop you off upriver for €30 so you can lazily paddle back.

The **Hosta Stud Farm** (Kobilarna Hosta; ☎ 031 220 059, 041 690 066; http://hosta-lipizzans.eu) in the village of Sela pri Šentjerneju, 7km west of Kostanjevica, is the second largest stud in Slovenia after the one at Lipica in Primorska and has 60 horses. It has riding tours of two hours, a full day and two days and boasts a riding school too.

The **Kostanjevica na Krki Balloon Club** (☎ 489 73 62, 040 883 007; www.balonarstvo.net) has 'flightseeing' trips in a hot-air balloon over Kostanjevica and surrounds for €100 per person.

Sleeping & Eating

Gostilna Žolnir (☎ 498 71 33, 041 626 717; www.zolnir-sp.si; Krška cesta 4; s/d/tr €30/48/60, apt €50-56; Ⓟ) This comfortable *gostilna*, about 700m northwest of the island, has 12 double rooms and an apartment for two or three people as well as a wonderful restaurant (starters €5.40 to €8.20, mains €8.30 to €11.90) open from 7am to 10pm daily. The owners are very serious about the food and wine they serve. A speciality of Kostanjevica is duck served with *mlinci* (thin dried flatbread) and, of course, Cviček wine.

our pick Gostilna Kmečki Hram (☎ 498 70 78, 031 369 750; www.gkh.si; Oražnova ulica 11; starters €5.50-6.50, mains €9.90-18; ⌚ noon-10pm Tue-Thu, noon-3am Fri, 9am-3am Sat, 9am-9pm Sun) This wonderful old-style inn, which has got a recent retro tarting-up, now really looks like the Peasant House it calls itself and offers excellent home cooking – among the best grilled dishes and roast lamb in Slovenia, locals say. Note the old wine press outside.

There's a **Mercator** (Ljubljanska cesta 4a; ⌚ 7am-3.30pm Mon-Fri, 7-11am Sat) supermarket next to the bus stop on the approach road to town.

Drinking

Rock Cafe (☎ 041 233 312; Talcev ulica 28; ⌚ 6am-midnight Mon-Fri & Sun, 6am-2am Sat) At the north-eastern end of the island, the Rock attracts a relatively raucous (for a comatose town) crowd and has wi-fi.

Bar Štravs (☎ 041 520 960; Talcev ulica 31; ⌚ 5.15am-midnight Mon-Thu, 5.15am-1am Fri & Sat, 6am-midnight Sun) Just across the street from Rock Cafe and fronting the Krka, this pleasant little bar and cafe is the ideal spot in which to while away a warm and lazy afternoon in Kostanjevica.

Getting There & Away

There are daily departures to from Kostanjevica to Novo Mesto (€3.10, 40 minutes, 25km, up to six a day), Brežice (€2.70, 30 minutes, 20km, four a day), Šentjernej (€1.80, 1¾ hours, 8km, six a day), Ljubljana (€9.20, 1½ hours, 97km) and Krško (€2.70, 2[illegible] minutes, 16km).

AROUND KOSTANJEVICA NA KRKI

Pleterje Monastery

Located 10km southwest of Kostanjevica na Krki, the enormous **Pleterje Monastery** (Samostan Pleterje; ☎ 308 12 29; www.kartuzija-pleterje.si; Drča 1; admission free; ⌚ 7.30am-6pm) belongs to the Carthusians, the strictest of all Roman Catholic monastic orders. The Gothic **Holy Trinity Church** (also called the Old Gothic Church or Stara Gotska Cerkev), 250m up a linden-lined path from the car park, is the only part of the complex open to the general public – there is a **multimedia display** (€4, including admission to the *skanzen* – an open-air museum displaying village architecture) in a side chapel on Sunday. But the monastery's location in a narrow valley between slopes of the Gorjanci Hills is so attractive and peaceful that it's worth a visit in any case. The **Pleterje Trail** (Pleterski Pot) is a 1½ hour walk in the hills around the complex.

Pleterje was built in 1407 by Herman II, one of the Counts of Celje, and its construction was supervised by English abbot Prior Hartman. The complex was fortified with ramparts, towers and a moat during the Turkish invasions and all but abandoned during the Protestant Reformation, which swept Dolenjska in the 16th century. The Carthusian order, like all monastic communities in the Habsburg Empire, was abolished in 1784. When French Carthusian monks returned to Pleterje in 1899, they rebuilt the complex to the plans of the order's charterhouse at Nancy in France.

You may catch a glimpse of some of the white-hooded monks quietly going about their chores – they take a strict vow of silence – or hear them singing their offices in the Gothic church at various times of the day. But the ubiquitous signs reading *Klavzura – Vstop Prepovedan* (Seclusion – No Entry) and *Območnje Tišine* (Area of Silence) remind visitors that everything apart from the church is off-limits.

Above the ribbed main portal of the aus-re church (1420) is a fresco depicting Mary eing crowned and the Trinity. Inside, the rib-aulted ceiling with its heraldic bosses and the arved stone niches by the simple stone altar re worth a look, but what is most interest-g is the medieval rood screen, the low wall cross the aisle that separated members of the rder from lay people.

There's a monastery **shop** (🕑 7.30am-5.30pm on-Sat) at the unattractive modern building o the left as you enter the complex, where the nonks sell some of their own products, in-luding packs of beeswax candles (€3), honey €5.50), propolis (€2 for a small flask), Cviček vine (€2.80 a litre) and various brandies, in-luding *sadjevec* (fruit; €7), *brinjevec* (juniper; 15), *slivovka* (plum; €8) and everyone's fa-ourite *hruška* (pear; €19). If you're wonder-ng how they got that pear into that seamless ottle, well, it's simpler than it first appears. n empty glass bottle is placed upside-down ver the immature fruit while it is still on the ree. When the pear ripens inside, the bottle nd pear are 'picked' and filled with brandy.

To the west of the monastery car park is the **leterje Open-Air Museum** (Muzej na Prostem; ☎ 308 10 0, 041 639 191; www.skansen.si, in Slovene; Drča 1; adult/hild/family €2.50/1.90/7; 🕑 10am-6pm Wed-Sun Apr-Oct, 0am-4pm Tue-Sat Nov-Mar), with about 10 differ-ent structures dating from the 19th century – hatched peasant houses, a pigsty, hayracks nd even an outhouse – moved here from the areas around Šentjernej. The *skanzen* also ents **bicycles** (per hr/day €3/10). See p223 for more on the open-air museum.

Šentjernej (population 1395), 3km north of Pleterje and 8km west of Kostanjevica, can be reached on some six Novo Mesto buses a day (€2.70, 30 minutes, 17km); return to Kostanjevica (€1.80, 12 minutes, 8km) on one of the same number of buses headed for Brežice. Buses stop along Prvomajska cesta just east of the main square (Trg Gorjanskega Bataljona), where you'll find a branch of Nova Ljubljanska Banka at No 2 and a **Mercator** (🕑 7am-7pm Mon-Fri, 7am-noon Sat) at No 10.

POSAVJE REGION

Most of what is called Posavje, the area 'on the Sava River' that extends as far as the border with Croatia, is in Štajerska. Historically and geographically, however, Posavje is closely tied to Dolenjska and easily accessible from many of its towns.

History

Posavje was settled early and, like the rest of Dolenjska, is rich in archaeological finds from the Hallstatt, Celtic and Roman periods. The Sava River, of course, was paramount, and the Romans built a major port here called Neviodunum near today's Drnovo.

Posavje took centre stage during the Turkish invasions starting in the 15th century – which explains the large number of heavily fortified castles in the region – and again a century later during the Slovenian-Croatian peasant uprisings and the Protestant Reformation. The arrival of the railway in 1862 linking Ljubljana and Zagreb helped the region develop industrially.

Posavje had more than its share of suffering during WWII. In a bid to colonise the area the occupying German forces engaged in a brutal program of 'ethnic cleansing' and expelled more than 15,000 Slovenes. Many of them were deported to Serbia, Croatia or Germany.

BREŽICE

☎ 07 / pop 6490 / elev 158m

Brežice is not the largest town in Posavje – that distinction goes to Krško, the energy capital of Slovenia 12km upriver – but from a traveller's point of view it is certainly one of the most interesting. One of the best museums in provincial Slovenia is here and a popular spa and water park just down the road.

History

Situated in a basin just north of where the Krka flows into the Sava, with the Orlica Hills to the north and the Gorjanci Hills to the south, Brežice was an important trading centre in the Middle Ages and was granted a town charter in 1354. Brežice's most dominant feature has always been its castle, mentioned in documents as early as 1249, with a strategic position some 400m from the Sava. In the 16th century the original castle was replaced with a Renaissance fortress to strengthen the town's defences against the Turks and later marauding peasants who, during one uprising, beheaded nobles at the castle and impaled their heads on poles. Today the castle houses the Posavje Museum.

Orientation

Brežice's main street is Cesta Prvih Borcev. Heading south it becomes Prešernova cesta and crosses the Sava. Going north it changes its name to Trg Izgnancev and then Cesta Bratov Milavcev. The main artery eastward is Bizeljska ulica.

The bus station is behind the big shopping centre on Cesta Svobode, 200m north of Bizeljska ulica and about 1km from the Posavje Castle. The train station is further afield on Trg OF, about 2.5km north of the town centre.

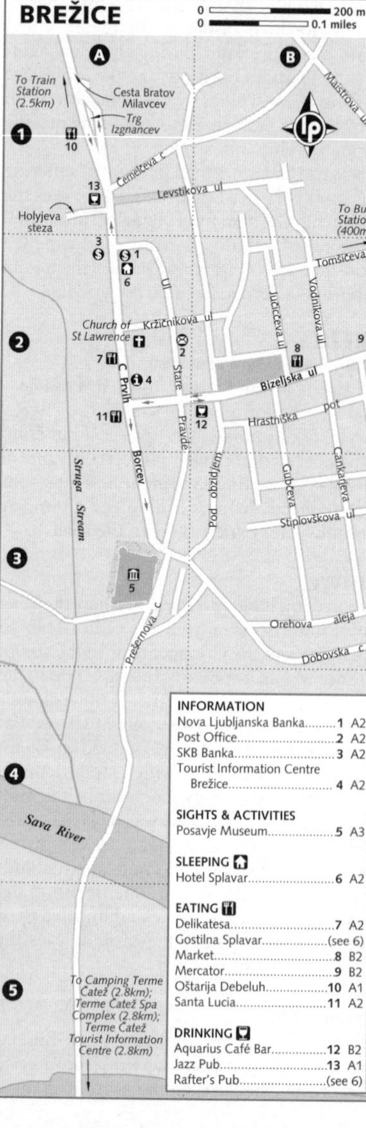

Information

Nova Ljubljanska Banka (Cesta Prvih Borcev 42)
Post office (Ulica Stare Pravde 34) In a new building behind the Church of St Lawrence.
SKB Banka (Cesta Prvih Borcev 39)
Tourist Information Centre Brežice (TIC; ☎ 496 69 95; www.visitbrezice.com; Cesta Prvih Borcev 22; 8am-4pm Mon-Fri) Terme Čatež Tourist Information Centre (☎ 493 67 57, 041 530 427; Topliška cesta 35; 8am-7pm Mon-Fri, 9am-4pm Sat, 9am-2pm Sun Jun-Aug, 9am-4pm Mon-Fri, 9am-noon Sat & Sun Sep-May)

Sights

Housed in Posavje Castle, the **Posavje Museu** (Posavski Muzej; ☎ 466 05 17; www.posavski-muz .si; Cesta Prvih Borcev 1; adult/student & child €2.5/ 8am-2.30pm Mon-Fri, 10am-2pm Sat & Sun) i one of provincial Slovenia's richest museums, particularly for its archaeological and ethnographic collections.

From the courtyard with arcades on the west side you ascend a staircase whose wall and ceiling are illustrated with Greek gods the four Evangelists and the Attems famil coat of arms. Rooms on the 2nd floor contai bits and pieces from early times to the arriva of the Slavs; be sure not to miss the skeleton from the 9th century BC unearthed nea Dobova, the 5th-century BC bronze horse bridle and the Celtic and Roman jewellery In the ethnographic rooms, along with the carved wooden bowls, decorated chests an plaited loaves of bread, there is a strange beehive in the shape of a soldier from the early 1800s.

Rooms on the 1st floor cover life in the Posavje region in the 16th century (focusing on the peasant uprisings in the area and the Protestant Reformation) and during the two world wars, with special emphasis on the deportation of Slovenes by the Germans during WWII. But the museum's real crowd-pleaser is the Knights' Hall (Viteška Dvorana), an Italian baroque masterpiece where everything except for the floor is painted with landscapes, gods and heroes from Greek and Roman mythology, allegories, the Muses and so on.

Activities

Rheumatics have been bathing in the thermal spring near Čatež ob Savi (population 355), situated 3km southeast of Brežice, since he late 18th century. Today, while the huge **erme Čatež** (☎ 493 67 00, 493 50 00; www.terme-catez.si; opliška cesta 35) complex still attracts those suffering from such aches and pains, it is every it as much a recreational area. The spa counts 0 thermal-water (27°C to 36°C) outdoor ools at the **Poletna Termalna Riviera** (Summer hermal Riviera; day pass adult/child Mon-Fri €10.50/9, Sat & un €13/11; 8am-8pm Jun-Aug, 9am-7pm Apr, May & Sep), ith massive slides, fountains and artificial aves all spread over an area of 10,000 sq metres. The indoor **Zimska Termalna Riviera** (Winter hermal Riviera; day pass adult/child Mon-Fri €12/10, Sat & Sun 12/15; 9am-9pm year-round) complex measures 800 sq metres with a water temperature of bout 32°C. The spa's **Sauna Park** boasts eight different saunas, a steam room, Roman bath, solarium, gym, a jogging track along the river, tennis courts and a naturists terrace.

You can rent a **bicycle** (per 2hr/5hr/day €4/6/8.50) from the Terme Čatež TIC. Ask at the TIC for a free copy of its *Cycling & Hiking Brežice Map*.

Festivals & Events

The **Seviqc Brežice** (www.seviqc-brezice.si) is a month-long series of concerts featuring ancient music and is held from late June to late July in various venues around the region, including the Knights' Halls in the castles at Brežice, Bizeljsko and Mokrice, and at the Hotel Toplice at Čatež ob Savi.

NATAŠA LUKEZIC

Nataša Lukezic works as a guide at the Pleterje Open-Air Museum (p220) at Drča near Šentjernej.

Local girl? I'm from Nova Gorica in Primorska; my grandfather was an Italian from Torino. I met the director (Simon Udvanc) and followed him here. Love brought me to Dolenjska and the *skanzen*.

What's the big idea? Living history or frozen in time? The place is supposed to show both young and old how our ancestors lived and we'd like to make it interactive. But we're limited by our location next to the monastery. In fact for that reason we may have to move, and we are now looking for a new site. As for frozen, well, until I came to Dolenjska I thought it only reached -15°C in winter in Russia!

What do local people think about the place? Young people studying things like history and ethnography find it interesting. And children love it, especially because of our animals – rabbits, cats, goats, mini-pigs and mini-goats. I learn a lot from some older people who tell me what this item was and how it was used. But middle-aged people can be problematical. 'Why should we pay to see a place like this?' they ask.

Why's that? Perhaps the museum is not big enough for them. More likely, they're too close to the time. These people know very well this way of living. It meant poverty and lots of work; some of the memories are not good. In fact, local farmers wanted to destroy the houses in the mid-1980s, which is why they were moved here and how the *skanzen* came about.

What's the worst thing about your job? Upkeep, especially thatching. We receive about 15,000 visitors a year and it's impossible to pay for repairs with the kind of money that brings in, especially with no help from the local or national government.

And the best thing? I feel the past here, especially when doing traditional things like baking bread in the 'black kitchen'. Since I came here I've lost all interest in material values. I have a degree in economics and could get a good job elsewhere but I prefer working here for next to nothing. I have found my peace here.

Anything to do with all that positive energy beaming down from the monastery? The monks are such positive people despite living almost in a desert. They are allowed to talk to one another only at lunch on Sundays and on walks on Mondays. And they get to see their families only once or twice a year. They have no contact with problems, no connection with the outside world. Still they retain their sense of humour and you can talk with them about anything – even relationship problems. As one brother once told me. 'We may be limited in a physical way, but not in a spiritual one.' There are no constraints on the mind.

Sleeping

Camping Terme Čatež (☎ 493 50 100; www.terme-catez.si; Topliška cesta 35, Čatež; per person €16-17.50; ⏰ year-round; P) The daily rate at this 3.6-hectare camping ground accommodating 550 guests at the Terme Čatež spa complex includes two day-long entrances to the outdoor swimming pools or one three-hour one to the Winter Thermal Riviera.

Hotel Splavar (☎ 499 06 30, 041 428 362; www.splavar.si; Cesta Prvih Borcev 40a; s/d €50/75; P) The Raftman with 16 rooms on Brežice's high street is above the Gostilna Splavar and popular Rafter's Pub. The rooms are in the back and dark but the staff are welcoming and friendly.

In addition to its popular (and five-star) camping ground, the **Terme Čatež spa complex** (☎ 493 50 00, 493 67 00; www.terme-catez.si; Topliška cesta 35) has some 15 apartments (one to three people €71 to €93, four to five people €85 to €1047) and three hotels. **Hotel Čatež** (s €86-94, d €138-154; P), a three-star place with some 1860 rooms and a modern addition, is generally reserved for those who are using the spa for medical reasons. **Hotel Toplice** (s €107-114, d €170-184; P) with 139-rooms and four stars has both a new and an old (1925) wing. The nicest of the three properties, the four-star **Hotel Terme** (s 114-122, d €184-200; P), in a somewhat isolated section of the complex has 149 rooms.

Eating

Santa Lucia (☎ 499 25 00, 041 624 596; Cesta Prvih Borcev 15; starters €4-5, pizza €5.50-7.80, mains €7-11; ⏰ 11am-11pm) This pizzeria with an over-the-top ceiling fresco does a roaring a trade in takeaway, as it does in eat-in pizza. There's both a front and back terrace.

Gostilna Splavar (Cesta Prvih Borcev 40a; starters €6-9, mains €7-17; ⏰ 7am-10pm Mon-Fri, noon-10pm Sun) A popular B&B, this *gostilna* is also a fine restaurant with a winter garden and summer terrace. The Laški Rizling, a slightly fruity, medium-dry wine from Bizeljsko, is not a bad accompaniment to the fish dishes on offer. It's also celebrated for the homemade ice cream (one/two/three scoops for €1/1.90/2.70).

our pick Oštarija Debeluh (☎ 496 10 70; Trg Izgnancev 7; starters €7.50-11, mains €18-22; ⏰ noon-4pm Mon-Sat) This attractive eatery, whose name roughly translates as Fatty's Inn, serves the best and most inventive – horse pâté with carpaccio (€6.50) – Slovenian and internationa dishes in Brežice. The all-Slovenian wine lis is admirable and the advice sage.

There's a supermarket called **Delikatesa** (Cest Prvih Borcev 23; ⏰ 7am-7pm Mon-Fri, 7am-noon Sat) diagonally opposite the Church of St Lawrence You'll find a much larger **Mercator** (Bizeljska ulic 23; ⏰ 7am-8pm Mon-Fri, 7am-1pm Sat, 7-11am Sun just beyond the produce **market** (Bizeljska ulic 5; ⏰ 7am-1pm Mon-Fri) in the direction of th bus station.

Drinking

Rafter's Pub (Cesta Prvih Borcev 40a; ⏰ 6am-10pm Mon-Fr 6am-11pm Sat, 8am-11pm Sun) This popular English style pub is below the Gostilna Splavar, it tables spilling out on to the high street.

Jazz Pub (Trg Izgnancev 2; ⏰ 6am-midnight Mon-Fri 7am-1am Sat, 8am-midnight Sun) This very attractive well decorated and friendly drinking spot i popular with students.

Aquarius Café Bar (☎ 499 25 05; Bizeljska ulica 4 ⏰ 7am-11pm Sun-Thu, 7am-1am Fri & Sat) Housed or three levels of Brežice's unmistakeable pink and half-timbered water tower (1914), this cafe-bar is decorated with old photos of the town and faux antiques.

Getting There & Around

Buses make the run to Terme Čatež (€1.30, five minutes, 3km) at least half-hourly Monday to Saturday. There are two regular daily buses (eight during the school year) to Bizeljsko (€2.70, 30 minutes, 18km), as well as up to four to Ljubljana (€10.70, 2¼ hours, 117km), and four to Kostanjevica (€2.70, 30 minutes, 20km) and Novo Mesto (€5.20, 70 minutes, 45km).

As many as 16 trains a day serve Brežice from Ljubljana (€6.50, two hours, 107km) via Zidani Most, Sevnica and Krško (€1.10, seven minutes, 9km). Many of these trains then cross the Croatian border near Dobova and carry on to Zagreb.

You can order a taxi on ☎ 041 611 391 or 041 790 842.

AROUND BREŽICE

Mokrice Castle

☎ 07 / elev 200m

Near Jesenice na Dolenjskem, about 10km southeast of Brežice, renovated **Mokrice Castle** is the loveliest fortress in the Posavje region and is now a luxury hotel. With one of Slovenia's handful of 18-hole golf courses, a 20-hectare

:nglish park' full of rare plants, a large orıard of pear trees and a small disused Gothic hapel with a vaulted ceiling and weddingıke plaster tracery, a trip to the castle makes delightful excursion from Brežice.

The castle as it stands today dates from ıe 16th century, but there are bits and ieces going back to Roman times (inscripon stones, part of a tower and so on) built ıto the structure. Like many other castles in ıe region, it was built as a defence against ıe Turks and later turned into a baronial ıanor. The castle is supposedly haunted by ıe ghost of a 17th-century countess named Barbara, who committed suicide by jumping :om one of the towers after her lover failed to eturn from sea. She is particularly active on ıer name day (4 December) when she spends nost of the night rolling cannonballs around he joint.

The green fee for a round at Mokrice's 18ıole, 71-par **golf course** is €39/48 weekdays/ veekends (nine holes: €26/32). A half-set of lubs costs €12.50 to rent.

The 29 rooms at the **Golf Hotel Mokrice Castle** (☎ 457 42 40; www.terme-catez.si; s €120-128, d €190-206, te from €250 P 💻) have beamed ceilings and eriod furniture, and the huge suites have fireılaces. The **Grad** (starters €5.85-9.20, mains €8.35-18.80; 🕑 7am-11pm) restaurant is a gorgeous venue vith fancy game and fish dishes, and classi:al music. The cellar has dozens of different Slovenian wines available by the glass or botle. Try some *viljamovka*, Mokrice's famous ›ear brandy.

You can reach Mokrice from Brežice on he infrequent bus to the border town of Obrežje (€1.80, 15 minutes, 8km) – though some Zagreb-bound buses stop here too – ›ut the ideal way to go would be by bicycle from Čatež, following the secondary road :unning parallel to route A2 (E70). Ask he TIC in Brežice or Terme Čatež for their *Cycling Booklet* with four itineraries.

Bizeljsko-Sremič Wine District

☎ 07 / elev to 175m

Cycling the 18km from Brežice to **Bizeljsko** (population 735) is a great way to see the Bizeljsko-Sremič wine country, but there are buses, allowing you to get off whenever you see a *gostilna, vinska klet* (wine cellar) or *repnica* (flint-stone cave for storing wine) that takes your fancy. In Bizeljsko, try some of the local medium-dry whites and reds at the **Vinska Klet Pinterič** (☎ 495 12 66, 041 520 481; Bizeljska cesta 115; 🕑 10am-7pm) or at **Gostilna Šekoranja** (☎ 495 13 10; Bizeljska cesta 72; 🕑 8am-11pm Tue-Sun). In the nearby village of Stara Vas visit the **Vinoteka Pri Peču** (☎ 452 01 03; 🕑 10am-midnight Wed-Mon) or **Repnica Pudvoi** (☎ 495 12 28, 031 484 003; 🕑 11am-7pm Sat or by appointment) cellars at house No 58 and No 89 respectively.

From Bizeljsko you can either return to Brežice or continue north for 8km to Bistrica ob Sotli past Bizeljska Vas and the ruins of the 15th-century **Bizeljsko Castle**, about 1.5km off the main road, whose **Klakočar-Wissell cellar** (☎ 495 12 55, 041 927 628; Bizeljska Vas 20; 🕑 Apr-Dec or by appointment) is open to the public all day and allows you a good look around the deteriorating central courtyard and the 18th-century rococo chapel undergoing a snail's-pace renovation. From here, buses head northwest to Kozje via the village of Podsreda (p240).

BELA KRAJINA

Bela Krajina has countless opportunities for active pursuits and relaxing stops along the heritage trails and wine roads. Ask the TIC in Metlika or Črnomelj for the excellent brochure-map *Kolesarske Poti Bela Krajina* (Bela Krajina Bike Trails), with 15 itineraries – some of them circular – outlined. Bela Krajina contains two important parks: the 259-hectare Lahinja Country Park and a large part of the 4332-hectare Kolpa Country Park.

Like Dolenjska, Bela Krajina is famous for its Hallstatt and Roman sites; a 3rd-century shrine to the god Mithra near the village of Rožanec (p231) is one of the best preserved in Europe. In the Middle Ages, Bela Krajina was the most remote part of Slovenia, and in some ways it still feels like that. Many of the peasant uprisings of the 15th and 16th centuries started here or just across the border in Croatia.

METLIKA

☎ 07 / pop 3480 / elev 167m

One of Bela Krajina's two most important towns, Metlika lies in a valley at the foot of the Gorjanci range of hills and is an excellent springboard for hiking and cycling in the area. It is surrounded by Croatia on three sides, and the Kolpa River and its 'beaches' lies about 1km to the south. There was a

major Hallstatt settlement here during the early Iron Age, and the Romans established an outpost in Metlika on the road leading to the important river port of Sisak in Croatia. During the Turkish onslaught of the 15th and 16th centuries, Metlika was attacked 17 times and occupied in 1578.

Orientation

Metlika's Old Town, consisting of three main squares, sits on a ridge between a small stream called the Obrh and the main street, Cesta Bratstva in Enotnosti, which translates as 'Ave of Fraternity and Unity'. The modern (and all-but-empty) bus station is 650m south of the Old Town on Cesta XV Brigade opposite a large shopping centre called Naselje Borisa Kidriča (NBK). The train station is on Kolodvorska ulica, another 600m southeast along Cesta XV Brigade.

Information

Metlika Public Library (Ljudska Knjižnica Metlika; ☎ 369 15 20, 305 83 70; Cesta Bratstva in Enotnosti 23; 11am-6pm Mon, 9am-3pm Tue-Fri Jul & Aug, 10am-6pm Mon, Wed & Fri, 7am-3pm Tue & Thu, 7.30-12.30pm Sat Sep-Jun) Free internet access.

Nova Ljubljanska Banka Trg Svobode (Trg Svobode 7); NBK shopping centre (NBK 2)

Post office (NBK 2) In the same shopping centre as the bank branch.

Tourist Information Centre Metlika (TIC; ☎ 363 54 70; www.metlika-turizem.si; Trg Svobode 4; 8am-5pm Mon-Fri, 9am-1pm Sat Jun-Aug, 8am-4pm Mon-Fri, 9am-noon Sat Sep-May)

Sights

TRG SVOBODE

Housed in **Metlika Castle** (Metliški Grad; Trg Svobod 4) with its splendid arcaded courtyard, th **Bela Krajina Museum** (Belokranjski Muzej; ☎ 306 3 70, 305 81 77; www.belokranjski-muzej.si; adult/chil student & senior €3.50/2.50/3; 9am-5pm Mon-Sa 10am-2pm Sun) houses a permanent collectio of archaeological finds taken from the area There are Hallstatt buckles, bracelets an amulets from Pusti Gradac (p232) south o Črnomelj and an early plaster cast of th Mithraic relief from the Roman period foun at Rožanec (p231) near Črnomelj, as well a items relating to the area's ethnology an agriculture: beekeeping, fruit cultivation viniculture, fishing and animal husbandry A 20-minute film introduces the collectio in four different languages.

Metlika was the first town in Slovenia t have its own fire brigade (1869), and th small building west of the castle entranc contains the **Slovenian Firefighters' Museum** (Slovenski Gasilski Muzej; ☎ 305 86 97; Trg Svobode 5; admission €1; 9am-2pm Tue-Sat, 9am-noon Sun). There ar old fire trucks with enormous wheels, ladders and buckets. Firefighters are considere the 'party animals' of Slovenia, hostin dances, fetes and other booze-ups outsid the *gasilski dom* (fire station) throughou the summer.

MESTNI TRG

This colourful, leafy square, where a dry-goods and produce market is held every first and third Tuesday, contains stunning 18th- and 19th-century buildings, including the neo-Gothic **town hall** (Mestni trg 24) dating from 1869 and **old cottages** at Nos 20 and 21. At the southern end of the square is the so-called **Commandery** (Komenda; Mestni trg 2), which once belonged to the Knights of the Teutonic Order (note the stone relief of a Maltese cross above the entrance). Its **defence tower** dates from the 16th century. To the northwest the **Parish Church of St Nicholas** (Farna Cerkev Sv Nikolaja) was built in 1759. On the ceiling are sobering contemporary frescoes of the Day of Judgment by Domenico Fabris, with some satyrlike devils leading sinners to damnation.

CESTA BRATSTVA IN ENOTNOSTI

Along this busy main street is the **Kambič Gallery** (Galerija Kambič; ☎ 305 83 32; Cesta Bratstva in

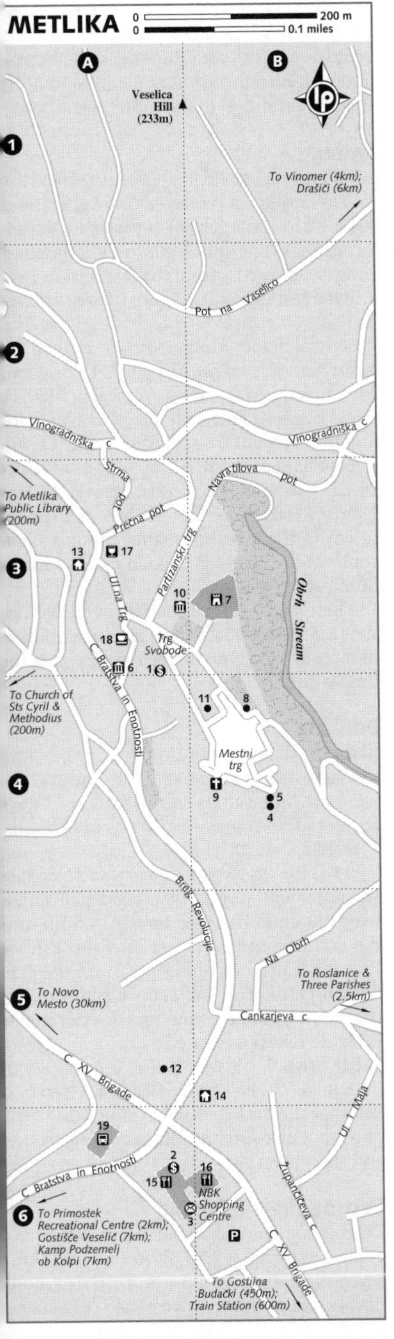

Enotnosti 51; admission free; 10am-4pm Tue-Sat, 10am-1pm Sun), which shows some 200 artworks donated by a university professor and stages cutting-edge temporary exhibits. The artist and sculptor Alojzij Gangl (1859–1935), who was born in Metlika, is given pride of place.

Southwest of the main street is the tiny Church of **Sts Cyril & Methodius** (Cerkev Sv Cirila in Metoda; Marentičeva ulica), one of just two Greek Catholic (Uniate) churches in Slovenia.

Activities

The Kolpa River is clean and very warm (up to 28°C to 30°C in summer), so you might want to go **swimming** at the Primostek or Podzemelj camping grounds.

The Kolpa is known for its grayling as well as carp and brown trout, but the area around Vinica, further south, is richer for **fishing**. You can purchase daily fishing licences at all camping grounds.

There are a lot of **hikes** and **walks** in the surrounding areas, including the 6.5km-long **St Urban's Trail** (Urbanova Pot) to Grabrovec and back via **Veselica**, a 233m-high small hill less than 1km north of Metlika, with great

INFORMATION
Nova Ljubljanska Banka........1 A3
Nova Ljubljanska Banka........2 A6
Post Office........3 A6
Tourist Information Centre Metlika........(see 7)

SIGHTS & ACTIVITIES
Bela Krajina Museum........(see 7)
Commandery........4 B4
Defence Tower........5 B4
Kambič Gallery........6 A3
Metlika Castle........7 B3
Old Cottages........8 B4
Parish Church of St Nicholas........9 B4
Slovenian Firefighters Museum........10 A3
Town Hall........11 B4
Vinska Klet........12 A5

SLEEPING
Hotel Bela Krajina........13 A3
Hotel Pri Belokranjcu........14 B5

EATING
Hotel Bela Krajina Restaurant........(see 13)
Julija Pizzeria........15 A6
Mercator Supermarket........16 B6

DRINKING
Bar Salon 1........17 A3
Grajska Klet........(see 7)
Slaščičarna Murn........18 A3

TRANSPORT
Bus Station........19 A6

views over the town. Another is the Učna Pot Zdence Vidovec from the village of Božakovo just east of Rosalnice (see p229) to the Zdence and Vidovec karst caves. Ask the TIC for brochures outlining the walks. It also has the *Kolesarske Poti Bela Krajina* (Bela Krajina Bike Trails) brochure-map.

Ask the TIC about organised wine tastings at the **Vinska Klet** (☎ 363 70 52; www.kz-metlika.si; Cesta XV Brigade 2; per person €2.50-8.50; ⏲ 8am-3pm Mon-Fri, 8am-noon Sat or by appointment), the 'Wine Cellar' run by the local wine cooperative, which usually requires a minimum 'group' of 10 people.

Festivals & Events

Metlika's main event is the **Vinska Vigred** (www.metlika-turizem.si) wine festival held on the third weekend of May.

Sleeping

Primostek Recreational Centre (Rekreacijski Centre Primostek; ☎ 305 85 28, 031 652 851; nada.frankovic@iskra-semic.si; campsite adult/child €7/3.50, bungalow per person €18-20; ⏲ May-Sep; P) This spruced up camping ground 2km southwest of Metlika has sites for tents and caravans as well as bungalows with up to eight beds.

Kamp Podzemelj ob Kolpi (☎ 306 95 72, 363 52 81; www.kamp-podzemelj.si; Podzemelj 16b; campsite adult/child €7.80/5.50, caravans for 4 €33-74; ⏲ May–mid-Sep; P) A larger and better-equipped camping ground with a 'beach' on the Kolpa 7km southwest of Metlika measures 2.5 hectares in size and can accommodate 70 tents and 250 guests. Without wheels, though, the only way to reach here is by train from Metlika and it's a 2km walk from the station at Gradac.

Gostišče Veselič (☎ 306 91 56; www.gostisce-veselic.com; Podzemelj 17; r per person €20; P) This *gostilna* in Podzemelj (house No 17), not far from the camping ground, has four rooms and its restaurant is a favourite of locals.

Hotel Pri Belokranjcu (☎ 302 84 44; 041 921 694; www.hotel.pribelokranjcu.si; Cesta Bratstva in Enotnosti 77; s/d/tr €38/55/78; P) This bright yellow box with green window frames and red shades, a former cop shop, is now a 10-room hotel offering adequate budget accommodation in the (almost) centre of Metlika. It is a branch of a hotel with the same name in Novo Mesto (p214).

Hotel Bela Krajina (☎ 305 81 23, 040 327 492; www.hotel-belakrajina.si; Cesta Bratstva in Enotnosti 28; s/d/tr €53/87/105; P) A nose-to-tail renovation has turned one of provincial Slovenia's socialist holdovers into the bell of Bela Krajina. Its 26 rooms have been pulled into the 21st century with air-conditioning, muted carpe and upgraded furnishings; the restaurant is welcome addition to the eating scene here.

Eating

Julija Pizzeria (☎ 305 9487; NBK 9; pizza €4.50-7.20 ⏲ 7am-midnight Sun-Thu, 7am-1am Fri & Sat) This pizzeria with a popular bar (open from 9am to 11pm daily) just opposite is in the large shopping centre across from the bus station.

Hotel Bela Krajina (Cesta Bratstva in Enotnosti 28; starters €5.20-9.50, mains €6.90-13.20; ⏲ 8am-10pm) This convivial place, which starts you off with a giant loaf of *belokranjska pogača* (local flat bread), is the best place for a meal in Metlika. Try the Bela Krajina-style *žlikrofi* (raviolis; €6) and the excellent trout in white wine (€8.50).

Gostilna Budački (☎ 363 52 00; Ulica Belokranjskeg Odreda 14; meals from €15; ⏲ 8am-10pm Mon-Fri, 8am-11pm Sat & Sun) One of the very few 'real' places to eat in the city limits, this *gostilna* 450m south of the centre gets good reviews for its home-style cooking.

There's a large **Mercator** (NBK 2; ⏲ 6.30am-7pm Mon-Fri, 6.30am-3pm Sat, 8-11am Sun) supermarket branch in the shopping centre opposite the bus station.

Drinking

Slaščičarna Murn (☎ 041 952 058; Ulica na Trg 3; ⏲ 8am-noon Tue, 9am-noon & 3-5pm Wed-Fri, 8am-1pm Sat, 8-10am Sun) This little cafe with the bankers' hours serves the best cakes and ice cream in town.

Grajska Klet (☎ 305 89 99, 031 632 470; ⏲ 7am-11pm Mon-Thu, 7am-midnight Fri, 8am-midnight Sat, 8am-noon Sun) If you want to try some Bela Krajina wine but don't have the time to get out into the country and can't get into the Vinska Klet (left), head for this *vinoteka* in the castle courtyard. You can sample pinot blanc, chardonnay, the rieslings and sweet rumeni muškat (yellow muscatel).

Bar Salon 1 (⏲ 040 309 970; Cesta Bratstva in Enotnosti 45; ⏲ 7am-11pm Mon-Thu, 7am-1.30am Fri & Sat) Opposite the Bela Krajina Hotel, this large pub is popular among Metlika's young bloods and stays open late.

Getting There & Around

Destinations served by bus from Metlika include Črnomelj (€2.70, 30 minutes, 16km, seven daily during the week, with five more during school term), Novo Mesto (€3.60, one our, 30km, five daily) and Vinica (€5.60, 1½ ours, 46km, three daily during the week and ix during school term).

Metlika is served by up to eight trains daily rom Ljubljana (€7.20, 2¾ hours, 122km) via Jovo Mesto and Črnomelj (€1.60, 20 minutes, 5km). Three to five trains a day head for Karlovac, 33km to the south in Croatia.

You can book a taxi on ☎ 041 708 733.

AROUND METLIKA

Rosalnice

☎ 07 / pop 395 / elev 138m

The **Three Parishes** (Tri Fare) in Rosalnice, 1.5km east of Metlika, is a row of three graceful little Gothic churches that have been important pilgrimage sites for seven centuries. Although they were originally built, according to Valvasor, in the late 12th century by the Knights Templar, today's churches date from the 14th and 16th centuries. The one to the north – the largest and oldest of the three – is the **Church of Our Lady of Sorrows** and has a Gothic presbytery and frescoes of scenes from the Old and New Testaments. The church in the middle, the 16th-century **Ecce Homo**, has a large tower rising above its porch. The one on the south with the buttresses and another Gothic presbytery is the **Church of Our Lady of Lourdes.** It dates from between the 16th and 19th centuries and is in the worst repair. The churches do not keep fixed opening hours. Seek the key from **house No 44** (☎ 306 00 51).

There is a train from Metlika to Rosalnice (€1.10, two minutes, 1km, daily at 3.21pm), but it is just as easy to walk from Metlika. Begin in the Old Town, head northeast along Navratilova pot and follow Ulica Janka Brodariča eastward for 600m, then turn south. After 200m turn east and continue straight on to the three churches.

Metlika Wine Area

☎ 07 / elev to 235m

The hills to the north and northeast of Metlika are one of the Bela Krajina wine districts' most important areas and produce such distinctive wines as Metliška Črnina, the ruby red 'Metlika Black' and a late-maturing sweet 'ice wine' called Kolednik Ledeno Vino. They are also superb areas for easy walking.

On the way to **Vinomer** and **Drašiči**, two important wine towns about 4km and 6km respectively from Metlika, you'll walk through *steljniki,* stands of birch trees growing among ferns in clay soil. They are the very symbol of Bela Krajina.

Drašiči is famous for its folk architecture, and you can sample local wines at several places, including the **Simonič farmhouse** (☎ 305 81 85, 041 572 596; Drašiči 56) and the **Prus farmhouse** (☎ 305 90 98, 041 690 112; Krmačina 6). Be sure to phone ahead. Ask the TIC in Metlika about wine tastings at the 250-year-old **Soseska Zidanica** (☎ 041 788 938; Drašiči 46; 🕑 by appointment), a vineyard cottage next to the Church of St Peter in the centre of Drašiči.

ČRNOMELJ

☎ 07 / pop 5930 / elev 163m

The capital of Bela Krajina and its largest town, Črnomelj (pronounced cher-*no*-mel) is on a promontory in a loop where the Lahinja and Dobličica Rivers meet. This relaxed town is the 'folk heart' of Bela Krajina', and its popular Jurjevanje festival attracts hundreds of dancers and singers from the region.

Črnomelj was settled very early on, and the Roman presence is evident from the Mithraic shrine at Rožanec (p231), about 4km northwest of the town. During the Turkish invasions in the 15th and 16th centuries, the town was attacked incessantly, but due to its strong fortifications and excellent hilltop lookouts at Stražnji Vrh and Doblička Gora to the west, it was never taken. After Italy's surrender in 1943, the town functioned for a time as Slovenia's capital.

Legend has it that Črnomelj (a corruption of the words for 'black miller') got its name when a beggar, dissatisfied with the quality of the flour she'd been given, put a curse on the local miller. The town's symbol today is a smiling baker holding a pretzel.

Orientation

Buses stop on Trg Svobode in front of Črnomelj Castle and near the Posojilnica, the old savings and loan bank building. The train station is about 1.5km to the north on Kolodvorska cesta.

Information

Nova Ljubljanska Banka Kolodvorska cesta (Kolodvorska cesta 32b); Posojilnica (Trg Svobode 2)

Post office (Kolodvorska cesta 30)

Tourist Information Centre Črnomelj (TIC; ☎ 305 65 30, 040 883 162; www.belakrajina.si; Trg Svobode 3; 🕑 8am-4pm Mon-Fri, 9am-noon Sat) On the ground floor of Črnomelj Castle.

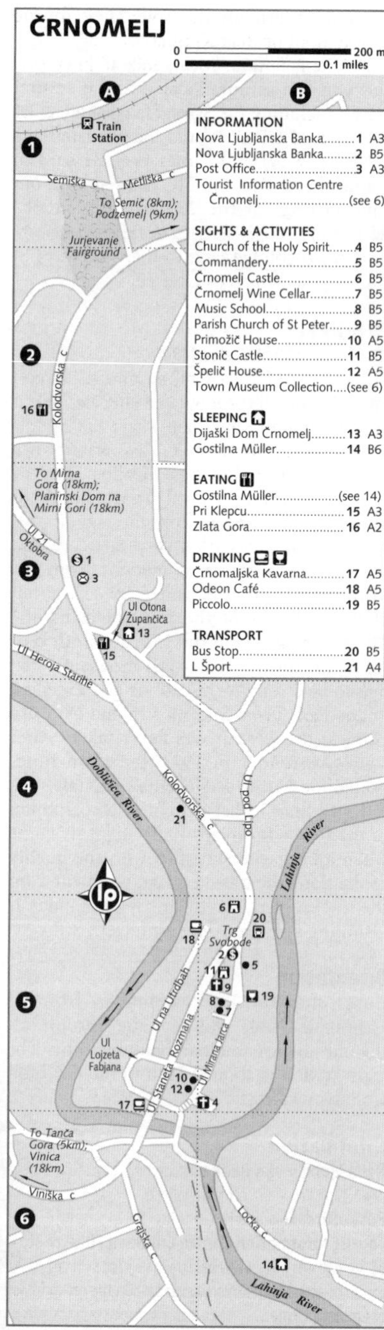

Sights & Activities

Črnomelj Castle (Črnomeljski Grad; Trg Svobode 3), par of which date from the mid-12th centur houses the **Town Museum Collection** (Mestna Muzejsk Zbirka; ☎ 305 65 30, 306 11 00; www.belokranjski-muzej.s adult/child €1/0.50; 🕒 8am-4pm Mon-Fri, 9am-noon Sa on the 1st floor, with items and document related to the history of Črnomelj and Bel Krajina from the 5th century AD onward.

The foundations of **Stonič Castle** (Stoniče Grad; Ulica Staneta Rozmana 4) to the south also g back nine centuries; this is where the town' original castle stood. The **Commandery** (Komend Trg Svobode 1) of the Teutonic Knights, the gre building across the square to the southeast, i a more recent structure, originally built in th mid-17th century and altered 200 years late On it is a stone relief of two knights and a inscription in German.

The **Parish Church of St Peter** (Cerkev Sv Petra; Ulic Staneta Rozmana), almost opposite Stonič Castle dates to the 13th century but what you'll se today is a standard-issue baroque structur with a single spire. You can still see Roma tombstones built into the walls, and on th western exterior above the main entrance i a fresco of St Christopher, the patron sain of travellers.

The desanctified **Church of the Holy Spiri** (Cerkev Sv Duha; www.csd.si, in Slovene; Ulica Mirana Jarca at the southeastern end of the Old Town wa built in 1487 and has just emerged from a decades-long renovation and is now used fo concerts and exhibitions. Opposite, in **Špeli House** (Špeličeva Hiša; ☎ 306 11 90, 040 238 714; Ulica Mirana Jarca 20; admission free; 🕒 8am-noon Mon, Wed & Fri), there is a gallery of Bela Krajina art and next door **Primožič House** (Primožičeva Hiša Ulica Mirana Jarca 18; 🕒 8am-4pm Mon-Fri, 9am-noon Sat has local arts and crafts (Easter eggs, napkins pottery, wickerwork) on display and for sale contact the TIC if it is shut.

The **Črnomelj Wine Cellar** (Črnomajska Klet; ☎ 305 65 30; Ulica Mirana Jarca), in the basement of the beautifully renovated music school, offers tastings of four wines from the Bela Krajina wine-growing district as well as nibbles on *belokranjska pogača* (local flatbread) and cheese for €7 (though you might have to join a group).

One of the most popular hikes in this part of Bela Krajina starts at the northern end of Ulica 21 Oktobra; it goes for 18km north-west to Mirna Gora (1047m), where you can stay 1000m high at Category III **Planinski Dom**

a Mirni Gori (306 85 73, 041 910 357; Tue-Sun), ›ith a total of 50 beds in nine rooms and ›ree dorms.

A wine road *(vinska cesta)* runs from Tanča ›ora, 5km southwest of Črnomelj, northward ›rough Doblička Gora, Stražnji Vrh and ›učetna Vas to **Semič** (population 2050). This ›tractive little town, 9km north of Črnomelj, ›as the ruins of a 13th-century castle and ›hurch. To the southeast lies the source of ›he Krupa River.

›estivals & Events

›urjevanje (www.jurjevanje.si), running for almost ›alf a century and Slovenia's oldest festival, › five days of music, dance and bonfires at ›he fairground near the train station and ›ther locations around town in mid-June. ›t's one of the most important and oldest ›elebrations of folklore in Slovenia. It is ›ased on the Zeleni Jurij (Green George), ›n early Slavic deity of vegetation, fertility ›nd spring.

›leeping

›amping grounds in the region of Črnomelj ›nclude those at Podzemelj (p228), 9km ›ortheast of Črnomelj, Adlešiči (p233), ›2km to the southeast, and Vinica (p233), ›9km to the south.

Dijaški Dom Črnomelj (306 21 60, 040 734 230; ›www.dd-crnomelj.si; Ulica Otona Župančiča 7; dm per person ›15; year-round; P) This HI-affiliated hos›el has 60 beds in 10 doubles and as many ›riples open to visitors in summer. A third ›f those are available year-round.

Gostilna Müller (356 72 00, 041 689 056; Ločka cesta ›; r per person €25; P) As the only game in town at ›resent, this B&B across the river to the south ›f the Old Town looks increasingly attractive. ›he four rooms are bright and attractive, and ›t's an easy walk into central Črnomelj.

›ating

›ri Klepcu (356 74 70; Kolodvorska cesta 24; pizza ›3.20-6.50; 9am-10pm Mon-Thu, 9am-11pm Fri, noon-11pm Sat, 4-10pm Sun) For pizza, try this place just ›outheast of the bank and post office. It's not ›he most authentic but it's cheap and central. ›nter from Ulica Otona Župančiča.

Zalata Gora (041 888 027; Kolodvorska cesta 53; ›tarters €1.50-3, mains €5.90-9.50; 8am-10pm Mon-Fri, ›am-11pm Sat, 11am-10pm Sun) Perhaps not the most ›uthentic place outside the Middle Kingdom, ›ut the Gold Mountain owned by a young couple from Beijing serves up some decent rice and noodle dishes (€4.60 to €5.20).

Gostilna Müller (Ločka cesta 6; starters €5-7.50, mains €7-12; 8am-10pm Tue-Fri, 11am-11pm Sat, 11am-10pm Sun) The restaurant at this guest house is just so-so these days but one of the few real options in Črnomelj. Try the cold meat platter.

Drinking

Odeon Café (305 22 86; Ulica na Utrdbah 2; 7am-11pm Sun-Thu, 7am-midnight Fri & Sat) This wonderful little place in a renovated old building just west of Črnomelj Castle overlooks the Dobličica River and has outside seating in the warmer months. The music (Putomayo world music) and literature (LP guides) for sale is very well chosen and there's wi-fi access for free.

Črnomaljska Kavarna (040 741 006; Ulica Lojzeta Fabjana 7; 7am-10pm Mon-Thu, 7am-midnight Fri-Sun) Known locally as 'the mayor's place' (his wife owns it), the Črnomelj Café is an upmarket pub-cafe serving hot and cold drinks just below the bridge over the Lahinja River.

Piccolo (305 32 96; Trg Svobode 1a; 7am-2am or 3am) Below a small (and now derelict shopping centre), this bar, complete with pool table, is a popular place for a drink till the wee hours.

Getting There & Around

Bus service is not very good to and from Črnomelj, although there are up to nine daily departures to Vinica (€2.70, 30 minutes, 19km) via Dragatuš depending on the season; two daily buses at 10.25am and 2.30pm to Adlešiči (€2.30, 30 minutes, 12km); one or two daily buses to Novo Mesto (€5.20, one hour, 43km); and a bus on weekdays to Ljubljana (€9.60, 2½ hours, 102km) via Semič, Muljava and Žužemberk.

Črnomelj is served by up to nine trains a day from Ljubljana (€6.50, 2½ hours, 107km) via Ivančna Gora, Novo Mesto and Semič. Three to five daily trains also depart Črnomelj for Karlovac, 45km to the south in Croatia.

You can hire bicycles from **L Šport** (305 24 81, 040 657 657; Kolodvorska cesta 13; per day €10; 8am-7pm Mon-Fri, 8am-noon Sat).

AROUND ČRNOMELJ

Rožanec

07 / pop 65 / elev 195m

About 4km northwest of Črnomelj just off the old Roman road (route No 216) is the little village of Rožanec; to reach it turn west just after Lokve. From a car park in the village centre, a sign points the way along a trail that leads about 400m to the **Mithraeum** (Mitrej), a temple in a cavern dedicated to the god Mithra, dating from the 2nd century AD. At first it appears to be no more than a natural hollow in the limestone set on a wooded hillside. But on one of the exposed limestone faces is a 1.5m-high carved relief of Mithra sacrificing the sacred bull, watched by Sol (the sun, at top left) and Luna (the moon, at top right), with a dog, serpent and scorpion at his feet.

Lahinja Country Park

☎ 07 / elev to 242m

This 259-hectare park, about 9km south of Črnomelj, is a protected karst area and the source of the Lahinja River, with trails criss-crossing the area. Two small swamps are home to a number of endangered plants and animals, especially birds like orioles, nightingales and kingfishers. The areas around **Pusti Gradac** and **Veliki Nerajec** are treasure-troves of prehistoric finds and caves. The **Lahinja Park Information Centre** (☎ 305 74 28, 031 705 519) is in Veliki Nerajec at house No 18a. There's also a shop here selling local folk art and crafts including pottery, musical instruments and distinctive 'kingfisher' whistles.

KOLPA VALLEY

☎ 07 / elev to 264m

The 118km-long Kolpa, which forms Slovenia's southeastern border with Croatia, is the warmest and one of the cleanest rivers in the country. As a result, it has become a popular recreational area for swimming, fishing and boating, especially around the village of **Vini** and to the northeast (and downstream) **Adleši** known for its folk culture and easy walks. Tl **Lahinja Park Information Centre** (☎ 305 74 28, 031 7(519) is in Veliki Nerajec at house No 18a.

Sights

In Vinica (population 220) the **Oton Županč Memorial Collection** (Spomninska Zbirka Otona Župančič ☎ 040 630 365, 041 703 609; www.belokranjski-muzej.: Vinica 6; adult/child €1.50/1; by arrangement), a branc of the Bela Krajina Museum in Metlika, housed in the cottage where the celebrate Slovenian poet was born in 1878.

In the village of **Žuniči**, about 10kr northeast of Vinica, keep your eyes ope for traditional rural architecture, especiall the farmsteads at Nos 2 and 5, which ar sometimes open to the public.

While passing through the village of **Purg** just north of Adlešiči (population 140), visi the **Čebelar Adlešič** (Adlešič Beekeepers; ☎ 307 02 3 Purga 5). The family will be happy to shov you their hives, explain all things apiaria and sell you their honey and *domača medic* (homemade mead). The ruins of 16th-centur **Pobrežje Castle**, on a steep rock above th Kolpa about 1km northeast of Purga, ar worth exploring.

Activities

Much of the Slovenian riverbank of the Kolp from Fučkovci, just north of Adlešiči, as fa southwest as Stari Trg ob Kolpi forms the 4332 hectare **Kolpa Country Park**, (Kolpa Krajinski Park; ☎ 35 52 40; www.kp-kolpa.si; information centre Adlešiči 15) a pro

MITHRA & THE GREAT SACRIFICE

Mithraism, the worship of the god Mithra, originated in Persia. As Roman rule extended into the west, the religion became extremely popular with traders, imperial slaves and mercenaries of the Roman army, and spread rapidly throughout the empire in the 1st and 2nd centuries AD. In fact, Mithraism was the principal rival of Christianity until Constantine, a convert, came to the throne in the 4th century.

Mithraism was a mysterious religion and its devotees were sworn to secrecy. What little is known of Mithra, the god of justice and social contract, has been deduced from reliefs and icons found in temples, such as the ones at Rožanec near Črnomelj and at Ptuj in Štajerska. Most of them portray Mithra clad in a Persian-style cap and tunic sacrificing a white bull in front of Sol, the sun god. From the bull's blood sprout grain and grapes and from its semen animals grow. Sol's wife Luna, the moon, begins her cycle and time is born.

Mithraism and Christianity competed strongly because of a striking similarity in many of their rituals. Both religions involved the birth of a deity on winter solstice (25 December), shepherds, death and resurrection and a form of baptism. Devotees of Mithraism knelt when they worshipped and a common meal – a 'communion' of bread and water – was a regular feature of the liturgy.

ɛcted area of natural wonders and cultural ıonuments. The **Žagar farmhouse** (☎ 306 44 41, 41 609 920; zvonko.zagar@volja.net) in Damelj (house lo 11), southwest of Vinica and in the heart f the park, rents canoes and minirafts (per day 15 to €18) and organises river excursions. The mbitious, however, will look into the rapid-vater kayak run from Stari Trg, 20km upriver and still in the park), to Vinica costing €20 nd organised by **Grand Kolpa** (☎ 305 51 01, 041 40 798; www.grandkolpa-sp.si; Stari Trg ob Kolpi 15). It also ents canoes and rafts. **Kamp Pezdirc** (see below) ents canoes for €5 per hour.

Fishing is especially good in the Kolpa round Dol pri Starem Trgu (grayling, red-potted trout, huchen); you can buy a daily shing licence at camping grounds for €15.

From Adlešiči, two easy **hikes** to nearby ills afford great views of the Kolpa, vine-ards and surrounding towns. To get to Aala Plešivica (341m), walk south along a ıarked trail for about half an hour. A short istance to the west is a sinkhole with a water ource called Vodenica; steps lead down to ıe source, where you'll find a large stone ault. Velika Plešivica (363m), topped with 12th-century church dedicated to St Mary Aagdalene, is about an hour's walk north-vest of Adlešiči. The *Tourist Destination 'ela Krajina* brochure available from the 'IC in Metlika and Črnomelj includes uggested itineraries.

leeping & Eating

amp Pezdirc (☎ 306 94 58, 040 306 051; www.kamp ‚riblje.com; Griblje 70; campsite per adult/child €6/3, dm €8; May-Sep; P) This very basic site at Griblje, 4km due east of Črnomelj, with spaces for 00 happy (or otherwise) campers as well as heap dormitory accommodation for 20 peo-le, has its own 'beach' on the Kolpa.

Camping Kolpa Vinica (☎ 031 513 060; www.kamp-kolpa i; Vinica 19a; per adult €6-7.50, child €4.50-5.50, chalets €48-); May-Sep; P) This camping ground hard y the Kolpa River and just metres from the Croatian border covers an area of about 1.5 ectares and has 60 tent and caravan sites as vell as in-place chalets for four people.

Pri Štefaniču farmhouse (☎ 305 73 47, 041 689 057; 'agatuš 22; d per person from €20; P) This farmhouse, vith a popular restaurant that serves produce lmost uniquely grown here (including buck-vheat ground at the nearby Klepčev mill), has ccommodation in four double rooms and is an excellent starting point for walks in Lahinja Country Park.

Grabrijanovi farmhouse (☎ 307 00 70, 040 391 286; Adlešiči 5; r per person €24; Mar–mid-Jan; P) This farmhouse, with five rooms and one apartment on the main road 500m from the Kolpa in Adlešiči, is one of the better choices in the area and the food gets rave reviews. Bikes are available for free to guests.

Raztresen farmhouse (☎ 307 05 16, 041 736 587; www.rim.si; Rim 5; half board €30-35; P) Along with accommodation, this inventive place 400m from the crossroads in Dolenjci, north of Adlešiči, offers courses in traditional crafts and trades such as weaving and basketry and has a shop and a gallery.

Gostilna Balkovec (☎ 305 76 32; starters €4.80-6.50, mains €7.20-9.50; 8am-11pm) This little *gostilna* in Mali Nerajec (house No 3), on the edge of Lahinja Country Park, specialises in *pečenka* (roast meat), especially *jagenjček* (roast lamb).

Gostilna Milič (☎ 307 00 19; Adlešiči 15; meals from €12; 11am-midnight Tue-Thu, 11am-1am Fri & Sat, 9am-10pm Sun) In the centre of Adlešiči, Milič is one of the oldest eateries in Bela Krajina. Its drawcard is a large baker's oven that produces anything and everything from pizza to roast suckling pig.

Shopping

The Lahinja Park Information Centre (see opposite) in Veliki Nerajec has a wide range of locally produced quality handicrafts for sale.

At Čebelar Adlešič you can buy honey, mead, beeswax, pollen and propolis, the sticky substance collected from certain trees by bees to cement their hives and considered an elixir.

Raztresen farmhouse contains a gallery of locally produced crafts for sale, including hand-woven linen from flax grown on the farm, painted Easter eggs, wicker baskets, even bee colonies. A visit to the gallery with demonstrations is €60 per person. It also has a range of local wines (including the sweet 'ice' variety) and brandies in beautifully crafted hand-blown bottles.

Getting There & Around

Depending on the season up to nine buses a day link Vinica with Črnomelj (€2.60, 30 minutes, 18km) via Dragatuš. There are a couple of buses a day from Adlešiči to Črnomelj (€2.20, 30 minutes, 11km).

Štajerska & Koroška

Štajerska (Styria in English), far and away Slovenia's largest province, gets a bum rap from other Slovenes. They dismiss the province as one huge industrial farm and tease the locals for being country bumpkins. It's true that Štajerska has more big agricultural land than any other part of Slovenia. And, along with wheat and potatoes, hops for making beer are an important crop, as are grapes for the province's excellent wines. But Štajerska is not the flat, seemingly endless plain that is Prekmurje. To the west are the Savinja Alps and to the north the Pohorje Massif, an adventure-land of outdoor activities. Those in search of culture will be drawn by three of the country's most historical centres: Maribor, Celje and that little gem, Ptuj.

In stark contrast is tiny Koroška (Carinthia in English), to the north of Štajerska and a mere shadow of what it was before being truncated after WWI. Basically just three valleys, Koroška is a region of forests, mountains and highland meadows and is tailor-made for outdoor activities, including skiing, mountain biking, horse riding and hiking.

HIGHLIGHTS

- Walk back into and through the past via the narrow back streets of medieval **Ptuj** (p243), the jewel of Štajerska
- Enjoy the wonderland (and the uncrowded skiing) that is **Rogla** (p257) in winter
- Watch the world walk (and maybe even sail) by from a cafe or bar in the waterfront Lent district of **Maribor** (p254)
- Stay with the locals on a farm holiday in **Logarska Dolina** (p266), the greenest of Štajerska's valleys
- Take the waters in style at the thermal baths of **Rogaška Slatina** (p240), one of the few true spa towns in Slovenia
- Pedal both above and underground at the spectacular **Mountain Bike Park** (p268) at Črna na Koroškem near Dravograd

ITINERARY

DOWN IN THE VALLEY

One Day / Štajerska

The destinations mentioned under Upper Savinja Valley in the Štajerska section of this chapter – from Mozirje to the entrance of the Logarska Dolina (Logar Valley) – fall along a 35km stretch of valley road that can be done by car or (in theory) bus but is perfect for bicycles. If you take the last option, arm yourself with the *Kolesarska Karta Zgornja Savinjska Dolina* (Upper Savinja Valley Cycling Map; €3).

From **Mozirje** (**1**; p264), where you won't want to miss one of the best botanical parks and flower gardens in Slovenia, head a couple of kilometres south along route 225 to **Nazarje** (**2**; p264), the town with the biblical name, castle below and monastery above it. From here it's another (relatively easy) 10km to the turn-off for the historical towns of **Radmirje** (**3**) and **Gornji Grad** (**4**; p265) but give them a miss – you've got 'miles to go before you sleep'.

Once you've passed **Ljubno ob Savinji** (**5**) on what is now route 428, the valley begins to feel – and smell – truly Alpine, with the mountains so close you can almost touch them, the houses built entirely of wood and the heady scent of pine in the air. The road continues along the winding Savinja River, past wooden bridges and hayracks. At **Struge** (**6**), 3km before Luče, there's a turn north along a forest road to **Snežna Jama** (**7**; Snow Cave; ☎ 839 35 55, 041 424 091; igor.ocvirk@h-rc.si; adult/child & student €9/7; 🕐 tour every 2hr, 9am-5pm daily mid-Jul–Aug, Sat & Sun Jun–mid-Jul & Sep, by appointment May & Oct), an ice cave some 1500m up toward Mt Raduha (2062m), where the temperature is a constant 0°C to 2.5°C.

Back on the main road, in a gorge 4km beyond **Luče ob Savinji** (**8**) is a rock tower called the Needle (Igla). Just before **Rogovilc** (**9**), the starting point for canoeing and kayaking on the Savinja, there's a turn south to **Robanov Kot** (**10**), a valley and park with trails and farmhouse accommodation.

Solčava (**11**), at 642m the highest town in the valley, has some lovely road markers with folk icons and painted barns. Continue along another 4km and you'll reach the start of the **Logarska Dolina.**

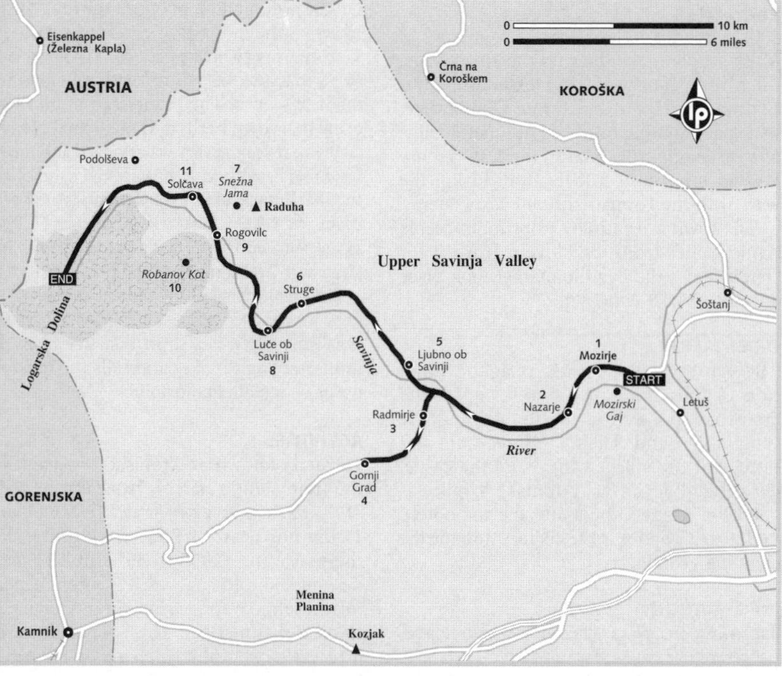

ŠTAJERSKA

Štajerska has been at the crossroads of Slovenia for centuries and virtually everyone has 'slept here' – Celts, Romans, early Slavs, Habsburgs and the Nazi occupiers. In the 14th century the German-speaking Counts of Celje were among the richest and most powerful feudal dynasties in Central Europe and they challenged the Austrian monarchy's rule for a century. Štajerska suffered more than most of the rest of Slovenia under the black leather boot of Nazism in WWII, when many of its inhabitants were murdered, deported or sent to labour camps.

KOZJANSKO REGION

Kozjansko is a remote region along the eastern side of the Posavje Mountains and the 90km-long Sotla River, which forms part of the eastern border with Croatia. It is an area of forests, rolling hills, vineyards, scattered farms and the site of one of Slovenia's three regional parks, with much to offer visitors in the way of spas, two important castles, hiking, cycling and excellent wine.

Podčetrtek

☎ 03 / pop 565 / elev 211m

Most people make their way to this village, on a little bump of land extending into Croatia, to relax at the Terme Olimia thermal spa. Looming overhead are the remains of a castle originally built in the 11th century and an important fortification during the wars with the Hungarians 300 years later.

The town's seemingly unpronounceable name comes from the Slovenian word for 'Thursday' – the day the market took place and the district court sat.

ORIENTATION

The centre of Podčetrtek is at the junction of four roads. All buses stop at the crossroads as well as at the spa and the camping ground. There are three train stations. For the village centre and the castle, get off at Podčetrtek. Atomske Toplice is good for Terme Olimia and the spa hotels. Podčetrtek Toplice is the correct stop for the camping ground.

INFORMATION

Banka Celje (Zdraviliška cesta 276) In the new shopping mall between the centre and spa complex.

Post office (Trška cesta 23; 🕑 8am-9.30am, 10am-5pm Mon-Fri, 8am-noon Sat) Some 200m north of the crossroac

Tourist Information Centre Podčetrtek (TIC; ☎ 8 90 13; www.turizem-podcetrtek.si; Cesta Škofja Gora 1; 🕑 8am-3pm Mon-Fri, 8am-1pm Sat) At the crossroads.

SIGHTS

The enormous Renaissance-style **Podčetrte Castle** (Grad Podčetrtek) atop a 355m-hig hill to the northwest of town went up som time in the mid-16th century but was badl damaged by an earthquake in 1974. The castl which is still not open to the public, can b easily reached by walking north along Tršk cesta and then west on Cesta na Grad fc about 1.5km.

The Minorite **Olimje Minorite Monaste** (Minoritski Samostan Olimje; ☎ 582 91 61; www.olim .com; Olimje 82), 3km southwest of Podčetrtel was built as a Renaissance-style castle in abou 1550. When Pauline monks took over wha was then called Wolimia in German about century later, they added the baroque **Churc of the Assumption**, which boasts its original cei ing paintings in the presbytery, one of th largest baroque altars in the country and th unbelievably ornate **Chapel of St Francis Xavie** On the ground floor of one of the four corne towers is the monastery's greatest treasure: 17th-century **pharmacy** (adult/child €1/0.50; 🕑 10am noon & 1-7pm Mon-Sat) painted with religious an medical scenes. The Franciscan monks her grow their own herbs and medicinal plants.

If you're feeling very waterlogged and time i weighing heavily on your puckered hands, hea for the **Museum of Farm Implements** (Muzej Kmečk Opreme; ☎ 810 92 56; Trška cesta 46; admission €1; 🕑 b appointment), with some 400 items on display in large barn 300m north of the post office.

Čokoladnica Olimje (Olimje Chocolate Boutique; ☎ 81 90 36; www.syncerus.si; Olimje 61; 🕑 10am-7pm Jun-Aug 10am-5pm Sep-May) is a short distance from th monastery and makes and sells the most fa mous chocolate in Slovenia.

ACTIVITIES

Formerly known as Atomske Toplice (thu the train station name), **Terme Olimia** (☎ 82 70 00; www.terme-olimia.com; Zdraviliška cesta 24), abou 1.2km northeast of Podčetrtek centre, ha thermal water (28°C to 35°C) full of magnesium and calcium, which is recommendec for those recovering from surgery or trying to cure rheumatism. These days, however, it places most of the emphasis on recreation

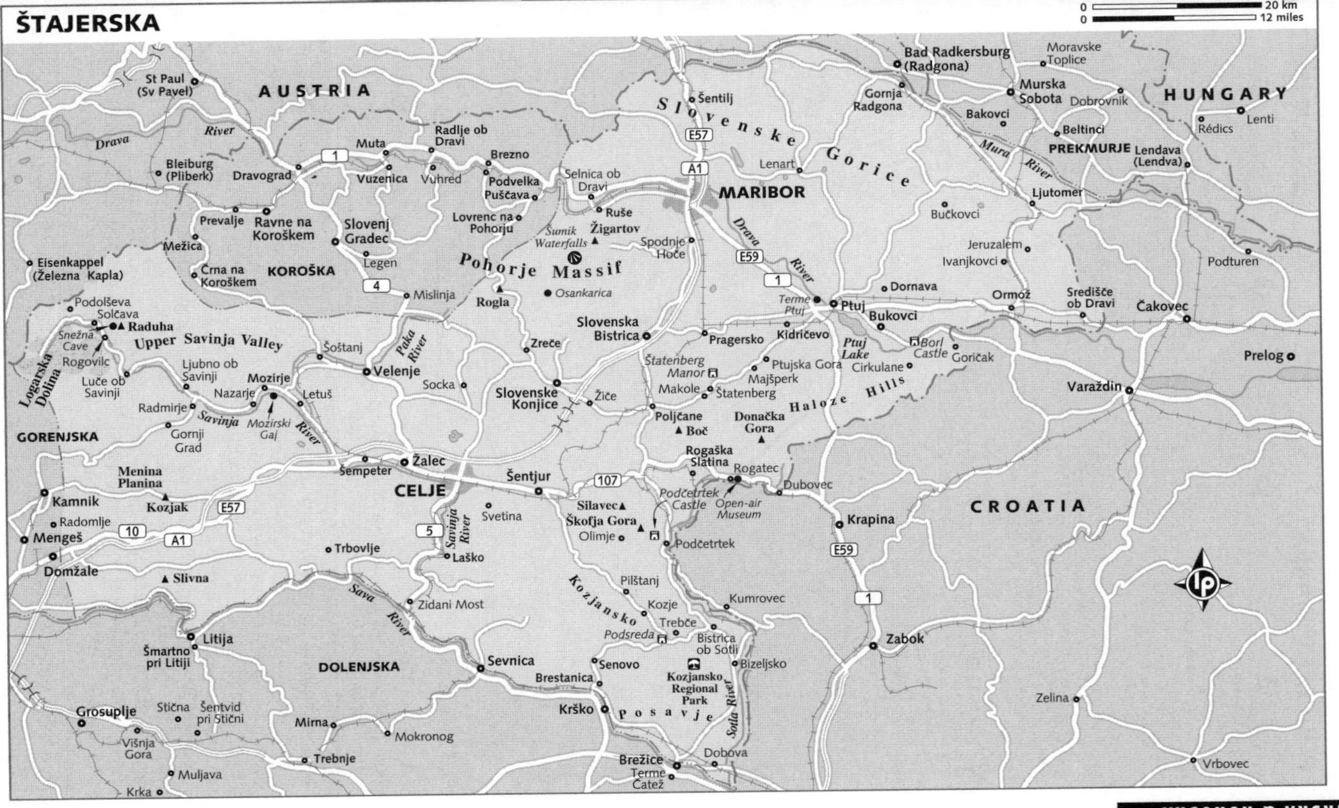
ŠTAJERSKA
0 20 km
0 12 miles
AUSTRIA
HUNGARY
CROATIA
St Paul (Sv Pavel)
Drava River
Bleiburg (Pliberk)
Dravograd
Muta
Vuzenica
Radlje ob Dravi
Vuhred
Brezno
Podvelka
Puščava
Selnica ob Dravi
Ruše
Lovrenc na Pohorju
Prevalje
Ravne na Koroškem
Slovenj Gradec
Legen
Mežica
Eisenkappel (Železna Kapla)
Črna na Koroškem
KOROŠKA
Mislinja
Pohorje Massif
Šumik Waterfalls
Žigartov
Osankarica
Rogla
Podolševa
Solčava
Raduha
Snežna Cave
Upper Savinja Valley
Rogovilc
Logarska Dolina
Luče ob Savinji
Ljubno ob Savinji
Nazarje
Mozirje
Letuš
Šoštanj
Paka River
Velenje
Socka
Zreče
Radmirje
Savinja River
Mozirski Gaj
Gornji Grad
GORENJSKA
Menina Planina
Kozjak
Kamnik
Radomlje
Mengeš
Domžale
E57
10
A1
Šempeter
Žalec
CELJE
Šentjur
Svetina
Savinja River
Laško
Trbovlje
Slivna
Sava River
Zidani Most
Litija
Šmartno pri Litiji
DOLENJSKA
Sevnica
Grosuplje
Stična
Šentvid pri Stični
Višnja Gora
Muljava
Krka
Mirna
Mokronog
Trebnje
Šentilj
Slovenske Gorice
Lenart
MARIBOR
Spodnje Hoče
Drava River
E59
1
4
5
107
Slovenska Bistrica
Slovenske Konjice
Žiče
Pragersko
Štatenberg Manor
Makole
Štatenberg
Poljčane
Boč
Terme Ptuj
Ptuj
Kidričevo
Ptujska Gora
Majšperk
Donačka Gora
Haloze Hills
Rogaška Slatina
Rogatec
Dubovec
Podčetrtek Castle
Open-air Museum
Silavec
Škofja Gora
Olimje
Podčetrtek
Kozjansko
Pilštanj
Kozje
Trebče
Podsreda
Bistrica ob Sotli
Senovo
Brestanica
Kozjansko Regional Park
Bizeljsko
Krško
Posavje
Sotla River
Brežice
Terme Čatež
Dobova
Kumrovec
Krapina
Zabok
Zelina
Vrbovec
Bad Radkersburg (Radgona)
Gornja Radgona
Moravske Toplice
Murska Sobota
Dobrovnik
Bakovci
Beltinci
Mura River
PREKMURJE
Lendava (Lendva)
Rédics
Lenti
Ljutomer
Bučkovci
Jeruzalem
Ivanjkovci
Dornava
Ormož
Središče ob Dravi
Čakovec
Podturen
Bukovci
Ptuj Lake
Borl Castle
Cirkulane
Goričak
Prelog
Varaždin

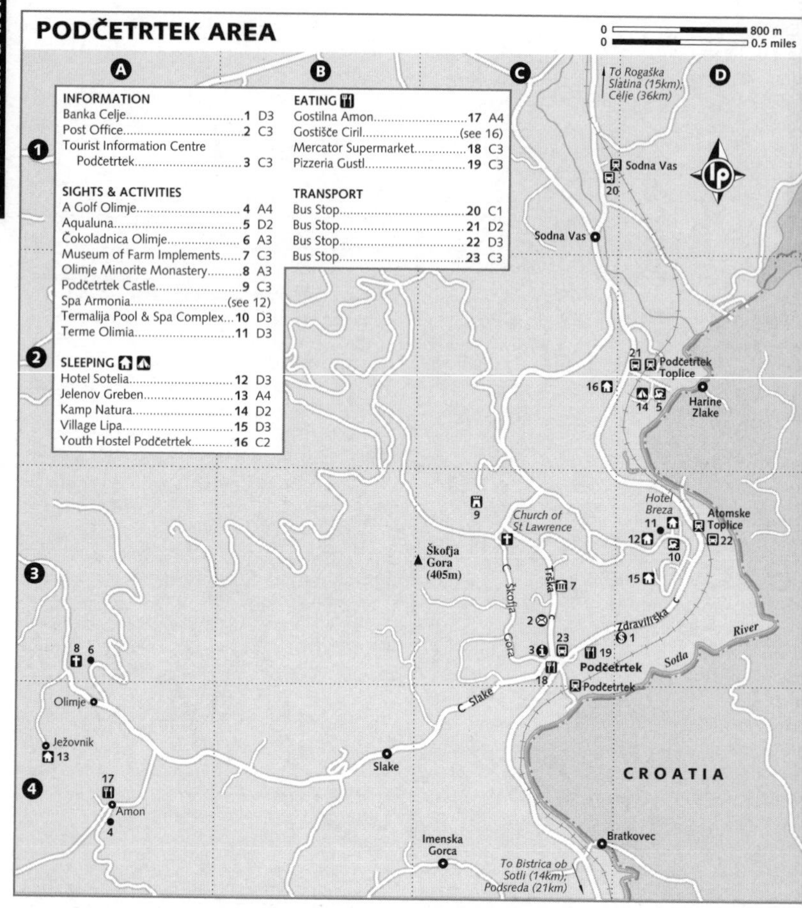

and beauty. The eight indoor and outdoor pools connected by an underwater passage at the **Termalija** (☎ 829 78 05; nonguests adult/child Mon-Fri €10.50/8, Sat & Sun €12.50/9.50; ⏰ 8am-10pm Sun-Thu, 8am-midnight Fri & Sat) pool and spa complex alone cover an area of 2000 sq metres. In addition, the complex has two wellness centres: the Spa Armonia at the Hotel Sotelia and the new (and quite luxurious) Orchidelia.

Next to the camping ground, about 1km north of the main Terme Olimia complex, is **Aqualuna** (☎ 829 77 00; adult/child Mon-Fri €10.50/8, Sat & Sun €9.50-12.50; ⏰ 8am-8pm Jun-Aug, 7am-6pm May & Sep), a water park with another eight outdoor pools over 3000 sq metres and the requisite spiral slides, Adrenaline Tower, wave machines and so on.

Some of the most rewarding **hikes** and **bik** trips in Slovenia can be made in this area. Th free 1:26,000-scale *Podčetrtek-Terme Olimi* tourist map lists and outlines two dozen excursions for walkers, cyclists and mountai bikers. The easiest walks on marked trails tak a couple of hours (though the 6.6km-long circuitous one northeast to the 18th-centur Church of St Emma at 345m lasts about fou hours), and there are bicycle routes all th way to Kozje (37km), Podsreda (41km) an Rogaška Slatina (31km).

A Golf Olimje (☎ 810 90 66; www.agolf.si; Olimje 24 18 holes adult/child Mon-Fri €30/15, Sat & Sun €35/17.50) is a nine-hole, 31-par golf course owned by and just south of the Gostilna Amon (opposite). Hiring half a set of clubs costs €6.

LEEPING

he TIC has a list of families offering private oms (per person from €20) in Podčetrtek nd Sodna Vas, 2km north of the spa complex n the main road.

Kamp Natura (☎ 829 70 00; www.terme-olimia om; campsite per person €7.70-8.80, with pools €12.30-.40; mid-Apr–mid-Oct) Owned and operated y Terme Olimia, this 1-hectare camping round with 200 sites is about 1km north of e main spa complex on the edge of the Sotla iver and next to Aqualuna water park.

Youth Hostel Podčetrtek (☎ 582 91 09; www iril-youthhostel-bc.si; Zdraviliška cesta 10; r per person 14-17; P) This hostel, above the popu-r Gostišče Ciril (right) on the main road ıst across from the entrance to the camp-ng ground and Aqualuna water park, has 5 basic rooms with two and three beds. Iolders of an HI card or equivalent get a 0% discount. It's pretty basic but comfort-ble enough and convenient to the area's ecreational facilities.

our pick **Jelenov Greben** (☎ 582 90 46, 041 317 093; www.jelenov-greben.si; Olimje 90; s €35-40, d €60-70, apt or 4 €65-75; P) This spectacular property, et on a ridge some 500m south of Olimje t Ježovnik, has 12 cosy rooms (some with alconies), four apartments and a popular estaurant (starters €4 to €10, mains €7.50 o €15, set menus €25 to €36, picnic lunches rom €7) that is open daily from 7am to 0pm and celebrated for its venison and vild mushroom dishes. There is also a shop elling farm products and souvenirs. 'Deer Ridge' is a working farm and a hundred ead of deer roam freely on the eight hec-ares of land. It also offers balloon rides.

Terme Olimia (☎ 829 70 00; www.terme-olimia.com; P) Along with its camping ground o the north, the spa complex offers accom-nodation in two hotels, an apartment com-plex and a tourist village. Package deals are endless at this place and those staying at any of the Terme Olimia properties may use all the pools for free.

The cheapest accommodation is at the **Village Lipa** (Vas Lipa; apt for 2 €80-88, apt for 4 €96-106), a tourist 'village' at the southern end of the complex that does not look unlike a cookie-cutter American suburban housing development. It has 25 houses with 136 apartments. The newest property is the 145-room **Hotel Sotelia** (s/d €99/170), a luxurious place that does packages exclusively. It's a very ecofriendly hotel whose undulating, very stylish design and colours seem to make it blend into the forest behind it.

EATING

Pizzeria Gustl (☎ 818 38 00; Zdraviliška cesta 229; pizzas €4.50-8.50; 9am-10pm Sun-Thu, 8am-11pm Fri, 9am-midnight Sat) This simple place attached to an 'aparthotel' in a shopping mall northeast of the centre has decent pizzas.

Gostišče Ciril (Zdraviliška cesta 10; starters €4-7, mains €7-9; 9am-9pm Mon-Fri, 9am-10pm Sat & Sun) This grill restaurant above a popular hostel is frequented by local Slovenes and their Croatian neighbours. The vine-covered terrace is lovely on a warm evening. It also does pizza (€4 to €7).

Gostilna Amon (☎ 818 24 80; Olimje 24; starters €7.30-12.70, mains €8-15; 11am-10pm Sun-Thu, 11am-11pm Fri & Sat) This Maison de Qualité establishment up on the hill south of Olimje, and opposite the golf course, is simply the best place for miles around. It offers high-quality food and organic wines. Set lunch from €9 to €16 is excellent value.

There's a branch of **Mercator** (Cesta Slake 1; 7am-7pm Mon-Fri, 7am-noon Sat & Sun) supermarket in Podčetrtek village.

GETTING THERE & AROUND

Two to five buses a day pass by Podčetrtek and Terme Olimia on their way to Bistrica ob Sotli (€2.30, 20 minutes, 14km) some of which pass by Podčetrtek and Terme Olimia from Celje (€4.70, one hour, 36km) on their way to Bistrica.

Podčetrtek is on the rail line linking Celje (via Stranje) with Imeno. Up to eight trains leave the main Podčetrtek station every day for Celje (€2.80, 50 minutes, 35km) and Imeno (€1.10, four minutes, 3km).

You can call a taxi on ☎ 041 173 700.

Kozjansko Regional Park

☎ 03 / elev to 685m

Established in 1999, 20,760-hectare **Kozjansko Regional Park** (Kozjanski Regijski Park; ☎ 800 71 00; www.kozjanski-park.si; Podsreda 45; 8am-4pm Mon-Fri), one of only three so designated in the country, stretches along the Sotla River, from the border with Dolenjska and Bizeljsko in the south to Podčetrtek in the north.

The forests and dry meadows of the park harbour a wealth of flora and fauna, notably butterflies, reptiles and birds, including corncrakes, kingfishers and storks. There are a number of trails in the park, including educational ones and the circular 32km-long **Podsreda Trail** (Pešpot Podsreda), which ends at the best-preserved Romanesque castles in Slovenia.

Podsreda Castle (Grad Podsreda; ☎ 580 61 18; adult/child €4/2.50; ⌚ 10am-6pm Tue-Sun Apr-Oct) looks pretty much the way it did when it was built in about 1200. A barbican on the south side, with walls 3m thick and a medieval kitchen, leads to a central courtyard with a sgraffito of a knight and a dungeon hidden beneath a staircase. The rooms in the castle wings, some with beamed ceilings and ancient chandeliers, now contain a glassworks exhibit (crystal from Rogaška Slatina, vials from the Olimje pharmacy, green Pohorje glass). The fabulous wood-panelled Renaissance Hall hosts exhibitions, classical concerts and, of course, weddings. Next to it is a wonderful collection of prints of Štajerska's castles and monasteries taken from *Topographii Ducatus Stiria* (1681) by Georg Mattäus Vischer (1628–96). There are exhibition spaces of art and photographs in the east and north wings. The tiny Romanesque chapel is under protracted renovation.

A rough, winding 5km-long road leads to the castle, but you can also reach it via a relatively steep 2km footpath from Stari Trg, less than 1km southeast of the village of Podsreda (population 200). In the village there's a bar near the park headquarters called the **Pod Gradom** (☎ 580 61 04; Podsreda 49; ⌚ 6.30am-10pm) and a **Tuš** (Podsreda 53; ⌚ 7am-4pm Mon-Fri, 7am-2pm Sat, 7am-noon Sun) supermarket around the corner.

You can reach Podsreda from Podčetrtek (€4.10, 50 minutes, 33km) on just one weekday bus at 11.11am though there's another one during school term at 4.12pm.

ROGAŠKA SLATINA

☎ 03 / pop 5050 / elev 228m

Rogaška Slatina is Slovenia's oldest and largest spa town, a veritable 'cure factory' with almost a dozen hotels and treatments and therapies ranging from 'pearl baths' to painful-sounding 'lymph drainage'. It's an attractive place set among scattered forests in the foothills of the Macelj range, and hiking and cycling in the area is particularly good.

Although the hot spring here was known in Roman times, Rogaška Slatina didn't make it on the map until 1574, when the governor of Styria, one Wolf Ungna took the waters on the advice of his physician. A century later a publication entitl *Roitschocrene* examined the curative properties of the springs and claimed they ha helped the ailing viceroy of Croatia. Th news spread to Vienna, visitors started arrive in droves and inns were opened. B the early 19th century Rogaška Slatina w an established spa town.

Orientation

The heart of Rogaška Slatina is the spa complex, an architecturally important group neoclassical, Secessionist and Plečnik-styl buildings surrounding a long landscaped garden called Zdraviliški trg, or Health Reso Sq. The hotels and central Terapija buildin to the north and northeast are late 1960s an '70s vintage and not in keeping with the re of the lovely square.

Rogaška Slatina's bus station is sout of Zdraviliški trg on Celjska cesta. Th train station is 300m farther south o Kidričeva ulica.

Information

Post office (Kidričeva ulica 3)
SKB Banka (Kidričeva ulica 11)
Tourist Information Centre Rogaška Slatina (TIC; ☎ 581 44 14; www.rogaska-slatina.si; Zdraviliški trg 1; ⌚ 8am-7pm Mon-Fri, 11am-5pm Sat & Sun Jul & Aug, 8am-4pm Mon-Fri, 8am-noon Sat Sep-Jun)

Activities

The mineral water (called Donat Mg) foun at the spa complex contains the larges amount of magnesium found in the worl and is primarily for drinking. The stuff is sol throughout Slovenia for both curative an refreshment purposes, but you might find th real thing here tastes a little bit too metalli and salty. The water, which also contains calcium, sulphates, lithium and bromide, is sai to eliminate stress, aid digestion and encourage weight loss. The magnesium alone, it i claimed, regulates 200 bodily functions.

You can engage in a 'drinking cure' o your own at the **Pivnica** (admission €1.50, 3-/5-day pass €7/11; ⌚ 7am-1pm & 3-7pm Mon-Sat, 7am-1pm & 4-7pm Sun), the round glassed-in drinking hal where mineral water is dispensed directly from the springs. It's just beyond the oval-shaped **bandstand** where concerts are staged in the warmer months.

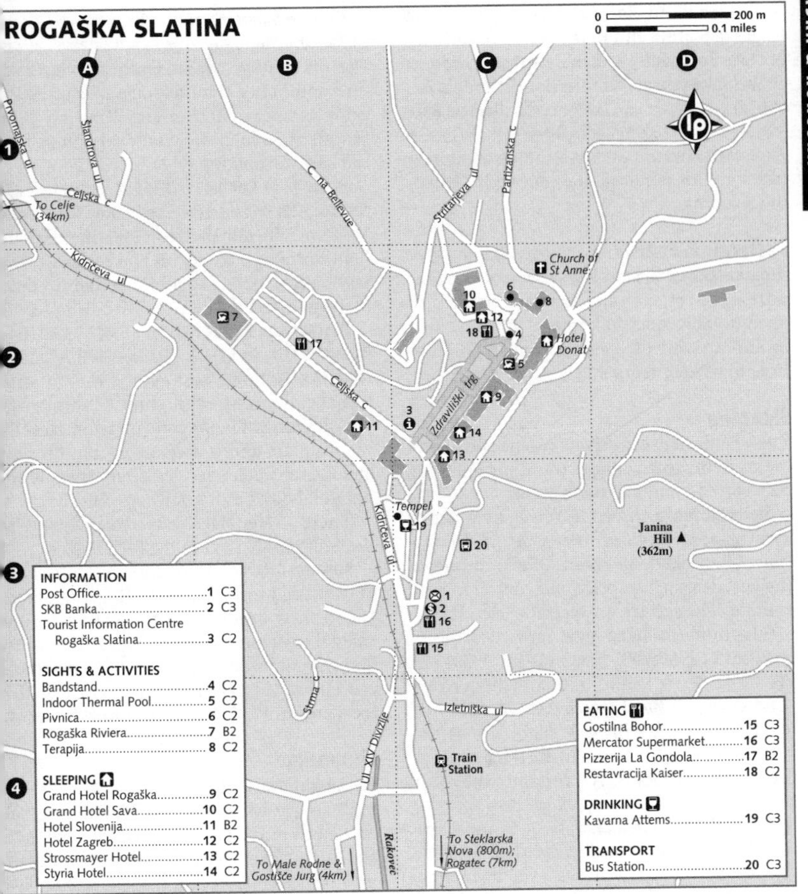

The centre of real action at the spa is the 12-storey **Terapija** (☎ 811 70 15; www.rogaska-medical.com; Zdraviliški trg 9; 7am-8pm Mon-Fri, 8am-noon & 3-7pm Sat, by appointment Sun) building where those pearl baths (€22) are being taken and all those lymph glands are being drained (€31). At the **Hotel Donat** (☎ 811 30 00; Zdraviliški trg 10) opposite the bandstand there's an **indoor thermal pool** (admission €7; 8am-8pm Mon-Sat, 9am-8pm Sun), sauna, steam room and gym. A 30-minute body massage costs €24. Most of the larger hotels have their own wellness centres, including the Grand Hotel Rogaška's Vis Vita and the Lotus Terme at the Sava.

The so-called **Rogaška Riviera** (☎ 818 19 50; Celjska cesta 5; day pass adult/child Mon-Fri €9/6, Sat & Sun €7.50/10; 9am-8pm Sun-Thu, 9am-11pm Fri & Sat) at the northern end of Celjska cesta has two indoor and two outdoor swimming pools that are all connected. There's also a whirlpool and saunas. Terme Rogaška hotels include free entry to these pools in their rates.

There are **walking trails** marked on the 1:25,000 *Rogaška Slatina* GZS map (€2.10) available from the TIC; they range from 2km to 15km and fan out from Rogaška Slatina into the surrounding hills and meadows. One leads 15km to the **Church of St Florian**, on a 818m-high hill northeast of the spa, and to Ložno, from where you can continue on another 4km to **Donačka Gora**. If you want to do it an easier way, take a bus or train to Rogatec (p243), then walk to Donačka Gora in about two hours.

The walk to **Boč** (979m) northwest of Rogaška Slatina and in the centre of the 886-hectare **Boč Country Park** (Krajinski Park Boč; www.boc.si) will take you about four hours though you can drive as far as Category III **Dom na Boču** (☎ 582 46 17, 041 609 615; gt-mali@volja.net; Tue-Sun year-round), a mountain hut a couple of kilometres south of the peak at 658m with 47 beds in 15 rooms.

Festivals & Events

Rogaška Musical Summer is a series of some four dozen concerts, from chamber music and opera to Slovenian folk music, which is held in and around the central bandstand from June to late September.

Sleeping

The TIC has a list of private rooms and apartments in the town and surrounding areas for between €12 and €20 per person,

Hotel Slovenija (☎ 811 50 00; www.terme-rogaska.com; Celjska cesta 5; s €56-62, d €80-96; P) is a flower-bedecked, 65-room hotel and one of the best deals for its price and central to everything. The service is especially friendly.

The modern **Grand Hotel Sava** (☎ 811 40 00; www.rogaska.si; Zdraviliški trg 6; s €62-101, d €100-202; P), and the attached older (and cheaper) **Hotel Zagreb** (s €62-70, d €100-116; P), each with four stars, are at the northwestern end of Zdraviliški trg and count a total of 276 rooms. It's certainly the most popular and active complex in town.

Grand Hotel Rogaška (☎ 811 20 00; www.terme-rogaska.com; Zdraviliški trg 10; s €94-119, d €116-216; P), along with its two branches, the contiguous Hotel Styria and Hotel Strossmayer (singles €58 to €72, doubles €84 to €112), on the eastern side of Zdraviliški trg with more than 350 beds among them, is a four-star property and *la crème de la crème* of accommodation in Rogaška Slatina. The Grand, with its spectacular public areas (especially the Crystal Hall), dates from 1913 while the other two were added in the mid-19th century.

Eating & Drinking

Gostišče Jurg (☎ 581 47 88; Male Rodne 20a; dishes €6.50-18; 11am-10pm Tue-Thu, 11am-11pm Fri & Sat, 11am-8pm Sun) This very swish farmhouse restaurant about 4km southwest of the centre gets rave reviews for its excellent homemade Slovenian dishes and stylish though traditional decor.

Gostilna Bohor (☎ 581 41 00; Kidričeva ulica 23; piz €4.90-6.60, mains €6.90-18; 8am-10pm Mon-Thu, 8ar 11pm Fri & Sat, 10am-10pm Sun) For hearty Slovenia fare and better-than-average pizza, try th popular local eatery. The Kmečka Pizz (Farmer's Pizza) has virtually everything fro the barnyard on top.

Pizzerija La Gondola (☎ 818 28 53; Celjska cesta dishes €7.50-9; noon-11pm Mon-Fri, noon-1am Sat, noo 10pm Sun) Beneath the Hotel Slatina, this de lightful cubby-hole serves good salads, pasta and pizzas, including a bizarre hybrid that half-pizza, half-kebab.

Restavracija Kaiser (☎ 811 47 10; Zdraviliški trg starters €8-13, mains €11-22; noon-11pm) Arguabl Rogaška Slatina's best eatery, this interna tional restaurant, with some Slovenian fa vourites thrown in for good measure, faces th main square and is accessible from the Sav and Zagreb hotels. Service is very friendly an helpful. Look out for daily specials.

There's a **Mercator** (Kidričeva ulica 13; 8am-7pr Mon-Fri, to 1pm Sat) next to the SKB Banka.

Kavarna Attems (☎ 051 200 600; Zdraviliški trg 2 8am-2am) Most visitors to Rogaška Slatin spend their evenings in the hotel bars an cafes; the Attems, in the renovated art nouveau Tempel building dating from 1904 at the south ern end of Zdraviliški trg, is popular with local crowd. We love the 'olde worlde' decor.

Shopping

Steklarska Nova (☎ 818 20 27; Steklarska ulica 1; 8am 7pm Mon-Fri, to 1pm Sat) Rogaška Slatina is as cel ebrated for its crystal as it is for its mineral wate and this outlet attached to the school where the making (and not breaking) of it is taught has a wide range of leaded crystal items for sale. It's about a kilometre south of the town centre.

Getting There & Around

Buses to Celje (€4.10, one hour, 34km) and Rogatec (€1.80, 10 minutes, 7km) leave Rogaška Slatina more or less hourly. There are buses to Maribor (€7.20, 1½ hours, 75km, three or four daily) and Dobovec (€2.30, 30 minutes, 15km, three to four daily) near the border with Croatia.

Rogaška Slatina is on the train line linking Celje (€2.95, 50 minutes, 36km, up to seven daily) via Rogatec (€1.10, 10 minutes, 6km) and Dobovec with Zabok in Croatia, where you can change for Zagreb.

Book a taxi in Rogaška Slatina on ☎ 041 720 824.

ROUND ROGAŠKA SLATINA

ogatec

☎ 03 / pop 1605 / elev 234m

his small town, about 7km east of (and ccessible by bus and train from) Rogaška latina, has two important sights worth ırrying over.

The **Rogatec Open-Air Museum** (Muzej na Prostem ɔgatec; ☎ 818 62 00; www.muzej-rogatec.si; adult/child/ nior & student/family €3/2.30/2.60/6, with Strmol Manor 5.40/4.10/4.60/10.80; 10am-6pm Tue-Sun Apr-Oct) is lovenia's largest and most ambitious *skanzen* open-air museum displaying village architecure). Some 10 original structures or replicas ave been relocated or built here to create a ypical Styrian farm of the 19th and early 20th enturies. The large farmhouse, barn, *toplar* double-linked hayrack), vintner's cottage nd Hungarian-style shahoof, or sweep-pole vell, are particularly interesting and there re often activities (weaving, stone-cutting, read-making etc).

Towering above Rogatec is **Strmol Manor** Dvorec Strmol; ☎ 810 72 22, 051 322 287; www.rogatec net; adult/child/senior & student/family €3/2.30/2.60/6, vith Strmol Manor €5.40/4.10/4.60/10.80; 10am-6pm ue-Sun Apr-Oct), a colossal, 15th-century castle ovingly restored in 2003 with exhibits on ive floors. Don't miss the restaurant on the st floor with its original open-hearth 'black itchen' *(črna kuhinja)*; the chapel, with its aroque and Renaissance murals just off the lecorative Small Hall (Mala Dvorana); and the memorable exhibit in the loft, which re-creates an early-20th-century country kitchen, complete with original furnishings and fittings.

PTUJ

☎ 02 / pop 19,015 / elev 224m

Rising gently above a wide, almost flat valley, compact Ptuj (Poetovio to the Romans) forms a symphony of red-tile roofs best viewed from across the Drava River. One of the oldest towns in Slovenia, Ptuj equals Ljubljana in terms of historical importance but the compact medieval core, with its castle, museums, monasteries and churches, can easily be seen in a day. There are so many interesting side trips and activities in the area that you may want to base yourself here for a while.

History

Ptuj, whose name in English sounds not unlike someone spitting, began life as a Roman military outpost on the south bank of the Drava River and later grew into a civilian settlement called Poetovio on the opposite side. Tacitus mentions it by name in his *Historiae* as having existed as early as 69 AD.

By the 1st century AD the largest Roman township in what is now Slovenia, Poetovio was the centre of the Mithraic cult (p232) and several complete temples have been unearthed in the area.

Ptuj received its town rights in 977 and over the next several centuries it grew rich through trade on the Drava. By the 13th century it was competing with the 'upstart' Marburg (Maribor), 26km upriver, in both crafts and commerce. Two monastic orders – the Dominicans and the Franciscan Minorites – settled here and built important monasteries. The Magyars attacked and occupied Ptuj for most of the 15th century.

THE HAYRACK: A NATIONAL ICON

Nothing is as Slovenian as the *kozolec*, the hayrack seen almost everywhere in the country except in Prekmurje and the Karst area of Primorska. Because the ground in Alpine and hilly areas can be damp, wheat and hay are hung from racks, allowing the wind to do the drying faster and more efficiently.

Until the late 19th century, the *kozolec* was looked upon as just another tool to make a farmer's work easier and the land more productive. Then the artist Ivan Grohar made it the centrepiece of many of his Impressionist paintings, and the *kozolec* became as much a part of the cultural landscape as the physical one. Today it is virtually a national icon.

There are many different types of Slovenian hayracks: single ones standing alone or 'goat hayracks' with sloped 'lean-to' roofs, parallel and stretched ones and double *toplarji* (hayracks), often with roofs and storage areas on top. Simple hayracks are not unknown in other parts of Alpine Central Europe, but *toplarji*, decorated or plain, are unique to Slovenia.

Hayracks were made of hardwood (usually oak) from the early 17th century. Today, however, the hayrack's future is in concrete, and the new stretched ones seem to go on forever.

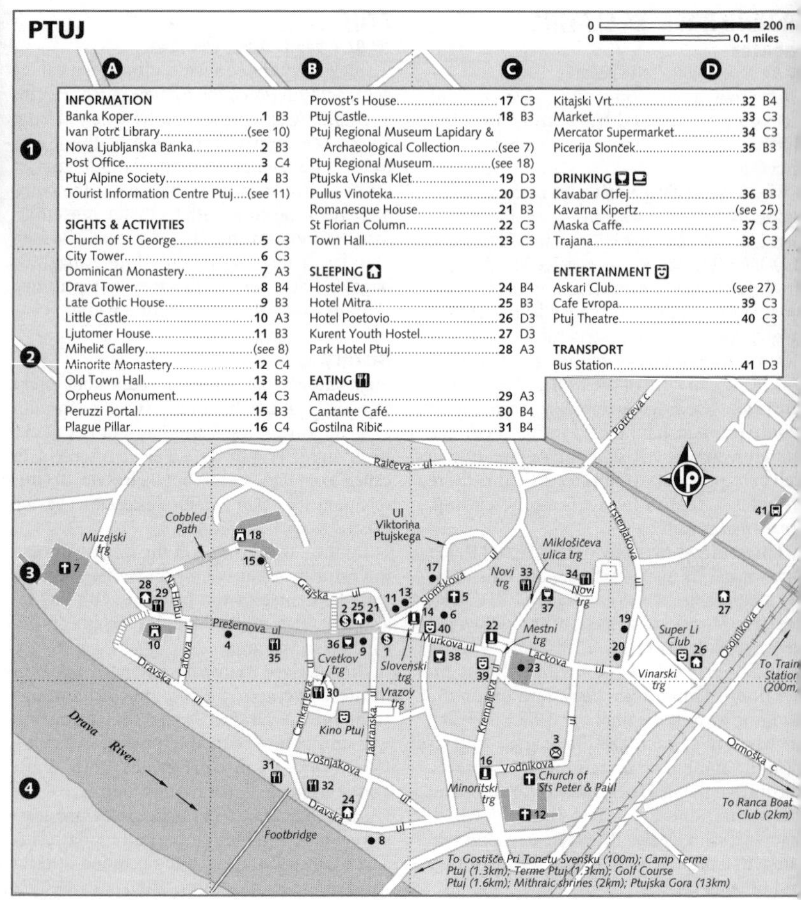

When the railroad reached eastern Slovenia from Vienna on its way to the coast in the mid-19th century, the age-old rivalry between Maribor and Ptuj turned one-sided: the former was on the line and the latter missed out altogether. The town remained essentially a provincial centre with a German majority until WWI.

Orientation

Ptuj lies on the left (north) bank of the Drava River. The castle, with its irregular shape and ancient walls, dominates the town from a 300m hill to the northwest. Most sites of historical interest lie on or near Slovenski trg, but Minoritski trg is the gateway to the Old Town.

The bus station is about 400m northeas of Minoritski trg at Osojnikova cesta 11. Th train station is another 250m farther alon at Osojnikova cesta 2.

Information

Banka Koper (Slovenski trg 3) Directly opposite the TIC.

Ivan Potrč Library (☎ 771 48 11; Prešernova ulica 33-35; per hr €0.90; 🕑 noon-7pm Mon, 8am-1pm Tue-Fr Jul & Aug, 8am-7pm Mon-Fri, 8am-1pm Sat Sep-Jun) Ten terminals with cheap internet access.

Nova Ljubljanska Banka (Prešernova ulica 6) Next door to the Hotel Mitra.

Post office (Vodnikova ulica 2)

Ptuj Alpine Society (☎ 777 15 11; Prešernova ulica 27; 🕑 2-4pm Tue, 5-7pm Fri) Information about hiking in the area.

urist Information Centre Ptuj (☎ 779 60 11; vw.ptuj-tourism.si; Slovenski trg 5; 8am-8pm May-p, 9am-6pm Oct-Apr) Wise counsel and advice in the th-century Ljutomer House.

ights

uj's Gothic centre, with its Renaissance and aroque additions, can be viewed on a 'walk-ng tour' if visited in the order below.

INORITSKI TRG & MESTNI TRG

)n the east side of **Minoritski trg**, which has a **'ague pillar** (1655) of Mary and the Infant Jesus n the centre, is the massive **Minorite monastery** Minoritski Samostan; ☎ 059 073 000; Minoritski trg 1; by ppointment), which was built in the late 13th entury. Because the Franciscan Minorites edicated themselves to teaching, the order vas not dissolved under the edict issued by Habsburg Emperor Joseph II in the late 18th entury, and it has continued to function in 'tuj for more than seven centuries.

The arcaded monastery, which dates from he second half of the 17th century, has a **sum-ner refectory** on the 1st floor, with beautiful tucco work and a dozen ceiling paintings of its Peter (north side) and Paul (south side). It lso contains a 5000-volume **library** of impor-ant manuscripts including an original copy of the New Testament translated by Primož Trubar in 1561.

About 150m west of the monastery is round **Drava Tower** (Dravski Stolp; Dravska ulica 4), a Renaissance water tower built as a defence against the Turks in 1551. It houses the **Mihelič Gallery** (Miheličeva Galerija; ☎ 787 92 50; admission free; 10am-5pm Tue-Fri, 2-6pm Sat & Sun), which hosts temporary exhibits of modern art.

At the end of Krempljeva ulica, which runs north from Minoritski trg, is **Mestni trg**, a rec-tangular square once called Florianplatz in honour of the **St Florian Column** (1745) stand-ing in the northwest corner. To the east is the neo-Gothic **town hall** (Mestni trg 1) dating from 1907.

A couple of hundred metres to the east, **Ptujska Vinska Klet** (Ptuj Wine Cellar; ☎ 787 98 10, 041 394 896; www.pullus.si; Vinarski trg 1; tours €9-12; 9am-3pm Mon-Fri) is one of the largest cellars in Slovenia and the place to go if you want to sample Štajerska wine, especially local tip-ple like Haloze chardonnay, Šipon or Laški Rizling. The cellar also stocks Zlata Trta, the 'Golden Vine' sweet wine dating from 1917 and the oldest vintage in Slovenia. The **Pullus Vinoteka** (☎ 787 98 27; Vinarski trg 11) just south has a wide range of labels for sale.

SLOVENSKI TRG

Murkova ulica, which has some interesting old houses on it, leads westward from Mestni trg to funnel-shaped **Slovenski trg**, the heart of old Ptuj. In the centre, the **City Tower** (Mestni Stolp) was erected in the 16th century as a belfry and later turned into a watch tower. Roman tombstones and sacrificial altars from Poetovio were incorporated into the tower's exterior walls in 1830; you can still make out reliefs of Medusa's head, dolphins, a man with grapes and a man on horseback.

In front of the City Tower stands the 5m-tall **Orpheus Monument** (Orfejev Spomenik), a Roman tombstone from the 2nd century with scenes from the Orpheus myth. It was used as a pillory in the Middle Ages; those found guilty of a crime were shackled to iron rings attached to the holes on the lower half.

Behind the City Tower is the **Church of St George** (Cerkev Sv Jurija), which reveals an array of styles from Romanesque to neo-Gothic. The church contains some lovely mid-15th-century choir chairs decorated with animals, a carved relief of the Epiphany dating from 1515 and frescoes in the middle of the south aisle and the **Laib Altar**, a three-winged altar painting (1460). Near the entrance is a carved 14th-century statue under glass of St George slaying the dragon.

On the northern side of the square are several interesting buildings, including the 16th-century **Provost's House** (Slovenski trg 10), the baroque **Old Town Hall** (Slovenski trg 6) and **Ljutomer House** (Slovenski trg 5), now housing the TIC, whose Mediterranean-style loge was built in 1565 by Italian workers who had come to Ptuj to fortify it against the Turks.

PREŠERNOVA ULICA

Pedestrian **Prešernova ulica**, the town's mar-ket in the Middle Ages, leads westward from Slovenski trg. The arched spans that look like little bridges above some of the narrow side streets are to support older buildings. The **Late Gothic House** (Prešernova ulica 1), dating from about 1400, has an unusual projection held up by a Moor's head. Opposite is the sombre **Romanesque House** (Prešernova ulica 4), the oldest building in Ptuj. The renovated yellow pile called the **Little Castle** (Mali Grad; Prešernova ulica

33-35) was the home of the Salzburg bishops and a number of aristocratic families over the centuries.

MUZEJSKI TRG

Just past Sunny Park (Sončni Park) in Muzejski trg is the former **Dominican Monastery** (Dominikanski Samostan; Muzejski trg 1) dating from the 13th century which contains the lapidary and archaeological collections of the **Ptuj Regional Museum** (☎ 748 03 60; adult/child/senior & student/family €4/2.50/3/8; 🕑 9am-5pm mid-Apr–Nov). The beautiful eastern wing has a cross-ribbed Romanesque window and Gothic cloisters with 14th-century frescoes of Dominican monks in their black and white garb. There's also a refectory with 18th-century stucco work, a chapter hall and a large Roman coin collection. But the main reason for coming is to see the Roman tombstones, altars and wonderful mosaics unearthed in Ptuj and at the **Mithraic shrines** (☎ 778 87 80; adult/child €1/0.50; 🕑 by appointment) at Spodnja Hajdina (key at house No 37a) and Zgornji Breg (key at Ulica K Mitreju 3), a couple of kilometres west of town.

PTUJ CASTLE

Parts of the **castle** (Grad Ptuj; ☎ 748 03 60, 787 92 45; Na Gradu 1) date back to the first half of the 12th century (eg the west tower), but it's mostly an agglomeration of styles from the 14th to the 18th centuries put into place by one aristocratic owner after another. The castle houses the **Ptuj Regional Museum** (Pokrajinski Muzej Ptuj; ☎ 787 92 30, 778 87 80; www.pok-muzej-ptuj.si; adult/child/senior & student/family €4/3/2.50/8; 🕑 9am-6pm Mon-Fri, 9am-8pm Sat & Sun Jul & Aug, 9am-6pm daily May-Jun & Sep–mid-Oct, 9am-5pm mid-Oct–Apr) on its three arcaded floors, but worth the trip mostly for the views of Ptuj and the Drava. The shortest way to the castle is to follow narrow Grajska ulica, which starts just east of the Hotel Mitra and leads to a covered wooden stairway and the castle's Renaissance **Peruzzi Portal** (1570).

As you enter the castle courtyard, look to the west at the red marble **tombstone of Frederick IX**, the last lord of Ptuj who died in 1438. The ground floor of one wing is devoted to an **arms collection** of some 500 weapons. The suits of armour are particularly fine. Also here is a fascinating **musical instruments collection** from the 17th to 19th centuries: some 300 flutes, horns, drums, lutes, violas, harps, clavichords and so on. As you approach each case, a tap plays the music the instruments make.

The 1st floor is given over to perio rooms – treasure-troves of original tap estries, painted wall canvases, portrait weapons and furniture left by the castle last owners, the Herbersteins (1873–194 or, as in the case of the wallpaper, broug from Dornava Castle, 8km to the northea of Ptuj. You'll probably notice a coat of arm containing three buckles and the motto 'Gri Fast' in English. It belonged to the Leslies, Scottish-Austrian family who owned the cas tle from 1656 to 1802. The **Chinoiserie Roor** is excellent.

Festival Hall contains Europe's largest co lection of **Turkerie portraits**, but they are c historical rather than artistic interest. The are portraits of Turkish and European aris tocrats, generals and courtiers commissione by Count Johann Herberstein in 1665 an painted in Štajerska. Partly because of thes paintings, Turkish dress became all the rag for a time in the early 18th century.

On the 2nd floor are Gothic statues an oil paintings from the 15th to the 18th cen turies. There's also a large collection of **Kuren masks** on this floor as well as a collection o works of the artist France Mihelič (1907–98 who lived here from 1936 to 1941.

Activities

Terme Ptuj (☎ 749 41 00; www.terme-ptuj.si; Pot v Toplice 9; adult €9-13, child €6-9; 🕑 7am-10pm Mon-Fri, 8am-10pm Sat & Sun), a thermal spa about 1.5km west of town on the south bank of the Drava, is primarily a huge (4200 sq metres) recreational Thermal Park (Termalni Park), with seven outdoor swimming pools, six indoor thermal ones (water temperature 32°C to 36°C), saunas, tennis courts and a gym. You can also rent **bicycles** (1hr/half-day/day €2/4/7) here.

About 300m west of Terme Ptuj is the 18-hole, par-71 **Golf Course Ptuj** (Golf Igrišče Ptuj; ☎ 788 91 10, 041 791 065; www.golf-ptuj.com; Mlinska cesta 13; 18 holes Mon-Fri €40, Sat & Sun €45, clubs hire €10; 🕑 mid-Mar–mid-Nov), by all accounts the most attractive links in Slovenia.

Licences for **fishing** in the Drava are available from the Hotel Poetovio (opposite) and the Gostišče Pri Tonetu Svenšku (opposite).

You can rent **rowing** and **sailing** boats from the **Ranca Boat Club** (Brodarsko Društvo Ranca; ☎ 041 791 005; www.ranca-ptuj.com, in Slovene), about 2km southeast of the centre on the Drava.

KURENT: PARTY TIME IN PTUJ

Ptuj – and many towns on the surrounding plain and in the hills – marks Shrovetide with Kurentovanje, a rite of spring and fertility that may date back to the time of the early Slavs. Such celebrations are not unique to Slovenia; they still take place at Mohács in Hungary and in Bulgaria and Serbia as well. But the Kurentovanje is among the most extravagant of these celebrations.

The main character of the rite is Kurent, god of unrestrained pleasure and hedonism – a 'Slovenian Dionysus'. The Kurents (there are many groups of them) are dressed in sheepskins with five cowbells dangling from their belts. On their heads they wear huge furry caps decorated with feathers, sticks or horns and coloured streamers. The leather face masks have eyeholes outlined in red, trunk-like noses and enormous red tongues that hang down to the chest.

The Kurents move from house to house in procession scaring off evil spirits with their bells and *ježevke* (wooden clubs) topped with quills taken from hedgehogs. A *hudič* (devil), covered in a net to catch souls, leads each group. Young girls present the Kurents with handkerchiefs, which they then fasten to their belts, and people smash little clay pots at their feet for luck and good health.

estivals & Events

urentovanje (www.kurentovanje.net) is a rite of pring celebrated for 10 days in February eading up to Shrove Tuesday; it's the most opular and best-known folklore event n Slovenia.

leeping

The TIC can arrange **private rooms** (per person 20-25) but most are on the other side of the Drava near Terme Ptuj or in the nearby vilage of Juršinci.

Hostel Eva (☎ 771 24 41, 040 226 522; info@bikeek si; Jadranska ulica 22; dm per person €12-17) If you're ooking for budget accommodation, look no further than this welcoming, up-to-date hostel connected to a bike shop (per-day rental €10) with six rooms containing two to six beds and a large light-filled kitchen.

Camp Terme Ptuj (☎ 749 45 80; www.terme-ptuj si; Pot v Toplice 9; adult €14.50-16.50, child €7.25-8.25; year-round; P) This 1.5-hectare camping ground next to the thermal spa and water park has 110 sites. Rates include entry to the park and use of pools and other recreational facilities. Terme Ptuj also has what it calls camp cottages (singles and doubles €65 to €80, triples and quads €85 to €110).

Kurent Youth Hostel (Mladinsko Prenočišče Kurent; ☎ 771 08 14, 051 319 186; www.csod.si, in Slovene; Osojnikova cesta 9; dm €17-18) This HI-affiliated dormitory situated near the bus station has 13 rooms with between two and six beds and is open all year. HI members get a 10% discount.

Gostišče Pri Tonetu Svenšku (☎ 788 56 83, 041 764 407; svensek.marjeta@amis.net; Zadružni trg 13; r per person €18; P) This guest house, with 24 beds in nine rooms and a popular restaurant (open 7am to 10pm Monday to Saturday, 8am to 10pm Sunday), is just over the footbridge on the south bank of the Drava. Ptuj's thermal baths and the golf course are nearby.

Hotel Poetovio (☎ 779 82 01; memorija@volja.net; Vinarski trg 5; s/d/tr €36/52/63; P) The 29-room Poetovio has small but bright and airy rooms and is handy to the bus and train stations. The huge Super Li club and its 'Yugorock' music is still too close for our comfort though.

our pick **Hotel Mitra** (☎ 787 74 55, 051 603 069; www.hotel-mitra.si; Prešernova ulica 6; s €48-64, d €88-98, ste €112-136; P) What we once called 'one of provincial Slovenia's more interesting hotels' has got a thorough makeover and is now even better. Each of the 25 generous-sized guest rooms and four humongous suites has its own name and story, there are lovely Oriental carpets on the original wooden floors and a wellness centre in an old courtyard cellar. Rooms at the top have mansard ceilings but there is now a lift.

Park Hotel Ptuj (☎ 749 33 00; www.parkhotel-ptuj.si; Prešernova ul 38; s €47-69, d €88-107, ste €116-126;) Giving the Hotel Mitra a run for its money, this lovely boutique hotel with 15 individually designed rooms and lots of original artwork on the walls is situated in an 18th-century town house. It's right in the thick of the action too, with cafes and bars in every direction.

Eating

Cantante Café (☎ 777 14 02; Cvetkov trg 6; dishes €3-9; 🕒 11am-midnight Sun-Thu, 11am-1am Fri & Sat) This popular place, in a quiet square south of Prešernova ulica and opposite the Kino Ptuj, attracts punters with its 150 cocktails as much as it does its Mexican dishes.

Picerija Slonček (☎ 776 13 11; Prešernova ulica 19; pizza €4.10-5.80; 🕒 9am-10pm Mon-Fri, 10am-10pm Sat) The cosy Little Elephant, with an interesting marble fountain out front, serves pizza and some meatless dishes as well as grills.

Kitajski Vrt (☎ 776 14 51; Dravska ulica 7; starters €2-3.50, mains €5.50-7.80; 🕒 11am-10pm Mon-Fri, 11am-11pm Sat & Sun) Ptuj's long-established Chinese restaurant is almost opposite the Ribič and has a fair few vegetable dishes on its menu.

Amadeus (☎ 771 70 51; Prešernova ulica 36; starters €3.50-13, mains €6.50-20; 🕒 noon-10pm Mon-Thu, noon-11pm Fri & Sat, noon-4pm Sun) This very pleasant *gostilna* (innlike restaurant) above a pub and near the foot of the road to the castle serves *štruklji* (dumplings with herbs and cheese; €3.50), steak and pork dishes, and fish.

our pick **Gostilna Ribič** (☎ 749 06 35; Dravska ulica 9; starters €6.50-11.90, mains €7.50-19; 🕒 10am-11pm Sun-Thu, 10am-midnight Fri & Sat) Arguably the best restaurant in Ptuj, the Angler Inn faces the river, with an enormous terrace, and the speciality here is – not surprisingly – fish, especially herbed and baked pike perch, or sander (€18.50). The seafood soup (€4) served in a bread loaf bowl is exceptional. Make sure to have the dessert speciality: chocolate fondant with ice cream (€5). There's live Slovenian music some nights.

The town's open-air **market** (Novi trg; 🕒 7am-3pm) sells fruit, vegetables and more. You'll find a large **Mercator** (Novi trg 3; 🕒 7.30am-7.30pm Mon-Fri, 7.30am-1pm Sat) supermarket in the same square as the market.

Drinking

Kavarna Kipertz (☎ 787 74 55; Prešernova ulica 6; 🕒 8am-11pm Mon-Thu, 8am-midnight Fri-Sun) Named after the very first man in Ptuj to roast coffee beans, this wonderful cafe in the Hotel Mitra attracts Ptuj's boho set with its very own coffee roast and rich desserts.

Kavabar Orfej (☎ 772 97 61; Prešernova ulica 5; 🕒 6.30am-11pm Mon-Thu, 6.30am-1am Fri & Sat, 10am-11pm Sun) The Orfej is the anchor tenant of Prešernova ulica and is usually where everyone starts (or ends) the evening.

Trajana (Murkova ulica 5; 🕒 6.30am-11pm Sun-Th 6.30am-1am Fri & Sat) This uber-designed ca and bar 100m east of Prešernova ulica h a good selection of wine and welcomes well-heeled clientele.

Maska Caffe (☎ 041 708 526; Novi trg 2; 🕒 7am-10p Mon-Thu, 7am-2am Fri, 8am-2am Sat, 3-10pm Sun) Th very trendy redder-than-red designer bar one of the top spots in town right now. Th front bar just goes on and on for days.

Entertainment

Ptuj Theatre (Gledališče Ptuj; ☎ 749 32 50; Slovenski trg 1 🕒 box office 9am-1pm Mon, Tue, Thu & Fri, 9am-5pm We Just beside the City Tower, this 18th-centur theatre stages a varied program year-round

Café Evropa (☎ 771 02 35; Mestni trg 2; 🕒 11am-10p Mon-Thu, 11am-3am Fri & Sat, 6-10pm Sun) By day an evening a popular cafe, the Evropa turns int one of Ptuj's hottest central clubs on Frida and Saturday nights.

Askari (☎ 041 371 782; Osojnikova cesta 9; 🕒 10pm 4am Fri & Sat) Next door to the Kurent Yout Hostel, this is the weekend-only club tha Ptuj's young-bloods anticipate week afte week. Dancing, pulling, falling down drunk it's got the lot.

Getting There & Around

Buses to Maribor (€3.60, 45 minutes, 27km) Majšperk (€2.30, 30 minutes, 14km) and Ormož (€3.60, 40 minutes, 26km) go every couple of hours, but count on far fewer a the weekend (if at all). One to two buses a day head for Stuttgart (€80, 11½ hours 704km, 9.15pm daily, 6.15pm Wednesday, Thursday, Saturday and Sunday) via Munich in Germany.

You can reach Ptuj up to eight times a day by train from Ljubljana (€8 to €13.60, 2½ hours, 155km) direct or via Zidani Most and Pragersko. Up to a dozen trains go to Maribor (€2.90 to €5.90, 50 minutes, 37km). Up to eight trains a day head for Murska Sobota (€4.90 to €8.90, 1¼ hours, 61km) via Ormož.

Book a taxi on ☎ 031 842 227, 041 798 788 or 051 681 400.

AROUND PTUJ

Ptujska Gora

☎ 02 / pop 355 / elev 342m

The pilgrimage **Parish Church of the Virgin Mary** (Župnijska Cerkev Sv Marije; ☎ 794 42 31; www.ptujska-gora.si; Ptujska Gora 40; 🕒 8am-7pm year-round) in this village 13km southwest of Ptuj contains one f the most treasured objects in Slovenia: a 5th-century carved caped Misericordia of ıe Virgin Mary and the Child Jesus.

The church itself, built at the start of the 5th century, is the finest example of a three-ave Gothic church in Slovenia. Among some f the other treasures inside is a small wooden **tatue of St James** on one of the pillars on the outh aisle and, under the porch and to the ight as you enter, 15th-century **frescoes** of the fe of Christ and of several saints, including St Nicholas and St Dorothy with the Child Jesus. ook behind the modern tabernacle in the hapel to the right of the main altar for faint rescoes of St Peter (right) and St Michael the rchangel (left).

The church, perched atop Black Hill (Črna Gora), is an easy 10-minute walk from where he bus headed for Majšperk will let you off. **ragica** (☎ 725 02 71, 031 556 633; Ptujska Gora 37; 🕑 8am-11pm Tue-Sun) is a small bar opposite the hurch with snacks and views.

Wine Roads

Ptuj is within easy striking distance of two mportant wine-growing areas: the **Haloze** district and the **Jeruzalem-Ljutomer** district. They are accessible on foot, by car and, best of all, by bike.

The Haloze Hills extend for about 30km from Makole, 18km southwest of Ptuj, to Goričak on the border with Croatia. The footpath taking in this land of gentle hills, vines, corn and sunflowers is called the **Haloze Highlands Trail** (Haloška Planina Pot). It is accessible from near **Štatenberg** (☎ 041 829 854; adult/child €2/1; 🕑 by appointment), an 18th-century manor at Makole, 9km southwest of Ptujska Gora in the Dravinja Valley. The manor has fabulous stucco work and frescoes in eight rooms with enormously high ceilings; don't miss the impressive paintings of the four elements as well as Peace, the Sciences and the Arts in the Knights' Hall. There's a **restaurant** (🕑 10am-10pm Wed-Fri, 10am-11pm Sat, 11am-10pm Sun) here.

The **Jeruzalem-Ljutomer wine road** begins at Ormož and continues for 18km north to Ljutomer (population 3610), the main seat in the area, via the hill-top village of Jeruzalem. There are quite a few cellars, small restaurants and pensions along this positively idyllic route where you can sample any of the region's local whites, especially around Ivanjkovci, including **Gostišče Taverna Jeruzalem Svetinje** (☎ 719 41 28; www.taverna-jeruzalem.si, in Slovene; Svetinje 21; s/d/tr €30/55/75). For guidance, visit the **Tourist Information Centre Jeruzalem** (☎ 719 45 45; www.jeruzalem.si; Jeruzalem 8; 🕑 10am-6pm), next door to the **Chateau Jeruzalem** (Dvorecc Jeruzalem; ☎ 719 48 05; Jeruzalem 8; s €75-95, d €130-170) with a wine cellar, romantic restaurant and 10 of the flashiest rooms in the district. The TIC rents **bicycles** (per hr/day/week €2/10/50).

MARIBOR

☎ 02 / pop 88,350 / elev 275m

Although it is the nation's second-largest city, Maribor has only about a third the population of Ljubljana and often feels more like a large provincial town than northeast Slovenia's economic, communications and cultural powerhouse. It really has no unmissable sights but oozes with charm thanks to its delightfully patchy Old Town along the Drava River. Pedestrianised central streets buzz with cafes and student life – Maribor has the country's only other university outside the capital – and in late June/early July the riverside Lent district hosts a major arts festival. Maribor is the gateway to the Maribor Pohorje, a hilly recreational area to the southwest, and the Mariborske and Slovenske Gorice wine-growing regions to the north and the east. Maribor is European City of Culture in 2012.

History

Maribor rose to prominence in the Middle Ages when a fortress called Marchburg was built on Piramida, a hill to the north of the city, to protect the Drava Valley from the Magyar advance. The settlement that later developed along the river grew wealthy through the timber and wine trade, financed largely by the town's small but wealthy Jewish community, and the waterfront landing (Pristan) in the Lent district became one of the busiest river ports in the country.

The town was fortified with walls in the 14th century and four defence towers still stand along the Drava. Though its fortunes declined in later centuries, the tide turned in 1846 when the railroad from Vienna reached here – the first town in Slovenia to have train connections with the imperial capital. Maribor became the centre of Slovene-speaking Styria – a kind of counter-balance to German-speaking Graz in Austria – and began to industrialise.

Air raids during WWII devastated Maribor, and by 1945 two-thirds of it lay in ruin.

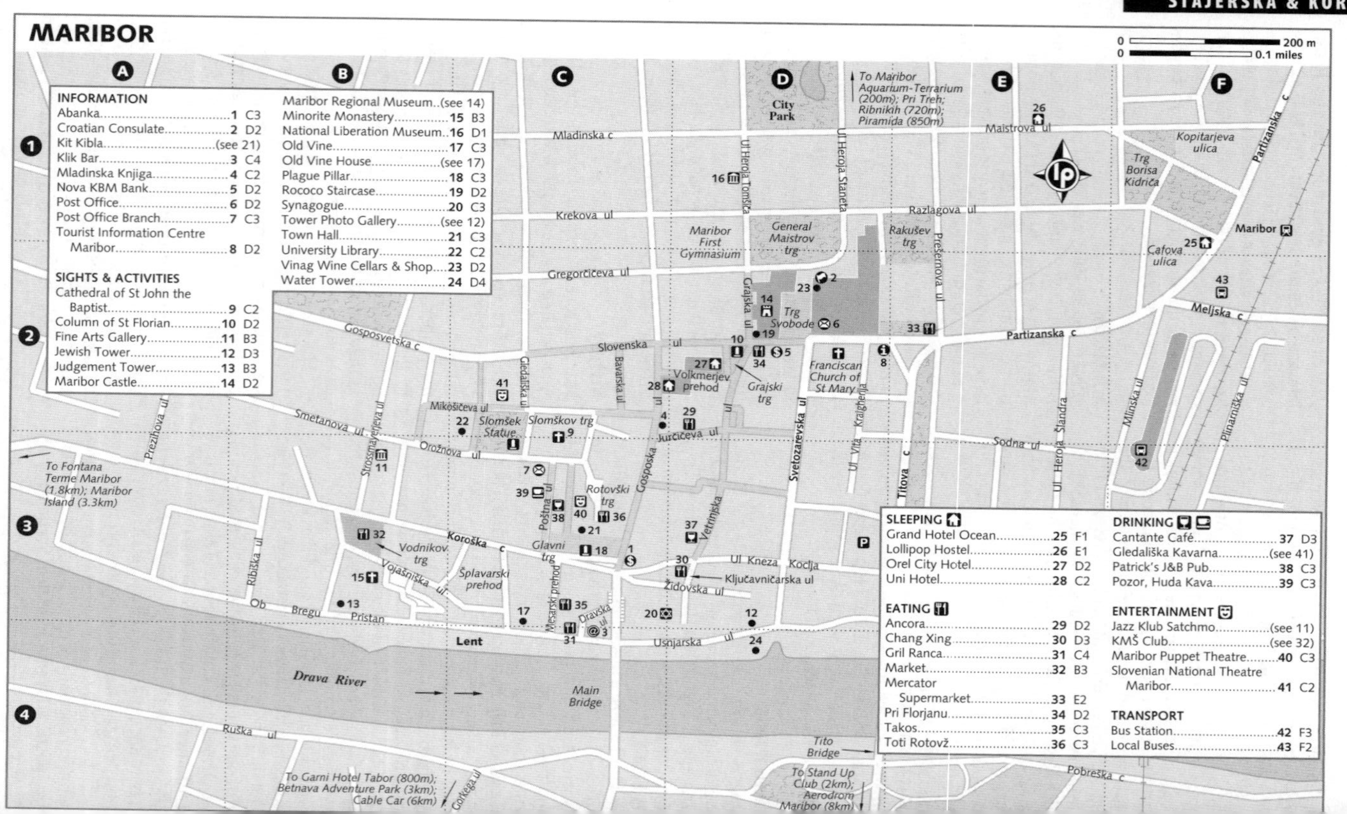
MARIBOR
0 200 m
0 0.1 miles
INFORMATION
Abanka 1 C3
Croatian Consulate 2 D2
Kit Kibla (see 21)
Klik Bar 3 C4
Mladinska Knjiga 4 C2
Nova KBM Bank 5 D2
Post Office 6 D2
Post Office Branch 7 C3
Tourist Information Centre Maribor 8 D2
SIGHTS & ACTIVITIES
Cathedral of St John the Baptist 9 C2
Column of St Florian 10 D2
Fine Arts Gallery 11 B3
Jewish Tower 12 D3
Judgement Tower 13 B3
Maribor Castle 14 D2
Maribor Regional Museum (see 14)
Minorite Monastery 15 B3
National Liberation Museum 16 D1
Old Vine 17 C3
Old Vine House (see 17)
Plague Pillar 18 C3
Rococo Staircase 19 D2
Synagogue 20 C3
Tower Photo Gallery (see 12)
Town Hall 21 C3
University Library 22 C2
Vinag Wine Cellars & Shop 23 D2
Water Tower 24 D4
SLEEPING
Grand Hotel Ocean 25 F1
Lollipop Hostel 26 E1
Orel City Hotel 27 D2
Uni Hotel 28 C2
EATING
Ancora 29 D2
Chang Xing 30 D3
Gril Ranca 31 C4
Market 32 B3
Mercator Supermarket 33 E2
Pri Florjanu 34 D2
Takos 35 C3
Toti Rotovž 36 C3
DRINKING
Cantante Café 37 D3
Gledališka Kavarna (see 41)
Patrick's J&B Pub 38 C3
Pozor, Huda Kava 39 C3
ENTERTAINMENT
Jazz Klub Satchmo (see 11)
KMŠ Club (see 32)
Maribor Puppet Theatre 40 C3
Slovenian National Theatre Maribor 41 C2
TRANSPORT
Bus Station 42 F3
Local Buses 43 F2
City Park
Trg Borisa Kidriča
Kopitarjeva ulica
Maistrova ul
Partizanska c
Maribor
Mlinska ul
Meljska c
Čafova ulica
Plinarniška ul
Ul Heroja Šlandra
Sodna ul
Titova c
Prešernova ul
Razlagova ul
Rakušev trg
Ul Heroja Staneta
General Maistrov trg
Trg Svobode
Franciscan Church of St Mary
Ul Vita Kraigherja
Svetozarevska ul
Ul Heroja Tomšiča
Grajska ul
Grajski trg
Maribor First Gymnasium
Volkmerjev prehod
Jurčičeva ul
Vetrinjska ul
Ul Kneza Koclja
Ključavničarska ul
Židovska ul
Usnjarska ul
Gosposka ul
Slovenska ul
Bavarska ul
Mladinska c
Krekova ul
Gregorčičeva ul
Rotovški trg
Slomškov trg
Poštna ul
Glavni trg
Mesarski prehod
Dravska ul
Gledališka ul
Slomšek Statue
Mikošičeva ul
Orožnova ul
Koroška c
Splavarski prehod
Lent
Vodnikov trg
Vojašniška ul
Strossmayerjeva ul
Smetanova ul
Gosposvetska c
Pristan
Ob Bregu
Ribiška ul
Prežihova ul
Ruška ul
Drava River
Main Bridge
Tito Bridge
Pobreška c
Gorkega ul
To Maribor Aquarium-Terrarium (200m); Pri Treh Ribnikih (720m); Piramida (850m)
To Stand Up Club (2km); Aerodrom Maribor (8km)
To Garni Hotel Tabor (800m); Betnava Adventure Park (3km); Cable Car (6km)
To Fontana Terme Maribor (1.8km); Maribor Island (3.3km)

rientation

Iaribor sits on both sides of the Drava River, vith the Lent waterfront district and other arts of the Old Town on the left (north) bank. here are several main squares, although Grajski trg is the historical centre.

Maribor's modern (and decrepit) bus staion is northeast of Grajski trg on Mlinska lica. The train station is about 350m further orth on Partizanska cesta.

One of only three international airports n Slovenia, **Aerodrom Maribor** (☎ 629 17 90; www naribor-airport.si; Letališka cesta 10) is at Orehova Vas, km southeast of the Old Town.

nformation

banka (Glavni trg 18) In the mall at the eastern end of lavni trg.

it Kibla (☎ 252 44 40; www.kibla.org/kit; Glavni trg 4; per 30/60min €0.70/1; 🕑 9am-10pm Mon-Sat) Cityun centre in the town hall with a dozen internet terminals.

lik Bar (☎ 040 167 191; www.klikbar.si; Dravska ulica ; free with drink; 🕑 9am-11pm Sun-Thu, 9am-1am Fri & at) Lively riverfront bar with internet terminals.

Iladinska Knjiga (☎ 234 31 13; Gosposka ulica 24; 🕑 9am-7pm Mon-Fri, 9am-1pm Sat) Bookshop, selling onely Planet guides as well as maps.

lova KBM Bank (Trg Svobode 2) Opposite Maribor Castle.

Post office (Partizanska cesta 1) Branch at Slomškov rg 10.

Tourist Information Centre Maribor (TIC; ☎ 234 56 11; www.maribor-tourism.si; Partizanska 6a; 🕑 9am-7pm Mon-Fri, 9am-6pm Sat & Sun) Very helpful TIC in kiosk opposite Franciscan church.

www.maribor.si Compliments of the boys and girls at city hall.

Sights

GRAJKSI TRG

The centre of the Old Town, this square is graced with the 17th-century **Column of St Florian**, dedicated to the patron saint of fire fighters.

Maribor Castle (Mariborski Grad; Grajski trg 2), on the square's northeast corner, is a successor to the Piramida fortress of medieval times. The 15th-century castle contains a **Knights' Hall** (Viteška Dvorana) with a remarkably disproportionate ceiling painting, the baroque **Loretska Chapel** and a magnificent **rococo staircase** (1759), with pink walls, stucco work and figures arrayed on the banisters and visible though two glass doors from the corner of Grajska ulica and Slovenska ulica.

The castle also contains the **Maribor Regional Museum** (Pokrajinski Muzej Maribor; ☎ 228 35 51; www .pmuzej-mb.si; adult/child €3/2.50; 🕑 9am-4pm Tue-Sat, 9am-2pm Sun), one of the richest collections in Slovenia. Be advised that at the time of research the museum was undergoing a protracted renovation and parts of the permanent collection may be off-limits.

On the ground floor there are archaeological, clothing and ethnographic exhibits, including 19th-century beehive panels painted with biblical scenes from the Mislinja and Drava Valleys, models of Štajerska-style hayracks, Kurent costumes and wax ex voto offerings from the area around Ptuj. Upstairs there are rooms devoted to Maribor's history and its guilds and crafts (glassware, wrought ironwork, clock-making), a complete 18th-century pharmacy, and altar paintings and sculptures from the 15th to the 18th centuries. Taking pride of place among the sculptures are the exquisite **statues by Jožef Straub** (1712–56) taken from the Church of St Joseph in the southwestern suburb of Studenci.

Two blocks north of the castle is a stunning 19th-century mansion housing the **National Liberation Museum** (Muzej Narodne Osvoboditve; ☎ 235 26 00; www.muzejno-mb.si; Ulica Heroja Tomšiča 5; adult/child €1.50/1; 🕑 8am-6pm Mon-Fri, 9am-noon Sat), whose collections document Slovenia's struggle for freedom throughout the 20th century, with particular emphasis on the work of the Pohorje Partisans during the Nazi occupation.

TRG SVOBODE

This fountain-cooled square east of Maribor Castle, along with leafy General Maistrov Trg and Rakušev trg to the north and northeast, would be unremarkable except for the honeycomb of wine cellars below that cover an area of 20,000 sq metres and can store 5.5 million litres of plonk.

The cellars, dating from the early 19th century, are managed by the wine export company **Vinag** (☎ 220 81 41, 051 680 430; www .vinag.si; Trg Svobode 3; admission €2.50; 🕑 visits noon-7pm Mon-Fri, noon-4pm Sat, shop 9am-7pm Mon-Fri, 8am-4pm Sat). They are filled with old oak barrels, steel fermentation tanks and an 'archive' of vintage wine – all kept at a constant temperature of 15°C. There's a small cellar open to the public with advance notice and a wine shop.

CITY PARK

North of Maribor's Old Town is City Park (Mestni Park), a lovely arboretum with 150 species of trees and three ponds. Here you'll find the small **Maribor Aquarium-Terrarium** (Akvarij-Terarij Maribor; ☎ 234 96 63; www.florina.si/akvarij-terarij; Ulica Heroja Staneta 19; adult/child €4/3.20; ⏲ 8am-7pm Mon-Fri, 9am-noon & 2-7pm Sat & Sun) with some 40 tanks filled with river, lake and sea fish as well as reptiles. To the northeast is **Piramida** (386m), where the titans of Marchburg once held sway and a chapel now takes pride of place.

SLOMŠKOV TRG

South of City Park is the square named after Anton Martin Slomšek (1800–62), the Slovenian bishop and politician who was beatified by the late Pope John Paul II in 1999, the first Slovene to earn such distinction.

Parts of the imposing **Cathedral** (Stolna Cerkev), which is dedicated to St John the Baptist, date from the 13th century and it shows elements of virtually every architectural style from Romanesque to modern (including some inept 19th-century attempts to 're-Gothicise' it). Of special interest are the flamboyant Gothic sanctuary and the gilded choir stalls with reliefs showing scenes from the life of the patron saint as well as the lovely modern stained glass. The grand building across the park to the west is the **University Library** (Univerzitetna Knjižnica; ☎ 250 74 00; www.ukm.uni-mb.si; Gospejna ulica 10). On the northern side of the square is the Maribor branch of the Slovenian National Theatre, housed in two mid-19th-century buildings and in a modern wing.

The Maribor **Fine Arts Gallery** (Umetnostna Galerija Maribor; ☎ 229 58 60; www.ugm.si; Strossmayerjeva ulica 6; adult/child/family €2/1.25/4; ⏲ 10am-6pm Tue-Sun), southwest of Slomškov trg, has a relatively rich collection of modern works by Slovene artists.

LENT

South of the Fine Arts Gallery and across Koroška cesta is Maribor's renovated market with tent-like stall awnings and the remains of the 13th-century **Minorite monastery**, closed by Joseph II in 1784 and used as a military barracks until 1927. To the south along the riverfront is the round **Judgement Tower** (Sodni Stolp), the first of four defence towers still standing, with curious friezes on the south side.

About 150m east along the Pristan embankment is the so-called **Old Vine** (Stara Trt Vojašniška ulica 8), the world's oldest living grape vine. It's still producing between 35kg and 55kg of grapes and about 25L of red wine per year some four centuries after it was planted. It is tended by a city-appointed viticulturist and the dark red wine called Žametna Črnina (Black Velvet) is distributed to visiting dignitaries as 'keys' to Maribor in the form of 0.25L bottles. Learn more about it and Slovenia viniculture at the adjacent **Old Vine House** (Hiša Stare Trta; ☎ 251 51 00; www.maribor-pohorje.si; Vojašniška ulica 8; admission free; ⏲ 10am-6pm Tue-Sun).

About 300m east is the pentagonal **Water Tower** (Vodni Stolp; Usnjarska ulica 10), a 16th-century defence tower now housing a *vinoteka* (wine-tasting cellar). Just north of it a set of steps lead to **Židovska ulica** (Jewish Street), the centre of the Jewish district in the Middle Ages. The 15th-century **synagogue** (☎ 252 7… 36; Židovska ulica 4; adult/child €1/0.50; ⏲ 8am-4pm Mon-Fri, 9am-2pm Sun) is now open to the public, and the square **Jewish Tower** (Židovski Stolp; Židovska ulica 6), dating from 1465, houses the **Tower Photo Gallery** (Fotogalerija Stolp; ☎ 620 97 13; www.galerijastolp.si; ⏲ 10am-1pm & 3-7pm Mon-Fri, 10am-1pm Sat).

GLAVNI TRG

Maribor's marketplace in the Middle Ages Glavni trg is just north of the river and the main bridge crossing it. In the centre of the square is Slovenia's most extravagant **plague pillar**. Designed by Jožef Straub and erected in 1743, it includes the Virgin Mary surrounded by a half-dozen saints. Behind it is the **town hall** (Glavni trg 14) built in 1565 by Venetian craftsmen living in Styria.

Activities

Maribor has several outdoor swimming pools, including several on **Maribor Island** (Mariborski Otok; ☎ 623 10 32; Na Otok 40; day ticket adult/child/family €5/4/15; ⏲ 9am-8pm Jun-Sep), a sand bank at the end of a dammed-off portion of the Drava River called **Maribor Lake** (Mariborsko Jezero), about 4km west of the Old Town. A sunbathing area is reserved for naturists. Local bus 15 from the train station will drop you off at the Kamnica stop, near the start of the footpath leading to the bridge and the island.

Fontana Terme Maribor (☎ 234 41 00; www.termemb.si; Koroška cesta 172; day pass adult/child €22/11, 4hr pass Mon-Fri €17/9, Sat & Sun €19/10; ⏲ 9am-10pm Sun-Fri, 10am-midnight Sat), a huge spa complex, is 2km est of the centre and accessible via bus 8 or 5. It offers thermal pools and whirlpools with water temperature of 33°C to 37°C, sauna, eam bath, fitness centre and massage.

estivals & Events

Iaribor hosts a lot of events throughout ie year, including the **Borštnik Meeting** (www orstnikovo.info), Slovenia's biggest theatre festival, in the second half of October and the new **estival Maribor** (www.festivalmaribor.si), a 10-day xtravaganza of 20 classical-music concerts. ut the biggest event on the city's calendar is ie **Lent Festival** (http://lent.slovenija.net), a two-week elebration of folklore, culture and music rom late June into July, when stages are set up hroughout the Old Town. Among the most olourful ceremonies here is the **harvesting of he Old Vine** for wine in early October.

leeping

The TIC can organise **private rooms** (from €25/40) nd apartments.

Lollipop Hostel (☎ 040 243 160; lollipophostel@yahoo com; Maistrova ulica 17; dm €20; 💻) This welcome new addition to Maribor's rather limited budget-accommodation, run by an affable English voman, has 10 beds in two rooms (choose the one with four facing the garden) and full kitchen a short distance from the train station.

Uni Hotel (☎ 250 67 00; www.termemb.si; Volkmerjev prehod 7; HI member/nonmember €24/29; 💻) This very central, almost luxurious 53-room 'residence hotel' affiliated with Hostelling International s run by, and attached to, the Orel City Hotel, where you'll find reception. It's home to full-time students and visiting professors during the academic year but lets out beds in singles and doubles to visitors during holidays.

Garni Hotel Tabor (☎ 421 64 10, www.hoteltabor .podhostnik.si; Ulica Heroja Zidanška 18; s €50-70, d €70-90, tr €90-100; P 💻 ♿) This friendly, 58-room hotel is housed in an uninspiring concrete block in Tabor 3km to the southwest of the centre across the Drava. It recently installed a lift. Reach the Tabor on bus 6 or 18.

Orel City Hotel (Orel Mestni Hotel; ☎ 250 67 00; www .termemb.si; Volkmerjev prehod 7; s €79-110, d €120-168, ste €220-260; P ❄ 💻 ♿) Still basking in the refit and scrub down that left it shiny and pretty and ready to kick ass, Maribor's most central hotel has 71 rooms and the price includes entry to the Fontana Terme Maribor (opposite).

Grand Hotel Ocean (☎ 059 077 120; www.hotelocean .si; Partizanska cesta 39; s/d/tr €118/132/142; ❄ 💻) This stunning new four-star boutique hotel is named after the first train to pass through Maribor city in 1846 and is the most exciting thing to happen here, well, since. It's got 22 rooms and the breakfast room on the top floor is a sun-drenched delight. Ask about their weekend packages.

Eating

Gril Ranca (☎ 252 55 50; Dravska ulica 10; grills €3.50-7; 🕑 8am-11pm Mon-Sat, noon-9pm Sun) This place serves simple but scrumptious Balkan grills like *pljeskavica* (spicy meat patties) and *čevapčiči* (spicy meatballs of beef or pork) pain full view of the Drava. Cool place on a hot night.

Ancora (☎ 250 20 33; Jurčičeva ulica 7; pizza €4-7.50; 🕑 9am-midnight Mon-Thu, 9am-1am Fri, 10am-1am Sat, 10.30am-10.30pm Sun) Located on the 1st floor of a very popular bar-restaurant, this place is the most popular pizzeria in town.

Chang Xing (☎ 250 15 90; Ključavničarska ulica ulica 2; starters €1.80-3.50, mains €5-8.50; 🕑 11am-11pm) The Long Prosperity, tucked away in a courtyard, is the place to go for simple rice and noodle dishes.

Toti Rotovž (☎ 228 76 50; Glavni trg 14 & Rotovški trg 9; mains €6-18; 🕑 9am-midnight Mon-Thu, 9am-2am Fri & Sat) This peculiar place behind the town hall, with a wine cellar below and a terrace in a lovely arcaded square, tries (not altogether successfully) to serve just about every cuisine under the sun – from Slovenian to Thai and Greek to Mexican.

Takos (☎ 252 71 50; Mesarski prehod 3; mains €6.90-12; 🕑 11am-midnight Mon-Thu, noon-2am Fri & Sat) This atmospheric Mexican restaurant in Lent serves excellent fajitas (€8.50 to €12) and enchiladas (€6.50 to €7.50), and turns into a snappy little night spot after the 11pm happy hour on Friday and Saturday.

Pri Florjanu (☎ 059 084 850; Grajski trg 6; starters €5.50-7, mains €9-18; 🕑 11am-10pm Mon-Thu, 11am-11pm Fri & Sat) A great new spot in full view of the Column of St Florian, this very stylish place has both an open front and an enclosed back terrace and a huge minimalist restaurant in between. It serves rather inspired Mediterranean food, with a good supply of vegetarian options.

Pri Treh Ribnikih (☎ 234 41 70; Ribniška ulica 9; mains €10-17; 🕑 11am-10pm Mon-Sat, 11am-9pm Sun) A great place for a meal if you want to get out of the city but don't feel like travelling is At the Three Fishponds in City Park. Oddly, its specialities are cheese *štruklji* (dumplings) and stuffed pork ribs, with fish all but banished from the menu. There's quite a good wine list.

There's a **market** (Vodnikov trg; ⌚ 6.30am-3pm Mon-Sat) selling produce just north of the former Minorite monastery. **Mercator** (Partizanska cesta 7; ⌚ 7am-7pm Mon-Fri, 7am-1pm Sat) supermarket has a branch on the corner of Prešernova ulica.

Drinking

Gledališka Kavarna (☎ 252 37 20; Slovenska ulica 27; ⌚ 8am-11pm Mon-Thu, 8am-midnight Fri, 10am-2pm Sat) The very upmarket Theatre Cafe next to the Slovenian National Theatre (enter from Slomškov trg) attracts a classy crowd.

Pozor, Huda Kava (☎ 251 71 58; Poštna ulica 3; ⌚ 7am-10pm Mon-Thu, to 11pm Fri & Sat, to midnight Sun) Making a play on words with the Slovenian 'Beware of the Dog' warning, 'Danger, Evil Coffee', it has a weekly guest coffee that will put hair on your chest (even if you don't want it). Linger for cocktails and canned reggae and funk in the evening.

Patrick's J&B Pub (☎ 251 18 01; Poštna ulica 10; ⌚ 8am-midnight Mon-Thu, 8am-2am Fri & Sat, 4-11pm Sun) Someone had better tell them that Paddy doesn't drink Scotch but what the heck? It's one of the liveliest places on pedestrian Poštna ulica.

Cantante Café (☎ 252 53 12; Vetrinjska ulica 5; ⌚ 8am-1am Mon-Thu, 8am-3am Fri, 9am-3am Sat, noon-1am Sun) This popular place with its Cuban/Hemingway feel does do Mexican and South American dishes, but we come here for the mojitos and 149 other cocktails on its extensive drinks list.

Entertainment

Slovenian National Theatre Maribor (Slovensko Narodno Gledališče Maribor; ☎ 250 61 00, box office 250 61 15; www.sng-mb.si; Slovenska ulica 27; ⌚ 10am-1pm & 5-7.30pm Mon-Fri, 10am-1pm Sat & 1hr before performance) This branch of the SNG in Ljubljana has one of the best reputations in the country, and its productions have received critical acclaim throughout Europe. The city's ballet and opera companies also perform here. Enter from Slomškov trg.

Maribor Puppet Theatre (Lutkovno Gledališče Maribor; ☎ 228 19 70, 031 614 533; www.lg-mb.si; Ratovški trg 2) Maribor's second-most famous theatre has productions year-round at its base in the lovely arcaded courtyard behind the town hall in Glavni trg.

Jazz Klub Satchmo (☎ 250 21 50; www.jazz-klub.si; Strossmayerjeva ulica 6; ⌚ 9am-2am Mon-Thu, 9am-3am Fri, 7pm-3am Sat, 7pm-midnight Sun) Maribor's celebrated jazz club meets in a wonderful cellar in the Fine Arts Gallery building.

KMŠ (☎ 228 29 33; www.klub-kms.si; Vodnikov t 4; ⌚ 4pm-4am Mon-Sat) This students' club, th original of the popular branch in Ljubljar (p98), is an equally raucous place with mus and dancers and parties all over the shop mo of the time. It's near the market.

Stand Up (☎ 070 993 399; www.standup.si; Tržaš cesta 38; ⌚ 7am-midnight Mon-Thu, 7am-5am Fri, 8am-5a Sat, 9am-midnight Sun) Maribor's most popular clu of the moment, this place a couple of kil metres south of the centre has less to do wi comedy and everything to do with Balka beats and turbo folk. Love the giant mirr watching me watching me watching me.

Getting There & Away

BUS

You can reach virtually any large town i Slovenia (and certain destinations in Austri Bosnia and even Germany) from Maribo The bus station is huge, with 30 bays, as we as a few shops, bars and cafes.

Bus services are frequent to Celje (€6.7, 1 hours, 65km, three to seven daily), Dravogra (€6.70, two hours, 61km, five daily), Lenda (€10.30, three hours, 111km, three to fo daily), Murska Sobota (€6.30, 1¼ hour 59km, 10 to 12 daily), Ptuj (€3.60, 45 minute 27km, hourly) and Radenci (€5.60, one hou 47km, seven to nine daily). For Ljubljan (€12.40, three hours, 141km) count on abo five buses a day.

Other destinations include Gornji Gra (€9.60, three hours, 101km, one daily Rogaška Slatina (€7.20, two hours, 75km one daily though more during school term and Slovenj Gradec (€7.20, two hours, 71km three daily).

For destinations in Bosnia there's a dai bus to Sarajevo (€59.40, 9½ hours, 533km) 9.15pm (5.15pm on Friday), and a bus fo times a week to Tuzla (€50.60, eight hour 451km, at 7pm Monday, and Wednesday Friday). There are daily buses to Munich (€4 7½ hours, 453km) at 6.50pm and 9.50pm and another at 8.12am Saturday. A daily bu departs for Vienna (€29, 4½ hours, 258km at 5.45pm.

TRAIN

From Ljubljana you can reach Maribor on th ICS express service (€13.60, 1¾ hours, 156km five trains daily), or any of 20 or so slow trains (€8, 2½ hours). About a dozen trair a day originating in Maribor go east throug ragersko to Ormož (€4.30 to €5.80, 1¼ ours, 59km), from where you can make your ay into Croatia. Connections can be made t Ormož for one of seven trains to Murska obota (€2.90 to €4.50, one hour, 39km).

Four daily trains head west for Dravograd €4.90, 1¾ hours, 64km) and other stops in oroška. These trains cross the Austrian order at Holmec, and one carries on to lagenfurt (Celovec) on weekdays. There re also services from Maribor to Zagreb €14, three hours, 119km, up to nine daily), ienna (€43, 3½ hours, 257km, four daily), elgrade (€47.40, 8½ hours, 518km, four laily), and Venice (€25, eight hours, 375km, hree daily).

etting Around

laribor and its surrounds are well served by ocal buses. They depart from the stands south f the train station near Meljska cesta.

Maribor Bike (☎ 234 66 11; per 2hr/1 day €1/5; 8am-8pm Apr-Oct) has bikes available from utside the TIC.

For a local taxi, ring ☎ 250 07 77 or 031 301 339.

MARIBOR POHORJE

☎ 02 / elev to 1347m

Maribor's green lung and its central playground, the eastern edge of the Pohorje Massif is known in these parts as the Maribor Pohorje (Mariborsko Pohorje). It can be easily reached by car, bus or cable car from Maribor. The area has countless activities on offer – from skiing and hiking, to horse riding and mountain biking.

Activities

There are heaps of easy **walks** and more difficult **hikes** in every direction from the Hotel Areh, but following a stretch of the marked Slovenian Mountain Trail, which originates in Maribor and goes as far as Ankaran on the coast, first west and then southwest for 5km will take you to the two **Šumik waterfalls** and **Pragozd**, one of the very few virgin forests left in Europe. Another 6km to the southwest is **Black Lake** (Črno Jezero), the source of the swift-running Lobnica River, and **Osankarica**, where the Pohorje battalion of Partisans was wiped out by the Germans in January 1943. PZS and GZS each produce their own 1:50,000-scale *Pohorje* map (€8.10 to €8.50).

The **Pohorje Sport Centre** (Športni Center Pohorje; ☎ 220 88 00; www.pohorje.org; Mladinska ulica 29) in Maribor organises most of the activities in the Maribor Pohorje. It can also offer excursions to the **Pohorje Adrenaline Park** (Adrenalinski Park Pohorje; ☎ 220 88 21, 031 655 665; adult/child from €17/15), a recreational area with all manner of towers, high-rope courses, swings and beams near Koča Luka, midway between the two cable-car stations.

Not quite in the Pohorje but on the way is the new **Betnava Adventure Park** (Pustolovski Park Betnava; ☎ 059 080 280; www.pustolovski-park.si; Streliška cesta 150; adult/child €15/10; 9am-9pm Jul, 9am-8pm Jun & Aug, by appointment Mar-May & Sep-Nov), which is a kind of adrenaline park in the forest at Betnava Castle for younger children about 3km south of the centre.

The Pohorje Sport Centre also operates the excellent **Bike Park Pohorje** (☎ 220 88 25, 040 645 054; adult/child with bike half day €19/14, full day €23/17), which starts at 1050m next to the upper cable-car station and wends its way down 4km through the forests, with more than 30 different obstacles such as table tops, hips, banks, step-downs and jumps up to 6m.

Cycling is an ideal way to explore the back roads and trails of the Maribor Pohorje. Make sure to ask the TIC for the 1:100,000 *Pohorje Cycling Map* and the simple but useful *Kolesarske Poti na Mariborskem Pohorju* (Cycle Trials in the Maribor Pohorje). The sport centre rents GT DHI Pro **mountain bikes** (per 4hr/day €40/50) from the lower cable-car station.

You can rent horses from **Koča Koča** (☎ 040 216 089), a restaurant in a hut 50m from the upper cable-car station, for €4 if you are content to twirl around the paddock three times; it costs €13/60 per hour/five hours to take one out on the trails. A trip in a horse-drawn coach will set you back €25/40 per half-hour/hour.

The **Maribor Pohorje ski grounds** (☎ 603 65 53; www.pohorje.org; day pass adult/child/student & senior €28/18/24) stretch from the Hotel Habakuk (336m) near the lower cable-car station to Žigartov Vrh (1347m) west of the Areh Hotel. With 80km of slopes (10km illuminated at night), 36km of cross-country runs and 20 ski lifts and tows (plus gondola), this is Slovenia's largest ski area. Ski equipment rentals are available from the upper cable-car station, and there's a ski and snowboarding school as well.

Festivals & Events

The annual **Women's World Cup Slalom and Giant Slalom Competition** – the coveted **Zlata Lisica** (Golden Fox; www.goldenfox.org) trophy – takes place on the main piste of the Maribor Pohorje ski grounds in mid-January.

Sleeping & Eating

There are plenty of places to stay in the Maribor Pohorje, including more than a dozen mountain lodges and holiday homes, some of them run by the Športni Center Pohorje who can provide you with a list and basic map. Places close to main roads are the Category III **Ruška Koča pri Arehu** (☎ 603 50 46, 041 666 552; year-round) with 36 beds at 1246m and the more swish Category III **Poštarski Dom pod Plešivcem** (☎ 822 10 55, 875 09 06; Wed-Mon) with 37 beds at 805m.

There are two camping sites at the foothills of the Maribor Pohorje near the cable car's lower station: **Camp Pohorje** (☎ 614 09 50; www.pohorje.org; Pot k Mlinu 57; adult/child €9/6; year-round), with only 20 pitches for tents and 10 for caravans; and the new **Camping Centre Kekec** (☎ 040 225 386; www.cck.si; Pohorska ulica 35; adult/child €9/6.50), with three-dozen pitches.

Hotel Areh (☎ 220 88 41; www.pohorje.org; Lobnica 32; per person half-board €35-45; P) At the summit of Areh peak (1250m), about 6km southwest of the upper cable-car station, this pleasant 84-bed ski lodge has wood-panelled rooms, a pleasant restaurant and helpful staff. It rents ski equipment and mountain bikes as well.

Hotel Zarja (☎ 603 60 00; www.hotel-zarja.si; Frajhajm 34; s €29-45, d €48-90, apt €80-115; P) Just east of the Hotel Areh and the ski fields, the chalet-like Zarja has 15 comfortable and airy rooms, a restaurant and a sauna.

Hotel Bolfenk (☎ 603 65 05; www.pohorje.si; Hočko Pohorje 131; per person half-board €45-75; P) This well-maintained property next to the Bellevue Hotel is an apartment hotel with 20 rooms, some of which are quite grand with living rooms and fireplaces.

Hotel Bellevue (☎ 607 21 00; www.termemb.si; Na Slemenu 35; s €90-140, d €130-230, ste €160-260; P) A Pohorje landmark, this very stylish place with 50 rooms and apartments within tumbling distance of the upper cable-car station is simply the poshest place in the region. Rates include entry to the hotel's fine wellness centre.

Almost everyone takes their meals in their hotels in the Maribor Pohorje; there are no independent restaurants except fo snack bars. Be on the lookout for dishe and drinks unique to the region, includin *pohorski lonec* (Pohorje pot), a kind of gou lash; *pohorska omleta*, a pancake filled wit fruit; and *boroničevec*, a brandy made wit forest berries.

Getting There & Away

You can drive or, if ambitious, cycle the 20kn from the Old Town in Maribor south pas the Renaissance-style Betnava Castle, turnin west at Spodnje Hoče before reaching a for in the road at a small waterfall. Go left an you'll reach the Areh Hotel after about 5km A right turn and less than 4km brings you t the upper cable-car station.

A much easier – and more exhilarating - way to get to the Bellevue and the heart o the Maribor Pohorje is to take the **cable ca** (vzpenjača; ☎ 041 959 795; Pohorska ulica) from the sta tion in Zgornje Radvanje, 6km southwest o Maribor's Old Town, though it was undergo ing a major overhaul when we last visited an ski lifts were transporting holiday-makers ir two stages. There are clamps on the outside of each of the cable car's cabins for mountair bikes and skis.

To reach the lower station from the trair station in Maribor take local bus 6 and ge off at the terminus. On weekdays the cable car runs every hour from 8am to noon and 6pm to 8pm; from 12.30pm to 5.30pm they go every half-hour. At the weekend departures are at 8am, 9am, 6pm, 7pm and 8pm and half-hourly between 9.30am and 5.30pm. The service is more frequent in winter.

CENTRAL POHORJE REGION

☎ 03 / elev to 1517m

Travellers can easily sample Pohorje's recreational offerings along its eastern edge from Maribor and its western fringes from Slovenj Gradec and Dravograd in Koroška. But the pear-shaped massif's highest and most beautiful area is in the centre. And although it's true that the Pohorje peaks can't exactly compete with those of the Julian and the Kamnik-Savinja Alps – most here barely clear the 1500m mark – hiking and trekking in the winter here is as good as it is in the summer.

Zreče (population 3015), about 40km southwest of Maribor, is the springboard for the central Pohorje region; indeed, the region is also ɪnown as the Zreče Pohorje (Zreško Pohorje). ʌlthough certainly not Slovenia's most at-tractive town – it's dominated by the tool-manufacturing company Unior – Zreče has modest spa and is within easy striking dis-ance of the ski and sport centre around **Rogla** 1517m), 16km to the north, where teams – in-luding the Slovenian Olympic one – train.

nformation

ıanka Celje (Cesta na Roglo 13b, Zreče) In the Zreče azaar (Zreški Bazar) shopping centre above the bus sta-ion 150m from the spa's main entrance. There's an ATM at he Dobrava 2000 Hotel.

'ost office (Cesta na Roglo 13b, Zreče) To the southeast f the bank.

'ourist Information Centre Zreče (TIC; ☎ 759 ɪ4 70; tic.zrece.lto@siol.net; Cesta na Roglo 13b, Zreče; 7am-3pm Mon, Tue, Thu & Fri, 7am-5pm Wed, 9am-ıoon Sat) In the Zreče Bazaar.

vww.rogla.si Useful website, especially for activities.

Activities

HIKING & MOUNTAIN BIKING

The 1:50,000 GZS *Pohorje* (€8.10) map out-lines various circular hiking trails that are as short as 2km (30 minutes) and as long as 32km (eight hours). The latter covers much of the hike described in the Maribor Pohorje section – Šumik waterfalls, Black Lake and Osankarica (p255) – but from the other side. Another good one is the 12km hike (three hours) that leads northwest to the **Lovrenc Lakes** (Lovrenska Jezera), a turf swamp with 20 small lakes that are considered a natural phenomenon. The free map/brochure *Rogla Terme Wanderwege/Footpaths* has eight hikes and walks of between 1km (15 minutes) and 32km (eight hours).

Mountain bikers should get hold of a copy of the free excellent 1:100,000 *Pohorje Cycling Map*, with a dozen trails outlined from Maribor in the east to Slovenj Gradec and Dravograd in the west. The spa's map/brochure (1:50,000) called *Rogla Terme Radfahrwege/Cycling Paths* is much more basic with nine trails linking Zreče, Rogla and Areh.

The **Rogla Cycling & Hiking Centre** (Kolesarsko in Pohodriško Center; ☎ 757 74 68; mountain bikes 1hr/half-day/day €8/14/18; 9am-7pm daily Aug, 9am-7pm Thu-Sun Jun & Jul) next to Pizzerija Planja (p258) organ-ises guided walks in season (per person €3 to €8) and rents mountain bikes. You can also rent bicycles for the same price from the Dobrava 2000 Hotel.

SKIING

The **Rogla ski grounds** (☎ 232 92 64, 757 61 55; www.rogla.eu; day pass adult/child/senior & student €28/18/25) has 12km of ski slopes (mostly intermediate) and 18km of cross-country trails served by two chairlifts and 10 tows. The season is a rel-atively long one – from the end of November to as late as April. There's also the **Rogla Ski School** (Smučarska Šola Rogla; ☎ 757 74 68; www.rogla.eu; 8.30am-4pm daily in season), in a little wooden cabin at the base of the ski lift where you can also learn to snowboard. You can rent equip-ment from the **Ski Servis** (☎ 757 74 89; skis per day adult/child €16/11; 8.30am-4.45pm) office at the Planja Hotel.

THERMAL SPA

While **Terme Zreče** (☎ 757 61 56; www.terme-zrece.si; Cesta na Roglo 15) is a serious treatment centre for post-operative therapy and locomotor disorders (especially those involving sports injuries), it is also a place where you can simply have fun. Along with an indoor **ther-mal pool** (the water temperature is 34.5°C), there are large covered recreational and outdoor **swimming pools** (adult/child 3hr Mon-Fri €8/6, Sat & Sun €8/9, all day Mon-Fri €10/7.50, Sat & Sun €12/9; 9am-9pm) covering an area of 1600 sq metres. **Sauna Village** (adult Mon-Fri €15, Sat & Sun €16; 11am-9pm Mon-Thu, 10am-9pm Fri-Sun) contains the usual assortment of saunas, Jacuzzis and steam rooms.

OTHER ACTIVITIES

The **Rogla Sport Hall** (Športna Dvorana Rogla; ☎ 757 71 00) has a covered stadium for all kinds of team sports (including basketball and volleyball), jogging tracks, lawn bowls, a squash court (per 45 minutes €10) and a badminton court (one hour €15), and indoor and outdoor **tennis courts** (1hr €16; 9am-9pm). The Planja Hotel has an **indoor swimming pool** (adult/child €8/5.50, with sauna admission €15; 9am-9pm). There's also a **climbing wall** (per hr €8).

Sleeping

The central Pohorje region abounds in farm-houses with rooms and apartments for rent, particularly along Cesta Kmečnega near Resnik, about 7km southwest of Rogla. One of the best is the four-room **Pačnik farmhouse** (☎ 576 22 02; Resnik 21; per person €23-28; Jul–mid-Sep, mid-Dec–mid-Mar; P). There are even more farmhouses accepting guests in Skomarje to the southwest.

Garni Hotel Zion (757 36 00; www.hotelzvon.biz; Slomškova ulica 2; r per person €40, apt €70-85; P) There's no particular reason for staying down in Zreče; all the fun is up in Rogla. But if you're a serious disciple of things thermal, the pension-like Bell is just opposite the entrance to the spa and has 15 spotless rooms and apartments.

Planja Hotel (757 71 00; www.terme-zrece.si; s €60-70, d €100-120; P) This four-star, 30-bed property, the poshest place to stay in Rogla, also has a three-star wing with 88 beds called the Rogla Hotel (singles €55 to €60, doubles €80 to €100). Its rooms, frankly, are brighter and more attractive than those in the main hotel. The Brinje Hotel (singles €45-50, doubles €70 to €80) is essentially just a poky annexe of the Planja with 22 apartments. The hotel's Jurgova Apartments (singles €40 to €45, doubles €60 to €70) are set off on their own.

Dobrava 2000 Hotel (757 60 00; www.terme-zrece.si; Cesta na Roglo 15; s/d €80/130; P) The spa's flagship hotel, this four-star place has 76 rooms at the entrance to the spa. Several rooms are adapted for guests with disabilities. Make sure you get one of the rooms with a balcony. The Dobrava Hotel (singles/doubles €70/110) is a slightly cheaper extension with 35 rooms. More pleasant (and still cheaper) are the Terme Zreče Villas (singles/doubles €60/100) in a small wooded area 150m from the main spa building, with 40 apartments and an equal number of double rooms.

Eating

Špajza (576 26 15; Cesta na Roglo 13b; pizza €4.20-5.50; 8am-9pm Mon-Fri, 8am-10pm Sat, noon-9pm Sun) If you feel like pizza in Zreče, try the friendly Pantry in the shopping centre.

Pizzerija Planja (757 72 50; pizza €4.40-6; 8.30am-8pm Jul & Aug, 8.30am-5pm Sep-Jun) Along with pizza, this place – just north of the Planja Hotel in Rogla and near the ski lift – does breakfasts and some Slovenian dishes.

Dom na Pesku (757 74 45; dishes €4.50-12.50; 7am-9pm Apr-Oct, 8am-7pm Nov-Mar) This mountain lodge (rooms per person €28) 3km north of Rogla on the unsealed road to Koroša is a popular place for hearty Slovenian fare, especially its celebrated mushroom soup with buckwheat goats (*gobova kremna juha z ajdovimi žganci*; €4.50) and *pohorski lonec* (Pohorje pot; €5), a kind of goulash.

Gostilna Jurček (041 686 725; Cesta na Roglo 4b; starters €5-8, mains €5.20-12; 7am-10pm Mon-Fri, 7am-11pm Sat, 9am-10pm Sun) This *gostilna* in Zreče on the main road to Rogla and opposite the shopping centre, is a friendly place for a quick meal.

Stara Koča (757 74 47; set lunch €12; 7am-midnight) The Old Hut is the main restaurant (and original structure) at the Planja Hotel and is retains its rustic mountain hut vibe.

There's a **Mercator** (Cesta na Roglo 11; 8am-8pm Mon-Sat, 8am-noon Sun) supermarket in the Zreče Bazaar shopping centre in Zreče. In Rogla you'll find the small **MBK** (8am-5pm) convenience store behind the Planja Hotel.

Getting There & Away

There are regular connections from Zreče to Celje (€3.60, 45 minutes, 26km, eight daily buses on weekdays) via Slovenske Konjice (€1.80, 10 minutes, 6km, eight to 10 on weekdays, two on Saturday). In winter two buses a day from Celje and a couple from Slovenske Konjice stop at Zreče and then carry on to Rogla. Local buses make the runs from Zreče bus station to Rogla.

In winter there are special ski buses from Zreče (five in each direction) as well as Celje and Slovenske Konjice. Terme Zreče runs buses hourly from 6am to 8.30pm or 9pm up to Rogla for its guests in winter, with up to four in each direction departing daily during the rest of the year.

CELJE

03 / pop 36,725 / elev 241m

With its time-warp historical centre, fabulous architecture, excellent museums and enormous castle looming over the picturesque Savinja River, Celje might appear to have won the tourism sweepstakes. But tell that to the city fathers… Slovenia's third-largest city can be a dispiriting place after dark, with even the simplest of places to eat and drink at a premium.

History

Celeia was the administrative centre of the Roman province of Noricum between the 1st and 5th centuries, and roads linked the town with other Roman settlements at Virunum (near Klagenfurt in Austria), Poetovio (Ptuj) and Emona (Ljubljana). In fact, it flourished to such a degree that it gained the nickname 'Troia secunda', the 'second Troy'.

Celje's second Camelot came in the mid-14th century when the counts of Celje took ontrol of the area. The counts (later dukes), ›ne of the richest and most powerful feudal lynasties in Central Europe, were the last on ›lovenian soil to challenge the absolute rule ›f the Habsburgs, and they united much of ›lovenia for a time. Part of the counts' emblem – hree gold stars forming an inverted triangle – ıas been incorporated into the Slovenian naional flag and seal.

Celje was more German than Slovene until he end of WWI, when the town government ›assed into local hands for the first time.

›rientation

Celje's compact Old Town is bordered by Levstikova ulica and Gregorčičeva ulica to he north and northwest, the area around the Lower Castle to the west, the train tracks to he east and the Savinja River to the south.

The town has two main squares: Glavni trg ıt the southern end of pedestrian Stanetova ılica and Krekov trg opposite the train staion. The main bus station is 300m north of the train station opposite the huge Celeia shopping mall on Aškičeva ulica. Local ›uses stop south of the train station on Ulica XIV Divizije.

Information

Abanka (Aškičeva ulica 10) Diagonally opposite the post office.

Banka Celje (Vodnikova ulica 2) In a building designed by Jože Plečnik in 1930.

Mladinska Knjiga (☎ 428 52 52; Stanetova ulica 3; ⌚ 8am-7pm Mon-Fri, 8am-noon Sat) Sells regional maps and guides.

Post office (Krekov trg 9) Purpose-built in 1898.

Tourist Information Centre Celje (TIC; ☎ 428 79 36, 492 50 81; www.celje.si) Celje Hall (Krekov trg 3; ⌚ 9am-5pm Mon-Fri, 9am-1pm Sat); Celje Castle (Cesta na Grad 78; ⌚ 9am-5pm Mon-Thu, 9am-7pm Fri, 11am-7pm Sat & Sun Jun-Aug, 9am-3pm Mon-Thu, 9am-7pm Fri, 11am-7pm Sat & Sun Apr, May & Sep, 10am-2pm Mon-Thu, 11am-3pm Sat & Sun Oct-Dec)

Sights

KREKOV TRG

Opposite the train station is the mammoth neo-Gothic **Celje Hall** (Celjski Dom; Krekov trg 3), built in 1907 and once the centre of social life for German-speaking *Celjani*. It now contains the year-round TIC and, in the lower ground floor, the **Children's Art Gallery** (Galerija Likovnih Del Mladih; ☎ 041 615 273; admission free; ⌚ 10am-6pm Tue-Sat), devoted to art produced by those under the age of 20 and the only such museum in all of Slovenia. To the south and connected to the Hotel Evropa is the 16th-century **Defence Tower** (Obrambni Stolp), and about 150m further on, the **Water Tower** (Vodni Stolp; Razlagova ulica 19), part of the city wall and ramparts and built between 1451 and 1473.

On the same street is the **Josip Pelikan Photo Studio** (Fotografski Atelje Josipa Pelikana; ☎ 548 58 91; www.muzej-nz-ce.si; Razlagova ulica 5; ⌚ 10am-2pm Tue-Fri, 9am-1pm Sat, 2-6pm Sun), the complete studio of an early 20th-century Celje photographer and part of the Museum of Recent History. It's a remarkable, err, snapshot of the past. Enter via the courtyard at Razlagova ulica 3.

SLOMŠKOV TRG & GLAVNI TRG

A few steps to the northwest of the tower is the **Abbey Church of St Daniel** (Opatijska Cerkev Sv Danijela), dating from the early 14th century. The church has some magnificent frescoes and tombstones, but its greatest treasure is a carved wooden **pietà** dating from 1415. The chapel has carved stone walls and vaults with remnants of frescoes from the early 15th century and carved effigies of the Apostles. Parts of Celje's **medieval walls** and **ramparts** can be seen along Ulica na Okopih, west of the church. In the southeast corner of Slomškov trg is the **Chapel of St Elizabeth** (Kapela Sv Elizabete) and the 15th-century **town almshouse** (mestni špital).

Contiguous with Slomškov trg is **Glavni trg**, the heart of the Old Town. It is filled with lovely town houses dating from the 17th and 18th centuries and, in the warmer months, outdoor cafes. In the centre of the square is the requisite **plague pillar** (1776) dedicated to Mary.

MUZEJSKI TRG

Overlooking the narrow park along the Savinja River's northern embankment is the 16th-century **Old County Hall** (Stara Grofija; Muzejski trg 1), a lovely Renaissance building with a two-level arcade around a courtyard, which contains the renovated **Celje Regional Museum** (Pokrajinski Muzej Celje; ☎ 428 09 50; www.pokmuz-ce; adult/child/student €3/1/2; ⌚ 10am-6pm Tue-Sun Mar-Oct, 10am-6pm Tue-Fri, 10am-noon Sat Nov-Feb).

Needless to say, the museum places much emphasis on Celeia and the Counts of Celje, right down to exhibiting 18 of the nobles'

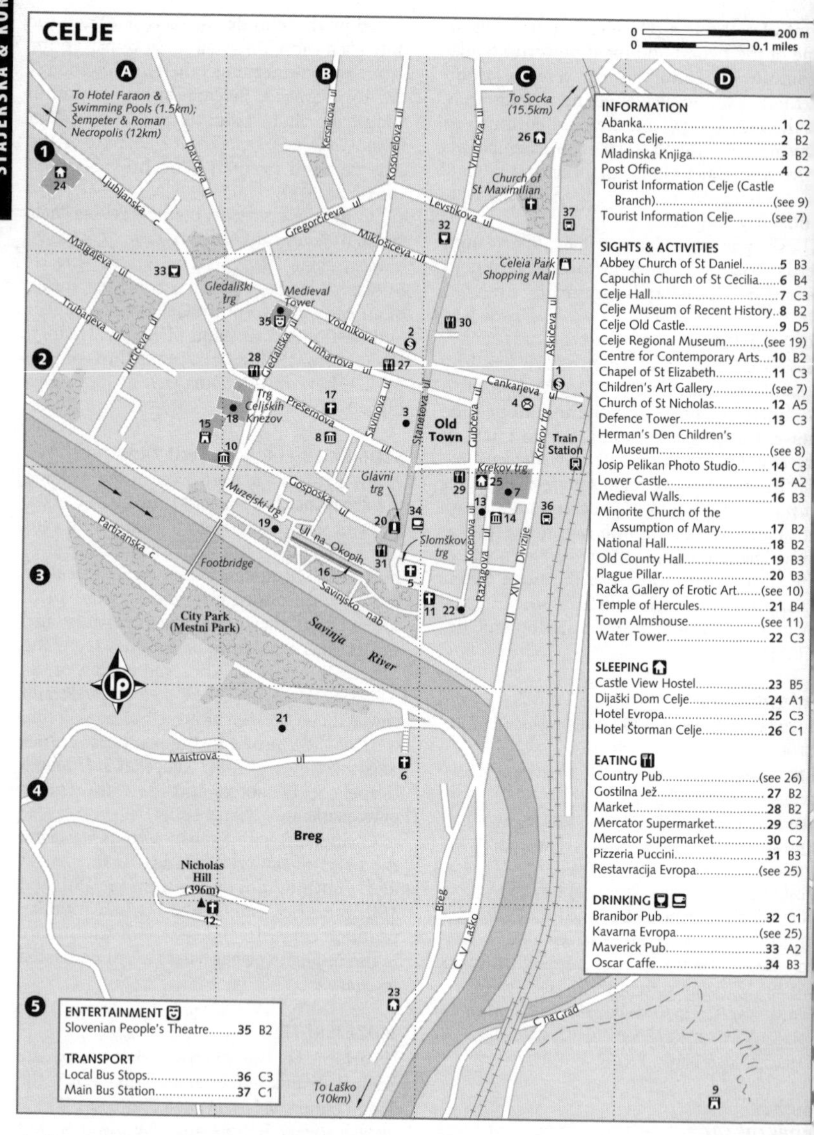

skulls in glass cases. (They were taken from the Minorite Church of the Assumption of Mary on Prešernova ulica in 1956 and are scheduled to be returned there soon.) The museum has a dozen rooms, many of them done up in styles from different periods (eg baroque, neoclassical, Biedemeier, Secessionist), painted with various scenes and filled with fine furniture. Don't miss the 18th-century cabinet with hunting scenes inlaid with ivory, the 20-drawer 'bank' desk with a secret compartment and the neoclassical combined clock and music box that still works. But the museum's main attraction is the **Celje Ceiling** (Celjski Strop), an enormous trompe l'oeil painting in the main hall of columns, owers, angels frolicking skyward, noblemen nd ladies looking down at you looking up. Completed in about 1600 by a Polish artist, he mural was meant to lift the ceiling up to he sky, and it does just that. Other panels epresent the four seasons and show scenes rom Roman and Greek mythology.

RG CELJSKIH KNEZOV

The funnel-shaped Square of the Celje Counts eads north from Muzejski trg. At the start s the **Lower Castle** (Spodnij Grad) built in he 14th century for the Celje Counts and oday containing the **Centre for Contemporary Arts** (Center Sodobnih Umetnosti; ☎ 426 51 60; Trg Celjskih Knezov 8; admission free; ⌚ 11am-6pm Tue-Fri, 10am-noon at, 2-6pm Sun), which contains the rather titillating **Račka Gallery of Erotic Art** (Galerija Erotike Račka), a first for Slovenia. To the north is the **National Hall** (Narodni Dom; Trg Celjskih Knezov 9), the cultural and social centre for Celje's Slovenes at the end of the 19th century and now the city hall.

PREŠERNOVA ULICA

Walking eastward along this street from Trg Celjskih Knezov, you'll pass the **Celje Museum of Recent History** (Muzej Novejše Zgodovine Celje; ☎ 428 64 10; www.muzej-nz-ce.si; Prešernova ulica 17; adult/child/senior & student/family €3/1.50/2/6; ⌚ 10am-6pm Mon-Fri, 9am-1pm Sat, 2-6pm Sun) in the former town hall building, which was built in 1830. The museum records the story of Celje from the late 19th century onwards and includes a re-creation of an early 20th-century street complete with tailor, hairdresser, clockmaker and goldsmith. It also contains the **Herman's Den Children's Museum** (Otroški Muzej Hermanov Brlog), the first children's museum in Slovenia.

BREG

On the south bank of the Savinja River a covered stairway with 90 steps at Breg 2 leads to the **Capuchin Church of St Cecilia** (Kapucinska Cerkev Sv Cecilije). The Germans used the nearby monastery (now apartments) as a prison during WWII. Between the church and **City Park** (Mestni Park; Partizanska cesta) is the reconstructed Roman **Temple of Hercules** (Heraklejev Tempelj; Maistrova ulica) dating from the 2nd century AD. Further south, you can walk up 396m-high **Nicholas Hill** (Miklavški Hrib), topped by the **Church of St Nicholas** (Cerkev Sv Miklavža), for a wonderful view of the castle, the Old Town and the Savinja.

CELJE OLD CASTLE

The largest fortress in Slovenia, this **castle** (Stari Grad Celje; ☎ 031 348 296; Cesta na Grad 78; admission €2; ⌚ 9am-5pm Mon-Thu, 9am-7pm Fri, 11am-7pm Sat & Sun Jun-Aug, 9am-3pm Mon-Thu, 9am-7pm Fri 11am-7pm Sat & Sun Apr, May & Sep, 10am-2pm Mon-Thu, 11am-3pm Sat & Sun Oct-Dec) is perched on a 407m-high escarpment about 2km southeast of the Old Town; the walk up via a footpath from Cesta na Grad takes about half an hour. The castle was originally built in the early 13th century and went through several transformations, especially under the Counts of Celje in the 14th and 15th centuries.

When the castle lost its strategic importance in the 15th century it was left to deteriorate, and subsequent owners used the stone blocks to build other structures, including parts of the Lower Castle and the Old County Hall. A surprisingly large portion remains intact, however, and has been restored, including the 35m-high **Frederick Tower** (Friderikov Stolp).

Activities

The TIC has brochures listing a number of **walks** and **hikes** into the surrounding countryside lasting between one and four hours. The longest one (28km) leads southeast to **Mt Tovst** (834m) and the picturesque village of Svetina via the **Celjska Koča** (☎ 059 070 400; www.celjska-koca.si), a mountain hut at 650m that has metamorphosed into a delightfully modern three-star hotel with adjacent skiing piste. It also distributes the brochure *Poti Primerne za Kolesarjenje* (Trails Suitable for Cycling), with 10 routes outlined for Celje and settlements to the north.

There are a couple of open-air **swimming pools** (☎ 547 30 10; Ljubljanska cesta 41; adult €5-6, child €3.50-4; ⌚ 9am-7pm daily Jun-Aug), including an Olympic-size one, on the Savinja just south of the Astor Hotel, about 1.5km west of the centre.

Sleeping

Castle View Hostel (☎ 070 220 069; www.elfa-sp.si; Breg 21; dm with/without HI card from €17/19; 💻) Smaller than the Dijaški Dom Celje, but closer to town and in the very shadow of the castle is the, well, Castle View, with eight beds in three rooms. It has a generous-sized kitchen and wi-fi in each room.

Dijaški Dom Celje (☎ 426 66 02, 041 621 266; www.ddcelje.si; Ljubljanska cesta 21; s/d/tr €19/34/45; ⌚ Jul & Aug) Northwest of the centre, this rather institutional 600-bed dorm accepts travellers for the most part in summer only, though between 60 and 100 beds are frequently available during the school year as well.

Hotel Štorman Celje (☎ 426 04 26; www.storman.si; Mariborska cesta 3; s €42-57, d €65-84, tr €90, ste from €100; P) The 52-room Štorman is in a canary-yellow, nine-storey block just north of the 15th-century Church of St Maximilian. The hotel is a favourite with businesspeople but eschew any of the rooms facing Mariborska cesta – it's a major and very busy highway.

Hotel Faraon (☎ 545 20 18; www.hotel-faraon.si; Ljubljanska cesta 39; s/d/tr €42/69/89; P) Another one to get a total facelift and not just a bit of botox, the Pharaoh has 26 modern rooms about 1.5km west of the Old Town and as close as you'll get to the Savinja River. It has its own swimming pool and casino. Good value.

Hotel Evropa (☎ 426 90 00; www.hotel-evropa.si; Krekov trg 4; s €62-98, d €98-124, ste €260; P) Located near the train station and in the centre of town, this 46-room historic hotel has been lovingly restored and is now a provincial favourite. We love the high-end cafe, the stunning new restaurant and the (as always) pleasant and helpful staff. Rooms on the 3rd and 4th floors are superior. Enter from Razlagova ulica.

Eating

Gostilna Jež (Linhartova ulica 6; dishes €4.20-6; 8am-5pm Mon-Sat) This very simple eatery is a great place for a cheap and filling lunch – as so many market-goers seem to think.

Pizzeria Puccini (☎ 544 29 25; Glavni trg 12; pizza €4.70-7.20; 10am-11pm Mon-Sat) This popular pizzeria with its retro decor and large glassed-in terrace overlooking a pretty square is always packed. Might be the pizzas, might be the dearth of alternatives in Celje.

Country Pub (☎ 426 04 14; Mariborska cesta 3; starters €7.50-9.20, mains €6.50-17.90; 6am-midnight) It's not often that we recommend hotel outlets but this pleasant pub-restaurant on the ground floor of the Hotel Štorman Celje is a viable option in a city with few choices. Go for one of the salads (€3.90 to €7.90) and a steak (€15.90 to €17.90).

Restavracija Evropa (Krekov trg 4; starters €6.80-9.90, mains €12.50-18.90; 11am-10pm Sun-Thu, 11am-midnight Fri & Sat) This stunning new eatery in the remade Hotel Evropa has superb international cuisine and some very inspired decor. We love th Manet-like portraits of film and rock stai (though we don't get the connection either)

There's an outdoor **market** (cnr Gledališki trg & Trg Celjskih Knezov; 6am-3pm) south of the theatr with fresh fruit, vegetables and other food stuffs. You'll find a large **Mercator** (Stanetov ulica 14; 7am-7pm Mon-Fri, 7am-3pm Sat, 8am-noo Sun) supermarket opposite the Art Deco Kin Metropol (Metropol Cinema; 1929) to th northeast. There's a more central **Mercato** (Prešernova ulica 1; 6am-6pm Mon-Fri, 7am-noon Sat branch next to the Hotel Evropa.

Drinking

Kavarna Evropa (☎ 496 90 00; Krekov trg 4; 7am-11pm Mon-Sat, 8am-10pm Sun) This 'olde worlde' caf in the Hotel Evropa – all dark wood panelling gilt mouldings and fusty chandeliers – is good place for a cup of coffee and a cake.

Oscar Caffe (Glavni trg 9; 8am-10pm) This ever so-cool cafe attracts the intelligentsia of Celje – at least that's what the retro decor and lots and lots of attitude suggests.

Branibor Pub (☎ 492 41 44; Stanetova ulica 27 6am-1am Mon-Thu, 6am-2.30am Fri, 7am-2.30am Sat 8am-1am Sun) This is one of the best pubs in town with jazz and other live music some nights.

Maverick Pub (Ljubljanska cesta 7; 6am-2am Mon-Thu, 6am-4am Fri & Sat, 6am-midnight Sun) One of several watering holes bunched up opposite Gledališki trg, this is a lively place with a large outdoor terrace for people-watching in the warmer months.

Entertainment

Slovenian People's Theatre (Slovenski Ljudsko Gledališče; ☎ 426 42 00, box office 426 42 08; www.slg-ce.si; Gledališki trg 5; 9am-noon Mon-Fri) The SLG, which encompasses part of a medieval tower once used as a dungeon on Vodnikova ulica, stages six plays between September and May.

Getting There & Away

BUS

Intercity buses, which leave from the main station, run at least once an hour (less frequently at weekends) to Mozirje (€4.10, 50 minutes, 31km), Rogaška Slatina (€4.10, one hour, 34km) and Rogatec and Zreče (€3.60, 40 minutes, 26km, up to four daily). Count on up to six buses on weekdays and two at the weekend to Ljubljana (€7.20, 1½ hours, 75km) and Maribor (€6.70, 1½ hours,

(65km). Other destinations accessible by bus from Celje and their frequencies include: Gornji Grad (€5.60, 1½ hours, 49km, two or three daily), Logarska Dolina (€7.20, two hours, 74km, 9.10am Monday to Friday April to October), Murska Sobota (€11.10, 2¾ hours, 124km, one daily at 6.55pm), Podsreda (€5.20, 1¼ hours, 43km, four on weekdays) and Solčava (€6.90, two hours, 67km, up to three daily).

For local destinations such as Šempeter (€2.60, 20 minutes, 12km, hourly), Škofja Vas, Šentjur, Prebold and Žalec, go to the bus stops south of the train station on Ulica XIV Divizije.

TRAIN

Celje is one of the few rail hubs in all of Slovenia, and for once you have a real choice between taking the train or the bus. Celje is on the main line between Ljubljana and Maribor; from Ljubljana (€5.90 to €9.90, 1½ hours, 89km) you can reach Celje up to two dozen times a day by regular train and six times a day by ICS express train.

Celje is also on the line linking Zidani Most (connections to and from Ljubljana and Zagreb) with Maribor (€4.90 to €8.90, one hour, 67km, half-hourly) and the Austrian cities of Graz and Vienna.

A spur line links Celje with Velenje (€2.90, one hour, 38km) via Šempeter up to nine times a day Monday to Saturday in each direction. A third line connects Celje with Zabok in Croatia via Rogaška Slatina (€2.90, 50 minutes, 36km), Rogatec and Dobovec. Up to seven trains arrive and depart on weekdays but only a couple at the weekend.

Getting Around

For a local taxi ring ☎ 544 22 00 or ☎ 031 464 646.

ŠEMPETER

☎ 03 / pop 2025 / elev 257m

Some 12km west of Celje and accessible by both local bus and by train, Šempeter is the site of a **Roman necropolis** (Rimska Nekropola; ☎ 700 20 56; www.td-sempeter.si; Ob Rimski Nekropoli 2; adult/child €4/3; 🕐 10am-6pm daily mid-Apr–Sep, 10am-3pm daily early Apr, 10am-4pm Sat & Sun Oct) reconstructed between 1952 and 1966. The burial ground contains four complete tombs and scores of columns, stellae and fragments carved with portraits, mythological creatures and scenes from daily life. They have been divided into about two dozen groups linked by footpaths.

The **Vindonius family tomb**, the oldest of them all, was commissioned by Gallus Vindonius, a Celtic nobleman who lived on a nearby estate in the 1st century. The largest tomb is, at 8m high, the **Spectacius tomb**, raised in honour of a Roman official, his wife and son. (Notice the kidnapping scene on the side relief.) The most beautiful is the **Ennius family tomb**, with reliefs of animals and, on the front panel, the priestess Europa riding a bull. If you compare these three with the more recent **Secundinus family tomb** erected in about 250 AD, it's obvious that Roman power and wealth was on the decline here in the mid-3rd century.

If you get hungry while touring around, **Gostišče Štorman** (☎ 703 83 00; www.storman.si; Šempeter 5a; mains €8-16.50, 🕐 7am-midnight), one of the first private restaurants to open in Slovenia under the former regime, is about 2km east of the site on the road to/from Celje.

UPPER SAVINJA VALLEY

The Upper Savinja Valley (Zgornja Savinjska Dolina) refers to the drainage areas and tributaries of the Savinja River from its source in the eastern Savinja Alps to a gorge at Letuš, 12km northwest of Šempeter. Bounded by forests, ancient churches, traditional farmhouses and Alpine peaks higher than 2000m, the valley is a land of breathtaking beauty. There are activities here to suit every taste and inclination – from hiking, mountain biking and rock climbing to fishing, kayaking and swimming in the Savinja.

The Savinja begins its rapid flow above Rinka – at 90m Slovenia's highest waterfall – then enters Logarska Dolina and continues past isolated hamlets and farmland. The region beyond the gorge at Ljubno is quite different, with a number of towns – really overgrown villages – of historical importance, including Radmirje, Gornji Grad, Nazarje and Mozirje.

The valley has been exploited for its timber since the Middle Ages, and until WWII the Savinja was used to power 200 sawmills. Rafters transported the timber from Ljubno to Mozirje and Celje and some of the logs travelled as far as Romania. The trade brought wealth to the valley, evident from the many fine buildings still standing here.

The free English-language brochure entitled *The Savinjska and Šaleška Valleys* is helpful if you intend spending a fair bit of time in the area. Serious hikers should pick up a copy of the 1:50,000 *Kamniško Savinjske Alpe* map (€8.10) by PZS. Cyclists will want the *Kolesarska Karta Zgornja Savinjska Dolina* (Upper Savinja Valley Cycling Map) available everywhere for €3.

Mozirje

☎ 03 / pop 2380 / elev 340m

The administrative centre of the Upper Savinja Valley lying on the Savinja's left bank, Mozirje is a town with a long history that has little to show for its past, except for a much rebuilt Gothic Church of St George at the at the western end of Na Trgu just after you cross the small Trnava Stream. Mozirje is really just a convenient stop on the way to Logarska Dolina, though the town's botanical garden opposite the bus station is worth a look and there's skiing in winter.

INFORMATION

Nova Ljubljanska Banka (Na Trgu 9)

Post office (Savinjska cesta 3) About 200m southwest of the bank.

Tourist Information Centre Mozirje (TIC; ☎ 839 33 34; www.ztksm-mozirje.si; Šmihelska cesta 2; 9am-5pm Apr-Oct, 8am-2pm Mon-Fri Nov-Mar) In the administration building near the Tuš supermarket.

SIGHTS & ACTIVITIES

Worth the short walk south of town and across the river is **Mozirski Gaj** (Savinja Grove; ☎ 583 27 19, 041 691 939; www.mozirskigaj.com; Hribernikova ulica 1; adult/child/student €5/2.50/4; 8am-7pm mid-Apr–Sep), a 7-hectare botanical park and flower garden with a small **open-air ethnographic museum**.

In winter, a cable car runs from Žekovec, 4km northwest of Mozirje, to the **Golte ski centre** (☎ 839 12 00; www.golte.si; day pass adult/child/student/senior €26/18/19/21), where there are 12km of slopes up to 1600m high and 15km of cross-country trails served by a gondola and a half-dozen lifts.

SLEEPING & EATING

Levc farmhouse (☎ 839 53 60; www.turisticna-kmetija-levc.com; Loke 19; r per person €20-26; P) About 800m southeast of Savinjski Gaj in Loke is this farmhouse with five guest rooms. The main activity here is cattle breeding.

Hotel Benda (☎ 839 37 00; www.hotel-benda.com; Loke 33; s/d €40/65; P) In the same settlement as the Levc farmhouse, the Benda is a pension with 36 rooms and a large restaurant.

Gaj (☎ 839 51 56; dishes €4.50-12; 10am-10pm) This restaurant at the entrance to the Mozirski Gaj botanical garden also does pizza (€... to €5.90).

Mercator (Savinjska cesta 4; 7am-8pm Mon-Sat, 8am-1pm Sun) This branch of the supermarket chain is at the start of the road to the botanical garden.

Nazarje

☎ 03 / pop 890 / elev 343m

At the confluence of the Savinja and Dreta rivers 2km south of Mozirje, 'Nazareth' is dominated by a 15th-century double-towered 'castle' (manor house, really) that houses a museum, a music school and offices of the Glin logging company, the industry that built Nazarje. In fact, the town's coat of arms bears a stylised image of the castle and three fir trees. There's an ATM at the **Nova Ljubljanska Banka** (Savinjska cesta 2) in the 1960s-style Culture House (Dom Kulture) opposite Vrbovec Castle.

SIGHTS & ACTIVITIES

Vrbovec Castle (Grad Vrbovec; Savinjska cesta 4) contains the **Forestry and Lumber Museum** (Muzej Gozdarstva in Lesarstva; ☎ 839 16 13, 040 345 630; www.muzej-vrbovec.si; adult/child €2/1; 9am-5pm Tue-Sun Mar-Nov, 8am-2pm Tue-Fri Dec-Feb), which is the industry that has kept bread on the tables of Nazarje for centuries (witness the huge pulp-processing plant just across the road).

Towering above the town on a hill called Gradišče is the **Franciscan monastery** (Frančiškanski Samostan; ☎ 583 19 93, 051 369 756; Samostanska pot 50) and its **Church of the Annunciation**, originally from the mid-17th century, all but flattened by Allied bombs in 1944 and now rebuilt. The twin-spired church has a choir loft with fine grill work; the original chapel, built by Bishop Tomaž Hren of Ljubljana in the early 17th century, now serves as the presbytery. Most people make the drive up to the monastery or climb its 200-odd steps to see the **library** (adult/child €1.50/1; by appointment), which has 16th-century manuscripts as well as priceless parchment incunabula dating from the 11th and 12th centuries.

The Ranč Burger Veniše (see p265) has **horses** (per hr riding €15, lessons €20) for hire.

SLEEPING & EATING

Three kilometres west of Nazarje, you'll find a couple of camping grounds on opposite sides of the river, including **Camping Menina** (☎ 040 25 266; www.campingmenina.com; Varpolje 105; adult €7.20-, child €3.60-4.50; year-round), a 7.5-hectare site on the north bank of the Savinja with cabins €80) for up to 10 people; and **Camping Savinja** (☎ 583 54 72, 041 528 098; www.sloveniaholidays.com/ng/camping-savinja; Spodnje Pobrežje 11; adult/child €6/3; May-Sep), with 80 sites on the south bank of the river.

Ranč Burger Veniše (☎ 839 25 50, 041 710 545; www.ranc-burger.com; Lačja Vas 22; s/d/tr €41/72/99) This 16-room hotel (with apartments too) and riding centre is in a beautiful valley 3km southwest of Nazarje.

Gostišče Grad Vrbovec (☎ 583 28 00; Savinjska cesta 4; starters €4.50-7, mains €7.50-13; 9am-9pm Mon-Fri, 11am-10pm Sat) This fine restaurant in Vrbovec Castle and overlooking the river is an excellent place to stop for lunch. Be sure to try the trout fried in buckwheat flour.

There's a **Tuš** (Savinjska cesta 1; 7.30am-3pm Mon-Fri, 7.30am-3pm Sat) supermarket near the centre.

Radmirje & Gornji Grad

Two kilometres before the town of Ljubno ob Savinji (population 1140), there's the option for a detour to two historical towns along route No 225. **Radmirje** (population 465), 1km to the southwest, is very picturesque with Štajerska-style hayracks and two important churches: the 16th-century **Church of St Michael** in the centre of town rebuilt after an earthquake in 1895, and the pilgrimage **Church of St Francis Xavier** on Straža Hill, containing a rich **treasury** (☎ 584 10 96; Radmirje 50; adult/child €1.70/0.60; by appointment) of Mass vestments donated by the kings of Poland and France and a gold chalice from Habsburg empress Maria Theresa.

Five kilometres further on in the Zadrečka Valley is **Gornji Grad** (population 915). The **former Benedictine monastery** (Attemsov trg 2) contains the small **Gornji Grad museum collections** (☎ 584 34 47, 041 531 442; admission €2; 3-5pm Sat, 9-11am & 3-5pm Sun Apr-Sep), with everyday objects relating to life on the Menina Planina, an area of mountain pastures and slopes south of town, and the **Štekl Gallery** (Galerija Štekl; ☎ 041 299 013; admission free; same as Gornji Grad), a 16th-century defence tower at the entrance to the complex with rotating exhibits. The large baroque **Cathedral of Sts Hermagoras and Fortunatus** (Katedrala Sv Mohorja in Fortunata) in the same complex was built in the mid-18th century (although parts go back to the 13th century) and modelled after the cathedral in Ljubljana. There's a **tourist information centre** (☎ 839 18 50, 041 447 330; www.gornji-grad.si; Attemsov trg 30) that keeps very erratic hours.

Logarska Dolina

☎ 03 / pop 95 / elev to 1250m

Most of the glacial Forester Valley, which is 7.5km long and no more than 500m wide, has been a country park of just under 2431 hectares since 1987. This 'pearl of the Alpine region', with more than 40 natural attractions – caves, springs, peaks, rock towers and waterfalls – as well as endemic flora (golden slipper orchid) and rare fauna (mountain eagles, peregrine falcons), is a wonderful place to explore for a few days. The **tourist office** (☎ 838 90 04, 051 626 380; www.logarska-dolina.si; Logarska Dolina 9; 9am-6pm Jul & Aug, 9am-3pm Apr-Jun & Sep) is in a small wooden kiosk opposite the Hotel Plesnik car park.

SIGHTS & ACTIVITIES

Logarska Dolina Country Park (Krajinski Park Logarska Dolina) is open year-round, but from April to September (and at weekends in October) cars and motorcycles entering the park must pay €6 and €4 respectively; pedestrians and cyclists always get in free. A road goes past a chapel and through the woods to the 90m **Rinka Waterfall** (Slap Rinka) at 1100m, but there are plenty of trails to explore and up to 20 other waterfalls in the area.

The bottom of the Rinka Waterfall is a 10-minute walk from the end of the valley road. The climb to the top takes about 20 minutes. It's not very difficult, but it can get slippery. From the top to the west you can see three peaks reaching higher than 2250m: Kranjska Rinka, Koroška Rinka and Štajerska Rinka. Until 1918 they formed the triple border of Carniola (Kranjska), Carinthia (Koroška) and Styria (Štajerska). Ask the tourist office for the *Trail around Logarska* brochure, which will take you through the valley for 7km and in two hours.

Opposite Dom Planincev is a trail leading to **Sušica Waterfall** and **Klemenča Cave**, both at about 1200m

Another magnificent and much less explored valley is 6km-long **Matkov Kot**, which runs parallel to Logarska Dolina and

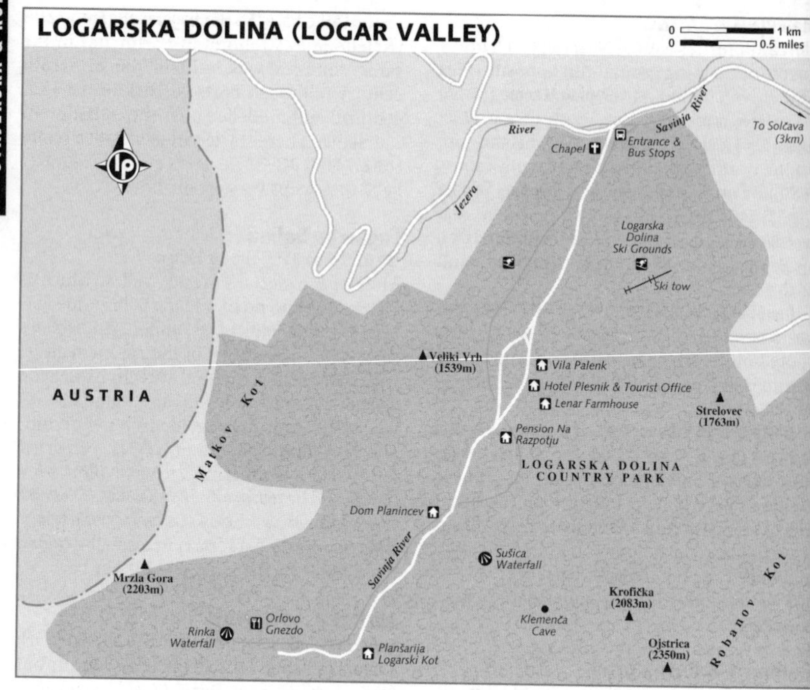

the border with Austria. You can reach here by road by turning west as you leave Logarska Dolina.

The tourist office can organise any number of activities – from guided mountaineering and rock climbing (per hour €25) to paragliding (€60). It also rents mountain bikes (per hr/day €3/12). The valley has the very basic **Logarska Dolina ski grounds** (☎ 838 90 04; www.logarska-dolina.si, day pass adult/child €10/7), a 1km-long slope and 15km of cross-country ski trails served by two tows.

SLEEPING & EATING

Dom Planincev (☎ 584 70 06, 070 847 639; www.domplanincev.si; Logarska Dolina 15a; per person €18; late Apr–Oct; P) This mountain hut 2.5km from Rinka has a relaxed, rustic feel to it and sleeps up to 32 people.

Planšarija Logarski Kot (☎ 838 90 30, 041 210 017; info@logarska.si; per person €18; late Apr–Oct; P) More isolated than the Dom Planincev but closer to the falls, this locally run hut has accommodation for two dozen hikers.

Lenar farmhouse (☎ 838 90 06; www.lenar.si; Logarska Dolina 11; r per person €22, apt for 3 €60; P) Another farmhouse with four rooms and a couple of apartments in a lovely peasant's cottage, Lenar is a couple of kilometres south from the entrance.

Pension Na Razpotju (☎ 839 16 50; www.logarska-narazpotju.si; Logarska Dolina 14; s/d €50/80; P) A very comfortable, relatively new pension set back from the main road, At the Crossroads has 21 beds and is a nice alternative to the Palenk complex, a short distance to the north.

Hotel Plesnik (☎ 839 23 00; www.plesnik.si; Logarska Dolina 10; s €89-96, d €144-154; P) A 30-room hotel in the centre of the valley with a pool, sauna, a fine restaurant (open 8am to 10pm) and lovely public area, the Plesnik pretty much *is* Logarska Dolina. Its annexe, the Vila Palenk (singles/doubles €79/126), with 11 rooms done up in generic 'Alpine style', takes the overflow.

The closest **Mercator** (7am-7pm Mon-Fri, 7am-noon Sat, 8-11.30am Sun) supermarket is in Solčava (house No 16).

In the valley itself, along with the restaurants at the Hotel Plesnik, Dom Planincev and Pension Na Razpotju, there's the **Orlovo** nezdo (Eyrie; ☎ 031 269 785; 10am-6pm), a simle cafe-pub with snacks in a tall wooden ower overlooking the falls and reached by steep set of steps.

etting There & Around

rom Mozirje, there is an hourly bus service o Celje (€4.10, 50 minutes, 31km) on weekays but few on Saturday. Other destinations re Gornji Grad (€2.70, 30 minutes, 18km, p to six a day) and Solčava (€4.70, 65 mintes, 36km, five on weekdays).

From Gornji Grad, buses go to Ljubljana €6, 1¾ hours, 52km, four daily Monday to riday, one at the weekend) and Kamnik €3.60, one hour, 26km, three on weekays, one or two at the weekend). There's 7.51am bus on Sunday to Logarska Dolina (€3.60, one hour, 30km) from une to September only. From Logarska Dolina you can reach Celje (€7.20, two ours, 74km, 12.41pm Monday to Friday April to October) on a daily weekday bus n season.

You can rent **bicycles** (per hr/day €3/12) from oth the park entrance and the tourist office. The latter also has **electric bikes** (per hr €14).

KOROŠKA

The truncated province of Koroška is essentially just three valleys bounded by the Pohorje Massif on the east; the last of the Karavanke peaks, Mt Peca, on the west; and the hills of Kobansko to the north. The Drava Valley runs east to west and includes the towns of Dravograd, Muta and Vuzenica. The Mežica and Mislinja valleys fan out from the Drava; the former is an industrial area with such towns as Ravne, Prevalje and Črna na Koroškem while the latter's main centre is Slovenj Gradec.

There is a reason why Koroška is so small. In the plebiscite ordered by the victorious allies after WWI, Slovenes living on the other side of the Karavanke, the 120-km-long rock wall that separates Slovenia from Austria, voted to put their economic future in the hands of Vienna while the mining region of the Mežica Valley went to Slovenia. As a result, the Slovenian nation lost 90,000 of its nationals (7% of the population at the time) as well as the cities of Klagenfurt (Celovec) and Villach (Beljak) to Austria.

Understandably, the results of that vote have never sat very well with the Slovenes on the southern side of the mountains. Still, Koroška holds a special place in the hearts and minds of most Slovenes. The Duchy of Carantania (Karantanija), the first Slavic state dating back to the 7th century, was centred here, and the word 'Carinthia' is derived from that name.

DRAVOGRAD

☎ 02 / pop 3310 / elev 362m

Situated mostly on the left bank of the Drava, Slovenia's second-longest river after the Sava, Dravograd is a sleepy place with few sights of its own (though students of history might make a trip here for its infamous WWII connections). It is, however, an excellent springboard for exploring the Kobansko Hills to the north and the Drava Valley to the east.

The town whose name means 'Drava Castle' is much smaller than its sister city, Slovenj Gradec, 12km to the south. It is just as old, however, with a recorded history dating back to the 12th century. It was at this time that the castle, the ruins of which can be seen on the hill to the north of town, was built. Located on a bend in the Drava at the point where the smaller Meža and Mislinja Rivers flow into it, the castle and the town were of great strategic importance for centuries and at the beginning of the 20th century as many as 2000 rafts sailed between here and Maribor, 60km to the east, each year. The river traffic came to a grinding halt in 1943 when the Dravograd hydro-power plant opened. Still, rafting upriver remains an option.

Orientation

Dravograd's historical centre and its main street, Trg 4 Julija, are on the north bank of the Drava. The bus and train stations are about 1km to the southeast on the south bank.

Information

Nova Ljubljanska Banka (Trg 4 Julija 44) Two doors east of the Church of St Vitus.

Post office (Trg 4 Julija 1) At the eastern end of Trg 4 Julija just before the bridge over the Drava.

Tourist Information Centre Dravograd (TIC; ☎ 871 02 85; info.dravograd@kanet.si; Trg 4 Julija 50; 10am-7pm May-Sep, 10am-2pm & 3-6pm Oct-Apr) Shares space with lovely art gallery next door to Church of St Vitus.

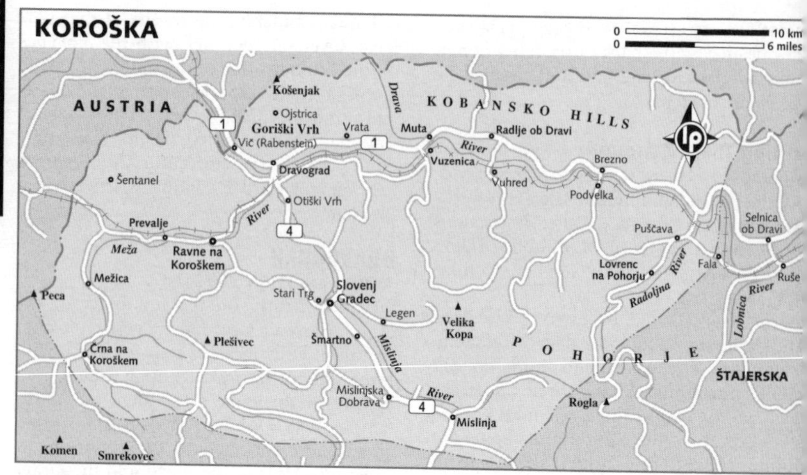

Sights & Activities

The **Church of St Vitus** (Cerkev Sv Vida), at the western end of Trg 4 Julija and opposite No 47, is one of the most important Romanesque buildings extant in Slovenia. Built in the second half of the 12th century and now renovated, it is a solid structure of light-brown stone with a high bell tower between the nave and the small circular presbytery.

The **town hall** (☎ 878 30 11; Trg 4 Julija 7; admission €1; 🕑 by arrangement) was used as a Gestapo prison and torture chamber during WWII, and the small museum in the basement can be visited; ask at the TIC. The hydroelectric dam on the Drava near Dravograd was built by German soldiers during the war, and many of them were lodged in town.

It's an easy hike north from Dravograd to the **castle ruins** (not much more than a wall); simply head up Pod Gradom, a lane just before Trg 4 Julija 22. The more energetic may want to carry on further into the **Kobansko Hills**, where you just might encounter some traditional charcoal burners. A circular section of the **Kozjak Mountain Trail** leads north past Goriški Vrh to Mt Košenjak (1521m) and returns to Dravograd via Ojstrica.

The TIC can help organise three-hour **rafting trips** (☎ 872 33 33; www.splaverjenje.com; per person €19.50) on the Drava, though they are usually available to groups only. The trip starts at Vrata, about 10km to the east, and carries on to Dravograd. The price includes food and drink.

Koroša is a centre for mountain bik ing. The adrenalin-pumping **Mountain Bik Park** (www.mtbpark.com) is situated near **Koro Farmhouse Bike Hotel** (☎ 870 30 60, 041 764 05; info@bikenomad.com; Jamnica 10; per person €29) nea Prevalje (population 4445), 15km south west of Dravograd. It sits at the centre of network of some 1000km of marked fores and mountain trails ranging in length fron 20km to 350km – some of which climl up to 1690m – and a downhill racecourse There's even a 5km trail through 300-year old Frederick Mine (Fridrihov Rov), which must be booked in advance. The hotel of fers single or multiday guided mountain bike tours and organises training camps and competitions. Mountain bikes cos €15/19 per day for front/full suspension and €84/112 per week.

Sleeping

There is a surfeit of farmhouse accommodation at Šentanel, a picturesque village in the Mežica Valley about 18km west of Dravograd, including the **Ploder farmhouse** (☎ 823 11 04, 041 867 375; kmetijaploder@hotmail.com; Šentanel 3; per person €20) with 10 rooms; and the **Marin-Miler farmhouse** (☎ 824 05 50, 041 654 886; marin@koroska.org; Šentanel 8; r per person €19) with six rooms and views of Mt Peca.

Planinski Dom Košenjak (☎ 878 35 04, 041 222 360; www.pddravograd.com; 🕑 Thu-Sun Mar–mid-Nov, Sat & Sun year-round) If you don your hiking boots and set out for Mt Košenjak, there is accommodation at this 43-bed Category II mountain lodge situated at 1169m, north of Dravograd.

Hotel Hesper (☎ 878 44 40, 878 30 73; www.hesper.si; Koroška cesta 47; s/d/tr €41/54/90; P) About 1.5km northwest of Trg 4 Julija in the Traberg shopping centre, this 24-room property is the only place to stay in central Dravograd, which is convenient and popular with *Avstrijci* from over the border.

Hotel Korošica (☎ 878 69 12; www.korosica.si; Otiški Vrh 25a; s/d €59/85; P) This popular hotel in Šentjanž pri Dravogradu on the Mislinja River about 3km southeast of Dravograd has 30 comfortable rooms and a very popular restaurant (starters €6 to €11.50, mains €10 to €18, open 7am to 10pm Monday to Thursday, 11am to midnight Friday and Saturday, 11am to 10pm Sunday).

Eating & Drinking

Pizza is as popular here as elsewhere in Slovenia and our man in Dravograd recommends the **Ribiški Dom** (☎ 878 00 93, 070 211 060; Ribiška pot 11) right on the Drava and **Pizzerija Bumerang** (☎ 051 642 902; Robindvor 103) a bit further afield.

Lovski Rog (☎ 878 32 88; Trg 4 Julija 37; dishes €6.50-9; 5.30am-11pm Mon-Thu, 5.30am-midnight Fri, 6am-10pm Sat, 7am-8pm Sun) Come to the Hunting Bugle for stick-to-the-ribs Slovenian dishes. It's most popular at breakfast and lunch.

Bistro Wolf (4 Trg Julija 36; 7am-11pm Mon-Thu, 7am-1am Fri & Sat) If time is weighing heavy in old Dravo, nurse a drink on the terrace of this old-style bistro and watch the world not pass by.

You'll find a **BA Center** (Trg 4 Julija 15; 7am-9pm Mon-Sat, 8am-8pm Sun) supermarket with extended hours in the centre of town, and a much larger but less central **Mercator** (Koroška cesta 48; 7.30am-8pm Mon-Fri, 7.30am-3pm Sat, 8am-noon Sun) next to the Hotel Hesper.

Getting There & Around

Count on frequent buses to Črna na Koroškem (€3.60, 50 minutes, 26km), Maribor (€6.70, two hours, 61km) via Radlje ob Dravi and Slovenj Gradec (€2.30, 20 minutes, 11km). Buses also serve Celje (€6.70, two hours, 65km, one at 2.45pm), Gornji Grad (€6.90, two hours, 67km, one at 1.10pm Monday to Saturday) and Ljubljana (€11.10, 2¼ hours, 121km, up to three daily).

Dravograd is on the rail line linking Maribor and Bleiburg (Pliberk) and Klagenfurt in Austria. Up to five trains a day on weekdays depart for Maribor (€4.90, 1½ hours, 64km) via Vuzenica and Vuhred. As many trains leave for Ravne na Koroškem and Prevalje (€1.60, 16 minutes, 11km), one of which crosses the Austrian border and carries on to Klagenfurt.

If you need a taxi, phone ☎ 878 57 57 or 041 621 938.

UNDER THE LINDEN TREES

If cities can have municipal animals – where would Rome be today without the she-wolf that suckled Romulus and Remus or Berlin without its bear – why can't a country have a national tree? Slovenia's is the linden (or common lime), and its heart-shaped leaf has become something of a symbol of Slovenia and Slovenian hospitality.

The stately linden *(lipa)* grows slowly for about 60 years and then suddenly spurts upward and outwards, living to a ripe old age. It is said that a linden grows for 300 years, stands still for another 300 and takes 300 years to die.

Linden wood was used by the Romans to make shields and, as it is easy to work with, artisans in the Middle Ages carved religious figures from it, earning linden the title *sacrum lignum*, or 'sacred wood'. Tea made from the linden flower, which contains aromatic oils, has been used as an antidote for fever and the flu at least since the 16th century. We're hooked. More importantly, from earliest times the linden tree was the focal point of any settlement in Slovenia – the centre of meetings, arbitration, recreation and, of course, gossip. The tree, which could never be taller than the church spire, always stood in the middle of the village, and important decisions were made by town elders at a table beneath it.

In fact, so sacred is the linden tree to Slovenes that its destruction is considered a serious offence. In discussing the barbarous acts committed by the Italians during the occupation of Primorska between the wars, one magazine article passionately points out that 'Kobarid had to swallow much bitterness…The fascists even cut down the linden tree…'

Slovenia's oldest linden is the 800-year-old Najevska Lipa under Koroška's Mt Peca, where Slovenian politicians meet in July. We give it another century.

AROUND DRAVOGRAD

An excellent bike trip follows the spectacular Drava Valley through the Pohorje and Kobansko Hills, 60km eastward to Maribor. The river, whose highest flow is reached at the start of the summer, is at its most scenic at Brezno and just above Fala, where it narrows into a gorge. Just before Maribor, the Drava widens into a lake with the help of a major dam.

You don't have to go that far to see some great scenery, however. Vuzenica and Muta, two very attractive villages, are just 14km from Dravograd and can be reached by train or on the Maribor bus.

Vuzenica

☎ 02 / pop 1670 / elev 338m

The **Church of St Nicholas** (Cerkev Sv Nikolaja; ☎ 876 40 34, 040 858 236) in Vuzenica, on the Drava's right bank, was built in the 12th century and expanded later; note the Gothic buttresses outside. Its outstanding features include a fabulous baroque gold altar, a star-vaulted ceiling typical of Koroška, 15th-century frescoes in the porch and an original fortified wall surrounding the churchyard. The ruins of a 16th-century castle can be seen on Pisterjev Vrh northeast of town.

Muta

☎ 02 / pop 2490 / elev 382m

A two-tier village across the Drava from Vuzenica, Muta has churches on both levels, but you want the one in Spodnja Muta (Lower Muta) near the main road. The austere **Rotunda of St John the Baptist** (Rotunda Janeza Krstnika; ☎ 876 11 77, 040 959 491) is one of the oldest churches in Slovenia – it was built while Pope Leo IX (1002–54) toured Carinthia and Styria in the mid-11th century. Its round shape, wooden-shingled roof and steeple are typical of the province, and the tiny church appears content with itself in a field with the hills far behind it. There are fragmented frescoes on the east side of the apse, and near the west entrance is a stone relief of an eagle dating from Roman times. If you can get the rotunda opened, you'll see 14th-century frescoes in the choir and the painted wooden ceiling in the presbytery from the 17th century.

SLOVENJ GRADEC

☎ 02 / pop 8340 / elev 410m

Slovenj Gradec is not the 'capital' of Koroška – that distinction goes to the industrial centre of Ravne na Koroškem to the northwest – but it is certainly the province's cultural and recreational heart. A large number of museums, galleries and historical churches line its main square, while the sporting opportunities in the Pohorje Massif to the east are many.

History

The history of Slovenj Gradec is closely tied to Stari Trg, a suburb southwest of the Old Town where there was a Roman settlement called Colatio that existed from the 1st to the 3rd centuries (though there is no trace of it now). At that time an important Roman road from Celeia (Celje) to Virunum (near Klagenfurt in Austria) passed through Colatio. Slovenj Gradec was an important trade centre in the Middle Ages and minted its own coins. Later it became an important cultural and artistic centre with many artisans and craft guilds. Among the prominent Habsburg nobles based in Slovenj Gradec over the centuries were members of the Windisch-Grätz family, a variant of the German name for the town (Windisch Graz).

Orientation

Slovenj Gradec's main street is Glavni trg, a colourful long 'square' lined with old town houses and shops. The bus station is at Pohorska cesta 15, about 500m northeast of the TIC. Slovenj Gradec is not on a train line.

Information

Mladinska Knjiga (☎ 881 22 83; Glavni trg 18; ⏰ 8am-6.30pm Mon-Fri, 8am-noon Sat) Stocks regional maps and guides.

Nova Ljubljanska Banka (Glavni trg 30)

Post office (Francetova cesta 1) At the northern end of Glavni trg.

Tourist Information Centre Slovenj Gradec (TIC; ☎ 881 21 16; www.slovenjgradec.si; Glavni trg 24; ⏰ 8am-4pm Mon-Fri, 9am-noon Sat & Sun) On the ground floor of the former town hall.

Sights

MUSEUMS

The former town hall, where the TIC is located, also contains two important museums. The **Koroška Regional Museum** (Koroški Pokrajinski Muzej; ☎ 884 20 55; http://gostje.kivi.si/muzej; Glavni trg 24; adult/child/family €2/1.50/5; ⏰ 9am-6pm Tue-Fri, 10am-1pm & 2-5pm Sat & Sun) has exhibits on the 2nd floor devoted to the history of Slovenj

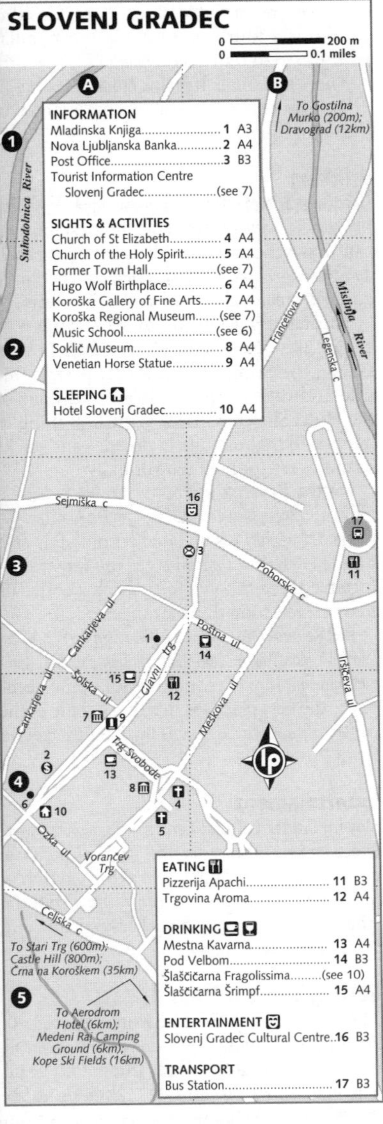

Gradec and the Koroška region – from local sport heroes' awards and farm implements to painted beehive panels and models of wartime hospital rooms and schools run by Partisans. There's also a very good archaeological collection focusing on the Roman settlement of Colatio. It includes jewellery and other effects taken from a Slavic burial ground at Puščava near Castle Hill (Grajski Grič) to the west.

The **Koroška Gallery of Fine Arts** (Koroška Galerija Likovnih Umetnosti; ☎ 884 12 83, 882 21 31; www.glu-sg.si; adult/student & child/family €2/1.50/5; 9am-6pm Tue-Fri, 10am-1pm & 2-5pm Sat & Sun) on the 1st floor has rotating exhibits but counts among its permanent collection African folk art, bronze sculptures by Franc Berneker (1874–1932) and naive paintings by Jože Tisnikar (b 1928). Tisnikar is among the most interesting and original artists in Slovenia, and his obsession with corpses, distorted figures and oversized insects is at once disturbing and funny. Don't miss *Rojstva in Smrt* (Birth and Death), *Ti, ki Ostanejo* (Those who Stay) and *Črička* (Crickets). The paintings are all very black and blue. Outside the town hall is the **Venetian Horse**, a life-size work by contemporary sculptor/designer Oskar Kogoj. It has become something of a symbol for Slovenj Gradec.

The items on display at the **Soklič Museum** (Sokličev Muzej; ☎ 884 15 05; Trg Svobode 5; by appointment) on the 2nd floor of the presbytery were amassed by Jakob Soklič (1893–1972), a priest who began squirreling away bits and bobs in the 1930s. Among the mediocre watercolours and oils of peasant idylls and the umpteen portraits of the composer Hugo Wolf (1860–1903), whose birthplace – now the town's **music school** (☎ 883 16 13; Glavni trg 40) – is nearby, are green goblets and beakers from nearby Glažuta (an important glass-manufacturing town in the 19th century), local embroidery and linen, religious artefacts and some 18th-century furniture.

CHURCHES

The sombre **Church of St Elizabeth** (Cerkev Sv Elizabete; Trg Svobode) was built in 1251 and is the town's oldest structure. But aside from the Romanesque nave and a couple of windows, almost everything here is baroque, including the massive gold altar and pulpit and the altar paintings done by local artist Franc Mihael Strauss (1647–1740) and his son Janez Andrej Strauss (1721–82). Far more interesting is the **Church of the Holy Spirit** (Cerkev Sv Duha; Trg Svobode) from 1494 to the south, with an interior covered with Gothic frescoes by Andrej of Otting. The 27 panels on the north wall represent the Passion of Christ; the scenes on the archway are of the Final Judgment. There's a peephole to view them (partially) when the church is locked.

Activities

The **Slovenian Alpine Trail** passes through Stari Trg and the centre of Slovenj Gradec before continuing up to Mala Kopa (1524m), where it meets the E6. There is a Category II 48-bed mountain hut at 1102m to the northwest called **Koča pod Kremžarjevim Vrhom** (☎ 884 48 83; 041 832 035; ⏰ Wed-Mon late Apr–Sep, Sat & Sun Oct–late Apr). The **E6** heads north through Vuhred and Radlje ob Dravi to Austria, and the Slovenian Alpine Trail carries on eastward to Rogla and Maribor. There is more accommodation on Velika Kopa at 1377m at the 68-bed **Grmovškov Dom pod Veliko Kopo** (☎ 883 98 60, 041 601 832; ⏰ year-round). If you are going to do a fair amount of hiking in the western Pohorje, pick up a copy of the 1:50,000-scale *Pohorje* GZS map (€8.50).

Three ski slopes are within striking distance of Slovenj Gradec, but the closest is **Kope** (☎ 882 27 40; www.pohorje.org; day pass adult/child/student & senior €26/18/23), with skiing up to 1542m above the Mislinja Valley on the western edge of the Pohorje Massif. The ski grounds have 8.5km of runs, 15km of cross-country trails and eight lifts on Mala Kopa and Velika Kopa peaks. To reach Kope, follow the Velenje road (No 4) for 3km south and then turn east. The ski area is another 13km at the end of the road.

Sleeping & Eating

Medeni Raj camping ground (☎ 885 05 00; www.aerodrom-sg.si; Mislinjska Dobrava 110; campsite per person €7, bungalows €40; ⏰ mid-Mar–mid-Oct) Sweet Paradise is a small, friendly place with sites for tents and caravans and six bungalows set among the pine trees of Turiška Vas, just beyond the Aerodrom hotel in Mislinjska Dobrava.

Hotel Slovenj Gradec (☎ 883 98 50; www.vabo.si; Glavni trg 43; s/d/tr €36/70/93; P) The only hotel option in town is this depressing 68-room property with rather gloomy rooms and long, dark corridors that seem to go on forever. It deeply and meaningfully cries out for a makeover.

Hotel Aerodrom (☎ 885 05 00; www.aerodrom-sg.si; Mislinjska Dobrava 110; s/d €52/75; P) It's a bit of a schlep 6km southeast of Slovenj Gradec, but the four-star Aerodrom with a dozen rooms is head and shoulders above any other accommodation in the area.

Pizzerija Apachi (☎ 883 17 84; Pohorska cesta 17b; pizza €4.50-6; ⏰ 7am-11pm Mon-Thu, 7am-1am Fri & Sat, noon-10pm Sun) This pizzeria with a 'cowboys and Indians' theme (go figure) is next to the bus station.

Gostilna Murko (☎ 883 81 03; Francetova cesta 24; meals from €18; ⏰ 8am-10pm) About 400m north of the centre on the Mislinja River, Gostilna Murko is a four-star roadside inn popular with Austrian tourists on the go.

There's a small **Trgovina Aroma** (Glavni trg 17; ⏰ 6am-8pm Mon-Sat, 8am-6pm Sun) supermarket on the main square.

Drinking

Šlaščičarna Šrimpf (☎ 884 14 82; Glavni trg 14; ⏰ 8.30am-8pm Mon-Sat, noon-8pm Sun) This long-established cafe draws the crowds with its fabulous cakes. Try the *zagrebska* (€1.70), a rich concoction of custard, cream, chocolate and flaky pastry.

Šlaščičarna Fragolissima (☎ 883 98 50; Glavni trg 43; ⏰ 6.30am-10pm Sun-Thu, 6.30am-midnight Fri & Sat) Giving the Šrimpf a run for its pastry, this cafe and cake shop on the ground floor of the Hotel Slovenj Gradec is the best thing to happen to that old pile in decades and packs in the sweet-toothed crowds daily.

Mestna Kavarna (☎ 884 51 09; Trg Svobode 7; ⏰ 7am-10.30pm Mon-Thu, 6.30am-1am Fri, 8am-1am Sat, 8.30am-10pm Sun) This updated yet old-style cafe on the corner of Glavni trg is the most comfortable place in town to tip back a coffee or maybe even something stronger.

Pod Velbom (☎ 041 654 843; Glavni trg 1; ⏰ 6.30am-midnight Mon-Thu, 6.30am-2am Fri, 9am-2am Sat, 4pm-midnight Sun) If you're looking for some company, the best place for meeting people in the centre of Slovenj Gradec is this pub-cafe; enter from Poštna ulica.

Entertainment

Slovenj Gradec Cultural Centre (Kulturni Dom Slovenj Gradec; ☎ 884 11 93; Francetova ulica 5) Classical music concerts are sometimes held at the Church of St Elizabeth and this centre, which also has a small cinema showing films between 7pm and 9pm Friday to Sunday.

Getting There & Around

There are buses to Črna na Koroškem (€4.70, 70 minutes, 39km, two daily), Dravograd (€2.30, 20 minutes, 11km, three daily) and Mislinja (€2.30, 20 minutes, 12km, up to six daily). Other destinations served by bus from Slovenj Gradec include Celje (€6, 1½ hours, 55km, 3.05pm daily), Gornji Grad (€6.30, 1½ hours, 57km, one at 1.31pm Monday to Saturday), Ljubljana (€9.90, two hours, 110km, up to three daily) and Maribor (€7.20, two hours, 71km, two or three daily).

You can call a taxi in Slovenj Gradec on ☎ 041 645 901.

Prekmurje

Prekmurje is Slovenia's 'forgotten' corner – mostly a broad farmed plain that extends for kilometres 'beyond the Mura River' (as its name suggests). Its isolation is rooted in history; until 1924 not a single bridge spanned the sluggish Mura River and crossings were made by ferry. As a result, Prekmurje has preserved some traditional music, folklore, architecture and a dialect unintelligible to other Slovenians.

Until the end of WWI, almost all of Prekmurje belonged to the Austro-Hungarian crown and a small Magyar minority still lives around the spa town of Lendava (Hungarian: Lendva), Slovenia's easternmost city, and Murska Sobota (Muraszombat). In many ways Prekmurje looks and feels more like Hungary than Slovenia, with its abundance of white storks (p278), large thatched farmhouses, a substantial Roma population and the occasional Hungarian-style *čarda* (inn) serving *golaž* (goulash) cooked with paprika.

For most Slovenes, Prekmurje brings to mind a rich pastry called *gibanica* and a people who are generally more volatile and quick-tempered than most others in the nation. For travellers the province is a springboard into Austria or Hungary and a place to relax and enjoy taking the waters at the thermal spas of Radenci, Moravske Toplice and Banovci.

HIGHLIGHTS

- Satisfy that sweet tooth with a helping of calorific *prekmurska gibanica*, pastry with poppy seeds, walnuts, fruit, cheese and cream
- Take the waters *au naturel* at the spa resort at **Banovci** (p276)
- Visit Prekmurje's last remaining **floating mill** (p279) on the Mura River near Veržej
- Admire the wonderful 14th-century **frescoes** (p276) at the Church of St Martin in Martjanci
- Marvel at the arrival of the **storks** (p278), those big white birds with long skinny legs so responsible for the population explosion

ITINERARY

GOING POTTY

One Day / Prekmurje

From **Murska Sobota** (**1**; opposite), head north along route 232 and from **Martjanci** (**2**; p276), with its important Gothic church, head east along route 442 to the thermal spa of **Moravske Toplice** (**3**; p279). **Tešanovci** (**4**), a couple of kilometres east, is noted for its *lončarstvo* (pottery).

About 2.5km further east is the village of **Bogojina** (**5**) and its Parish Church of the Ascension, which was redesigned by Jože Plečnik around 1926. To the original Romanesque and baroque structure, Plečnik added two asymmetrical aisles and a round tower reminiscent of a crow's nest on a ship. The interior is an odd mixture of black marble, brass, wood and terracotta; the oak-beamed ceiling is fitted with Prekmurje ceramic plates and jugs, as is the altar.

Filovci (**6**), 2km past Bogojina, is famed for its *črna keramika* (black pottery). **Keramika Bojnec** (☎ 041 330 987; www.bojnec.com; Filovci 20; admission €2.50), 200m southwest of the main road, asks visitors to watch them work here at the ancient kiln in the *skanzen* (open-air museum displaying village architecture) over the road, where there's a Pannonian homestead with two thatched buildings and a small shop.

Carry on southeast to **Dobrovnik** (**7**), which has a couple of decent roadside *gostilne* (p280) and, in one of those 'only-when-travelling' moments, a large nursery called **Ocean Orchids** (☎ 02-573 73 05; www.oceanorchids.si; admission free; 8am-5pm Mon-Fri, to 4pm Sat) at house No 297 with a *tropski vrt* (tropical garden) worth a detour.

From here route 439 leads southwest to **Beltinci** (**8**), known to philatelists as the place where one of the 1918 provisional stamps was overprinted on Hungarian stamps by the Serbian occupation forces in WWI. Southwest at **Ižakovci** (**9**) is one of the last floating mills (p279) on the Mura, the **Island of Love Mill** (Otok Ljubezni Mlin; ☎ 02-541 35 80; www.beltinci.si; Mladinska ulica 2; admission €2.50; 9am-6pm Apr-Jun, Sep & Oct, to 8pm Jul & Aug), including a small museum and a raft ride across the Mura. Murska Sobota and its 16th-century castle are just 8km to the northwest of Beltinci.

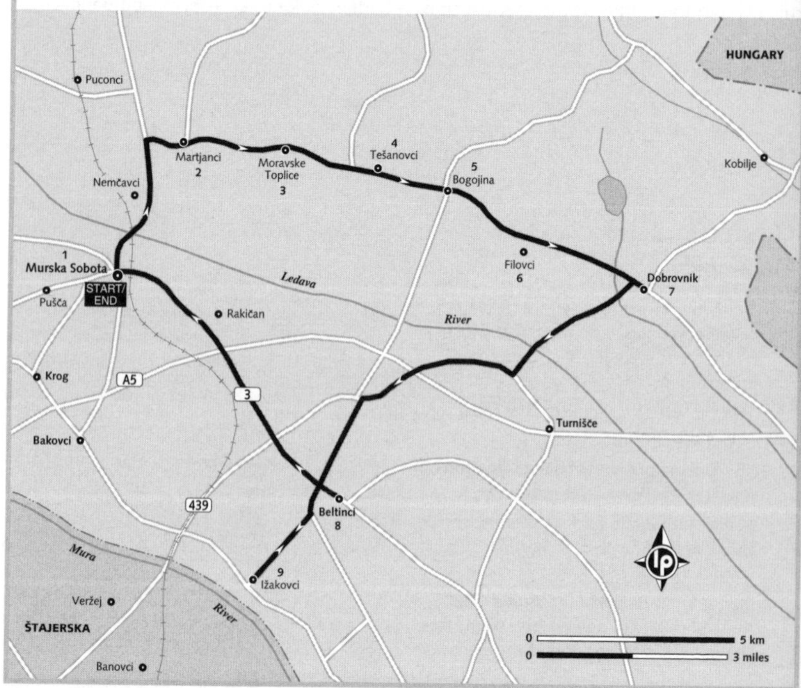

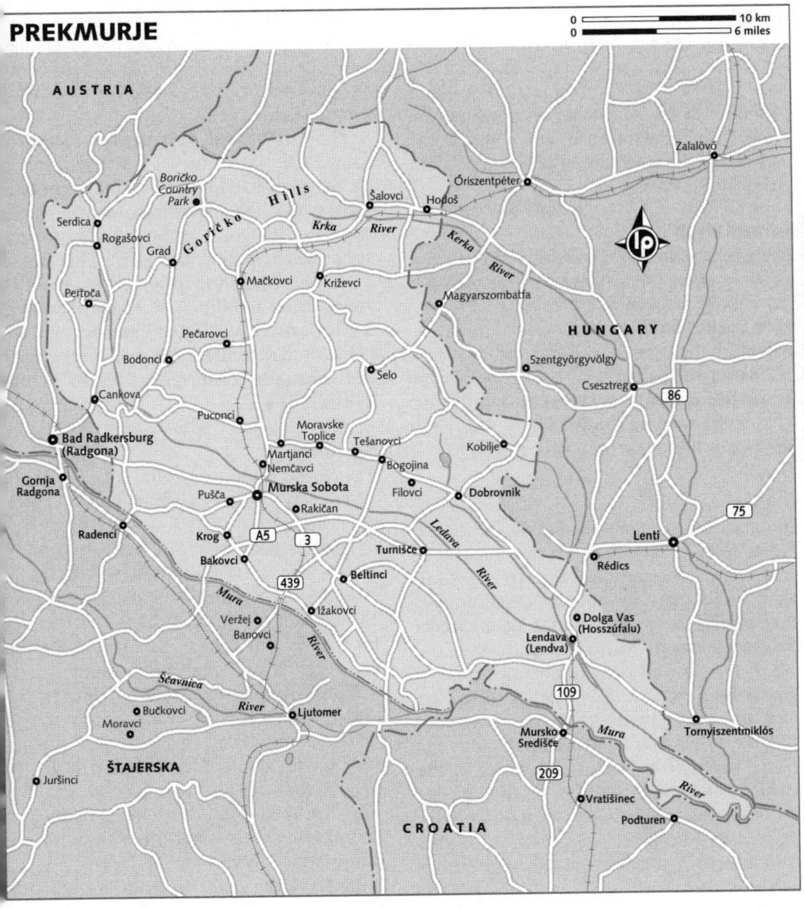

MURSKA SOBOTA

☎ 02 / pop 12,135 / elev 189m

Slovenia's northernmost city, Murska Sobota is unusual in mostly Alpine Slovenia because it is situated on a plain flatter than a *palačinka,* a pancake filled with jam or nuts and topped with chocolate that is so popular here. Today, the capital and administrative centre of Prekmurje itself has little to recommend it except for its odd architectural mix of neoclassical, Secessionist and 'socialist baroque' buildings. But the surrounding countryside, potters' villages and an embarrassment of thermal spas make it an enviable springboard for the entire surrounding region.

History

The town of Murska Sobota was once little more than a Hungarian market town – its name in both Slovene and Hungarian (Muraszombat) means 'Mura Saturday', which indicated the day when the market took place – until two pivotal events last century. The first was the opening of the railway in 1907, which linked Murska Sobota with Hungary proper via Šalovci to the northeast. The second event was ultimately even more significant for the city. With the formation of the Kingdom of Serbs, Croats and Slovenes in 1918 and the transfer of territory, Murska Sobota found itself more or less in the centre of Prekmurje and development really then took off.

Orientation

Trg Zmage (Victory Sq), the centre of Murska Sobota, lies southeast of large, shady Mestni Park (City Park). The bus station is 400m to the south on Slomškova ulica behind the Hotel Diana. The train station is 600m southeast of Trg Zmage at the eastern end of Ulica Arhitekta Novaka.

Information

Dobra Knjiga (☎ 522 37 22; Lendavska ulica 1; ⌚ 7am-6pm Mon-Fri, 8am-noon Sat) Central bookshop with regional maps for hiking in Prekmurje.
Nova Ljubljanska Banka (Trg Zmage 7)
Post office (Trg Zmage 6)
SKB Banka (Kocljeva ulica 9)
Tourist Information Centre Murska Sobota (☎ 534 11 30; tic.sobota@siol.net; Zvezda ulica 10; ⌚ 9am-7pm Mon-Fri, 8am-1pm Sat) Just north of the bus station.

Sights

Renaissance-style **Murska Sobota Castle** (Grad Murska Sobota), a sprawling manor house with an arcaded courtyard in the centre of Mestni Park and dating from the mid-16th century, now houses the award-winning **Murska Sobota Regional Museum** (Pokrajinski Muzej Murska Sobota; ☎ 527 17 06; www.pok-muzej-ms.si; Trubarjev drevored 4; adult/student & child €3/2; ⌚ 9am-5pm Tue-Fri, 9am-1pm Sat & Sun Sep-Jun, 10am-4pm Tue-Fri, 9am-noon Sat & Sun Jul & Aug), which tells the story of life along the Mura River, from prehistoric times to the early 1990s in 15 ground-floor rooms. The ethnographic exhibitions will look familiar to anyone who has visited such collections in southern Transdanubia over the border in Hungary.

At the eastern entrance to Mestni Park the **Victory Monument** is an impressive (if anachronistic) grouping of heavy artillery and Yugoslav partisans and Soviet soldiers in stone that somehow remained while the rest of Slovenia was 'spring cleaning' after independence. Opposite the park is the neo-Gothic **Evangelical Church** (1910), the main Lutheran seat in Slovenia (the majority of Slovenian Protestants, who number about 18,000, live in Prekmurje). The interior, painted with geometric shapes and floral motifs in muted shades of blue, green, brown and gold, is a welcome change from the overwrought baroque gold and marble decor found in most Catholic churches here.

The **Murska Sobota Gallery** (Galerija Murska Sobota; ☎ 522 38 34; www.galerija-ms.si; Kocljeva ulica 7; admission varies; ⌚ 10am-6pm Tue-Fri, 9am-noon Sat Sep-Jun, 10am-4pm Tue-Fri, 9am-noon Sat Jul & Aug), the best galler in Prekmurje, has a permanent collectio of 550 works (mostly sculpture) as well a rotating exhibits.

The **Parish Church of St Martin** in **Martjan** (pop 520), 4km north of Murska Sobot on the road to Moravske Toplice, contain wonderful 14th-century frescoes by Johanne Aquila of Radgona, painted on the sanctu ary's vaulted ceiling and walls. They depic angels bearing inscriptions, the Apostles scenes from the life of St Martin and eve a self-portrait of Master Johannes himsel Look for the centuries-old graffiti on the eas wall, including a Hungarian visitor Matija Vörös in 1644.

Sleeping

The closest camping ground is Camp Term 3000 at Moravske Toplice (p280), 7km to the northeast.

Terme Banovci (☎ 513 14 00; www.terme-banovci.s campsite per person €13; ⌚ late Mar-Oct; Ⓟ) Som 59 of the 130 sites at this small spa near Verže 13km south of Murska Sobota, are reserve for naturists. The price includes entry to th spa's thermal and swimming pools.

Dijaški Dom Murska Sobota (☎ 530 03 10; ww .d-dom.ms.edus.si; Tomšičeva ulica 15; dm per person €18 ⌚ late Jul–Aug; Ⓟ) This student dormi tory southwest of the centre with 40 tri ple rooms accepts travellers in summe only, although there is usually a handful o rooms available at other times as well. It ha laundry facilities.

Hotel Zvezda (☎ 539 15 73; www.hotel-zvezda.si, i Slovene; Trg Zmage 8; s/d €31/52) After well over decade in the wilderness, this 36-room cara vanserai has reopened and it's more of th same – just a bunch of rooms above a pub restaurant of the same name. Still, the pric is right.

Hotel Štrk (☎ 525 21 58; www.gostilna-lovenja .com; Polana 40; s/d €35/60; Ⓟ) Th accommodation part of the Lovenjakov Dvo (Lovenjak Court) tourist house (opposite) this guest house situated 4km northeast o Murska Sobota has two dozen rooms tha boast remarkable special features – from furnishings taken from a nearby castle (No 24) and views of nesting storks (No 21), to waterbeds, balconies and old tile stoves The thermal water in the pool comes from Moravske Toplice.

Hotel Diana (☎ 514 12 00; www.hotel-diana.si; ɔvenska ulica 52; s/d/ste €47/76/162; P ✕ 💻 ♿) he 95 rooms in Murska Sobota's anchor otel are bright and airy but get no points ɔr decor; they're in a nondescript concrete lock in the centre of town. It has a glassed-ı swimming pool, sauna and fitness room s well as a decent pizzeria (pizzas €5 to €7) pen seven days of the week.

ating

krepčevalnica Grill (☎ 524 18 50; Kocljeva ulica 5; dishes ɔm €3.50; ⏰ 6am-6pm Mon-Fri, 6.30am-1pm Sat) This ıexpensive *bife* (snack bar) in the market outh of Trg Zmage serves fish dishes as well s Balkan-style grills.

Mini Restavracija Rajh (☎ 523 12 38; Cvetkova ulica 1; starters €4-7, pizza & pasta €4.80-7.30; ⏰ 10am-10pm ue-Fri, from 11.30am Sat, from 4pm Sun) A self-styled mini-restaurant' on the corner of Lendavska ılica, Rajh is an upmarket *špagetarija* nd *picerija*.

Zlati Petelin (☎ 523 17 90; Lendavska ulica 39e; tarters €1.60-3.20, mains €4-9.20) The Golden Cock s a Chinese restaurant on the main drag nto town that serves up the usual range of rather toned-down Chinese dishes amid garish surroundings.

our pick **Gostilna Lovenjak** (☎ 525 21 53; starters €6.50-12.70, mains €7.50-16.10; ⏰ 11am-10pm Mon-Thu, 11am-midnight Fri & Sat, 11am-6pm Sun) This excellent, very atmospheric *gostilna* in the Lovenjakov Dvor tourist house serves such Prekmurje favourites as *bograč golaž* (Hungarian-style goulash soup), roast suckling pig served with noodles, Gypsy-style pork with garlic, Prekmurje ham, fresh Dalmatian fish and seafood at the weekend and, for dessert, the indecently rich *prekmurska gibanica*. Be sure to book for the Sunday buffet lunch and grab a table under the grape arbour. There's live music at the weekend.

Gostilna Rajh (☎ 543 90 98; Soboška ulica 32; meals from €20; ⏰ 10.30am-10pm Tue-Sat, 11am-4pm Sun) In Bakovci, a village 5km to the southwest, this *gostilna* (inn-like restaurant) specialises in local dishes and boasts a large cellar of regional wines.

There's a **Mercator** (Lendavska ulica 21; ⏰ 7am-9pm) northeast of the centre and open till late daily.

MURSKA SOBOTA

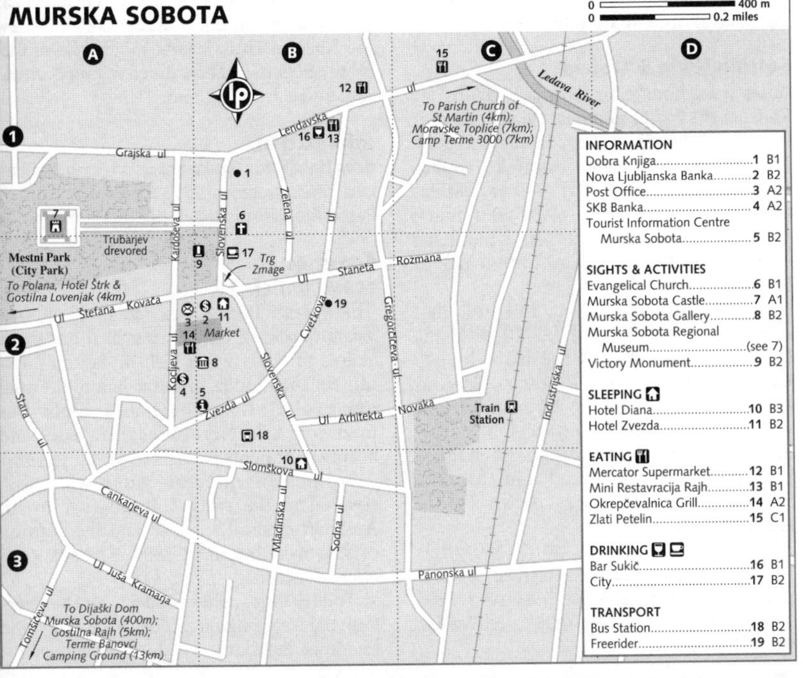

WHITE STORKS

The white stork (*Ciconia cicconia*), or *beli štrk* in Slovene, is Prekmurje's most beloved symbol. Country people consider it an honour for a pair to nest on the rooftop, and the distinctive birds with black-and-white feathers and long bills and legs are thought to bring good luck (not to mention babies). The storks arrive in spring – usually March or April – and spend the warm summer months here. When mid-August arrives, instinct tells the birds – some of them just a few months old – to fly south for a two- or three-year, 12,000km trek to sub-Saharan Africa, from where they return to Prekmurje when they are ready to breed.

Storks build their nests on church steeples, rooftops or telephone poles, and normally return to the same one every year. The nest is repaired or rebuilt every year, and some can weigh as much as 500kg. Storks live on a diet of worms, grasshoppers, frogs and small rodents, which are most easily found in the region's meadows. If food is scarce, however, it is not unknown for parents to turf their fledglings out of the nest.

The number of storks in Slovenia – currently 235 pairs with 37% (87 pairs) breeding in Prekmurje – has grown over the past two decades as it has throughout Europe. Nevertheless, the white stork remains a vulnerable species primarily because its hunting and breeding grounds – the meadows – are being destroyed, dried out and regulated.

Drinking

City (Slovenska ulica 27; 7am-9pm Mon-Fri, to 1pm Sat & Sun) Essentially a stylish cafe with drinks, City also serves snacks and is a convenient distance to the museum.

Bar Sukič (☎ 523 12 58; Lendavska ulica 14; 5.30am-10pm Mon-Fri, 6am-3pm Sat) This convivial cafe-bar has a large open terrace fronting the main thoroughfare into town.

Getting There & Around

Buses leave hourly for Gornja Radgona via Radenci (€2.75, 20 minutes, 19km), Maribor (€6.30, 1¼ hours, 59km), Lendava (€3.60, 30 minutes, 29km) and Moravske Toplice (€1.80, 15 minutes, 10km). Other destinations include Dobrovnik (€2.70, 30 minutes, 18km, up to seven a day) and Ljubljana (€16.80, 4¼ hours, 199km, one a day at 5.45am via Maribor and Celje).

Murska Sobota is on a rail link that connects it with Ormož (€2.90 to €5.90, 45 minutes, 39km) on the main line to Ljubljana (€11 to €16, 4¼ hours, 216km) and Maribor (€6 to €7.50, 1¾ hours, 98km) and Vienna. There are up to eight departures a day, and the train stops at Beltinci, Ljutomer and Veržej. From Murska Sobota the train carries on to Hodoš and Budapest.

You can order a taxi on ☎ 051 300 601.

You can rent bikes from **Freerider** (☎ 524 15 68; www.freerider-on.net, in Slovene; Cvetkova ulica 2; regular/mountain bikes per hr €3/5, per day €10/18; 10am-6pm Mon-Fri, 10am-1pm Sat).

RADENCI

☎ 02 / pop 2200 / elev 208m

Radenci is best known for its health resort, parts of which still feel like a full-of-itself 19th century spa town. Indeed, as one Slovenian wag put it: 'Radenci remains the preserve of highbrow intellectuals and rumble-tumble chamber music'. But when most Slovenes hear the name they think of Radenska Tri Srca – the 'Radenci Three Hearts' mineral water that is bottled here and consumed in every restaurant and cafe in the land.

Information

Nova Ljubljanska Banka (Panonska cesta 7) Near the main entrance to the spa.

Post office (Panonska cesta 5) Next door to the bank.

Activities

TERME RADENCI

The **Radenci Thermal Spa** (☎ 520 27 20; www.zdravilisce-radenci.si; Zdraviliško naselje 12) has three claims to fame: water rich in carbon dioxide for drinking; mineral-laden thermal water (41°C) for bathing; and sulphurous mud from Lake Negova for therapeutic and beauty treatments.

Springs of mineral water were discovered in the early 19th century by an Austrian medical student, and the bottling of Radenska began in 1869. The spa itself opened in 1882.

Today, thoroughly modern blocks overlook the few remaining older Victorian-style buildings and a large wooded park with paths, chapel and pavilions. The 1460-sq-metre wimming complex has 10 **pools** (🕑 9am-9pm n-Thu, to 10pm Fri & Sat) of varying sizes, including rge indoor and outdoor thermal pools with mperatures of 30°C to 33°C, and glassed-in wimming pools with normal water. Guests an use the pools at will; outsiders pay €9.50 er day, €7.50 for three hours, and €6 after pm. There are also a half-dozen different ypes of **sauna** (per 3hr/day €13/17.50; 🕑 4-9pm Mon-u, 2-10pm Fri & Sat, 2-9pm Sun) and the new **Corrium ellness Centre**.

THER ACTIVITIES

he seven outdoor and indoor **tennis courts** st southeast of the hotel complex can be ented for €6/10 per hour during the day/ ight from May to September; they're a niform €16 per hour the rest of the year. ackets (€2) and balls are available from the **ennis school** (🕑 9am-9pm), which offers lessons t €25 per hour.

The spa rents **bicycles** for €2.50/5.50/8.50 er hour/three hours/day. Excellent **cycling xcursions** can be made into the surrounding wine country; head southwest along he *vinska cesta* (wine road) for about km to Janžev Vrh and an old vineyard ottage called Janžev Hram or maybe ven further south to Kapelski Vrh and vanjski Vrh. The region's most celebrated wine is a sparkling one – Zlata Radgonska Penina (p50).

leeping

There are lots of private rooms available on Panonska cesta to the west and south of the pa's main entrance; **house No 23** (☎ 565 15 77) harges from €20 per person.

Consolidation and renovation have reduced the number of **spa hotels** (☎ 520 27 20; www.zdravilisce-radenci.si; P ✖ 💻 ♿) open to the public recreationally to two: the three-star **Hotel Izvir** (s €66-71, d €112-122), with 128 rooms; and the 286-room, four-star **Hotel Radin** (s €70-75, d €120-130).

Eating & Drinking

Restavracija Park (☎ 520 10 00; set lunch/dinner €8.50/19; 🕑 10am-9pm Tue-Sun) In the heart of the resort's large wooded park and serving local specialities, the aptly named Park is a pleasant place for a meal in summer.

Pub Kavarna Vikend (☎ 566 93 95; Panonska cesta 2; 🕑 7am-11pm Mon-Thu, 7am-midnight Fri, 8am-midnight Sat, 9am-11pm Sun) This convivial pub-cafe with a large open-air terrace is just opposite the bank and post office, and around the corner from the main entrance to the Terme Radenci.

You'll find a **Mercator** (Panonska cesta 145; 🕑 7am-7pm Mon-Fri, 7am-noon Sat) supermarket on the main road near the bank and post office.

Getting There & Away

The bus station is opposite the main entrance to the spa. There are daily buses to Gornja Radgona (€1.80, eight minutes, 7km, hourly), Ljubljana (€16, four hours, 187km, two a day at 5.58am and 6.08am) via Maribor (€5.60, one hour, 47km) and Celje (€10.30, 2¼ hours, 112km). Murska Sobota (€2.30, 15 minutes, 12km) is served by six buses a day.

Passenger trains do not run on the Ljutomer–Gornja Radgona line that passes through Radenci; it is used for freight only.

You can order a taxi on 🕑 031 457 777 or 031 671 076.

MORAVSKE TOPLICE

☎ 02 / pop 760 / elev 201m

The thermal spa of Moravske Toplice, 7km northeast of Murska Sobota, boasts the hottest water in Slovenia: 72°C at its source but cooled to a body temperature of 38°C for use in its many pools and basins. Though it's one of the newest spas in the country – the spring was discovered in 1960 during exploratory oil drilling – many young Slovenes consider the clientele too geriatric for their liking, preferring

MURA MILLS & THRILLS

Floating mills, which date back to Roman times, were very popular on rivers that changed their course abruptly or swelled rapidly after rainfall, as they allowed millers to move to the best possible spots for milling. In Slovenia, floating mills were largely built on the Mura River; there were dozens of them in operation up to WWII. Today, the only ones left are the Island of Love Mill (p274) at Ižakovci southwest of Beltinci and the Babič Mill at Veržej. But even the latter cannot be classified as a fully 'floating mill' as only the mill wheel is in the water. The rest of it is firmly tethered to the riverbank.

the small partly *au naturel* spa at Banovci to the southwest. But Moravske Toplice is every bit a health resort geared for recreation, with enough upgraded sport facilities to cater to every taste.

Information

Nova Ljubljanska Banka (Kranjčeva ulica; 8am-noon & 3-5pm Mon-Fri) At the entrance to the Terme 3000 spa.
Post office (Kranjčeva ulica 5; 8-9.30am & 10am-6pm Mon-Fri, 8am-noon Sat) Next to the TIC.
Tourist Information Centre Moravske Toplice (TIC; 538 15 20; www.moravske-toplice.com; Kranjčeva ulica 3; 8am-8pm Mon-Fri, 7am-3pm Sat, 8am-2pm Sun Jul & Aug, 8am-6pm Mon-Fri, 7am-3pm Sat, 8am-2pm Sun Sep-Jun) On the main road northwest of the entrance to the Terme 3000 complex.

Activities

The **Terme 3000** (512 22 00; www.terme3000.si; Kranjčeva ulica 12; 8am-9pm May-Sep, 9am-9pm Oct-Apr) spa complex has 26 indoor and outdoor pools filled with thermal water, six slides, a water tower and – wait for it – sound and light special effects spread over a surface area of 5000 sq metres. The thermal water is recommended for relief of rheumatism and certain minor skin problems. Guests at the resort have free use of the pools and saunas; otherwise they cost €11.90/8.20 (after 3pm €9.90/7.70) per adult/child. The resort also has an 18-hole golf course, three tennis courts, a fitness room and saunas.

Terme Vivat (538 21 29; www.vivat.si; Ulica ob Igrišču 3; full day/after 3pm adult €10/3.50, child €6/5; 8am-8pm Mon-Thu, 8am-11pm Fri & Sat, 8am-9pm Sun), a much smaller and newer spa, has thermal indoor and outdoor pools (connected by a swimming channel), saunas and an ambitious wellness centre.

Sleeping

The TIC can organise private rooms for around €17 per person, while apartments for two work out to be from €30 to €50, depending on the length of stay.

All the accommodation here at **Terme 3000** (512 22 00; www.terme3000.si) shares the same contact numbers; prices vary according to the season and all prices quoted here except the camping ground are half board. The spa's 7-hectare camping ground, **Camp Terme 3000** (p person €16-17), can accommodate 800 guests an is open year-round. Use of the swimming poc nearby is included in the price. The attractiv **bungalows** (s €52-66, d €102-110;) at the re sort's Prekmurje Village (Prekmurska Vas) a done up to look like traditional peasant cot tages, with thatched roofs, cool whitewashe walls and a total of 78 double rooms. At th **Hotel Termal** (s €78-84, d €132-144;) about half of the 116 rooms have balconies The 151-room **Hotel Ajda** (s €91-96, d €154-16) is in a large, three-winge modern building of little interest but, wit four stars. Much better is the new **Hotel Livad Prestige** (s €100-105, d €170-182, ste €115-290) nex door, with 122 five-star rooms.

Eating

Opposite the spa's main entrance, **Gostiln Kuhar** (548 12 15; Kranjčeva 13; meals from €15; 9am 11pm Tue-Sun) is a decent and convenient place i which to sample Prekmurje's cuisine. It als has accommodation.

Two eateries with meals from €15 tha come highly recommended by locals includ **Gostilna Marič** (538 14 90; Sebeborci 46a; 8am 11pm Tue-Sun), with excellent *bograč* and mush room dishes in the village of Sebeborci, 4km t the northwest; and **Gostišče Oaza** (051 383 141 8.30am-10pm Tue-Thu, 8.30am-midnight Fri & Sat, 10am 10pm Sun), overlooking a tiny lake in Mljatinc just south of the pottery village Tešanovc about 3km southeast of Moravske Toplice.

Further afield in **Dobrovnik** (pop 1050) about 12km southeast of Moravske Toplice, there are a couple of decent roadside *gostilna* where a meal should cost less than €12. They are **Pri Lujzi** (579 90 06; Dobrovnik 273a; starters €4-7, mains €5-12; 7-1am Mon, Wed & Thu, 7-2am Fri & Sat, 8-1am Sun), with a small terrace overlooking the main road; and the larger **Lipot** (579 11 47; starters €4-6, mains €5-10; Dobrovnik 277a; 7am-10pm Tue-Thu, 7am-midnight Fri & Sat, 8am-9pm Sun).

Getting There & Around

Buses leave from Kranjčeva ulica up to six times a day for Murska Sobota (€1.80, 10 minutes, 7km) and Dobrovnik (€2.70, 10 minutes, 19km).

The TIC rents bicycles for €2/9 per hour/day.

Directory

CONTENTS

ACCOMMODATION

Accommodation in Slovenia runs the gamut from riverside camping grounds, hostels, mountain huts (for details see the boxed text, p65), cosy *gostišča* (inns) and farmhouses, to elegant castle hotels in Dolenjska and Štajerska, and five-star hotels in Ljubljana. Slovenia counts just over 82,500 beds in total – well over a third of them in hotels – so you'll usually have little trouble finding accommodation to fit your budget, except at the height of the season (July and August) on the coast, at Bled or Bohinj, or in Ljubljana.

Accommodation listings throughout this guide are ordered by price – from the cheapest to the most expensive. Very roughly, budget accommodation means a double room under €50, midrange is €51 to €100 and top end is anything over €100. Unless otherwise indicated, rooms include en suite toilet and bath or shower and breakfast.

Virtually every municipality in the land levies a tourist tax of between €0.50 and €1 per person per night. For stays of less than three nights, many pensions and almost all private rooms charge 30% to 50% more, although the percentage usually drops on the second night.

Camping

You'll find a conveniently located *kamp* (camping ground) in virtually every corner of the country, but there are about 40 registered ones; seek out the Slovenian Tourist Board's *Camping in Slovenia* brochure. And you don't always need a tent; a few grounds have inexpensive bungalows available for hire.

Camping grounds generally charge per person, whether you're in a tent or caravan. Prices vary according to the site and the season, but expect to pay anywhere from €5 to €17.50 per person (children are usually charged 20% to 50% of the adult fee). Most of the official camping grounds offer discounts of 5% to 10% to holders of the Camping Card International (CCI; see p285).

Almost all sites close between mid-October and mid-April. Camping 'rough' is illegal in Slovenia, and this is enforced, especially around Bled.

Farmhouses

Hundreds of working farms in Slovenia offer accommodation to paying guests, and for a truly relaxing break they can't be beaten. You stay either in private rooms in the farmhouse itself or in Alpine-style guesthouses somewhere nearby. Many of the farms offer activities such as horse riding, kayaking, trekking or cycling and allow you to help out with the farm chores if you feel so inclined. This is how your humble author first discovered Slovenia.

Expect to pay about €15 per person in a room with shared bathroom and breakfast (from €20 for half-board) in the low season (September to mid-December and mid-January to June), rising in the high season (July and August) to

PRACTICALITIES

- Use the metric system for weights and measures (see inside front cover for conversions).
- Plug your hairdryer or laptop into a standard European adapter with two round pins before connecting to the electricity supply (220V, 50Hz AC).
- Read any of the following: *Slovenia Times* (www.sloveniatimes.com; €4.80), a fortnightly English-language magazine usually distributed for free; *Sinfo* (www.ukom.gov.si), a free government-produced monthly magazine about Slovenian politics, environment, culture, business and sport; and *Slovenian Business Report* (www.sbr.si), a quarterly publication with a cover price of €12 but usually available for free at top-end hotels.
- Listen to the news bulletin broadcast in English year-round at 10.30pm on Radio Slovenija 1 (88.5, 90.0, 90.9, 91.8, 92.0, 92.9, 94.1, 96.4 MHz FM and 918 kHz AM). In July and August Radio Slovenija 1 and Radio Slovenija 2 (87.8, 92.4, 93.5, 94.1, 95.3, 96.9, 97.6, 98.9 and 99.9 MHz FM) broadcast a weather report in English at 7.10am and Radio 2 broadcasts traffic conditions after each news bulletin from Friday afternoon to Sunday evening. In summer Radio Slovenia International (RSI) has hourly news bulletins in English and German on 91.1, 93.4, 98.9 and 102.8 MHz FM. Visit the RTV Slovenija (www.rtvslo.si) website.

a minimum €17 per person (from €25 for half-board). Apartments for groups of up to eight people are also available. There's no minimum stay, but you usually must pay 30% more if you stay fewer than three nights.

For more information, contact the **Association of Tourist Farms of Slovenia** (Združenje Turističnih Kmetij Slovenije; ☎ 03-425 55 11, 041 435 528; www.farmtourism.si; Trnoveljska cesta 1, 3000 Celje) or check out the Slovenian Tourist Board's *Friendly Countryside* brochure, which lists upwards of 300 farms with accommodation.

Hostels & Student Dormitories

Slovenia's growing stable of hostels includes Ljubljana's trendy Celica (p90), the stunning Situla (p214) in Novo Mesto and the three branches of the Alibi chain (p183) in Piran. Throughout the country there are *dijaški dom* (college dormitories) or *študentski dom* (student residences) moonlighting as hostels for visitors in July and August. Unless stated otherwise hostel rooms share bathrooms. Hostels usually cost from €15 to €22; prices are at their highest in July and August and during the Christmas break.

Some three dozen hostels nationwide are registered or affiliated with the Maribor-based **Hostelling International Slovenia** (Popotniško Združenje Slovenije; ☎ 02-234 21 37; www.youth-hostel.si; Gosposvetska cesta 84). In Ljubljana contact Erazem (p75). You are not required to have a Hostelling International (HI) card to stay at hostels in Slovenia, but it sometimes earns you a discount or cancellation of the tourist tax.

Hotels

Rates at Slovenia's hotels vary seasonally with July and August the peak season an September/October and May/June the shoulder ones. Ski resorts such as Kranjska Gor and Maribor Pohorje also have a peak seaso from December to March. In Ljubljana price are generally constant throughout the year though weekends are often cheaper at top-en hotels. Many resort hotels, particularly on th coast, are closed in winter.

There's a new crop of destination hotels - places you'd travel a great distance just t stay in. These include Ljubljana's Allegr (p91) and Antiq (p91) hotels, Dobra Vil (p151) in Bovec and the Hotel Balnea (p210 in Dolenjske Toplice. Other fine and/or romantic places to stay include the country' castle hotels such as those at Otočec (p216 and Mokrice (p224).

Mountain Huts

Mountain huts are ranked according to category in Slovenia. A hut is Category I if it is a a height of over 1000m and is more than on hour from motorised transport. A Categor II hut is within one hour's walking distanc from motorised transport. A Category III hu can be reached by car or cable car directly.

A bed for the night runs from €18 to €27 i a Category I hut, depending on the numbe of beds in the room, and from €12 to €20 in Category II. Category III huts are allowed t set their own prices but usually cost less tha Category I huts.

For more details see Bedding Down on High boxed text, p65, in the Slovenia Outdoors chapter.

Pensions & Guest houses

Pensions and guest houses go by several names in Slovenia. A *penzion* is, of course, a pension, but more commonly it's called a *gostišče* – a rustic (or made to look rustic) restaurant with *prenočišče* (accommodation) upstairs or somewhere in a separate building. They are more expensive than hostels but cheaper than hotels, and they might be your only option in small towns and villages. Generally speaking, a *gostilna* serves food and drink only, but some might have rooms as well. The distinction between a *gostilna* and a *gostišče* isn't very clear – even to most Slovenes.

Private Rooms & Apartments

You'll find private rooms and apartments available through tourist offices and travel agencies in most towns. Make sure you understand exactly where you'll be staying; in cities, some private rooms are located quite far from the centre. The Slovenian Tourist Board's brochure *Rates for Accommodation in Private Rooms and Apartments* is useful, as it provides a photo and the location of the house along with the rates of its rooms and/or apartments.

You don't have to go through agencies or tourist offices; any house with a sign reading 'Sobe' or 'Zimmer frei' means that rooms are available. The only advantage to this is that, depending on the season, you might save yourself a little money by going directly.

In Slovenia, *registered* private rooms and apartments are rated with from one to four stars. Prices vary greatly according to the town and season, but typical rates range from around €15 to €30 for a single and €25 to €40 for a double.

> **BOOK ACCOMMODATION ONLINE**
>
> For more accommodation reviews and recommendations by Lonely Planet authors, check out www.lonelyplanet.com/hotels. You'll find the true, insider lowdown on the best places to stay. Reviews are thorough and independent. Best of all, you can book online.

The price quoted is usually for a minimum stay of three nights. If you're staying a shorter time, you'll have to pay 30% and sometimes as much as 50% more the first night and 20% to 30% extra the second and third. The price of a private room never includes breakfast (from €4 to €6 when available) or tourist tax.

Some agencies and tourist offices also have holiday apartments available that can accommodate up to six people. One for two/four people could go for as low as €35/50.

ACTIVITIES

Known as 'Europe's activities playground', Slovenia offers an extensive range of outdoor activities, from skiing, climbing and cycling to bird-watching, diving and 'taking the waters' at one of the nation's many spas. For details, see the Slovenia Outdoors chapter (p63).

BUSINESS HOURS

With rare exceptions, the *delovni čas* (opening times) of any concern are posted on the door. *Odprto* means 'open' while *zaprto* is 'closed'.

Grocery stores and supermarkets are usually open from 8am to 7pm on weekdays and 8am until 1pm on Saturday. In winter they may close an hour earlier. Some branches of the Mercator supermarket chain open from 8am to 11am or noon on Sunday.

Restaurant hours vary tremendously across the country but essentially are from 10am or 11am to 10pm or 11pm daily. Bars are equally variable but are usually open 11am to midnight Sunday to Thursday and to 1am or 2am on Friday and Saturday.

Bank hours vary, but generally they're from 8am or 8.30am to 5pm weekdays (often with a lunchtime break from 12.30pm to 2pm) and (rarely these days) from 8am until noon or 1pm on Saturday. The main post office in any city or town (almost always the ones listed in this book in the Information sections of the individual towns and cities) is open from 8am to 6 or 7pm weekdays and 8am until noon or 1pm on Saturday.

Museums are usually open from 10am to 6pm Tuesday to Sunday. Winter hours may be shorter (or they may open at weekends only) outside the big cities and towns.

CHILDREN

Travelling with children in Slovenia poses very few problems: the little ones receive discounts on public transport and entry to museums and attractions; shops like DM, the nationwide German-owned health and cosmetic store with five dozen branches across the country, stock basic supplies for children; and the general public attitude to kids is enthusiastic. Outside upmarket hotels, baby sitters are almost impossible to organise however.

All car-rental firms in Slovenia have children's safety seats for hire for around €35 per rental. Make sure you book them in advance; by law children must use such seats until age 12. The same goes for highchairs and cots (cribs); they're standard in some restaurants and hotels, but numbers are often quite limited.

When touring around don't try to overdo things; even for adults, packing too much into the time available can cause problems. And make sure the activities include the kids as well. Although the Slovenian Ethnographic Museum (p81) in Ljubljana has wonderful and very colourful hands-on exhibits for kids, balance a morning there with an afternoon at the Ljubljana Zoo (p84) on Rožnik Hill or at the huge Atlantis water park (p87) in the BTC City shopping mall. Include children in the trip planning; if they've helped to work out where you will be going, they'll be much more interested when they get there. Lonely Planet's *Travel with Children* is a good source of information.

CLIMATE CHARTS

In general, Slovenia is temperate with four distinct seasons, but the topography creates three individual climates. The northwest has an alpine climate with strong influences from the Atlantic and abundant precipitation. Temperatures in the alpine valleys are moderate in summer but cold in winter. The coast and a large part of Primorska as far as the Soča Valley has a Mediterranean climate with warm, sunny weather much of the year, and mostly mild winters (although the *burja*, a cold and dry northeast wind, can be fierce at times). Most of eastern Slovenia has a Continental climate with very hot summers and cold winters.

Depending on the region, Slovenia gets most of its rain off and on from late spring to autumn; precipitation varies but averages about 820mm in the east, 1200mm in the centre (Ljubljana), 750mm on the coast and 1500mm in the Alps. January is the coldest month, with an average temperature of -3°C to 5°C, and July is the warmest (17°C to 24°C). The mean average temperature is 12°C in Ljubljana, 7.5°C in the mountains and 14.5°C on the coast. The number of hours of sunshine per year ranges from 1900 to 2500, with Ljubljana at the low end of the scale and Portorož at the top. For more information on how the climate might affect your travel plans, see p16.

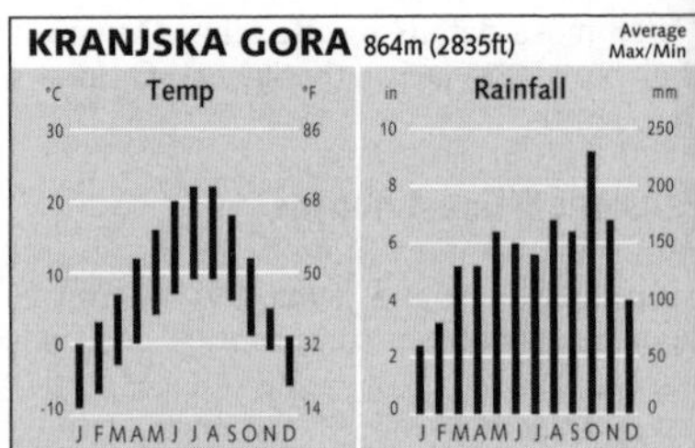

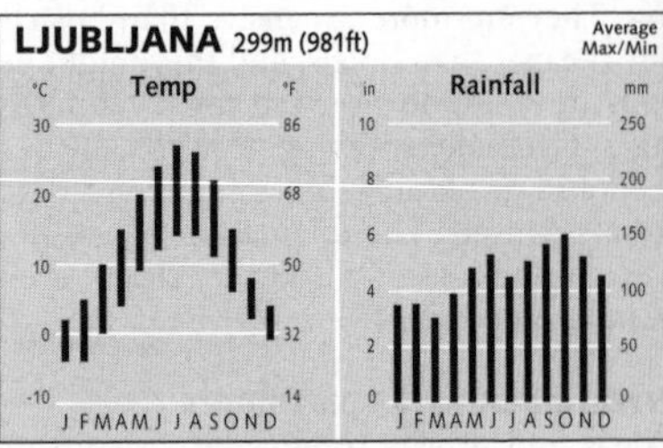

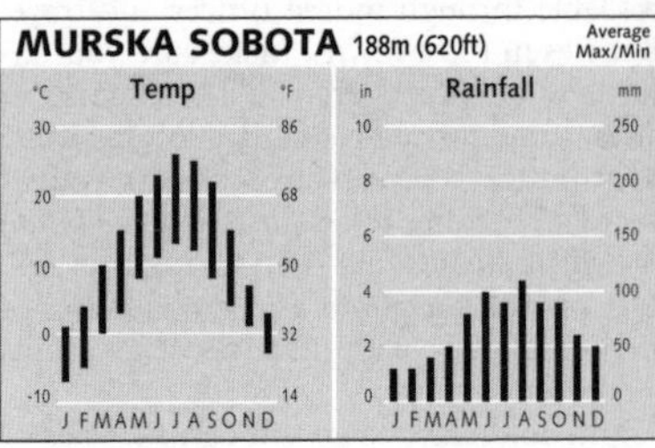

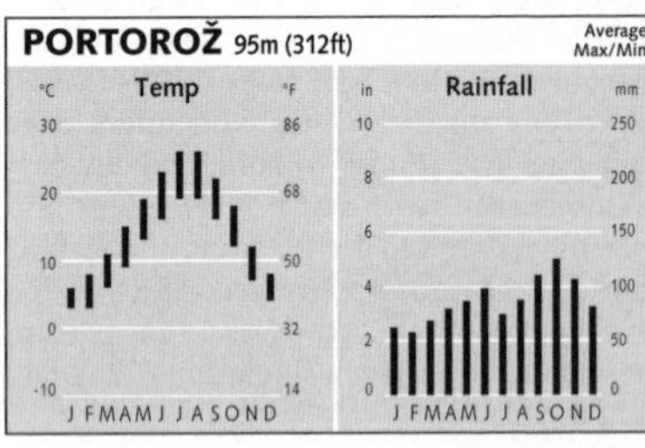

COURSES

The most famous and prestigious place to learn Slovene is the **Centre for Slovene as a Second/Foreign Language** (Center za Slovenščino kot Drugi/Tuji Jezik; Map p77; ☎ 01-241 86 47, 01-241 86 77; www.centerslo.net; 2nd fl, Kongresni trg 12) at the University of Ljubljana. There are a number of courses available, including a two-week (18 hours) winter course in January/February for €400, two- and four-week summer ones in July of 40 and 80 hours respectively for €530 and €900, and an intensive 12-week course running from September to December (240 hours; €1200) and a 14-week one (260 hours) from February to May (€1300). Prices do not include room and board. The centre also sponsors free 1½-hour introductory lessons in Slovene for tourists on at 5pm on Wednesday from May to September at the Slovenian Tourist Information Centre (p291) in Ljubljana.

Private schools offering courses in Slovene in Ljubljana include the academic **Miklošič Educational Centre** (Map pp72-3; ☎ 01-230 76 02; www.ism.si; Miklošičeva cesta 26), with courses of 30/85 hours starting at €240/590, and **Mint International House Ljubljana** (Map pp72-3; ☎ 01-300 43 00; www.mint.si; 1st fl, Kersnikova ulica 1), with courses of 51/63 hours costing from €277/333. Individual lessons cost from €33 an hour.

CUSTOMS REGULATIONS

Duty-free shopping within the European Union was abolished in 1999, and Slovenia, as an EU member since 2004, now adheres to those rules. You cannot buy tax-free goods in, say, Austria, Italy or Hungary and take them to Slovenia. However, you can still enter Slovenia with duty-free items from countries outside the EU (eg Australia, the USA, Croatia etc). The usual allowances apply: 200 cigarettes, 50 cigars, 100 cigarillos or 250g of loose tobacco; 2L of wine and 1L of spirits; 50g of perfume and 250cc of eau de toilette. The total value of the listed items must not exceed €175/90 for those over/under 15 years of age.

DANGERS & ANNOYANCES

Slovenia is not a violent or dangerous society. Police say that 90% of all crimes reported in Slovenia involve theft, so take the usual precautions. Be careful of your purse or wallet in busy areas like bus and train stations, and don't leave it unattended on the beach, or in a hut while hiking. Lock your car at all times, park in well-lit areas and do not leave valuables visible. Bike theft is also on the increase. Secure it at all times.

One rather irksome law here is that alcohol may not be purchased from a shop, off-license or bar for consumption off the premises by anyone of any age between the hours of 9pm and 7am. Of course you can drink to your heart's content in restaurants, bars, pubs and clubs until closing time, but not buy it and take it away. The 2003 ruling follows a number of horrific car accidents involving young people who had consumed alcohol bought at popular round-the-clock convenience stores.

DISCOUNT CARDS

For details about the excellent-value Ljubljana Card, see p71.

Camping Card International

The **Camping Card International** (CCI; www.campingcardinternational.com), which is basically a camping-ground ID, is available free from local automobile clubs, local camping federations such as the UK's **Caravan Club** (www.caravanclub.co.uk) and sometimes on the spot at selected camping grounds. They incorporate third-party insurance for damage you may cause, and many camping grounds in Slovenia offer discounts of 5% or 10% if you sign in with one. For a list, contact the **Caravaning Club Slovenije** (CCS; www.ccs-si.com).

Hostel Card

No hostel in Slovenia requires you to be a Hostelling International (HI) cardholder or member of related hostel association, but they sometimes offer a discount if you are. Hostelling International Slovenia (see p282) in Maribor and Erazem (p75) in Ljubljana sell hostel cards for those aged up to 15 (€5.50), 16 to 29 (€7.50) and over 30 (€9.20).

Student, Youth & Teacher Cards

The **International Student Identity Card** (ISIC; www.isic.org; €10), a plastic ID-style card with your photograph, provides bona fide students many discounts on certain forms of transport and cheap admission to museums and other sights. If you're aged under 26 but not a student, you can apply for ISIC's International Youth Travel Card (IYTC; €10) or the Euro<26 card (€17) issued by the European Youth Card Association (EYCA), both of which offer the same discounts as the student card. Teachers can apply for the International Teacher Identity Card (ITIC; €12).

EMBASSIES & CONSULATES

Selected countries with representation in Ljubljana appear below. If telephoning from outside the capital but still within Slovenia, remember to dial 01 first. From outside Slovenia dial 386-01 then the number.

Australia Consulate (off Map pp72-3; ☎ 425 42 52; Dunajska cesta 50; 🕒 9am-1pm Mon-Fri)
Austria Embassy (Map pp72-3; ☎ 479 07 00; Prešernova cesta 23; 🕒 8am-noon Mon-Thu, 8-10am Fri) Enter from Veselova ulica.
Canada Consulate (Map pp72-3; ☎ 252 44 44; 12th fl, Trg Republike 3; 🕒 9am-noon Mon-Fri)
Croatia Embassy (Map p85; ☎ 425 62 20; Gruberjevo nabrežje 6; 🕒 9am-1pm Mon-Fri); Consulate (Map p250; ☎ 02-234 66 86; Trg Svobode 3, Maribor; 🕒 10am-1pm Mon-Fri)
France Embassy (Map pp72-3; ☎ 479 04 00; Barjanska cesta 1; 🕒 8.30am-12.30pm Mon-Fri)
Germany Embassy (Map pp72-3; ☎ 479 03 00; Prešernova cesta 27; 🕒 9am-noon Mon-Thu, 9-11am Fri)
Hungary Embassy (off Map pp72-3; ☎ 512 18 82; Ulica Konrada Babnika 5; 🕒 8am-5pm Mon-Fri)
Ireland Embassy (Map pp72-3; ☎ 300 89 70; 1st fl, Palača Kapitelj, Poljanski nasip 6; 🕒 9.30am-12.30pm & 2.30-4pm Mon-Fri)
Italy Embassy (Map pp72-3; ☎ 426 21 94; Snežniška ulica 8; 🕒 9-11am Mon-Fri); Consulate (Map p173; ☎ 05-627 37 49; Belveder 2, Koper; 🕒 8.30am-noon Mon-Fri)
Netherlands Embassy (Map pp72-3; ☎ 420 14 61; 1st fl, Palača Kapitelj, Poljanski nasip 6; 🕒 9am-noon Mon-Fri)
New Zealand Consulate (off Map pp72-3; ☎ 580 30 55; Verovškova ulica 57; 🕒 8am-3pm Mon-Fri)
South Africa Consulate (Map pp72-3; ☎ 200 63 00; Pražakova ulica 4; 🕒 3-4pm Tue) In Kompas building.
UK Embassy (Map pp72-3; ☎ 200 39 10; 4th fl, Trg Republike 3; 🕒 9am-noon Mon-Fri)
USA Embassy (Map pp72-3; ☎ 200 55 00; Prešernova cesta 31; 🕒 9-11.30am & 1-3pm Mon-Fri)

FESTIVALS & EVENTS

For a list of Slovenia's most important, useful and/or enjoyable festivals and events, see p20.

FOOD & DRINK

Slovenia has a highly developed and varied cuisine and a wine-making tradition that goes back to the time of the Romans. For details see the Food & Drink chapter (p49).

EMERGENCY NUMBERS

Ambulance (Reševalci) ☎ 112
Fire brigade (Gasilci) ☎ 112
First aid (Prva Pomoč) ☎ 112
Police (Policija) ☎ 113 (emergencies)
Road emergency or towing (AMZS) ☎ 1987

In terms of cost, very roughly, a two-course sit-down meal for one person with a drink for under €15 in Slovenia is 'budget' (though you can eat 'cheaply' for less than that). A 'moderate' meal will cost up to €30. An 'expensive' meal is anything over that. Many restaurants offer an excellent-value set menu of two or even three courses at lunch.

GAY & LESBIAN TRAVELLERS

Slovenia has no sodomy laws. There's a national gay rights law in place that bans discrimination in employment and other areas on the basis of sexual preference, and homosexuals are allowed in the military. In recent years a highly visible campaign against homophobia has been put in place across the country. Outside Ljubljana, however, there is little evidence of a gay presence, much less a lifestyle.

Roza Klub (Map pp72-3; ☎ 01-430 47 40; Kersnikova ulica 4) in Ljubljana is made up of the gay and lesbian branches of **ŠKUC** (www.skuc.org), which stands for Študentski Kulturni Center (Student Cultural Centre) but is no longer student-orientated as such. It organises the gay and lesbian **Ljubljana Pride** (www.ljubljanapride.org) parade in late June and the **Gay & Lesbian Film Festival** (www.ljudmila.org/siqrd/fglf) in late November/early December. The gay male branch, **Magnus** (skuc magnus@hotmail.com), deals with AIDS prevention, networking and is behind the Kulturni Center Q (Q Cultural Centre) in Ljubljana's Metelkova Mesto (p98), which includes Klub Tiffany (p98) for gay men and Klub Monokel (p99) for gay women. Lesbians can contact the Ljubljana-based (and ŠKUC-affiliated) **LL** (www.ljudmila.org/lesbo) through the latter.

Kiss Legebrita (www.drustvo-legebitra.si), affiliated with the Student Organisation of the University of Ljubljana (Študentska Organizacija Univerze Ljubljani; ŠOU) is a youth group for lesbians, gays, bisexuals and transsexuals under 26. **Lingsium** (www.lingsium.org) is a similar and even more organised gay youth group in Maribor.

The website of the **Slovenian Queer Resources Directory** (www.ljudmila.org/siqrd) contains a lot of stuff, both serious and recreational, but it's often out of date and/or in Slovene only. Much more up to date and reliable for entertainment venues and parties is the **Slovenia for Gay Travellers** (www.sloveniaforgaytravelers.com) website. **Out in Slovenia** (www.outinslovenija.com), the first sports and recreational group for gays and lesbians in Slovenia is where to go for the latest on outdoor activities and events. A new monthly publication called **Narobe** (Upside Down; www.narobe.si) is in Slovene only, though you might be able to at least glean from the listings.

It's not a helpline as such but for advice ring **Mavrična Svetovalnica** (Rainbow Counselling; ☎ 031 258 585; 🕑 6-8pm Mon, Wed & Fri)

HOLIDAYS

Slovenia celebrates 14 *prazniki* (holidays) each year. If any of them fall on a Sunday, then the Monday becomes the holiday.

New Year's holidays 1 & 2 January
Prešeren Day (Slovenian Culture Day) 8 February
Easter & Easter Monday March/April
Insurrection Day 27 April
Labour Day holidays 1 & 2 May
National Day 25 June
Assumption Day 15 August
Reformation Day 31 October
All Saints Day 1 November
Christmas Day 25 December
Independence Day 26 December

Although it's not a public holiday, St Martin's Day (11 November), the day that fermenting grape juice officially becomes new wine, is almost marked as such (p53), and just about everyone has to have a sip or three.

On the eve of St Gregory's Day (11 March), all the children in certain Gorenjska towns and villages – Železniki is the most famous – set afloat hundreds of tiny boats bearing candles.

On Palm Sunday (the Sunday before Easter), people carry a complex arrangement of greenery, wood shavings and ribbons called a *butara* to church to be blessed. These bundles end up as home decorations or are placed on the graves of relatives.

Many towns celebrate Midsummer's Night (Kresna Noč; 23 June) with a large bonfire, and St John's Eve (30 April) is the night for setting up maypoles and more bonfires. A *žegnanje* is a fair or celebration held on the feast day of a church's patron saint. Naturally a lot of them take place throughout Slovenia on 15 August, the feast of the Assumption of the Virgin Mary.

INSURANCE

A travel insurance policy to cover theft, loss and medical problems is a good idea. There is a wide variety of policies available, so check the small print. EU citizens on public health insurance schemes should note that they're generally covered by reciprocal arrangements in Slovenia; see p302.

Some insurance policies specifically exclude 'dangerous activities', which can include motorcycling and even trekking, so check the small print.

You may prefer a policy that pays doctors or hospitals directly rather than you having to pay on the spot and claim later. If you have to claim later, make sure you keep all documentation. Some policies ask you to call back (reverse charges) to a centre in your home country, where an immediate assessment of your problem can be made. Check that the policy covers ambulances or an emergency flight home.

Paying for your airline ticket with a credit card often provides limited travel accident insurance, and you may be able to reclaim the payment if the operator doesn't deliver. Ask your credit-card company what it will cover.

For information on vehicle insurance, see p299.

INTERNET ACCESS

The internet has arrived in a very big way in Slovenia; some 56% of the population uses it regularly with 58% of all households having access to it. The useful **e-točka** (e-points; www.e-tocke.gov.si, in Slovene) website lists free access terminals, wi-fi hotspots and commercial internet cafes where you can log on across the nation.

Virtually every hotel and hostel in the land now has internet access – a computer for guests' use (free or for a small fee), wi-fi – or both. Most of the countries tourist information centres offer free (or very cheap) access and many libraries in Slovenia have free terminals and most cities and towns have at least one internet cafe (though they usually only have a handful of terminals). Check the Information section of cities and towns throughout the book.

If you have your own laptop and can't access a free server, log onto to Mobitel's wi-fi network **NeoWLAN** (☎ 041 700 700; www.neowlan.net), which has hotspots all over the country. You pay by prepaid NeoWLAN scratch cards available from kiosks and post offices or by credit card but it's not cheap: €3 for 30 minutes, €9 for two hours in one day and €15/19 for 24 hours over three/six days.

LAUNDRY

With a full 97% of all Slovenian households owning a washing machine – well, good luck trying to find a self-service laundrette! The best place to seek out do-it-yourself washers and dryers is at hostels, college dormitories and camping grounds; more and more such places now have them. There are a few commercial laundries in Ljubljana (p74) that will do your laundry reasonably quickly, but they are expensive, charging from €4.20 per kilogram. Hotel laundry service is even more costly.

LEGAL MATTERS

Persons violating the laws of Slovenia, even unknowingly, may be expelled, arrested or imprisoned. Penalties for possession, use or trafficking in illegal drugs in Slovenia are strict, and convicted offenders can expect heavy fines and even jail terms. The permitted blood-alcohol level for motorists is 0.05%, and it is strictly enforced, especially on motorways.

The age of consent for all sexual activity (ie heterosexual and homosexual) is 15 years.

MAPS

The **Geodesic Institute of Slovenia** (Geodetski Zavod Slovenije or GZS; www.gzs-dd.si), the country's principal map-making company, which also runs the Kod & Kam (p71) shop in Ljubljana, produces national (1:300,000; €8.10) and regional maps. Some two-dozen excursion maps at scales of 1:50,000 or 1:70,000 (€8.10) cover the whole country, and there are city plans with scales of 1:8000 to 1:20,000 (€5.45 to €7.70) for all the major towns. GZS's *Ljubljana* map (1:20,000; €7.70) with street index is excellent. The **Alpine Association of Slovenia** (Planinska Zveza Slovenije or PZS; www.pzs.si) produces 30 hiking maps (€8.10) with scales as large as 1:25,000.

Anyone planning to do a lot of driving in the country should pick up a copy of the 1:300,000 *Turistični Atlas Slovenija* (Tourist Atlas of Slovenia; €18.60) from GZS, which includes 14 city plans, or the more detailed 1:100,000 *Avtoatlas Slovenija* (Road Atlas of Slovenia; €28.90), with 73 1:12,500 maps of Slovenian cities and towns.

MONEY

Slovenia now uses the euro as its legal tender.

One euro is divided into 100 cents. There are seven euro notes in different colours and sizes; they come in denominations of €5, €10,

ADDRESSES & PLACE NAMES

Streets in Slovenian towns and cities are well signposted, although the numbering system can be a bit confusing with odd and even numbers sometimes running on the same sides of streets and squares.

In small towns and villages, streets are usually not named and houses are just given numbers. Thus Ribčev Laz 13 is house No 13 in the village of Ribčev Laz on Lake Bohinj. As Slovenian villages are frequently made up of one road with houses clustered on or just off it, this is seldom confusing.

Places with double-barrelled names such as Novo Mesto (New Town) and Črna Gora (Black Hill) start the second word in lower case (Novo mesto, Črna gora) in Slovene, almost as if the names were Newtown and Blackhill. This is the correct Slovene orthography, but we have opted to go with the English-language way of doing it to avoid confusion.

Slovene frequently uses the possessive (genitive) case in street names. Thus a road named after the poet Ivan Cankar is Cankarjeva ulica and a square honouring France Prešeren is Prešernov trg. Also, when nouns are turned into adjectives they often become unrecognisable. The town is 'Bled', for example, but 'Bled Lake' is Blejsko Jezero. A street leading to a castle *(grad)* is usually called Grajska ulica. A road going in the direction of Trieste (Trst) is Tržaška cesta, Klagenfurt (Celovec) Celovska cesta and Vienna (Dunaj) is Dunajska cesta. The words 'pri', 'pod' and 'na' in place names mean 'at the', 'below the' and 'on the' respectively.

20, €50, €100, €200 and €500. The designs on he recto (generic windows or portals) and erso (imaginary bridges, a map of the EU) re exactly the same in all 15 countries and ymbolise openness and cooperation.

The eight coins in circulation are in denominations of €1 and €2, then one, two, five, 0, 20 and 50 cents. The 'heads' side of the oin, on which the denomination is shown, s identical throughout the euro zone; the ails' side is particular to each member-state, hough euro coins can be used anywhere vhere euros are legal tender, of course.

In Slovenia, the €1 coin (silver centre with rassy outer ring) portrays the Protestant eformer and translator Primož Trubar 1508–86) and the Latin inscription Stati Inu Obstati (To Exist and Persevere). The verso of the €2 coin (brassy centre ringed with silver) shows the poet France Prešeren (1800–49) and a line from his poem *Zdravljica* (A Toast), which forms part of the Slovenian national anthem.

On the three lowest-denomination coins – €0.01, €0.02 and €0.05 (all copper) – are a stork, the stone where the 8th-century Carantanian dukes were installed, and *The Sower* by painter Ivan Grohar (1867–1911). The other three coins are brass. On the €0.10 coin is a design for a parliament by architect Jože Plečnik (1872–1957) that was never built and the words 'Katedrala Svobode' (Cathedral of Freedom). The €0.20 coin features a pair of Lipizzaner horses prancing. The stunning and very symbolic €0.50 coin shows Mt Triglav, the Cancer constellation (under which independent Slovenia was born) and the words 'Oj Triglav moj dom' (O Triglav, my home).

Exchange rates are given on the inside front cover of this book. For a general idea on what you might spend while visiting Slovenia, see p17.

ATMs

Automated teller machines (ATMs) – called *bančni avtomat* – are ubiquitous throughout Slovenia. If you have a card linked to either the Visa/Electron/Plus or the MasterCard/Maestro/Cirrus network and a PIN (personal identification number), then you can withdraw euros from almost any ATM in the country. Both Abanka and SKB Banka ATMs are linked to both networks; all banks mentioned in this guide have an ATM unless otherwise indicated.

Credit Cards

Visa, MasterCard/Eurocard and American Express credit cards are widely accepted at hotels, restaurants, shops, car-rental firms, petrol stations and travel agencies. Diner's Club is also accepted but less frequently.

Visa cardholders can get cash advances from any Abanka branch, Eurocard/MasterCard holders from a Nova Ljubljanska Banka or SKB Banka. American Express clients can get an advance from the main office of **Atlas Express** (Map pp72-3; ☎ 01-430 77 20; Slovenska cesta 56; 8am-5pm Mon-Fri) in Ljubljana, but the amount is usually limited to €600 in travellers cheques for Green Card holders, €1200 for Gold Card holders and €3600 for Platinum Card holders. American Express customers who want to report a lost or stolen card or travellers cheques should also call here or on ☎ 01-568 0300. They can both replace cards (although you must know the account number) and make refunds for lost or stolen American Express travellers cheques.

If you have problems with your Visa card, call the **A Banka Visa Centre** (☎ 01-471 81 00) in Ljubljana. Eurocard and MasterCard holders should call **Nova Ljubljanska Banka** (☎ 01-525 01 55) or **SKB Banka** (☎ 01-433 21 32). **Diners Club** (☎ 01-589 61 33) is based in Bežigrad, a northern suburb of Ljubljana.

Moneychangers

It is easy to change cash and travellers cheques at banks, post offices, tourist offices, travel agencies and private exchange offices. Look for the words *menjalnica* or *devizna blagajna* to guide you to the correct place or window. Most banks take a *provizija* (commission) of 1% on travellers cheques but usually nothing at all on cash. Tourist offices, travel agencies and exchange bureaus usually charge around 3%. Hotels can take as much as 5%.

Taxes & Refunds

Value-added tax (known as *davek na dodano vrednost* or DDV in Slovenia) is applied to the purchase of most goods and services at a standard rate of 20% (eg on alcoholic drinks, petrol and so on) and a reduced rate of 8.5% (eg on hotel accommodation, food, books, museum entrance fees etc). It is usually included in the quoted price of goods but not always, so beware.

Visitors who are not residents of the European Union can claim refunds on total purchases of around €65 (not including tobacco products or spirits) issued on one or more receipts by the same retailer/shop on the same day as long as they take the goods out of the country (and the EU) within 90 days. In order to make the claim, you must have a DDV-VP form or Global Tax-Free Shopping refund cheque correctly filled out by the salesperson at the time of purchase and have it stamped by a Slovenian customs officer at the border. You can then collect your refund – minus handling fee – from selected offices or have it deposited into your credit-card account. For information and the location of refund offices contact **Global Refund** (☎ 01-513 22 60; www.globalrefund.com; Goriška ulica 17) in Ljubljana.

Tipping

When a gratuity is not included in your bill, which may or may not be the case, paying an extra 10% is customary. If service is outstanding, you could go as high as 15%. With taxi drivers, you usually just round up the sum.

POST

The Slovenian postal system (Pošta Slovenije), recognised by its bright yellow logo, offers a wide variety of services – from selling stamps and telephone cards to making photocopies and changing money. The queues are never very long, but you can avoid a trip to the post office if you just want to mail a few postcards by buying *znamke* (stamps) at newsstands and dropping your mail into any of the yellow letterboxes on the street. Staff at post offices can sell you boxes.

Postal Rates

Domestic mail costs €0.20 to €0.30 for up to 20g depending on the size, €0.41 for up to 50g and €0.48 for up to 100g. Postcards are a uniform €0.26. For international mail, the rate is €0.45 for 20g or less, €0.92 for up to 100g and €0.35 for a postcard.

Sending & Receiving Mail

Look for the sign 'Pisma – Paketi' if you've got a *pismo* (letter) or *paket* (parcel) to post.

Poštno ležeče (poste restante) is kept at the main post office of a city or town. In the capital, address it to Glavni Pošta, Slovenska cesta 32, 1101 Ljubljana, where it will be held for 30 days.

SHOPPING

Although Ljubljana has a nice array of cra and souvenir shops, in general it's best to g to the source where you'll find the real thin and not mass-produced kitsch. In Gorenjsk go to Bohinj for carved wooden pipes wit silver lids and to Kropa for objects mad of wrought iron. Both Idrija and Železnik in Primorska specialise in lace. Ribnica i Dolenjska is famous for its *suha roba* ('dr goods' – wooden household utensils Rogaška Slatina in Štajerska for its crysta and Prekmurje for its Hungarian-style blac pottery. Some people think they're tacky, bu traditional *panjske končnice* (beehive panels painted with folk motifs make original an unusual souvenirs – especially the one show ing a devil sharpening a gossip's tongue o a grindstone.

The silver-filigree jewellery you'll se for sale in shops all over the country, bu especially on the coast, is not distinctivel Slovenian but a good buy nonetheles Almost all of the shops are owned and run b ethnic Albanians who brought the craft he from Kosovo.

Ski equipment and ski-wear are of ver high quality. Skis and snowboards are mad by **Elan** (www.elan.si) in Begunje na Gorenjsken near Bled, and ski boots and trekking shoe by **Alpina** (www.alpina.si) at Žiri, northea of Idrija.

Natural remedies, herbal teas, sea salt an apian products, such as beeswax, honey, po len, propolis and royal jelly, can be found i speciality shops around the country.

A bottle of quality Slovenian wine makes great gift. Buy it from a *vinoteka* or a deale with a large selection, such as Vinotek Movia or the Wine Cellars of Sloveni (Vinske Kleti Slovenije) in Ljubljana. A couple of the monasteries in Dolenjska the Cistercian one at Stična near Ivančn Gorica and the Carthusian one at Pleterje sell their own brand of firewater made fro fruits and berries. It's fragrant and ver potent stuff.

An excellent and very well-illustrated wor on the arts and crafts of Slovenia is *Craf and Treasures of Slovenia* (101 Zaklad) by th ethnologist Janez Bogataj. Other sources c information include the **Slovenian Chamber Craft & Small Businesses** (Obrtna Zbornica Slovenije; ww .ozs.si) and **Art & Craft Slovenija** (Rokodelstvo Slovenij www.rokodelstvo.si, in Slovene).

USEFUL TELEPHONE NUMBERS

Domestic directory assistance ☎ 1188
International directory assistance ☎ 1180
International operator/collect calls ☎ 115
Time/speaking clock (in Slovene) ☎ 195

ELEPHONE

ublic telephones in Slovenia don't accept pins; they require a *telefonska kartica* or *telkartica* (telephone card) available at all post ffices and some newsstands. Phonecards cost 2.70/4/7.50/14.60 for 25/50/100/300 *impulv* (impulses, or units). A three-minute local ll will cost just under €0.09 during peak mes (7am to 7pm weekdays) and €0.07 at ff-peak times.

A three-minute call from Slovenia to ustria, Croatia, Italy or Hungary will cost).37; to much of Western Europe, including e UK, as well as Canada and the USA, it's).42; to Australia €1.15; and to New Zealand, uth Africa and most of Asia €1.71. Rates are % cheaper on most calls between 7pm and m every day. Slovenian call boxes do not splay their telephone numbers, so it's impossble for the other party to phone you back.

To call Slovenia from abroad, dial the inrnational access code, ☎ 386 (the country de for Slovenia), the area code (minus the itial zero) and the number. There are six area des in Slovenia (01 to 05 and 07), and these e listed at the beginning of each city and wn section in this book. To call abroad from ovenia, dial ☎ 00 followed by the country d area codes and then the number. Numbers ginning with 80 in Slovenia are toll-free.

obile Phones

ore than half of all Slovenes – 58% to be ecise – have mobile phones, and network verage amounts to more than 95% of the untry. In fact, even certain businesses only ote mobile numbers, identified by the prefix 30 and 040 (SiMobil), 031, 041, 051 and 071 Aobitel) and 070 (Tušmobil).

Slovenia uses GSM 900, which is compatle with the rest of Europe and Australia it not with the North American GSM 1900 the totally different system in Japan. SIM rds with €5 credit are available for €12 om **SiMobil** (www.simobil.si) and for €17.50 from **Mobitel** (www.mobitel.si). Newcomer **Tušmobil** (www.tusmobil.sil) has them for under €10. Top-up scratch cards available at post offices, newsstands and petrol stations, cost €5, €10 and €20.

All three networks have outlets throughout Slovenia, including in Ljubljana:

Mobitel Centre (Mobitelov Center; Map p77; ☎ 01-472 24 76; www.mobitel.si; Trg Ajdovščina 1; 🕑 8am-8pm Mon-Fri, 8am-1pm Sat); Trubarjeva cesta (Map pp72-3; ☎ 031 357 555; Trubarjeva cesta 40; 🕑 9am-7pm Mon-Fri)

SiMobil (Halo Centre; Map pp72-3; ☎ 01-430 01 77; www.simobil.si; Slovenska cesta 47; 🕑 8am-7pm Mon-Fri); Čopova cesta (Map p77; ☎ 01-426 71 02; Čopova cesta 4; 🕑 8am-7pm Mon-Fri, 9am-1pm Sat)

Tušmobil (off Map pp72-3; ☎ 01-600 6000; www.tusmobil.sil; Bratislavska cesta 9; 🕑 9am-9pm Mon-Fri, 8am-9pm Sat, 9am-3pm Sun) In the BTC City shopping mall.

TIME

Slovenia lies in the Central European time zone. Winter time is GMT plus one hour while in summer it's GMT plus two hours. Clocks are advanced at 2am on the last Sunday in March and set back at the same time on the last Sunday in October.

Without taking daylight-saving times into account, when it's noon in Ljubljana, it's 11pm in Auckland, 1pm in Bucharest, 11am in London, 2pm in Moscow, 6am in New York, noon in Paris, 3am in San Francisco, 9pm in Sydney and 8pm in Tokyo.

Like some other European languages, Slovene tells the time by making reference to the next hour – not the previous one as in English. Thus 1.15 is 'one-quarter of two', 1.30 is 'half of two' and 1.45 is 'three-quarters of two'.

TOURIST INFORMATION

The **Slovenian Tourist Board** (Slovenska Turistična Organizacija, STO; ☎ 01-589 18 40; www.slovenia.info; Dunajska cesta 156) based in Ljubljana is the umbrella organisation for tourist promotion in Slovenia, and it can handle requests for information in writing or by email. The STO produces a number of excellent brochures, pamphlets and booklets in English, 17 of which can be ordered on its website. The site itself is not open to the public.

Walk-in visitors in Ljubljana can head to the **Slovenian Tourist Information Centre** (STIC; Map pp72-3; ☎ 01-306 45 75; www.slovenia.info; Krekov trg 10; 🕑 8am-9pm Jun-Sep, 8am-7pm Mon-Fri, 8am-3pm Sat Oct-May). In addition, the STO oversees another five dozen or so local tourist offices and bureaus called 'tourist information centres' (TICs) across the country; there are smaller, independent or community-run offices in other cities and towns. In the unlikely even that the place you're visiting doesn't have either, seek assistance at a branch of one of the nationwide travel agencies (eg Kompas) or from hotel or museum staff.

The best office in Slovenia for face-to-face information is the **Ljubljana Tourist Information Centre** (TIC; Map p77; ☎ 01-306 12 15; www.ljubljana-tourism.si; Kresija Bldg, Stritarjeva ulica; 8am-9pm Jun-Sep, 8am-7pm Oct-May) run by the Ljubljana Tourist Board (Zavod za Turizem Ljubljana). The staff know everything about the capital and almost as much about the rest of Slovenia. In summer the TIC employs students who are very enthusiastic about their country and your interest in it. There's a branch at the train station (p75).

TRAVELLERS WITH DISABILITIES

Disabled facilities found throughout Slovenia include public telephones with amplifiers, pedestrian crossings with beepers, Braille on maps at city bus stops, occasional lifts in pedestrian underpasses, sloped pavements and ramps in government buildings, and reserved spaces in many car parks. An increasing number of hotels (mostly top-end, although not always) have at least one room designed especially for disabled guests (bathrooms big enough for a wheelchair user to turn around in, access door on bath tubs, grip bars alongside toilets etc). These are noted in the text throughout the book with an icon (♿).

The **Paraplegics Association of Slovenia** (Zveza Paraplegikov Republike Slovenije; ☎ 01-432 71 38; www.zveza-paraplegikov.si; Štihova ulica 14) in Ljubljana looks after the interests and special needs of paraplegics and tetraplegics, and produces a special guide for its members in Slovene only (although their English-language website is fairly complete). Another active group is the Ljubljana-based **Slovenian Association of Disabled Students** (Društvo Študentov Invalidov Slovenije; ☎ 01-565 33 51; www.dsis-drustvo.si; Kardeljeva ploščad 5). Some towns and cities produce useful brochures describing which local sights and attractions are accessible by wheelchair. Ask the TIC.

VISAS

Virtually everyone entering Slovenia mu have a valid passport, although citizens the EU as well as Switzerland need only pro duce their national identity card on arriv for stays of up to 30 days. It's a good idea t carry your passport or other identificatio at all times.

Citizens of virtually all European countri as well as Australia, Canada, Israel, Japa New Zealand and the USA do not requi visas to visit Slovenia for stays of up to 9 days. Those who do require visas (includin South Africans) can get them at any Slovenia embassy or consulate for up to 90 days. The cost €35 regardless of the type or length validity. You'll need confirmation of a hot booking plus one photo and may have to sho a return or onward ticket.

Your hotel, hostel, camping ground or pr vate room arranged through an agency w register your name and address with the m nicipal *občina* (government) office as require by law. That's why they have to take yo passport away – at least for the first night. you are staying elsewhere (eg with relatives friends), your host is supposed to take care this for you within three days.

If you want to stay in Slovenia long than three months, the easiest thing to d is simply cross the border into Croatia an return (it won't work with Austria, Italy Hungary as they are all EU countries too Otherwise you will have to apply for a ten porary residence permit at the Ministry the Interior's **Department for Foreigners** (Oddel za Tujce; Map pp72-3; ☎ 01-306 32 61; Tobačna ulica 8am-noon & 1-3pm Mon & Tue, 8am-noon & 1-6p Thu, 8am-1pm Fri, 8am-noon Sat) just south of Pa Tivoli in Ljubljana.

WOMEN TRAVELLERS

Travelling as a single woman in Slovenia no different from travelling in most Weste European countries. If you can handle yours in the very occasional less-than-comfortab situation, you'll be fine.

In the event of an emergency call the **poli** (☎ 113) any time or the **SOS Helpline** (☎ 080-55; www.drustvo-sos.si; noon-10pm Mon-Fri, 6-10p Sat & Sun).

Transport

CONTENTS

GETTING THERE & AWAY

ENTERING THE COUNTRY

Border formalities with Slovenia's three fellow European Union neighbours – Italy, Austria and Hungary – are now virtually nonexistent. However, as a member state that forms part of the EU's external frontier, Slovenia must implement the strict Schengen border rules, so expect a somewhat closer inspection of your documents – national ID (for EU citizens) or passport and, in some cases, visa (opposite) when travelling to/from Croatia.

Passport

Virtually everyone entering Slovenia must have a valid passport, although citizens of the EU as well as Switzerland need only produce their national identity card on arrival for stays of up to 30 days. It's a good idea to carry your passport or other identification at all times.

For information on visas, see opposite.

AIR

Airports & Airlines

Slovenia's only international airport receiving regular scheduled flights – Aerodrom Maribor does limited charters only – is Ljubljana's renamed **Jože Pučnik Airport** (LJU; ☎ 04-206 19 81; www.lju-airport.si) at Brnik, 27km north of Ljubljana. In the arrivals hall you'll find a branch of the **Slovenia Tourist Information Centre** (STIC; 11am-11pm Mon, Wed & Fri, 10am-10pm Tue & Thu, 10.30am-10.30pm Sat, 12.30pm-12.30am Sun), a hotel-booking telephone and an ATM. In the departures area there is an information desk, a **post office** (8-9.30am, 10am-3.30pm & 4-6pm Mon-Fri, to noon Sat), a branch of **Nova Ljubljanska Banka** (☎ 8am-3pm Mon-Fri) and a branch of **Mobitel** (☎ 04-206 50 15; 6am-8pm Mon-Fri, 6am-noon Sat), where you can rent mobile phones and buy SIM cards and prepaid 'top up' vouchers. Some nine car-rental agencies, including Atet, Avis, Budget, Europcar and Hertz have outlets in the parking garage just opposite the terminal.

From its base at Brnik, the Slovenian flag-carrier, **Adria Airways** (JP; ☎ 01-239 19 13, ☎ toll-free 080 13 00, ☎ airport 04-259 40 00; www.adria-airways.com; Gosposvetska cesta 6; 8.30am-6pm Mon-Fri), serves some 30 European destinations on regularly scheduled flights, with some two-dozen holiday spots covered by charter flights in summer. Adria connections include three to four daily from Munich and Paris (Roissy Charles de Gaulle), two to four per day from Frankfurt and Zürich, once or twice daily from Amsterdam, daily from Istanbul and London (Gatwick), twice weekly from Manchester, and useful connections to Ohrid (Macedonia), Pristina (Kosovo) and Tirana (Albania).

Other airlines with regularly scheduled flights to and from Ljubljana include:

Air France (AF; ☎ 01-244 34 47; www.airfrance.com/si) Daily flights to Paris (CDG).

ČSA Czech Airlines (OK; ☎ 04-206 17 50; www.czechairlines.com) Flights to Prague.

> **THINGS CHANGE**
>
> The information in this chapter is particularly vulnerable to change. Check directly with the airline or a travel agent to make sure you understand how a fare (and ticket you may buy) works, and be aware of the security requirements for international travel. Shop carefully. The details given in this chapter should be regarded as pointers and are not a substitute for your own careful, up-to-date research.

TRANSPORT

CLIMATE CHANGE & TRAVEL

Climate change is a serious threat to the ecosystems that humans rely upon, and air travel is the fastest-growing contributor to the problem. Lonely Planet regards travel, overall, as a global benefit, but believes we all have a responsibility to limit our personal impact on global warming.

Flying & Climate Change

Pretty much every form of motor travel generates carbon dioxide (the main cause of human-induced climate change) but planes are far and away the worst offenders, not just because of the sheer distances they allow us to travel, but because they release greenhouse gases high into the atmosphere. The statistics are frightening: two people taking a return flight between Europe and the US will contribute as much to climate change as an average household's gas and electricity consumption over a whole year.

Carbon Offset Schemes

Climatecare.org and other websites use 'carbon calculators' that allow jetsetters to offset the greenhouse gases they are responsible for with contributions to energy-saving projects and other climate-friendly initiatives in the developing world – including projects in India, Honduras, Kazakhstan and Uganda.

Lonely Planet, together with Rough Guides and other concerned partners in the travel industry, supports the carbon offset scheme run by climatecare.org. Lonely Planet offsets all of its staff and author travel.

For more information check out our website: www.lonelyplanet.com.

easyJet (EZY; ☎ 04-206 16 77; www.easyjet.com) Low-cost flights to London Stansted.
Finnair (AY; ☎ 080 13 00, 04-259 42 45; www.finnair.com) Four fights a week to Helsinki.
Lufthansa (LH; ☎ 434 72 46; Gosposvetska cesta 6; www.lufthansa.com) Code-shared flights with Adria.
JAT Airways (JU; ☎ 01-231 43 40; www.jat.com) Five weekly flights to Belgrade.
Malév Hungarian Airlines (MA; ☎ 04-206 16 65; www.malev.hu) Daily flights to Budapest.
Montenegro Airlines (YM; ☎ 04-259 42 52; www.montenegroairlines.com) Daily flight to Podgorica.
Turkish Airlines (TK; ☎ 04-206 16 80; www.turkishairlines.com) Flights to Istanbul.

Australia

Flights to Ljubljana from Australia generally involve a combination of airlines, passing through one of the main European hubs. Return low-season fares from Sydney from around A$2100 and slightly higher from Melbourne.

The following are well-known agents for competitive fares:
STA Travel (☎ 134 782; www.statravel.com.au)
Flight Centre (☎ 133 133; www.flightcentre.com.au)

Continental Europe

Return flights from Frankfurt and Munich on an Adria-Lufthansa joint flight cost around €212. From Paris on Adria or Air France expect to pay about €208, and from Vienna (Adria or Austrian Airlines) from €210.

A few recommended travel agent include:
France Nouvelles Frontières (☎ 01 49 20 65 87; www.nouvelles-frontieres.com, in French)
Germany STA Travel (☎ 069-743 032 92; www.statravel.de)
Netherlands NBBS Reizen (☎ 0180-39 33 77; www.nbbs.nl, in Dutch)

UK

Adria flies nonstop daily from London Gatwick and once or twice a week from Manchester and Dublin from May to September. The cheapest return ticket is currently around UK£200.

If your schedule is flexible and your are travelling light consider **easyJet** (EZY; (☎ in the UK 0905 560 7777), which flies once or twice daily to Ljubljana from London's Stansted airport. Depending on the season and the day of the week, return fares can go as low as UK£40 including taxes.

An alternative budget option to Slovenia from London, especially if you want to concentrate on the coast, is **Ryanair** (FR; ☎ in the UK at 10p per min 0871 246 0000; www.ryanair.com), which links London Stansted with Trieste's **Ronchi dei Legionari Airport** (www.aeroporto.fvg.it) for a ow as UK£60 all in. Trieste may (still) be in taly, but it's much closer to Primorska than jubljana. From the coach station in Trieste here are buses every half-hour (with a dozen n Sunday) to Koper (one hour, 56km), Izola 1¼ hours, 61km), Piran and Portorož (1½ ours, 69km).

Competitive travel agencies in the UK nclude the following:

bookers (☎ 0871 223 5000; www.ebookers.com)
TA Travel (☎ 0871 230 0040; www.statravel.co.uk)
railfinders (☎ 0845 058 5858; www.trailfinders.com)

JSA & Canada

A return flight from New York to Ljubljana via Paris with Air France and Adria costs from JS$1500. Return fares from Toronto start at about C$2300.

Competitive travel agents include:

Council on International Educational Exchange (☎ 1-800-407 8839; www.ciee.org)
TA Travel (☎ 1-800 781 4040; www.statravel.com)
Travel CUTS (☎ 1-866 246 9762; www.travelcuts.com)

LAND

Slovenia is well connected by road and rail with its four neighbours. Note that bus and train timetables sometimes use Slovenian names for foreign cities (p314).

Bus

Most international buses arrive and depart from **Ljubljana bus station** (Map pp72-3; ☎ 234 46 00, ☎ information 090 93 42 30; www.ap-ljubljana.si; Trg OF 4; 6am-9pm Mon-Sat, 8am-8pm Sun).

Car & Motorcycle

Slovenia maintains some 150 border crossings with its neighbours, but not all are open to citizens of 'third countries' (ie those not from either side). On country maps and atlases, those marked with a circle and a line are international ones; those with just a circle are local ones.

Train

Slovenian Railways (Slovenske Železnice, SŽ; ☎ 01-291 33 32; www.slo-zeleznice.si) links up with the European railway network via Austria (Villach, Salzburg, Graz, Vienna), Germany (Munich, Frankfurt), Czech Republic (Prague), Croatia (Zagreb, Rijeka), Hungary (Budapest), Italy (Venice), Switzerland (Zürich) and Serbia (Belgrade). SŽ trains are clean and punctual; in recent years the acquisition of new rolling stock, including high-speed InterCity (ICS) tilting trains, has brought the network firmly into the 21st century.

The international direct trains include EuroCity (EC) ones linking Ljubljana with Vienna as well as Salzburg and Munich. InterCity (IC) trains connect Maribor with Vienna and Graz, and Ljubljana with Villach, Zagreb and Belgrade. Express trains run via Ljubljana between Zürich and Belgrade, Vienna and Zagreb and Munich and Zagreb and Rijeka. EuroNight (EN) between Budapest and Venice go via Ljubljana and Zagreb.

Seat reservations (€3.50), compulsory only on trains to and from Italy, is included in the ticket price. On night trains, sleepers and couchettes are available.

ROAD DISTANCES (KM)

	Bled	Bovec	Celje	Črnomelj	Koper	Kranj	Kranjska Gora	Ljubljana	Maribor	Murska Sobota	Nova Gorica	Novo Mesto	Postojna	Ptuj	Slovenj Gradec
Bled	---														
Bovec	83	---													
Celje	131	207	---												
Črnomelj	147	223	130	---											
Koper	156	161	185	193	---										
Kranj	27	102	105	123	131	---									
Kranjska Gora	39	45	161	178	186	58	---								
Ljubljana	59	134	76	93	107	33	89	---							
Maribor	181	257	54	198	234	156	212	126	---						
Murska Sobota	245	320	118	266	298	219	275	189	64	---					
Nova Gorica	156	72	185	193	90	131	168	107	236	299	---				
Novo Mesto	127	202	95	32	171	101	157	69	151	246	173	---			
Postojna	102	131	131	139	59	77	133	53	182	245	60	118	---		
Ptuj	184	260	58	179	237	159	215	129	29	64	238	148	183	---	
Slovenj Gradec	164	188	50	191	217	138	185	108	71	135	218	146	163	75	---

DISCOUNTS & PASSES

Undiscounted international tickets on SŽ trains are valid for two months. Certain fares bought at special offer are valid for one month, while others are valid only for the day and train indicated on the ticket; see the destinations following for details. Half-price tickets are available to children between the ages of six and 12 years.

A Global Pass from **Inter Rail** (www.interrailnet.com) covers some 30 European countries and can be purchased by nationals of European countries (or residents of at least six months). A pass offers 1st-/2nd-class travel for five days within a 10-day period (€289/219), 10 days within a 22-day period (€429/315), 22 continuous days (€549/409), or one month (€709/525). Discounts are available for those under 26.

Inter Rail now offers a 'One Country Pass' valid for rail travel in Slovenia only. For details see p301.

It would be impossible for a standard **Eurail pass** (www.eurailnet.com) to pay for itself in Slovenia. But if you are a non-European resident, you may consider one of its combination tickets allowing you to travel over a fixed period for a set price. These include the Hungary N' Slovenia/Croatia and Austria N' Slovenia/Croatia passes, offering five/10 days of travel within two months on those countries' rail networks for adults US$258/421 and youths US$214/349; children aged four to 11 travel half-price. Buy the pass before you leave home.

Croatia, Bosnia & Hercegovina, & Serbia

BUS

Koper, Piran and Portorož are the ports of entry from Croatian Istria and points farther south by bus. A bus leaves Koper daily on Monday and Friday at 10.10am for Rijeka (€12.50, two hours, 84km) and there are buses at 7.30am weekdays and again at 2pm daily to Pula (€16.50, 2½ hours; 101km) via Poreč, Umag and Rovinj.

From Ljubljana count on at least two daily departures to Belgrade (€38.70 to €40.70, eight hours, 549km, 10am and 7.45pm daily, 10.25pm Sunday to Friday). Buses depart from Ljubljana at 3.30pm and 7.40pm daily for Rijeka (€16.70 to €25.70, 2½ hours, 136km); the second one carries on to Split (€43.20, 10 hours, 528km), where you can change for Dubrovnik (€20.40, 4½ hours, 212km). A bus for Banja Luka (€27.20, 5½ hours, 336km) leaves twic[e] a day at 12.57pm and 4pm. There's a daily bu[s] at 8pm for Sarajevo (€44.70 to €48.70, 9½ t[o] 12 hours, 554km) and another one at 7.15p[m] on Monday, Wednesday and Friday).

TRAIN

There are seven trains a day to Ljubljan[a] from Zagreb via Zidani Most (€12.20, tw[o] hours, 141km), two a day from Rijek[a] (€12.60, two hours, 135km) via Postojn[a] and five a day from Split (€47.80, eight t[o] 12 hours, 456km), with a change at Zagre[b]. There are five trains a day from Belgrad[e] (€44.20, nine to 10 hours, 569km) vi[a] Zagreb. There are also two trains a day fro[m] Sarajevo (€43.20, 12 hours, 670km) with [a] change at Zagreb.

Germany, Austria & Czech Republic

BUS

Deutsche Touring (☎ in Frankfurt 069-790 35 01; ww[w].deutsche-touring.com) operates a daily overnight bu[s] between Frankfurt and Ljubljana (adult on[e] way/return €90/136, under 26/student €81/12[3] 11½ hours, 777km), leaving Frankfurt a[t] 12.30pm and picking up passengers at Stuttga[rt] (4pm), Ulm (5.15pm) and Munich (7.45pm[)]. The northbound bus leaves Ljubljana at 6.30p[m] Sunday to Friday and at 9.30am on Saturday.

There is a daily bus from Maribor acros[s] Austria to Munich, Stuttgart and Frankfu[rt] (€91, 12½ hours, 778km) at 6.50pm.

TRAIN

There are three direct trains a day betwee[n] Ljubljana and Munich (€72.40, six hours[,] 441km) via Villach and Salzburg; one o[f] them – the 9.27am – carries in to Frankfu[rt] (€144.40, 10 hours, 859km). There is also [a] train from Salzburg (€19, four hours, 290km[)] to Ljubljana and another just from Villac[h] (€18.20, two hours, 102km).

To get to Vienna (€61.80, six hours, 441km[)] from Ljubljana choose the direct EC *Emon[a]* or five other trains which require a change a[t] Maribor. To get to Graz (€31.40, three hours[,] 221km) you have a choice of up to six connections per day with a change at Maribor (wit[h] the exception of the EC *Emona*).

While fares to Vienna and Graz fro[m] Ljubljana and Maribor are high, so-calle[d] SparSchiene fares as low as €19 (valid fo[r] travel in one direction in 2nd class) appl[y] on certain trains at certain times. Also, [a] raga Spezial fare is available for only €29 to ıose travelling to Prague via Salzburg on the C 212/112 and EC 100. Be aware that the umber of these discounted tickets per train limited.

ungary

US

he Hungarian town of Rédics is only km to the north of Lendava, in northeastrn Slovenia, which can be reached from lurska Sobota (€3.60, 30 minutes, 29km). wo buses a day link Murska Sobota and jubljana (€16, four hours, 195km). From édics trains go to Zalaegerszeg (795Ft, 1¼ ours, 49km, up to nine a day), which is :ached by trains from Budapest (3380Ft) 4890Ft, four to five hours, 252km), all of hich require at least one change (usually t Boba).

RAIN

he EN *Venezia* links Ljubljana directly ith Budapest (€49.80, nine hours, 507km) ıa Zagreb. The IC Citadella goes via Ptuj nd Hodoš in Slovenia's northeast. There re Budapest Spezial fares available as low as 29/39 oneway/return on certain trains and t certain times.

taly

US

uses from Koper to Trieste (€3, one our, 23km, up to 13 daily) run along the oast via Ankaran and Muggia Monday to aturday. There's a direct year-round serv:e from Ljubljana to Trieste (€11.60, 2½ ours, 105km, 6.25am Monday to Saturday). wo daily buses at 5.10am and 8.15am link jubljana with Mestre (€25, four hours, 40km) near Venice.

Hourly buses link the train stations in the alian city of Gorizia with Nova Gorica (€1, 5 minutes) just across the border.

RAIN

he EN *Venezia* runs between Ljubljana and enice (four hours, 244km) and though the ormal one-way fare €25, there's also a few o-called Smart Price tickets available for 15 on some trains. Another possibility is) go first to Nova Gorica (€8, three hours, 53km, up to six daily), walk to Gorizia then ıke an Italian train to Venice (about €8, ¼ hours).

Switzerland

TRAIN

The overnight MV414/415 links Ljubljana directly with Zürich (€89.60, 14½ hours, 730km) via Schwarzach-St Veit; the SparSchiene (€29) and SparNight (with couchette; €39) offer enormous savings on the standard fare.

SEA

The **Prince of Venice** (☎ 05-617 80 00; portoroz@kompas.si) is a 39.6m-long high-speed catamaran that runs day trips between Izola and Piran and Venice from April to October. It departs Izola at 8am (Piran at 7.30am) and arrives in Venice at 11am; the return journey departs at 5pm and arrives back at Izola/Piran at 8pm. The schedule changes according to the season, but essentially there are sailings on Saturday from mid-April to October, with between seven and 15 sailings a week from May to September. Less-frequent sailings to/from Piran are between late June and mid-September. An adult return ticket costs €50 to €65 (children aged three to 14 pay half-price) depending on the season and day, including a tour of Venice, and there are various family packages available. An adult single costs €35 to €45. Tickets can be purchased at **Kompas** (www.kompas.si) and various other travel agencies along the coast.

From late May to late September, **Venezia Lines** (☎ in Italy +39 41 272 2646; www.venezialines.com) runs a similar service from Piran, departing at 8.30am and returning at 7.30pm on selected Wednesdays, Thursdays and Saturdays. Tickets, which cost from €46/89 oneway/return for an adults (children aged three to 13 pay half-price), are available through several travel agencies in Piran and Portorož, including **Maona Tourist Agency** (www.mao na.si).

A third vessel, the 42m-long catamaran **Dora** (☎ 05-674 71 60; www.topline.si), sails from Piran to Venice at 8am on Saturday from early May to late September returning at 5pm. The adult fare is €65, with children aged three to 13 paying half-price.

A service run by **Trieste Lines** (☎ in Italy +39 923 873 813; www.triestelines.it) links Portorož and Trieste between one and four times a day from May to September. Buy tickets (oneway /return €7.10/13.10) from the Atlas Express in Portorož or the TIC in Piran.

GETTING AROUND

AIR

Slovenia has no scheduled domestic flights, but a division of Adria Airways called **Aviotaxi** (☎ 04-236 34 60, 041 636 420; www.adria-airways.com) flies chartered four-seater Piper Turbo Arrows on demand to airports and aerodromes around the country. Sample return fares for three passengers from Brnik airport are €95 to Bled, €134 to Bled and Bohinj, €172 to Slovenj Gradec and €369 to Portorož or Maribor.

BICYCLE

Cycling is both a popular leisure pastime and a means of transport in Slovenia, and bikes can be transported for €2.80 in the baggage compartments of IC and regional trains. On buses you can put your bike in the luggage compartment as long as there is space. Cycling is permitted on all roads except motorways. Many larger towns and cities, including Ljubljana, Maribor, Celje, Ptuj, Novo Mesto, Kranj and Murska Sobota, have dedicated bicycle lanes and traffic lights.

Bicycle rental places are generally concentrated in the more popular tourist areas such as Ljubljana, Bled, Bovec and Piran though a fair few cycle shops and repair places hire them out as well. Expect to pay from €1/5 per hour/day; some places may ask for a cash deposit or a piece of ID as security. Look in the Getting Around sections of the relevant towns for details.

BUS

You can buy your ticket at the *avtobusna postaja* (bus station) or simply pay the driver as you board. In Ljubljana you should book your seat (€1.20/3.70 domestic/international) one day in advance if you're travelling on Friday, or to destinations in the mountains or on the coast on a public holiday. Bus services are severely restricted on Sunday and holidays (less so on Saturday).

A range of bus companies serve the country, but prices are uniform: €3.10/5.60/9.20/16.80 for 25/50/100/200km of travel. For sample domestic bus fares from the capital, see p101.

Some bus stations have a *garderoba* (left-luggage office) and charge €2 per hour. They often keep banker's hours; if it's an option, a better bet is to leave your things at the train station, which is usually nearby and kee longer hours. If your bag has to go in th luggage compartment below the bus, it wi cost €1.25 extra.

BUS TIMETABLE ABBREVIATIONS

D	workdays (Mon-Fri)
D+	Mon-Sat
N	Sun
NP	Sun & holidays
So	Sat
SoNe	Sat & Sun
SoNP	Sat, Sun & holidays
Š	Mon-Fri when schools are in session
ŠP	Mon-Fri during school holidays
V	daily

Bus Timetables

Timetables in the bus station, or posted on wall or column outside, list all destinatio and departure times. If you cannot find yo bus listed or don't understand the schedul get help from the *blagajna vozovnice* (infor mation or ticket window), which are usuall one and the same. *Odhodi* means 'departure while *prihodi* is 'arrivals'.

CAR & MOTORCYCLE

Automobile Association

Slovenia's national automobile club is th **AMZS** (Avto-Moto Zveza Slovenije; off Map pp72-3; ☎ 5 53 00; www.amzs.si; Dunajska cesta 128) based i Ljubljana. For emergency roadside assistanc call the ☎ 19 87 anywhere in Slovenia. A accidents should be reported to the police o ☎ 113 immediately.

Driving Licence

Foreign driving licences are valid for one ye after entering Slovenia. If you don't hold European driving licence and plan to driv here, obtain an International Driving Perm (IDP) from your local automobile associatio before you leave.

Fuel

Petrol stations, which accept almost eve credit card, are usually open from abo 7am to 8pm Monday to Saturday, thoug larger towns have 24-hour services o the outskirts.

The price of *bencin* (petrol), once a rela-ve bargain here, is now on par with the ·st of Continental Europe: EuroSuper 95/ uperPlus98 costs €1.10/1.17 per litre, with iesel at €1.05.

ire

enting a car in Slovenia is recommended nd can even save you money as you can ac-ess cheaper out-of-centre hotels and farm or illage homestays. Car rentals from interna-onal firms such as Avis, Budget, Europcar nd Hertz (all have offices in Ljubljana and in ome provincial cities) vary in price. Expect pay from €40/210 a day/week, including nlimited mileage, collision damage waiver CDW), theft protection (TP), Personal ccident Insurance (PAI) and taxes. Some maller agencies (p101) have somewhat more ompetitive rates; booking on the internet is lways cheaper.

nsurance

hird-party liability insurance is compulsory Slovenia. If you enter the country in your wn car and it is registered in the EU, you are overed; Slovenia has concluded special agree-ients with certain other countries, including roatia. Other motorists must buy a **Green Card** vww.cobx.org) valid for Slovenia at the border.

arking

ou must pay to park in the centre of most ovenian towns. In general you'll have to buy special 'pay and display' parking coupon from €0.30 per hour) from vending machines no change) and display it on the dashboard. n Ljubljana there are underground car parks here fees are charged (€1.50 to €1.70 for the rst hour and €0.50 to €1.50 per hour after hat depending on the time of day).

oad Conditions & Tolls

oads in Slovenia are generally good, well naintained and rapidly improving as road onstruction and expansion continues at a ever pitch. Driving in the Julian Alps can be air-raising, with a gradient of up to 18% at the orensko Sedlo Pass into Austria, and a series f 49 hairpin bends on the road over the Vršič ass from Gorenjska into Primorska. Many nountain roads are closed in winter and some vell into early spring. Motorways and high-vays are very well signposted, but secondary nd tertiary roads not always so; be sure to have a good map or atlas (see p288) at the ready or hire a GPS navigation device (from €12/60 a day/week) from your car-rental agency.

Investments worth upwards of €6 billion have been earmarked over a 10-year period to 2013 for the expansion of Slovenia's motor-way network – from 228km in 1990 to 580km by the start of 2007. There are two main motorway corridors – between Maribor and the coast (via the impressive flyover at Črni Kal) and from the Karavanke Tunnel into Austria to Zagreb in Croatia – intersecting at the Ljubljana ring road, with a branch from Postojna to Nova Gorica. Motorways are numbered from A1 to A10 (for *avtocesta*).

Major international roads are preceded by an 'E'. The most important of these are the E70 to Zagreb via Novo Mesto, the E61 to Villach via Jesenice and the Karavanke Tunnel, the E57 from Celje to Graz via Maribor, and the E59 from Graz to Zagreb via Maribor. National highways contain a single digit and link cities. Secondary and tertiary roads have three digits.

Private-car ownership in Slovenia almost equals that of the UK (501 vs 504 vehicles per 1000 inhabitants), so expect a lot of traffic con-gestion, especially in summer and on Friday afternoons when entire cities and towns head for the countryside. Work is being carried out on major roads throughout the country and roundabouts being installed so factor in the possibility of delays and the occasional *obvoz* (diversion).

Tolls are no longer paid separately on the motorways, Instead a law introduced in 2008 requires all cars to display a *vinjeta* (road-toll sticker) on the windscreen. They cost €15/30/95 for a week/half/full year for cars and €7.50/25/47.50 for motorbikes and are available at petrol stations, post offices and certain newsstands and tourist information centres. These stickers will already be in place on a rental car, but if you are driving your own vehicle, failure to display such a sticker risks a fine of up to €800.

Road Rules

You must drive on the right. Speed limits for cars and motorcycles (less for buses) are 50km/h in towns and villages, 90km/h on secondary and tertiary roads, 100km/h on highways and 130km/h on motorways.

The use of seat belts is compulsory, and motorcyclists must wear helmets. As in neighbouring Hungary all motorists must illuminate their headlights throughout the day – not just at night. The permitted blood-alcohol level for drivers is 0.05%.

HITCHING

Hitchhiking remains a popular way to get around for young Slovenes, and it's generally easy – except on Friday afternoon, before school holidays and on Sunday, when cars are often full of families. Hitching from bus stops is fairly common. Otherwise use motorway access roads or other areas where the traffic will not be disturbed.

Hitching is never entirely safe in any country in the world, and we don't recommend it. Travellers who decide to hitch should understand that they are taking a small but potentially serious risk. People who do choose to hitch will be safer if they travel in pairs and should let someone know where they are planning to go. In particular, it is unwise for females to hitch alone; women are better off hitching with a male companion.

TOURS

Many local travel agencies organise excursions and tours for both individuals and groups. **Kompas** (☎ 051 371 849; www.kompas-online.net) is just one example that has half-day and day trips to Bled (€46), Postojna Cave and Predjama Castle (€52), Lipica and Škocjan Caves (€60) and Maribor and Ptuj (€69). Tours last for between five and nine hours and include transport, guide and entrance fees.

Roundabout (☎ 041 786 168; www.roundabout.si) offers a series of a hop-on, hop-off bus trips, including what it calls an Alpine Fairytale trip (Škofja Loka, Bled and Bohinj; €42) on Monday, Wednesday and Friday and a Karst & Coast Mystery one (Predjama, Škocjan, Lipica and Piran; €46) on Tuesday, Thursday, Saturday and Sunday. You can either do the trip in one go or get off and wait for the next bus. There's also an Emerald River trip (€55) on the same days as the Karst & Coast Mystery tip that takes in Bled, Kranjska Gora, Bovec via the Vršič Pass and Kobarid. The Way to Bled trip (€55; Alpine Fairytale schedule) includes rafting. A more ambitious trip is the two-day West Roundy one departing on Monday, Wednesday and Friday that takes in Bled, Bohinj, Kranjska Gora, Bovec (where you stay overnight), Kobarid, Nove Gorica, Štanjel, Lipica, Piran and the Škocjan Caves before heading back to Ljubljana. The trip alone cost €95; with multibed apartment/hotel accommodation in Bovec added on it's €120/140. Ticket are available from tourist offices, hostels an selected hotels in Ljubljana.

TRAIN

Slovenian Railways (☎ 01-291 33 32; www.slo-zeleznic .si) runs trains on 1228km of track, about 40% of which is electrified. Very roughly, figure on covering about 60km/h to 65km/h except on the ICS express trains, which hurtle between Ljubljana and Maribor (€13.60, 1¾ hours) at an average speed of 90km/h. In the summer months an ICS train links Koper with Maribor (€23.80, four hours) via Ljubljana (€13.60, two hours).

The provinces are served by *regionalni vlaki* (regional trains) and *primestni vlaki* (city trains), but the fastest are InterCity trains (IC), which levy a surcharge of about €1.54.

An 'R' next to the train number on the timetable means seat reservations are available. If the 'R' is boxed, seat reservations are obligatory.

Purchase your ticket before you travel at the *železniška postaja* (train station) itself; buying it from the conductor on the train costs an additional €2.50. An invalid ticket or trying to avoid paying will earn you a fine of €40.

A *povratna vozovnica* (return ticket) costs double the price of a *enosmerna vozovnica* (one-way or single ticket). A 1st-class ticket costs 50% more than a 2nd-class one.

Travelling by train in Slovenia is about 35% cheaper than going by bus. In rough terms a 100km journey costs €6.03 in 2nd class; see p102 for sample domestic fares out of the capital.

You'll find luggage lockers at train stations in Celje, Divača, Koper, Ljubljana, Maribor, Nova Gorica, Postojna and Sežana. The charge

TRAIN TIMETABLE SYMBOLS

- ⊗ Mon-Fri (except public holidays)
- ⚒ Mon-Sat (except public holidays)
- ● Mon-Sat and public holidays
- Ⓥ Sat & Sun
- ● Sat, Sun & public holidays
- Ⓟ Sun and public holidays
- 7 No Sun service
- † Public holidays

NATIONAL RAIL NETWORK

; €2, €3 or €8 per day, depending on the size f the locker.

rain Timetables

)epartures and arrivals are announced by oudspeaker or on an electronic board and are lways on a printed timetable somewhere in ne station. The yellow one with the heading *)dhod* or *Odhodi Vlakov* means 'Departures', nd the white one with the words *Prihod* or *'rihodi Vlakov* is 'Arrivals'. Other important vords that appear often are *čas* (time), *peron* platform), *sedež* (seat), *smer* (direction) and *'r* (rail).

If you expect to use the train a lot in lovenia, buy a copy of the official timetable, *'ozni Red Slovenske Železnice* (€4.20), which as explanatory notes in Slovene and German. n abridged version listing main routes only n Slovene costs €1.

Discounts & Passes

There's a 30% discount on return weekend and ICS fares.

SŽ sells the new One Country Pass Slovenia from **Inter Rail** (www.interrailnet.com), which is valid for rail travel in Slovenia only and available to residents of any European country (excluding Slovenia). The pass, which includes travel on ICS trains, is available for three/four/six/eight days of travel within one month for €49/69/99/119; those under 26 years of age pay €32/45/64/77.

Steam Trains

SŽ has a stock of five steam locomotives and antique rolling stock – a trainspotter's dream come true – and several of them dating as far back as 1919 are put to good use in summer when the Old Timer Train *(Muzejski Vlak)* excursions depart. For details see p128.

Health

CONTENTS

Travel health depends on your predeparture preparations, your daily health care while travelling and the way you handle any medical problem that develops while you are on the road. Although the potential dangers might seem frightening, in reality few travellers experience anything more than an upset stomach.

BEFORE YOU GO

A little planning before departure, particularly for pre-existing illnesses or conditions, will save trouble later. See your dentist before a long trip, carry a spare pair of contact lenses or glasses, and take your optical prescription with you. Bring medications in their original, clearly labelled, containers. A signed and dated letter from your physician describing your medical conditions and medications, including their generic names, is also a good idea.

INSURANCE

EU citizens on public-health insurance schemes should note that they're generally covered by reciprocal arrangements in Slovenia. They should, however, carry their European Health Insurance Card. In the UK, application forms for such cards are available from any post office branch or online from the **Department of Health** (www.dh.gov.uk/travellersh.gov.uk). In addition, citizens of certain non-EU countries, including Croatia and Macedonia, are guaranteed emergency medical assistanc or subsequent treatment provided they submit the appropriate documentation. Citizen of other countries should check with thei Ministry of Health or equivalent before settin out. Everyone else is entitled to emergenc medical treatment in Slovenia, but they usually must pay for it. Check the website of th **Health Insurance Institute of Slovenia** (www.zzzs.s for more information.

If you do need health insurance whil travelling (p287), we strongly advise yo to consider a policy that covers you for th worst possible scenario, such as an acciden requiring an ambulance or an emergency flight home.

INTERNET RESOURCES

The World Health Organization's (WHO online publication *International Travel and Health* is revised annually and is available a www.who.int/ith.

Other useful websites:

www.ageconcern.org.uk Advice on travel for the elderly.

www.fitfortravel.scot.nhs.uk General travel advice for the layperson.

www.mariestopes.org.uk Information on women's health and contraception.

www.mdtravelhealth.com Travel-health recommendations for every country; updated daily.

It's usually a good idea to consult your government's travel health website before departure, if one is available:

Australia (www.smarttraveller.gov.au)
Canada (www.travelhealth.gc.ca)
UK (www.dh.gov.uk/en/home)
USA (www.cdc.gov/travel)

IN TRANSIT

DEEP VEIN THROMBOSIS (DVT)

Blood clots may form in the legs (deep vein thrombosis or DVT) during plane flights, chiefly because of prolonged immobility. The longer the flight, the greater the risk. The chief symptom of DVT is welling or pain in the foot, ankle or alf, usually – but not always – on just ne side. When a blood clot travels to ne lungs, it may cause chest pain and reathing difficulties. Travellers with any f these symptoms should seek medical ttention immediately.

To prevent the development of DVT n long flights, you should walk about the abin, contract the leg muscles while sitng, drink plenty of fluids and refrain from rinking alcohol.

ET LAG & MOTION SICKNESS

To avoid jet lag, which is common when rossing more than five time zones, try rinking plenty of nonalchoholic fluids and ating light meals. Upon arrival, get expoure to natural sunlight and readjust your chedule (for meals, sleep and so on) as oon as possible.

Antihistamines such as dimenhydrinate Dramamine) and meclizine (Antivert, Bonine) are usually the first choice for reating motion sickness. A herbal alternaive is ginger.

IN SLOVENIA

AVAILABILITY & COST OF HEALTH CARE

Medical care in Slovenia corresponds to European standards and is very good. Every large town or city has a *zdravstveni dom* (health centre) or *klinični center* (clinic) that operates from 7am to at least 7pm. Treatment at a public outpatient clinic costs little or nothing; doctors working privately will charge from €30 per consultation.

Pharmacies are usually open from 7am to 8pm, and at least one in each community is open round the clock. A sign on the door of any *lekarna* (pharmacy) will help you find the nearest 24-hour one.

ENVIRONMENTAL HAZARDS

Insect Bites & Stings

Tick-borne encephalitis (TBE) is spread by *klop*, the annoying little insect that burrows under the skin. In recent years, it has become a common problem in parts of Central and Eastern Europe, especially eastern Austria, Germany, Hungary, the Czech Republic and Slovenia. Encephalitis is a serious infection of the brain, and vaccination is advised for campers and hikers who intend on staying in the woods for prolonged periods between May and September. Two doses of vaccine will give a year's protection, three doses up to three years'. For up-to-date information, log on to www.masta.org.

Lyme disease is another tick-transmitted infection not unknown in Central and Eastern Europe. The illness usually begins with a spreading rash at the site of the tick bite and is accompanied by fever, headaches, extreme fatigue, aching joints and muscles and mild neck stiffness. If untreated, these symptoms usually resolve over several weeks, but over subsequent weeks or months disorders of the nervous system, heart and joints might develop.

Mosquitoes can be a real annoyance, especially around lakes and ponds in the warmer months in Slove nia. The bloodthirsty beasties might not carry malaria, but they can still cause irritation and infection. Just make sure you're armed with a DEET-based insect repellent *(prašek proti mrčesu)* and wear long-sleeved shirts and long trousers around dusk

Bee and wasp stings cause real problems only to those with a severe allergy (anaphylaxis) who should carry an 'epipen' or similar adrenaline injection.

Water

Tap water is 100% safe everywhere in Slovenia. If you are hiking or camping in the mountains and are unsure about the water, the simplest way of purifying it is to boil it for 10 minutes. Chlorine tablets will kill many pathogens. Iodine is more effective and is available in tablet form. Follow the directions carefully, and remember that too much iodine can be harmful.

RECOMMENDED VACCINATIONS

While Slovenia does not require any vaccination of international travellers, the World Health Organization (WHO) recommends that all travellers be covered for diphtheria, tetanus, measles, mumps, rubella and polio, regardless of their destination. Since most vaccines don't produce immunity until at least two weeks after they're given, visit a physician or clinic at least six weeks before departure.

TRAVELLING WITH CHILDREN

All travellers with children should know how to treat minor ailments and when to seek medical treatment. Make sure the children are up to date with routine vaccinations, and discuss possible travel vaccines well before departure as some vaccines are not suitable for children younger than a year.

Children should be encouraged to avoid and mistrust any dogs or other mammals because of the risk of rabies and other diseases. Any bite, scratch or lick from a warm-blooded, furry animal should immediately be thoroughly cleaned. If there is any possibility that the animal is infected with rabies, immediate medical assistance should be sought immediately.

WOMEN'S HEALTH

If using oral contraceptives, remember that some antibiotics, diarrhoea and vomiting can stop the pill from working and lead to the risk of pregnancy. Time zones, gastrointestinal upsets and antibiotics do not affect injectable contraception.

Travelling during pregnancy is usually possible but always consult your doctor before planning your trip. The riskiest times for travel are during the first 12 weeks of pregnancy and after 30 weeks.

SEXUAL HEALTH

Emergency contraception is most effective if taken within 24 hours after unprotected sex. The **International Planned Parent Federation** (www.ippf.org) can advise about the availability of contraception in different countries.

When buying condoms, look for a European CE mark, which means they have been rigorously tested, and then keep them in a cool dry place; otherwise they might crack and split.

The numbers of registered AIDS cases in Hungary and those who are HIV-positive are very low (just under 320), though Slovenian epidemiologists say the number of unreported cases could be double that number. For information about testing contact the Ljubljana-based organisation **ŠKUC-Magnus** (☎ 01-430 4 40; skucmagnus@hotmail.com).

anguage

ONTENTS

lovene *(slovenščina)* is the official language f the Republic of Slovenia. The forebears f today's Slovenes brought the language, ith its roots in Old Church Slavonic, from ieir original homeland beyond the Car-athian Mountains. Slovene belongs to the outh Slavic language family, along with roatian and Serbian (although it is much oser to Croatia's northwestern and coastal ialects). It also shares some features with ie more distant West Slavic languages rough contact with a dialect of Slovak, om which it was later separated by the rrival of the Hungarians to Central Europe the 9th century.

Virtually every adult over the age of 25 more than 92% according to a 2007 gov-rnment poll – speaks at least one other nguage, most commonly (73%) Croatian r Serbian. Some 48% are conversant in nglish, 29% in German, and just under 0% speak Italian. German, once the lan-uage of education and the elite, is generally poken by older Slovenes these days, mostly Koroška, Štajerska and northern Goren-ka. English is definitely the preferred lan-uage of the young, with the vast majority f students claiming knowledge of it. Most peak English very well indeed. Italian is eally only useful in Primorska and small arts of Notranjska.

The fact that you'll rarely have difficulty making yourself understood and that you'll probably never 'need' Slovene shouldn't stop you from learning a few words and phrases of this rich and wonderful language. More than anything else, Slovene has kept the Slovenian *narod* (nation) alive and united as a culture over centuries, so any effort on your part to speak it will be rewarded a hundred-fold.

For a list of food and drink terms, check out the food glossary on p312. For a more in-depth guide to the language, pick up a copy of Lonely Planet's *Eastern Europe* phrasebook.

PRONUNCIATION

The sounds in Slovene are not difficult for a speaker of English to learn. If you follow the pronunciation guides (explained in the lists below) that are included next to the Slovene phrases throughout this chapter, you'll have no problems being understood.

Vowels

Note that we've used the symbols **oh** and **ow** to help you pronounce vowels followed by the letters *l* and *v* in written Slovene – when they appear at the end of a syllable, these combinations sometimes produce a sound similar to the 'w' in English, eg *pol* (poh), *nov* (noh), *ostal* (os·*tow*), *prav* (prow).

a	as in 'father'
ai	as in 'aisle'
e	as in 'red'
ee	as in 'bee'
o	as in 'pot'
oh	as the 'o' in 'note'
oo	as in 'moon'
ow	as in 'cow'
uh	as the 'a' in 'ago'

Consonants

Most Slovene consonant sounds are pronounced more or less as they are in English. Don't be intimidated by the vowel-less words such as *trg* (square) or *vrt* (garden) – just try pronouncing a slight 'uh' sound before the *r*, which serves as a semi-vowel between the two other consonants.

ch	as in 'chip'
ly	as the 'lli' in 'million'
ny	as in 'canyon'
r	as in 'red' but rolled
sh	as in 'ship'
ts	as in 'cats'
zh	as the 's' in 'pleasure'
'	a slight 'y' sound

Word Stress

Slovene has no fixed rules for word stress, ie it can fall on any syllable within a word. You don't need to worry about this though, as in our pronunciation guides the stressed syllable is indicated with italics.

ACCOMMODATION

I'm looking for a/the ...	*Iščem ...*	eesh·chem ...
campsite	*kamping*	*kam*·peeng
guesthouse	*gostišče*	gos·*teesh*·che
hotel	*hotel*	ho·*tel*
youth hostel	*mladinski hotel*	mla·*deens*·kee ho·*tel*

Do you have a ...?	*Ali imate prosto ...?*	*a*·lee ee·*ma*·te *pro*·sto ...
bed	*posteljo*	*po*·ste·lyo
cheap room	*poceni sobo*	po·*tse*·nee *so*·bo
double room	*dvoposteljno sobo*	dvo·*po*·stel'·no *so*·bo
room with a bathroom	*sobo z kopalnico*	*so*·bo z ko·*pal*·nee·tso
single room	*enoposteljno sobo*	e·no·*po*·stel'·no *so*·bo

How much is it ...?	*Koliko stane ...?*	ko·*lee*·ko *sta*·ne ...
per night	*na noč*	na noch
per person	*na osebo*	na o·*se*·bo

I'd like to share a dorm.
Rad/Rada bi delil/delila spalnico. (m/f) — rad/*ra*·da bee *de*·leew/de·*lee*·la *spal*·nee·tso

Is breakfast included?
Ali je zajtrk vključen? — *a*·lee ye *zai*·tuhrk *vklyoo*·chen

May I see the room?
Lahko vidim sobo? — lah·*ko vee*·deem *so*·bo

Where is the bathroom?
Kje je kopalnica? — kye ye ko·*pal*·nee·tsa

Where's the toilet?
Kje je stranišče/WC? — kye ye stra·*neesh*·che/ve tse

I'm/We're leaving today.
Danes odhajam/odhajamo. — *da*·nes od·*ha*·yam/od·*ha*·ya·mo

MAKING A RESERVATION

(for written and phone inquiries)

To ...	*Do ...*
From ...	*Od ...*
Date	*Datum*
I'd like to book ...	*Rad/Rada bi rezerviral/rezervirala ...* (m/f)
in the name of ...	*v imenu ...*
from ...	*od ...*
to ...	*do ...*
credit card type	*vrsta kreditne kartice*
number	*številka*
expiry date	*datum poteka*
Please confirm availability and price.	*Prosim da potrdite rezervacijo in ceno.*

CONVERSATION & ESSENTIALS

Good day.
Dober dan. — *do*·ber dan

Hello.
Zdravo. — *zdra*·vo

Goodbye.
Na svidenje. — na *svee*·de·nye

Bye.
Adijo. — a·*dee*·yo

Please.
Prosim. — *pro*·seem

Thank you (very much).
Hvala (lepa). — *hva*·la (*le*·pa)

You're welcome. (Don't mention it.)
Ni za kaj. — nee za kai

Yes.
Da/Ja. (pol/inf) — da/ya

No.
Ne. — ne

Excuse me.
Dovolite mi, prosim. — do·*vo*·lee·te mee *pro*·seem

Sorry. (Forgive me.)
Oprostite. (pol) — o·pro·*stee*·te
Oprosti. (inf) — o·*pro*·stee

What's your name?
Kako vam je ime? (pol) — ka·*ko* vam ye ee·*me*
Kako ti je ime? (inf) — ka·*ko* tee ye ee·*me*

My name's ...
Jaz sem ... — yas sem ...

Where are you from?
Od kod ste/si? (pol/inf) — od kot ste/see

I'm from ...
Sem iz ... — sem eez ...

May I?
Ali lahko? — *a*·lee lah·*ko*

No problem.
Brez problema. brez pro·*ble*·ma
I'd like ... (to do something)
Rad/Rada bi ... (m/f) rad/*ra*·da bee ...
I like ... (something)
Mam rad/rada ... (m/f) mam rad/*ra*·da ...
I don't like ...
Ne maram ... ne *ma*·ram ...

brother	*brat*	brat
daughter	*hči*	hchee
father	*oče*	*o*·che
husband	*mož*	mozh
mother	*mama*	*ma*·ma
sister	*sestra*	*ses*·tra
son	*sin*	seen
wife	*žena*	*zhe*·na

DIRECTIONS

I'm lost.
Izgubil/Izgubila sem se. (m/f) eez·*goo*·beew/eez·goo·*bee*·la sem se
Where is ...?
Kje je ...? kye ye ...
What's the address?
Kakšen je naslov? *kak*·shen ye na·*sloh*
Please write it down.
Prosim, napišite naslov. *pro*·seem na·*pee*·she·te na·*sloh*
How do I get to ...?
Kako pridem do ...? ka·*ko pree*·dem do ...
Is it near/far?
Ali je blizu/daleč? *a*·lee ye *blee*·zoo/*da*·lech
(Go) Straight ahead.
(Pojdite) Naravnost naprej. (poy·*dee*·te) na·*rav*·nost na·*prey*

Turn left/right at the ...	*Obrnite levo/desno pri ...*	o·*buhr*·nee·te *le*·vo/*des*·no pree ...
corner	*vogalu*	vo·*ga*·loo
traffic lights	*semaforju*	se·ma·*for*·yoo

behind	*za/zadaj*	za/*za*·dai
far (from)	*daleč (od)*	*da*·lech (od)
here	*tu*	too
in front of	*spredaj*	*spre*·dai
near (to)	*blizu (do)*	*blee*·zoo (do)
opposite	*nasproti*	nas·*pro*·tee
there	*tam*	tam

north	*sever*	*se*·ver
south	*jug*	yoog
east	*vzhod*	ooz·*hod*
west	*zahod*	za·*hod*

SIGNS

Vhod	Entrance
Izhod	Exit
Odprto	Open
Zaprto	Closed
Informacije	Information
Carina	Customs
Policija	Police
Prepovedano	Prohibited
Postaja	Station
Železniška Blagajna	(Train) Ticket Office
Avtobusno Postajališče	Bus Stop
Proste Sobe	Rooms Available
Zasedeno	Full (No Vacancies)
Stranišče	Toilets
Moški	Men
Ženske	Women

beach	*plaža*	*pla*·zha
bridge	*most*	most
castle	*grad*	grad
cathedral	*stolnica*	*stol*·nee·tsa
church	*cerkev*	*tser*·kev
hospital	*bolnišnica*	bol·*neesh*·nee·tsa
lake	*jezero*	*ye*·ze·ro
main square	*glavni trg*	*glav*·nee tuhrg
market	*tržnica*	*tuhrzh*·nee·tsa
palace	*palača*	pa·*la*·cha
ruins	*ruševine*	roo·she·*vee*·ne
tower	*stolp*	stolp

EATING OUT

Do you have a menu in English?
Ali imate jedilni list v angleščini? *a*·lee ee·*ma*·te ye·*deel*·nee list v an·*glesh*·chee·nee
Is service included in the bill?
Ali je postrežba všteta v ceno? *a*·lee ye pos·*trezh*·ba *vshte*·ta v *tse*·no
I'm a vegetarian.
Vegetarijanec sem. ve·ge·ta·ree·*ya*·nets sem
I don't eat meat/chicken/fish).
Ne jem meso/piščanca/ribo. ne yem me·*so*/pish·*chan*·tsa/*ree*·bo
Do you have some typical Slovenian dishes?
Ali imate kakšne pristne slovenske jedi? *a*·lee ee·*ma*·te *kaksh*·ne *preest*·ne slo·*ven*·ske ye·*dee*
What is the house speciality?
Kaj je domača specialiteta? kai ye do·*ma*·cha spe·tsee·a·lee·*te*·ta
I'm hungry.
Lačen/Lačna sem. (m/f) *la*·chen/*lach*·na sem
I'm thirsty.
Žejen/ Žejna sem. (m/f) *zhe*·yen/ *zhey*·na sem

LANGUAGE

EMERGENCIES

Help!
Na pomoč! — na po·*moch*
There's been an accident!
Nesreča se je zgodila! — ne·*sre*·cha se ye zgo·*dee*·la
Could you please help me?
Mi lahko pomagate? — mee lah·*ko* po·*ma*·ga·te
Go away!
Pojdite stran! — poy·*dee*·te stran

Call ...!	*Pokličite ...!*	po·*klee*·chee·te ...
a doctor	*zdravnika*	zdrav·*nee*·ka
the police	*policijo*	po·lee·*tsee*·yo

I'd like the set lunch, please.
Rad/Rada bi meni, prosim. (m/f) — rad/*ra*·da bee me·*nee* *pro*·seem
I'd like some ...
Rad/Rada bi nekaj ... (m/f) — rad/*ra*·da bee *ne*·kai ...
Another one, please.
Še enkrat, prosim. — she *en*·krat *pro*·seem
The bill, please.
Račun, prosim. — ra·*choon* *pro*·seem

HEALTH

I'm sick.
Bolan/Bolna sem. (m/f) — bo·*lan*/*boh*·na sem
Where's the nearest doctor?
Kje je najbližji zdravnik? — kye ye nai·*bleezh*·yee zdrav·*neek*
Where's the nearest hospital?
Kje je najbližja bolnica? — kye ye nai·*bleezh*·ya *bol*·nee·tsa
I'm diabetic/epileptic/asthmatic.
Sem diabetik/epileptik/astmatik. — sem dee·ya·*be*·teek/e·pee·*lep*·teek/ast·*ma*·teek
It hurts here.
Tukaj boli. — *too*·kai bo·*lee*

I'm allergic to ...	*Alergičen/Alergična sem na ...* (m/f)	a·*ler*·gee·chen/a·*ler*·geech·na sem na ...
antibiotics	*antibiotike*	an·tee·bee·*o*·tee·ke
nuts	*orehe*	o·*re*·he
peanuts	*kikiriki*	kee·kee·*ree*·kee
penicillin	*penicilin*	pe·nee·tsee·*leen*

antiseptic	*antiseptik/razkužilo*	an·tee·*sep*·teek/raz·koo·*zhee*·lo
aspirin	*aspirin*	as·pee·*reen*
condoms	*kondomi*	kon·*do*·mee
contraceptive	*kontraceptivno sredstvo*	kon·tra·tsep·*teev*·no *sret*·stvo
diarrhoea	*driska*	*drees*·ka
medicine	*zdravilo*	zdra·*vee*·lo
nausea	*slabost*	sla·*bost*
sunblock cream	*krema za sončenje*	*kre*·ma za *son*·che·nye
tampons	*tamponi*	tam·*po*·nee

LANGUAGE DIFFICULTIES

Do you speak English?
Govorite angleško? — go·vo·*ree*·te an·*glesh*·ko
Does anyone here speak English?
Ali kdo tukaj govori angleško? — *a*·lee gdo *too*·kai go·vo·*ree* an·*glesh*·ko
I (don't) understand.
(Ne) Razumem. — (ne) ra·*zoo*·mem
Could you repeat that, please?
Lahko ponovite? — lah·*ko* po·no·*vee*·te
Could you write it down, please?
Lahko to napišete? — lah·*ko* to na·*pee*·she·te
Can you show me (on the map)?
Mi lahko pokažete (na mapi)? — mee lah·*ko* po·*ka*·zhe·te (na *ma*·pee)
How do you say ... (in Slovene)?
Kako se reče ... (po slovensko)? — ka·*ko* se *re*·che ... (po slo·*ven*·sko)
What does ... mean?
Kaj ... pomeni? — kai ... po·*me*·nee

NUMBERS

0	*nula*	*noo*·la
1	*en/ena* (m/f)	en/*e*·na
2	*dva/dve* (m/f)	dva/dve
3	*trije/tri* (m/f)	*tree*·ye/tree
4	*štirje/štiri* (m/f)	*shtee*·ree·ye/*shtee*·re
5	*pet*	pet
6	*šest*	shest
7	*sedem*	*se*·dem
8	*osem*	*o*·sem
9	*devet*	de·*vet*
10	*deset*	de·*set*
11	*enajst*	en·*naist*
12	*dvanajst*	*dva*·naist
13	*trinajst*	*tree*·naist
14	*štirinajst*	*shtee*·ree·naist
15	*petnajst*	*pet*·naist
16	*šestnajst*	*shest*·naist
17	*sedemnajst*	*se*·dem·naist
18	*osemnajst*	*o*·sem·naist
19	*devetnajst*	*de*·vet·naist
20	*dvajset*	*dvai*·set
21	*enaindvajset*	*e*·na·een·dvai·set
22	*dvaindvajset*	*dva*·een·dvai·set
30	*trideset*	*tree*·de·set
40	*štirideset*	*shtee*·ree·de·set
50	*petdeset*	*pet*·de·set

LANGUAGE

)	*šestdeset*	*shest*·de·set
0	*sedemdeset*	*se*·dem·de·set
)	*osemdeset*	*o*·sem·de·set
)	*devetdeset*	de·*vet*·de·set
00	*sto*	sto
01	*sto ena*	*sto e*·na
10	*sto deset*	*sto* de·*set*
000	*tisoč*	*tee*·soch

'APERWORK

ate/place of birth	*datum/kraj rojstva*	*da*·toom/krai *roy*·stva
iven name	*ime*	ee·*me*
ıale/female	*moški/ženska*	*mosh*·kee/*zhen*·ska
ationality	*državljanstvo*	duhr·zhav·*lyan*·stvo
assport	*potni list*	*pot*·nee leest
urname	*priimek*	pree·*ee*·mek

UESTION WORDS

ow?	*Kako?*	ka·*ko*
ow much/ many?	*Koliko?*	ko·*lee*·ko
/hat?	*Kaj?*	kai
/hat is it?	*Kaj je to?*	kai ye to
/hen?	*Kdaj?*	gdai
/here?	*Kje?*	kye
/hich?	*Kateri/ Katera?* (m/f)	ka·*te*·ree/ ka·*te*·ra
/ho?	*Kdo?*	gdo
/hy?	*Zakaj?*	za·*kai*

HOPPING & SERVICES

/here is /the ...?	*Kje je ...?*	kye ye ...
bank	*banka*	*ban*·ka
bookshop	*knjigarna*	knyee·*gar*·na
chemist	*lekarna*	le·*kar*·na
church	*cerkev*	*tser*·kev
consulate	*konzulat*	kon·zoo·*lat*
embassy	*ambasada*	am·ba·*sa*·da
exchange office	*menjalnica*	me·*nyal*·nee·tsa
grocery store	*špecerija*	shpe·tse·*ree*·ya
hospital	*bolnica*	*bol*·nee·tsa
laundry	*pralnica*	*pral*·nee·tsa
market	*tržnica*	*tuhrzh*·nee·tsa
museum	*muzej*	moo·*zey*
newsagency	*kiosk*	*kee*·yosk
police	*policija*	po·lee·*tsee*·ya
post office	*pošta*	*posh*·ta
public phone	*javni telefon*	*yav*·nee te·le·*fon*
public toilet	*javno stranišče*	*yav*·no stra·*neesh*·che
restaurant	*restavracija*	rest·tav·*ra*·tsee·ya
supermarket	*samopostrežna*	sa·mo·pos·*trezh*·na
telephone centre	*telefonska centrala*	te·le·*fon*·ska tsen·*tra*·la
tourist office	*turistični urad*	too·*rees*·teech·nee oo·*rad*

What time does it open/close?
Kdaj se odpre/zapre? gdai se od·*pre*/za·*pre*

I'd like to buy ...
Rad/Rada bi kupil/ kupila ... (m/f) rad/*ra*·da bee *koo*·peew/ koo·*pee*·la ...

I'm just looking.
Samo gledam. sa·*mo gle*·dam

How much is it?
Koliko stane? ko·*lee*·ko *sta*·ne

I don't like it.
Ni mi všeč. nee mee vshech

It's too expensive for me.
Predrago je zame. pre·*dra*·go ye *za*·me

It's cheap. (ie good value)
Poceni je. po·*tse*·nee ye

May I look at it?
Ali lahko pogledam? *a*·lee lah·*ko* po·*gle*·dam

I'll take it.
Kupil/Kupila bom. (m/f) *koo*·peew/koo·*pee*·la bom

more	*več*	vech
less	*manj*	man'
bigger	*večje*	*vech*·ye
smaller	*manjše*	*man'*·she

I'd like to change some ...	*Rad/Rada bi zamenjal nekaj ...* (m/f)	rad/*ra*·da bee za·*me*·nyow *ne*·kai ...
money	*denarja*	de·*nar*·ya
travellers cheques	*potovalnih čekov*	po·to·*val*·neeh *che*·koh

Do you accept credit cards?
Ali vzamete kreditno kartico? *a*·lee *vza*·me·te kre·*deet*·no *kar*·tee·tso

I want to make a telephone call.
Rad/Rada bi telefoniral/ telefonirala. (m/f) rad/*ra*·da bee te·le·fon·*nee*·row/ te·le·fon·*nee*·ra·la

Where can I get internet access?
Kje lahko dobim internet povezavo? kye lah·*ko do*·beem *een*·ter·net po·*ve*·za·vo

TIME & DATES

What time is it?
Koliko je ura? ko·*lee*·ko ye *oo*·ra

It's (one) o'clock.
Ura je (ena). *oo*·ra ye (*e*·na)

half past seven (literally 'half eight')
pol osem pol *o*·sem

LANGUAGE

quarter past (one)
četrt čez (ena) — che·*tuhrt* chez (*e*·na)
quarter to (one)
četrt do (ena) — che·*tuhrt* do (*e*·na)

yesterday	*včeraj*	*vche*·rai
today	*danes*	*da*·nes
in the morning	*zjutraj*	*zyoot*·rai
in the evening	*zvečer*	zve·*cher*
tonight	*nocoj*	no·*tsoy*
tomorrow	*jutri*	*yoo*·tree

Monday	*ponedeljek*	po·ne·*de*·lyek
Tuesday	*torek*	*to*·rek
Wednesday	*sreda*	*sre*·da
Thursday	*četrtek*	che·*tuhrt*·tek
Friday	*petek*	*pe*·tek
Saturday	*sobota*	so·*bo*·ta
Sunday	*nedelja*	ne·*de*·lya

January	*januar*	*ya*·noo·ar
February	*februar*	*fe*·broo·ar
March	*marec*	*ma*·rets
April	*april*	a·*preel*
May	*maj*	mai
June	*junij*	*yoo*·neey
July	*julij*	*yoo*·leey
August	*avgust*	av·*goost*
September	*september*	sep·*tem*·ber
October	*oktober*	ok·*to*·ber
November	*november*	no·*vem*·ber
December	*december*	de·*tsem*·ber

TRANSPORT

Public Transport

What time does the … leave?	*Kdaj odpelje …?*	gdai od·*pe*·lye …
boat	*ladja*	*la*·dya
bus	*avtobus*	*av*·to·boos
ferry	*trajekt*	tra·*yekt*
plane	*avion*	a·vee·*on*
train	*vlak*	vlak

I want to go to …
Želim iti … — zhe·*leem ee*·tee …
Can you tell me when we get to …?
Mi lahko poveste kdaj pridemo …? — mee lah·*ko* po·*ves*·te gdai *pree*·de·mo …
The train has been delayed.
Vlak ima zamudo. — vlak ee·*ma* za·*moo*·do
The train has been cancelled.
Ta vlak je odpovedan. — ta vlak ye od·po·*ve*·dan
Stop here, please.
Ustavite tukaj, prosim. — oos·*ta*·vee·te *too*·kai *pro*·seem

How long does the trip take?
Koliko traja potovanje? — ko·*lee*·ko *tra*·ya po·to·*va*·nye
Do I need to change?
Ali moram presesti? — *a*·lee *mo*·ram pre·*ses*·tee

1st class	*prvi razred*	*puhr*·vee *raz*·red
2nd class	*drugi razred*	*droo*·gee *raz*·red
one way	*ena smer*	*e*·na smer
return	*povratna*	pov·*rat*·na
the first	*prvi*	*puhr*·vee
the last	*zadnji*	*zad*·nyee

platform number	*številka perona*	shte·*veel*·ka pe·*ro*·na
ticket office	*prodaja vozovnic*	pro·*da*·ya vo·*zov*·neets
timetable	*spored*	spo·*red*
train station	*železniška postaja*	zhe·*lez*·neesh·ka pos·*ta*·ya
bus station	*avtobusno postajališče*	*av*·to·boos·no po·sta·ya·*leesh*·che

Private Transport

I'd like to hire a …	*Rad/Rada bi najel/najela …* (m/f)	rad/*ra*·da bee na·*yel*/na·*ye*·la …
4WD	*terenski avto*	te·*ren*·skee *av*·to
bicycle	*kolo*	ko·*lo*
car	*avto*	*av*·to
guide	*vodiča*	vo·*dee*·cha
horse	*konja*	*ko*·nya
motorcyle	*motorno kolo*	mo·*tor*·no ko·*lo*

Is this the road to …?
Ali je to cesta za …? — *a*·lee ye to *tses*·ta za …
Where's a service station?
Kje je bencinska črpalka? — kye ye ben·*tseen*·ska *chuhr*·pal·ka
Please fill it up.
Napolnite prosim. — na·*pol*·nee·te *pro*·seem
I'd like … litres.
Prosim … litrov. — *pro*·seem … *leet*·roh

diesel	*dizel*	*dee*·zel
leaded petrol	*benzin z svincem*	ben·*zeen* z *sveen*·tsem
unleaded petrol	*benzin brez svinca*	ben·*zeen* brez *sveen*·tsa

(How long) Can I park here?
(Koliko časa) Lahko tukaj parkiram? — (*ko*·lee·ko *cha*·sa) lah·*ko too*·kai par·*kee*·ram
Where do I pay?
Kje plačam? — kye *pla*·cham

ROAD SIGNS

Cestnina	Toll
Dajte Prednost	Give Way
Ena Smer	One Way
Izhod	Exit
Nevarnost	Danger
Obvoz	Detour
Prepovedan Vhod	No Entry
Prepovedano Parkiranje	No Parking
Prepovedano Vstavljanje	Keep Clear
Vhod	Entry
Vozite Počasi	Slow Down

need a mechanic.
Potrebujem mehanika. po·tre·*boo*·yem me·*ha*·nee·ka

he car/motorbike has broken down (at ...).
Avto/motor se je pokvaril (pri ...). *av*·to/mo·*tor* se ye pok·*va*·reel (pree ...)

he car/motorbike won't start.
Avto/motor noče vžgati. *av*·to/mo·*tor* *no*·che vuhzh·*ga*·tee

have a flat tyre.
Zračnica mi je počila. *zrach*·nee·tsa mee ye *po*·chee·la

ve run out of petrol.
Nimam več benzina. *nee*·mam vech ben·*zee*·na

ve had an accident.
Imel/Imela sem nesrečo. (m/f) ee·*mel*/ee·*me*·la sem ne·*sre*·cho

TRAVEL WITH CHILDREN

I need a ...	*Potrebujem ...*	po·tre·*boo*·yem ...
baby change room	*prostor za previjanje dojenčka*	*pro*·stor za pre·*vee*·ya·nye do·*yench*·ka
(English-speaking) babysitter	*otroško varuško (ki govori angleško)*	ot·*rosh*·ko va·*roosh*·ko (kee go·vo·*ree* an·*glesh*·sko)
car baby seat	*sedež za dojenčka*	*se*·dezh za do·*yench*·ka
child-minding service	*nekoga, da mi čuva otroka*	*ne*·ko·ga da mee *choo*·va ot·*ro*·ka
children's menu	*otroški meni*	ot·*rosh*·kee me·*nee*
disposable nappies/diapers	*papirnate plenice*	pa·*peer*·na·te ple·*nee*·tse
highchair	*visoki stol*	vee·*so*·kee stoh
infant milk formula	*mleko za dojenčka*	*mle*·ko za do·*yench*·ka
potty	*kahlico*	*kah*·li·tso
stroller/pusher	*otroški voziček*	ot·*rosh*·kee vo·*zee*·chek

Do you mind if I breastfeed here?
A lahko tukaj dojim? a lah·*ko* *too*·kai do·*yeem*

Are children allowed?
Ali je dovoljeno za otroke? *a*·lee ye do·*vo*·lye·no za ot·*ro*·ke

Also available from Lonely Planet:
Eastern Europe phrasebook

LANGUAGE

Glossary

Can't find the word you're looking for here? Try the Language chapter (p305) or the Slovene-English Glossary in Food & Drink (p49).

AMZS – Avto-Moto Zveza Slovenije (Automobile Association of Slovenia)
avtocesta – motorway, highway

bife – snack and/or drinks bar
bivak – bivouac (most basic form of shelter in the mountains)
breg – river bank
burja – bora (cold northeast wind from the Adriatic)

c – abbreviation for *cesta*
čaj – tea
čakalnica – waiting room (eg in station)
cena – price
cerkev – church
cesta – road

DDV – davek na dodano vrednost (value-added tax, or VAT)
delovni čas – opening/business hours
dijaški dom – student dormitory, hostel
dolina – valley
dom – house; mountain lodge
Domobranci – anti-Partisan Home Guards during WWII
drevored – avenue
dvorana – hall
dvorišče – courtyard

fijaker – horse-drawn carriage

gaj – grove, park
garderoba – left-luggage office, coat check
gledališče – theatre
gora – mountain
gostilna – innlike restaurant
gostišče – innlike restaurant usually with accommodation
gozd – forest, grove
grad – castle
gradbišče – building site, road works
greben – ridge, crest
GRS – Gorska Reševalna Služba (Mountain Rescue Service)
GZS – Geodetski Zavod Slovenije (Geodesic Institute of Slovenia)

Hallstatt – early Iron Age Celtic culture (800–500 BC)
hiša – house
hrib – hill

izhod – exit
izvir – source (of a river, stream etc)

jama – cave
jedilni list – menu
jezero – lake
jug – south

kamnolom – quarry
Karst – limestone region of underground rivers and caves in Primorska
kavarna – coffee shop, cafe
klet – cellar
knjigarna – bookshop
knjižnica – library
koča – mountain cottage or hut
kosilo – lunch
kot – glacial valley, corner
kotlina – basin
kozolec – hayrack distinct to Slovenia
kras – karst
krčma – drinks bar (sometimes with food)
krožno križišče – roundabout

La Tène – late Iron Age culture (450–390 BC)
lekarna – pharmacy
LPP – Ljubljanski Potniški Promet (Ljubljana city bus network)

mali (m) **mala** (f) **malo** (n) – little
malica – midmorning snack
menjalnica – private currency exchange office
mesto – town
morje – sea
moški – men (toilet)
most – bridge
muzej – museum

na – on
nabrežje – embankment
narod – nation
naselje – colony, development, estate
nasip – dike, embankment
novi (m) **nova** (f) **novo** (n) - new

bčina – administrative division; county or commune; city r town hall
bvoz – detour (road sign)
bvoznica – ring road, bypass
dhod – departure
dprto – open
krepčevalnica – snack bar
svobodilne Fronte (OF) – Anti-Fascist Liberation ront during WWII
tok – island

anjska končnica – beehive panel painted with lovenian folk motifs
eron – train-station platform
ivnica – pub, beer hall
ivo – beer
lanina – Alpine pasture
lanota – plateau
od – under, below
odhod – pedestrian underpass (subway)
olje – collapsed limestone area under cultivation
opravek – correction/clear (on ATM)
ot – trail
otok – stream
otovanje – travel
otrditev – enter/confirm (on ATM)
razniki – holidays
rehod – passage, crossing
rekinitev – cancel (on ATM)
rekop – canal
renočišče – accommodation
revoz – transport
ri – at, near, by
rihod – arrival
ZS – Planinska Zveza Slovenije (Alpine Association of lovenia)

egija – province, region
eka – river
estavracija – restaurant
ini – push (on door)
ob – escarpment, edge

amopostrežna restavracija – self-service estaurant
amostan – monastery
ecessionism – art and architectural style similar to rt nouveau
edežnica – chairlift
edlo – pass, saddle
ever – north
IT – international currency code for tolar (Slovenia's urrency from 1992 to 2007)
kanzen – open-air museum displaying village rchitecture

slaščičarna – shop selling ice cream, sweets
smučanje – skiing
SNTO – Slovenska Nacionalna Turistična Organizacija (Slovenian National Tourist Office)
sobe – rooms (available)
soteska – ravine, gorge
sprehajališče – walkway, promenade
stari (m) **stara** (f) **staro** (n) – old
stena – wall, cliff
steza – path
stolp – tower
STP – Slovenian Tourist Board
štruklji – dumplings
Sv – St (abbreviation for saint)
SŽ – Slovenske Železnice (Slovenian Railways)

terme – Italian word for 'spa' used frequently in Slovenia
TIC – Tourist Information Centre
TNP – Triglavski Narodni Park (Triglav National Park)
toplar – double-linked hayrack unique to Slovenia
toplice – spa
trg – square

ul – abbreviation for *ulica*
ulica – street

vas – village
večerja – dinner, supper
veliki (m) **velika** (f) **veliko** (n) – great, big
vhod – entrance
vila – villa
vinoteka – wine bar
vinska cesta – wine road
vinska klet – wine cellar
vleci – pull (on door)
vozni red – timetable
vozovnica – ticket
vrata – door, gate
vrh – summit, peak
vrt – garden, park
vrtača – sinkhole
vzhod – east
vzpenjača – gondola, funicular

zahod – west
zaprto – closed
zavetišče – mountain 'refuge' with refreshments and sometimes accommodation
zdravilišče – health resort, spa
zdravstveni dom – medical centre, clinic
žegnanje – a patron's festival at a church or chapel
ženske – women (toilet)
žičnica – cable car
zidanica – a cottage in one of the wine-growing regions
znamenje – wayside religious shrine

ALTERNATIVE PLACE NAMES

Abbreviations

(C) Croatian, (Cz) Czech, (E) English, (G) German, (H) Hungarian, (I) Italian, (P) Polish

Avstrija – Austria (E), Österreich (G)

Beljak – Villach (G)
Benetke – Venice (E), Venezia (I)
Bizeljsko – Wisell (G)
Bohinj – Wochain (G)
Brežice – Rhain (G)
Budimpešta – Budapest (H)

Čedad – Cividale (I)
Celovec – Klagenfurt (G)
Celje – Cilli (G)
Cerknica – Cirkniz (G)
Črna Gora – Montenegro (E)
Črnomelj – Tschernembl (G)

Dolenjska – Lower Carniola (E)
Dunaj – Vienna (E), Wien (G)

Gorenjska – Upper Carniola (E)
Gorica – Gorizia (I)
Gradec – Graz (G)
Gradež – Grado (I)

Hrvaška – Croatia (E), Hrvatska (C)

Idrija – Ydria (G)
Istra – Istria (E)
Italija – Italy (E), Italia (I)
Izola – Isola (I)

Jadran, Jadransko Morje – Adriatic Sea (E)

Kamnik – Stein (G)
Kobarid – Caporetto (I)
Koper – Capodistria (I)
Koroška – Carinthia (E), Kärnten (G)
Kostanjevica – Landstrass (G)
Kranj – Krainburg (G)
Kranjska – Carniola (E), Krain (G)
Kras – Karst (E)
Kropa – Cropp (G)
Krnski Grad – Karnburg (G)

Lendava – Lendva (H)
Lipnica – Leibnitz (G)
Ljubljana – Laibach (G), Liubliana (I)

Madžarska – Hungary (E), Magyarország (H)
Metlika – Möttling (G)
Milje – Muggia (I)
Murska Sobota – Muraszombat (H)

Notranjska – Inner Carniola (E)
Nova Gorica – Gorizia (I), Görz (G)

Otočec – Wördl (G)
Oglej – Aquileia (I)

Piran – Pirano (I)
Pleterje – Pletariach (G)
Pliberk – Bleiburg (G)
Portorož – Portorose (I)
Postojna – Adelsberg (G)
Praga – Prague (E), Praha (Cz)
Ptuj – Pettau (G)

Radgona – Bad Radkersburg (G)
Radovljica – Ratmansdorf (G)
Reka – Rijeka (C), Fiume (I)
Ribnica – Reiffniz (G)
Rim – Rome (E), Roma (I)
Rogaška Slatina – Rohitsch-Sauerbrunn (G)
Rosalnice – Rosendorf (G)

Seča – Sezza (I) Peninsula
Sečovlje – Sicciole (I)
Škocjan – San Canziano (I)
Štajerska – Styria (E), Steiermark (G)
Soča – Isonzo (I)
Srbija – Serbia (E)
Sredozemlje – Mediterranean (E)
Sredozemsko Morje – Mediterranean Sea (E)
Štajerska – Styria (E), Steiermark (G)
Stična – Sittich (G)
Strunjan – Strugnano (I)

Trbiž – Tarvisio (I)
Trst – Trieste (I)
Tržaški Zaliv – Gulf of Trieste (E), Golfo di Trieste (I)
Tržič – Monfalcone (I)

Varšava – Warsaw (E), Warszawa (P)
Videm – Udine (I)
Vinica – Weinitz (G)

Železna Kapla – Eisenkappel (G)

Behind the Scenes

THIS BOOK

This 6th edition of Lonely Planet's *Slovenia* guide was written by Steve Fallon. Steve also wrote the previous two editions. The Health chapter was adapted from material written by Dr Caroline Evans. This guidebook was commissioned in Lonely Planet's London office and was produced by the following:

Commissioning Editor Paula Hardy
Coordinating Editor Jeanette Wall
Coordinating Cartographer Brendan Streager
Coordinating Layout Designer Aomi Hongo
Managing Editor Brigitte Ellemor
Managing Cartographers Alison Lyall, Herman So
Managing Layout Designer Sally Darmody
Assisting Editors Justin Flynn, Alan Murphy
Assisting Cartographers Peter Shields
Cover Research Marika Mercer, lonelyplanetimages.com
Internal Image Research Jane Hart, lonelyplanetimages.com
Project Managers Craig Kilburn, Michelle Lewis
Language Content Annelies Mertens, Branislava Vladisavljevic

Thanks to Lucy Birchley, Chris Girdler, Indra Kilfoyle, Rebecca Lalor, Trent Paton, Averil Robertson, Lyahna Spencer, Clifton Wilkinson, Juan Winata, Glenn van der Knijff

THANKS

STEVE FALLON

A number of people assisted in the research and writing of *Slovenia,* in particular my dear friends and fonts-of-all-knowledge at the Ljubljana Tourist Board: Verica Leskovar, Tatjana Radovič, Petra Stušek and new-kid-in-town Jan Oršič. I appreciate the assistance of the Slovenian Tourist Board, too; thanks especially to Lucija Jager for all her help. Slovenian Railways' Marino Fakin, Vojko Anzeljc and Tone Plankar at the Ljubljana bus station and Tomaž Škofic of Adria Airways all assisted with transport matters and I am very grateful. Five people raised their Local Voices and shared a bit of their Slovenian lives with you all: Dušan Brejc of the Wine Association of Slovenia; writers Andrej Blatnik and Erica Johnson Debeljak; canyoning maestro Robert 'Bob' Žerovec; and *skanzen* guide Nataša Lukezic.

It was wonderful catching up with old mates Aleš Hvala of the Hotel Hvala and Restavracija Topli Val in Kobarid; Lado Leskovar of UNICEF based in Ljubljana; and Aleksander Riznič of Radio Odeon in Črnomelj. Domen Kalajžič of 3glav Adventures in Bled and mountain guide Marjan Manfreda got me up and then down Triglav. Thanks to them I can finally say: *Jaz tudi sem slovenec* (I too am a Slovene).

THE LONELY PLANET STORY

Fresh from an epic journey across Europe, Asia and Australia in 1972, Tony and Maureen Wheeler sat at their kitchen table stapling together notes. The first Lonely Planet guidebook, *Across Asia on the Cheap,* was born.

Travellers snapped up the guides. Inspired by their success, the Wheelers began publishing books to Southeast Asia, India and beyond. Demand was prodigious, and the Wheelers expanded the business rapidly to keep up. Over the years, Lonely Planet extended its coverage to every country and into the virtual world via lonelyplanet.com and the Thorn Tree message board.

As Lonely Planet became a globally loved brand, Tony and Maureen received several offers for the company. But it wasn't until 2007 that they found a partner whom they trusted to remain true to the company's principles of travelling widely, treading lightly and giving sustainably. In October of that year, BBC Worldwide acquired a 75% share in the company, pledging to uphold Lonely Planet's commitment to independent travel, trustworthy advice and editorial independence.

Today, Lonely Planet has offices in Melbourne, London and Oakland, with over 500 staff members and 300 authors. Tony and Maureen are still actively involved with Lonely Planet. They're travelling more often than ever, and they're devoting their spare time to charitable projects. And the company is still driven by the philosophy of *Across Asia on the Cheap*: 'All you've got to do is decide to go and the hardest part is over. So go!'

As always, my efforts here are dedicated to my partner, Michael Rothschild, who has finally done the Grand Tour of God's own country and is converted.

OUR READERS

Many thanks to the travellers who used the last edition and wrote to us with helpful hints, useful advice and interesting anecdotes:

Karen Abell, Brooke Babcock, Chrys & Peter Baldwin, Laura Barron, Michael Beck, Jo Bertram, Bogdan Bevk, Bogdan Bevk, Iain Bisset, Stuart Bleazard, Nick Boag, Evert Boshoven, Philippe Bouchery, Tina Brelih, Paul Bristow, Alexis Broulis, Rob Brown, Helen Burton, Mihai Ciobanu, Neal Cook, Geert Cromphout, Justin Curran, Guy Debulpaep, Victor Del Arco Cristià, Christopher Fletcher, Matjaz Francelj, Colin Gamblin, Jim Gillard, Dalit Ginossar, Marilyn Goebel, Leah Gold, Kevin Gordon, Raoul Gunning, Gareth Hamilton, Jan Heeringa, Gerard Helmink, Alison Hood, Mulle Harbort, Boris Jansen, Luka Jeglic, Louise Jones, Tony Jowett, Bernar Karo, Regina Koehler, Edward Kollar, Matej Kosir, Harry Kriewaldt, András Kugler, Rebecca Leone, Matic Leskosek, Jorn Lund, Ursa Malovrh, Prof. Marschner Arnulf, Preseren Marta, Damjana Mavrič, Ken Merk, Ivan Mikulin, Peter Moselund, Janet Nicolas, Miriam Novak, Yoav Ossia, Peter Palan, Thomas Parker, Katja Pavlic, Cindy Pavlik, David Peck, Kent Pettersson, Igor Plahuta, Tim Plenderleith, John Pot, David Pumphrey, Barbara Rajgelj, Celina Rebola, Vesna Resnik, Peter Roth, Joseph Sanderson, Gerhard Schweng, Lado Sencar, Anle Shen, Vladimir Silak, Chris Sim, Jackie Spratt, Toma Strle, Mladen Stropnik, Julie Teague, Rosy Turnbull, Sheila Turner, Jon Tydeman, Ivan Valencic, Vesteinn Valgardsson, Annelies Van Baelen, Roger Van De Sompel, Meg Viezbicke, Šilak Vladimir, Kelly Vogel, Sue Walker, Jan Walmsley, Ian Wilkins, Tony Williams, Noam Zevit

LONELY PLANET AUTHORS

Why is our travel information the best in the world? It's simple: our authors are passionate, dedicated travellers. They don't take freebies in exchange for positive coverage so you can be sure the advice you're given is impartial. They travel widely to all the popular spots, and off the beaten track. They don't research using just the internet or phone. They discover new places not included in any other guidebook. They personally visit thousands of hotels, restaurants, palaces, trails, galleries, temples and more. They speak with dozens of locals every day to make sure you get the kind of insider knowledge only a local could tell you. They take pride in getting all the details right, and in telling it how it is. Think you can do it? Find out how at **lonelyplanet.com**.

ACKNOWLEDGMENTS

Many thanks to the following for the use of their content:

Globe on title page ©Mountain High Maps 1993 Digital Wisdom, Inc.

SEND US YOUR FEEDBACK

We love to hear from travellers – your comments keep us on our toes and help make our books better. Our well-travelled team reads every word on what you loved or loathed about this book. Although we cannot reply individually to postal submissions, we always guarantee that your feedback goes straight to the appropriate authors, in time for the next edition. Each person who sends us information is thanked in the next edition and the most useful submissions are rewarded with a free book.

To send us your updates – and find out about Lonely Planet events, newsletters and travel news – visit our award-winning website: **lonelyplanet.com/contact**.

Note: we may edit, reproduce and incorporate your comments in Lonely Planet products such as guidebooks, websites and digital products, so let us know if you don't want your comments reproduced or your name acknowledged. For a copy of our privacy policy visit lonelyplanet.com/privacy.

Index

ABBREVIATIONS

Bel	Bela Krajina
Dol	Dolenjska
Gor	Gorenjska
Kor	Koroška
Lju	Ljubljana
Not	Notranjska
Pre	Prekmurje
Pri	Primorska
Šta	Štajerska

000 Map pages
000 Photograph pages

A

B

C

D

E

F

000 Map pages
000 Photograph pages

INDEX

000 Map pages
000 Photograph pages

INDEX

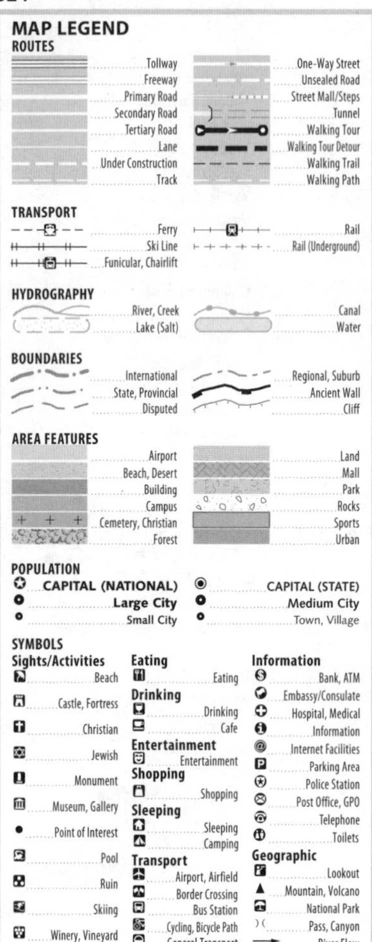

LONELY PLANET OFFICES

Australia (Head Office)
Locked Bag 1, Footscray, Victoria 3011
☎ 03 8379 8000, fax 03 8379 8111
talk2us@lonelyplanet.com.au

USA
150 Linden St, Oakland, CA 94607
☎ 510 250 6400, toll free 800 275 8555
fax 510 893 8572
info@lonelyplanet.com

UK
2nd fl, 186 City Rd,
London EC1V 2NT
☎ 020 7106 2100, fax 020 7106 2101
go@lonelyplanet.co.uk

Published by Lonely Planet
ABN 36 005 607 983

Cover photograph: Ljubljana at sunset from Castle Hill, Sloveni Guy Edwardes/Getty Images. Many of the images in this guic are available for licensing from Lonely Planet Images: lone planetimages.com.

Printed by China Translation and Printing Services Ltd
Printed in China

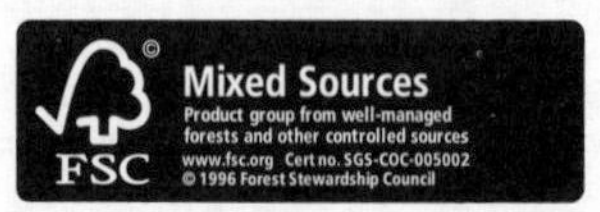